The Profits of Charity

The Profits of Charity

International Perspectives on the Law Governing the Involvement of Charities in Commerce

Kerry O'Halloran

OXFORD
UNIVERSITY PRESS

OXFORD
UNIVERSITY PRESS

Oxford University Press is a department of the University of Oxford. It furthers the University's objective of excellence in research, scholarship, and education by publishing worldwide.

Oxford New York
Auckland Cape Town Dar es Salaam Hong Kong Karachi Kuala Lumpur Madrid Melbourne Mexico City Nairobi New Delhi Shanghai Taipei Toronto

With offices in
Argentina Austria Brazil Chile Czech Republic France Greece Guatemala Hungary Italy Japan Poland Portugal Singapore South Korea Switzerland Thailand Turkey Ukraine Vietnam

Published in the United States of America by
Oxford University Press
198 Madison Avenue, New York, NY 10016

Library of Congress Cataloging-in-Publication Data
O'Halloran, Kerry.
The profits of charity / Kerry O'Halloran.
p. cm.
Includes bibliographical references and index.
ISBN 978-0-19-976771-7 ((hardback) : alk. paper)
1. Charity laws and legislation. 2. Charitable uses, trusts, and foundations. 3. Charities—Government policy. 4. Gifts—Law and legislation. 5. Charities—Taxation—Law and legislation.
I. Title.
K797.O38 2012
344.03'17—dc23
2012009275

9 8 7 6 5 4 3 2 1

Printed in the United States of America on acid-free paper

Note to Readers

This publication is designed to provide accurate and authoritative information in regard to the subject matter covered. It is based upon sources believed to be accurate and reliable and is intended to be current as of the time it was written. It is sold with the understanding that the publisher is not engaged in rendering legal, accounting, or other professional services. If legal advice or other expert assistance is required, the services of a competent professional person should be sought. Also, to confirm that the information has not been affected or changed by recent developments, traditional legal research techniques should be used, including checking primary sources where appropriate.

(Based on the Declaration of Principles jointly adopted by a Committee of the American Bar Association and a Committee of Publishers and Associations.)

This book is dedicated to Elizabeth.

GENERAL TABLE OF CONTENTS

DETAILED TABLE OF CONTENTS

PREFACE

The Profits of Charity identifies, examines, and assesses the applicable rules and principles governing charity's current engagement with commerce. The "working hypothesis" is that for reasons stemming from demographic trends and falling levels of manufacturing, among others, governments in the developed world are keen to negotiate with the nonprofit sector a sharing of responsibility for the future provision of some public benefit service.

This book focuses broadly on matters of government policy, law, and practice, and in particular on the issues that generate the most significant case law. In doing so, it explores the pressures and policies driving charity to be involved in trading and commerce, and compares and contrasts the related experience of leading common law nations, as well as taking into account the very relevant developments occurring in continental Europe.

Is the relevant law changing and, if so, where, how, and why is this now taking place? As the leading nonprofits, charities must be positioned to step up to the plate. This requires that certain changes happen, including enabling and allowing charities to overcome the traditional constraints on profit making. The recent and widespread spate of national charity law reform processes is relevant. Only by examining the nuts and bolts of current law in this area, and the nature of any changes taking place, can some light be shed on the policies as they are developed and implemented.

The perennial debate—what "welfare" responsibilities should rest with the citizen and the family, what should be shouldered by government or shared with the market, and what should be left to charity—has become livelier in recent years. Although culturally determined (and in some countries politically imposed), the current balance seems increasingly open to question as threats to civil society from international terrorism, global recession, and domestic social unrest have increased.

The public benefit principle could become more instrumental in rebalancing the division of "welfare" responsibilities and in shaping related social policy. But as always, how best to ensure that the necessary funding—authorized by law and enabled by tax privileges—reaches these entities to allow public benefit activity to be pursued remains the significant open question.

Arguably, we are seeing a convergence of public and private trading interests as capitalism morphs into public benefit (Chrysler, AIG, leading banks, etc., in receipt of state bailouts), hedge funds sprout philanthropic foundations, and charity moves into banking (the Big Society Bank). The evermore complex cross-sector linkages, and fee-paying service facilities (mainly in health care and education) are blurring the traditional public/private divide. Where does this leave "altruism"? Is "charity," as long known to the common law, now in danger of losing its identity? What are the implications arising for charities, for the sector, and more broadly, for the market? What is "public benefit"? What is "private benefit"?

In the stress of these times, there is a general willingness to question inherited positions and, perhaps, a general edging toward convergence. In the United States, health care reforms have triggered a widespread acknowledgment that although America is not a "welfare state," more needs to be done for its socially disadvantaged citizens. In the U.K., government has for some years now been winding down the "welfare state", privatizing public utilities and cultivating a partnership with charities to deliver public benefit services. To a lesser degree, other common law countries such as Canada, Australia, and New Zealand have been experiencing a not dissimilar dynamic. In continental Europe, those countries emerging from totalitarian regimes seek to redress a balance customarily fixed by government and find common ground with their more egalitarian E.U. partners.

Charities have responded to the opportunities provided by the changing role of the state with enthusiasm. The vigor with which they have entered the marketplace—competing and merging with other nonprofits, forging alliances with business, taking on the ownership of public service utilities devolved by local government, and simply switching legal status to become full-blooded for-profit commercial entities—has come as a surprise to many. Something along the same lines is occurring in all the developed nations of the common law world and elsewhere. It seems appropriate to explore:

- whether the driving forces are the same;
- what the outcomes are for the main players (government, business, and the nonprofit sector); and
- whether the outcomes differ according to political context, and, if so, how and why?

Given that charities and other nonprofits are granted tax-exempt status because of their supposedly unique socioeconomic contribution, the changes now being made to that role do give rise to significant questions. They have traditionally occupied the space between the public and for-profit sectors on the basis that they supplement the core public service provision of the former and substitute for the absence of any such non-profitable provision that might be made by the latter. That space has allowed for a contribution based on such public benefit activity as education, health care, and poverty relief. Increasingly, however, the need to generate earned income to augment the diminishing flow from customary funding sources is driving these organizations to make considerable inroads into the remit of both public and for-profit sectors. The steady expansion of charities and nonprofits into mainstream public benefit services and into mainstream commercial activity is weakening their claim to a unique role, and perhaps also to automatic tax-exempt status as the earning of funds rather than its distribution grows in importance.

But the boundary infringements are not solely attributable to incursions from the nonprofit sector as for-profits poach exploitable aspects of public benefit provision, and government sets up proxy arrangements whereby it wholly controls the activities of some charities and other nonprofits. A complex web of intersectoral strands is now being woven in many jurisdictions.

From the perspective of a charity lawyer, a key concern relates to the principles involved in charity assuming this new role: just how free are charities (subsidized by taxpayers, donors, and volunteers; bearing a government-conferred and privileged status, and licensed to pursue a specified public benefit) to exploit such opportunities? What are the legal risks for a charity if it allows its autonomy to be compromised or becomes otherwise dependent upon externalities? What exactly are the rules governing charities and profit? Where do we or should we draw the line between public benefit and private profit?

The Profits of Charity suggests that these issues should now be of concern not just to academics, lawyers, charity managers, and business entrepreneurs but to all with a concern for "civil society."

Interest in such questions has been sharpened by recent events, in particular by the sudden rush to charity law reform in the leading common law jurisdictions; the impact of new regulatory constraints on charities resulting from government action against the threat of international terrorism; and the consequences of economic recession for the dynamics of the marketplace, for the public benefit principle, and for the future role of charity. In the teeth of economic recession, presaged by the collapse of some of the nosier engines of capitalism, now seems a good time to inquire as to how charity is holding up.

The following comparative jurisdictional analysis of the law governing charities and profit aims to make a contribution to our understanding of these issues.

The Profits of Charity consists of 13 chapters, arranged in three parts under the headings "Background," "Contemporary International Perspectives," and "New Directions." The jurisdiction-specific chapters carry a heavy concentration of case law as, in the general absence of legislation, it is only by examining the judicial rationale that it is possible to identify and compare the legal rules governing the trading activities of charity and other nonprofits. Although the focus remains on "charity" throughout the book, it seems necessary to refer, as appropriate, to other nonprofits and to the sector more generally in recognition of their often common interests.

Part I of the book, in four chapters, explores the background to the subject and formulates key themes to be tracked through the policy, law, and practice of the jurisdictional study that constitutes Part II, and which later forms the basis of the comparative analysis that begins Part III. It identifies and examines the rules governing trading by charities, explaining their traditional function and why such legal constraints are now a matter of pressing concern across the developed common law world. It explores the principles involved, the tension between public and private interests, and the relevance of the political context.

Part II, the core of the book, consists of six chapters that each deal with a jurisdiction or region that is currently engaged in, or has just completed, a process of charity law reform intended to improve the regulatory framework and address contemporary patterns of social need. To a varying degree, these reform processes broadened the scope of matters designated as charitable purposes to allow charities to assume greater levels of responsibility for public benefit provision. Some also facilitated the creation of new legal structures, thereby enabling charities to act in partnership with government and business entities. The objective of this section is to examine the current law relating to charities and trading, within a political context, in each jurisdiction. The inquiry focuses on the ways and means by which each jurisdiction is addressing the future capacity of charity to operate as a trading entity, whether doing so independently or acting in partnership with government or business, and to consider how this works in practice as illustrated by contemporary case law. It identifies, weighs, and evaluates their distinctive characteristics. This exercise is facilitated by uniformly applying a loosely designed template that permits the systematic gathering of information in respect of England and Wales, Australia, New Zealand, the European Union, the United States, and Canada.

Part III, in three chapters, draws from the findings in Part II to consider the significance of the established facts, trends, and anomalies and their implications for the future relationship among charity, law, and trading. *The Profits of Charity* concludes by reflecting on how the Titmuss concept of "the gift relationship" fits with contemporary developments in the law governing trading by charities: the nexus between altruism and profit.

Kerry O'Halloran
White Park Bay
Winter 2011/12

ACKNOWLEDGMENTS

Heartfelt thanks are due to Professor Myles McGregor-Lowndes[1] without whose support, advice, and friendship—given patiently under the pressure of many other competing claims on his time—completing *The Profits of Charity* would have been a much greater struggle. For his companionship and that of other colleagues at the Australian Centre for Philanthropy and Nonprofit Studies, and for all their many acts of friendship to my wife and self during our visits to the Centre, I remain extremely grateful.

A considerable debt of gratitude is owed to those who made room in their busy lives to offer comment on particular draft chapters. In particular thanks are due to the helpful feedback received from: Myles McGregor-Lowndes (Australia); Professor Evelyn Brody[2] and Putnam Barber[3] (United States); Dr. Alison Dunn[4] (U.K.); Dr. Michael Gousmett[5] (New Zealand); and Stefan Ingerfurth[6] together with Elly Mariani[7] (Europe). A special tribute must be paid to Laird Hunter Q.C.[8] (Canada) who kindly undertook his task while on the Saint Jacques-de-Compostelle pilgrimage, thus adding immeasurably to his penitence.

I am very thankful to Oxford University Press for the vote of confidence that resulted in the publication of this book.[9] The scrupulous and challenging editorial

[1] Director, the Australian Centre of Philanthropy and Nonprofit Studies, Queensland University of Technology, Brisbane, Australia.

[2] Chicago-Kent College of Law and Reporter, American Law Institute's Project on Principles of the Law of Nonprofit Organizations.

[3] Renowned Seattle-based writer and commentator on public policy issues affecting the work of nonprofits.

[4] Director, Postgraduate Research, Newcastle Law School, Newcastle University, U.K.

[5] Founding Trustee, The New Zealand Third Sector Educational Trust.

[6] University of Mannheim, Department of Business Administration, Public & Nonprofit Management.

[7] University of Amsterdam, Philanthropic Studies, Researcher, Tax regulation on charitable giving.

[8] Recognized by Lexpert as one of Canada leading practitioners in charity and nonprofit law and retained by some of Canada's leading charitable foundations, Laird served a two-year term as a member of The Charities Advisory Committee.

[9] The *Profits of Charity* was completed during my tenure at the Australian Centre of Philanthropy and Nonprofit Studies, and there may be some overlap of material with other books also written during that period such as *The Politics of Charity* (Routledge, 2011), *Modernising Charity Law* (Elgar, 2010) *and Charity Law & Social Policy* (Springer, 2008).

input of Blake Ratcliff,[10] ably overseen by Kevin Pendergast,[11] has been much appreciated; it has been a pleasure to work with both. Despite their editorial diligence, some mistakes, inconsistencies, and other faults of omission or commission may have found their way into print, in which case, responsibility for same, and for all views expressed, must rest exclusively with me.

Finally, thank you as always, Elizabeth, for... everything.

[10] Associate Developments Editor, Oxford University Press, New York.

[11] Acquisitions Editor, Oxford University Press, New York.

PART 1

Background

1

THE COMMON LAW: CONCEPTS, DEFINITIONS, AND STRUCTURES FOR CHARITY

I. INTRODUCTION

This chapter explains the basic conceptual framework underpinning charity law in all common law jurisdictions. It provides a baseline from which to track the unfolding themes that comprise this book and permits a clear grasp of developing jurisdictional differences in the law governing charity involvement in commerce.

Beginning with the essence of charity—"the gift relationship"[1]—the chapter briefly explores the origins and social significance of "charity," based on the altruism[2] of the individual, generating the voluntary contribution of many for the public good. It then turns to examine the hallmarks of "charity" as interpreted within the common law: the public benefit principle; charitable intent; the exclusiveness rule; and the nongovernmental, independent, and nonpolitical requirements. It defines and assesses the significance of matters designated by government as "charitable purposes" initially in the Preamble to the Charitable Uses Act of 1601[3] and as subsequently developed by the judiciary, and broadly accepted throughout the common law world.

The chapter closes by considering the importance of legal structures as a means of housing and giving effect to charitable purposes: the traditional reliance on the trust form in the U.K. and Ireland as opposed to an early preference for incorporation in the United States, Australia, and elsewhere. It provides a brief taxonomy of

[1] See Titmuss, R. A., *The Gift Relationship: From Human Blood to Social Policy*, London, Allen and Unwin, 1970.

[2] Meaning an unselfish concern for the welfare of others: a private act for public benefit. It was Comte's Philosophy of the Sciences (translated by George Lewes, 1890) that first introduced the word "altruism" (from the French "alteri huic") into the English language.

[3] The Statute of Charitable Uses 1601, also known as the Statute of Elizabeth; 43 Eliz 1, c 4.

relevant legal structures and reflects on their relative advantages and disadvantages as vehicles for charity.

II. THE "GIFT RELATIONSHIP"

"Profit" and "charity" are not readily reconciled. The difficulties in so doing exercised Titmuss in his seminal and widely quoted work, *The Gift Relationship*,[4] in which he examined the nature of the relationship between donor and recipient in the context of two models of blood donation that prevailed in the 1960s: the philanthropic exchange model in the U.K. and the commercial service model in the United States. The former relied upon an act of "giving": blood being donated by the voluntary and altruistic act of an individual, constituting ethically based behavior. The latter relied upon a commercial system: Blood donation was an organized service, and individual behavior was motivated by self-interest. The U.K. National Blood Transfusion Service provided a service to which blood donors made anonymous contributions, without financial or other reward, and from which recipients took according to need, incurring no cost, and without knowing the identity of the donor. The corresponding U.S. service, on the other hand, reduced people's willingness to donate blood because the transaction had become tarnished by commercialism, causing such adverse consequences as the repression of expressions of altruism and an erosion of a sense of community. In Titmuss's view, the free gift of blood in the U.K. left the relationship between giver and recipient uncompromised by any "contract of custom; legal bond; functional determinism; situations of discriminatory power; nor by domination, constraint or compulsion."[5] In essence, "profit" and "charity" were worlds apart.

The gift relationship, it has been argued, is something that can bond us as a society. Indeed, as Titmuss himself pointed out: "the social relations set up by gift exchange are among the most powerful forces which bind a social group together."[6] His claim that altruism lay at the heart of that relationship—and that activities which allowed opportunities for altruism were of value to the individuals concerned and to society generally because ethical conduct was good in itself, generating a sense of shared morality and civic responsibility that served to bond society—seemed persuasive.

A. The Giver

Titmuss took the view that altruism was the reason people donated blood without direct reward, at a cost of their own time and effort, to another with whom they would have no direct contact. A regard for the needs of others was the principle that motivated their action. Donors showed a high sense of awareness of belonging to

[4] Titmuss, *The Gift Relationship*.

[5] Titmuss, *The Gift Relationship*.

[6] Titmuss, *The Gift Relationship*, at p. 73.

a community and of social responsibility. It followed that it was important for the state to provide the opportunity for individuals to express their commitment to the community in which they lived; indeed, he developed this theme in his final chapter, "The Right to Give." In his view, the substitution of profit for altruism inhibited the freedom to give or not to give; material incentives destroyed rather than complemented moral incentives. The freedom of choice, enabling individuals to give for the benefit of others, coupled with constraints preventing them from doing so on a basis that may discriminate on grounds of country, religion, gender, locality, etc., was to be valued in a democracy:[7]

> It was the explicit or implicit institutionalization of separateness, whether categorized in terms of income, class, race, colour or religion, rather than the recognition of the similarities between people and their needs which causes much of the world's suffering. By not doing something—by not giving donors a "right" to prescribe the group characteristics of recipients—the Service thus presumes an unspoken shared belief in the universality of need.

The gift was to be valued both for its own sake and because its demonstration of altruism would also encourage others to give themselves. The act of giving modeled ethical conduct, and generated a sense of shared morality and civic responsibility in more caring communities.

Titmuss acknowledged that the altruistic motive of the giver could, perhaps, be accompanied by a degree of self-interest. The fact of anonymity in the blood donation process removed the possibility of donors being motivated by the desire for social approval, although clearly this could be a factor in other forms of giving. The concern to help another, however, may, to a varying extent, be attributable to a desire to see that person lead an independent and useful life and relieve the giver of further concern for that person's welfare. Giving, of course, can also be more firmly motivated by personal gain or for the common good, as, for example, in the gift of medicines to prevent the spread of infectious disease. Whether utility or unalloyed altruism was the driving factor for a particular giver in relation to the equally particular gift and recipient was not a significant issue for Titmuss. The two factors were compatible, conducive to promoting socially responsible behavior and at risk of negation by the profit motive.

B. The Gift

The gift is twofold: from the donor and from the state. The first is uncontroversial: In a democracy, any persons of sound mind (subject to the rights of dependants) are free to give their property to whomsoever they choose; this can be by way of charity.

[7] Titmuss, *The Gift Relationship*, at p. 238. The author gratefully acknowledges observations made by Anne Robinson (Solicitor Director, Prolegis Lawyers, Sydney) on this matter.

The second, when the charity vehicle is used and the state adds considerably to the value of the gift by exempting it from tax, is hedged about with conditions that can give rise to controversy (see, further, below). To be charitable any such gift need not be restricted to the poor: The public utility of gifts and organizations that contribute to enhancing the public good through the building of bridges, harbors, etc., was recognized in the Preamble and in such early case law such as *Jones v. Williams*,[8] where a bequest to fund the supply of good spring water to the town of Chepstow was found to be a charitable gift. As Lord Camden LC then explained:

> definition of charity; a gift to a general public use, which extends to the poor as well as to the rich: many instances in the statute 43 Eliz carrying this idea, as for building bridges etc. The supplying of water is necessary as well as convenient for the poor and the rich.

Titmuss would still recognize the altruism that underpins modern charity and his defense of the right to give remains valid. However, although the parties to the gift relationship remain much the same, the nature of the gift itself has changed considerably, with such nontraditional or intangible gifts of capital assets, time, opportunity, and information now having gained in popularity in recent years.

1. Of Capital Assets

The traditional gift of funds and/or food and shelter still has its place in societies, and in many communities within developed nations, where real poverty persists. Increasingly, however, use is now made of assets with potential for achieving more long-term and sustainable improvement. The strategic value of a workshop, farm, or manufacturing plant can be an effective exit gift in situations where those who are to use it, and thereby secure their future independence, have received the necessary preparatory training, and appropriate support systems are in place. For example, in New Zealand the provision of a creamery to assist a small new rural community to become economically viable was found to be charitable.[9]

2. Of Time

A charitable gift may involve the giving of time as well as or instead of a gift of money or other forms of property. Volunteering lies at the heart of charitable activity. Indeed, the gift of personal skill, time, and energy for the benefit of others is now valued as being of greater charitable worth than the giving of funds. By engaging concerned individuals in ameliorating the disadvantages of others, charities generate a healthy, caring, and responsible sense of community. As a consequence it is

[8] (1767) ER 652.

[9] Re Tennant [1996] 2 NZLR 633.

often the policy of governments[10] to develop and support the contribution of volunteers in order to foster a sense of civic responsibility and promote the growth of social capital.[11]

3. Of Opportunity

The provision of such tangible forms of assistance as volunteered time and money is seldom sufficient to lift a person, family, or community from circumstances of dependency. Providing opportunities for the unemployed to acquire appropriate skills and training, followed by opportunities to enter the job market and receive the support necessary to sustain that achievement, has become a particularly important development in charitable activity. Similarly, creating the legal structures necessary for private business and government bodies to join in partnership with charities to establish enterprises that afford opportunities for individuals, groups, and communities to engage in mainstream social activity is now also recognized as strategically important, even if this does entail a mix of both charity and profit.

4. Of Information

Many large charities now run or fund very professional research departments that generate and disseminate authoritative data to identify, measure, and assess causal relationships between social need and effective resource deployment. The archives of such data, sometimes accumulated over many generations and available on both a jurisdiction-specific and on a global bases, equip charities to advise governments and lead the development of socially disadvantaged communities in a more informed manner than ever before. The responsibility that comes with information places a heavy onus on both charities and governments to give or intervene in ways that effect enduring change.

C. The Recipient

In a common law context, the categories of those from whom charitable requests may legitimately be received have long since been embedded in charity law. The *Pemsel* case,[12] together with such new categories as can fit within the "spirit and intendment" rule,[13] has served to identify charitable purposes, the bodies upon

[10] See, e.g., *Giving Time, Getting Involved—A Strategy Report by the Working Group on the Active Community* (the Warner Report), Home Office, London, 1999.

[11] See Puttnam, R., *Bowling Alone*, Simon and Schuster, New York, 2000.

[12] Income Tax Special Purposes Commissioners v. Pemsel [1891] AC 531.

[13] This rule refers to the common law practice of extending by analogy a recognition of charitable purpose to those activities that, although not enumerated in the Preamble to the Statute of Charitable Uses 1601, are judicially viewed as being so close to those listed that they can be construed as coming within the intention of that legislation.

which charitable status is to be conferred, and ultimately those entitled to charitable resources. In *Pemsel*, Macnaughten L.J. classified charitable purposes into four divisions or "heads": (1) to relieve poverty; (2) to advance education; (3) to advance religion; and (4) for "other purposes beneficial to the community not falling under any of the preceding heads." The *Pemsel* heads of charitable purposes, now statutorily enlarged and incorporated into the law of the U.K.[14] and Irish[15] jurisdictions, have considerably extended the list of possible charity recipients.

Traditionally, the position of the recipient in the gift relationship has been complicated. The gift, intended to meet a need, also provides a measure and social confirmation of inadequacy whereas its nature and the manner of giving are clearly matters that may ultimately affect its utility. For the recipient, to receive was to accept not just the benevolence of others, but to recognize that a failure to be self-sufficient had acquired a level of social exposure. The fact that the recipient recognized and was comforted by the inherent virtue of the giver (who may well have given anonymously) and valued and used the gift as intended, did not necessarily mean that the recipient thereby became better equipped to cope. For the recipient, the psychological dynamics of the gift relationship all too often served to confirm inadequacy and induce long-term compliant dependency.

Although this traditional approach, together with the compromised position of the recipient, continues to be the main vehicle for the gift relationship, it is now, to some degree, being gradually displaced by other more innovative models. Newly emerging hybrid partnerships, in which charity has a more discrete presence, where overtly commercial enterprises offer opportunities for the disadvantaged to engage in mainstream social activity without any connotations of failure are more acceptable and sustainable for contemporary recipients. To the extent that hybrids subordinate profit motive to mission, they would seem able to achieve some compatibility with charity.

D. The Charitable Organization

The infinite variety of nonprofit organizations together represents the collective moral strength of a sector that makes a nonexploitive contribution to society. A nonprofit organization may be similar, in many cases, to a charitable organization, but in law the two are distinct. Many nonprofits, for example, have objects and activities that are to benefit the community in which the members reside. Another group of nonprofits exist to provide programs and services that are to provide benefits to their members—chambers of commerce, trade organizations, cooperatives, golf clubs, and so forth are some examples of this group. Where the benefits are restricted by geography, by membership, by mutuality, and where they allow for "user" involvement in determining benefit distribution, then these organizations

[14] See: in England and Wales, the Charities Act 2011, s.3(1); in Scotland, the Charities and Trustees Investment Act (Scotland) 2005, s.7(2); in Northern Ireland, the Charities Act (Northern Ireland) 2008, s.2(2).

[15] Charities Act 2009, s.3(11).

cannot be charitable because they have accepted the interposing of a nexus that restricts the "public" dimension of the public benefit principle, thereby compromising the signature legal characteristic of charity. All nonprofits have one key element in common—they do not distribute any profits to their members.

Within that range of organizations, charities are distinctive because they cleave to the public benefit principle as their raison d'être and have the capacity to channel the value of donors' gifts to their intended purposes across many generations. The trust and specialized knowledge that charities build up in the process of mediating between giver and recipient places them in a crucially important strategic position between state and market, as broker on behalf of the socially disadvantaged, and vests them with the responsibility to work with both to reduce disadvantage. Their registration as such confirms the special status of charities as organizations dedicated to furthering the public benefit of the disadvantaged, and in the eyes of society confers upon them the stamp of virtue.

Free from the exigencies of government, and to some extent also from the competitive pressures of the commercial marketplace, unaccountable to shareholders or constituency and yet entrusted with funds from private donors and the public purse, the charitable organization bears the responsibility to promote the interests and publicly champion the cause of those it represents. In theory, the independence, resources, and knowledge of a charitable organization operating from within a centuries-old charitable sector of enormous wealth should enable it to have some impact on social disadvantage.

E. The State

From the state's perspective, endorsing the gift relationship affirms a value system that encourages altruism, reinforces a sense of obligation, stimulates social capital, provides a basis for community bonding, and builds a more ethical society. The state only stands to gain from a sector that generates a vibrant and diverse participative form of democracy; attracts the involvement of an army of volunteers; bolsters civic responsibility and thereby fosters the growth of social capital; strengthens the community's "moral tie";[16] and consolidates civil society.[17] In addition to being a catalyst

[16] See De Tocqueville, A., *Democracy in America*, trans. George Lawrence, New York, Harper Collins, 1988 [1835]:

> "Despotism may govern without faith, but liberty cannot. How is it possible that society should escape destruction if the moral tie is not strengthened in proportion as the political tie is relaxed?".

[17] See, e.g., Bothwell, J., "Indicators of a Healthy Civil Society", in Burbridge, J. (ed.), *Beyond Prince and Merchant: Citizen Participation and the Rise of Civil Society*, Institute of Cultural Affairs International, Brussels.

See also Turnour, M., "Modernising Charity Law: Steps to an Alternative Architecture for Common Law Charity Jurisprudence," in McGregor-Lowndes, M. and O'Halloran, K. (eds), *Modernising Charity Law: Recent Developments and Future Directions*, Elgar, Cheltenham, 2010.

for a more civil and morally based society, the encouragement of altruistic conduct also has the happy consequence of reducing state expenditure.

However, some of the criticism leveled by Titmuss against the influence of commerce on altruism applies equally to that exercised by the welfare state.[18] Both commerce and the welfare state inhibit individual acts of altruism, in the latter case because of the collective pact that taxes are paid and public service systems exist to address the needs of the socially disadvantaged. This results in the worth of an individual gift being devalued by the collective provision of the welfare state, which, in turn, may well have a correspondingly negative effect on moral values as a binding social influence.

Arguably, if charity is to find a credible role in modern society, one that sits respectably alongside social justice, human rights, and politics, this will have to involve the realignment of "need" and "gift" that form the twin core components of the gift relationship. This will require a reworking of that relationship to make room for the profit motive. In the purity of the Titmuss model lies its greatest limitation: It is too removed from the reality of mainstream social life; it fosters a separate approach—one that, however regrettable, is not representative of the social interactions of the majority in a modern democratic society. The "need" for today's disadvantaged is to belong and share in mainstream social life. The "gift" must be one that literally "buys them in." Commerce and charity have to work in tandem if the right doors are to be opened for the socially marginalized to be drawn into full participation in society. The idealistic Titmuss model of social exchange must make way for a profit component. It falls to charity law to balance the extent to which "profit" can be allowed to compromise "charity."

III. CHARITY AND CHARITY LAW

For the best part of four hundred years, both legislature and judiciary have chosen to ignore opportunities to define the precise legal meaning of "charity." For practical purposes, however, a "charity" may be understood as any organization that is established for and giving effect to charitable purposes, as defined by the Preamble to the Statute of Charitable Uses 1601[19] or subsequently found to be within its spirit and intendment, and as organized under the four *Pemsel* heads[20] or any statutory extension thereof; that is registered as such with the appropriate regulatory body, whether that be the tax collecting authority or a charity specific government agency; and that may be housed in a variety of different legal structures.

"Charity" is an activity undertaken by bodies that vary greatly in type, size, legal form, longevity, and in resources. Over the past four centuries, the concept of charity has with very little legislative interference continued to judicially evolve within the

[18] See, e.g., Bartholomew, J., *The Welfare State We're In*, Methuen, London, 2006.

[19] Also known as the Statute of Elizabeth; 43 Eliz 1, c 4.

[20] Income Tax Special Purposes Commissioners v. Pemsel [1891] AC 531.

common law tradition. During this time, charity law has taken root throughout the nations that formerly comprised the British Empire. Together these nations have contributed to building a body of jurisprudence that now, with varying emphases and subject to certain jurisdictional differences, constitutes charity law in the common law tradition. This is a history that has very largely been written by the judiciary in England and Wales as their rulings have with few exceptions been followed by their counterparts in all other common law countries. Although this leadership role has gradually weakened in recent years, it remains the case that the precedents set over the centuries by the decisions of the higher courts in that jurisdiction continue to underpin charity law in all others that share the same legal tradition, and new decisions are at least regularly cited, and most often are followed, in those same courts.

A. Origins of Charity

Charities predate the 1601 Act and have existed for at least the last millennium.[21] However, it is customary to date the emergence of charity's current social role to the dissolution of the monasteries by Henry VIII. This Act had several important consequences for charities. First, it had the immediate effect of removing the single most important source of housing, care, and education for the poor; the homeless and destitute were left to roam the towns in search of alms and shelter. Second, it ended the possibility of making grants of property to the Church in exchange for spiritual benefits. Third, it broke the Church's hold on charities, leading to the secularization of the objects of charity as the majority of English society "reflected less on their souls and became more concerned with the worldly needs of their fellow men."[22]

By the end of the 16th century much of the power, land, and monasteries had been stripped from the Catholic Church. The Elizabethan era began with the pressing need to both forestall further social unrest by filling the social care gap left by the dissolution of the monasteries and by soliciting the funds necessary to repair the damage caused by the ravages of war. The introduction in 1601 of a statute to "cure the widespread misappropriation of funds given to charitable uses and thus to mobilise the resources of private benefaction in the task of national rehabilitation"[23] marked the beginning of a new approach to charity and the birth of charity law as we now know it.

[21] See Picarda, H., *The Law and Practice Relating to Charities* (3rd ed.), Butterworths, London, 1999.

[22] See Jones, G., *History of the Law of Charity 1532–1827*, Wm. W. Gaunt & Sons, Holmes Beach, FL, 1986, at p. 10; see also Leonard, E. M., *The Early History of the English Poor Relief*, Cambridge University Press, Cambridge, 1900, at p. 9.

[23] See Brady, J., "The Law of Charity and Judicial Responsiveness to Changing Need," in *Northern Ireland Legal Quarterly*, Vol. 27, No. 3, 1976, at p. 199.

1. Legal

The law relating to charities is of ancient origin,[24] and its roots most likely lie in the *parens patriae*[25] responsibilities of the King of England that protected the interests of charities, wards, and lunatics. Although equity and the law of trusts undoubtedly formed the underpinning principles, it is to the Statute of Charitable Uses 1601 that the common law nations trace the origins of their charity law. Entitled "an act to redress the Mis-employment of lands, Goods, and Stocks of Money heretofore given to Charitable Uses," its intent—to specify matters regarded as charitable and to provide a regulatory system to prevent their abuse—was quite explicit. The Preamble sets out the following charitable purposes:[26]

> The relief of aged, impotent and poor people; the maintenance of sick and maimed soldiers and mariners, schools of learning, free schools and scholars of universities; the repair of bridges, havens, causeways, churches, sea banks and highways; the education and preferment of orphans; the relief, stock or maintenance of houses of correction; marriages of poor maids; supportation, aid and help of young tradesmen, handicraftsmen and persons decayed; the relief or redemption of prisoners or captives and the aid or ease of any poor inhabitants concerning payments of fifteens, setting out of soldiers, and other taxes.

These purposes were treated from the outset as being illustrative rather than definitive, though initial judicial uncertainty prevailed as to whether they could be construed disjunctively. The courts would not regard a purpose as charitable unless it could be defined as coming within "the spirit and intendment" of the Preamble. An element of public benefit was also crucial. A broadened interpretation of the purposes identified in the Preamble provided the basis for charity law throughout the common law world (see also chapter 3).

[24] See, e.g., Westlake, H. F., *The Parish Gilds of Mediaeval England*, London, Society for Promoting Christian Knowledge, 1919, where mention is made of "the gild of the Blessed Virgin Mary in the parish church of St Botolph at Boston founded in 1260 gave a yearly distribution of bread and herrings to the poor in alms for the souls of its benefactors"; cited in Brady, J. J., *Religion and the Law of Charities in Ireland*, W & S Magowan, Belfast, 1975, at p. 14.

[25] A parental jurisdiction inherently vested in the monarch, exercised by the Chancellor, delegated to the Court of Chancery and then administered by the High Court and the Attorney General. See Seymour, J., "Parens Patriae and Wardship Powers: Their Nature and Origins," *Oxford Journal of Legal Studies*, Vol. 14, No. 2, 1994.

[26] As noted in Tudor, O., *Charities* (9th ed.), Sweet & Maxwell, London, 2003, at 3, the wording of the Preamble closely resembles a passage in The vision of Piers Plowman.

2. Social

The driving forces for launching charity law in Elizabethan times were much the same as the factors that drove charity law reform four centuries later: social instability, concern that public finances could not meet the cost of burgeoning social need, and realization that something needed to be done to restore the confidence of the citizens in the state's capacity to ensure their care and protection. As has been pointed out, however, there are differences in the two social contexts:[27]

> The fear of general revolution in the days of the Preamble driving State intervention has been replaced by the loss of political power for public goods not delivered at the right cost to taxpayers. The changing shape of modern government has impacted on the boundaries of charity. The Preamble's list of schools, universities, hospitals, roads, bridges, jetties and prisons once provided by charity are now regularly provided by consortia in which big business and international financiers play a leading role; and charity plays little, if any, in many jurisdictions. This is particularly the case in the U.K. where government experimentation with public–private finance initiatives has brought the finances, skills, competitiveness, and profit motive of the business world to bear on areas of utility and service provision that were once the heartland of charity.

The fact that the role played by charity in such public benefit provision is neither as prominent nor as exclusive as previously does not, however, mean that charity's role as a service provider has necessarily diminished. The other main contextual difference is the current diversification in charitable activity, which includes services provided by charities that are often only tenuously related to their charitable purposes.[28] The single most obvious area of difference is the role now played by commerce in the provision of public benefit services that for so long had been the raison d'être of charity: Profit and charity have become much more closely intertwined than could have been foreseen by Titmuss.

IV. THE LEGAL HALLMARKS OF "CHARITY"

The core legal requirements for a charity to be recognized as such are that an entity must (1) be confined exclusively to charitable purposes, (2) be for the public benefit, (3) be independent, (4) be forbidden from distributing profits, and (5) be nonpolitical. There are some jurisdictional variations in the interpretation of these attributes, and donor intention can also be relevant, but throughout the common law world these have long been held to be the legal hallmarks of charity.

[27] See McGregor-Lowndes, M. and O'Halloran, K. (eds.), *Modernising Charity Law*, at p. 6.

[28] See Weisbrod, B. A. (ed.), *To Profit or Not to Profit: The Commercial Transformation of the Nonprofit Sector*, Cambridge University Press, Cambridge, 1998.

A. Charitable Intent

Judicial support for those who choose to donate private wealth for the public benefit has a considerable history, as the courts have long considered they were bound to give effect to a valid charitable gift in the terms as expressed by the donor. Sir John Romilly M.R. summarized the judicial approach in *Philpott v. St George's Hospital*:[29]

> If the testator has, by his will, pointed out clearly what he intends to be done, and his directions are not contrary to the law, this Court is bound to carry that intention into effect, and has no right, and is not at liberty to speculate upon whether it would have been more expedient or beneficial for the community that a different mode of application of the funds in charity should have occurred to the mind of the testator, or that he should have directed some different scheme for carrying his charitable intentions into effect. Accordingly instances of charities of the most useless description have come before the Court, but which it has considered itself bound to carry into effect.

Motive is important, but the presence or absence of charitable intent is not by itself determinative. In most common law jurisdictions (but not in Ireland),[30] the test judicially applied to ascertain a donor's intention is an objective one: the fact that a donor believed when making the gift that it was charitable will not prevent the courts from ruling otherwise, and vice versa, because "the court cannot inquire into the motives of the donor if the gift is in its nature a charity."[31] In all jurisdictions and in all cases, however, charitable intent is by itself insufficient: An altruistic motive will not transform a non-charitable purpose into a charitable one, and vice versa. No matter how charitable the donor's intention may be, this will not make charitable a gift that does not satisfy the other requirements of the common law definition of "charity," that has no intrinsic merit,[32] that breaches the law,[33] or that is contrary to public policy. Where the donor's intention is malicious, is charitable but the gift has no intrinsic merit,[34] or is given for non-charitable purposes or could possibly be so used, then again the gift would be deemed to be not charitable.[35]

[29] (1859) 27 Beav. 107 at 111.

[30] In Ireland the test is subjective (i.e., "if he intended to advance a charitable object recognized as such by the law, his gift will be a charitable gift"), as stated by Keane J. in Re the Worth Library [1994] 1 ILRM 161, at p. 193.

[31] See Hoare v. Osborne (1866) LR 1 Eq, 585 per Kindersley VC, at p. 588.

[32] Re Pinion [1965] Ch 85.

[33] See, e.g., National Anti-vivisection Society v. IRC [1948] A.C. 31.

[34] Re Pinion [1965] Ch 85.

[35] See, e.g., Anglo-Swedish Society v. Commissioners of Inland Revenue (1931) 16 T.C. 34.

B. Charitable Purposes

Charitable purposes were first identified and listed in the 1601 statute, subsequently classified in *Pemsel,*[36] and intermittently broadened by the judiciary applying the spirit and intendment rule.[37] Under the common law, the courts required that gifts be given exclusively for purposes recognized in law as charitable (as per *Pemsel* and related case law) and not be contrary to public policy or otherwise illegal.[38] The courts have readily acknowledged that the test of what may or may not be lawful will "vary from generation to generation as the law successively grows more tolerant."[39] Therefore, the fact that a purpose was previously judicially found to be non-charitable will not prevent it from becoming charitable in the future, and vice versa.[40] The common law approach to charitable purposes and its definition thereof, has, in some jurisdictions, been significantly affected by the outcomes of recent charity law reform processes (see part 2).

In practice, the fact and nature of a charitable purpose is most often determined by reference to the objects stated in the charity's relevant governing instrument (viz. declaration of trust, company memorandum, and articles or constitution). However, there have been occasions when the courts have considered it necessary and appropriate to take background information into account in order to determine the true purpose for which an organization was established.[41] Occasionally, for example, when the objects are not specified or are inadequately described, then in order to decide whether an organization's purposes were charitable and for the public benefit, the courts have examined the circumstances in which the organization

[36] Income Tax Special Purposes Commissioners v. Pemsel [1891] AC 531.

[37] As explained by Wilberforce L.J. in Scottish Burial Reform and Cremation Society v. Glasgow Corporation [1968] AC 138, [1967] 3 All ER 215:

> "For the purposes in question to be charitable, must be shown to be for the benefit of the public, or the community, in a sense or manner within the intendment of the Preamble to the statute, 43 Eliz. 1 c.4."

[38] See, e.g., National Anti-Vivisection Society v. IRC [1948] AC 31 and Re Pinion, [1965] Ch 85.

[39] See Lord Wright in National Anti-Vivisection Society v. Inland Revenue Commissioner, [1948] AC 31, at p. 42. In Re Foveaux [1895] 2 Ch 501 Chitty J. had considered that the abolition of vivisection was charitable because the intention was to benefit the community, and it was not for the court to examine whether or not the community would in fact derive any benefit. In coming to the opposite conclusion 50 years later in National Anti-Vivisection Society v. IRC, the House of Lords repudiated the Chitty J. approach, stating that the intention of the testator was not determinative of public benefit; this was for the court to decide.

[40] National Anti-Vivisection Society v. Inland Revenue Commissioner, [1948] AC 31.

[41] For example, Smith v. Kerr [1902] 1 Ch. 774 (Court of Appeal), Incorporated Council of Law Reporting v. Attorney-General [1972] Ch. 73 (Court of Appeal), McGovern v. Attorney-General [1982] Ch. 321 (Chancery Division) and Southwood v. Attorney-General [2000] WL 877698 (Court of Appeal (Civil Division)).

came into existence and the sphere in which it operated,[42] and whether[43] or not[44] the wording of the governing document was ambiguous. Moreover, in recent years there have been strong indications that in some jurisdictions the judiciary and/or charity regulators are becoming more willing to impose an "activities test" to clarify the actual purposes of a charity. The Charity Commission, for example, which regulates registered charities in England and Wales, has placed great emphasis in its various public benefit guidance documents on examination of a charity's activities, as opposed to its objects, when it comes to satisfying the public benefit requirement. The rationale for this approach was succinctly expressed by Gummow J. in the *Aid/Watch* case:[45] "It is one thing to have objectives. Another question is what you are actually doing"; or, as expressed by Kiefel J. during the course of the appeal hearing in the High Court, "Whether an organization has charitable purposes is determined by reference to the natural and probable consequences of its activities, as well as its stated purposes."[46]

C. The Public Benefit Principle

The voluntary redistribution of private wealth for public benefit underpins the history of charity. The moral and fiscal rationale for the state to exempt a charitable trust from certain tax and other financial impositions rests on the premise that a donor has chosen not to confer a private benefit upon a personally selected recipient, but instead to make an altruistic gift for the public good. Altruism has long and often been judicially upheld as the key component of charity, as expressed by MacDermott L.J:[47]

> There can be no doubt that unselfishness and benevolence are still the essence of legal charity...The principle...is that a valid charity must be substantially altruistic.

The public benefit test, a mandatory hurdle for a gift to attain charitable status, requires a real verifiable benefit to accrue to the public or to a significant section of it. This critical component, aided by the "spirit and intendment" rule, has proven to be an essential aspect of the common law regime. In the absence of legislative

[42] Incorporated Council of Law Reporting v. Attorney-General [1972] Ch. 73 (Court of Appeal), Sachs J., at p. 91.

[43] McGovern v. Attorney-General [1982] Ch. 321 (Chancery Division), Slade J., at p. 348.

[44] Southwood v. Attorney-General [2000] WL 877698 (Court of Appeal (Civil Division)), Chadwick L.J.

[45] Commissioner of Taxation v. Aid/Watch Incorporated [2009] FCAFC 128 (Sept. 2009).

[46] Commissioner of Taxation v. Aid/Watch Incorporated [2010] HCA 42 per Kiefel J., at para. 67.

[47] National Deposit Friendly Society Trustees v. Skegness UDC [1959] AC, 293, at p. 315. See also Re Cranston [1896] 1 IR 431 per Fitzgibbon L.J., at p. 446 and Waterson v. Hendon BC [1959] 1 WLR 985 per Salmon J., at p. 991.

initiative, it provided the only means whereby new interpretations of charitable purposes could be introduced to develop the concept of charity, enabling it to accommodate newly emerging and local manifestations of social need.

To be charitable, the gift must satisfy both arms of the "public benefit test": it must (1) confer an objectively verifiable "benefit," and (2) it must do so in favor of sufficient members of the "public." The test has been applied unevenly across the four *Pemsel* heads of charity,[48] falling most onerously upon the last category.

1. Public

Although it is certain that a gift conferred on a very limited number of identifiable people would be found to be private and therefore not charitable, it is less certain as to what number of persons or other criteria would be sufficient to satisfy a definition of "public" and justify charitable status. It will not be justified where the gift is to a closed class[49] (see chapter 2).

2. Benefit

Traditionally, the benefit was required to be one that was recognized as charitable within the *Pemsel* classification or could be found to be so on the grounds that it came within the "spirit and intendment" of the Preamble. For all but the small minority of common law nations that have now substituted a legislative regime for the common law approach, this continues to be the case (only some within that minority have extended the *Pemsel* heads of charitable purposes).

The issue of public benefit has been particularly contentious in relation to gifts made to, or for the use of, a closed contemplative religious order[50] or for the saying of a private mass.[51] Such gifts have been found not to be charitable because intercessory prayers and the example set by leading pious lives were viewed as being too vague in terms of their benefit to the public.[52] Although the courts in the U.K. and Canada have taken the view that the public benefit requirement for charitable status

[48] Generally presumed to be satisfied in respect of the first three heads but requiring proof in relation to the fourth.

[49] See Re Hobourn Aero Components Ltd's Air Raid Distress Fund [1946] Ch 194.

[50] See, e.g., the English case Cocks v. Manners [1871] 12 Eq 574, where a contemplative order of nuns was found to be not charitable, in contrast to the Irish case Maguire v. Attorney General [1943] I.R. 238, where a similar convent was held to be a "spiritual powerhouse" and a bequest to it was charitable.

[51] See, e.g., Kehoe v. Wilson (1880) 7 L.R. Ir. 10. See also Re Hetherington's Will Trusts [1990] Ch. 1, where it was held that the celebration of a religious rite in private does not contain the necessary element of public benefit.

[52] Gilmour v. Coates [1949] AC 426. See also Trustees of the Congregation of Poor Clares of the Immaculate Conception v. The Commissioner of Valuation [1971] NI 114 at 169 per Lowry L.J.:

> "an Order which has no other purpose other than to achieve its own santification by private prayer and contemplation is not an association with charitable objects."

is absent in such circumstances because private piety in a convent does not tend, directly or indirectly, to edify the public, the opposite view has prevailed in Ireland and Australia.

3. The Public Benefit Test

The essentially subjective quality of the public benefit test has allowed this crucial benchmark of charitable status to be applied in accordance with the eye of the judicial beholder. The result has been an accumulated baggage of disparate case law and doubtful precedent, leaving the test exposed to accusations that it is not always serving the best interests of Western society in the third millenium. For example, it has been argued that providing amenities for a privileged minority such as public school education, private hospital care, opera houses, and concert halls, etc., is a doubtful interpretation of public benefit. Similarly, organizations that reinforce sectoral differences by ensuring affiliation to a particular religion arguably also provide membership benefits only to specified groups and are thereby discriminatory, emphasizing social divisions and possibly reinforcing existing social inequity (see chapter 2). This approach, however, may be countered by a broad view argument that charitable status is an appropriate stamp of approval for the activities of organizations that enrich the texture, health, and general good of society, promoting diversity rather than stultifying it by protecting homogeneity.

D. Exclusively Charitable

Case law in the common law jurisdictions has long established that for a trust to be charitable, it must be confined exclusively to charitable purposes. The courts look for an exclusive charitable intent and have resolutely declined to save gifts as charitable where the donor had failed to unequivocally and unambiguously state such intent or had expressed mixed intentions, some charitable and some not. If a donor's gift included both charitable and non-charitable purposes, and allowed for the possibility of trustees to use at their discretion some or all of the gift for non-charitable purposes, then the courts would refuse to recognize it as charitable.[53] In *AG of the Cayman Islands v. Wahr—Hansen*,[54] for example, the Privy Council determined that a trust from which the income was to be paid to "any one or more religious charitable or educational institution or institutions operating for the public good," was in breach of the exclusivity rule and therefore void and not charitable. The term "public good" was considered to be wider than the public benefit test for charitable purposes and like "philanthropic" and "benevolent" could not therefore be construed as exclusively charitable.

[53] See, e.g., Boyle v. Boyle (1877) I.R. 11 Eq 433.

[54] [2000] 3 All E.R. 642.

E. Independent

Traditionally, under common law, a charity was required to be a freestanding, independent entity, founded by and bound to fulfill the terms of the donor's gift. The duty resting on trustees to honor the terms of their trust and ensure that the objects of the charity prevail has always been seen as the primary means whereby the integrity of the donor's gift could be protected.[55] Fulfilling this duty has required trustees to be resolutely committed to the charity's objects and free from any influence that may deflect from that focus, most clearly represented in the endowed foundation, which has, with its present and future funding secured, and its management legally required to pursue certain charitable objectives, the capacity to act independently. When, as is often the case with charities delivering public benefit services, they are managed by boards that include or are sometimes totally comprised of government appointees, their independence is inevitably compromised. Much the same dilemma arises when charities develop a commercial arm or enter into partnership arrangements with commercial enterprises.

F. Nongovernmental

Some charities are routinely contracted by government departments to deliver health and social services. Such charities are clearly vulnerable to pressure to become government agents in the delivery of a government agenda. When providing public benefit services, such bodies are constrained in their capacity to do so by their political masters and cannot act independently in marshalling resources to satisfy user-identified need.

G. Nonpolitical

The current restrictions on advocacy and political activity by charities are a relatively recent addition to the common law. In England during the Victorian era, many important initiatives resulting in policy changes by government were led by charities. The protests against the conditions suffered by children employed in factories or as chimney sweeps were led by charities such as Barnardo's and the NSPCC. However, it is now generally the case that charities must abide by certain constraints on political activity if they are to retain their charitable status. The crucial issue is whether an organization intends to pursue political activity as its principal objective, or whether it is merely pursued ancillary to and in support of a main objective which is not itself political; the former would definitely be incompatible with charitable status. Charities may

[55] The essence of a trust is that the appointed trustee should exercise good stewardship in respect of the assets entrusted to him or her. See, e.g., Hallows v. Lloyd (1888) 39 Ch.D. 686.

engage in limited campaigning for political change but only as an incidental means to achieving a genuine charitable end.[56]

When faced with a charity that is campaigning on policy issues arising from action or inaction by the government or Parliament, the judicial dilemma remains as stated by Simons L.J.: "it is not for the court to judge and the court has no means of judging."[57] Subsequently, the ruling of Slade J. in the seminal case of *McGovern v. Attorney General*,[58] also known as the *Amnesty International* case, has served to generally underpin the traditional common law approach to political activity by charities. This was approved and followed in Canada, Ireland, and other countries, though not expressly in Australia, and now presents a considerable roadblock for charities wishing to engage in public advocacy or political campaigning.

Essentially, the *Amnesty International* court and others have taken the view that matters of law and policy are for Parliament or government to determine: Any organization with a purpose of changing or supporting existing law or policy cannot be a charity as there is no way of establishing whether such activity would in fact be compatible with the public benefit test.[59] This approach is open to question, as it is not immediately obvious why a court should not be able to test the boundaries of law and policy. Arguably, the whole point of the common law was that the judiciary could and did interpret the law in accordance with contemporary social conditions. By so doing, for four centuries they allowed charity law to develop through established case law precedents without intervention from Parliament or government.

H. Nonprofit Distributing

A charity does not compromise its legal status by making a profit. In general, the common law rule is that charities may make profits (or gains) or accumulate surpluses, provided these are not used for the profit or gain of its individual members or for distribution to its owners or members, or to any other person, either while operating or upon winding up.[60] The recent emergence of social entrepreneurs in the field of charitable activity owes much to the available profit-making margins.

[56] See, e.g., Webb v. O'Doherty (1991), The Times, 11 February [1991] 3 Admin LR 731, when Hoffmann J. granted an injunction restraining the officers of a students' union, which was an educational charity, from making payments to a national campaign to Stop War in the Gulf, and stated:

> "There is . . . a clear distinction between the discussion of political matters, or the acquisition of information which may have a political content, and a campaign on a political issue. There is no doubt that campaigning, in the sense of seeking to influence public opinion on political matters, is not a charitable activity."

[57] Webb v. O'Doherty, at p. 62.

[58] [1982] 1 Ch 321.

[59] See, e.g., National Anti-Vivisection Society v. Inland Revenue [1948] AC 31.

[60] See, e.g., Midland Counties Institution of Engineers v. IRC (1928) 14 T.C. 285; General Nursing Council for England and Wales v. St Marylebone BC [1959] AC 540; and Incorporated Council of Law Reporting for England and Wales v. Attorney-General [1972] Ch 73.

However, any commercial venture must remain incidental and ancillary to the pursuit of the organization's overall charitable purpose. A crucial and well-established principle is that any profit gained must not accrue to the benefit of individuals but be directed toward the fulfillment of the charity's objects: There must be benefit for the community or a section of the community.[61]

V. LEGAL STRUCTURES FOR CHARITY

The legal structure for charitable activity has been heavily influenced by the common law legacy, which brought with it a reliance upon the trust as the preferred legal structure for charity and a corresponding regulatory emphasis on charitable purpose, thereafter reflected in charity law case precedents. This has been most evident in the U.K. and Irish jurisdictions and least apparent in the United States, whereas Australia, New Zealand, Canada, and other common law jurisdictions have retained some usage of the trust form but have switched at an early stage toward a preference for incorporated structures and have since further developed that commitment. Jurisdictions where the trust structure prevails also invariably have a statutory regulatory system for supervising all incorporated organizations. Parallel reporting requirements have thus been unavoidable for the many charities structured as companies. Issues as to the continued appropriateness of charities being variously constituted as unincorporated associations, companies, or as charitable trusts or foundations, and the complications involved in transferring from one to another, have arisen in many of the leading common law countries. Some of these have opted to introduce new statutory models specifically designated for charitable activity and designed to balance corporate form and trust principles; these are intended to displace traditional structures, accommodate social entrepreneurship, and assist partnership arrangements with government and commercial bodies (see chapter 2). Additionally, all have experimented with variations of the "public finance initiative" but perhaps none with as much enthusiasm as successive governments in England and Wales.

However, whether an organization is constituted as an unincorporated association, charitable trust, charitable company, foundation; as a friendly society or an industrial and provident society, or as one of the variety of new entrepreneurial and hybrid structures, it is equally entitled to recognition in law as a charity. Whether established for centuries or for only a few weeks, whether operating from a one-room office with part-time volunteers or from a multistory company building with hundreds of professional staff, whether servicing need in a local housing estate or across several continents, an organization may still be a charity. Nonetheless, it is an

[61] In Commissioners of Inland Revenue v. Oldham Training and Enterprise Council (1996) 69 T.C. 231, the Council provided various services to businesses, persons intending to set up businesses, and trainees. Its purposes were not wholly charitable because they extended to promoting the interests of individuals engaged in trade, commerce, or enterprise, and to providing benefits and services to them.

inescapable fact that many hybrids are now choosing to avoid charity registration as the price of submitting to the accompanying common law and statutory constraints is too high; they are still able to survive and thrive even while foregoing the benefits of that long-favored status.

A. Traditional Structures for Charity

In England and Wales (unlike the United States, Canada, and Australia), the legal structures mainly relied upon for charity have been the charitable trust and the unincorporated association, which have brought an emphasis on protecting the integrity of charitable purposes and policing eligibility for charitable status rather than on formal governance arrangements and requirements for accountability, transparency, and reporting. This reliance has not proved conducive to promoting the growth of charities in the modern world, as the trust or foundation is not an attractive structure for social entrepreneurs. Charitable companies, long favored as the preferred structure in the United States and elsewhere, have also been present in the U.K. and Ireland, but in recent years have become more prevalent. However, regardless of whether it is constituted as a trust or as an incorporated entity, a charity remains quite legally distinct from other nonprofit but mutual-benefit organizations such as co-operatives, friendly societies, and industrial and provident societies.

Drawing a line between entities that are charitable and organized for public benefit, as opposed to those organized for mutual benefit, has proved difficult. Legal issues tend to arise in circumstances where an entity is ostensibly dedicated to the charitable purpose of promoting commerce, but its modus operandi is in fact closer to that of a trade organization. Determining the balance struck between the proportion of benefit flowing to the public as a consequence of innovation and entrepreneurial flair brought to a commercial enterprise, and the proportion that actually adheres to the members themselves, is a challenge that has often exercised the judiciary and regulators.[62]

It is well established that the "public" component of the test will not be met where the gift is solely for member benefit, which necessarily limits beneficiaries to those comprising a personal nexus, meaning the gift is therefore insufficiently "public,"[63] a restriction which can compromise the status of self-help groups or localized community development projects.[64]

[62] See, e.g., Re Dutton (1878) 4 Ex D 54; IRC v. Yorkshire Agricultural Society]1928] 1 KB 611; Fairtrade Foundation (1994) 4 Decisions 1; the Concrete Society Ltd [1976] Ch Com Rep 16 (paras. 50–53).

[63] See, e.g., Oppenheim v. Tobacco Securities Trust Co Ltd [1951] AC 297 (HL).

[64] See Re Hobourn Aero Components Ltd's Air Raid Distress Fund [1946] Ch 194.

1. Unincorporated Association

Defined as "an association of persons bound together by identifiable rules and having an identifiable membership,"[65] an unincorporated association is not a legal entity and has no separate existence in law. It is not the aggregate of its members—it is merely a collection of individuals. Very often charities commence as unincorporated associations, and many small or local organizations remain as such; others incorporate as they grow in organizational complexity. No formalities are required to create an unincorporated association. They are formed by and depend upon the contractual relationships established between members.

2. Charitable Trust

A charitable trust is a public trust, made with a charitable intention, to give effect to purposes designated in common law or by statute as charitable purposes, and which purposes satisfy the public benefit test. Its governing instrument is a deed of trust.

Establishing a properly constituted charitable trust requires adherence to the same requirements common to all trusts in a particular jurisdiction, and the legislation governing the technical requirements for creating trusts in general has an equal application to charitable trusts. What distinguishes the setting up of such trusts from other legal forms is the relative speed, simplicity, and lack of cost involved. However, the requirements regarding the substance of the trust have a distinctive application when charities are concerned. For a trust to be properly constituted as a charitable trust, the law requires it to satisfy the "three certainties test":[66]

a. Certainty of Subject Matter

The trust property must be clearly identified, as must the entitlements of the beneficiaries in that property. The obligation to identify with some precision the exact property that a donor intends to give to charity can pose problems. This can often be the case with testamentary dispositions of residual property to religious or charitable causes.

b. Certainty of Intention

It must be clear that the donor intended for the property to be received by the trustee, that the property is to be held in trust, and that this was to be a binding obligation. The language used must be imperative and without ambiguity.

[65] See Re Koeppler's Will Trusts [1984] Ch. 243, [1984] 2 All E.R. 111. See also Conservative and Unionist Central Office v. Burrell [1982] 1 W.L.R. 522 per Lawton L.J., at p. 525.

[66] It was Lord Langdale MR in Knight v. Knight (1840), 3 Beav 148 who outlined the three certainties test.

c. Certainty of Objects

The beneficiaries or purposes for which the trust property is held must be clearly identified. In ordinary trust law, the beneficiaries must have a legal personality; they can be natural persons or corporations, but in the case of a charitable trust this requirement is relaxed. As Viscount Simonds explained:[67]

> a gift can be made to persons (including a corporation) but it cannot be made to a purpose or object; so also a trust may be created for the benefit of persons as *cestuis que trust* but not for a purpose or object unless the purpose or object be charitable. For a purpose or object cannot sue but, if it be charitable, the Attorney-General can sue to enforce it.

3. Foundations

The term "foundation" most commonly refers to a body established by an initial endowment that may or may not be dedicated to charitable purposes. A charitable foundation acquires a legal personality upon incorporation, although the charitable purpose to which the endowment is addressed will always remain as stated by the founder in the governing instrument. Commercial companies, particularly in the U.K., are beginning to appreciate the advantages of the foundation model and are creating charitable foundations to assist their strategic corporate responsibility programs.

There are a number of variations on this theme, including foundations based in local communities or particular religious groupings, or distinguished by their funding source such as livery companies, appeal trusts, or public subscription trusts, etc. In recent years a particularly interesting variant has emerged: the endowed charitable foundation established by a wealthy private individual dedicated to pursuing its own program of intervention in respect of a specific area of social need (e.g., the Bill & Melinda Gates Foundation, and AIDS in Africa). Again, there is the corporate foundation, also known as a company-sponsored foundation, which is a private foundation that receives its primary funding from a profit-making business.

a. Endowed Foundations

This type of charitable organization is a grant-making institution that does not itself conduct direct charitable activity. It is typically established by a single individual or family, and receives more than two-thirds of its support from its founders or from investment income earned by an endowment. Traditionally established by a successful business, it has most often served as a grant-making body providing financial assistance to projects that come within its designated purposes (e.g., the

[67] Leahy v. Attorney General for New South Wales [1959] AC 457.

Ford, Nuffield, Carnegie, and Rockefeller Foundations). The endowed foundation, when established within the boundaries of charity law, is a powerful member of the charity family. Even when not established as a charity—and many donors choose not to accept the limitations of this legal structure (e.g., because of the constraints regarding political activity)— it is still a powerful institution. But it is not a typical charitable trust.

With its financial base secured by an endowment, such a foundation is uniquely free from the fundraising concerns that drive the management of other charities. This gives these foundations an independence and capacity for strategic long-term intervention that often attracts pioneering social entrepreneurs. Although essentially a private trust, the endowed foundation has always attracted particular regulatory attention because of its potential to accumulate considerable asset reserves, the resulting removal of any need to solicit the goodwill and funds of government or the general public, and its capacity to thereby acquire a great deal of independence. Charities that accrue wealth through donor endowment tend to be viewed by regulators as susceptible to donor control, and are thus invariably subject to more rigorous statutory controls regarding governance, accounting, and reporting arrangements, while also forced to comply with mandatory requirements for a high level of annual income dispersal. This legal structure is most commonly found in the United States.[68]

b. Community Foundations

This type of charitable trust, used to support local community causes, was first established in the United States in 1914, emerged in the U.K. in the 1980s, and has since become widespread in over 35 countries. As Anheier and Leat explain,[69] "community foundations are rooted in, and emphasise, building local communities; they encourage and provide vehicles for corporate giving; they are governed locally; they encourage citizen-donor involvement and "democratise" giving by enabling smaller donors to create what are, in effect, their own mini-foundations (i.e., donor-advised funds) within an established infrastructure; and they seek to work with rather than apart from local government and businesses."

[68] In 1999, there were over 50,000 foundations in the United States with a total of $448 billion in assets. When the federal government launched its War on Poverty, foundations' assets were then valued at less than $30 billion. The Bill & Melinda Gates Foundation, which started in 1999 with $21 billion, is now the biggest U.S. foundation. John Walters, publisher of *Philanthropy Magazine*, estimates that foundation assets alone may easily grow to between $4 trillion and $5.9 trillion by 2035. See further John Waters, "Come the Revolution? Will Philanthropy Live up to Its Potential?" *Philanthropy* (July/August 1999), http://www.philanthropyroundtable.org/topic/excellence_in_philanthropy/come_the_revolution.

[69] Anheier, H. and Leat, D., *Creative Philanthropy: Toward a New Philanthropy for the 21st Century*, London, Routledge, 2005, at p. 149.

B. Incorporated Structures

A company is a body that is registered as such and whose memorandum of association and articles of association are lodged with the companies' regulator. It is a separate legal entity with an existence independent from that of its members. Many unincorporated associations, as they grow in size and organizational complexity, make the transition to company status. This is usually prompted by the need to avail of the protection afforded by the corporation's limited liability, and also because certain grants are only available to incorporated organizations. Religious organizations are also often established as corporations. In the United States, religious corporations have a long history; they have charitable status and are exempted from the public benefit test as are their activities and gifts to them. This is also the case in Ireland, Canada, and Australia, whereas in the U.K. they have traditionally been exempted[70] from the normal regulatory requirements imposed by the Charity Commission.[71]

A charitable company is one whose objects, as stated in its constitutive documents, are exclusively charitable. Of the three main types of company—companies limited by shares, companies limited by guarantee, and unlimited companies—charities generally incorporate as a company limited by guarantee.

1. Company Limited by Guarantee

Such companies may or may not have share capital, and each member gains a stake in the company by means of guaranteeing a set sum of money to the company. This sum is fixed, so there is no possibility of profit by the members by means of selling their stake. The maximum liability of the members is the amount of their guarantee. This is the preferred structure because it grants limited liability and therefore restricts the liability exposure of its members, and yet also restricts the possibilities for trading ownership of the company by selling shares.

The capacity of a charitable company is limited in the sense that its powers are restricted to those required to give effect to its charitable purposes. Strictly speaking, it is legally bound to use its powers within the parameters set by its objects as stated in its constitution; it may only operate outside those parameters if it is reasonably necessary to do so in pursuance of matters ancillary to its objects. Directors act as the agents of the company; they are subject to its control as exercised through annual general meetings and are unable to act with full discretion. Actions taken that fall outside such limited capacity would be ultra vires of the company's authority and may be challenged by injunction. The company itself could deny liability for the consequences whereas its directors could be held directly and personally liable.

[70] See the Charities Act 1993, Schedule 2.

[71] This will change when provisions introduced by the Charities Act 2006 take effect.

2. Specialized Charitable Companies

In recent years some jurisdictions, such as the U.K. and Ireland, have introduced new legal structures designed exclusively for charities and intended to make available all the advantages of incorporation while removing the necessity for duplicate regulatory accountability (e.g., the charitable incorporated organization; see chapter 5). Importantly, the direction of market-induced innovation has not always been set by a charity seeking to adapt itself to opportunities presented by commerce. In a reverse dynamic, there is a developing trend of large-scale commercial companies opting to establish charitable foundations, funded and staffed from their profits. This evidence of commercial corporations acting to further a social responsibility agenda highlights the need for new legal structures to facilitate the operations of charity and commerce in the area of public benefit provision where, increasingly, the interests of both are converging.

C. Marrying Public and Private: New Models for Cross-Sector Trading

Charity law provides an intriguing framework for holding in balance the private interests of a donor to exercise his or her discretionary right to make a gift to a chosen charitable purpose, on one hand, and on the other the public interest in ensuring that the value of the gift is protected and vests in the rightful beneficiaries without private benefit, reward, or profit accruing to others. This is encapsulated in the concepts of "charitable trust" and "charitable purpose" which lie at the heart of charity law and have always served as markers on the line separating charity from other forms of transaction. Their capacity to continue doing so, however, has become increasing threatened in recent years by the challenge of new models for financing public goods, which are designed to mix public and private interests and allow for an element of private benefit. Charity has been severely challenged by these innovations. Arguably its traditional legal hallmarks have not always succeeded in insulating it, and concessions have been made in response to contemporary marketplace pressures.

1. Public Finance Initiatives (PFI)

Essentially, PFI is a procurement method for giving effect to a public/private partnership by securing private funding for the construction and maintenance of public infrastructure in return for part-privatization. Ostensibly, it transfers risks and responsibility, but not accountability, for the delivery of public services to private companies, and provides much-needed public facilities in the short-term at a cost deferred by a schedule of long-term repayments. The initial finance for projects is provided by the private sector, which then leases the facilities back to the public sector, typically for up to 30 years. In addition, the contract often designates the private sector as the service provider in the new facility. The repayment schedule is "locked in," and its critics claim that ultimately it can prove to be an inflexible and inordinately expensive method of financing any such facility.[72] Given that it deals with public benefit facilities, the use of PFI is open to political abuse by a government wishing to gain credit with the electorate for providing such goods while passing on the bulk of their cost to beyond the government's likely term of office. Undoubtedly the fact that PFI contracts are generally kept "off the balance sheet," meaning that they do not show up as part of the public debt, can also be an attraction for government.

The private finance initiative was developed in Australia in the late 1980s, when it was applied to toll road and railway projects, and first adopted in England and Wales by the conservative government in 1992 (see chapter 5). It has since become a preferred government option (although with variable interpretation) in a number of countries, including the common law jurisdictions of Ireland, Canada, and the United States.

The implications of PFI for charity may not be immediately apparent, as the primary parties involved are government and for-profit companies. However, as the middle ground between "public" and "private" enterprises becomes muddied by the emergence of new bodies and consortiums designed to balance the interests of both, charities are being drawn into projects that have a PFI component. In England and Wales, this has occurred in relation to the many housing, hospital, and leisure trusts with charitable status. Such involvement does present risks for charity in respect of the possibility of jeopardizing its independence and even its assets.

2. Hybrid Legal Structures

Housing for charitable activity is not confined to charitable trusts, companies, unincorporated associations, and foundations: Charities may also assume, or be subsumed into, other legal structures. The middle ground between charity and commerce is increasingly spawning new entities such as social enterprises designed to pursue both social mission and profit and thereby link the two sectors (see chapter 2).

D. Legal Structures: Trust Principles and Company Requirements

Centuries ago, the Courts of Equity had taken the view that the "gift" at the heart of the gift relationship could be best secured by a combination of trust principles, the fiduciary duties and moral obligations of the trustees (as reinforced by the *parens*

[72] See, e.g., Monbiot, G., *Captive State—The Corporate Takeover of Britain*, Macmillan, London, 2000.

patriae jurisdiction of the Attorney General),[73] and ultimately by the powers of the High Court. In particular, the protection of a charity in trust form was seen as best assured by being placed in the hands of a board of independent and unpaid trustees. With the assumption that trust law would always be available to secure the donor's gift, regulatory attention shifted instead to the purpose for which the donee used the gift. In due course, as all common law jurisdictions acquired the trust as a legal structure for charities, though some to a much lesser extent than others, those jurisdictions also adopted a regulatory focus on purpose. The weight of case law, largely emanating from the English courts, clearly reveals the extent to which the body of charity law jurisprudence, shared among all the common law nations, grew and solidified around issues relating to charitable purposes.

In many jurisdictions, however, the trust was only ever nominally present, and in all it is gradually being displaced in favor of incorporated entities. The case law, being largely derived from trust issues, was consequently never very representative of charity law as experienced in the United States and other jurisdictions where companies rather than trusts have always provided the predominant legal structure for charitable activity. This is reflected in the virtual absence of any significant contribution from the U.S. judiciary to charity law jurisprudence. It was not that charity issues did not arise in this most litigious of common law nations, but rather that charity was very largely treated as just another species of nonprofit, and issues were mainly addressed on an administrative rather than on a judicial basis, either within a company law framework by the companies regulator or within a tax framework by the IRS. Legal structure determined type of arbiter and regulator, with a consequent sharp division between those common law nations (primarily the U.K.), which dealt with charity issues from a perspective conditioned by trust principles and definitional matters, and those (primarily the United States) that did so within company law and tax frameworks; a division present within as well as between jurisdictions. This fairly fundamental bifurcation, the nonalignment of trust principles and corporate regulation, continues to obstruct efforts to formulate a coherent policy for charity and the nonprofit sector as a whole, particularly in the ways that the law relates to charity in the common law world.

1. Regulating Charity: The Common Law Complications

In England and Wales the dominance of the trust form, together with the size and wealth of the charitable sector and the significance of its contribution to social

[73] The powers of *parens patriae* are best understood as the paternal rights and duties of the monarch in respect of those of his subjects who, being without legal capacity and therefore unable to defend their interests, had a right to his protection. This jurisdiction, as exercised by the Lord Chancellor on behalf of the Crown, came to be administered by the Court of Chancery and was used to determine issues relating to trusts, charitable and otherwise, long before the introduction of the 1601 Act. See further, Seymour, J., "Parens Patriae and Wardship Powers: Their Nature and Origins," *Oxford Journal of Legal Studies*, Vol. 14, No. 2, 1994, at pp. 159–88.

infrastructure, resulted in lead regulatory responsibility being assigned to a charity-specific body. Over a period of a century and a half, the Charity Commission[74] operated a regulatory regime for charities that primarily policed the interpretation of trust objects to ensure conformity with charitable purpose, advised and supervised trustees in their management of trust property, and used cy pres in a flexible manner to transfer assets and change purposes. This was largely a supportive regime that aimed to maximize the appropriate and effective use of charity assets while safeguarding the rights of beneficiaries. It had no particular brief for charity involvement in commerce, other than to ensure that trustees did not take risks that could jeopardize charity assets and beneficiary entitlement, and, until relatively recently, matters relating to earned income would have been the responsibility of the Revenue. Indeed, the trust form itself militated against any such involvement. Where the trust prevailed, so too did the attendant problems: ensuring limited liability for trustees while also equipping the charity to enter into contractual relations with third parties, and ensuring modern management models were available and the reciprocal rights and duties of directors and staff properly addressed. Reliance upon the responsibilities of trustees proved to be an insufficient basis for ensuring that standards of good governance, transparency, and accountability were maintained.[75]

In the United States, Canada, and Australia where there was never the same commitment as in England and Wales to trusts as the preferred legal structure, incorporation was always viewed as a more secure basis for charitable activity, and an early reliance upon the charitable corporation became a distinctive feature in the development of their charity law. In the United States, corporations for charitable purposes flourished to become the dominant legal form[76] and grew to become the most common legal vehicle for charitable activities; this also occurred in Canada, Singapore, and Australia. In those jurisdictions, the Revenue was the lead regulatory agency. As its focus was on income, with no particular brief for charitable purposes other than as a threshold for tax exemption, it provided a regulatory regime conducive to dealing with earned income that accommodated the commercial ventures of all types of entities.

In short, the jurisdictional differences between the trust led U.K. regulatory regime for charities and its corporate- and tax-led counterpart in the United States (shared if to a lesser extent with other common law jurisdictions) carried significant

[74] Following the success of the Brougham Inquiry 1819–1837, the government in England passed the Charitable Trusts Act 1853, amended in 1855 and 1860, to establish a permanent Charity Commission to supervise charitable activity.

[75] See Brakman R. D., "For Profit Philanthropy," 77 *Fordham Law Review* 2437, 2472, 2009; and Sugin, L., "The Increasing Resemblance of Nonprofit and Business Organizations Law: Resisting the Corporatization of Nonprofit Governance: Transforming Obedience into Fidelity," 76 *Fordham Law Review* 893, 2007.

[76] See Fishman, J. J., "The Development of Nonprofit Corporation Law and an Agenda for Reform," *Emory Law Journal*, Vol. 34, 1985, at pp. 619–83, 631.

implications for the future involvement of charity in commerce. When, at the turn of the century, that involvement began to escalate—as governments in all developed nations scaled back on grant-aiding charities and on public service provision, contracted with charities to bear a greater share of responsibility for such provision, and fund-raising revenue streams to charity dried up—so too did the problems escalate arising from jurisdictional differences in the regulatory regimes.

VI. CONCLUSION

Within the common law tradition, the basic conceptual and legal foundations of charity can be traced back to at least the 16th century, and indeed some existing charitable trusts long predate 1601 (the oldest being, it is claimed, King's School, Canterbury founded in 587). The many rules and principles applied by the judiciary over the centuries, since initially defined by the Preamble and the decision in *Pemsel,* have contributed to the present body of judicial precedents that has grown to form charity law in the nations of the common law world. Of all these concepts and constraints none is more important than the principle that charity must be for the "public benefit": This lies at the heart of the legal definition of "charity," and it has strong associations with altruism.

The Titmuss theory of "the gift relationship," anchored on the idea of "altruism," does much to explain the social transaction that constitutes an act of charity. He may well have been right to conclude that this relationship encapsulates significant jurisdictional differences in the approach of the U.K. and the United States to charitable activity, but it is not the only measure of such difference, and these are not confined to those jurisdictions. The exploration of jurisdictional differences in the role played by altruism in contemporary charity law, an important theme of this book, is not as amenable to study as when Titmuss formulated his theory. It now seems a good deal more difficult to be certain of the parameters of "public benefit" and to be confident of the circumstances in which public benefit and private interest are in conflict. In all jurisdictions studied, the mutual interests of government and charity in public benefit service provision are being recalibrated as government, and the nonprofit sector and business adjust their respective boundaries. The chapters that follow are intended to identify and analyze the many different ways in which jurisdictions make room for altruism as they apply the law, tweak the tax system, and revise the regulatory framework in relation to charity.

2

TRADING AND PROFIT

I. INTRODUCTION

Initially interpreted, for charitable purposes, in terms of the redemption of one's soul in the next life, "profit" is now defined in terms of the distribution of surplus in this one. The focus in this chapter is on how, in the competitive marketplace characteristic of modern society, "profit" fits alongside the ethos of "charity." It begins by considering the traditional and overriding duty of the trustee to protect and preserve trust assets, and includes references to the case law that illustrates the importance long attached to this duty. Any prospective trading venture can only be undertaken subject to this fundamental common law constraint. It then traces the unfolding relationship between charity law and trading law: the governing principles; the presumption of public benefit in services for purposes that relieve poverty, or advance education or religion; and the types of services and forms of trading. It examines the role of a charity as a competing entity in the marketplace: the rules relating to profit, the ancillary and incidental rule, and the constraints on private benefit; and the reality of competition. It also analyzes the law relating to "unfair" competition. It reflects on the crunch issue for modern charity law: the extent to which it may accommodate restrictions on access to charity services that favor those who can pay.

The chapter then outlines the types of commercial activity pursued for charitable purposes and the range of organizational forms and their related tax liability, giving particular attention to subsidiary trading companies. It concludes by examining the law relating to overseas charitable trading and the fraught issues associated with international aid and trade.

II. THE DUTY TO PRESERVE CHARITY ASSETS, MISSION, AND INDEPENDENCE

A charitable trust may continue in perpetuity[1] and with it will continue the role of trustees, although individual trustees will change. Their duties are of crucial importance if the assets, mission, and independence of the trust are to be preserved for the benefit of the beneficiaries intended by the donor. It is, therefore, not surprising that a core principle, forged by the judiciary in the Courts of Chancery and subsequently given effect in charity law,[2] has been that the assets and intentions of a donor entrusted to others for charitable purposes must not be abused. Any action that places a donor's gift at risk has traditionally provided grounds for intervention by the Attorney General. It is an approach with direct contemporary relevance for charities engaged in trading.

The charitable trust, traditionally the preferred legal structure for charity in England and Wales, as in Ireland, is now giving way to the corporate forms long preferred in the United States, Australia, and other common law countries. This is being accompanied by a corresponding switch in the emphasis of regulatory attention from the role of trustees to that of corporate boards as guardians of good governance. However, as many of the older established charities (which are often also the wealthier and more powerful) commenced as and have chosen to remain charitable trusts, the role of trustees and the capacity of charity law to ensure their proper supervision will continue to be important.

A. Charity Assets

The essence of a trust is that the appointed trustee should exercise good stewardship in respect of the funds or other assets entrusted to him or her. This requires, in the first instance, that the trustee gather in and account for all trust property, inspect all relevant documents (ensuring that they are in order),[3] and ascertain whether the trust property is subject to any form of liability.[4] The trustee must conserve and manage the property in such a way as to promote the best interests of the intended beneficiaries.

Two broad principles govern all trustee duties. In executing the terms of the trust, the trustee is required to demonstrate both loyalty to the objects as set out in the governing instrument and impartiality when negotiating between the interests of trust beneficiaries. A trustee has little scope for discretion; he or she is bound by the donor's directions. Insofar as the directions are realizable, they must be followed to

[1] See, e.g., the Bridge House Trust initiated in 1097, which currently makes grants of £15 million a year to charitable projects benefiting the inhabitants of Greater London. Renamed the City Bridge Trust in 2007, the City of London Corporation is its sole trustee.

[2] And also embodied in the Trustee Act 1893.

[3] Macnamara v. Carey [1867] I.R. 1 Eq 9.

[4] See, e.g., Hallows v. Lloyd (1888) 39 Ch D 686.

the letter.[5] Instances where the actions of trustees have failed to meet this standard include: the substitution of a more practical site for a hospital instead of the location specified by the donor;[6] the broadening of a donor's gift of a chapel to a school to permit the conferring of revenues upon villagers who were accustomed to the use of the chapel;[7] and the destruction of a church, the maintenance for which the donor had left funds.[8] Where the trustee is given discretion, this must be exercised fairly.[9] When a discretionary decision is taken jointly by a majority of trustees, this will be binding on the remainder.[10]

1. To Manage Trust Assets

Trustees have a duty to manage trust funds so as to minimize risk exposure and ensure an equitable distribution of proceeds among all beneficiaries. When a fund is intended to subsist for future generations of beneficiaries, this will entail taking such measures as may be necessary to avoid first-generation beneficiaries benefiting at the expense of those with a future entitlement. The duty of a trustee to give effect to the purposes for which the trust was established can sometimes conflict with the more pressing obligation to be prudent in the management of trust assets.

a. Investments

The obligations of a trustee may entail investing or reinvesting trust funds and, when doing so, there is an onus to exercise due care. When the investing trustee is acting in relation to charitable funds, then, arguably, the law will require a higher standard of care than would be expected from the private management of personal funds. In the words of Lindley L.J.:[11]

> The duty of the trustee is not to take such care only as a prudent man would take if he had only himself to consider: the duty rather is to take such care as an ordinary prudent man would take if he were minded to make an investment for the benefit of other people for whom he felt morally bound to provide.

However, trustees can sometimes be faced with a difficult balancing act. On the one hand, they must approach investment options objectively, making decisions that are

[5] See Robertson v. Robertson's Executors 1914 AD 503, which reaffirms the Roman law principle that a testator's last wishes, as recorded in a will, must be carried out—*voluntas testatoris servanda est.*

[6] Re Weir Hospital [1910] 2 Ch. 124.

[7] Attorney-General v. Earl of Mansfield (1827) 2 Russ 501.

[8] Ex parte Greenhouse (1815) 1 Madd 92; on appeal sub-non Ludlow Corp. v. Greenhouse (1827) 1 Bligh nS 17.

[9] Re Beloved Wilkes Charity (1851) 20 L.J. Ch. 588.

[10] Re Whiteley [1910] 1 Ch. 600, 608.

[11] See Learoyd v. Whitely (1886) 33 Ch D 347, at p. 355.

most likely to safeguard and increase trust assets. On the other hand, they and the trust are established to further purposes designated by the donor in the originating trust instrument. In juggling these priorities the trustee is required to be guided by the best interests of the beneficiaries, rather than personal bias.[12] This tension was illustrated in *Harries v. Church Commissioners*,[13] where it was alleged that the commissioners were more concerned with managing their investment portfolio than furthering the purposes of the charitable trust. The plaintiffs argued that investment decisions which did not accord with the central purpose of promoting the Christian faith should not be pursued. The court disagreed, with Nicholls V.C. explaining that trustees:[14]

> must not use property held by them for investment purposes as a means for making moral statements at the expense of the charity of which they are trustees.

Where loss is incurred, not because of poor judgment or bad luck, but as a result of decisions taken by trustees acting outside the scope of their authority, then they will be liable to make good the loss to the trust property. They will not escape personal liability by claiming to have relied upon expert advice, where that advice is wrongheaded and perverse.[15]

2. To Apply Trust Assets for the Benefit of Beneficiaries

In addition to prudent stewardship of trust assets, the trustee must also make appropriate arrangements to distribute those assets (and/or the related income) to the intended beneficiaries. Where a foundation has been established by donor endowment, then the obligation is to preserve the value of the capital entrusted to the foundation. It is the income from investing the capital that is available for distribution; in some jurisdictions, problems can arise when a foundation seeks to "grow" its capital rather than distribute the income. This distribution must be both in keeping with the donor's intentions and in accordance with the law: A failure on either count will amount to a breach of trust. There is a long-standing general rule that a person holding a fiduciary office must not acquire or seek to acquire any personal gain or advantage in the course of executing the responsibilities of that office. As Lord O'Hagan stated in *Armstrong v. Armstrong*:[16]

> I think it is plain that a trustee, so making a commodity of his position, and gaining a profit which but for it he would not have secured, must be held, on general

[12] See, e.g., Cowan v. Scargill [1985] Ch. 270. See also Buttle v. Saunders [1950]. 2 All E.R. 193 where it was stated that trustees: "have an overriding duty to obtain the best price which they can for their beneficiaries" per Wynn-Parry J.

[13] [1992] 1 W.L.R. 1241.

[14] Harries v. Church Commissioners [1992] 1 W.L.R. 1241, at p. 1247.

[15] *See* Re Beddoe [1892] 1 Ch. 547 per Bowen L.J., at p. 562.

[16] (1880) 7 LR Ir 207, at p. 218.

> principles and for the safety of *cestius que trusts*, to retain that profit for the benefit of the trust estate.

This is an approach supported by Sullivan M.R. in *Attorney-General v. Kelly*:[17]

> This Court seeks to aid a testator's wishes, not to control them. It is a different thing to oust the control of this Court over charities; where the testator vests in his friend a sum of money to administer to pious uses, this Court never dreams of controlling this man in the administration of the fund, so long as it is within pious uses; but if the trustee puts it in his pocket the Court will interfere.

A characteristic feature of the office of trustee is an acceptance by the latter that the appointment is one of honor, carrying with it an obligation to serve the interests of the trust in a selfless manner; arguably, this is accentuated in the context of a charitable trust. In addition to bearing the responsibilities that have traditionally accompanied the role of trustee, there is now the possibility of assuming additional duties, by agreement, and for those services only, the trustee can receive reasonable payment.

It is in the nature of an appointment to the office of trustee that the latter undertake their responsibilities on the basis of trust personally vested in him or her: A delegate must not delegate or *delegatus non potest delegare*, and a trustee can never be a mere delegate or representative of any appointing or funding body. Trustees are honor-bound to personally assume and give effect to their duties. This principle has been expressed by Lord Langdale in *Turner v. Corney* as follows:[18]

> [T]rustees who take on themselves the management of property for the benefit of others have no right to shift their duty on to other persons; and if they employ an agent, they remain subject to the responsibility towards their *cestius que trust*, for whom they have undertaken the duty.

However, this principle is not inflexible, and the courts have conceded that delegation may occur in circumstances of "legal necessity" or "moral necessity."[19]

B. Charity Mission

The duty to protect the charitable status and respect the integrity of the purpose a charity has been directed to advance is vested in its trustees. It is a well-established, often-repeated rule that charities must not stray from their objectives in pursuit of funding. This is also a rule that in practice is often honored more in breach than in compliance as in order to compete for contracts, trustees creatively reconfigure

[17] (1877) 11 I.L.T.R. 131.
[18] (1841) 5 Beav 515, at p. 517.
[19] Ex parte Balchier (1754) Amb 218.

their charity's objectives and purposes to fit with government policy. Trustees have no authority to act in this way. They are required to honor the terms of their charity's purpose, which licenses its entitlement to donations and tax exemption privileges and directs its activities. Where those objectives have become impossible or impractical to fulfill, then the trustees may make a cy-pres application to the court or regulator for authority to change them but, otherwise, the trustees must adhere to the objectives and thus to the mission that their charity was established to pursue.

1. Mission Drift

The principles of equity, which have informed trusts for centuries and underpin the modern concept of charity, require its trustees to accept and respect the terms on which a trust was set up, was awarded charitable status, and subsequently attracted public donations and tax exempt privileges, by remaining within the confines of its charitable purpose. Failure to do so not only jeopardizes the right to charitable status but also exposes the organization to "mission drift" as it constantly adapts to meet the requirements of the next government contract, and loses both its mandate with stakeholders and its market niche as uncertainty comes to surround its identity.

In recent years, most notably in jurisdictions where the charitable trust is not and has not been the dominant legal structure such as the United States and Australia, the elasticity of this rule has come under severe strain as the nonprofit sector generally experiences a trend toward increased commercialization. The pressure on charities to tender for contracts poses a threat to their mission, and for some it threatens their survival, as they may not be best equipped to compete in a ruthless marketplace.[20]

C. Charity Independence

Again, it rests with trustees to ensure that a charity remains totally committed to its donor's intention, is uncompromised in its capacity to pursue its charitable purpose, and is an honest and effective advocate on behalf of its beneficiaries. The role played by trustees in the governance arrangements for a trust are often crucial to the trust's survival in the current economic climate. A key element differentiating charity from other nonprofits is the obligation of trustees to assert the independence of their charity, ensuring that in sharing the functions of government the charity does not become merely a government agency, and to protect the charity's fiduciary base.

[20] See, e.g., Weisbrod, B., "The Pitfalls of Profits," in 2(3) *Stanford Social Innovation Review* (2004).

It may at one time have been possible to confidently assert that "the independence of the sector is virtually enshrined in the fact that voluntary and charitable organisations should be governed by independent, unpaid boards of trustees,"[21] but this is no longer the case. The traditional protective role of trustees has to some extent depended on the prevalence of the trust as the preferred legal structure for charities. As the latter has diminished, so too has the relative significance of the trustee model of governance. Moreover, in recent years legislation has adjusted the traditional fiduciary and other obligations of trustees. For example, the age-old duty of a trustee to act gratuitously[22] has been undermined in some jurisdictions by a statutory entitlement to payment when the trustee provides goods or a service to the charity over and above the normal trustee duties. In addition, the governance arrangements for charities are often not what they seem as the board can be comprised of (or sometimes consist entirely of) government appointees. The effectiveness of trustees as protectors of charities has faded considerably in recent years in many common law jurisdictions.

The unique identity of charity and the integrity of charitable purposes, set within a common law legacy that has endured for four centuries and been shared fairly uniformly among the many nations that formerly constituted part of the British Empire, are increasingly in danger of being undermined by pressures from government and indeed from commerce. As across the developed common law nations, much of the burden of public service provision is shunted from government to the nonprofit sector, so are charities drawn into closer association with government, and in so doing are compromising their objectives and their independence.

D. Regulatory Constraints

The long-standing common law constraints on trustees, who by fault or default place the assets of beneficiaries at risk, continue to have a place in contemporary charity law. This traditional set of controls is now supplemented by statutory powers vested in various regulators and by the usual criminal law sanctions.

1. Control of Trustees

Traditionally, the power to remove and/or replace trustees was exercised in the U.K. by the Court of Chancery using its inherent jurisdiction. This power was, and continues to be, available in circumstances where trustees behave with incompetence or dishonesty, or obstruct the purposes of the trust. The courts have also long had statutory powers to control or remove trustees.[23]

[21] Seddon, N., *Who Cares?*, Civitas, London, 2007, at p. 149.

[22] This duty probably dates from the decision in Robinson v. Pett (1734) 3 P Wms 249.

[23] Traditionally, and currently in Ireland, under s.25 of the Trustee Act 1893 a court could remove and replace a trustee.

a. Breach of Trust

Trustees will be liable to a charge of breach of trust if they either fail to discharge the duties of their office or if their actions are in excess of the authority conferred by their office. Any loss incurred to the trust property resulting from such a breach of trust must be made good by the trustee;[24] any improper profits gained, whether or not loss resulted to the trust, must be made over to the trust. Liability for a breach of trust is actionable even though the trustee has since retired; if the trustee is dead, the action will lie against the estate of the deceased. Breaches of trust or mismanagement may provide grounds for judicial removal of trustees. However, in the words of Lindley L.J. in *Re Chapman*:[25]

> trustees acting honestly, with ordinary prudence and within the limits of their trust, are not liable for mere errors of judgment.

Where trustees act improperly[26] or corruptly,[27] the court will hold them fully accountable. Otherwise, the traditionally rigorous approach to trustees, with strict liability imposed for the consequences of a lapse in diligence, has now been generally statutorily moderated to provide for trustees to be excused where by fault or default they have caused loss to their trust.

b. Conflict of Interest

Acceptance of appointment brings with it a duty that trustees, directors, and other officials will not place themselves in a position where a conflict might arise between their personal interests and those of the organization.[28] This does not prevent a public authority from nominating or appointing trustees, or even being a trustee in its corporate capacity. Where a public authority becomes trustee of a charity in its corporate capacity, any funding agreement between the authority and the charity would constitute self-dealing unless mechanisms are put in place to manage such a conflict of interest.

There is a presumption that any acquisition by a trustee of benefits from beneficiaries will be presumed to derive from the former exercising undue influence over

[24] See, e.g., Murphy v. Allied Irish Banks Ltd [1994] 1 I.L.R.M. 220.

[25] [1896] 2 Ch. 763, at p.776.

[26] Att.-Gen. v. Boucherett (1858) 25 Beav. 116.

[27] See Att.-Gen. v. Glegg (1738) Amb. 584; Att.-Gen. v. Governors of Harrow School (1754) 2 Ves. Sen. 551; Waldo v. Caley (1809) 16 Ves. 206, 212; Ex parte Berkhampstead Free School (1813) 2 V. & B. 134, 138; and Re Bedford Charity (1833) 5 Sim 578.

[28] See, e.g., Bray v. Ford [1896] A.C. 44.

the latter.[29] Where that trustee is a solicitor, the rule applies with particular force.[30] A trustee is, however, entitled to remuneration for all out-of-pocket expenses reasonably incurred[31] and is now generally statutorily entitled to enter into a service agreement with the charitable organization and receive reasonable and proportionate remuneration for the service provided. This does not introduce a trustee entitlement to payment for trustee services: Trustee responsibilities remain non-remunerative. These most basic obligations require company directors to conduct themselves with honesty when dealing with a charity's internal and external affairs.

2. Fraudulent Trading

Trustees are as subject as anyone else to the sanctions of the criminal law for fraudulent conduct. To sustain an allegation of fraudulent trading, there has to be evidence of an intent to defraud creditors, the burden of proof for which rests on the applicant. In *R v. Grantham*,[32] for example, the judge clarified that an intention to defraud could be inferred if a person incurred a debt, for example by obtaining credit, without knowing that there was a good prospect of being able to meet the debt payments as they fell due.

The court may order any person, knowingly a party to carrying on the business of a company with intent to defraud creditors, to make a contribution to the company's assets. For an insolvent charitable company, senior management, and not just the trustees, could also be made liable for fraudulent trading.

3. Wrongful Trading

Statute law introduced the concept of wrongful trading to protect creditors from the negligence of directors. It covers situations where there has been a failure to exercise proper diligence in managing the company and to take corrective action when insolvency loomed, even though directors may not have acted in bad faith or fraudulently. A director will be guilty of reckless or wrongful trading where he or she: in the carrying on of the business, having regard to the general knowledge, skill and experience that might reasonably be expected of a person in this position, ought to have known that his or her actions or those of the company would cause loss to the creditors, and/or allowed the contracting of a debt by the company and did not honestly believe on reasonable grounds that the company would be able to pay the debt when it fell due for payment as well as its other debts. There must be evidence that at some time before the company went into insolvent liquidation, the directors

[29] Provincial Bank of Ireland v. McKeever [1941] I.r. 471.

[30] Edwards v. Meyrick (1842) 2 Hare 60. But also see the rule in Cradock v. Piper (1850) 1 Mac. & G. 664, which provides for an exception to the principle that a solicitor-trustee cannot charge the trust for services rendered as solicitor.

[31] Courtney v. Rumley (1871) Ir 6 Eq 99.

[32] [1984] QB 675.

or shadow directors continued trading although they knew or ought to have known that there was no reasonable prospect of the company avoiding that fate, and did nothing to protect the interests of creditors. As Knox J. commented in *Re Produce Marketing Consortium Ltd (No 2)*:[33]

> the facts which a director of a company ought to know or ascertain, the conclusions which he ought to reach and the steps which he ought to take are those which would be known or ascertained, or reached or taken, by a reasonably diligent person having both—
>
> 1. the general knowledge, skill and experience that may reasonably be expected of a person carrying out the same functions as are carried out by that director in relation to the company, and
> 2. the general knowledge, skill and experience that that director has.

In short, less expertise is expected of a director in a small company than one in a large company with sophisticated procedures.

In wrongful trading, liability is limited to company officers: its directors, secretaries, shadow directors, auditors, liquidators, and receivers. Liability is unlimited for all debts of the company where it is apparent that, while an officer, the person was knowingly a party to the carrying on of the business of the company in a reckless manner.

III. TRADING AND CHARITY LAW

Trading, or commerce as it is more commonly known in the United States, is not a charitable purpose. An organization established for such a purpose cannot acquire charitable status,[34] and a charity that has allowed such activity to become its sole purpose cannot hope to retain it.

Many forms of income may, however, be derived from sources other than commercial activity. Not all forms of gifts, grants, donations, or income from passive investments constitute commerce. Even where this actually occurs—as in raffles, auctions, charity dinners, and the sale of goods or services for charitable fundraising—these may be discounted for tax purposes if they are "once off" or only very occasional activities. Again, where goods or services are supplied entirely by volunteer labor, or through the use of freely donated materials, and the proceeds are wholly dedicated to the organization's charitable purpose, this will not fall within the tax definition of "trading." Selling donated goods is not considered to be

[33] (1989) 5 BCC 569.

[34] See Luxton, P., *The Law of Charities* (1st ed.), Oxford, Oxford University Press, 2001, at 20.2 (citing refusal of Charity Commission of England and Wales to register as charities entities with such objectives). See also Tudor, O., *Charities* (9th ed.), Sweet & Maxwell, London, 2003, at 7.039.

a commercial activity because businesses do not depend on donations, and selling them does not expose a charity to the level of risk usually associated with running a business, although if donated goods are remanufactured, then any sale of the resulting products would constitute commerce.

This does not detract from the fact that a charity may also engage fully and deliberately in commercial activity. This can be quite legally compatible with charity, and increasingly many charities are developing trading activities to complement their charitable purposes.

The right to engage in commercial activity, conditional though it may be, is important for many charities, but there are limits to the extent they can allow their purposes to be diluted or distorted by the drive to secure and deliver on what can often be a succession of short-term, narrowly defined service contracts. Charities seeking contracts are susceptible to developing compliant relationships. The concern that short-term government contracts "may lead to unhealthy dependencies"[35] has been highlighted but, in reality, all involvement in commerce is likely, to a greater or lesser extent, to compromise a charity's independence. In terms of the "gift relationship," it has to be conceded that the altruism quotient is at least diluted for both parties when commerce intervenes.

A. Trading: Governing Principles

A charity engaged in commerce must ensure both that any resulting profits flow back to promote its designated primary charitable purpose (rather than accrue to the benefit of individuals), and that in pursuing this activity the charity is not in breach of that purpose. Up until fairly recently, as McGregor-Lowndes has explained, "the boundary between charity and business has been relatively clear with the bright line of the non-distribution constraint combined with a core purposes test."[36] However, the current charity experiments in setting up commercial arms housed in subsidiary companies, with hybrid legal structures deliberately designed to circumvent these boundaries, is now threatening to undo long-accepted ground rules.

In determining whether a charity engaged in trading is eligible for tax exemption, the rules relating to "public benefit" and "exclusively charitable" are of crucial importance.

[35] See the Commission on the Future of the Voluntary Sector in England, *Meeting the Challenge of Change: Voluntary Action into the 21st Century*, NCVO Publications, London, 1996 (also referred to as the Deakin Report), and the Commission on the Future of the Voluntary Sector in Scotland, *Head and Heart*, SCVO, Edinburgh, 1997 (also referred to as the Kemp Report), at p. 47, para. 6.5.5. See also Charity Commission 37 and Seddon, *Who Cares?*.

[36] See McGregor-Lowndes, M., "Introduction," in McGregor-Lowndes, M. and O"Halloran, K. (eds.), *Modernising Charity Law: Recent Developments and Future Directions*, Elgar, Cheltenham, 2010, at p. 3.

1. Public Benefit

Charity is altruistic and intends social value or utility. Although the benefit need not be for the whole community, it must be at least for an appreciable section of the public.

a. Poverty and Charity

Poverty has never been a necessary precondition for acts of charity as defined by the common law, and the case law of recent years illustrates just how far its development has been dictated by a much broader interpretation of matters judicially held to constitute the public benefit. Many charities now have no relationship whatsoever with poverty and indeed, it could be argued, some of those associated with facilities accessed by the wealthy (fee-paying schools, clinics, hospitals, opera houses, the British National Lottery, etc.) exacerbate its effects.

Restricting the proportion of the public who may potentially benefit by directing that preference toward a class of potential beneficiaries,[37] or by charging fees for goods, services, or other benefits that are provided for a purpose that is otherwise charitable, is unlikely, on its own, to prevent the provider from being found to be charitable.[38] However, if the objective in doing so (rather than being an incident of carrying out a charitable purpose) is to confer benefits on people by way of fee,[39] by way of contractual right,[40] through common action for mutual gain,[41] or as part of

[37] Re Koettigen's Will Trusts [1954] Ch. 252.

[38] The Abbey, Malvern Wells Ltd v. Minister of Town and Country Planning [1951] 2 All E.R. 154 (school charging fees for students); Le Cras v. Perpetual Trustee Co. Ltd and others [1969] 1 A.C. 51; Far West Children's Health Scheme and others v. Perpetual Trustee Co. Ltd and others [1967] 3 All E.R. 915 (hospital charging fees).

[39] Comments of Rowlatt J. in The Commissioners of Inland Revenue v. The Society for the Relief of Widows and Orphans of Medical Men (1926) 11 T.C. 1, 70 Sol. Jo. 837 and The Commissioners of Inland Revenue v. The Medical Charitable Society for the West Riding of Yorkshire (1926) 11 T.C. 1 at 22, as clarified by comments of Peter Gibson J. in Joseph Rowntree Memorial Trust Housing Association Ltd and others v. Attorney-General [1983] 1 All E.R. 288.

[40] Doust v. Attorney-General (1904) 4 S.R. (NSW) 577 (employee accident fund); In Re Harris Scarfe Limited [1935] S.A.S.R. 433 (employee superannuation fund); Over-Seventies Housing Association v. Westminster City Council (1974) 21 RRC 48 (tenants' association).

[41] Braithwaite v. Attorney-General [1909] 1 Ch. 550 (friendly society); Re Trusts of Hobourn Aero Components Ltd's Air Raid Distress Fund; Ryan and others v. Forrest and others [1946] 1 All E.R. 501 (subscribers fund); Lord Nuffield as Ordinary Trustee of the Nuffield Foundation v. Commissioners of Inland Revenue; Trustees of the Nuffield Provident Guarantee Fund v. Commissioners of Inland Revenue (1947) 28 T.C. 479 (mutual insurance association).

carrying on a particular business,[42] then the provider is unlikely to be found to be charitable. In these situations, even if the benefit is of a kind conventionally provided by charities, the provider would not be a charitable entity.

b. Member Benefit

A charity does not compromise its standing by making a profit "so long, at any rate, as all the profits must be retained for its purposes and none can enure to the benefit of its individual members."[43] If the benefits to members are merely ancillary and incidental to a purpose of benefiting the community, they do not jeopardize the charitable status of an organization. Benefits are ancillary if they are conferred merely as a means to help carry out an organization's charitable purpose.[44] However, the greater the benefits received by members, the greater the concern that in fact the purpose is not to provide for the community, but to provide benefits mainly for members. In this context any limitation imposed by the donor of the gift on the class of persons who may benefit from it will be relevant and taken into account in determining whether such limitation is justified and reasonable.

In *Commissioners of Inland Revenue v. White and others and Attorney-General*,[45] for example, an association's main objectives were to advance and encourage craftsmanship in crafts ancient and modern. Its principal activities were the conversion and maintenance of two workshops for craftsmen (including a clock maker, silversmith, bookbinder, and diamond mounter). The craftsmen were not necessarily members of the association. This endeavor was motivated by increasing pressure from property developers to convert into office premises areas traditionally occupied by some of the best craftsmen in London. The view of the founders of the association was that there would be considerable loss to the community if craftsmen were forced to leave the area. In the particular circumstances of the association, the court found the association's purposes were charitable, with any benefits to the craftsmen merely incidental; this approach was also adopted in *FC of T v. The Triton Foundation*.[46]

42 Re Producers' Defence Fund [1954] V.L.R. 246 (assistance to rural producers especially with employment disputes); The Corporation of Foreign Bondholders v. Inland Revenue Commissioners [1944] 1 All E.R. 420 (protection of foreign bondholders); Re Davis (deceased); Watts v. Davis & Westralian Farmers Co-operative Limited [1965] W.A.R. 25 (assistance to cooperatives).

43 Incorporated Council of Law Reporting for England and Wales v. Attorney-General [1972] Ch 73 (CA) 90 per Sachs L.J.

44 Bona fide remuneration for services provided (say, as an employee, contractor, officeholder or consultant) would not, of course, be inconsistent with a charitable purpose.

45 (1980) 55 T.C. 651.

46 2005 A.T.C. 4891; (2005) 60 A.T.R. 451.

2. Exclusive

To be a charity, an entity must have a primary charitable purpose and that purpose must be directed exclusively toward charitable objects[47] (see chapter 1). Any other purpose or purposes must be of lesser importance and support the dominant charitable purpose or purposes. In the form of words long favored by the judiciary throughout the common law world, "a body is a charity even if some of its incidental and ancillary objects, considered independently, are non-charitable."[48] In addition—charities like other organizations—are restricted by the doctrine of ultra vires. They cannot act beyond their legal power or authority. For those established by statute, this can be a significant restraint. Acts done by the management committee of a charitable incorporated association that are outside of its objectives are voidable.

a. Mixed Purposes

The problems associated with the exclusivity rule have most often arisen in situations where the organization or donor has a mixture of purposes.

Although an entity will not be denied charitable status simply because it also has purposes other than charitable ones, the status will be denied if any such other additional non-charitable purpose is so independent and substantial as to put into question whether the declared main purpose is in fact the one to which the entity is committing its resources. The requirement is not just that objectives or purposes described as ancillary, incidental, or concomitant to a main charitable purpose are merely minor, as in of lesser importance: They must also lack substance in their own right, and amount to no more than something that tends to assist (or that naturally goes with) the achievement of the main purpose.[49]

b. Trading Activity and Charitable Purpose

Although commercial activity is not incompatible per se with charitable purpose, it may in certain circumstances become so: Much depends on the application of

[47] See Commissioners of Inland Revenue v. Yorkshire Agricultural Society [1928] 1 K.B. 611, Inland Revenue Commissioners v. City of Glasgow Police Athletic Association [1953] A.C. 380 and Commissioner of Inland Revenue v. Royal Naval and Royal Marine Officers' Association (1955) 36 T.C. 187. It should be noted that the case law is bedeviled by a laissez faire approach to any distinction among "purpose," "object," and "power"—terms that are often randomly assigned, resulting in inconsistency and some confusion.

[48] As stated by Dixon C. J. McTiernan, Williams and Fullagar J.J. in Congregational Union of NSW v. Thistlethwayte (1952) 87 C.L.R. 375, at p. 442. See dicta to the same effect in: Re White; White v. White [1893] 2 Ch. 41; Salvation Army (Vic) Property Trust v. Fern Tree Gully Corporation (1952) 85 C.L.R. 159.

[49] (1949) 2 All E.R. 537 and In re Harpur's Will Trusts (1962) 1 Ch. 78, at p. 87.

certain rules such as the "destination of income" test and the "ancillary and incidental" principle. The destination of income test is determinative in Australia for the purposes of the charitable tax exemption,[50] whereas the ancillary and incidental principle continues to underpin the established view in the U.K. that raising funds is itself not charitable.[51] The different jurisdictional approaches to this crucial issue present an interesting challenge for all common law nations as well as a focus of inquiry in the jurisdictions studied (see chapter 12).

B. *Pemsel*, Types of Services, and the Public Benefit Presumption

Contemporary commercial activity pursued for charitable purposes has grown from and remains closely aligned to the range of service provision long associated with charities, which is developed under the four *Pemsel* heads. As detailed in chapter 1, the constituency of charity was shaped by the services that evolved under the categories of poverty relief and the advancement of religion and education. The presumption of public benefit judicially held to apply in respect of the organizations, donations, and bequests governed by these three heads facilitated the emergence of certain types of service provision that duly spread to those established under the fourth head, some of which are now becoming commercialized (see chapter 3). However, public benefit is a relative concept: The test remains governed by prevailing social values. The fact that a trust or gift is judged to be for the public benefit at one point in time provides no guarantee that it will continue to be so.[52]

1. Relief of Poverty

Of the four *Pemsel* heads of charity, the judicial interpretation as to whether trusts or gifts to them can satisfy the public benefit test has applied with most leniency in respect of those made toward the relief of poverty. For poverty alleviation, both the "public" and the "benefit" requirements have always been construed in a more relaxed and generous fashion. This approach has had a significant effect on the number and range of charities created not only for the poor[53] but also for the provision of facilities and services for "the impotent"—the elderly, the ill, and the disabled.[54]

[50] Commissioner of Taxation of the Commonwealth of Australia v. Word Investments Ltd (2008) 236 CLR 204.

[51] Oxfam v. City of Birmingham DC [1976] AC 126 (HL); Blackpool Marton Rotary Club v. Martin [1988] STC 823, aff'd [1990] STC 1 (CA).

[52] National Anti-Vivisection Society v. IRC [1948] AC 31, HL.

[53] Att-Gen v. Goulding (1788) 2 Bro C.C. 428; Bristow v. Bristow (1842) 5 Beav. 289.

[54] Re Lewis [1955] Ch. 104.

2. Advancement of Education

Gifts or trusts made simply for "educational purposes" have invariably been prima facie charitable, though this charitable aim has always attracted judicial scrutiny to ensure that the "benefit" arm of the test is not breached by being political, biased, or propagandist, and is in fact genuinely "educational."[55] A wide range of activities have gradually acquired charitable status under this head, including: schools and colleges, preschool playgroups, adult learning, research bodies, think tanks, professional institutes, museums, and libraries; in addition, sport facilities have usually also been accommodated. The general cultural enrichment of society owes a good deal to the broad legal definition given to this charitable purpose, as zoos, opera houses, ballet, art galleries, and museums have now also been endowed and provided for under an educational aim.

3. Advancement of Religion

Once again, a gift or trust for religious purposes has been construed as prima facie charitable, as the public benefit test was presumed to be satisfied.[56] The contribution of religious organizations to total charitable activity, to the work of the wider voluntary sector, and to statutory services provision in all common law jurisdictions is inestimable. Ireland, Australia, New Zealand, and Canada in particular are indebted to the religious organizations that laid much of the foundations for their present systems of health and education and often provided the staff and resources for their functioning and maintenance.

4. Other Purposes Beneficial to the Community

There has never been any presumption that gifts or trusts made under this fourth *Pemsel* head satisfy the public benefit test, and the judiciary has applied the test with some rigor in this context. Nevertheless, the volume and variety of gifts and organizations found to be charitable under this residual *Pemsel* head increased exponentially in the last years of the 20th century. In this vein, the courts have extended charitable status to include, for example, specialized accommodations for the mentally ill, the disabled, children, the elderly and infirm, single mothers, and more recently to provide local general and specialized housing.

That commerce could be incorporated under charity was demonstrated by the enthusiasm with which it was extolled in the founding charter of the Royal Philanthropic Society, which was established in 1788 to "unite the spirit of society with the principles of trade, and to erect a temple to philanthropy on the foundations

[55] Re Ward [1941] Ch. 308.

[56] Re Ward [1941] Ch. 308; Re Watson [1973] 1 WLR 1472.

of virtuous industry."[57] This early declaration, asserting the compatibility of charity with the contemporary entrepreneurial flair of the marketplace, resonates with current attitudes toward the new era promised by the advent of venture philanthropy and social enterprise.

5. Activities Test

The issue as to whether it may be permissible to determine charitable status by reference to an organization's activities in addition to the purposes and objectives declared in its governing instruments has been contentious. In the first instance, it is to the stated objectives and purposes that a regulator or court will look to ascertain compatibility with charitable status. Where there is doubt after such an inquiry, however, then it has become more acceptable that attention also be given to the body's actual activities: The more removed those activities are from its stated objectives and purposes, the more difficult it will be to satisfy the test. It was Lord Normand who perhaps first explained the rationale for and nature of an activities test:[58]

> [I]n order to ascertain what the purposes of an association are, the court is not limited to consideration of its rules or its constituent documents…I begin with the rules…But it will not do to stop there…The question is what are the purposes for which the association is established, as shown by the rules, its activities and its relation to the police force and the public.

This was a view shared by MacDermott L.J.:[59]

> it is permissible to look some distance beyond the expressed objects for the purpose of seeing where they lead. The trouble, as ever, is to draw the line in the right place and distinguish between what is and what is not too remote.

In England and Wales, the Charity Commission has been ambivalent in its approach to the test,[60] whereas the judiciary and regulators in other modern common law jurisdictions have experienced difficulty in determining the outer limits of

[57] See Lansley, J., "Changing Concepts of Charity 1700–1900," paper presented at the NCVO conference, Birmingham, September 2000; as cited by as cited by Deakin, N., *In Search of Civil Society*, Palgrave, London, 2001, at p. 28.

[58] Inland Revenue Commissioners v. City of Glasgow Police Athletic Association [1953] 1 All ER 747, at pp.751–52, in finding the Association was not a charity.

[59] Baptist Union of Ireland (Northern) Corporation Ltd v. Commissioners of Inland Revenue (1945) 26 TC 335, at p. 348.

[60] See the difference in advice given by the Charity Commission in 1966 and 1996 (respectively, [1966] Ch Com Rep para. 34 and [1996] Ch Com Rep 79).

"remoteness."[61] This is a dilemma in the context of charities and trading—one that necessarily brings into play issues of intent and altruism.

C. Non-Trading Activity

From the outset, the law governing charity and trading activity contained a conundrum. On the one hand, charities are required by law to pursue charitable purposes and deliver public benefit outcomes; their purpose must not be to acquire profits. On the other, the Preamble expressly includes an exhortation to provide for the "aid and supportation of young tradesmen, [and] handicraftsmen," which gave recognition to the validity, in charity law terms, of a linkage between charity and trade and to the legitimacy of a charitable purpose that aimed to equip beneficiaries to become proficient in the marketplace. Charity and profit-making have ever since coexisted in an uneasy relationship.

Charities are also required to safeguard their assets for the future benefit of intended beneficiaries by protecting the assets from any untoward risk. Moreover, as a matter of public policy, charities should not enter into unfair tax-subsidized competition with taxpaying businesses. This is not to say that charities should not engage with commerce: Not all forms of involvement in the world of commerce necessarily constitute trading. Charities are well versed in modes of engagement with businesses, which modes have long been accepted by the tax authorities as not compromising charitable status. Broadly these are activities that, in terms of scale or duration, do not quite meet the definition of "carrying on a business."

1. Fund-Raising

Fund-raising events at times can closely resemble business activities: They typically involve the sale of goods or services for the purpose of obtaining income. For most purposes, they are redeemed from being classified as trading because the objective of a fund-raising event is not to accrue private profit. Holding the event is not an end in itself. Moreover, true market conditions are most often absent: The service/goods are usually offered at below-market cost, if only because the labor costs are defrayed by numbers of volunteers, but also there are often product subsidies involved, and the "customers" are self-selecting as they are motivated primarily by a wish to support the charitable cause rather than solely to benefit from the transaction. Ultimately, a substantial percentage of the gross revenue from the event is actually applied to a charitable purpose. Most critically, however, fund-raising very rarely constitutes "carrying on" a business: fund-raisers tend to be one-off amateur events, of limited duration; each with a definite beginning and end, which occur without any pattern of frequency, regularity, or uniformity.

[61] See, e.g., Hadaway v. Hadaway [1955] 1 WLR 16, 20 (PC) where it was found that "between a loan to an individual planter and any benefit to the community the gulf is too wide."

However, as fund-raising becomes more professional, and more part of the entertainment service industry, it is liable to cross the line and be treated by tax authorities as a form of trading. This is most obviously the case when professional fund-raisers are involved, when telethons, or lavish entertainment programs are held, and when such events occur with a predictable regularity. Increasingly some larger charities are being drawn into global fund-raising/entertainment events that approximate, and at times clearly wholly conform to, the process of carrying on a business.

2. Investing

Deriving income from investments can also be different from carrying on a business. Indeed, the passive investment of funds has traditionally been the preferred way for trustees to protect and marginally enhance the value of their charity's assets. The long-term investment in "safe" institutional bonds and pension funds, the low risk being accompanied by a low dividend, has been routinely accepted as part of a trustee's responsibilities. The overriding duty to safeguard charity assets has generally acted as a sufficient restraint to prevent more adventurous investment strategies, and the tax authorities have most usually accepted such practice as not endangering charitable status.

However, charity trustees proved to have little more immunity than bankers from the cavalier attitudes that prevailed in the financial institutions of the leading developed nations in the early years of the 21st century. As the banking collapse in 2008 revealed, many U.K. charity trustees had abandoned a risk-averse strategy and sought the relatively high rates of return offered by Icelandic banks (and subsequently ardently campaigned for government reimbursement to compensate for losses incurred following the collapse of those banks). In such circumstances, it is not impossible that the tax authorities will detect an intention to "carry on a business." Distinguishing between investments that are compliant with charitable status and investments that constitute carrying on a business involves a question of fact. The type of asset is not always a reliable guide—although there are many kinds of assets more typically associated with investments (such as common or preferred shares and bonds), there are other assets (such as real estate and royalty interests) that may equally well be used by trustees undertaking bona fide investments and trustees carrying on a business. Evidence of active trading is one indicator of the dividing line having been crossed: The buying and selling of an asset to maximize profit constitutes business dealings, with the frequency of such dealing betraying a profit motive.

For most purposes, charity investments will lie outside any legal or tax definition of trading. It has long been accepted that charities need to invest their capital, and any funds not required for their current operations, both to safeguard the value and to generate a modest income. Charity law dictates that a charity's assets be managed so as to obtain the best return within the bounds of prudent investment principles. As long as a charity manages its investments prudently, this function would generally be regarded as a necessary administrative function rather than a business activity.

3. Partnerships

In the increasingly complex world of mixed public and private finance initiatives, which involves a myriad of hybrid legal structures, charities are often caught up in partnership arrangements with other government and business organizations in a common public benefit service provision venture. Such arrangements differ from fund-raising and passive investment in that the normal legal rules governing principal and agent come into play. Where the partnership is one between a charity and a business, they are jointly engaged in the undertaking and the business modus operandi is imputed to the charity; even though the charity may play no active role in the business it is still fully complicit in "carrying on a business." The most common charity partnerships involve a charity and a government body, whereby the former undertakes contractual service provision duties as funded by the latter; this is inescapably trading and will also be treated as such by the tax authorities. Where such a partnership is not of such a contractual nature but is focused on policy development or planning and organizing (but not implementing) service delivery programs, then although it avoids business connotations the charity concerned may still run afoul of the principal/agency rules, which arguably pose a greater threat to its charitable status as the trustees have knowingly surrendered their independence—which is a required attribute of any charity.[62] Partnerships are thus a suspect option for charities.

D. Types of Trading Activity

Commercial ventures, undertaken to make profit, are in general permissible where they are clearly either part of or incidental to carrying out the charitable purpose. The circumstances in which charities may engage in commercial activities can be broadly grouped, in charity law terms, as "primary purpose trading" (or "related business activity" as it is known in the United States), "non-primary purpose trading" (or "unrelated business activity" in the United States), and ancillary trading.[63]

1. Primary Purpose Trading

Where the charitable purpose is itself being carried on in a way that is commercial, this is known in England and Wales as "primary purpose trading," and as "related business activity" in the United States. For example, the following activities have

[62] See further Colombo, J. D., "Commercial Activity and Charitable Tax Exemption," in *William and Mary Law Review*, Vol. 4, 2002, at pp. 487–567.

[63] See Charity Commission, CC35, *Charities and Trading*, London, 2001.

been found to constitute primary purpose trading: the preparation and sale of law reports;[64] the manufacture and sale of animal vaccines;[65] and the provision of cremation services.[66]

Trading conducted by the beneficiaries of a charity is generally associated with primary purpose trading. A charity for the blind selling goods made by its blind members in its workshops for the blind[67] is perhaps the classic illustration of this form of trading, as would be the sale of farm produce from a farm operated by the students of an agricultural college or the profits from a restaurant that is associated with a catering college. Thus, it has been held that trading in the inevitable produce of a training farm established for delinquent boys did not mean that the lands in question were not being used exclusively for charitable purposes.[68]

In circumstances such as those listed above, where no private benefits accrue to charity trustees, the trading activity is a natural extension of the charitable purpose and remains no more than a means for achieving it.[69] The charity is then wholly and safely compliant with established principles.

2. Non-Primary Purpose Trading

Non-primary purpose trading, or "unrelated business activity" in the United States, refers to business activities undertaken by a charity that are not directly related to the achievement of the body's charitable purpose. A typical example of non-primary purpose trading arises when a charity engages in business activity to raise funds for its charitable purpose. Such unrelated activity may take the form of selling promotional goods in a charity gift shop, running sideline businesses such as funeral services or investment services, or any one of a range of activities that seem opportune at that time and place. The compatibility of that activity with charitable status under charity law will usually depend on the extent of the activities rather than the ultimate destination of the income. Where this is undertaken on a scale that would involve significant risk to the assets of the charity, it may well be prohibited by the regulator in case the costs of the trading venture exceed turnover, forcing the

64 The Incorporated Council of Law Reporting of the State of Queensland v. FC of T (1971) 125 C.L.R. 659.

65 McGarvie Smith Institute v. Campbelltown Municipal Council (1965) 11 LGRA 321. See also Dean Leigh Temperance Canteen v. IRC (1958) 38 TC 315 (coffee shop run by charity, in a locality with many public houses, as a method of giving effect to its purpose of promoting temperance).

66 Scottish Burial Reform and Cremation Society Ltd v. Glasgow City Corporation [1967] 3 All E.R. 215.

67 Belfast Association for Employment of Industrious Blind v. Commissioner of Valuation for Northern Ireland [1968] NI. 21.

68 Salvation Army (Vic) Property Trust v. Shire of Ferntree Gully (1952) 85 C.L.R. 159.

69 Royal British Legion Attendants Company v. Commissioner of Valuation [1979] NI 138.

charity to finance the shortfall out of those assets, resulting in a depletion of funds intended for beneficiaries.[70]

3. Ancillary Trading

A business or commercial enterprise merely incidental to the carrying out of a purpose otherwise charitable is known as "ancillary trading"[71] and does not itself prevent that purpose from being charitable.[72] Similarly, the receipt of private benefits by members—such as free admission to shows, access to reading rooms, reduced fees for analysis of manures and foodstuffs, special railway facilities, and the like—was held not to disqualify a society from being regarded as charitable.[73]

To be ancillary, activities must serve and be subordinate to the charity's purposes. They cannot, therefore, be undertaken as an end in themselves, and must not be allowed to dominate the main activities that the charity undertakes to carry out its charitable purposes. In *Scottish Burial Reform and Cremation Society Ltd v. Glasgow City Corporation*,[74] for example, the House of Lords held as being a society established for charitable purposes a non–profit-making company whose main purpose was carrying out cremation by operating a crematorium. The court came to this conclusion by analyzing decided cases that had used the "repair of churches" mentioned in the Preamble and deciding that the maintenance of burial grounds in a church was indeed charitable, and that the maintenance of a cemetery extended from a churchyard was thus charitable. In what was considered to be a reasonable extension or analogy with these cases, it was held that the company's purposes were charitable as they, too, were concerned with the disposal of the dead.

However, if an objective is or becomes divorced from the charitable purpose, with its own goals, then it has been transformed into an end in itself, breaching the exclusivity rule with fatal consequences for charitable status. In such an example, contractual powers to produce, distribute, rent, or otherwise deal in film production were unanimously held to be more than ancillary to an expressed purpose of promoting the arts of "drama, dance, singing and music" and instead to be independent, "seemingly ridiculous objects," of a non-charitable nature that breached the exclusivity rule.[75] It may be, however, that a purpose or objective which, if viewed in isolation would be non-charitable, could be charitable due to the degree of its integration with essential

[70] 21 CCEW, CC-35 "Trustees, Trading and Tax: How Charities May Lawfully Trade," at C8 (April 2007).

[71] See, e.g., Salvation Army (Victoria) Property Trust v. Fern Tree Gully Corporation (1952) 85 CLR 159 (home for neglected boys that also provided training through its farm); and Trustees of the Dean Leigh Temperance Canteen v. Commissioners of Inland Revenue (1958) 38 TC 315 (the promotion of temperance through the running of a canteen).

[72] See, e.g., Commissioner of Taxation v. Word Investments Ltd [2006] FCA 1414.

[73] Commissioners of Inland Revenue v. Yorkshire Agricultural Society [1928] 1 K.B. 611.

[74] [1967] 3 All E.R. 215.

[75] Tennant Plays Ltd v. IRC (1948) 1 All E.R. 506 per Macnaghten J., at p. 509.

aspects of carrying out a charitable purpose.[76] Where there is uncertainty regarding a change in the balance between charitable purpose and commercial activity, it is usually best to seek the advice of the relevant regulator before the latter intervenes to challenge entitlement to charitable status.

It is clear that that a social element will not detract from a charitable purpose if it is merely incidental to it.[77] In relation to the advancement of education, for example, it can be difficult to discern the point where a legitimate charitable objective such as the study of ornithology shades into the private hobby of bird-watching, or music therapy into entertainment. A distinction, however, must be made between those gifts that directly enhance the capacity of a body to achieve charitable objectives and gifts that would enable it to either cater to ancillary objectives or contribute toward its general effectiveness.[78] This distinction is not readily made, and the case law is replete with illustrations of quixotic gifts and exoteric judicial rulings. For example, a testator's bequest to provide for the distribution of sweets, on every bank holiday, to all children below the age of 14 and resident in a named parish, was judged not to be a charitable gift that advanced education, because the sweets were not restricted to school children,[79] and neither was one to establish a college for the study of spiritualist mediums as no public benefit could be identified,[80] but a gift for the provision of a rose garden on a university campus did advance that purpose as "it must of its very nature be conducive to the inspiration in all but the most blasé of students of a state of mind better attuned to the academic tasks ahead."[81]

IV. CHARITIES, TRADING, AND PROFIT

Charities may engage in commercial activities to make a profit.[82] Entering fully into the commercial marketplace by engaging in trading, competitive practices, mergers and management takeovers, etc., has for many charities become a necessity. Although this is permissible, it has traditionally been subject to the condition that such profit-making activity remains incidental to the carrying out of a purpose that is otherwise charitable. When an organization's purpose has in fact become one of carrying on a commercial enterprise to generate profit, then the rule dictates that

[76] London Hospital Medical College v. Inland Revenue Commissioners and another [1976] 2 All E.R. 113.

[77] See, e.g., Barralet and others v. Attorney-General and others [1980] 3 All E.R. 918 and Re Mariette; Mariette v. Aldenham School Governing Body [1914–1915] All E.R. Rep 794.

[78] See, e.g., Incorporated Council of Law Reporting for England and Wales v. Att-Gen [1972] 1 Ch. 73.

[79] Re Ward's Estate (1937) 81 Sol Jo 397.

[80] Re Hummeltenberg [1923] 1 Ch 237.

[81] McGrath v. Cohen [1978] 1 NSWLR 621.

[82] Note, however, that the absence of a profit motive will not necessarily indicate that a charity is not in fact trading: see Re Duty on Estate of Incorporated Council of Law Reporting for England and Wales (1888) 22 QBD 279.

neither the purpose nor the organization will be considered charitable. The rule has, however, acquired considerable elasticity in some jurisdictions.[83] Also, although there is no legal bar on charities using their own funds to subsidize or supplement public services, they must only do so when it is within their objectives and powers, and is in the interests of the charity and its beneficiaries to do so.

A. Public Benefit and Private Profit

When a charity's activities constitute a commercial undertaking, any element of private profit must be modest in scale relative to the corresponding public benefit.[84] In *Hadaway v. Hadaway*,[85] for example, Viscount Simonds took the view that a bequest to set up a bank for the purpose of providing low interest loans to "planters and agriculturalists" was not charitable as the benefit was intended to be primarily private with any public benefit being of a speculative nature. Similarly, in the *Oldham* case,[86] the private profit element was judged to negate charitable status. In *Incorporated Council of Law Reporting v. Attorney General*,[87] Buckley J. considered that although the publication of law reports supplied lawyers with the tools of their trade this did not irredeemably compromise the public benefit nature of the charitable purpose of the organization concerned. As he explained:[88]

> The benefit which the council confers on members of the legal profession in making accurate reports available is that it facilitates the study and ascertainment of the law. It also helps the lawyer to earn his livelihood but that is incidental to or consequential on the primary scholastic function of advancing and disseminating knowledge of the law, and does not detract from the exclusively charitable character of the council's objects.

Private benefit is generally permissible if it is a necessary and incidental consequence of bona fide charitable activity, if it is not disproportionate in amount, and if no other criteria unrelated to the purpose are imposed to further limit potential beneficiaries.[89] It is not permissible where the benefit is confined to a "closed" group such as the employees of a particular company or any organization with a fixed

[83] See, e.g., Commissioner of Taxation v. Word Investments Ltd [2006] FCA 1414.

[84] The nature of the "profit" may be intangible, as in Royal Choral Society v. IRC [1943] 2 All ER 101 where it was held that the personal satisfaction enjoyed by choir members did not prevent their joint enterprise from being charitable.

[85] [1955] 1 WLR 16 (PC).

[86] Inland Revenue Commissioners v. Oldham Training and Enterprise Council (1996) STC 1218.

[87] [1972] Ch 73 (CA) 90.

[88] [1972] Ch 73, at p. 103.

[89] See, e.g., Springhill Housing Action Committee v. Commissioner of Valuation [1983] NI 184.

membership, or where potential beneficiaries are linked by a personal nexus (subject to the poor relations anomaly[90]).

B. Paying for Charity

Restricting access to charitable services to those who can afford to pay may be controversial on moral grounds, but in charity law terms it is quite straightforward. In the words of Sachs J.:[91]

> [I]t is clear that the mere fact that charges on a commercial scale are made for services rendered by an institution does not itself bar that institution from being held to be charitable—so long, at any rate, as all the profits must be retained for its purposes and none can enure to the benefit of its individual members.

A charity does not compromise its status by making a profit.[92] It may make profits (or gains) or accumulate surpluses provided, generally speaking, these are not used for the profit or gain of its individual members or for distribution to its owners or members, or to any other person, either while the charity is operating or on winding up.

1. Fees and the Public Benefit Test

The fact that access to services is controlled by a compulsory fee payment, thereby debarring the poor who are often in greatest need of them, does not necessarily mean that the services cannot be charitable. The law has been quite clear on this issue since at least the decision in *Scottish Burial Reform and Cremation Society Ltd. v. Glasgow Corporation*[93] when the House of Lords ruled that the provision of cremations did not cease to be a charitable purpose merely because fees were charged. Again, in *Joseph Rowntree Memorial Trust Housing Association Limited v. AG*[94] it was held that a charity's beneficiaries could be required to pay and, provided they fell within the beneficiary class, their economic circumstances did not have to be modest. It has been widely accepted among the common law nations that the public

[90] A type of trust where the donor or testator intends to make a gift for the benefit of poor relatives, which has been recognized as an exception to the "public" constraint in a line of decisions stretching back to the 18th century. See, e.g., Issac v. Defriez (1754) Amb 595; Gillam v. Taylor (1873) L.R. 16 Eq. 581; and Re Scarisbrick [1951] Ch. 622. The principle governing the exception of "poor relations" was extended to trusts for "poor employees" by cases such as Re Gosling (1900) 48 W.R. 300 and Gibson v. South American Stores (Gath & Chaves) Ltd. [1950] Ch. 177. But see also Re Koettigen's Will Trusts [1954] Ch 252.

[91] Incorporated Council of Law Reporting for England and Wales v. Attorney-General [1972] Ch 73 (CA) 90, per Sachs L.J.

[92] See, e.g., Re Resch's Will Trusts [1969] AC 514 and Joseph Rowntree Memorial Trust Housing Association Limited v. AG [1983] Ch 159 (ch).

[93] [1968] AC 138. See also Brighton College v. Marriott [1926] AC 192 (HL).

[94] [1983] Ch 159 (Ch).

benefit test is not necessarily breached by charities imposing fees for the services they provide. However, there is considerable debate as to whether there are limits to this principle, as will be seen in the following jurisdiction-specific chapters.

One argument in defense of this principle rests on the view that charity has never been limited to the poor: The elderly or the blind, for example, do not need to bear the additional burden of poverty in order to qualify as potential beneficiaries for a charity dedicated to the relief of their disability. As Danckwerts J. put it:[95] "[i]t has never been suggested that poor people must be aged to be objects of charity, and there is no reason for holding that aged people must also be poor to come within the meaning of the Statute." Deaf persons, for example, whether rich or poor will have the same need for hearing aids, which bear a cost that each might be expected to defray to some extent.

However there is a weight of judicial opinion that, while conceding the above point, would add the caveat that any such approach that had the effect of excluding the poor could not satisfy the public benefit test. In the words of Lindley L.J.:[96]

> I am quite aware that a trust may be charitable though not confined to the poor: but I doubt very much whether a trust would be declared to be charitable which excluded the poor.

This view received support from the decision in *Re Resch*,[97] which confirmed that an organization, wholly excluding the poor from any benefits—direct or indirect—could not be for the benefit of the public and therefore would not be a charity.

2. Private Education

For a school to be a charity, the education it provides must be available to the public or a sufficient section of the public.[98] However, many charities whose aims include advancing education also charge fees for the services or facilities they provide. The same approach can be seen in relation to private hospitals.[99]

[95] Re Glynn [1950] 69 (2) TLR 500.

[96] In re Macduff [1966] 2 Ch. 451, at p. 464.

[97] [1969] 1 AC 514. See also Charity Commission, Review Decision made on the application for registration of Odstock Private Care Limited, September 25, 2007.

[98] See De Mandeville, B., *Essay on Charity Schools* (1723), which questioned both the motivations behind legacies for the establishment of such schools and their impact on the children of the poor.

[99] Re Resch's Will Trusts [1969] AC 514.

Although it is compatible with charitable status to restrict the "benefit" to a section of the public, as defined by social circumstances or charitable need, any such restriction should be reasonable[100] (see chapter 5).

3. Private Hospitals and Other Forms of Health Care

The issue of compatibility between a hospital's charitable status and the payment of fees for accessing its services has a long history. For example, in 1756 the Foundling Hospital, a charitable institution in London, received a grant of £10,000 on condition that, inter alia, it opened up access to all infants under a certain age.[101]

It would seem that a hospital would satisfy the public benefit test most convincingly when its wards are open as of right to all members of the public on the basis of need, supported wholly or partially by public funds, and subject to a form of public control. It would not do so if maintained entirely by fees levied in respect of all admissions.[102] The status of a hospital as a voluntary or state institution has never been a factor affecting the validity of a charitable gift to it, and the presence of some fee-paying patients has been held not to compromise the charitable status of a hospital,[103] but a hospital restricted to fee-paying patients was refused entitlement to charitable status.[104] In the United States, there has been considerable debate[105] and a mounting body of case law[106] on the issue of what should the charitable quotient be regarding the services offered by a hospital if it is to acquire or retain charitable or nonprofit status.

[100] See Charity Commission, *The Advancement of Education for the Public Benefit* (December 2008), at para. E3, which advises that it "must be legitimate, proportionate, rational and justifiable given the aim of the organization."

[101] A Royal Charter was granted to Thomas Coram for the creation of the Foundling Hospital in 1739. See further Owen, D., *English Philanthropy 1660-1960*, Oxford University Press, London, 1965, at pp. 52–57.

[102] See Needham v. Bowers 21 QBD 436 (1888) where a lunatic asylum that was unendowed and received no appreciable subscriptions, but was maintained entirely out of fees received, was held not to be a charity for the purposes of the 1838 Act.

[103] Relying on Verge v. Somerville [1924] AC 496.

[104] Nuffield (Lord) v. Inland Revenue Commissioners (1946) 175 L.T. 465. See also Morris, D., "Fee-Paying Hospitals and Charitable Status: A New Dawn or Lost Opportunities?" in *Kings Law Journal*, Vol. 18, 2007, at p. 455.

[105] See, e.g., Fox, D. M. and Schaffer, D. C., "Tax Administration as Health Policy: Hospitals, the Internal Revenue Services and the Courts," in *Journal of Health Politics, Policy, and Law*, Vol. 16, 1991, at pp. 251, 255–56; Rev. Rul. 69–545, 1969–2 C.B. 117 (citing Restatement (Second) of Trusts § 368 and § 372 (1959)); Stevens, R., *In Sickness and in Wealth* 17–51, Basic Books, New York, 1989.

[106] See E. Ky. Welfare Rights Org. v. Schultz, 370 F. Supp. 325, 326 (D.D.C. 1973); E. Ky. Welfare Rights Org. v. Simon, 507 F.2d 1278, 1290 (D.C. Cir. 1974); Lugo v. Miller, 640 F.2d 823, 831 (6th Cir. 1981); Provena Covenant Med. Ctr. v. Dep't. of Revenue, 384 Ill. App. 3d 734 (App. Ct. 2008).

4. Unfair Competition

The courts have maintained a vigilant watch on charities that engage in any form of commerce. This wariness springs from a perceived need to safeguard private enterprise from unfair competition by tax-subsidized charities seeking to exploit their standing as registered public benefit organizations to gain a market advantage. The main bar to a charity undertaking permanent non-primary purpose trading is the general view of government that the resulting tax-exempt profits would constitute unfair competition with the private sector.

C. Gambling for Charity

The association between gambling (high risk for high personal profit) and charity (public benefit) is not merely somewhat ironic—given their close but antithetical ties to poverty—it is also well established, highly productive, and now very often viewed mainly as a professional and multinational form of entertainment. It is an association that favors utility over altruism.

1. Lotteries

Charities everywhere have probably always had occasional recourse to lotteries for fund-raising purposes. Relatively new, however, is the phenomenon of "National Lotteries" that now are featured in many developed nations, the proceeds of which are channeled toward charities and other public benefit organizations or services. This method of exploiting the private profit motive for public benefit purposes has since been joined by various other highly professional forms of public entertainment (game shows, etc.), which similarly provide "games of chance" aimed at generating funds for charity.

V. CHARITABLE TRADING, LEGAL STRUCTURES, AND TAX

The common law rule is that charities may make profits (or gains) or accumulate surpluses, provided these are not used for the profit or gain of its individual members or for distribution to its owners or members, or to any other person, either while the charity is operating or on winding up; the charging of fees for services is normally construed as consistent with the nonprofit requirement. This has acted as a considerable constraint on the contemporary trading ventures of charities. In order to ease the tensions emanating from this constraint, there has been a tendency for charities with a growing investment in commerce to establish a separate trading arm in which all commerce-related activity is housed and designated ancillary and incidental, thereby leaving the organization free to concentrate on its main charitable purpose or purposes. The choice of legal structure as the trading vehicle for a charity is important for many reasons, not least because of the resulting tax implications.

A. Charitable Foundations

In some jurisdictions more so than in others, the traditional charitable trust has been reinterpreted to allow it to play a key role in leveraging funds from business for application in a nonprofit context. Charitable foundations have been so adapted. Generally this is a foundation with an asset base, often in the form of an endowment, which uses the income generated from that fund for grant disbursements to further charitable purposes. Whereas this structure has traditionally taken the form of family foundations or private foundations, its more recent incarnation as a corporate foundation or community foundation is of interest for present purposes.

1. Community Foundations

This is a locally based independent charity that aims to create an endowment by fund-raising from a variety of donor sources with a common interest in the welfare of that particular geographic area. It brings together a diverse range of stakeholders in rural and metropolitan communities and provides them with resources and tools to initiate key social, environmental, and cultural activities. Over time it builds up a collection of endowed funds from many donors in the community, provides services to the community and its donors, makes grants, and undertakes community leadership and partnership activities to address the needs in that area. It serves as a vehicle for local donors who wish to contribute their cash, trusts, bequests, or real property to create permanent endowments that will benefit the community in perpetuity. Using the investment earnings on each endowed fund, a community foundation makes and builds capacity within the community to address local needs and opportunities. Its task is to build substantial, permanent funds from which grants are made to local charitable and community organizations. A community foundation is generally incorporated, and its governing body would normally be a board comprised of local people acting in a voluntary capacity.

Community foundations were first established in the United States in 1914. They emerged in the U.K. in the 1980s and now have a presence in at least 35 countries. As Anheier and Leat explain:[107]

> community foundations are rooted in, and emphasise building, local communities; they encourage and provide vehicles for corporate giving; they are governed locally; they encourage citizen-donor involvement and "democratise" giving by enabling smaller donors to create what are, in effect, their own mini-foundations (e.g. donor-advised

[107] See Anheier, H. and Leat, D., *Creative Philanthropy: Toward a New Philanthropy for the 21st Century*, Routledge, London, 2005, at p. 149.

funds) within an established infrastructure; and they seek to work with rather than apart from local government and businesses.

2. Corporate Foundations

This is a foundation that derives the majority of its income from a profit-making company, usually by investment income on assets originally given by a company; regular donations from a company; or an endowment linked to a company's profits, in lieu of shares; or from donations given by a company's customers or employees. These foundations may be established for a variety of reasons, including: to create a vehicle for corporate giving that is at arm's length from core business activity, to ensure focused and structured giving, to ensure continuity of giving, to further the personal motivations of the owner or founder, to obtain reputational benefits, or to provide a company with a credible way of engaging with the sector. A corporate foundation must be established as a separate entity from its parent company and is subject to the same rules and regulations as other foundations. These foundations are becoming more popular as a means whereby for-profit companies can "give something back," and are particularly effective when targeted toward supporting unpopular social issues.

B. Trading Subsidiary

Many charities can and do undertake trading activity in furtherance of their primary purposes, most often by setting up a subsidiary company to do so on the charity's behalf. These can be large-scale commercial enterprises, free to engage in commercial activities unrelated to the charitable purposes of their parent charity, but to the promotion of which purposes all activities of the trading arm must remain dedicated. These organizations are not themselves charities but are limited companies, the shares in which are owned by the parent charity. They can be owned by one charity or jointly by several, and can seek investment from sources other than their parent charity. For example, "Café Direct," the trading arm of Oxfam, is a trading subsidiary established on a commercial basis unrelated to the core business of its parent charity, to which all profits are returned. There are, however, real dangers for the charitable status of an organization that establishes a commercial trading arm.[108] In particular, where the latter is in reality a large commercial organization with a small attached charity, its commercial activity is not "incidental," the methods and products of that activity may well not be "ancillary," and the organization itself will have so compromised its status that it may no longer be considered charitable.

[108] See the Charity Commissioners *War on Want Inquiry* (1991), which found that the trading arm of this organization was not entitled to receive an interest-free loan from the parent charity as this constituted an application by the latter of charitable funds for non-charitable purposes.

Although such a subsidiary trading company is not itself a charity, and is fully taxable on its profits, it can donate those profits back to its parent charity. This arrangement is encouraged by the Charity Commission in England and Wales as a strategy for reducing risk to a charity's assets and minimizing its tax liabilities while allowing the trading subsidiary to make donations to its parent charity as "Gift Aid," thereby reducing or eliminating the profits of the subsidiary that are liable to tax.[109] As Breen indicates, setting up a separate trading company has a number of advantages for a charity:[110]

> First, by distinguishing between a charity's main mission and its trading operations, a subsidiary can create both financial and organisational clarity for a charity. Second, an independent non-charitable subsidiary will not be constrained in its trading activities or the levels of profits that it makes from its business activities. Third . . . the use of separate structures may be tax efficient since the trading company can potentially eliminate its tax liabilities on trading profits donated back to the charity.[111]

Breen goes on to point out that there are also downsides to establishing a trading subsidiary:[112]

> Subsidiaries can be costly to set up and maintain for charities. They require separate administrative structures and when charity trustees sit on their boards, conflict of interest issues may arise. Moreover, these subsidiaries do not themselves enjoy charitable tax-exempt status. In setting up such entities, charity trustees are required to ensure that any charity money advanced by way or loan or otherwise to capitalize the subsidiary is invested in accordance with the charity's investment powers and properly secured so as not to risk the capital. The charity trustees are also subject to the broader charity legal obligations relating to prudent investment and diversification of investment assets.

Another difficulty facing trustees who are contemplating advancing a loan to their trading subsidiary, which is construed as investing in it, is that they must ensure that in so doing they are not thereby gratuitously favoring that entity. Normal commercial practice and rates should apply; if not, the charity trustees are open to the

[109] See Charity Commission leaflet CC35—*Trustees, Trading and Tax: How Charities May Lawfully Trade* (Version April 2007).
[110] See Breen, O., "Holding the Line," in McGregor-Lowndes, M. and O'Halloran, K. (eds.), *Modernising Charity Law*, Elgar Publishing, Cheltenham, 2010, at pp.149–50.
[111] The position in the U.K. differs in this regard from the position in the United States, where a percentage limitation is imposed on the amount that a corporation can deduct from its tax liability through charitable contributions, c.f. I.R.C. §170(b)(2) restricting charitable donations by corporations to 10 percent of the corporation's taxable income in any given tax year.
[112] Breen, "Holding the Line," at p. 150.

challenge of reckless investment by permitting an avoidable loss.[113] The charity cannot simply give away any part of its assets to the subsidiary.

The relevant regulatory provisions tend to focus on ensuring that trading is not compromising an organization's charitable status, and on determining eligibility for tax exemption on trading profits, and on the post-tax use of those profits. The courts, as Picarda has noted, have carefully scrutinized the activities that come within the legal definition of "trade"[114] and have been keen to ensure that "when a trade is carried on by a charity, tax is chargeable on the profits of the trade notwithstanding that the profits are, and can only be, applied to the purposes of the charity."[115]

C. Modern Types of Trading Organizations

The pace of government withdrawal from public service provision in recent years has led to a rapid growth in intersectoral activity as various forms of commercial and non-profit organizations compete or cooperate to fill the gap. Governments in all leading common law nations now experiment with variations of public–private finance initiatives. As a consequence, a number of hybrid organizations have come into being designed to provide more appropriate legal vehicles for the intersectoral delivery of public benefit services. In what is perhaps a further stage of evolution beyond what has been termed the "third sector,"[116] Billitteri has drawn attention to:[117]

> an emerging "Fourth Sector" of social enterprise organizations that combine charitable missions, corporate methods, and social and environmental consciousness in

[113] See Rosemary Simmons Memorial Housing Association Ltd v. United Dominion Trust Ltd [1986] 1 WLR 1440 where the view was expressed (obiter) that, by providing a guarantee for a loan acquired by its subsidiary company on the open market, a charity was unlawfully giving away its assets.

[114] Picarda, H., *The Law and Practice Relating to Charities* (3rd ed.), Butterworths, London, 1999, at p. 741. Citing Coman (Surveyor of Taxes) v. Governors of Rotunda Hospital, Dublin [1921] 1 A.C. 1 (letting out rooms for entertainment); Grove v. Young Men's Christian Association (1903) 88 L.T. 696 (running a restaurant open to outsiders); Religious Tract and Book Society of Scotland v. Forbes (1896) 3 T.C. 415 (bookselling); Brighton College v. Marriott [1926] A.C. 192 (carrying on a public school); IRC v. Glasgow Musical Festival Association (1926) 11 T.C. 154 (promoting a music festival to which the paying public was admitted); Income and Corporation Taxes Act 1988, s.510—Royal Agricultural Society of England v. Wilson (1924) 9 T.C. 62 (running an agricultural show); and British Legion Peterhead Branch, Remembrance and Welcome Home Fund v. IRC (1953) 35 T.C. 509 (arranging regular public dances).

[115] Picarda, H., *Law and Practice Relating to Charities*, at p. 741, citing St. Andrew's Hospital, Northampton v. Shearsmith (1887) 19 Q.B.D. 624; Psalms and Hymns Trustees v. Whitwell (1890) 3 T.C. 7; and Davis v. Superioress Mater Misericordiae Hospital Dublin [1933] I.R. 480.

[116] A term probably first introduced in Etzioni, A., in "The Third Sector and Domestic Missions," in *Public Administration Review*, No. 33, 1973, at pp. 314–23.

[117] Billitteri, T., "Mixing Mission and Business: Does Social Enterprise Need a New Legal Approach?" *Highlights from an Aspen Institute Roundtable*, January 2007. See further the Aspen Institute Google Groups listserv called Hybrid Legal Forms and Tax Structures (HLFTS) established to help people who run or support hybrid organizations share their knowledge and introduce new ideas.

> ways that transcend traditional business and philanthropy. This new generation of hybrid organizations is taking root in a fertile space between the corporate world, which is constrained by its duty to generate profits for shareholders, and the non-profit world, which often lacks the market efficiencies of commercial enterprise.

He goes on to define such "hybrid" organizations as those that:

> typically work within the capitalist system, earning income and operating in a businesslike manner, but their goals are not purely financial and their duty is far broader than serving just the interests of shareholders. They strive not only to succeed financially but also to do good, using a blend of traditional corporate methods and progressive social approaches such as sharing governing power with employees and community members and hewing to rigorous outcome standards. Some groups are tax-exempt while others are for-profit organizations...they may seek to develop a unique charitable "brand"...their financing might come from a blend of traditional business sources, such as bank loans and stock offerings, and philanthropic sources, such as foundation investments.

Billitteri is led to posit the following questions: Are wholly new legal forms and tax structures needed to accommodate the next generation of social enterprise organizations? Is the growth of social enterprise being hindered by the limitations of traditional corporate structures and nonprofit tax laws?

Various contenders have surfaced as possible new legal structures for the "fourth sector."

1. Social Enterprises

These are businesses with primarily social objectives, the surpluses of which are principally reinvested for that purpose in the business or in the community, rather than extracted to maximize profit for shareholders and owners. They are mission-driven organizations that trade in goods or services to achieve a social goal. They aim to accomplish targets that are social and environmental in nature as well as financial. Social enterprises are profit-making businesses set up to tackle a social or environmental need, and can include local community enterprises, social firms, mutual organizations such as cooperatives, and large-scale organizations operating nationally or internationally. They may take the form of: companies limited by guarantee, industrial and provident societies, and companies limited by shares; some organizations are unincorporated associations and others are registered charities; some are housing associations, credit unions, or the trading arms of registered charities. Although social enterprises can acquire charitable status, and many do, this is only possible if they satisfy the usual requirements (by being established exclusively for charitable purposes and for the public benefit, etc). As has been said: "in many ways the expression 'social enterprise' is simply a relatively new term for what some charities have been doing for years, namely promoting their social purposes through a sustainable business model."[118]

2. The Limited Liability Company

Some countries have introduced custom-made incorporated legal structures tailored to bridge the gap between nonprofits and commerce. In England and Wales, the community interest company (CIC) is an example of such a structure, and is designed to function as the trading arm of a charity (see chapter 5).

3. Low-Profit Limited Liability Companies

Also known as an L3C,[119] this is seen as offering an attractive investment opportunity for foundations, as well as individuals and government agencies, through the purchase of an equity position or other means, such as loans. Such investments could provide capital for socially beneficial activities such as keeping a small-town factory in business or building low-cost housing. Modest dividends would accrue to its investors, who, in the case of foundations, could then use that money to make more program-related investments or traditional grants. If an L3C stopped pursuing its charitable mission, a foundation investor would have to divest its stake. By Spring 2010, five U.S. states had passed legislation enabling companies to incorporate as an L3C, and Vermont, the first state to pass such legislation, already has more than 80 companies so incorporated[120] (see chapter 13).

4. Venture Philanthropy

Venture philanthropy is an ill-defined term that broadly refers to the nonprofit sector's application of certain practices used by venture capitalists when investing in new business ideas.[121] It emerged in the United States in the 1970s and grew as venture capital

[118] Lloyd, S. and Walker, A. F., *Charities, Trading and the Law* (2nd ed), Jordans, Bristol, 2009, at p. 2.

[119] See further Wikipedia at: en.wikipedia.org/wiki/L3C.

[120] Established in Michigan, Wyoming, Utah, and Illinois, as well as the Crow Indian Nation and the Oglala Sioux Tribe. L3Cs are recognized in all 50 states.

[121] See Emerson, J. and Twersky, F., *New Social Entrepreneurs: The Success, Challenge and Lessons of Nonprofit Enterprise Creation*, The Roberts Foundations, San Francisco, 1996; Letts, C., Ryan, W., and Grossman, A., "Virtuous Capital: What Foundations Can Learn from Venture Capitalists," in *Harvard Business Review*, March/April 1997, at pp. 36–44; Reis, T. and Clohsey, S.J., "Unleashing New Resources and Entrepreneurship for the Common Good: A Philanthropic Renaissance," in Schluter, A., Then, V., and Walkenhorst, P. (eds.), *Foundations in Europe, Society, Management and Law*, Directory of Social Change, London, 2001; Breiteneicher, C. K. and Marble, M. G., "Strategic Programme Management," in Schluter, Then, and Walkenhorst, (eds.), *Foundations in Europe, Society, Management and Law*.

investment ballooned into a multibillion dollar industry in the 1990s. At the heart of the venture capital model "is the concept of treating funding as an investment rather than as the traditional concept of a charitable grant, with corresponding expectations of return on investment, operating efficiencies, and management oversight that this shift requires."[122] It is an approach that utilizes funds leveraged from private equity combined with private finance expertise to maximize the long-term social impact of charity. It allows for funds to be invested in projects and a return to be gained or reinvested by the investor on the basis of the resulting social impact evaluation. It requires measurable indices to quantify return on investment and an exit strategy.

Venture philanthropy may also be used more loosely to refer to all kinds of charitable endeavors that involve risk-taking, innovation, and entrepreneurship. Specifically it includes "funding social entrepreneurs in organisations with scale-up potential. Support it long-term and the funder makes substantial commitments to a few rather than smaller commitments to many."[123]

Venture philanthropy represents a significant step away from the "gift relationship" approach, away from personifying altruism, and away from the stigma of "charity." In the traditional supplicant/benefactor relationship, the nature of the gift was defined and confined by an exchange mechanism that imposed restrictions on its utility. It had to be requested from someone in evident distress, to address a pressing need as perceived from that person's circumstantially compromised vantage point. It was given by a donor to meet the terms of the request. It was specific, short-term, and limited to the parties involved. To be considered charitable, it had to conform to a *Pemsel* charitable purpose.

Venture philanthropy, instead, opens up the transaction to take into account matters of context, strategy, means, and impact. It need be neither triggered by a specific request nor addressed by a single donor, and should not be constrained by the usual limitations of time, resources, or problem specification. One advantage of venture philanthropy is that it may choose to operate outside the confines of *Pemsel* purposes, instead being engaged in social enterprises and thus avoid the restrictions of charity law. It is an approach that takes donor control much further—involving participation in governance and management of funded organizations. Venture philanthropists tend to focus on efficiency, effectiveness, and performance, but some nonprofits would argue that this fails to take into account the importance of user participation and process that are central to the concepts of civil society and social capital.

[122] See Sievers, B., "If Pigs Had Wings: The Appeals and Limits of Venture Philanthropy," the Waldemar A. Nielsen Issues in Philanthropy Seminar Series, Center for Public & Nonprofit Leadership, Georgetown University, Washington, DC, November 16, 2001.

[123] See Reis and Clohsey, "Unleashing New Resources," at p.477.

D. Trading and Tax

Since the first taxation statute, the Income Tax Act 1799,[124] charities have been tax exempt in the U.K. The Act stated that "no corporation, fraternity, or society of persons established for charitable purposes only, shall be chargeable under this Act, in respect of the income of such corporation, fraternity, or society." Eligibility for a range of tax exemptions has ever since been a primary reason for acquiring charitable status. Trading, however, is a taxable activity, and charities engaged in trade will be liable for income tax on any profits that accrue unless specifically exempted. Charity trading profits are generally exempt from tax (income tax or corporation tax in England and Wales) in the case of primary purpose trading, ancillary trading, trading within the terms of the "small scale exemption," or a lottery, or when connected with certain fund-raising events. In all these cases, the exemption is subject to the condition that the profits are applied solely to the purposes of the charity. This means that all such profits are wholly dedicated to furthering the purpose of the charity concerned and as then determined in accordance with the type of trading (see above).

1. Primary Purpose Trading

The profits from such trading are exempt from tax when carried on directly by the charity as a means of giving effect to one or more of its objectives and thereby fulfilling the charitable purpose as stated in its governing instrument. Examples of such trades would include: an art gallery or museum holding an exhibition and charging an admission fee, a school providing an educational service on a fee-paying basis, a theater selling tickets for a production it is staging, or a hospital providing health care services on a fee-paying basis. As a charity may have more than one primary purpose, it may therefore have multiple forms of primary purpose commerce. Primary purpose trading also includes trade mainly carried out by the beneficiaries of a charity.

It is then necessary to prove that the greater part of the trade carried on by a charity is undertaken by the beneficiaries, particularly where there are others involved (e.g., volunteer workers who are not beneficiaries). A charity conducting commercial activity may pay wages or a salary to its beneficiaries (i.e., in effect treat them as employees). On the understanding that such individuals can still clearly qualify as beneficiaries of the charity, the profits of the trade will continue to be exempt from tax.

2. Non-Primary Purpose Trading

Non-primary purpose trading is intended to raise funds for the charity, as distinct from trading that furthers the charity's objectives, and is the U.K. equivalent of

[124] 39 Geo III c 13, s 5.

"unrelated business activity" in the United States. It most often occurs when a charity engages in commerce to raise funds to offset its running costs. The profits from such trading will normally be fully taxable, but may qualify for exemption in certain circumstances. Essentially, the profits of such trading will be tax exempt only where that part of the trade, which is not a primary purpose activity, is small relative to overall trading activity. Otherwise those profits will be liable to tax regardless of the ultimate destination of the income, and such trading may also, depending upon the scale of this activity, threaten the charitable status of the organization. Charities often engage in both primary purpose and non-primary purpose forms of trading and, when they do, rules of apportionment may then apply (see chapter 5).

3. Ancillary Purpose Trading

Commercial activity may also qualify for tax exemption if it is ancillary, contributing indirectly to the carrying on of a charity's primary purpose. Examples of such trades would include: a theater selling food and drink in a bar and/or restaurant to members of the audience attending a staged performance; a school providing accommodation for students on a rental basis; a hospital selling papers, flowers, and toiletries to patients and their visitors; or a museum or art gallery selling food in a coffee shop to visitors attending an exhibition. The need is for a demonstrably clear relationship between the primary purpose of the charity and the nature of the ancillary trading.

4. Trading in Other Circumstances

In practice, the profits arising from other small-scale charitable fund-raising activities will not be taxed where the trading activities are not carried on regularly, are not in competition with other commercial traders, and have public support because the profits are claimed to be for application to charitable purposes only (and the profits are in fact applied for charitable purposes only). In the decision on what is "small-scale," the following factors will be considered: the level of both turnover and profit; the degree of commercial organization involved; the level of input by outside bodies including professional fund-raisers and well- known personalities including individuals giving their services voluntarily; and the number of people attending.

Normally, relief extends to all the profits of such an activity, including admission charges, sale of refreshments, sale of programs, and sale of advertisements. Every source of income must form part of the overall event and contribute to the total profits earned. In any case where a source of income constitutes a separate profit-making activity, the profits will be taxable.

5. Charity Shops

The sale of donated goods is not regarded as being a trade for tax purposes and does not attract tax liability. Only if the donated goods are subject to a major refurbishment or are fundamentally reconstituted will their sale be regarded as constituting taxable commerce.

VI. CHARITY, OVERSEAS AID, AND TRADE

In terms of charity law, it matters little whether a charity chooses to commit its resources to furthering its charitable purposes within the country where it is established or on an international basis. In terms of scale, however, the bilateral government-to-government aid budgets of Western nations drawn up in response to the plight of developing nations dwarf any possible resource input by charities, although nongovernmental charities are often both funded by governments and used by them to channel their aid budget to recipient nations. More important is the pronounced and inescapable political dimension that distinguishes the international and domestic roles of charity. Although in many respects the Titmuss concept of the "gift relationship"[125] would appear to hold equally well for charitable transactions conducted on an international basis, the political context is then particularly revealing, and also perhaps serves to illuminate the dynamics of domestic charitable transactions.

A. Political Context

A government's choice as to which states receive bilateral aid is a political matter. The decision will be at least influenced by current strategic policies taken in conjunction with obligations entered into through international trade agreements, loans, and tariffs, and will also be vulnerable to cutbacks in times of economic recession.[126] Charities can find themselves under considerable pressure to channel resources in directions that are compliant with the policies that have determined the direction of government trade. Only those that are large enough, structured as financially independent foundations, and have political leverage in donor and recipient nations will be able to withstand government constraints or inducements and decide for themselves where, when, and how they may best contribute to the amelioration of hardship overseas.

1. Aid and Trade

The likely impact of charitable resources has to be calculated within the boundaries set by government trade agreements. For example, the Common Agricultural Policy of the European Union has set the parameters for the 27 Member States in

[125] See Titmuss, R. A., *The Gift Relationship: From Human Blood to Social Policy*, Allen and Unwin, London, 1970.

[126] The U.K. government announced in October 2010 that it would honor the commitment made in the 1970s to spend 0.7 percent of GDP on overseas aid by 2013.

relation to trade in agricultural produce with developing nations.[127] This has led to massive distortions in the real marketplace price for certain staple goods such as sugar. This in turn creates difficulties for those charities that are furthering their purposes (such as promoting commerce or preventing poverty) by investing in the development of an indigenous trading capacity.

There is also the fact that whatever injection of aid is made to the fragile economies of developing nations may have a disproportionate impact on existing patterns of commerce. The distortion caused by bilateral aid to local chains of supply and demand through gratuitous acts of benevolence has in the past caused serious long-term disruption to established family, tribal, and community networks, though many NGOs have since learned to operate with the awareness and sensitivity necessary to minimize interference with customary coping mechanisms. The irony is that this is usually coupled with crippling long-term debt repayments, often to the same developed nations that are providing the overseas aid. The net result can simply de-incentivize the recipient nation.

B. Intervention and Sustainable Growth

Although there are, unfortunately, many examples of situations where foreign charity input has been effectively negated by foreign government aid and trade skewing local market conditions, there are also instances where charity and trade have had a demonstrably positive impact on a recipient nation's economy.

1. Charitable Impact

The Fairtrade Foundation[128] illustrates what charitable activity in a trading context can achieve. Created in the Netherlands in the late 1980s, by September 2004 Fairtrade had grown to include 422 certified producer groups in 49 producer countries selling to hundreds of Fairtrade registered importers, licensees, and retailers in 19 countries. Such numeric measures of its success, however, belie the broader significance of the Fairtrade initiative. It has demonstrated that a form of intervention based on collaborative skill development can offer a more viable strategy for breaking the dependency dynamic that often accompanies "the gift relationship" model practiced by donor nations: The recipient is more likely to achieve a greater measure of self-affirmation, self-reliance, and long-term sustainability than by relying on

[127] The Common Agricultural Policy (CAP) is a system of European Union agricultural subsidies and programs. It represented 48 percent of the EU's budget, €49.8 billion in 2006 (up from €48.5 billion in 2005). See further, Grant, W., *The Common Agricultural Policy,* Macmillan Press, Basingstoke (U.K.), 1997.

[128] Established in the U.K. in 1992, the Fairtrade Foundation is a charity that works to empower disadvantaged producers in developing countries by ensuring that products retailed in the U.K. have been produced in accordance with internationally agreed Fairtrade standards. See further at: http://www.fairtrade.org.uk/.

handouts. Many international charities have developed trading arms that provide the vital service of finding and managing markets for locally produced goods. To support this service, they often have organizational infrastructure, in particular developing nations. The protection of that investment may at times arise as a factor influencing choice of destination for aid.

In recent years, the emergence of wealthy and highly skilled charities, with a focus on intervention in developing nations, show considerable potential for effecting lasting change. The Bill and Melinda Gates Foundation,[129] Make Poverty History,[130] and other philanthropic initiatives are perhaps beginning to achieve an even larger impact on health and well-being in Sub-Saharan Africa than was ever achieved through the many preceding decades of government aid and charity input. It may well be that any breakthrough made in combating malaria, polio, and AIDS will come from the private initiatives of charity rather than from government intervention.

2. Aid/Trade

An alternative model for effecting sustainable growth on a government-to-government basis is currently being demonstrated by China's involvement in Africa.[131] The many decades of aid and trade involvement in Sub-Saharan Africa by the United States, U.K., and France have in the course of the past few years been wholly eclipsed by the impact of Chinese investment. Unlike the Western powers, China is a restrained donor, giving little in the way of direct aid and canceling the bilateral debts of some 30 African countries, while making available credit, loans, and development assistance. It has made a considerable and growing commitment to putting in place basic infrastructure such as roads, bridges, dams, railways, and power plants. However, there can be no doubt that China is seeking a return on its investment in terms of oil, timber, minerals, and agricultural produce. Equally, there can be no doubt that China is also focused on gaining land, mineral, and fishery rights to secure natural resources at low cost and on expanding markets for its products. Moreover, China rarely attaches labor, human rights, environmental, or governance standards to its investments or loans, which brings into question the sustainability of its projects. Arguably, it is rapidly depleting natural resources that need careful management as these are often the main revenue streams of African countries. There is also concern that Chinese involvement has hampered, or is undermining, Western efforts to gain political and economic reforms across Sub-Saharan Africa. Although this may be interpreted as respectful nonintervention in established forms of governance, it can also have the effect of entrenching corrupt

[129] See further, at: http://en.wikipedia.org/wiki/Bill_%26_Melinda_Gates_Foundation.

[130] Launched in 2005, this was the biggest and most media-promoted antipoverty campaign in history. See further at: http://www.makepovertyhistory.org/takeaction/.

[131] Tull, D. L., "China's Engagement in Africa: Scope, Significance and Consequences," in *Journal of Modern African Studies*, Vol. 44, No. 3, 2006, at pp. 459–79.

ruling elites. Notwithstanding these serious caveats, this combination of trade and investment in infrastructure over the past 10 to 15 years has allowed many developing African countries to make significant and sustained socioeconomic progress that they had been unable to achieve during previous decades of Western aid/trade involvement.[132]

3. Building Trust and Promoting Independence

International altruistic activity is useful in itself, and it demonstrates good faith. Aid and trade, however, is at best a compromised means for pursuing such goals. Although there can be little doubt that altruism is no more the driving force for the involvement of China in Africa than it was for its Western predecessors, as trade policies and long-term strategic political and economic interests similarly color the motivation for involvement, China is also engaged in a range of capacity-building initiatives. This may result in recipients being able to avoid the "culture of dependency" or "clientism" that characterized their relationships with previous donors. Alternatively, it may prove to be a particularly pernicious distortion of the "gift relationship."[133]

VII. CONCLUSION

There are real dangers for the charitable status of an organization that engages in commercial activity. The traditional constraints were largely embodied in the common law "incidental and ancillary" rule, which operated to ensure that the relationship between a charity and its trading arm did not grow to the point where the latter was no longer simply a means to assist in achieving the former's charitable objects, but had instead become an end in itself. The rule guards against commercial activity that may have either grown so disproportionate in scale that it could no longer be defined as "incidental" or have grown so far away in nature from the charitable purpose that it could not be defined as "ancillary"; either way, it would have subverted the charitable purpose and invalidated any right to continued charitable status. Although it remains relevant, this rule no longer operates as the main common law gatekeeping mechanism in determining whether trading activity is compliant with charitable status. The legal and tax relationship between charity and trading has acquired additional complexity in recent years with considerable jurisdictional variation.

[132] The author acknowledges with gratitude the contribution of Blake Ratcliff (The Fletcher School of Law and Diplomacy, University of Connecticut School of Law) to this section.

[133] See further The Munk Debates, *Does the 21st Century Belong to China?*, Aurea Foundation, Toronto, 2011.

3

CHARITY AND THE NONPROFIT SECTOR

I. INTRODUCTION

This chapter identifies and considers the ways in which charity represents the nonprofit sector as a whole. It begins by drawing attention to its roots in particular areas of service provision, such as education, hospitals and other health care facilities, day care, social housing, etc. It examines the evidence indicating that these long-established services have always been areas of crucial importance to the sector and to government. It suggests that the contemporary strategic significance of charity, as provider of key services and sector representative along the public benefit frontier, is growing in all leading common law jurisdictions. It then considers the significance of the nonprofit sector for government as the locus for generating social capital, serving as a conduit for consolidating civil society, and promoting responsible civic engagement. This view is countered by the newly emerged characterization of the sector as the weak link in the government-led international fight against global terrorism.

The chapter considers the lengths that some governments have gone to, in recent years, to build formal links with the nonprofit sector. Following the lead provided by the U.K. with compacts, accords, protocols, and the Office of the Third Sector, the governments of several other countries such as Ireland, Singapore, New Zealand, Australia, and Canada have, with varying success, also sought to construct similar links. The chapter concludes with the theory that the existence of a thoroughly negotiated understanding between government and the sector is probably a prerequisite for any subsequent managed transfer of public benefit service provision from government to charity. Without that platform in place, the probability arises that market forces would be left to determine the future provision of such services.

II. BACKGROUND: CHARITIES, THE NONPROFIT SECTOR, AND EVOLVING SOCIAL SERVICE PROVISION

In the U.K., as elsewhere in the common law world, the social services brief of charity was first formally sketched in the provisions of the Statute of Charitable Uses 1601.[1] The Preamble laid down government's expectations as to the contribution that should be made by charity to furthering the public benefit:

> Releife of aged impotent and poore people, some for Maintenance of sicke and maymed Souldiers and Marriners, Schooles of Learninge, Free Schooles and Schollers in Universities, some for Repaire of Bridges Portes Havens Causwaies Churches Seabankes and Highwaies, some for Educacion and prefermente of Orphans, some for or towardes Reliefe Stocke or Maintenance of Howses of Correccion, some for Mariages of poore Maides, some for Supportacion Ayde and Helpe of younge tradesmen Handicraftesmen and persons decayed, and others for reliefe or redemption of Prisoners or Captives, and for aide or ease of any poore Inhabitantes concerninge paymente of Fifteenes, setting out of Souldiers and other Taxes...

The categories and expectations identified there were subsequently classified in *Pemsel*[2] and extended by the judiciary, with a considerable degree of uniformity across all common law nations. Those principles have come to constitute the contemporary social agenda of charity, and mark out the very heart of the nonprofit sector.

There is, of course, more to charity and the nonprofit sector than the brief for social services provision. The Preamble also implied that charity should have a role in supporting social norms and references to assisting the "Mariages of poore Maides" and the "Maintenance of Howses of Correccion," which indicated a legislative intent to promote a congruity between the agendas of charities and government on the assumption that both shared a common interest in activities that conformed with and tended to preserve the values of contemporary society. Further, the suggestion of government endorsement for provision that maintains social order and defends the status quo is implied in the language "setting out of Souldiers." That the institutions of government and charity should over time jointly engage in arrangements that are resistant to change and serve instead to strengthen "the establishment," induce conformity, and dampen dissent has arguably been a significant but largely overlooked strand to their relationship.

[1] Statute of 43 Eliz. 1 Cap. 4.

[2] Commissioners for Special Purposes of Income Tax v. Pemsel [1890] AC 531.

A. Social Service Provision

In the U.K., from at least the time of the Reformation until local authorities were established in 1929,[3] the responsibility for meeting the needs of the poor, the ill, the disabled, and those otherwise disadvantaged fell mainly to charities. It was in the Preamble to the 1601 Act, however, that legislative recognition was first given to charity's core business, and the current pattern of charitable social service provision clearly originated from this blueprint. Although a similar pattern of provision evolved in other common law nations it was nowhere as embedded, sophisticated, and diversified as in the U.K. In some nations, most notably the United States, the level and range of charity social service provision was low and variable, with private enterprise responsible for more and government for less than their U.K. counterparts. This initially crude, shared, but growing ever more dense specification of services and public utility provision has afforded a basis for the sense of solidarity and civil society awareness that now links third sector representatives and institutions (academics, practitioners, and regulators) across the developed common law nations. It also facilitates the comparative analysis of themes and trends in contemporary sector development within and between those nations.

1. Health Care

The "releife of aged impotent and poore people," the first purpose declared charitable in the Preamble, gave rise to a wide range of health care and related services. Charities provided the hospitals,[4] almshouses,[5] infirmaries or dispensaries,[6] asylums for the blind,[7] the care services of nurses and almoners, and the long-term support needed by the impoverished ill, unmarried mothers, and abandoned children. In 1739, for example, Thomas Coram established a hospital for foundling children; it survived into modern times.[8] Charities also provided support services for the carers including rest homes for

[3] The Local Government Act 1929 (19 & 20 Geo V c.17) abolished all boards of guardians for poor-law unions; responsibility for public assistance was transferred to county councils and county boroughs. The local authorities took over infirmaries and fever hospitals, while the workhouses became public assistance institutions. See further Bartholemew, J., *The Welfare State We're In*, Politico's Publishing, London, 2006.

[4] Pelham v. Anderson (1764) 2 Eden 296.

[5] Harbin v. Masterman [1894] 2 Ch. 184.

[6] See Pelham v. Anderson (1764) 2 Eden 296; A-G v. Gascoigne (1833) 2 My & K 647; and Biscoe v. Jackson (1887) 35 Ch D 460 CA.

[7] Henshaw v. Atkinson (1818) 3 Madd 306.

[8] Followed in due course by Dr Barnardo who established his first home for orphans and abandoned children in Stepney in 1870 and the National Society for the Prevention of Cruelty to Children, which was founded in 1884; both still provide services in respect of children orphaned, abandoned, or abused.

nurses,[9] for the relief of the disabled or sick,[10] or for the "sick and wounded."[11] Many gifts were construed as charitable under this head: For example, a gift for the aged[12] had to either expressly aim to relieve poverty or to relieve infirmities associated with aging (e.g., lack of mobility, ill health, etc.).

However, the development of health and social care services also owes much to charitable activity pursued under the fourth *Pemsel* head—especially gifts to a hospital, bequests for patients in named hospitals,[13] and gifts for the endowment of hospital beds.[14] Gifts for the relief of the "impotent," or persons impaired by a physical disability, were commonly accorded charitable status under this head, as also were the development of related aids (e.g., braille for the blind) whether or not the ultimate beneficiaries were rich or poor,[15] as well as gifts to promote the curing of alcoholics or drug addicts or to assist in the prevention of such addictions.[16]

2. Education

The link between education and charity was established in the Preamble with its reference to "schools of learning, free schools and scholars of universities; . . . the education and preferment of orphans." Thereafter the history of the development of education in England has been one in which separate provision made by church and the wealthy prevailed initially instead of an encompassing state system.[17] State intervention into traditional charity areas such as education (to introduce public secular education for young children in England) began in the 19th century[18] and continued with the National Insurance Act 1911, which laid the first foundations of the welfare state. Private education had been available to those who could afford it at least a century earlier when the church and other charities maintained a patchwork of schools for poor children. Significantly, charities also developed services judged to have a long-term uplifting effect, such as apprenticeships[19] and training.

For most of the 19th century, the state contribution took the form of grants aiding the education provided by church-based and nonconformist schools. The "public

[9] See Re White's Will Trusts [1950] 1 All E.R. 528.

[10] See Re Lewis [1955] Ch 104 and Re Elliott (1910) 102 LT 528.

[11] See Re Hillier [1944] 1 All ER 528.

[12] It is unlikely that the courts would still concur with the view of Kay, J. in Re Wall (1889) 42 Ch D 510 that "men and women not under fifty years of age" adequately satisfies any modern definition of "aged."

[13] See Re Roadley [1930] 1 Ch 524.

[14] See A-G v. Belgrave Hospital [1910] 1 Ch 73.

[15] See John Brunyate (1945) 61 LQR 268, at p. 272.

[16] See Re Hood [1931] 1 Ch 240; IRC v. Falkirk Temperance Café Trust 1927 SC 261.

[17] See Bartholemew, *The Welfare State We're In*, at Chap. 4.

[18] In 1856 a Department of Education was established, and the Education Act 1870 finally laid the foundations for a system of mandatory primary education, which was to be secular and freely available to poor children.

[19] A-G v. Minshull (1798) 4 Ves 11 and A-G v. Wansay (1808) 15 Ves 231.

school" system, educating the children of a wealthy elite, was established during this period and consolidated in the early decades of the 20th century. Until the latter half of the 19th century, such schooling as existed for all others was provided by the church and other charitable organizations.

More recently, the practice of privately endowing fellowships,[20] scholarships,[21] and university chairs has become a well-worn route for establishing charitable trusts for educational purposes. Gifts have routinely been confirmed to be charitable when given to found new departments or faculties within a college,[22] to endow a college library,[23] or to benefit learned societies[24] or institutions for the advancement of science.[25] Facilities such as zoos,[26] public libraries,[27] museums,[28] and botanical gardens[29] have also been recognized as appropriate objects for charitable trusts for the advancement of education.

3. Housing

Providing a place of shelter or refuge for the destitute, the homeless, and the abandoned children was perhaps one of the first and most basic acts of charity, one traditionally available from religious organizations.[30] Charities gradually acquired a reputation for providing more specialist accommodation such as flats for the poor elderly,[31] children's homes,[32] homes for ladies in reduced circumstances,[33] homes for working young women,[34] and for female teachers.[35] The provision of a rest home, as a support service for a defined group of persons with a need for such a service,[36] has

[20] Attorney-General v. Whorwood (1750) 1 Ves 537.

[21] R v. Newman (1684) 1 Lev 284.

[22] Davenport v. Davenport Foundation, 222 P. 2d 11 (1950).

[23] See A-G v. Marchant (1866) LR 3 Eq 424, at p. 430 and see also Re Good [1905] 2 Ch. 60.

[24] British Museum Trustees v. White (1826) 2 Sim & St 594.

[25] Weir v. Crum-Brown [1908] AC 162.

[26] Re Lopes, Bence-Jones v. Zoological Society of London [1931] 2 Ch. 130.

[27] See Abbott v. Fraser (1874) LR 6 PC 96; Re Russell Institution [1898] 2 Ch. 72; Re Jones [1898] 2 Ch. 83; and Re Pitt-Rivers [1902] 1 Ch. 403, CA.

[28] See Re Holburne (1885) 53 L.T. 212; Re Spence [1938] 2 Ch. 96; British Museum v. White (1826) 2 Sim. & St. 594; and Re Allsop (1884) 1 TLR 4.

[29] Townley v. Bedwell (1801) 6 Ves 194 and Harrison v. Southampton Corporation (1854) 2 Sm & G 387.

[30] See, e.g., , Brady, J. C., *Religion and the Law of Charities in Ireland*, W&S Magowan, Belfast, 1975.

[31] Re Cottam's Will Trusts [1955] 1 W.L.R. 1299.

[32] Re Sahal's Will Trusts (1958) 1 WLR 1243.

[33] See Re Douglas (1887) 35 Ch D 472; Re Lacy [1899] 2 Ch. 149; and Spiller v. Maude (1881) 32 Ch D 158n.

[34] Rolls v. Miller (1884) 27 Ch D 71.

[35] See Re Estlin (1903) 72 LJ Ch 687.

[36] See Re James [1932] 2 Ch 25, at p. 31, per Farwell, J.

long been charitable, though, as is often observed, a trust to establish a rest home for millionaires would fail.

In the U.K., as the era of the Poor Laws gave way to the welfare state at the beginning of the 20th century, a number of charities developed an interest in providing housing in general and residential care facilities in particular.

4. Public Utilities

The government intention that charities should play a role in the provision and maintenance of public utilities was clearly stated in the Preamble (repair of bridges, ports, highways, etc.) and recognized by Sir William Grant as coming within the legal definition of charitable ("objects of general public utility").[37] There being no requirement for either poverty or necessity on the part of prospective users, this interpretation of "charity" has attracted considerable controversy over the centuries but has nonetheless made an important contribution to the physical infrastructure and to enriching the texture of modern society. It has been the means for erecting or restoring not just facilities for general public use such as bridges and parks[38] but those such as concert halls and art galleries that serve a narrower and, arguably, more privileged sector of the public. It has permitted the judiciary, by analogy with public utility items listed in the Preamble, to extend charitable status to: the advancement of agriculture;[39] the national defense;[40] the provision of Internet services;[41] the advancement of the merchant navy,[42] and the police force.[43] The protection of lives and property has also been found to be charitable: for example, lifeboats[44] and a fire brigade.[45]

Interestingly, from an early stage the promotion of commerce had been recognized under this head as a charitable purpose in its own right, subject to the satisfaction of the public benefit test. In *Commissioners of Inland Revenue v. Yorkshire Agricultural Society*[46] the advancement of agriculture was found to be charitable, whereas in *Crystal Palace v. Minister of Town Planning*[47] the promotion of industry, commerce, and art was also so found. Indeed, it is difficult to ascertain the parameters for containing the

37 Morice v. Bishop of Durham (1804) 32 ER 656, 9 Ves. J. 399.

38 Note that the Mortmain and Charitable Uses Act 1888, s.6, provided for charitable status to be extended to parks created for public recreation.

39 Pig Marketing Board v. Commissioners of Inland Revenue (1945) NI 155 and Commissioners of Inland Revenue v. Yorkshire Agricultural Society (1928) KB 611.

40 Re Good (1905) 2 Ch. 60 and Re Gray (1925) Ch. 362.

41 Vancouver Regional Freenet Assoc. v. Minister of National Revenue [1996] 137 DLR 4th 406.

42 Re Corbyn (1941) Ch. 400.

43 Inland Revenue Commissioners v. City of Glasgow Police Athletic Association (1953) AC 380.

44 Johnston v. Swann (1818) 3 Mad. 457.

45 Re Wokingham Fire Brigade Trusts (1951) Ch. 373.

46 (1928) KB 611.

47 (1951) Ch. 132.

spread of charitable status for public utility service provision: Internet eligibility could conceivably pave the way for other similar services such as electricity, street lighting, highways, and drinking water.

5. Social Control Facilities

In addition to the services and utilities listed above, available to the general public on a consensual basis, the Preamble also gave permission for the charitable provision of more specialized facilities restricted to the use of clearly defined minority groups and accessible only on a compulsory basis.[48] The suggestion that charity should be engaged in the provision of such social control facilities as "Howses of Correccion" has allowed the charitable provision of facilities such as detention centers, asylums, and youth training units, and, in recent years, prisons.

6. Defraying Government Expenditure

Whereas the provision of self-evidently socially beneficial facilities, such as hospitals and schools, merit charitable status on the *Pemsel* grounds of relieving poverty or advancing education, other forms of social service provision may similarly qualify simply by the fact that they spare the government the expense of establishing equivalent facilities.[49] This approach has been considerably developed in recent years, particularly in the U.K. and the United States.

III. CHARITY, OTHER NONPROFITS, AND THE SECTOR

There is more to the nonprofit sector than charity; indeed the proliferation of new forms of non-government organizations in recent years has made charity, numerically, a minority entity in almost all common law jurisdictions, and certainly in the U.S. In fact, the sector has long provided a home for various other forms of non-government organizations such as cooperatives, non-provident bodies, and other mutual benefit entities. In recent years community foundations and social enterprises have come to prominence. New hybrid structures, seeking an optimal fusion of commerce and public benefit, are now constantly emerging as a consequence of

[48] See McIntosh, M. K., "Poverty, Charity and Coercion in Elizabethan England," in *Journal of Interdisciplinary History*, Vol. 35, No. 3, 2005, p. 458.

[49] It has for some time been recognized that a charity providing a service that relieves local or general taxation is pursuing a legitimate charitable purpose provided it is for the benefit of the public; see, e.g., AG v. Bushby (1857) 24 Beav 299. See, e.g., Charity Commission, "Public Service Delivery by Charities—Commission Decision in (i) Trafford Community Leisure Trust and (ii) Wigan Leisure and Culture Trust," at p. 6., where "it was accepted as a good charitable purpose to relieve the community from general or local taxation provided that such purpose was applied for the benefit of a sufficient section of the community."

experimentation in entities and arrangements designed to facilitate cross-sector functioning. Although its diversity, in terms of type and size of organizations and their disparity of life spans, makes the nonprofit sector somewhat unwieldy and incoherent, its present physical composition is only part of the story.

A. Sector Origins

The nonprofit sector's raison d'être lies in principles that first prompted the emergence of organizations to pursue objectives for which, it was perceived, neither government nor the market held solutions. Principles that, thereafter: informed their collective sense of purpose and direction, differentiated the nonprofit sector from others, and constituted an important legacy that gave the sector its current distinctive ethos. Although charitable purposes, the gift relationship, and the central concept of altruism made a significant contribution to sector origins, much was also owed to forces that operated alongside charity.

1. Associations and Rights

The history of collective action for the common good, particularly during the colonial era in countries such as the United States, Ireland, and Australia, probably has its roots as much in the struggle for rights of association and freedom of expression as in charity. The compassion, benevolence, and resources contributed by charity were complemented, or countered, from an early stage by associations formed to articulate, protect, and advance some of the more basic rights we now take for granted. Among the first of such rights was the freedom to form associations. This, along with the rights to peacefully assemble and freedom of expression, have for centuries been recognized as fundamental attributes of democratic citizenship. The organizations, groups, and movements responsible for ensuring that such rights were eventually integrated into our legal system have brought a proud tradition of advocacy and independent action, and a capacity to assertively campaign for social change, in order to form a distinctive strand in the makeup of the modern nonprofit sector.

2. Voluntary Organizations and Self-Help

Following the revolutions in France and America, socialist principles began to mix with philanthropy in England, giving rise to both theoretical and very practical expressions of a new liberal activism[50] that spread through the common law world and laid the basis for a principled and practical approach that looked inward to the community rather than out to the state for resources. By the time the 18th century drew to a close, the traditional role of charity had come to be viewed by some as unsatisfactory, as a

[50] See, e.g., John Stuart Mill, *Principles of Political Economy* (1848), Longmans, Green and Co., London [1909].

pernicious corollary to persisting structural divisions in society, complicit with and ultimately serving to reinforce the position of the wealthy.[51] This coincided with the final collapse of the state's Poor Law system.[52]

In England, examples of such self-help initiatives would include the Magdalen Hospital for Penitent Prostitutes, established in 1758 to provide respite and care for prostitutes and encourage their "reformation," and the Royal Philanthropic Society, founded in 1788, which directed its efforts toward training destitute street children for service in the cottage industries. Then there was the Charity Organisation Society,[53] launched in 1869, which sought to address poverty in a methodical fashion. It provided little in the way of direct gifts or grants but instead strove to build mentoring relationships between its lady "visitors" and the wives and mothers of destitute families, through which habits of thrift, frugality, healthy eating, and hygiene could be imparted. The Charity Organisation Society's principal aim was rehabilitation: to restore the destitute to a more self-sufficient and productive life. It was quite opposed in principle to providing doles or alms, as this was believed to encourage dependency.[54]

3. Collectivism

Collectivism emerged in England toward the end of the 19th century as a basis for organized mutual support through initiatives such as those that launched the Friendly Societies.[55] Prominent liberal activists, including Mary Wollstonecraft,[56] Mary Carpenter,[57] and Octavia Hill,[58] generated public awareness of contemporary issues of social inequity. A new pattern of social activism emerged that was most fully embodied in the creation of Associational Charities.[59] Leadership for a new approach was provided by "chocolate philanthropists" from the Quaker confectionary families

[51] See, e.g., observations made by George Bernard Shaw.

[52] The Poor Law regime had collapsed by the end of the 19th century but was not formally laid to rest until the local authorities were set up by the Local Government Act 1929.

[53] Its full name was the Society for Organising Charitable Relief and Suppression of Mendicity.

[54] See further Whelan, R., *Helping the Poor,* Civitas, London, 2001, at pp. 9–24. Another such organization was the Marine Society, a charity established in 1756 to provide apprenticeships in seamanship for young destitute teenage boys.

[55] The 1874 report of the Royal Commission on Friendly Societies offered support for the new forms of intervention into the circumstances of the poor.

[56] See, e.g., Gordon, L., *Mary Wollstonecraft: A New Genus,* Little Brown, London, 2004.

[57] See Carpenter, M., *Reformatory Schools for the Perishing and Dangerous Classes and for the Prevention of Juvenile Delinquency,* Charles Gilpin, London, 1851.

[58] Founder member of the Charity Organisation Society; see Hill, O., *Homes of the London Poor,* Macmillan, London, 1875.

[59] See Hitchcock, T., "Paupers and Preachers: The SPCK and the Parochial Workhouse Movement," in Davison, L. et al. (eds.), *Stilling the Grumbling Hive: The Response to Social and Economic Problems in England, 1689–1750,* Sutton, Stroud, U.K., 1992, at pp. 145–66.

of Fry, Cadbury, and Rowntree. Their construction of model villages[60] that enabled whole communities to be self-sufficient and mutually supportive offered a new and challenging interpretation of philanthropy: an initiative which, in diverting the profits of commerce to fund charitable activity, was designed to leverage structural change in disadvantaged communities. These efforts presaged the intervention of venture philanthropists a century later. This approach contrasted sharply with the previous centuries of alms, the workhouse, and ignominious dependency, and provided a tangible example of the public benefit outcomes possible in a fortuitous marriage of charity and profit. It was an ethos that gave birth to organizations formed to provide sustained economic security for their members, such as cooperatives, guilds, mutual benefit associations, and the Credit Union movement.[61] This era first saw the emergence of "social economy,"[62] a concept developed by writers such as Herbert Spencer,[63] Kirkman Gray,[64] and the Fabian socialism of the Webbs.[65] By the close of the 19th century, myriad forms of voluntary action had taken root, and these were to flower prolifically through the 20th century in the U.K., the United States, and throughout the common law world.[66]

B. The Modern Sector

The nonprofit sector is a fluid, amorphous, ragbag entity of uncertain size and components:[67] There is no way of establishing reliable data due to the many categories of organizations that are not legally required to register the fact and purpose of their existence, and increasingly its boundaries overlap other sectors. From the Salvation Army to al-Qa'ida, from a local train-spotting club to the Bill and Melinda Gates

60 In 1900, the Bournville Village Trust was established to manage the village. The trust focused on providing schools, hospitals, museums, public baths, and reading rooms.

61 Organizations set up for the mutual benefit of members have, of course, consistently been refused charitable status: see, e.g., Nuffield (Lord) v. Inland Revenue Commissioners (1946) 175 LT 465.

62 The middle ground between the public and private sectors, or between the economic interests of government and market, is referred to as the "social economy." It is territory occupied by organizations with an economic role to provide public benefit services in collaboration with those in need and to do so through methods that allow for minimal private profit. Such organizations would include cooperatives, building societies, development trusts, and credit unions. They typically share a mission to provide new and innovative solutions to issues (whether they be socially, economically, or environmentally based) and to satisfy the needs of members and users that have been ignored or inadequately fulfilled by the private or public sectors.

63 See Spencer, H., *Man versus the State*, the Contemporary Review, London, 1884.

64 See *Philanthropy and the State*, B. L. Hutchins, London, 1908.

65 See Webb, S. and Webb, B., *The Prevention of Destitution*, Longmans, London, 1911.

66 See, e.g., Lake, P. and Pincus, S., "Rethinking the Public Sphere in Early Modern England," in *Journal of British Studies*, Vol. 45, 2006, at pp. 270–92.

67 See, e.g., Lyons, M., *The Third Sector*, Allen & Unwin, Australia, 2001, pp. 5–26.

Foundation, whether neighborhood-based or multinational, nonprofit organizations share little in common other than belonging to neither government nor commerce and having an uneven entitlement to tax exemption (differing according to status). Some are totally reliant on a handful of volunteers; others rely wholly on salaried professional staff; most have a mix of both. Although by far the majority enrich society and add a participative dimension to the workings of our modern democracies, others such as the Mafia and paramilitary groups corrode society. As Lyons noted, "it is also important to recognize that the third sector has a dark side."[68]

The disparate components of the modern nonprofit sector—varying immensely in size, activities, spread, and duration—often have little in common and so are unable to act in a coordinated fashion in pursuit of long-term collective goals. To a large extent, the capacity to do so is culturally determined. In the U.K. and Irish jurisdictions, the sector, with its trust and welfare state heritage, has achieved considerable autonomy, cohesion, and maturity as a political entity and is now able to negotiate internally and externally as a coherent entity. This is less the case in other jurisdictions. The sector varies from being large but fragmented with a pronounced religious and service delivery orientation in Australia, to being diffuse and focused largely on supplementing welfare benefits, improving fund-raising, and reducing tax liability in Canada and the United States.

1. Mutual Benefit Organizations

The range of organizations established to promote and share acquired benefits among their members is considerable; it includes: cooperatives, friendly societies,[69] building societies, industrial and provident societies,[70] credit unions, and trade associations. Some of these may occasionally qualify for charitable status, but for the most part they do not as benefits derived from their activities are restricted to members rather than made available for distribution to the public.

2. Self-Help Organizations

Many mutual benefit organizations are clearly also self-help in nature. Any difference will lie in the probability that the latter will be more short-term with a single-issue focus and that its governance arrangements will be heavily weighted in favor of user

[68] Lyons, *The Third Sector*, at p. 21.

[69] Established in England and Wales under the Friendly Societies Act 1896, these include mutual insurance and assurance bodies, benevolent societies, and other societies formed for purposes such as the promotion of science, literature, and education.

[70] Established in England and Wales under the Industrial and Provident Societies Acts 1893–1978, these organizations (usually commercial) are formed "for carrying on any industries, businesses or trades," which includes agricultural producers, group water schemes, and housing cooperatives.

representation. Housing associations, community development organizations, and training-for-employment associations can be readily recognized as essentially self-help in nature. Organizations dedicated to furthering or resisting some project or cause, which may entail antisocial or even illegal activity, including paramilitary bodies, must also be acknowledged as falling within this classification. The social enterprise phenomenon often has a strong self-help element.

3. Lobbying/Campaigning Organizations

Again this is obviously not a classification that excludes any of the above or, necessarily, charities. The tradition of advocacy and dissent, of mediating on conflicts of interest and of championing worthy causes, is represented in the modern nonprofit sector by bodies such as trade unions, law centers, citizens' advice bureaus, and indeed by political parties.

C. Charities

Distinct, for the most part, from all the above, charities (including charitable trusts or foundations) exist for the public benefit, which they pursue by giving effect to legally defined charitable purposes. For many reasons, they have been and remain the most powerful players in the nonprofit sector.

1. Role in the Sector

Charities are at the heart of the nonprofit sector, controlling most of its assets, generating much of its income, and contributing longevity and consistency while deploying the majority of its volunteers (which constitute a significant proportion of the national workforce) across most sector activities. As employer, manager of assets, and generator of income, charities add significant fuel to the engines of national economy. Over long periods of time, sometimes for centuries, charities have provided the key components of our social infrastructure: religious organizations and their churches, together with universities and hospitals and an array of varied institutions comprising the fabric of our communities; all had and continue to have charitable status. They have played a particularly prominent role in health and social care service provision, education, and culture (including sport and recreation in some jurisdictions).

Through their activities in the areas of poverty, education, and religion, and in such other areas of benefit to the community as health and social care, charities ameliorate hardship, address issues of fundamental concern, and facilitate the growth of civil society. They contribute to the alleviation of poverty and facilitate the articulation of grievance, and by so doing, charities reduce social tensions. By reinforcing the standing of religion and education, charities have helped provide the means for both to become more generally pervasive and to build their institutional infrastructures.

2. Leadership

In recent years, the nonprofit sector has generally become more organized and has produced high-profile umbrella bodies able to speak for it on sector-wide issues. Simultaneously, it has also become more diversified, accommodating an ever-broadening range of organizations. It has developed a research capacity, has its own dedicated banking and finance facilities, uses sophisticated multimedia techniques to communicate, and, with its well-established policy units, is often called upon to assist in the framing of policy to guide government intervention on behalf of the socially disadvantaged.

Of all nonprofit sector entities, charities are best placed to strategically act as a bridge between government and the community by representing a wide range of groups and causes. Because they may exist in perpetuity, charities are able to cultivate trusted, long-term relationships with their respective beneficiaries and serve as intermediaries on their behalf with successive governments. Their longevity and specialized interest in specific charitable purposes enables them to compile data archives that can inform government policy makers in search of practical and acceptable solutions to problems affecting related groups of beneficiaries.

In the current fluctuating and uncertain socioeconomic environment, charities, with their wealth, longevity, and established relationships with those who avail of public benefit services and utilities, are natural leaders, and as such have given some stability, continuity, and cohesion to the nonprofit sector.

3. Autonomy

Charities could once be counted upon to exercise leadership on breaking social issues and to be at the forefront of movements for social betterment. Today, they are no longer quite so prominent. Government funding, which some suggest[71] is being employed as a tool to facilitate government colonization of the sector, has compromised the independence of charities[72] as it has that of all the larger public benefit service providers in the nonprofit sector. Arguably, however, the predations of commerce are also a cause of the current muting of dissent in the sector and the blurring of its boundaries.

[71] See, e.g., Morris, D., "Paying the Piper: The 'Contract Culture' as Dependency Culture for Charities," in Dunn, A., (ed.), *The Voluntary Sector, the State and the Law,* Hart Publishing, Oxford, 2000, at pp. 123–41.

[72] See Advisory Group on Campaigning and the Voluntary Sector, *Report of the Advisory Group on Campaigning and the Voluntary Sector,* London, 2007; *Speaking Truth to Power: A Discussion Paper on the Voluntary Sector's Relationship with Government,* Baring Foundation, London, 2000; and the Commission on the Future of the Voluntary Sector in England, *Meeting the Challenge of Change: Voluntary Action into the 21st Century,* NCVO Publications, London, 1996.

IV. GOVERNMENT, CHARITY, AND THE SECTOR

The Preamble agenda, as developed through principles and precedents established by charity law over centuries, and largely pooled between the common law nations, shaped a core code for mediating responsibility between government and charity on matters of public benefit provision. In modern times, largely due to the absence of any other platform, this has come to play a role of some political significance as the government for various reasons endeavors to bridge the gap between it and the sector. Among the more pressing of these push factors are the need to: reduce government public service expenditure; consolidate civil society by generating a greater sense of civic responsibility and engaging more directly with the electorate; and regulate the sector to safeguard against fiscal abuse, promote better governance arrangements, and supervise the flow of funds to prevent their use by terrorists.

A. Reducing Government Public Benefit Service Provision

The last decades of the 20th century witnessed the general retreat of the state as a public benefit service provider, accompanied by a steady increase in the devolving of responsibility for that provision to commercial entities, charities, other nonprofits, and to various combinations or mutations of such bodies. Falling birthrates,[73] increased longevity, outsourcing of manufacturing capacity, the need to devote resources to combating the threat of global terrorism and manage the turmoil in banking and other financial institutions, all served to accelerate the erosion of tax revenues. There was also the perennial concern in some states to further reduce the costs of service provision and its related bureaucracy. This resulted in an acceptance among the developed nations of the common law world that the future capacity of government to meet the rising costs of public benefit service provision was becoming irretrievably compromised. Consequently, the first decade of the new century saw considerable policy debates on the appropriate balance to be struck between the state, commerce, and the sector with regard to their respective shares of such responsibility. In the main, this was resolved through a combination of letting market forces decide, strengthening the brief of charities, and imposing government controls on service providers.

[73] As Judt, T., notes in *Postwar: A History of Europe Since 1945*, Vintage Books, London, 2010: "Within a few years of the reforms of the Seventies, *no* west European country except Ireland had a birthrate sufficient to replace the previous generation" (at p. 490). Whereas 30 years ago a total of 23 countries in Europe had fertility rates that exceeded those for morbidity, now none do.

1. Market Forces

In the U.K., an acute need to reduce government spending led to a retraction of state provision not only in health, education, and social care, but in many other areas that until then had been regarded as core public services. In that jurisdiction and elsewhere in the common law world, the privatization of social utilities and social infrastructure components has enabled the state to leave the market to provide, at a price, services such as roads, railways, housing, prisons, airports, sanitation electricity, gas, and tap water. It was, however, primarily in the area of public utilities that government experimentation with market forces was most adventurous and opportunistic. From the early 1990s, a proliferation of private finance initiatives resulted in responsibility for the provision of such services being devolved to or being shared with charities, other nonprofits, and commercial organizations.

2. The Charity Remit

Government policy in the U.K. to withdraw from much direct public service provision was planned to ensure that much of the responsibility devolved where feasible to nonprofits. In community care, health, and education, these organizations were invariably charities, and their close working relationship with the government meant that many were already positioned as service delivery agents and could then rapidly become primary service providers. To some extent the roles of government and charity had already been adjusted as government had replaced direct grants to organizations for core funding with short-term contracts for service delivery. This policy of aligning charities with specific areas of public benefit provision was taken a big step further through measures such as: reconstituting community-based health care services into consortiums with charitable status; hiving off-council facilities such as leisure centers and setting them up as independent but wholly government-funded charities;[74] and similarly encouraging scores of schools to leave the local authority framework to become independent academies with charitable status. This has been coupled with a vast increase in the contribution of charities established specifically for the purpose of generating funds for hospital facilities and other public services.[75] In short, the strategy to shift the burden of service provision was expedited in some instances by simply redesignating government services as charities—following the financial inducements necessary to ensure nominal independence, at least in terms of governance arrangements.

[74] See, e.g., Charity Commission and Applications for Registration of (i) Trafford Community Leisure Trust and (ii) Wigan Leisure and Culture Trust (April 21, 2004).

[75] See Paines, A., "Grant-Making Charities and the NHS," in Garton, J. and Mitchell, C., (eds.), *Charities and the NHS, King's Law Journal*, Vol. 18, No. 3, Hart Publishing, London, 2007, at p. 508, where she notes that in March 2004 there were 309 NHS-linked charities in England with total assets of some £1.643 billion.

3. Controls

Although the state withdrew from direct provision of public benefit services, it did not relinquish its control. The exercise of government control over an entity need not in itself be a barrier to the latter acquiring or retaining charitable status.

a. Government Control by Statute

Direct government control was found to be compatible with charitable status in the *British Museum* case, which concerned the establishment of that institution by the British Museum Act 1753. Despite it being entirely a creature of statute, wholly defined by and limited to its statutory functions, the museum was found to be a charity.[76] Again, in *Construction Industry Training Board v. A-G,*[77] direct ministerial control was held to be not incompatible with charity status. More recently, the Charity Commission has advised that:[78]

> it is not a bar to charitable status that a new body has been created with a view to discharging a function of central or local government, provided that the new body was established for exclusively charitable purposes (which may coincide with a governmental authority's function) and not for furthering the non charitable purposes of securing and implementing the policies of any governmental authority."

b. Government Control by Funding

Government funding has frequently been found insufficient to indicate an inappropriate level of control over a charity's affairs. The fact that a body is largely or even wholly funded by government would not necessarily prevent it from being a charity.[79]

Where government control was not exercised directly through funding or management arrangements it was retained by arrangements for government scrutiny. The services hived off or franchised out were made subject to statutory regulations that specified benchmarks for standards of quality, and to government powers of monitoring and inspection; a new range of regulatory bodies, ombudsmen, and human rights commissioners were in place to scrutinize, audit, and ensure value for money.

[76] See the British Museum v. White (1826) 2 Sim & St 594; 57 ER 473.

[77] [1973] Ch 173.

[78] Charity Commission RR7, *The Independence of Charities from the State*, London, 2001.

[79] See, e.g., Charity Commission and Applications for Registration of (i) Trafford Community Leisure Trust and (ii) Wigan Leisure and Culture Trust (April 21, 2004). See also Central Bayside (VCA) [2005] VSCA 168.

B. Charity, the Sector and the "Gift Relationship"

The temptation to treat charities as just another sector entity is misplaced. Charity law, together with a history of principles, practice, precedents, and institutions stretching back many centuries, differentiates a "charity" from all other nonprofits. The indices of difference, judicially defended throughout the common law world, make it problematic for charities to engage fully in the challenges and opportunities that now face the nonprofit sector. This can be seen in terms of certain aspects of the "gift relationship."

1. The Constraints of the "Gift Relationship"

In the "gift relationship," the donor is required to give exclusively and the trustees are thereafter bound to honor the terms of the gift, with any adjustment or deviation being limited to cy pres occasions. This poses serious difficulties where a charity enters into an arrangement with other parties, or is part of a consortium, and avails itself of a funding stream that is subject to conditions. To do so may not only dilute or skew the charitable purpose to which the original donor assigned his or her gift (if only by necessitating a creative interpretation of the charity's objects), but will also entail sacrificing some degree of independence and control over the charity contrary to trustee duties. A charity, however, is not permitted to cede control. Moreover, the value of the gift is to be protected and restricted to the use of intended beneficiaries, present and future. Any trustee decision that entails undue exposure to risk or to the possibility of charity resources being partially expended on persons or causes that fall outside the objects, or that allows for a degree of private benefit, would again be in breach of trustee duties. The opportunities available to other nonprofits, acting perhaps jointly with social enterprises or for-profit bodies, to develop broad strategies or to exploit a gap in the market, may well be denied to charities that are legally restricted to pursuing their tax-exempt charitable purpose. Such constraints should in effect debar charities from engaging in precisely the sort of cross-sectoral arrangements—where PFI, venture philanthropy, or social enterprises are involved—now being initiated to address public benefit service provision.

There is also a sense in which the nature of the "gift" may distance a charity from the collective interests of the sector. Charities are most often associated with purposes and objects that clearly address a social need, thus plugging a hole in the provision made by the public and business sectors. However, within the confines of the Preamble and *Pemsel*, donors have a long tradition of meeting the public benefit test by establishing charities for purposes construed as being for the public good, but being additional to it rather than a necessary component of it. Some are esoteric, such as the recent, if failed, attempt to secure charitable status for a body dedicated to reintroducing wolves to Scotland, and others such as provision for public parks or the distribution of educational pamphlets are about broadening the quality and texture of social life. Most often the nature of the gift can serve to distance charity from the business sector, and from its collaborative endeavors with the nonprofit sector or with government, when the activity is directed toward remedying areas of need caused by deliberate neglect or abuse. Charities established to alleviate poverty, preserve flora and fauna, or improve medical treatment for the ill, may find it impossible to work jointly with those for-profit or government bodies perceived as having created the situation in the first place through exploitation or neglect.

Charity law requires that all parties remain permanently tied to the purpose of a gift, which is held in trust for the benefit of others: The ownership of assets, and the discretionary freedom of decision making that goes with ownership, is not as fully available to a charity. The motives and mission of those responsible for giving effect to a charitable gift is not, in law, the same as that of their counterparts in business, government, or other nonprofits, and their resources cannot always be aligned in pursuit of an agreed common objective. These and other legal difficulties (not least the constraints on political purposes) can distance charities from other sector bodies, but it also empowers them to remain steadfast, allowing them not be swept along in a competitive rush to seize the latest market opportunity.

C. Consolidating Civil Society

The concept of "civil society" means different things to different people. Bothwell has usefully suggested that the literature on the subject has revealed four distinctively different approaches:[80]

> First, scholars such as Robert Putnam, Larry Diamond and Francis Fukuyama focus on what they see as the results of a strong civil society—the behaviours they believe healthy civil society produces including trust, reciprocity, tolerance and inclusion (traits and networks that add to a society's social capital)...Second, other students of civil society, such as Rajesh Tandon, David Brown and John Clark focus on the preconditions that must be met before a healthy civil society can come about (e.g. freedom of speech, freedom of association, rule of law etc)...Third, many who have considered what is a healthy civil society have sought to define it as a desirable state of all society (e.g. free public education and health care available to all)...Fourth, most who write about civil society define it in terms of its composition (e.g. including religious organisations, social clubs and movements, community based organisations etc but excluding family, tribe, clan, political parties etc).

[80] See Bothwell, J., "Indicators of a Healthy Civil Society," in Burbridge, J. (ed.), *Beyond Prince and Merchant: Citizen Participation and the Rise of Civil Society*, Institute of Cultural Affairs International, Brussels, 1997.

These four are not discrete mutually exclusive categories, as it would be quite feasible to subscribe to some or all without losing much of the concept's egalitarian essence. As has been emphasized "the boundaries of the space in which civil society activities take place are permeable."[81] For the purposes of charity law, however, the concept is perhaps best seen as represented by the preconditions of the second approach leading to the goals of the first. Regardless of the approach adopted, the concept of civil society would seem to rest on the free association of people in the pursuit of aims that complement the public benefit efforts of the state and result in a more coherent and engaged body politic. It is then most usually envisaged as being given effect by a myriad of non-governmental bodies that influence, supplement, or counterbalance the institutional infrastructure of the state.

The concepts of "civil society" and "social capital" have, in recent decades, generated a considerable body of work and have now been adopted as the modern hallmarks, or perhaps the slogans, of democracy.[82]

1. Civic Responsibility

Charities are viewed by government as having significant potential to strengthen the rights and benefits of citizenship and to assist in the consolidation of civil society. They are distinctive among nonprofit organizations for characteristics that are uniquely relevant to this task: Underpinning principles require charitable bodies to strive with a "moral mission" to improve the circumstances of the socially disadvantaged,[83] to maintain independent governance,[84] and in the process, to refrain from distributing any profits[85] for private gain. Given the incidences of increased social dysfunction—evidenced, for example, in the growth in prison populations, civil unrest, climbing rates of family breakdown, child abuse, and suicides—governments have become alert to the possibility of using the good offices of organizations, with credibility in disadvantaged communities, to broker modes of intervention designed to effect positive and sustainable change. In that context, the proven capacity of charities to harness armies of committed volunteers, reach the socially marginalized, and

[81] See Deakin, N., *In Search of Civil Society*, Palgrave, Hampshire, 2001.

[82] See, e.g., Cohen, L. and Arato, A., *Civil Society and Political Theory*, MIT Press, Cambridge, MA, 1992; Seligman, A.B., *The Idea of Civil Society*, Princeton University Press, Princeton, NJ, 1992. Putnam, R., "Bowling Alone: America's Declining Social Capital," in *Journal of Democracy* Vol. 6, No. 1, January 1995, at pp. 65–78; and *Bowling Alone: the Collapse and Revival of American Community*, Simon and Schuster, New York, 2000.

[83] As specified in the Preamble and in the four *Pemsel* heads. See further Mitchell, C. and Moody, S., (eds.), *Foundations of Charity*, Hart Publishing, Oxford, 2000.

[84] See, e.g., Charity Commission, CC10—"The Hallmarks of an Effective Charity" (July 2008) where it states that a charity must ensure that it "is independent and recognises that it exists to pursue its own purposes and not to carry out the policies or directions of any other body." See further at: http://www.charitycommission.gov.uk/Publications/cc10.aspx#h3.

[85] See Commissioners of Inland Revenue v. Oldham Training and Enterprise Council (1996) 69 T.C. 231.

deliver value-for-money public benefit outcomes, has undoubtedly been an attraction for contemporary governments in the developed common law nations committed to policies of generating social capital, increasing community capacity, and embedding a broad sense of civic responsibility

The pressing need to share responsibilities for public benefit service provision, reduce social alienation, and promote harmony in the face of increasing cultural diversity has, in recent years, prompted a number of governments to reflect on the bridging role of charities and to initiate processes of charity law reform in order to maximize the latter's potential. Charitable purposes as legally defined are essential components for establishing and sustaining an equitable, inclusive, and stable society and for promoting a truly contemporary interpretation of matters constituting the public benefit. In the view of government and others, to promote charitable purposes is to promote civil society.

2. Engaging the Electorate

Allied to the government's wish to generate and harness a stronger sense of civic responsibility is its need to engage more directly with an increasingly apathetic electorate. Baroness Kennedy's observation that "the public's disengagement from organized politics has gathered pace as they have lost faith in the more traditional forms of political engagement" holds true not just for the U.K. but for a number of leading common law nations.[86] To bridge this gap, and ostensibly to revive and re-energize democracy but as much to win party political advantage, governments in the U.K. and elsewhere have been experimenting with opening direct lines of engagement to their constituencies and developing "third way"[87] strategies. Moreover, encouraging the use of charities and their cohorts of volunteers in public service provision was itself viewed by government as a means of promoting civic engagement and building social capital, and thereby enhancing the capacity of democratic politics.

[86] See the Advisory Group on Campaigning and the Voluntary Sector *Report of the Advisory Group on Campaigning and the Voluntary Sector*, London, 2007, at p. 2.

[87] The Third Way is a political position that tries to reconcile right-wing and left-wing politics by advocating a synthesis of mostly right-wing economic and some superficially left-wing social policies. Third Way approaches are commonly viewed from within the first- and second-way perspectives as representing a centrist compromise between free market capitalism and democratic socialism. However, proponents of third way philosophies see it as something beyond free market capitalism and democratic socialism. This claim is embodied in the alternative description of the Third Way as the Radical center. See further, Giddens, A., *The Third Way: The Renewal of Social Democracy*, Cambridge, Polity Press, 1998. See also the Labour Party's publication "Building the Future Together," 1997 and Blair, T., *The Third Way: New Politics for the New Century*, Fabian Society, London, 1998.

D. Regulating the Sector

In the view of government, the sector was not only the answer to some of its problems but also a likely cause of others. By the early years of the 21st century, it had become clear that tighter regulatory control was indicated to achieve greater compliance with government policy, safeguard against fiscal abuse, promote better governance arrangements, and monitor the flow of funds so as to prevent their use by terrorists.

1. Compliance through Funding Arrangements

By replacing core funding with short-term service provision contracts, government has succeeded in leading charities to invest its resources in targeted areas of public benefit provision. One consequence of government directly shaping the charity remit through such funding arrangements has been the steady growth in those charities favored with contracts in certain government-selected areas of service provision and the relative decline or disappearance of those that have not been so fortunate. The extent of funding to charities is such that in some circumstances the latter's service delivery is now little more than government provision by proxy. This places charity in the position of being seen as a public benefit service provider and as being accountable for service deficiencies while the government in fact exercises control through funding and by regulating standards.[88]

However, whether channeled through short-term contract arrangements, direct grant aid, funded research projects, national lottery grants, or by other means, the proportion of a charity's income that comes from government has grown considerably in recent years in most leading common law nations.[89] With government controlling much of its income, and this being tied to government-designated service provision and to tacit approval of government policy, the traditional role of charity as independent entity and sector leader is becoming increasingly compromised. This has had a major impact upon the sector, on charities, and on the relationships between charities and other nonprofit organizations.

Ostensibly the mouthpiece for the socially disadvantaged, the larger charities have grown to become dependent upon contract renewal, which is undoubtedly inhibiting their capacity to challenge government policy where this negatively impacts upon the needs of the disadvantaged.[90] Their place as vigorous independent

[88] See, e.g., Seddon, N., *Who Cares?*, Civitas, London, 2007; O'Halloran, K., *The Politics of Charity*, Routledge, London, 2011.

[89] See, e.g., National Council for Voluntary Organisations, *Voluntary Sector Almanac*, London, 2009, which shows that over a five-year period the level of contract income earned by charities rose from £3.8 billion (in 2001) to £7.8 billion (in 2006).

[90] See, e.g., Seddon, *Who Cares?*, at p. 4.

advocates for social change now often falls to those nonprofits that have chosen not to seek charitable status and thereby avoid compromising their autonomy.

2. Preventing Fiscal Abuse

At the turn of the century the fact that no common law jurisdiction, except England and Wales, had in place a regulatory system specifically for the purpose of routinely auditing and inspecting the accounts of charities, was readily recognized as providing opportunities for fiduciary abuse. Nor indeed, with the exception of that same jurisdiction, did common law states have mandatory registers for charities. Such a register is clearly a prerequisite for a regulatory regime: Without it, government is not in a position to formally know of the existence of a charity within the jurisdiction, let alone its location, the nature, and scale of its activity, or the identity of its executive officers. Company law and revenue requirements provided some access to information in respect of charities that happened to be incorporated, but otherwise there was no basis for a charity-specific regulatory framework. The impetus for charity law reform came as much from the widespread realization that preventing fiscal abuse required, as a first step, a procedure for mandatory registration. The tracking of charity funds, the capacity to impose a regime for auditing income and inspecting charity affairs, and the ability to compare and coordinate information with other agencies within and between jurisdictions all depended on the existence of a charity-specific registration system.

3. Promoting Better Governance

The widespread media coverage given to corporate scandals in the United States (e.g., Enron) had a ripple effect that awakened a general concern to ensure that adequate standards of propriety prevailed in the boardrooms of corporations and trusts. The fact that, at the turn of the century, the law relating to charity governance remained conditional upon legal structure was widely acknowledged to be a considerable weakness in preventing the spread of abusive practices. There was little logic to support, but considerable consequences resulting from, the different governance arrangements for charities depending on their structure as trusts or companies. Although the latter were subject to standard registration requirements imposed upon all incorporated entities, this did nothing to ensure that their governance arrangements were appropriate to give effect to charitable purposes in accordance with charity law principles. Trusts, on the other hand, while required to comply with governance arrangements that at least in the U.K. and Irish jurisdictions had changed little since the Trustee Act 1893, were exempt from basic regulatory requirements imposed upon their incorporated counterparts.

With the exception of England and Wales, the lack of any charity-specific regulatory system to regulate all charities, whatever their legal structure, ensuring consistency of objects and activities and monitoring the number and creditworthiness of executive officers, was a recognized legal anomaly that added to the push for charity law reform.

4. Antiterrorism

Following the terrorist attacks of 9/11 and in the wake of subsequent incidents, most common law nations and others have in recent years introduced antiterrorism legislation.[91] New powers requiring the registration of nongovernmental organizations and permitting covert surveillance of their funds, activities, and staff have been sometimes accompanied by other new police powers of arrest and deportation. The "chilling" effect of such measures on charities in general cannot be denied: They have inhibited and slowed the overseas movement of funds and other resources.[92] However, the existence of a link between some fund-raising bodies, whether or not registered as charities, and the use of some of those funds by terrorist organizations is also undeniable. Striking a proportionate response, targeted and effective but not too generally restrictive, has proven difficult.

V. GOVERNMENT AND SECTOR PARTNERSHIPS

For all the reasons given above, and perhaps in some jurisdictions driven particularly by the need to win support from an increasingly apolitical constituency, governments in several leading common law nations have recently been going to considerable lengths to build formal links with the nonprofit sector. This strategy and the means for giving effect to it are of significance as it signals government recognition of the rising political importance of the sector and positions the latter more favorably than in other jurisdictions to develop and carry future public benefit service responsibilities.

A. Partnership

The initiative to build institutional, legal, and procedural bridges with the nonprofit sector was triggered in England and Wales close to the quatrocentenary of the initial demarcation in that jurisdiction between government and charity responsibilities for public benefit provision. Indeed, arguably, on both occasions government was responding to much the same set of conditions. Despite the rhetoric of

[91] Required by the United Nations Security Council Resolution 1373.

[92] See the Advisory Group, *Campaigning and the Voluntary Sector*, London, 2007, in which Baroness Helena Kennedy QC warns of this "chilling effect." Evidence of the need for surveillance was provided by the recent Charity Commission disclosure that its revised counterterrorism strategy had resulted in 16 investigations into suspected terrorist activity among charities during the period 2010–2011 (see further at: http://www.thirdsector.co.uk/news/1129301/charity-commission-looked-16-cases-suspected-terrorist-activity-2010-11/).

partnership[93] it may simply be the case, as McGregor-Lowndes argues, that "the fear of general revolution in the days of the Preamble driving state intervention has been replaced by the loss of political power for public goods not delivered at the right cost to taxpayers."[94] Doubt as to political motivation, however, should not distract from acknowledgment of the two major steps taken in that jurisdiction that have set out the route for other common law jurisdictions to achieve partnership: creating bridging institutional infrastructure and launching charity law reform.[95]

1. Institutional Infrastructure

The governments of the U.K., closely followed by Ireland, then by New Zealand and Australia, and to a lesser extent by Singapore and more recently by Hong Kong, have gradually but systematically assembled to varying degrees a framework of concordats, protocols, partnerships, and agencies to bridge the gap between their respective governments and the nonprofit sector. This system of institutional linkages has often been designated as an area of ministerial responsibility, an elevation of status that both signifies its newly acquired importance as a government priority and strengthens the suspicions of those who perceive a government intent to harness rather than facilitate the sector. The effect of such bridging architecture, together with the reasons for its absence and the resulting consequences in jurisdictions such as the United States and Canada, are among the matters that will be examined in the following jurisdiction-specific chapters.

2. Charity Law Reform

By the end of the 20th century, most leading common law nations were struggling with the limitations of a benign regulatory framework for charities that until then had seemed sufficient to facilitate and monitor the workings of a not particularly significant aspect of the nonprofit sector. The principles and the parameters set by the Preamble and *Pemsel* were by that stage being impacted by a broad range of developments, including: the law relating to matters such as human rights, equity, equality and discrimination; the retreat of the state from public benefit provision; the increased socioeconomic weight and political leverage of the nonprofit sector; the concerns of government regarding possible terrorist exploitation of a poorly regulated sector; and the need to address new manifestations of social disadvantage. It

[93] See further, Kendall, J. and Taylor, M., "On the Interdependence between Politics and Policy in the Shaping of English Horizontal Third Sector Initiative," in Gidron, B. and Bar, M. (eds.), *Policy Initiatives towards the Third Sector in International Perspective*, Springer Publishing, The Netherlands, 2009, at p. 198.

[94] See McGregor-Lowndes, M., "Introduction," in McGregor-Lowndes, M. and O'Halloran, K. (eds), *Modernising Charity Law: Recent Developments and Future Directions*, Elgar Publications, Cheltenham, 2010, at p. 6.

[95] See also, O'Halloran, *The Politics of Charity*, 2011.

was with a view to addressing such matters, and others referred to above, that in the early years of the 21st century, Canada,[96] Australia,[97] New Zealand,[98] the United States,[99] Singapore,[100] Scotland,[101] Northern Ireland[102] and more recently Hong Kong[103] followed the example set by England and Wales[104] and embarked upon a protracted period of charity law reform intended by all to at least strengthen regulatory processes and by some to also statutorily define and encode common law concepts.

a. The Regulatory Framework

In all modern common law jurisdictions, neither the courts nor the Attorney General any longer played the role traditionally required for effective monitoring of charities. In all, except England and Wales, the Revenue exercised such rudimentary regulatory control as was feasible, treating charities as just another income-generating entity and taking no account of any charity-specific characteristics. In short, the traditional mechanisms for developing charitable purposes and ensuring relevance, accountability, and transparency in relation to charitable activity were outdated, had fallen into disuse, or were otherwise no longer fit for purpose.

[96] See *An Accord between the Government of Canada and the Voluntary Sector*, December 2001.

[97] See the Charity Law Reform Committee Report *Inquiry into the Definition of Charities and Related Organisations*, Canberra, June 2001.

[98] See Ministry of Social Policy, *Communities and Government—Potential for Partnership Whakatopu Whakaaro*, 2001. The Office of Ethnic Affairs, Auckland, 2001.

[99] See Panel on the Nonprofit Sector, *Strengthening Transparency, Governance, Accountability of Charitable Organisations*, final report to Congress and the Nonprofit Sector, Washington, DC, 2005.

[100] See for Singapore, the final report of the Inter-Ministry Committee on the *Regulation of Charities and Institutions of Public Character*, 2006.

[101] See for Scotland the Scottish Charity Law Review Commission report, *Charity Scotland*, Edinburgh, 2001.

[102] See for Northern Ireland the Charities Branch, Voluntary & Community Unit, Department for Social Development *Consultation on the Review of Charities Administration and Legislation in Northern Ireland*, Belfast, 2005.

[103] See for Hong Kong the Law Reform Commission of Hong Kong, the *Charities Sub-Committee Consultation Paper*, June 2011. See further at: http://www.hkreform.gov.hk/en/publications/charities.htm.

[104] See for England and Wales the National Council for Voluntary Organisations, Commission on the Future of the Voluntary Sector, *Meeting the Challenge of Change: Voluntary Action into the 21st Century*, London 1996; the National Council for Voluntary Organisations, *For the Public Benefit? A Consultation Document on Charity Law Reform*, London, 2001; and *Private Action, Public Benefit, a Review of Charities and the Wider Not-For-Profit Sector*, London, September 2002.

b. Common Law Concepts

As the number of charities increased, so too did evidence of a general failing in the common law system for renewing the interpretation of charitable purposes and maintaining the ongoing adjustment of charity law necessary to ensure its continuing relevance to contemporary social circumstances. The four heads of *Pemsel* no longer provided an appropriate and sufficient classification of purposes for a rapidly expanding range of charitable activity: New manifestations of social need were constantly emerging, and, in effect, the law was constricting the development of more relevant charitable purposes. The traditional public benefit test was open to challenge: The presumption of satisfaction in relation to organizations and gifts that could fit within the first three *Pemsel* heads was controversial, particularly in respect of religion; the requirement to prove public benefit for all organizations and gifts under the fourth head, was arguably discriminatory; and there was uncertainty as to the thresholds of proof for both the "public" and the "benefit" components of the test.

c. Commerce

Among the areas where the law was misaligned with practice was its failure to provide for the increasing fusion of commerce and charitable purposes. There was growing pressure to broaden the categories of bodies qualifying for charitable status, and thereby permit charities to undertake new forms of activity, including commercial activity, and to extend recognition to bodies with such activities.

B. Partnership and the Law Reform Processes

Following the U.K.'s lead in building an institutional framework, governments of several other countries (e.g., Ireland, Singapore, New Zealand Australia, and Canada) also sought, with varying success, to emulate that example and construct similar links (see Part 2).

1. Political Leverage of Umbrella Bodies

The success or otherwise of a government/sector partnership would seem to be at least related to, if not wholly dependant upon, the existence of umbrella or "apex" bodies capable of representing the sector. Umbrella organizations[105] (or "peak bodies" as they are known in Australia) have been defined as "nonprofit organisations

[105] See further, Anheier, H. and Toepler, S. (eds), *International Encyclopedia of Civil Society*, Vol. 3, "Umbrella Organizations," Springer, New York, 2010, at pp. 1577–82.

whose members are themselves nonprofit organisations"[106] and they can operate at local, national or international levels. Although they vary greatly, all tend to provide services such as information dissemination, membership support, coordination, advocacy, and representation together with research, policy development, and capacity building for their members. Some emphasize their role in developing, not merely implementing, government policy that can give rise to issues regarding the legitimacy of their mandate and accusations of undermining the functions of elected representatives in modern democracies. They can adopt any one of a variety of organizational structures depending on factors such as the power balance between member bodies, their agreed purpose and intended duration, particularly whether or not they are single-issue oriented, but they all invariably face considerable internal management and external organizational challenges. It has been estimated that over "80 countries around the world currently have national NGO umbrella organizations, though these vary widely in size, capacity and scope; at least 20 of these national associations are in sub-Saharan Africa."[107] In the United States, it is believed that approximately one-fifth of all nonprofits belong to an umbrella organization.[108]

A level of sector cohesion is a necessary prerequisite for the emergence of such bodies. This requires the sector to have acquired a sense of identity as an independent entity with its own identifiable set of interests. As has been said:[109]

> An independent voluntary sector is a distinct and important element of any democracy. It is a vehicle for direct public participation, with its autonomy enabling it not just to participate, but to maintain a check upon the State.

Not until there is an acceptance of shared concerns, and a willingness to address these through coordinated and cooperative action, will key nonprofit bodies coalesce into umbrella or "apex" organizations with a mandate to negotiate on behalf of the sector's collective interests. These have the capacity to neutralize the fragmentary effect of special interest groups such as powerful religious organizations, employers or trade union bodies, or professional associations and instead speak for the broad long-term best interests of the sector. They promote sector inclusiveness.

Such bodies can assume a mediatory role between government and sector, acting as advocates for the sector and as "pressure groups" shaping government policy on sector-related issues. The leadership they provide is crucially important to the developmental process of coordinating, organizing, and politicizing this "loose,

[106] See Young, D., "Organizational Identity and the Structure of Nonprofit Umbrella Organizations," *Nonprofit Management & Leadership*, Vol. 11, No. 3, at p. 290.

[107] See Gugerty, M. K. and Prakash, A. (eds), *Advocacy Organizations and Collective Action*, Cambridge University Press, New York, 2010.

[108] See V. A. Hodgkinson et al, "A Portrait of the Independent Sector," the *Independent Sector*, Washington DC, 1993.

[109] Dunn, A. (ed), *The Voluntary Sector, the State and the Law*, Hart Publishing, Oxford, 2000, at p.1.

baggy monster."[110] Without umbrella bodies there is no driving force to pull together the disparate sector components, forge a unity of vision, and push for the attainment of agreed common goals. With such bodies, the sector then has a voice and policies to which government can relate and begin to negotiate. The success of the government/sector partnership in the U.K. and Ireland, relative to the lack of it in Canada and Singapore or its weakness in Australia, is largely attributable to the presence of well-established, politically mature, sector umbrella bodies.

2. Nonprofits, Charity Law, and Public Benefit Provision

Throughout the common law world the principal means of orchestrating not just the balance to be struck between government and charity in relation to responsibility for public benefit service provision, but also the relationship between government and the nonprofit sector, has continued to rest on charity law. This has been by default as no other legal framework has yet been devised to govern a relationship only recently formally acknowledged in a few jurisdictions and yet to be fully developed in any.[111] The government agenda, as initially embodied in the Preamble and thereafter maintained in the body of charity law, set the only parameters available for negotiating the responsibility for future public benefit service provision. In all jurisdictions, the Preamble parties had been extended from government and charity to include the broad nonprofit sector and commerce whereas the Preamble range of public benefit services and utilities, embraced through the concept of "charitable purpose," had also been greatly extended by case law and to some extent by statute (e.g., sports and recreational activity).

However, the charity law reform processes revealed considerable jurisdictional variation in sector capacity to use charity law as a platform for negotiating the sector's relationship with government and its role in the future provision of public services. In some jurisdictions, the political leverage of the sector was virtually nullified by government either choosing not to facilitate sector engagement (Singapore) or to give only token regard to it (Australia under the liberal administration). In others, that leverage was, perhaps, compromised by dependency on government funds whether through direct grants or through contracts (U.K. and Ireland). In the United States the prospect of government/sector negotiations never arose, whereas in Canada various attempts at different levels largely ended in stalemate. The process in New Zealand started promisingly, produced anodyne outcomes, but may proceed through tax law adjustments and Commission initiatives

[110] See Kendall, J. "Revisiting the Loose and Baggy Monster," in *Charity Finance*, November 2003, at pp. 30–32.

[111] Some academics have called for a sector wide legal framework: see, e.g., Garton, J., "The Future of Civil Society Organizations: Towards a Theory of Regulations for Organized Civil Society" and Turnour, M., "Modernising Charity Law: Steps to an Alternative Architecture for Common Law Charity Jurisprudence," in McGregor-Lowndes, M. and O'Halloran, K. (eds), *Modernising Charity Law: Recent Developments and Future Directions*, Elgar Publications, Cheltenham, 2010.

to a further stage of government/sector negotiations. A determining factor in the jurisdictional progress of charity law reform was the relative strength of the respective sector umbrella bodies.

VI. CONCLUSION

The moral authority, socioeconomic value, and, although indifferently realized, the political leverage of the nonprofit sector comes in part from its record of providing public benefit services pursued essentially for reasons of altruism rather than private benefit. In the main, however, this status is traceable back to the sector's history as the birthplace of our most basic civil liberties: Through its associational life the rights of freedom of expression, equality, and nondiscrimination were first asserted, and charities were always to the fore in the struggle for legal affirmation of such rights. Ownership of this history, in respect of matters so fundamental to securing and promoting social well-being, gives charities and the nonprofit sector as a whole its credibility and has served to bind the sector with a shared sense of direction and purpose and define its role in relation to government and commerce.

This identity is now in danger of being eroded. As the sector becomes increasingly susceptible to commercialization, the focus of intersectoral boundary disputes, and ever more complicit in the working out of a government agenda for future public benefit service provision, there are good reasons to be concerned for its future. Although these challenges pose clear dangers for the sector, they present a more fundamental challenge to "charity" as it is drawn into arrangements that at best fudge, and at worst corrupt, the clarity of roles and purpose underpinning the initial terms of the "gift relationship." There are, however, also opportunities for charities and the sector more broadly to now demonstrate moral leadership and restore a sense of civic responsibility as the public and private sectors recover in the aftermath of institutional collapse.

4

CHARITY AT THE MARGINS

I. INTRODUCTION

This chapter considers the space left to charity in contemporary Western society: the parameters set by other forces, the areas that it is poised to enter, and the terms of its engagement with government and business. The central axis of this chapter, and of the book, is the relationship between government and charity. This chapter deals primarily with that relationship, examining how and why this is now undergoing change.

Beginning with the sources of support to which an individual in need has traditionally reached—the family and religion—consideration is given to why these are no longer relied upon as much as formerly and how charity, or the nonprofit sector more broadly, has to some extent taken their place. This leads into a review of the growing importance of the boundary between charity and legal rights and the effects of social justice: in particular, the considerable displacement of charity in all modern nations by a raft of equity, equality, and human rights legislation. Then an assessment is made of the charity/government boundary: The traditional terms of engagement between the two parties are examined and the underlying political frame of reference, evidenced in the Preamble, is considered in a contemporary context. The reasons this boundary is now changing are explained: the rolling back of the "welfare state"; governments retreating from providing to regulating public benefit services; and the push for more joined up, transparent, and holistic provision that is community-based rather than left to the monopoly of institutionally based specialized professions.

The chapter then focuses on the charity/business boundary, generally most evident in education and health care facilities. It explains why charity is now a growing presence in the marketplace. Next, there is an assessment of the significance of: corporate philanthropy and the role of private interests, the nature and effect of protection given to charities by law, the partnerships between charity and business, the "feeder" organizations, the public/private finance initiatives, the challenge of social entrepreneurship, and the role played by private insurance. Other boundaries are also noted. The significance of jurisdiction is examined, particularly with regard to the impact of global anti-terrorism provisions and economic recession, the difficulties presented by federation, the interface between common law and civil law, and the complexities of transnational charities, aid/trade, etc.

This chapter concludes with the notion that charity, consigned to the margins of society until the late 20th century, is now poised to assume a more mainstream role. Arguably, given the social consequences of market-led, private profiteering in the banking and financial sector, the climate is now set fair for a more ethics-compliant, charity-led nonprofit sector to develop a prominent public benefit, service provision profile that will assist the broad consolidation of civil society. The ideological context is explored: The connections between the fall of communism, the rise of capitalism, and the consequent implications for public benefit service provision are briefly considered.

II. CHARITY AND THE BOUNDARIES BETWEEN INDIVIDUAL/FAMILY/RELIGION

For most, in our developed common law jurisdictions, the time when individuals were born into and remained largely within various sets of relationships that had seemingly proved sufficient and sustaining for previous generations has now long passed. The ties of family, church, locality, social class, culture, and even of race and gender that were once assumed at birth and continued thereafter can no longer be taken for granted, and for many some of these are now barely relevant. As the traditional sources for our sense of belonging, of sharing in a collective identity with all the security that offered, have melted away, there has been a corresponding adjustment to the social role of charity. Charity was once confined to the margins of family and church, operating to salvage society's victims, the poor, the frail and the failed, restoring them as far as possible to their place in society, thereby helping to maintain social values and institutions. It is now a much more diffuse entity and no longer defined mainly by its relationship to the helpless.

A. Charity and Family

The meltdown of the clan, or network of extended family members, to the nuclear family unit occurred remarkably quickly, perhaps in the space of two or three generations. This transition directly led to today's dominant and spreading pattern of serial parenting arrangements for the children of a household, who may often be only tenuously related to each other.

1. Changes in the "Family"

The Victorian family model—characterized by the monogamous, lifelong union of a heterosexual couple and their parenting of the children of their marriage—has not, for some time, been the ubiquitous norm it once was.[1] Developments in medicine and law have had a great impact upon parenting: Increasing the extent to which maternity is now a chosen option as pregnancy may be achieved due to the introduction of techniques of artificial insemination and surrogacy, or avoided through the use of improved contraceptives, or terminated by abortion, while decreasing the relevance of paternity and rendering obsolete any residual traces of patriarchy. Families have become more nuclear, impermanent, and mobile, often featuring transient and serial parenting arrangements. Such developments together with a decline in the rates of both fertility and marriage in modern Western nations, with childbirth being less dependent upon marriage, has led to a general loosening of the relationship between family and state.

The collapse of the customary buffers between family and state—the kith and kin support networks and good neighbor relationships of settled communities—increases the likelihood that individuals in difficulty will turn instead to either charity or the church.

2. Charity, Professional Services, and Family Support

There are now a great many charities that offer a wide variety of support or mediatory services in the general area of family relationship breakdown. Marriage guidance counseling is perhaps the most obvious, but family planning, parental guidance, day-care centers, and bodies providing financial support are among the list of those now claiming charitable status under the fourth, catch-all *Pemsel* head. It would seem that as the traditional sources of family support weaken or disappear, their functions are often being displaced onto charity or absorbed into the commercial sector. In either case, this results in family problems being passed to professionals as the private becomes more public and opportunities for profit margins determine whether the professionals are employed by charity, a commercial entity, or by some hybrid structure that combines the two. It may also increase the probability of breakdown being irretrievable as objective, disinterested professionals assist individuals to decide what's best for each rather than for the family as a whole, and the safe anonymity of professional rather than family intervention avoids the involvement of other family members. Escape from exposure to family relationship sanctions, which may have previously exercised a restraining influence on individual action, is now readily achieved in our more mobile society where relocation to

[1] See, for example, Wohl, A. S. (ed), *The Victorian Family: Structure and Stresses*, Croom Helm, London, 1978.

a similar but safely anonymous form of employment, housing, and lifestyle can be swiftly organized.

One of the more significant 20th century developments affecting the relationships among citizen, family, and the state was the rise of the professional as the mediator of issues occurring within that relationship context. Although the advocacy role on behalf of those in need—articulating, negotiating, and advising—to facilitate access to appropriate resources has undoubtedly been of great value, it has come at a price. There is a sense in which personal problems are now "owned" by relevant professionals who are expected to have the skills and solutions that might once have been found within the family. Moreover, the professionals are in many senses removed from those with the problems, including being physically situated in an entirely different and carefully manicured setting and being devoid of associational relationships to distress; this requires the problem to be brought to the professional. By mediating in that space between citizen, family, and state, the professional has, perhaps, confirmed those boundaries, increased social fragmentation, deskilled or demoted the family, and further distanced the individual from traditional sources of support. To that extent, the increased presence of the nonprofit sector may offer a counterbalance to professionalism and a more holistic, comfortable, and readily accessible resource.

3. State and Family Support

In recent years, the state has been withdrawing from consensual intervention in family affairs. The unfortunate current correlation in developed Western nations between demographic trends that result in an increasing proportion of the population requiring public benefit services and falling public revenues that result in the diminishing state provision of such services, is leading to a greater proportion of the population being denied the public support services to which they had previously grown accustomed. Perhaps this is most evident at either end of the age spectrum as care of the greater numbers of elderly is increasingly privatized whereas support for more fluid and vulnerable parenting becomes largely reduced to child protection. Instead of using its permissive powers to assist families in need, the state is retreating to coercive intervention thresholds and saving its resources for deployment through the use of compulsory powers to ensure the care and protection of family members from abuse or neglect.

B. Charity and Religion

Religion's positive role in the evolution of our contemporary societies is immeasurable: contributing cultural values; building or supporting the building of the institutional infrastructure; and determining and delivering the health, social care, and education services that have raised living standards for all citizens. There is, however, a balance to be struck between religion's capacity to generate social cohesion (e.g., instilling values of compassion and altruism) and its tendency to promote social divisions (e.g., polarizing communities and accentuating differences). Further, the secularization of the social infrastructure, together with the introduction of an ever-expanding raft of national and international legislation underpinning entitlements to human rights, equity, equality, and nondiscrimination, in contemporary developed nations has undermined or displaced the traditional social role of religion.

1. Changes in "Religion"

"Religion," like the "family," is no longer the social force it once was, though this is perhaps more true of Europe than elsewhere (certainly religion is growing in strength in the Middle East and is arguably undergoing a resurgence in the United States and Australia). An indication of religion's diluted social standing is apparent in the changes imposed upon it by recent charities legislation in the U.K. jurisdictions. Before the reforms, the essential requirements for a religious organization, or for a donation to such an organization, to be legally recognized as charitable, were broadly the same in all common law nations: a belief in a "Supreme Being" and a shared commitment to faith and worship,[2] though these requirements were assisted by the legal presumption that such organizations and gifts to them were for the public benefit.[3] In addition, importance has traditionally been attached to "the laws, canons, ordinances and tenets of the religion concerned."[4] Since then the new legislative definition has: excised any need for a belief in a God, and allows for philosophical belief and belief in multiple gods;[5] removed the need for worship or

[2] See Charity Commission, "Analysis of the Law Underpinning *Public Benefit and the Advancement of Religion*," February 2008 at para. 2.14, where the Commission concluded that the definition of a religion in English charity law was characterized by a belief in a supreme being and an expression of that belief through worship. See also Charity Commission in Church of Scientology of California v. Customs and Excise Comms. [1980] CMLR 114, [1979] STC 297; [1979] T.R. 59; aff'd [1981] 1 All ER 1035; [1981] STC 65, Ca., where it concluded that "belief in a supreme being remains a necessary characteristic of religion for the purposes of English charity law. It would not, however, in their view, be proper to specify the nature of that supreme being or to require it to be analogous to the deity or supreme being of a particular religion."

[3] The advancement of religion has been presumed to be for the public benefit in all common law jurisdictions; in some, such as Ireland, this presumption has statutory endorsement.

[4] It was Wickens V-C in Cocks v. Manners (1871) L.R. 12 Eq. 574, who initially suggested that the "benefit" quotient of a religious organization for the "public" lay in its moral and spiritual values, which could be found in its beliefs, doctrines and practices (at p. 585).

[5] See the Charities Act 2011, s.3(2)(a) "religion" includes—

(i) a religion which involves belief in more than one god, and

(ii) a religion which does not involve belief in a god.

Also, Charities and Trustee Investment (Scotland) Act 2005, s.7(2A)(e); and the Charities Act (Northern Ireland) 2008, s.2(3)(a)(i).

liturgy;[6] and reversed the public benefit presumption so that any such organization or gift must now demonstrably satisfy the public benefit test.[7] It is not impossible that other common law countries will in due course, either explicitly by statute or by following case precedents, accept the changes made by the U.K. jurisdictions.

These changes are symptomatic of a general decline in the role of established religions and the traditional powerful position of organized religion in most developed Western societies: Fewer people now have religious convictions or belong to an organized religion; respect for religious organizations has been greatly damaged by revelations of systemic child abuse,[8] while the impact of social justice principles worked through by legislators and judiciary, in combination with recent advances in scientific research (genetic programming and genome structures, for example), are perhaps also making their own contribution to the general displacing of deity-based morals by a more secular approach. Paradoxically, this is being accompanied by a resurgence in reliance upon faith-based social facilities (mainly schools) and a higher social profile for non-Christian religions, particularly Islam. The community cohesion that religion and its institutions can generate when members conspicuously belong to the same faith is now reversed to some degree as all Western societies include citizens affiliated with a variety of religions, some of whose adherents parade their differences and stimulate public controversy regarding their sites for worship, religious dress, and ornaments. This gives rise to doubt as to the future capacity of religion to promote equity, equality, and pluralism; to deliver public benefit rather than advance member benefit; and to further social cohesion instead of fostering social divisions. The complexities of this intriguing relationship between religion and charities, and the changes in the religious nature of Western societies, is not a topic that can or need be fully explored for present purposes.

2. Charity and Faith-Based Provision

Any sense in which private piety can be interpreted as a public good tends to disappear when that piety manifests itself in a facility that represents beliefs not shared by the community within which it is located. Whether it takes the form of a "closed" convent, a mosque, a school for children of a specific religion, a halal butcher's

[6] There is no mention of any such requirement in U.K. charity legislation. In Ireland, the Charities Act 2009 leaves the common law requirement unaltered. In determining whether an organization has purposes that are religious, the regulatory body will examine "the laws, canons, ordinances and tenets of the religion concerned" as required, previously by the 1961 Act and now in identical terms by the 2009 Act, s.3(6).

[7] See the Charities Act 2011, s.4:

> (2) In determining whether that requirement is satisfied in relation to any such purpose, it is not to be presumed that a purpose of a particular description is for the public benefit.

[8] See, e.g., the *Report of the Commission to Inquire into Child Abuse* (the "Ryan Report"), Dublin, May 2009.

shop, or any one of a number of such religion-specific facilities, its social significance, as excluding those who do not subscribe to the relevant belief system, can be deeply divisive. Similarly, but in reverse, where the facility is wholly secular but operates a service that offends the piety of religious people in the community, then again the effect can be divisive for that community. This, for example, can occur in circumstances where a particular registrar in a registry office refuses to officiate in marriage services for gay/lesbian couples[9] or where the services of abortion clinics are opposed by those with deeply held religious beliefs.[10] Again, community polarization may well flow from the differentiating, if not discriminating, restrictive practices of religious bodies such as those that rent halls for wedding receptions but refuse to do so for gay/lesbian couples,[11] or adoption agencies[12] or foster care agencies[13] that refuse to place children with such couples. Controversies caused, for example by an abortion clinic, a registry office offering marriage services for gay or lesbian couples, or an adoption agency that will place children with such couples, have been known to have deadly consequences. Clearly, where private piety and its social manifestations of difference can be accommodated within a cultural setting that welcomes and values such diversity, then it is in itself very much a public good, but this is possible only when religion preaches tolerance and politics cultivates pluralism. Otherwise emblematic representations of religious difference can too easily become a trigger for social discord.

However, it must be acknowledged that this is an area of boundary permeability, particularly between business and religion. The spread of faith-based schools in the United States[14] and the U.K., and the growing involvement of religious organizations in health care, nursing homes, and residential homes for the elderly, etc. all indicate a more diffuse capacity that enables religion to penetrate and become an integral part of commonplace social facilities, as will become evident in the following jurisdiction-specific chapters.

[9] See, e.g., Ladele v. London Borough of Islington [2009] EWCA (Civ) 1357 (December 15, 2009).

[10] See, e.g., Dalliare v. Les Chevaliers de Columb 2011 HRTO 639.

[11] See, e.g., the Canadian case Smith and Chymshyn v. Knights of Columba and others, 2005 BCHRT 544 (CanL11).

[12] See Catholic Care v. The Charity Commission for England and Wales, First-tier Tribunal (Charity), April 26, 2011.

[13] See, e.g., OW & OV v. Members of the Board of the Wesley Mission Council [2010] NSWADT 293 (December 10, 2010).

[14] The Welfare Reform Act 1996 (known as the PWRORA), facilitated the rise of faith-based organizations as providers of publicly funded services as the federal government reached out to organizations through the Charitable Choice clause in the 1996 Act, enabling them to assist in the welfare reform effort.

C. Charity, the Sector, and the Citizen

As the buffers of family and religion have dissolved, more so in some jurisdictions than others, charity has become enveloped in an ever-expanding and mutating non-profit sector offering endless opportunities for alternative forms of support to be selected and discarded as and when the individual feels the need to do so. Whereas family and religion required loyalty of its members, gave them a sense of affiliation, and built for them a collective value base and enduring identity, the nonprofit sector offers individuals a shopping mall and recycling depot for identity accessories. Local community support networks that used to be localized, organized around a sense of belonging to a congregation and focused on the parish church, are now likely to take the form of very individualized attachments to an eclectic array of nonprofit bodies, some accessed solely by the Internet. Although the sector provides diverse "belonging" opportunities, it also opens the door for individuals to lend their weight to mission-driven collaborative enterprises that demand commitment, obey definite principles, and strive to achieve beneficial outcomes for their members or for others who are more disadvantaged. None of this should distract from acknowledging the growing caring capacity of the sector, led by charities, as it assumes a role alongside religion as a buffer between citizen and government.

III. THE CHARITY/LEGAL RIGHTS BOUNDARY

The extent to which legal rights have come to displace charity is an important measure of social progress. Instead of being viewed as mutually exclusive, charity and legal rights have gradually assumed roles that are now more often complementary, the realignment varying in accordance with the pace of jurisdictional recognition of citizens' rights. It is a development that could not have been predicted four centuries ago, is still imperfectly realized in common law countries, and has not yet happened in many countries such as China. However, even in some of the more-developed common law nations, poverty, inequality, discrimination, and other forms of inequity are still very much in evidence. As such societies now struggle to cope with the additional stresses imposed by economic recession, the protection afforded by legal rights, and the entitlement they bring to access basic social services and preserve self-respect, is growing in importance relative to the discretionary contributions of charity.

A. Charity and Legal Rights

Legal rights and charity once functioned in an obverse relationship similar to justice and mercy. It was a relationship forever associated with corresponding stereotypical attitudes: benefits won through adversarial assertion on basis of merit, accompanied by a sense of achievement; and benefits conferred through discretionary patronage on a supplicant, accompanied by deference, gratitude, and compliant dependency. Possibly a downside to the modern development of a rights-conscious culture, where an "ambulance chasing" mentality and readiness to litigate can fuel self-righteous attitudes, is a diminution in the traditional give-and-take approach to community relationships, a reduced willingness to share, and fewer acts of compassion to strangers.

Although there is a sense in which they may now operate in a manner that can be mutually complementary, it remains important that a line can still be drawn between needs to be addressed by charity and needs addressed by legal rights.

1. Charity

Charity, as known to the common law, provides the means for discretionary gifts or activities to be given for charitable purposes, as defined under charity law, by individuals or organizations, for the public benefit. It was never intended to provide an answer to poverty; indeed, although permitted to alleviate its effects, charity has traditionally been debarred from addressing its causes.[15] Nor can charity deal with the needs of those suffering from the many, often complex and interwoven systemic forms of contemporary social disadvantage. It can provide defined opportunities for those who wish to make a contribution for the public benefit. It serves to ameliorate hardship, demonstrate altruism, enrich the fabric of society, and generate social cohesion. Although charity continues to carry vestiges of the traditional model, which rested on private acts of gratuitous benevolence favoring impoverished or otherwise dependent beneficiaries, it has long since spread to accommodate the ever-growing range of organizations, activities, and gifts that, in a contemporary sophisticated Western society, conform to a charitable purpose and satisfy the public benefit test.

Whereas acts of charity may well be, and perhaps most often are, located in the nexus of personal relationships and therefore remain confined to private law, charitable purposes and charitable organizations and the broad practice of modern philanthropy are now defined and governed by public charity law. Most important, charity rests on donor discretion, recipient eligibility is dependent upon the recipient's needs fitting within the designated charitable purpose, and the public benefit test must be satisfied.

2. Rights

For most developed common law nations, the displacing of charity by rights was a phenomenon that gathered pace through the last half of the 20th century. International conventions and national legislation began to assert basic entitlements

[15] See, e.g., Gurin, M. G. and Van Til, J., "Philanthropy in Its Historical Context," in Van Til, V. and Assocs. (eds.), *Critical Issues in American Philanthropy, Strengthening Theory and Practice*, Jossey-Bass, San Francisco, 1990 where a distinction is drawn between charity (person-to-person alleviation of need) and philanthropy (strategic approach to social problems).

and displace reliance upon charitable acts of gratuitous compassion. Litigation, or the threat of it, pushed aside the controls of price or grace and favor that had hitherto determined access to some of the more basic necessities of life. The rights approach is one that provides for assertive action in the courts by individuals for alleged breach of an entitlement as established in legislation. Legal rights and corresponding legal duties, usually underpinned by moral authority and enforced by legal powers, form the basis for: a formal recognition of individual entitlement, objective adjudication on alleged breach and appropriate recompense, and a process for enforcement.[16] Where need can be met by established legal rights, charity has no role: Need is then entitled to a legal remedy.

a. Legal Rights

A legal rights approach specifies entitlements, and the grounds under which they may be claimed, within a range of legislation that includes human rights, equity, and nondiscrimination provisions. Many everyday aspects of life, now taken for granted as governed by universally applied rights (to maternity leave, holiday pay, health and safety standards in the workplace, etc), and by processes for enforcing them (legal aid, etc.), have only become so relatively recently.

b. Human Rights

Certain rights have gained recognition as being of greater importance and of a more fundamental nature than others and are embodied in international conventions[17] or in national constitutions. They include many civil, economic, social, minority, and gender-specific rights, most notably the freedom of association and assembly, of expression, of religion, of access to justice, and the right to family life. By giving formal recognition and protection to the most basic and accepted of rights they reinforce the standing of corresponding charity law principles while also clarifying those parameters of charity that interface with legal rights.[18]

[16] See Hart, H. L. A., *The Concept of Law* (2nd ed.), Clarendon Law Series, Oxford University Press, Oxford, 1994.

[17] See, e.g., the European Convention for the Protection of Human Rights and Fundamental Freedoms 1950, which is now binding upon all 27 Member States of the European Union, many of which have legislated to incorporate all or most of the rights into national law.

[18] See, e.g., in the United States, the Bill of Rights comprising the first 10 amendments to the Constitution; Canada, the Charter of Rights and Freedoms (schedule B to the Canada Act 1982) and the Human Rights Act 1985; Ireland, the Constitution 1937 and the Human Rights Act 2003 (which gives effect to the European Convention); the U.K. jurisdictions, the Human Rights Act 1998 (which gives effect to the European Convention); Australia, the Human Rights and Equal Opportunity Commission Act 1986; and New Zealand, the Bill of Rights Act 1990 and the Human Rights Act 1993 (amended in 2001).

c. Social Justice

In contrast to an approach based on the rights of the individual, social justice requires universal standards of equity, equality, and nondiscrimination to be entrenched in legislation and applied uniformly across society, largely through the procedures and practice of government agencies, with a right of recourse to the courts. All modern Western societies have now put into place much the same raft of legislation to ensure the provision of equal opportunities for citizens regardless of factors such as gender and age. Many national laws now apply similar principles to prohibit discrimination in relation to disability, race, religion or belief, or sexual orientation, and to promote equal pay and fair employment, etc., while also requiring more general social legislation to be proofed against those principles and providing for an independent overview by regulatory bodies, commissions, or tribunals coupled with power of referral to the court. It is a collective approach to do justice and is most apparent in national legislation dealing, for example, with civil liberties and freedom of information, but is also reinforced by international conventions.

B. The Contemporary Charity/Legal Rights Boundary

The shift from rights won by trade unions, negotiated by the parties in a contract or otherwise tied to ownership of property, to rights established in national or international law with universal applicability to a class of persons, is of fundamental importance in any democratic society. It is a constantly unfolding process and one which, as has been demonstrated in recent antiterrorism legislation,[19] can roll back as well as forward.

1. The Right to Give

For charity, this right is clearly also of fundamental importance. In charity law, however, it has been constrained by the requirement that it is exercised in accordance with the public benefit test and that the gift fit within the *Pemsel* definition of a charitable purpose. Other common law constraints, such as the restrictions on political activities, have also served to confine a donor's right to give. The right is also, increasingly, subject to fairly direct government influence. The direction of donor giving can be and often is set by donor incentive schemes, by national lotteries with government-designated charities as recipients, and by selection of charities for grant aid or service delivery contracts. As the 20th century drew to a close, the common law processes for developing charitable purposes to keep pace with emerging forms of social need were no longer able to do so, thereby limiting donor giving capacity;

[19] See the Advisory Group, *Campaigning and the Voluntary Sector*, London, 2007, in which Baroness Helena Kennedy QC noted the "chilling effect" caused by the use of powers such as to "stop and search" under the Terrorism Act 2000, s.44.

this became a driving force impelling some governments to embark on charity law reform.

One effect of all such constraints is that a decreasing number of charities are now sufficiently strong and independent to champion the cause of the disadvantaged, direct resources toward new socially marginalized groups, or lobby for changes to government policy. As the availability of charity's mediatory services decline, the option of seeking to remedy social disadvantage through the enforcement of legal rights becomes more attractive.

2. The Right to Receive

Legislative recognition and processes for accessing and enforcing legal rights are imperfectly provided for by national legislatures, and even where they exist they may produce imperfect results. This is only too clearly evidenced by the referrals made to international bodies, particularly to the European Court of Human Rights, alleging breaches of rights. In all modern common law jurisdictions the volume of appeals being made to supervening sources of authority (Conventions, constitutions, etc.), usually on matters of human rights, speaks to the failings of national processes. However, the fact that such appeals are now routinely made, together with the growing proportion of national laws and processes becoming compliant with the standards set by such authorities, is resulting in the recognition of an ever-broadening range of matters in respect of which persons may hold legal rights, even though the exercise of such rights remain vulnerable to the vagaries of politics as evident in the practice of "extraordinary rendition," the use of drones, and the treatment of asylum seekers. Some of this expansion of rights is at the price of reducing the areas left to charity. The extent to which there will be further rights incursions into the realm of charity, or a retraction of such rights in the face of the new antiterrorism political imperative, is unknown, but inevitably the charity/legal rights boundary is one that will be continuously changing.

IV. THE CHARITY/GOVERNMENT BOUNDARY

The Preamble, as expanded by *Pemsel*, broadly identified the matters that would thereafter constitute the main themes in the agenda set by government for its relationship with charity. In the intervening four centuries, charity law in the common law nations remained largely immune from further direct legislative interference by government. The Preamble agenda therefore continued with some legislative additions (notably in relation to sport and recreation) and a judicial widening of definitional matters, while a range of new legal structures were absorbed. Ultimately, the charity/government boundary remained recognizably close to its Elizabethan parameters.[20]

[20] See Bromley, B., "The 1601 Preamble: the State's Agenda for Charity," in *Charity Law & Practice Review*, Vol. 7, No. 3, 2002.

A. Boundary Setting: Government, Charity, Tax, and Public Benefit Services

There is, clearly, an important issue of cost for public benefit services and the consequences that then flow for charitable status and more broadly for charities. This is more straightforward where the services are pre-paid by way of taxes or paid for at point of delivery by the user. It becomes a good deal more complex, and at times suspect, when obscured by the magical accountancy of "internal markets," and the contracting out of service provision to commerce or service delivery to charity, both sometimes coupled with a means-tested contribution to be paid at point of use.

At the root of the difficulty is the distinction between service provision as the mandatory statutory duty of government officials, paid for from public taxes, and the provision of the same or a substitute service by a charity where the market cost has been partially offset by donations, by reliance on volunteers, and by tax exemption. Although the activities of both government and charity are legally required to conform to the same public benefit principle, those of the latter are ultimately discretionary. The recipients, those meeting a statutory definition of social need, have a legal right to access statutorily authorized and tax-funded public services and not to be left reliant upon the discretionary choices of independent agencies where funding and authority to disburse funds are essentially sourced in the choices of private citizens. That legal right, however, is only exercisable in respect of available public services, which, in turn, are a product of wealth redistribution taxes and the associated political ideology.

1. The Welfare State

In the U.K., the establishment of a National Health Service in 1948 provided for the nationwide delivery of health and social care services to a uniform specification and standard that was free at point of access, available as of right, and in accordance to individual need. This together with other forms of public service provision similarly launched in 1948[21] constituted the "welfare state," defined the charity/government boundary in the U.K., and thereafter shaped expectations in that jurisdiction regarding the separation of government and charity responsibilities for health and social care services.

[21] The legislative authority for the "welfare state" came in the form of a package of statutes: the National Insurance Act 1946, which implemented the Beveridge scheme for social security; the National Health Service Act 1946, which nationalized relevant charitable provision and introduced nationwide health and social care services; the National Assistance Act 1948, which repealed and replaced the Poor Law regime (all of which came into effect in July 1948); and the Children Act 1948.

However, in a common law context, the Beveridge fully fledged welfare state[22] model, wholly dependent upon wealth redistribution taxes, never really transcended its U.K. origins. The Labour party, which in 1945 formed the first post-war U.K. government, sought to make health, social care, housing, education, welfare benefits, etc. as much the responsibility of government as the provision of such public utilities as roads, street lighting, tap water, and other services. It removed public benefit service provision from the discretion of charities by conferring rights on citizens to basic services and consigning charity to a secondary role of supplementing government provision. It provided that which the market could not or would not deliver. In theory it therefore served as a government guarantee that its citizens would not be deprived of public benefit services by any failure on the part of charity or market. The immediate post-war period in Britain was a time of national reconstruction when a high level of social solidarity gave a Labour government the mandate to impose the high level of taxation necessary to fund universal public health and welfare services. These conditions simply did not apply in other common law countries.

Although aspects of Beveridge's template for organizing the national delivery of health and social care services to a uniform specification and standard that was free at point of access were successfully if variably adopted in some jurisdictions such as Ireland, that model was rejected in the United States. Only in the U.K., therefore, has there been a sharp distinction between government-provided services to be availed of as of right—health, education, housing, welfare benefits—and other services accessible at private choice and expense. This has been accompanied by a general acceptance of the necessity for wealth redistribution taxes but also by a corresponding understanding that provision of such services was a responsibility that fell to government.

2. The United States

Other than in the U.K., governments have not stepped in to assume so much of the responsibility for public benefit services, and a fluid pick-n-mix of public and private provision has been the norm. In the United States, the intrusion into private life, necessitated by a "welfare state" approach to service provision and by the accompanying wealth redistribution taxes, has been continuously rejected by a significant proportion of its citizens. From the earliest days of the republic, freedom from the oppression of such taxes has been upheld as a constitutional right. As James Madison, sometimes referred to as father of the Constitution, wrote, "I cannot undertake to lay my finger on that article of the Constitution which granted

[22] See William Beveridge (1879–1963) and the 1942 Beveridge Report (*The Report of the Inter-Departmental Committee on Social Insurance and Allied Services,* the single most instrumental step in founding the British welfare state), which led to the establishment of a National Health Service in 1948, with free medical treatment for all, and a national system of welfare benefits.

a right to Congress of expending, on objects of benevolence, the money of their constituents."[23]

Consequently, in the United States there never has been a commonly shared view of what should be core government services or of what should be the remit of charity. Even as the state pursues some health care reform today, in the United States there is uncertainty as to the essential components of a public health[24] or education service; different providers deliver in accordance with state or local market conditions; and a competitive and varied range of services can be availed of at individual initiative and expense.

B. The Contemporary Charity/Government Boundary

Despite the welfare state, charities in the U.K. maintained a presence in health and social care services, training for employment, education, and housing, and in the general alleviation of those in impoverished circumstances. Although their profile was not as prominent as in other common law countries, charities were never wholly displaced by the welfare state. Since the 1970s, following recurring economic crises, they have steadily became more prominent in all those areas as state provision receded.

In recent years, governments in the U.K. and in such other places as New Zealand, Canada, and Australia have moved more toward the boundary set in the United States. In the U.K. this has, arguably, been largely achieved by stealth: the incremental shedding of responsibility for the delivery of core public benefit provision to both the for-profit and the nonprofit sectors, coupled with a vast increase in the contribution of charities established specifically for the purpose of generating funds for hospital facilities and other public services. In general, however, the observation made in relation to Canada that "principally, the contraction of the welfare state has meant that much that was previously done by government agencies is now done by charities or other non-profit groups"[25] applies with equal validity to all the developed common law nations, though less so in the United States where government simply never undertook a similar spread of welfare state responsibilities.

Much of the cost for new public utilities, or for renewing old ones, in the U.K. is increasingly being passed to the private sector whereas costs for meeting basic health and social care provision is at least defrayed by charity. Government has also used its funding power to encourage charities to deliver services it formerly provided, thereby creating an array of "captive" nonprofits that must compete with for-profit

[23] James Madison, *Annals of Congress*, House of Representatives, 3rd Congress, 1st Session, at p. 170.

[24] See the controversy preceding health care reform in the United States in 2010, which was enacted in the Patient Protection and Affordable Care Act (March 23, 2010) shortly thereafter amended by the Health Care and Education Reconciliation Act of 2010 (H.R. 4872).

[25] See Phillips, J., Chapman, B. and Stevens, D. (eds), *Between State and Market: Essays on Charities Law and Policy in Canada*, McGill-Queen's Press, Montreal, 2001, at p. 3.

firms in artificially created service markets.[26] Such efforts, often aided and abetted by fund-seeking charities, to assimilate the latter into public service provision, risk compromising the identity of "charity," the integrity of "charitable purpose," and the loosening of de Tocqueville's "moral tie"[27] between giver and receiver, with adverse consequences for altruism, social capital, and civil society.

In short, the charity/government boundary in the U.K. is being peremptorily and radically readjusted to ensure that government bears less direct responsibility for future public benefit service provision, as has long been the case elsewhere.

1. Public and Private Interests

In the U.K., the transfer of responsibility for public benefit services to form the welfare state at least ensured that government, charity, and citizens had a clear understanding of the forms of provision that could be construed as core public benefit services, a recognition that never fully transferred to other jurisdictions. For the first 50 years or so of the welfare state, the public/private division was represented by the roles of government and charity respectively.[28] Unlike Australia, where the government grant aided but never sought to replace charity, in the U.K. government largely absorbed and augmented the existing patchwork of charitable education and health care provision and undertook to ensure a nation wide framework of services freely and uniformly accessible to all on a needs basis. Where leading charities were already well established or had developed services that supplemented state provision, the state would then support the continuation of that role through a program of grant aid.[29] Such grant-aided charities maintained their independence while being valued for their capacity to innovate. They were not as encumbered with bureaucratic systems and prescriptive policies and procedures as their statutory counterparts, and could rely upon a pool of volunteers, which allowed them to develop more flexible types of intervention. Consequently, charities soon acquired a reputation as the pioneers of new forms of services that government would in time emulate.

[26] See Handy, C., "The Privatisation of Social Housing: Capture and Commercialisation of the Voluntary Sector," in Dunn, A., (ed.) *The Voluntary Sector, the State and the Law*, Hart Publishing, Oxford, 2000, at pp.107–19.

[27] See de Tocqueville, A., *Democracy in America*, 1835 (trans. George Lawrence, New York, Harper Collins, 1988, ch. 17):

> Despotism may govern without faith, but liberty cannot. How is it possible that society should escape destruction if the moral tie is not strengthened in proportion as the political tie is relaxed? And what can be done with a people who are their own masters if they are not submissive to the Deity?

[28] See Home Office, *Efficiency Scrutiny of Government Funding of the Voluntary Sector, Profiting from Partnership*, HMSO, London, 1990.

[29] See Beveridge, W. H., *Voluntary Action: A Report on Methods of Social Advance*, Allen and Unwin, London, 1948. See also Wolfenden, J., *The Future of Voluntary Organisations*, Croom Helm, London, 1978 and the Home Office, *The Government and the Voluntary Sector*, London, 1978.

The previously clear public/private divide created by the welfare state became more blurred as government responded to the intractable problems resulting from demographic trends, falling revenue, and massive public debt with cutbacks in public spending, a broadening involvement of nonprofits, and increased privatization.[30] This shift in public service provision from government to commerce and the nonprofit sector began in the U.K. in the 1980s, was well advanced in all modern common law jurisdictions by the turn of the century, and has done much to intensify the blurring of the public/private boundary in health, education, housing, and social care services. Government retreat from service provision, however, was accompanied by the introduction of increased regulatory powers and retention of control over policy (and to a lesser degree also over funding).

V. THE CHARITY/BUSINESS BOUNDARY

Charities, as outlined in chapter 2, were never wholly business averse. The range of income-generating activity associated with long-established charities is considerable, and ranges from service delivery charities contracted to government departments; universities charging admission fees; and hospitals, clinics, nursing homes, and other health or social care charities charging for their services. In recent years, however, following the method adopted in the United States, other common law countries are now witnessing a surge in the commercial activities of charity. As economic recession reduces the inward flow of funds from government and from fund-raising while simultaneously increasing the outward flow of resources to those in need, charities are left with little option other than to rapidly develop entrepreneurial ventures in order to subsidize the operating costs of their charitable activities. Failure to do so is to run the risk of being bypassed as the new wave of social enterprises and entrepreneurs, driven by a "profits for social purpose" idealism, challenges charity and its seemingly arcane baggage for the position of champion of the socially oppressed and disadvantaged in today's world. The scale of this engagement is difficult to judge as so many of the charity/business links are not very visible. The existence of dense ties between the two sectors emerges on occasions such as the banking crisis in Iceland, which revealed that very many U.K. charities had high levels of financial exposure due to investments in overseas commercial companies. This level of engagement brings with it complex difficulties in terms of appropriate legal structures and the management of consortiums of charities and commercial entities, and in ensuring that regulatory controls are in place to monitor governance arrangements, provide adequate levels of transparency, and facilitate accountability.

[30] See Charity Commission for England and Wales, RS15 *Stand and Deliver—The Future for Charities Providing Public Services* (Version February 2007).

A. Patrolling the Boundary: Law and Tax

The commercial ventures of charity have always attracted scrutiny by tax regulators. At either extreme the application of law and tax is straightforward: a charity operating a business that functions at or below cost does not need income tax exemption, and, if it is operating a business that totally dwarfs its charitable activity, it will forfeit charitable status and be wholly liable for tax. The difficulties lie between these extremes and, increasingly in recent years they have also attracted judicial scrutiny. Further complications are added by the range of taxes, dividends, interest, rents, and royalties from which charities and other nonprofits may or may not gain exemption: In particular, the rules regarding exemption from rates on property can be of considerable importance to charities; in some jurisdictions the rule is that the entire property must be used for charitable purposes, in others apportionment is permissible.

Essentially, however, the main area of concern in all common law jurisdictions is the same: Has the blending of commerce and charity been such as to affect the tax-exempt status and/or the charitable status of the organization? The degree to which commercial involvement will threaten charitable status is the crucial issue and one which courts and regulators in the common law world are increasingly having to resolve.[31]

In addition to established common law principles and the law relating to types of trading (see chapter 2), there are certain rules which have come to play a critical bearing in determining such issues; these are applied by tax authorities with varying consistency across the main common law jurisdictions. Their primary significance probably lies in their relative capacity to reduce any unfair competitive advantage to be gained by charities and other nonprofits at the expense of purely commercial entities, with the "level playing field" principle a matter of political importance, particularly in the United States.

1. The Nondistribution Constraint

Fundamentally, all nonprofit corporations including charities are distinguishable from their for-profit counterparts by the prohibition on the distribution of earnings among their officials, or what Henry Hansmann has called "the nondistribution constraint":[32]

> A nonprofit organization is, in essence, an organization that is barred from distributing its net earnings, if any, to individuals who exercise control over it, such as members, officers, directors, or trustees. By "net earnings" I mean here pure

[31] For example, in the United States, see Provena Covenant Med. Ctr. v. Dep't. of Revenue, 384 Ill. App. 3d 734 (App. Ct. 2008); in the U.K., see the Charity Commission ruling on five public schools in 2009, two of which were denied charitable status.

[32] Hansmann, H., "The Rationale for Exempting Nonprofit Organisations from Corporate Income Taxation," in *Yale Law Journal*, Vol. 91, No. 1, 1981, at pp. 54–100.

> profits—that is, excess of the amount needed to pay for services rendered to the organization; in general, a nonprofit is free to pay reasonable compensation to any person for labor or capital that he provides, whether or not that person exercises some control over the organization. It should be noted that a nonprofit is barred from earning a profit. Many nonprofits in fact consistently show an annual accounting surplus. It is only the distribution of these profits that is prohibited. Net earnings, if any, must be retained and devoted entirely to financing further production of the services that the organization was formed to provide.[33]

As a starting point, Revenue authorities will be alert to any indication that a nonprofit has compromised its legal status by arrangements that allow for the distribution of net earnings to any of its stakeholders.

2. The Commensurate Test

Introduced by the IRS in the United States in 1964,[34] the commensurate test requires charities to conduct charitable activities commensurate in scope with their resources. It was customarily applied by monitoring the flow of income at its destination. Since 2008, the IRS has demonstrated a fresh interest in the potential usefulness of this test and has shifted its focus (see chapter 7).

3. Destination of Income Test

Basically, this test operates on the basis that the source of the income is irrelevant. Regardless of whether an organization is a charity or a wholly commercial entity, if all its income is being channeled toward a charitable purpose then it will be treated as tax exempt. This approach licensed a wave of commercial enterprises, the activities of which often bore little or no relationship to the charitable purpose of the organization receiving the income generated. Following controversy generated by so-called "feeder organizations" in the *Macaroni*[35] and *Trinidad*[36] cases in the United States, this test was replaced by the unrelated business income tax regime (UBIT) in 1950.[37] It has never played such a determinative role in U.K. tax law. As Pollock M.R. warned in *Brighton College v. Marriot*:[38]

> under income tax law the fact that profits when made are to be devoted to the advancement of the charity will not include an exemption. Profits when made are subject to the tax, and their destination does not seek immunity for them.

[33] Hansmann, H., "The Role of Nonprofit Enterprise," in *Yale Law Journal*, Vol. 89, No. 5, 1980, at pp. 835–902.

[34] IRS ruling 64–182, 1964–1 CB 186.

[35] C. F. Mueller Co. v. Commissioner of Internal Revenue, 190 F.2d 120 (3rd Cir. 1951).

[36] Trinidad v. Sagrada Orden de Predicadores, 263 U.S. 578 (1924).

[37] Strictly speaking, the test disappeared with the introduction of s.502 of the IRC in 1954.

[38] [1925] 1 KB 312; aff'd [1926] AC 192.

The test reemerged with the recent Australian decision in the *Word Investments* case[39] (see chapters 7, 9, and 12).

4. Primary Purposes Test and Unrelated Business Income

Tax exemption is generally available in respect of related business income, or income derived from activities ancillary to the carrying out of a charity's primary purpose. In the United States, this is known as the primary purpose test and basically permits an organization to be tax exempt:[40]

> although it operates a trade or business as a substantial part of its activities, if the operation of such trade or business is in furtherance of the organisation's exempt purpose or purposes and if the organisation is not organised or operated for the primary purpose of carrying on an unrelated trade or business.

If the trade or business in fact constitutes an overwhelming majority of the organization's activities (i.e., if it in fact operates as a business with a relatively insignificant attached charity), then it will forfeit its eligibility for charitable status. If the direct conduct of commercial activity is "related" to the charitable purpose forming the basis of the organization's tax-exempt status—for example, education delivered by a university—it does not jeopardize the organization's tax-exempt status, and is not taxed.

If the direct conduct of commercial activity is "unrelated" to the organization's charitable purpose it will not jeopardize the overall exemption if the organization is not operated for the primary purpose of carrying on an unrelated business, but the net income will be subject to the UBIT if the activity is "regularly carried on." In effect, it prohibited exemption for any feeder organization that operates a business and contributes the profits to charity as its primary activity rather than itself conducting inherently charitable activities. These changes in the law made the destination of income test virtually obsolete.[41]

5. Commerciality Doctrine

In the United States in particular, the IRS will take an overview of the nature and scale of activity in order to estimate whether, in aggregate, an organization's actions

[39] Commissioner of Taxation of the Commonwealth of Australia v. Word Investments Ltd [2008] HCA 55.

[40] Treas. Reg. s.1.501)c)(3)–1(e)(1).

[41] See further, Brody, E., "Business Activities of Nonprofit Organizations," in Cordes, J. J. and Steuerle, C. E. (eds.), *Nonprofits and Business*, The Urban Institute Press, Washington, DC, 2009.

give the impression of commerciality.[42] No particular attention is given to the destination of income. Attention will instead be given to the manner in which an organization's activities are conducted, the commerciality of those activities, the competition with commercial firms, and the existence and amount of annual or accumulated profits.[43] These will each be taken into account as evidence in determining whether an organization has developed commercial interests to such an extent that its activities are no longer exclusively dedicated to its charitable purpose but instead constitute a substantially different and taxable purpose. Where the cumulative picture is one indicating that the organization has come to resemble any other commercial enterprise, then that will be sufficient to warrant removal or denial of charitable status. This approach has enabled the IRS to deny tax exemption to a range of nonprofits engaged in a variety of activities including adoption, insurance, financial services, religious publishing, conference centers, low-income housing, and retreats for caretakers—all on the general basis of their resemblance to similar for-profit businesses. It has application also to the growing phenomenon of "whole hospital" joint ventures, involving charities acting in a consortium with commercial entities, which obscures tax liability and forces the IRS to make a broad judgment on the enterprise as a whole. Charities may jeopardize their entitlement to charitable status by becoming immersed in such taxable ventures unless they are able to sanitize their area of involvement.

6. Private Benefit and Inurement

Linked to the commerciality doctrine, and central to the nondistribution constraint, is the prohibition on private benefit.[44] Where there is evidence that an entity's operations are of an overwhelming commercial nature, and of private benefit (accruing to charity outsiders) or private inurement (charity insiders), this will confirm a substantial nonexempt purpose. For example, in *Rameses School of San Antonio, Texas v. Commissioner*,[45] the revocation of a school's tax-exempt status was upheld because its founder and executive director received a private benefit from the school by using school funds for personal expenses and drawing a salary in excess of the amount approved by the board.

[42] See Hopkins, B. R., "The Most Important Concept in the Law of Tax Exempt Organizations Today: The Commerciality Doctrine," in *Exempt Organisation Tax Review* 459, 1992; and Sanders, W. M., "The Commerciality Doctrine Is Alive and Well," in *Taxation of Exempts* Vol. 16, 2005, at pp. 209, 210.

[43] See, e.g., Living Faith, Inc. v. Commissioner, 950 F.2d 365, 371 (7th Cir. 1991).

[44] See Inland Revenue Commissioners v. Oldham Training and Enterprise Council (1996) STC 1218.

[45] T.C. Memo. 2007–85 (April 10, 2007).

B. Blurring the Boundary: New Structures, Arrangements, and Management Systems

The need for the above rules, and their changeability, is in large part due to the ingenuity with which new structures, consortiums, or arrangements of mutual convenience are being created that enable charities, other nonprofits, and for-profit entities to work together. In some ways, philanthropy at the end of the 20th century seemed to be echoing a synergy with commerce previously experienced in the U.K. at the end of the 18th century. At that time, the introduction of joint stock companies for furthering commerce inspired philanthropic effort that saw the founders of the Royal Philanthropic Society in 1788[46] establish charitable associations that adopted the form, the management systems, and the funding mechanisms of the new trading companies. Now it would seem that philanthropy is being caught up in the new world of high finance—with its venture capitalism, hedge funds, and derivatives—and is similarly intent on cloning and customizing new vehicles for channeling philanthropic effort. As regulators in all leading common law jurisdictions scramble to catch up, there are real dangers that charity may overreach itself by placing at risk its autonomous, mission-led identity. Alternatively, it may be simply bypassed as the challenge of social entrepreneurship proves itself by providing the flexibility, partnership opportunities, and access to funds and finance management skills that charity, confined by purposes and common law constraints, is having difficulty accessing.

1. From Charity to Business

Charities developing business interests is far from new, but the volume of charities now doing so and the scale of some of their business ventures has been a dramatic change from established practice. Some simply opt to transfer from charitable to for-profit status whereas others build disproportionately large business enterprises within the protective shell of charitable status. As charities increasingly resort to joint ventures with businesses, the potential for a degree of private profit to infiltrate practice and negate charitable tax exemption is becoming a more common hazard. There will also be issues regarding the possibility of private benefit or inurement, and perhaps also issues regarding the subversion of charitable purpose, with consequences for charitable status. As more charities straddle the boundary with commerce, this will be an area of recurring difficulty.

In normal circumstances a charity wishing to raise funds to offset its running costs by commercial activity may well choose to establish a subsidiary company for that purpose. In that case, both entities have separate legal identities but the subsidiary company could qualify for tax exemption in its own right. If, however, the

[46] See A History of the Royal Philanthropic Society 1788–1988; see further at: www.redhill-reigate-history.co.uk/philanth.htm.

charity decides to pursue the same ends by way of working with a consortium or with an arrangement of different entities, then because that grouping does not have a separate legal identity and no separate tax liability any income that passes through to the charity will be liable for tax. In that event there will also be issues regarding the possibility of private benefit or inurement and perhaps also ones regarding the subversion of charitable purpose, with consequences for charitable status. As more charities straddle the boundary with commerce this will be an area of recurring difficulty.

2. From Business to Charity

The reverse development, whereby established commercial entities decide to extend their activities into the charity arena, has become a noticeable phenomenon in recent years. Brody has identified higher education and hospitals as two subsectors where that form of interaction between nonprofits and commerce has lately been highly visible.[47] She draws attention to the fact that this is often low-profile but intensive traffic in which

> businesses provide financing to nonprofit projects, such as loans and investments in tax credit partnerships, and businesses enter into a myriad of contracts with nonprofits. For example...proprietary businesses fill niches in classroom teaching, provide tutoring and remedial education; supply computers and software; design curricula; and provide food services, transportation, maintenance, and security. Finally, charities might outsource administrative functions, such as asset management and online membership enrollment—and even donor solicitation.[48]

3. Public Service Management

The charity/business boundary has, in recent years, become blurred by "New Public Management," which applies to public services the techniques and practices of management developed in the private sector; it has become a respected and globally established approach to the dynamics of public benefit service provision.[49] Oriented toward increasing outcomes and efficiency through better management of public funds and by introducing competition, New Public Management incorporates an

[47] See Brody, "Business Activities of Nonprofit Organizations," at pp. 83–129.

[48] Citing Ben-Ner, A., "Outsourcing by Nonprofit Organisations," in Young, D. (ed.), *Effective Economic Decision-Making by Nonprofit Organisations*, The Foundation Centre, New York, 2004, at pp. 67–83.

[49] See, e.g., Austin, R. P., "The Impact of the Human Rights Act on Administrative Law," in *Current Legal Problems*, 1999, pp. 200–10. See also, R v. Panel on Takeovers and Mergers, ex parte Datafin [1987] QB 815 (CA).

open market approach. The transfer of much public benefit service provision from the public to the nonprofit sector included this approach as part of the package.

Charities have proved to be an enthusiastic convert to New Public Management though, once enveloped in the contract culture they probably had little option other than to fully participate. Consequently, in terms of service administration, management systems, and professional careers, adherence to New Public Management has played a not-insignificant part in further blurring the boundaries between charity, business, and government.

4. Private Insurance

Insurance rather than government funding is increasingly determining the income flow into the health care system. In the United States, as Brody has noted, insurance schemes such as Medicaid and Medicare now contribute so much to hospital running costs that in practice it is of little relevance whether a hospital is a charity or a for-profit entity.[50] In the U.K., also, as the NHS is slowly eroded, so too is its customer base as people increasingly turn to insurance schemes to access private hospitals and clinics. There is a sense in which this represents a broad shift in responsibility for insuring public health and social care from government to the private sector. This transition in the fiscal fundamentals of the economic environment has been noted by Tanzi:[51]

> In the phenomenal increase in public spending that took place in industrial countries from the first to the second half of the 20th century, the government became a huge insurance company and intermediary for the citizens. In this de facto insurance company, the citizens as a group paid fees in the form of high taxes; in turn, they were compensated with free or highly subsidized public services.

Demographic trends put paid to that. Now, as governments peer over the financial abyss and examine their unfunded future liabilities in public pensions and health care, it may indeed seem that, as Tanzi says, "these programmes have become public examples of Ponzi schemes—payments to future beneficiaries are to be covered by the future contributions of new members."[52] The relentless need to continuously rebalance this "beneficiaries and new members equation" makes the past position of the government as "insurer of last resort" untenable for the future. As these changes become more pronounced and government expeditiously makes more room for private insurance, so too will the charity/business boundary in health care become ever more difficult to discern.

[50] See, Brody, "Business Activities of Nonprofit Organisations," at p. 86.

[51] See Tanzi, V., *Government versus Markets: The Changing Economic Role of the State*, Cambridge University Press, Cambridge, 2011, at p. 13.

[52] Tanzi, *Government versus Markets*, at p. 19.

VI. CHARITY AND JURISDICTIONAL BOUNDARIES

Frontiers impose their own finite limits. Charity, in keeping with every other aspect of law, must remain subject to national courts. Charitable status, tax liability, and fund-raising are among the matters that may give rise to issues requiring regulatory accountability or juridical adjudication within a charity's jurisdiction of origin. To some extent this operates as a constraint. In an age when global movements of people and funds and the relocation of businesses are commonplace, charities cannot just ignore jurisdictional boundaries. Again, however, this boundary is one that is by no means as firm as it once was.

A. Jurisdictional Boundaries and Charitable Status

There is a long-standing common law rule that a charity must be amenable to the courts and laws of its jurisdiction of origin,[53] which means that it must be "established" within it. The rule is generally interpreted as meaning that a charity must have its administrative offices, or at least a main branch of the organization, located within that jurisdiction. In any case, it would in practice be difficult for a court to attempt to exercise any control over an entity that had no physical presence or assets within the jurisdiction but was amenable to a foreign court.[54]

For most purposes, however, charities recognized as such in one common law jurisdiction have been accustomed to readily gaining equivalent recognition in another; although, unless "established" in the second, a charity has had to seek recognition by applying for registration there. This is still the case even in the U.K. and Irish jurisdictions where very many charities operate across territorial boundaries. Following recent national charity law reforms, and the introduction of differences in the definition and application of certain key common law concepts, it is likely that such reciprocal status recognition among common law countries will in the future become more complicated.

1. Reciprocal Recognition: Common Law and Civil Law; Federated Jurisdictions

For some years now charities and other nonprofits operating across European borders have been experiencing considerable difficulties in getting reciprocal government recognition for their legal status; this is not dissimilar to the problems occurring in federated jurisdictions such as Australia, Canada, and the United

[53] See Construction Industry Training Board v. Attorney-General [1971] 1 WLR 1303, 1308; aff'd [1973] Ch 173 (CA).

[54] See Gaudiya Mission v. Brahmachary [1997] 4 All ER 957 (CA).

States. The root of the European difficulty, however, lies in the innate differences between common law and civil law bodies of jurisprudence. Given that the EC is wholly premised on the free movement of people and goods between member states,[55] it was inevitable that these difficulties would eventually come before the courts. The cases *Centro di Musicologia Walter Stauffer v. Finanzamt München für Körperschaften*[56] and *Hein Persche v. Finanzamt Ludenscheid*[57] are instances where this matter was brought in front of the ECJ. *Stauffer* concerned an Italian charitable foundation (tax exempt in Italy) that received rental income from property in Germany. The ECJ held that German domestic law constituted an obstacle to the free movement of capital, which could not be justified under Article 58(1)(a) of the EC Treaty because the objects of the Stauffer foundation would have been recognized as charitable in Germany had it been established there. In *Hein Persche,* a German tax advisor, Mr. Persche, sought a ruling on the deductibility for German tax purposes of a gift he had made to a retirement home and children's center in Portugal after the German tax authorities refused to grant him a tax deduction as the recipient was not a German charity. The court concluded that Germany's tax law constituted a constraint. This was because a charitable gift made in Portugal, by a German citizen, was being treated differently by the German taxation authority than a similar one given in that citizen's homeland. The two decisions confirm that the traditional interpretation of "establishment" operates as a constraint that is discriminatory in effect, and breaches the EC requirements for free movement of goods across the jurisdictions of member states (see chapter 6).

B. Jurisdictional Boundaries and Tax Liability

Unlike the standard jurisdictional requirement that a body corporeal must be within the court's jurisdiction or be brought within it before that court can exercise any powers in relation to it, the tax laws adopt a slightly different approach.

1. An Overseas Charity Operating within the Jurisdiction

Any such charity, established in one jurisdiction but operating within another, must pay tax in the latter on any income derived from trading there. It was in the leading U.K. case of *Camille and Henry Dreyfus Foundation Inc. v. IRC*[58] that Jenkins L.J. first laid down the rule that tax exemption must be restricted to charities "established"

[55] See the EC Treaty: Articles 43 and 48, guaranteeing the freedom of establishment; Articles 39 and 43, guaranteeing freedom of movement and freedom from discrimination; and Article 12, guaranteeing freedom from discrimination.

[56] (C386/04).

[57] [2008] ECJ C318/07. This account is taken from a case note prepared at QUT, see further at: https://wiki.qut.edu.au/display/CPNS/Hein+Persche+v+Finanzamt+Ludenscheid.

[58] [1955] 3 All ER 97.

within the jurisdiction. The rule has been taken to apply in respect of "any body of persons or trust established for charitable purposes." As Jenkins L.J. explained in the course of his judgment in *Dreyfus,* which concerned an organization incorporated in New York that had no physical presence within the U.K. and had undertaken no activities there:

> The phrase to be construed is the whole phrase "body of persons or trust established for charitable purposes only",[59] and it must be construed in its context. Whether the claim for exemption is made on behalf of a body of persons or on behalf of a trust, the body or trust must be shown to be established for charitable purposes only, and that requirement must have the same quality in the case of a body of persons as it has in the case of a trust. I have already expressed the view that "trust" in an Act of the United Kingdom means a trust taking effect and enforceable under the law of the United Kingdom. It follows that, in my opinion, a "trust established for charitable purposes only" must mean here a trust taking effect and enforceable under the law of the United Kingdom and creating an obligation enforceable in the Courts of the United Kingdom to apply its funds for purposes which are, according to the law of the United Kingdom, exclusively charitable. I can attribute no different meaning to the phrase "established for charitable purposes only" when applied to a body of persons. So applied, I think it is only satisfied by a body of persons which is under the law of the United Kingdom subject to an obligation enforceable in our Courts to apply its funds for purposes which are according to that law exclusively charitable.

In more recent years, the courts have tended to the view that "established" need not be restricted to imply a requirement that the charity be represented by having at least a main branch within the jurisdiction.[60] Instead, whether an organization is established within the jurisdiction where it has its administrative center, or whether it merely has a presence in it but is established in another jurisdiction where it actually has an administrative center, it will generally be entitled to charitable status in the first jurisdiction, although its tax exemption will obviously be restricted to income derived from its activities there. In jurisdictions with a statutory, charity-specific, registration requirement (in states such as the U.K., Ireland, New Zealand, and Singapore) this approach now forms part of and is governed by the terms of registration.

[59] Income Tax Act 1918, s.37(1)(b), citing also the fact that an exemption substantially in this form had appeared in income tax legislation ever since 1799, at which date there was no question of taxing, and therefore none of exempting nonresident foreigners.

[60] See, e.g., the Irish case Revenue Commissioners v. Sisters of Charity of the Incarnate Word [1998] 2 I.R. 553.

2. A Charity within the Jurisdiction Operating Overseas

The *Dreyfus* rule clearly does not imply that a charity's funds may only be applied within the jurisdiction. Many charities, based within one jurisdiction and claiming tax exemption there, apply their funds for charitable purposes abroad in another. Such charities are wholly amenable both to the judicial and tax authorities within the first jurisdiction.[61]

C. Jurisdictional Boundaries and the Flow of Funds

Charities have long been required to have a swift and decisive capacity to act globally in coordinating the transfer of personnel, resources, and funds for disaster relief in jurisdictions often far removed from any sources of aid. In recent years, however, their freedom to do so has become somewhat compromised.

1. Charitable Fund-Raising

The abrupt change in the nature and methods of fund-raising caught the legislatures of most common law jurisdictions by surprise. Laws and regulatory frameworks established to deal with raffles, church collections, and door-to-door and street collections proved ill-equipped to cope with modern professional and entertaining fund-raising techniques with the capacity to attract within a very short period a large volume of funds. As the Internet allowed charitable causes to become global in scope and facilitated the flow of an ever-increasing volume of funds across continents, issues of probity suddenly became more pressing. This has been most obvious in the context of concerns regarding international terrorism, as has been a great deal of national legislation introduced to monitor the international movement of funds (See chapter 12). The volume, the speed, the frequency, the distances, the risks associated with misuse, and the glamour of celebrity-led fund-raising benefits could not be managed within customary frameworks.

In particular, although traditional forms of fund-raising continue to play their part in generating volunteers and stimulating the generosity of local communities, charities have more recently come to rely heavily upon the mass media, on professional entertainment events, and on trading ventures for generating resources. Professional fund-raisers, electronic media such as telethons and telemarketing, and global fund-raising initiatives (e.g., campaigns such as "Make Poverty History") all have involved the general public in fund-raising and promoted awareness of deserving causes. Powerful national and multinational televised appeals attracting a great volume of funds in a concentrated period have brought with them complex legal problems.

[61] See, e.g., Re Vagliano [1905] WN 179; and Re Robinson [1931] 2 Ch 122, 129.

Other developments have also had an impact on orthodox fund-raising. National lotteries, where government bodies determine the list of recipient charities for the proceeds generated, with adverse consequences both for all other charities and for traditional charitable fund-raising activities, have become a familiar feature in all modern common law nations. This has been accompanied by considerable controversy regarding the contradiction between the responsibilities of government to control gambling as a pernicious source of social evil while simultaneously promoting it as a funding source for remedial social intervention. Again, donor incentive schemes have enabled governments, particularly in Australia and Singapore, to intervene in traditional patterns of gratuitous giving by channeling individual and corporate donations toward government-designated charitable purposes. The thresholds set for the associated tax relief schemes have come to play an important part in some jurisdictions, such as the United States, in attracting more charitable donors. That jurisdiction has also led the way in generating a greater volume of contributions from "high value donors." The Gates charitable foundation would seem to have set an example for other successful industrialists in the United States, Australia, and elsewhere to similarly devote their wealth, entrepreneurial skill, and high finance expertise toward the creation of new models of targeted, proactive intervention in areas blighted by habitual poverty and disease.

2. Economic Recession

There is some evidence that the increasing domestic poverty within the developed common law nations, which has demanded a higher proportion of charitable resources, is decreasing the outward flow of funds for the alleviation of hardship overseas. This is not unexpected. However, the current economic recession is unlike others in two important respects.

First, the recession is commonly perceived to be a consequence of the excesses of capitalism: The gross profits of a few have been at the expense of the majority, and the latter have been disproportionately affected by shrinking employment opportunities and remedial government action to reduce national debt by cutting social services. As governments acknowledge the urgency of the situation and demonstrate their capacity to act swiftly and collectively by nationalizing the engines of capitalism, and through measures such as "quantitative easing," there is a general disquiet regarding their seeming inability or reluctance to respond similarly to poverty and social disadvantage. Why should the former be government business and the latter be left to charity?

Second, this recession has awakened a broad awareness of the importance of good governance. It is problematic on many different levels that the "high finance champagne culture" that prevailed before and precipitated the fact of recession should remain virtually intact after it. For charities and other nonprofits there are difficulties in weathering a public perception that they are being asked to make good the shortfall caused by a systemic abuse of principles of good governance by those in a privileged position to oversee the workings of a crucial part of our social infrastructure. That governments should stand aside and allow that culture and its adherents to continue indicates, perhaps, a willingness to condone willful failures of governance. The reluctance to prosecute those responsible for reckless corporate management, to demand some fiscal redress from those who profited excessively, and to require regulators to answer for their failings are among the long list of government omissions that cause ongoing citizen disquiet. A disenchanted general public, with less disposable income, is likely to remain poorly motivated in terms of trusting corporate entities with donations for overseas aid until its faith in corporate governance is restored.

VII. CHARITY AND POLITICAL BOUNDARIES

Finally, the current shift in the boundaries between state, business, and nonprofits must also be seen in a historical context, set against a broad political background. Although the move toward charity law reform is explicable in its own terms, as governments sought to better regulate the nonprofit sector and broaden its public benefit remit, it can in addition be viewed as an incidental by-product of more fundamental political change. The link between the collapse of communism and charity law reform may seem a bit of a stretch, but it was the ending of the Cold War and the consequent ascendancy of the market that prepared the ground for government reviews of their public benefit responsibilities and how to pay for them. The abrupt dissolution of a lengthy and paralyzing ideological stalemate permitted a general recalibration of politics that included not only a rebalancing of private and public interests in the former communist regimes, but also licensed entrepreneurial capitalism to extend its reach on a domestic and international basis. Arguably, it was the latter's sudden freedom to push beyond the previously constraining boundaries, both geographical and ideological, bringing resources and a belief in the capacity of private profit margins to displace the state's duty—as arbiter of public goods availability—that allowed governments to consider the renegotiation of public benefit responsibilities now incorporated in the law reform outcomes.

A. The Fading Significance of Ideology

The consequences of the collapse of communism are still being worked through. The implosion of the most potent, dominant, and enduring ideology of the past century had several immediate and obvious outcomes: It has taken with it the accustomed reference points for socialism and left-wing politics in general, leading inevitably to a melting away of organized political power on a domestic and international basis from that quarter; it has freed up governments in the leading democratic nations and licensed them to demonstrate the benefits of the open market; competitive commerce and entrepreneurial activity have been given both a political boost and unrestrained access to markets without frontiers; and forms of associational activity that may serve as vehicles for community benefit have acquired a growing legitimacy in recognition of their potential to generate nonprofit sector coherence. As the potency of socialist ideology faded so also did that of its organizing forums, particularly the trade unions,[62] and its unifying programs that had prescribed the rationale and resources for public benefit provision.

1. Some Consequences for Democracy

That the collapse of communism has done more to bolster the forces of capitalism than the principles of democracy can be seen, for example, in the emergence of millionaires amid the endemic poverty and neglected social infrastructure of Russia and other former communist countries where the attainment of public office is often by processes that fail to fully comply with the normal standards of Western democracies. In the latter there is now a generalized resistance to the "welfare state" approach, and government cutbacks on unemployment and disability benefits are the norm, whereas political campaigns to drive down taxes are becoming increasingly common. It has been evident also in the resulting rise of neoconservatism in the United States, and to some degree in the U.K. and Australia; the more general drift of left-wing politics to the center ground as illustrated most obviously in the "third-way" approach for the Blair administration in the U.K.; and the move from a "Cold War" footing to an active and spreading engagement in war.

In retrospect, an important consequence of the collapse of communism may have been the free rein given to entrepreneurial capitalism, as reflected in the market excesses that led to the financial crisis of 2008. Indeed, it would be hard not to construe a causal link between the demise of the enemy of capitalism and the latter's ensuing rampant and reckless exploitive practices that were, after all, politically endorsed until they culminated in global economic recession. This saga has yet to run its course, and any attempted analysis of its long-term significance for the workings of democracy would at this stage be premature. In the short-term at least, however, the balance between capitalism and democracy is likely to undergo serious stress tests as citizens in many developed nations respond to the effects of austerity programs imposed by government to limit the social harm caused by a financial elite and restore stability to domestic banking. On an international basis, the crisis has convincingly demonstrated the interdependency of national banking and financial systems. As the EU struggles to contain the threat to its currency and to the continued economic integration of its 27 Member States, the implications for the balance between capitalism and democracy of imposing financial management

[62] The traditional power of trade unions has also been eroded in all "developed" nations in recent years by the outsourcing of manufacturing: the employer threat to transfer production overseas effectively "capping" the pay-bargaining negotiating capacity of the unions.

strategies on the democratically elected governments concerned will undoubtedly become more apparent.

As the "Arab Spring"[63] phenomenon continues on its uncertain path, it perhaps remains to be seen whether the eventual realignment of oil producing nations, Islamic power, and Western interests proves conducive to promoting democracy as well as capitalism in that region. The probability of any such outcome is, however, being compromised by the serial military intervention of Western powers in Islamic countries, usually entailing "regime change," in conjunction with their continued financial support for the military capacity of Israel. It currently seems at least as likely that it will instead open up a new ideological cold war front. The added complications that may flow from China, driven by its own singular ideology, extending into Europe and North America the investment practices it has rehearsed in Africa, can only be guessed at. Nor is it possible to foresee how the entrée of India, with the world's largest democratic population, into the ranks of the developed nations will impact upon accepted interpretations of "democracy" and "capitalism."

Geopolitics would seem to be undergoing a process of quite fundamental change, and there is no good reason to suppose that "democracy," with the institutional checks and balances customarily associated with it, will survive in a form familiar to previous generations. The chances of it doing so will probably be dependent upon capitalism and the ascendancy of the market being curbed by effective regulatory constraints.

2. Some Consequences for Charity

An important characteristic of former communist and other totalitarian regimes differentiating them from the developed democratic nations was the principle of basic public benefit provision as a duty and prerogative of the state. Such provision, together with state control over the disposal of "private" property, ensured that charity as a legally sanctioned, organized means of redistributing private wealth for public good could not constitute a formal part of social life. Donor choice, discretion, and the very concept of a "gift relationship" endangered the authority of the state. So, for example, the fact that the recipient must be a stranger to the donor, without any legal or moral obligation or any form of personal nexus between them, would undermine the state's right to determine public benefit entitlement and distribution of property; a nongovernmental organization dedicated to the promotion of public benefit purposes, providing the formal conduit for channeling a donor's gift to the recipient, would be outside government control and displace the need for state service provision; whereas the freedom of citizens to form, join, or not to join

[63] The social revolutions that began in December 2010 then spread from Tunisia, Egypt, and Libya to prompt civil uprisings in Bahrain, Syria, and Yemen. Major protests have also occurred in Algeria, Iraq, Jordan, Morocco, and Oman. Civil unrest has been evident in Kuwait, Lebanon, Mauritania, Saudi Arabia, Sudan, and Western Sahara.

associations, a hallmark of democracy,[64] would be viewed as a potential source of civil unrest and a threat to social order.

The transition to democracy had the incidental effect of opening the door to organized "charity" or philanthropy in the many countries concerned. This opportunity has been accompanied by the challenge to ensure that charitable intervention meets the needs of the citizenry as well as that of the governments of these new or incipient democratic states. It will take time before it becomes clear how nonindigenous charities will, for example accommodate the restrictions of working within very corporatist systems, transcend an immediate role of dealing with the effects of poverty and assisting government to adopt the legal and social infrastructure of democracy, maintain established levels of functioning in the face of reduced resources and increased domestic demand, and respond to government as it wrestles with the unfamiliar problems associated with addressing the collective strength of charities and other nonprofits.

The collapse of communism was also not without domestic consequences for charities in the jurisdictions that comprise this study, not least of which has recently been the need to spread their resources that much further at a time of economic recession. Advocacy in particular has grown in importance. As ideologically based campaigning forums have largely closed or lost their bargaining position, and trade unions (whether or not socialist controlled) become emasculated, the responsibility for articulating the grievances of the growing numbers of the socially disadvantaged, and lobbying for change on their behalf, should logically have fallen to charities. This, however, is a responsibility they are now less able to bear due to being compromised by their relationship with government[65] and by judicial enforcement of the rule prohibiting their political activity.[66] Consequently, issue-specific campaigning by special interest groups, without the added leverage of shared principles or any collective sense of direction and purpose, now threaten to displace the advocacy role once borne by charity.

The role of charity has also come under threat from commerce, particularly regarding its core public benefit contribution in health, social care, and education. The boost to entrepreneurial capitalism has led to charity losing some of its traditional constituencies as inroads are carved out by the poaching predations of private business. Granted this has had a variable impact across the "developed" and developing nations, with much of "corporatist" continental Europe so far remaining relatively immune to private business intrusion, but for most of the countries

[64] The International Covenant on Civil and Political Rights (ICCPR) and the Universal Declaration of Human Rights both guarantee freedom of association internationally, as does the Helsinki Accords of the Organisation (former Conference) on Security and Cooperation in Europe (OSCE). See also the Freedom of Association and Protection of the Right to Organise Convention, 1948 (No. 87) and the Right to Organise and Collective Bargaining Convention, 1949 (No. 98).

[65] In the U.K., see, e.g., Seddon, N., *Who Cares?*, Civitas, London, 2007.

[66] In Australia, for example, see the prolonged judicial process that culminated in Aid/Watch Incorporated v. Commissioner of Taxation [2010] HCA 42; [2009] FCAFC 128.

studied the general trend toward a closer involvement of business in public benefit provision is unmistakable.

In the long run, however, it may be that the proliferation of faith-based charities, especially those involved in education, will be seen as a particularly significant consequence. It does not seem too farfetched to suggest a link between the collapse of communist ideology, the fading attraction of socialism, and the filling of the resulting vacuum by a resurgence of religiously motivated entities, and indeed by a belief in the web of principles and institutions held to constitute "civil society."

B. The Changing Nature of "the State"

The functions of the state must be configured in relation to prevailing circumstances sufficient to address the priority needs of its citizens at any point in time, and flexible enough to take into account significant emerging domestic and external pressures. For the developed nations, and many of those in the process of "developing," the virtual evisceration of socialism has been the most significant change in circumstances to be faced by the state in the past generation. It has largely removed ideology from politics. The former communist states no longer coercively control their artificial internal markets, the welfare states are a good deal less committed to "cradle to grave" public benefit provision, and corporatist states are making more room for commercial and other external influences. Relieved of the need to constantly engage in ideological positioning, and faced with the global trends and pressures now plunging many of the developed nations into recession, government in those nations has been left mainly with its age-old duty to ensure the protection of its citizens and borders while also addressing the growing contemporary need to manage domestic and international economic matters.

1. Economics Rather than Ideology

As ideology receded, managing the economy came to the fore as the primary business of the state.[67] This was largely necessitated by the increasing weight of public service responsibility that fell to government. Throughout the 20th century and well into the first decade of the 21st, the proportion of national GDP spent by government on public benefit provision rose steadily in all developed countries, including those in this study. It has been calculated that "between 1913 and 2000, the share of public spending in gross domestic product for the groups of industrial countries for which data are available rose by about a factor of four."[68] By 1999, public expenditure in some countries (e.g., Belgium, Italy, the Netherlands, Norway, and Sweden) exceeded 50 percent of GDP, in others (e.g., Austria, Canada, France, Germany, Ireland, New Zealand, and

[67] See, e.g., Stiglitz, J., *The Economic Role of the State*, Basil Blackwell, Oxford 1989; see also Tanzi, *Government versus Markets*, at pp. 305–35.

[68] See Tanzi, *Government versus Markets*, at p. 239.

Spain) it was 40–50 percent, whereas in some (e.g., Australia, Japan, Switzerland, the U.K., and the United States) it was reaching toward 40 percent.[69] This can be traced to the steady buildup in government spending on such staple public services as education, health, housing, welfare benefits, and state pensions.

However, as the first decade of the 21st century progressed the evidence that such levels of expenditure were unsustainable accumulated: The established problems of demographic trends, the cost of pensions and health care for ageing populations, etc., were exacerbated by the drain of financing foreign wars, meeting rising fuel costs, and paying the price for the decline or outsourcing of domestic manufacturing and production. In the lead-up to the 2008 financial crisis, governments in most developed nations were cutting back on public expenditure and, notwithstanding the sudden spike of increased spending—triggered by measures to bailout banks, underpin national currencies, and ameliorate the social suffering caused by a surge in unemployment—such cutbacks can only be increased as global politics are brought to bear on the new imperative to stabilize international financial systems and restore normal market functioning. As market failure requires state intervention, it is likely that the economy will continue to be the primary preoccupation of government for the foreseeable future. The pressing need to introduce more efficient regulatory controls and greater global coordination and for national governments, like banks and other financial institutions, to plan and manage for surplus revenues, all within the constraints of democracy, are set to become the driving force shaping politics in the "developed" nations. An unknown factor, of course, is whether a worsening economic crisis will jolt society along ideological fault lines and reawaken ideology as a challenge for government.

2. Social Policy and Taxation

In most of the countries studied, government where feasible now chooses to advance its public benefit–related social policy objectives by discretely manipulating the tax system, rather than do so by policy declaration and legislation, as this is less politically compromising. Funding for welfare-type services is often raised by "tax expenditures" that enable government to sidestep the policy confrontation that would be invited if tax revenues were overtly used to directly fund public-benefit deficits. So, in practice, the tax exemption privileges for charities and their legally established purposes are supplemented by government use of a sophisticated and varied range of tax expenditure devices—including national lotteries and tiered tax exemption for certain categories of charities and other nonprofits, together with a range of donor incentive schemes and corporate tax exemptions—all of which serve to direct private funds toward the achievement of government-selected public-benefit purposes.[70] This approach forms a

[69] Tanzi, *Government versus Markets*, at p. 232.

[70] See further, Zelinsky, E., "Are Tax 'Benefits' Constitutionally Equivalent to Direct Expenditures?," in *Harvard Law Review*, Vol. 112, No. 2, 1998, at pp. 400–09.

somewhat opaque part in the economic management role of the modern state but has significant implications for the funding of charity and for government relations with the nonprofit sector.

3. The State, Charity, and Public Benefit Provision

It is clear that, despite globalization, the line between the public benefit provision of government and charity will be drawn differently in accordance with a nation's culture, history, and prevailing economic circumstances. However, when considering in the following chapters the choices made by different governments. it is worth bearing in mind Judt's observation:

> Only a state can provide the services and conditions through which its citizens may aspire to lead a good or fulfilling life. These conditions vary across cultures. They may emphasize civic peace, solidarity with the less fortunate, public facilities of the infrastructural or even the high cultural sort, environmental amenities, free health care, good public education, and much else...only the state can adjudicate with reasonable impartiality between competing demands, interests, and goods. Most important, only the state can represent a shared consensus about which goods are positional and can be obtained only in prosperity, and which are basic and must be provided to everyone in all circumstances. These are things the market—much less the global market—cannot do.[71]

VIII. CONCLUSION

The role of charity in contemporary society has been steadily constrained by parameters in many different forms: displaced by family, church, and professionals; and restricted by legal rights, social justice, and antiterrorism measures. Recent changes in the way it interfaces with government, however, are now pushing charity into assuming a more mainstream role in society. As grant aid has given way to contracts, charities have been forced into the market to seek funding through public-benefit service provision and from trading. For many, the current state of flux in the permeable boundaries separating charities from the business and the government sectors presents real opportunities if the traditional common law constraints imposed by rules relating to trading and profit can be overcome. As nonprofit enterprises take on ever-more flexible legal structures, allowing affiliation with business, charities have had every reason to feel boxed in. This has generated considerable experimentation, particularly in the U.K. and the United States, as charities and other nonprofits explore new ways of working with government and commerce in their pursuit of mission and funding.

[71] Judt, T., *Reappraisals*, Vintage Books, London, 2008, at p. 423.

PART 2

Contemporary International Perspectives

5

ENGLAND AND WALES

I. INTRODUCTION

Within the common law world, England and Wales has historically carried the lead role, forging ahead with developments in the field, including experimenting with charities and trading. Within that world, it has also taken further and longer its investment in a centralist welfare state model, and consequently has had to deal with a more extreme form of withdrawal from government service provision. The recent history of government/charity relations in England and Wales offers a particularly interesting example of a political strategy developed to allow the responsibility for future public benefit service provision to be shared more broadly, and delivered in a manner tailored to meet local community need, between government and its chosen partners in the charity and business sectors. Although the outcome of the recent charity law reform process demonstrates the strength of the government/charity partnership, and reveals key elements of the government strategy, it also indicates some serious pitfalls that need to be avoided or overcome if the partnership is to prevail and succeed in covering the government retreat from the high ground of the welfare state.

This chapter focuses on England and Wales, rather than on the U.K. as a whole, because the remit of the Charity Commission, the regulatory body for charities, has always been limited to that jurisdiction. Although very recently the other jurisdictions have each acquired their own Commission, this focus is compromised to some extent by statistical material, legislation, and judicial and regulatory rulings that are U.K.-wide. It begins with a brief sector profile: It considers contemporary data and trends, distinguishing between the role of charities and other nonprofits. It then examines the government/charity relationship first in relation to the institutional and other structures put in place to bridge the gap between the parties, and second with regard to the impact of charity law reform outcomes. Attention then moves to the changes introduced by the coalition government and its "Big Society" policy, focusing in particular on the steps taken to pass more responsibility for public service delivery toward the nonprofit sector and the introduction of new legal structures to facilitate such a transfer. The chapter concludes by taking stock of the present situation in this jurisdiction: identifying the main components in the legal framework for charitable trading; assessing the related case law; and reflecting on the scale and nature of changes taking place in the government/charity relationship at a time when severe economic pressures are forcing the pace in terms of government withdrawal from its position as the main public benefit service provider.

II. SECTOR PROFILE

England and Wales comprise one jurisdiction of the three[1] that constitute the United Kingdom and of those three it is the one with the most significance for charity law mainly because the rulings of its higher courts are binding on the others, and because for the last 150 years it alone had a Charity Commission. Currently, it has a population of approximately 53 million, or 89 percent of the total U.K. population.[2] Since the late 1990s, immigration has significantly increased, which, together with a rise in the birthrate,[3] is now an important factor in sustaining population growth.

Over the past two decades, government had greatly reduced public ownership and contained the growth of social welfare programs. However, the U.K. economy, the sixth largest in the world, suffered a serious setback when it became entangled in the global financial crisis that began in 2008. The outgoing Labour government sought to stabilize the country's finances by measures that included nationalizing parts of the banking system, cutting taxes, repeated bouts of "quantitative easing," suspending public sector borrowing rules, and moving forward public spending on capital projects. In 2010, the incoming Conservative/Liberal Democrat coalition government took further steps to retrieve a situation that had markedly deteriorated in 2009 as output slowed and unemployment increased. By 2010 the U.K. had the biggest budget deficit in the G20, public sector debt stood at £952.8 billion (or 64.6 percent of GDP), GDP hovered around a 0.7 percent growth rate with even lower rates applicable to output from manufacturing, construction, and services industries, while unemployment reached its highest point for 17 years.[4] The new

[1] The other jurisdictions are Scotland and Northern Ireland.

[2] See Office for National Statistics at: http://www.statistics.gov.uk/hub/population/index.html.

[3] Office for National Statistics at: http://www.statistics.gov.uk/hub/population/index.html, which shows that the birthrate has been rising steadily over the past decade. In 2009 the birthrate attained a 35-year high, but still failed to reach a "replacement rate."

[4] See further the National Institute of Economic and Social Research 2011 report at: http://www.niesr.ac.uk/

coalition government then launched its Big Society[5] initiative and, simultaneously, embarked upon the most radical and comprehensive program of post-war cuts in public spending.[6]

It is against this background that the socioeconomic significance of the nonprofit sector and the role of charity must be measured.[7]

A. The Nonprofit Sector

The National Council of Voluntary Organizations in its latest survey[8] estimates that the U.K. sector consists of approximately 870,000 entities, including charities, universities, cooperatives, housing associations, independent schools, industrial and provident societies, faith groups, sports clubs, and many more. It assesses the sector's total income to be £116 billion, and its workforce as consisting of over 1.3 million people. It notes that "organizations involved in social services, culture and recreation, and health activities make up the majority of the sector's economic activity with social services organizations receiving one-quarter of the sector's income." It draws attention to the significant role played by cooperatives and social enterprises. In 2007/2008 it estimates there were over 4500 cooperatives, with an overall income of £26.3 billion. There are also, at present, at least 50,000 social enterprises generating approximately £18 billion in annual turnover and employing over 775,000 people.[9] In 2003 the Social Enterprise Coalition was formed, an organization comprised of some 8000 social enterprises, ranging from housing associations and credit unions to registered charities, a coffee company, and a newspaper published by homeless people. This coalition promotes a unified voice for social enterprise companies, lobbies government in favor of policies that

[5] See Launch of "Big Society" program by Cameron, D. P. M. , *Building the Big Society*, Cabinet Office Press Office (May 18, 2010); further at: www.cabinetoffice.gov.uk/media/407789/building-big-society.pdf.

[6] See Comprehensive Spending Review, published in September 2010. HM Treasury, Comprehensive Spending Review 2010; see further at: http://www.google.co.uk/search?q=Comprehensive+Spending+Review%2C+UK+September+2010&ie=utf-8&oe=utf-8&aq=t&rls=org.mozilla:en-US:official&client=firefox-a.

[7] For further more detailed statistical data, see, e.g., the Commission on 2020 Public Services, the final report *From Social Security to Social Productivity: A Vision for 2020 Public Services*, the 2020 Public Services Trust, London, 2010, at Chapter 2, pp. 18–21.

[8] See NCVO, the *UK Civil Society Almanac 2010*, NCVO Publications, London, 2010. See also NCVO, *The Reform of Public Services: The Role of the Voluntary Sector*, NCVO Publications, London, 2005.

[9] See Department of Trade and Industry, *The Small Business Service: Social Enterprise Survey across the UK*, July 11, 2007. Almost two-thirds of those surveyed (64 percent) stated that they had charitable status. Of those that were not registered with the Charity Commission, 5 percent were exempt or had exempted status, and 5 percent were in the process of registering. The NCVO, alternatively, calculates that social enterprise activity in 2007/2008 amounted to £82 billion (71 percent) accounting for most of the sector's income.

support them, and identifies best practices among those engaged in social enterprise work. Its work will be advanced further when the Public Services (Social Enterprise and Social Value) Bill 2010/2011 becomes law.[10]

The sector has, in recent years, become more organized, and important umbrella bodies have been created that are able to speak for it on sector-wide issues. It has also become more diversified and, with the surging growth in social enterprises, now accommodates an ever-broadening range of nonprofits. It has developed a research capacity, has its own dedicated banking and finance facilities, uses sophisticated multimedia techniques to communicate, and, with its well-established policy units, has become adept at formulating and negotiating on policy issues affecting sector interests.

1. Sector Umbrella Bodies

In this jurisdiction there are a number of well-established umbrella or "apex" organizations accustomed to coordinating and leading nonprofit bodies, acting as effective advocates on sector-related matters, and contributing to government policy. They provide a forum for collecting data, articulating concerns, sifting and channeling issues to appropriate government bodies, and relaying government views back to the sector. They organize focused research and arrange for the findings to be disseminated and used for advocacy purposes. The leadership provided by organizations such as the NCVO,[11] ACEVO,[12] ACF,[13] NAVCA[14] and CAF[15] in England and Wales has been vital to the maturation of the nonprofit sector and to the development of its present considerable political leverage.

[10] The Bill, which had its second reading in the House of Lords in January 2012, aims to strengthen the social enterprise business sector and make the concept of "social value" more relevant and important in the placement and provision of public services.

[11] The National Council of Voluntary Organizations, which commenced in 1919 as the National Council of Social Services, is the umbrella body for the voluntary and community sector in England. Equivalent organizations elsewhere in the U.K. would be the Wales Council for Voluntary Action, the Northern Ireland Council for Voluntary Action (NICVA) and in Scotland, the Scotland Council for Voluntary Organizations (SCVO).

[12] The Association of Chief Executives of Voluntary Organizations was established in the early 1990s.

[13] The Association of Charitable Foundations formed in 1989 and became a charitable company limited by guarantee registered in England and Wales in 2005. It is a U.K.-wide support organization with a membership of over three hundred including many large independent foundations, local and community trusts, family trusts, corporate foundations, and broadcasting appeals.

[14] The National Association of Voluntary and Community Action, previously known as the National Association of Councils for Voluntary Service (NACVS), was renamed and relaunched as NAVCA in June 2006. It is the national body for local support and development organizations in England.

[15] The Charities Aid Foundation, an offshoot of the NCVO, was established in 1974 to provide services and assistance to U.K. and international charities and their donors, as well as to promote donations to charity generally.

2. Charities

Only a minority of the entities that comprise the nonprofit sector are charities. This minority, however, includes the largest, most professional, powerful, and enduring organizations with a well-established role as sector leaders.

The Charity Commission report[16] noted that at the end of June 2010 there were 180,000 charities on its Register with a total income of £52 billion. Not all charities are registered. They are not required to do so if: they have an annual income of £5000 or less, have their head office in another jurisdiction, or are "exempt" or "excepted" from the requirement to register.[17] "Excepted" charities are those with an annual income of less than £100,000, most of which are connected with certain churches and chapels belonging to various Christian denominations, charitable service funds of the armed forces, or scout and guide groups; they will continue to be "excepted" until 2012. "Exempt" charities are those, such as universities, that are supervised by another organization or body. The Commission profiles the wealth of charities as follows: 45 percent of registered charities have an income of not more than £10,000 and contribute less than 0.5 percent of the total income recorded; 1.1 percent of charities receive £5 million or more in annual income, which is 66.9 percent of the total annual income recorded. It has been estimated that in 2010, registered charities held nearly £78 billion in investment assets.[18]

3. Charitable Giving

The Civil Society Almanac estimates that individual donations remain the single most important funding stream for the entire voluntary sector, accounting for £13.1 billion (37 percent) of its total £35.5 billion annual income in 2007/2008.[19] Its data on charitable giving shows that a small number of donors continue to generate a large proportion of the total amount donated. In 2008/2009, two million people (7 percent of donors) gave more than £100 per month, but they generated almost half (49 percent) of the total. Charitable giving is still crucial to the sector, it says, particularly to the 78 percent (133,074) of charities that receive no government funding at all and rely on donations. The government's Citizenship Survey recorded a slight fall in volunteering levels over the 2009/2010 period.

[16] See Charity Commission, Annual Report, 2009–2010.

[17] Certain charities were "excepted" or "exempt" from the requirement to register by the Charities Act 1993.

[18] Chair of Charity Commission on launch of *Consultation on Charity and Investment Matters*, December 2010.

[19] See NCVO, the *UK Civil Society Almanac 2010*, which aims to provide a comprehensive statistical breakdown of Civil Society based on figures from the 2007/2008 financial year.

B. Financing the Sector

The latest available figures show that the sector in 2007/2008 had an income of £33.2 billion of which 36 percent (£12.8 billion) came from statutory (government) sources, including £586 million from the National Lottery. It had an operating expenditure of £31.2 billion and total assets of £91.3 billion, and employed 634,000 people, with 37 percent working part-time.[20]

1. Government Funding

In England and Wales, the sector has a long-term dependency upon government funding. In particular, under the Labour government there were a series of public policy initiatives that directed funding streams toward the sector.[21] The most recent data shows that government spending on the sector accounts for 2 percent of the overall national budget,[22] but this simple statistic belies the complicated nature of the financial relationship between government and the sector. Although much attention is given to the change in funding streams from grant aid to service contracts, less note is taken of the fact that only 25 percent of nonprofits actually have any direct financial relationship with government and that public money in total accounts for no more than approximately 36 percent of sector income compared to 37 percent from donations by individuals.[23]

Undoubtedly government funding has a significant impact on the nonprofit sector, but it is differentiated in its effect with much greater significance for some subsectors than others, and virtually none for most nonprofits. For example, from 2000 to 2008, the following subsectors all closely aligned to government service provision received particularly high levels of statutory income: employment and training (70 percent), education (51 percent), law and advocacy (51 percent), social services (50 percent) and housing (50 percent).[24] In trying to wean itself off dependency on government, the sector has had some success in developing self-financing sources.

[20] See NCVO, the *UK Civil Society Almanac 2010.*

[21] See, e.g., the "Futurebuilders," "Capacitybuilders" and "Together We Can" programs, all of which aimed to fund increased sector capacity.

[22] See NCVO, *The UK Civil Society Almanac 2010.*

[23] The National Survey of Third Sector Organizations, which closed in December 2008, estimated that nearly a third of voluntary and community organizations receive funding from local government and that this provides the largest source of statutory income (47 percent) to the U.K. sector; see further, Cabinet Office, *Office of the Third Sector's National Survey of Third Sector Organizations,* London, 2009.

[24] See NCVO, *The UK Civil Society Almanac 2010.*

2. Self-Financing

It would be a mistake to underestimate the sector's self-financing capacity. During 2007/2008, for example, it received grants, donations, and legacies worth £13.6 billion, equivalent to 41 percent of total income for that year. Recently the sector has acquired an important new capacity to fund nonprofits at below-market rates. In part this has been made possible by the emergence of socially minded investors willing to fund, at preferred rates, socially minded businesses and enterprises.

a. The Charities Aid Foundation

The Charities Aid Foundation was established as a separate entity from its parent organization, the NCVO, in 1974.[25] In 1986 it set up the CAF Bank[26] to provide banking services exclusively for U.K. charities. In 1992, the CAF Bank became the Charity Bank and was subsequently registered as a charity. It now uses its funds to finance other charities and nonprofit entities. It also provides funds for community projects in a manner similar to the private finance initiative used in many major public sector building contracts.

In 2002 CAF launched Venturesome,[27] a social investment fund, to provide the capital investment necessary for charities and social enterprises to deal with cash flow difficulties and expand their organizations. Venturesome is not limited to registered charities but applicant organizations must have a clearly defined charitable purpose.

b. The Big Society Bank

This bank was first proposed by the Labour government and is now due to be launched in Summer 2012 by the coalition government with funds of between £60 million and £300 million from dormant bank accounts,[28] in order to become a wholesale provider of finance to nonprofit or social entrepreneurs.[29] Government has declared that the bank is intended to play a central role in providing working

[25] Barclays, HSBC, Lloyds, RBS, and Santander UK are to commit a total of between £1billion and £1.5billion over a two-year period to augment the bank's funds.

[26] See further at: www.cafonline.org/can.

[27] See further at: http://www.venturesome.org.

[28] See further at: http://www.cabinetoffice.gov.uk/news/big-society-bank-gets-green-light.

[29] The Charities Aid Foundation derived from the Charities Department instituted by the National Council of Social Service in 1924 to encourage efficient giving to charity. It is a registered charity that, among other things, delivers banking services at minimum rates for charities and social enterprises.

capital for those charities and other nonprofits wishing to "run public services and deliver the big society."[30]

It should make a substantial contribution to the sector's finances, both through use of its own funds and by leveraging additional private capital.

III. CHARITIES AND GOVERNMENT: ARCHITECTURE FOR PUBLIC SERVICE PARTNERSHIP

Since the Thatcher administration in the 1980s, the U.K. government has been resolutely committed to reducing the size of the public sector. Despite party political changes, the government has consistently viewed the nonprofit sector, and charities in particular, as the key to its policy of shrinking the scale of government public benefit provision and sharing the costs of future services with other providers. The early years, which saw a fire-sale approach to shedding responsibility for core utilities largely to the private sector, has been replaced by a more nuanced but equally determined resolve to outsource, or at least reduce the government share of, traditional public benefit services.[31] Similarly, earlier government/sector links have since been expanded, formalized, and reinforced with policies and protocols to become a complex, institutional partnership framework.

The coalition government that was installed in 2010, in *Our Programme for Government*,[32] made a commitment to: "support the creation and expansion of mutuals, co-operatives, charities, and social enterprises, and enable these groups to have much greater involvement in the running of public services." This, as the Prime Minister later explained when launching the "Big Society" policy, will require the government to "foster and support a new culture of voluntarism, philanthropy, social action . . . open up public services to new providers like charities, social enterprises and private companies so we get more innovation, diversity and responsiveness to public need."[33] Although the "Big Society" may, perhaps, provide a broad policy context for future government/sector relationships, the architecture of that relationship was built largely by the previous Labour government and must be viewed in conjunction with the charity law reform outcomes.

[30] Now to be known as Big Society Capital Group, it will be constituted as a group of three entities: the Big Society Trust, which is responsible for ensuring that the group is true to its mission; Big Society Capital Limited, which is the operating company of the group; and Big Society Foundation, which will be a charitable foundation able to receive philanthropic donations.

[31] See, e.g., the Partnership Improvement Programme (PIP), which builds on a scheme piloted in 2005/2006 and is designed to improve cross-sector partnership working among local authorities, other public sector bodies, and local nonprofits.

[32] See HM Government, *The Coalition: Our Programme for Government*, London, May 20, 2010. See further at: http://www.cabinetoffice.gov.uk/news/coalition-documents.

[33] From transcript of a speech by the Prime Minister on the "Big Society," Liverpool, July 19, 2010.

A. Government Bodies and the Sector: Structural Links

Over a period of some decades, governments of differing political hues have gradually added to and formalized their links with the sector. It was during the Blair-led Labour government, however, that the links were packaged and institutionalized until they began to resemble a treaty with a foreign country. The framework was later further augmented, by the coalition government, to become the centerpiece of its "Big Society" policy.

1. Ministerial Responsibility for the Sector

Government recognition that certain matters in the public interest have attained a new and challenging level of political importance is invariably signaled by the appointment of a minister to assume responsibility for it. In the U.K., the appointment in 2010 of the Minister for Civil Society to lead the new Office for Civil Society (formerly the Office of the Third Sector) and "act as a champion of the voluntary sector in the heart of government" signified the new government's wholehearted endorsement of the elevated political salience acquired by the sector under Labour.[34]

2. The Office for Civil Society

This strategically important government office is located in the Cabinet Office and "leads work across government to support voluntary and community groups, social enterprises, charities, co-operatives and mutuals."[35] It oversees partnership arrangements and coordinates the involvement of the Commission for the Compact and the Charity Commission.

a. Strategic Partners Program

The Office of the Third Sector launched its strategic partners program in 2006. By 2008 this had expanded to include several new partners in a Social Enterprise Coalition. In August 2010, the Minister for Civil Society announced that, as part of government public spending cuts, the strategic partners program was to be slimmed down from £12.1 million to a maximum of £7.5 million and from 40 partners to a maximum of 15.

[34] As explained in a letter to voluntary organizations prior to the election campaign, signed by both the now-Minister for Civil Society, Nick Hurd, and the new Minister for the Cabinet Office, Francis Maude. In fact, this 2010 initiative amounted to little more than a name change: Government recognition of the sector's political importance, as represented by the creation of the ministerial post and office, was already established.

[35] See http://www.thecompact.org.uk/information/100018/101234/101495/officeofthethird-sector/. In 2006 the government established the Commission for the Compact, an independent body to champion the Compact and promote good relations between sector and government.

3. The Compact

The Compact initiative, first introduced in England and Wales, is a framework document and a process negotiated initially between central government and a cross section of representatives of the voluntary and community sector (i.e., national and local charities, other nonprofits and community bodies), which sets out the principles under which partnerships between public authorities and voluntary and community bodies should be developed. In particular it seeks to entrench the independence of voluntary bodies and ensure that the relationship is genuinely one of partnership. The Compact for England and Wales, launched in 1998 and accompanied by Codes of Practice, provided a set of principles to govern working relationships between government and the sector[36] with application to all government departments and primary agencies. It was a model duly adopted in all U.K. jurisdictions,[37] eventually replicated in all local authorities and monitored by means of annual reviews. The Compacts have introduced a nationwide framework for monitoring the government/sector relationship in operational terms.

a. Local Strategic Partnerships

The implementation of policy for embedding a government/nonprofit sector working relationship at the local community level was expedited by incorporating local strategic partnerships in virtually all local government offices.[38] First established in 2000, they were intended to bring together representatives from the local statutory, voluntary, community, and private sectors to address local problems, allocate funding, and discuss strategies and initiatives.

4. The Charity Commission

Commissioners are statutorily entrusted, as restated in the 1993 Act and more recently in the 2006 Act, and now the Charities Act 2011, with the duty of "promoting the effective use of charitable resources."[39] Further, the Commissioners are required

[36] See the *Compact on Relations between Government and the Voluntary and Community Sector in England* Cm 4100 London, Home Office, 1998. The Compact has codes of good practice for Black & Minority Ethnic Groups, Community Groups, Consultation & Policy Appraisal, Funding & Procurement, and Volunteering. See further at: http://www.thecompact.org.uk.

[37] The *Scottish Compact* was published in October 1998, the English Compact *Getting It Right Together* and the *Compact for Wales* were both published in November 1998. In Northern Ireland, *Building Real Partnership—Compact between Government and the Voluntary and Community Sector in Northern Ireland* was laid before Parliament in December 1998.

[38] See, e.g., Office of the Third Sector, "Principles of Representation: A Framework for Effective Third Sector Participation in Local Strategic Partnerships," 2008.

[39] Section 14(4) of the Charities Act 2011.

to encourage and facilitate the better administration of charities,[40] as stated in the 2011 Act, s.15(1)(2). The 2006 Act also established the Charity Tribunal, which was transferred to the First–tier Tribunal (Charity) on September 1, 2009, following the reform of the Tribunal system by the Tribunals Courts and Enforcement Act 2007. The Charity Commission is the lynchpin of the newly formulated government/sector partnership. As an outcome of recent charity law reform processes, each of the U.K. jurisdictions now has a similar Charity Commission with virtually identical statutory powers, functions, and procedures.

B. Government Policy: Charity Law Reform

The process of charity law reform in England and Wales[41] concluded with some important adjustments to the regulatory framework but, for present purposes, the more significant changes are those made to some core definitional matters.[42] In the main, these have taken the form of a reworking of "public benefit," an expanded list of charitable purposes, and their embodiment in legislation.

1. Public Benefit

The 2006 Act, now the Charities Act 2011, reversed the public benefit presumption traditionally granted to the first three *Pemsel* heads[43] to give the public benefit test an unequivocal mandatory application in respect of all charitable purposes in England and Wales.[44] This reversal had potentially important implications for the Commission's

[40] Previously, s.1(4) of the Charities Act 1993 as amended by the Charities Act 2006,s.7.

[41] Concluded with the introduction of the Charities Act 2006. This omitted any change to the rules governing trading by charities (proposals for same having been made earlier in the Strategy Unit Review report *Private Action, Public Benefit* (2002) were rejected in the Home Office report *Charities and Not for Profits: A Modern Legal Framework*, HMSO, London, 2003).

[42] The need for a statutory definition of matters constituting "charity" had been recommended by the Royal Commission on the Income Tax 1920 (Cmd 615) and by the Royal Commission on the Taxation of Profits and Income 1955 (Cmd 9474).

[43] All three U.K. jurisdictions and Ireland have modified this common law test by introducing statutory rules to guide interpretation and provide powers for further guidance to be supplied by the regulator.

[44] Under what is now the Charities Act 2011, s.3(1):

> A purpose falls within this subsection if it falls within any of the following descriptions of purposes—
>
> (a) the prevention or relief of poverty;
> (b) the advancement of education;
> (c) the advancement of religion;
> (d) the advancement of health or the saving of lives;
> (e) the advancement of citizenship or community development;
> (f) the advancement of the arts, culture, heritage or science;
> (g) the advancement of amateur sport;
> (h) the advancement of human rights, conflict resolution or reconciliation or the promotion of religious or racial harmony or equality and diversity;

role. Given that this ostensibly independent body is already within the ambit of government influence (wholly government funded, staffed by government-approved appointees, and, if not directly accountable to government ministers, subject to government oversight), it could be vulnerable to party political pressure to apply the test to the benefit or detriment of facilities such as private schools, hospitals, and other health and social care facilities with expensive admission fees—depending on the political stripe of the government of the day.[45]

2. Charitable Purposes

This jurisdiction has introduced legislative provisions that list a new set of "*Pemsel* plus" charitable purposes in addition to the existing *Pemsel* heads. Although these largely simply give statutory recognition to purposes already judicially established as charitable, many are central to government's new partnership agenda with charity. As has been recently explained,[46] this legislation identifies new purposes that clearly reveal the matters central to government's intended partnership arrangement with charity, among which are some that are targeted on trading. Of the latter, the most relevant of the newly stated charitable purposes in s.3(1) of the 2011 Act are subsections (d) the advancement of health or the saving of lives; (e) the advancement of citizenship or community development; (f) the advancement of the arts, culture, heritage, or science; and (g) the advancement of amateur sport. A clear message has been given to the nonprofit sector that government will encourage organizations to become established in these areas and will reward them with charitable status and

(i) the advancement of environmental protection or improvement;
(j) the relief of those in need by reason of youth, age, ill-health, disability, financial hardship or other disadvantage;
(k) the advancement of animal welfare;
(l) the promotion of the efficiency of the armed forces of the Crown, or of the efficiency of the police, fire and rescue services or ambulance services;
(m) any other purposes—
  (i) that are not within paragraphs (a) to (l) but are recognised as charitable purposes by virtue of section 5 (recreational and similar trusts, etc.) or under the old law,
  (ii) that may reasonably be regarded as analogous to, or within the spirit of, any purposes falling within any of paragraphs (a) to (l) or sub-paragraph (i), or
  (iii) that may reasonably be regarded as analogous to, or within the spirit of, any purposes which have been recognised, under the law relating to charities in England and Wales, as falling within sub-paragraph (ii) or this sub-paragraph.

[45] This, indeed, is what Luxton alleges has occurred; see further, Luxton, P. "Making Law? Parliament v The Charity Commission," Politeia, London, 2009. An alternative view would be that s.6 of the 2006 Act (inserting 1A(4) into the 1993 Act) and expressly providing that the Commission is not subject to the direction or control of a Minister, addresses this situation (as pointed out by Alison Dunn in a note to author, September 22, 2011).

[46] See McGregor-Lowndes, M. and O'Halloran, K. (eds.), *Modernising Charity Law*, Elgar, Cheltenham, 2010.

tax exemption. Of even greater significance is the fact that all charitable purposes are now placed on the statute book, thereby enabling any future government to swiftly and directly delete, amend, or add charitable purposes by simply amending the legislation. This *Pemsel*–plus list creates a new statutory platform that facilitates the contribution of charity to specific public benefit activity and clarifies the terms of reference of government's intended partnership with the sector.

One aspect of the changes made to charitable purposes concerns the advancement of religion. A statutory definition of "religion" now forms part of charity law in this jurisdiction, including an express reference to faiths that do not profess belief in a god as well as to polytheistic religions, while advancing religion is itself subject to the public benefit test. Although it is difficult at this stage to predict the ramifications that could flow from the reversal of the presumption, it may be safe to assume that such a fundamental opening up of the interpretation of "religion" can only expand the number of organizations able to avail themselves of charitable status and develop an associated trading capacity.

IV. THE "BIG SOCIETY," PUBLIC SERVICE RETRACTION, AND THE SECTOR

The "Big Society," whether policy or slogan, was launched in the pre-election Conservative manifesto and then relaunched in July 2010. It aimed "to create a climate that empowers local people and communities, building a big society that will 'take power away from politicians and give it to people.'"[47] It stated that its priorities were to give communities more powers; encourage people to take an active role in their communities; transfer power from central to local government; support co-ops, mutuals, charities, and social enterprises; and publish government data.[48] Its emphasis on a greater role for charity, social enterprise, and community ownership attracted praise and controversy[49] from the outset. There was considerable suspicion that the government, having already committed to substantial devolution of health care commissioning,[50] had designed this policy as a smokescreen to obscure its intention to proceed with a wholesale dismantling of the welfare state.

[47] See "Government Launches 'Big Society' Programme," 10 Downing Street Web site, May 18, 2010.

[48] See *Building the Big Society*, Cabinet Office, May 18, 2010.

[49] See, e.g., Charlesworth, L., "England's Early 'Big Society': Parish Welfare under the Old Poor Law," in *History & Policy*, December 2010, comparing the system to the Old Poor Law, and suggesting that "any voluntary system for the relief of poverty is purely mythical." See further at: http://www.historyandpolicy.org/papers/policy-paper-108.html.

[50] As indicated in the report of the Commission on 2020 Public Services, launched in December 2008 and chaired by Sir Andrew Foster. See the Interim Report *Beyond Beveridge: Principles for 2020 Public Services* (March 2010) and the final report *From Social Security to Social Productivity: A Vision for 2020 Public Services*, the 2020 Public Services Trust, London, 2010.

A. Public Benefit Service Provision: The Policy

Of all the common law jurisdictions, the perception that there exists a spectrum of services for the public benefit, customarily construed as being pre-paid through taxes and therefore the responsibility of government to provide, is greatest in England and Wales, due to the legacy of the welfare state. Even so, by 2010 considerable inroads had been made into the nation's sense of accustomed public service entitlement.

1. Privatization

The privatization of basic utilities such as water supplies, electricity, etc. had prepared the ground for the subsequent erosion of services in sectors such as public housing, transport, prisons, and most recently education and health care. The Royal Mail, the Tote,[51] part of the student loan portfolio, the air traffic control, and the state forests had also been identified as targets for privatization. Expectations of further and more radical surgery on the monolithic public sector came with publication of Sir Philip Green's Government Efficiency Review[52] in October 2010 and the report of the Commission on 2020 Public Services.[53]

The Commission on 2020 Services was launched in 2008 under a Labour administration, and presented its report in 2010 to the coalition government. The central dilemma facing government as it planned the future shape of public services was described in the report in the following terms:[54]

> We need a new deal between citizen, society and the state. This rejects both old statist models of universal service delivery and the new public management models of consumerism. Instead a new settlement for public services should be based on the principle of social citizenship. As citizens we should have a duty to contribute as well as a right to receive support—responsibility and reciprocity are essential characteristics of a more resilient society.

This message resonated with that underpinning the coalition government's Green Paper *Modernising Commissioning: Increasing the role of charities, social*

[51] Formerly the Horserace Totalisator Board, this facility has a monopoly on organizing and managing all high street betting shops and racetracks associated with horseracing in the U.K. and has recently diversified into other sports, as well as casino and online bingo. Owned since its formation in 1928 by the U.K. Government, the Tote was sold to a private commercial company in July 2011.

[52] Cabinet Office, *Efficiency Review by Sir Philip Green*, London (October 11, 2010). See further www.cabinetoffice.gov.uk/ . . . /efficiency-review-sir-philip-green-key-findings-and-recommendations.

[53] See Public Services Trust, *2020 Vision: A Far-Sighted Approach to Transforming Public Services*, London, June 16, 2010.

[54] Public Services Trust, *2020 Vision*, at p. 9.

enterprises, mutuals and cooperatives in public service delivery, which was launched in 2010.[55] This outlined plans to "create and promote new opportunities for citizens, communities and public service workers to set local priorities, steer local public spending decisions and deliver services in more targeted and responsive ways." The questions it raised focused on how commissioning could be reformed to support the coalition government's commitment to enhance the role of civil society organizations in running public services.

2. Welfare Benefit Cuts

In tandem with its policy to shrink government public benefit services, the coalition also embarked on a policy to reduce welfare benefits.[56] The Comprehensive Spending Review presented in 2010 an overall picture of stringent fiscal rectitude with significant cuts to government spending in most areas.[57] From January 2011, the government has sought considerable welfare savings by measures such as capping the level of total benefit received per household, reducing Working Tax Credits and council tax benefit, placing caps on housing benefit entitlement, and ending Child Benefit payments to households that include a higher-rate tax payer. Subsequent court cases brought by plaintiffs alleging hardship due to service retraction failed in their efforts to challenge this policy where government service providers could demonstrate they acted with procedural propriety and with due regard for the plaintiffs' circumstances. Although upholding the principle that lack of resources is no excuse for unlawful or unfair decision making, no matter how pressing economic problems may be,[58] the courts tended to find that in the absence of evidence of unreasonableness, the local government service providers were entitled to

[55] Cabinet Office, December 2010. Followed early in 2011 by a *Public Service Reform* White Paper, which explored how the following could drive reform further in a range of service areas: promoting independent provision in key public services; developing new rights for communities and public employees to buy and run services; attracting external investment and expertise into the public sector to deliver better and more efficient services; extending innovative payment and funding mechanisms, such as personal budgets and payment by results commissioning in more areas; and maintaining continuity of service and managing risks in light of these reforms.

[56] The findings of a study, published by the Institute for Fiscal Studies in December 2010 (commissioned by the Joseph Rowntree Foundation), estimated that the government's tax and benefit reforms will plunge 800,000 people into relative poverty by 2013/2014.

[57] See further HM Treasury, *Overview of the Impact on the Spending Review 2010 on Equalities*, London, 2010, at: http://www.hm-treasury.gov.uk/spend_sr2010_equalities.htm.

[58] See R v. Gloucestershire CC ex parte Mahfood (1997) 1 CCLR 7, R v. Gloucestershire CC, ex parte Barry [1997] AC 584 and R (Savva) v. Royal Borough of Kensington and Chelsea [2010] EWCA Civ 1209; (2011) 14 CCLR 75.

implement policy designed to reduce services to those in need.[59] As one judge put it "the economic reality was that to meet imperative needs of reducing expenditure it would be extraordinarily difficult to avoid an adverse effect on adult social care."[60]

B. Sector Capacity Building

Given the above evidence of endeavors by successive governments to shrink expenditure on public benefit services, it is unsurprising that there also exists evidence of a simultaneous strategy to prepare the ground for the sector to undertake such service provision.

1. Charities and Government Funding

Whether channeled through short-term contract arrangements, direct grant aid, funded research projects, national lottery grants, or by another means, the proportion of a charity's income that comes from government has grown considerably in recent years.[61] This has had a major impact upon the sector, on charities, and on the relationships between charities and other nonprofit organizations.

Increasingly, charity is being led toward investing its resources in government-targeted areas of public benefit provision, a direction facilitated by the absence of any general legal prohibition on charities delivering public services under a funding agreement with a public authority, or using their own funds to do so, even if the authority has a legal duty to provide the service. The government lead is apparent in its pattern of funding for charities, whether through preferentially awarded direct grant aid, service delivery contracts, or hiving off public facilities to the charity sector.

Among measures designed to strengthen the capacity of the nonprofit sector, government has put in place and thereafter adjusted certain funding mechanisms.

a. Communitybuilders

The Communitybuilders fund is a £70 million investment fund, managed jointly by the Department for Communities and Local Government and the Office for

[59] See, e.g., R (Domb) v. Hammersmith and Fulham LBC [2009] EWCA Civ 941; R (Harris) v. Haringey LBC [2010] EWCA Civ 703, [2011] PTSR 931; R (McDonald) v. Kensington and Chelsea LBC [2011] UKSC 33, [2011] PTSR 1266; and D and S, R (on the application of) v. Manchester City Council [2012] EWHC 17 (Admin) (January 12, 2012).

[60] See JG and MB v. Lancashire CC [2011] EWHC 2295 (Admin), per Parker J. at [48] to [51].

[61] See, e.g., National Council for Voluntary Organizations, *Voluntary Sector Almanac*, London, 2007, which estimates that public sector income grew from 28 percent of the nonprofit sector's total income in 1995, to 38.5 percent, or £10.7 billion, in the financial year 2004–2005. Large national charities—those with annual incomes of over £10 million—obtained 32.7 percent of their income from the public sector in 2003–2004, whereas those with incomes of between £1 million and £10 million received 40.1 percent from public sources.

Civil Society, which commenced its investment program in June 2009.[62] It invests in the sustainability of multipurpose, inclusive, community-led organizations that provide and run local services; stimulate community involvement and enterprise, and generate independent sources of income. It aims to help community anchor organizations attain long-term financial stability so they can meet the needs of their communities for future generations.

b. Futurebuilders

The Futurebuilders fund, now the responsibility of the Office for Civil Society, began operations in 2003.[63] It is the largest social investor in the U.K. with the £125 million Futurebuilders (England) Fund at the heart of its program. Its purpose is to:

> provide loan financing, often combined with grants and professional support, to third sector organizations in England that need investment to help them bid for, win and deliver public service contracts. The aim of the Fund is to substantially improve the financial and strategic capability of the third sector so that it can play an ever greater role in improving the lives of the people and communities it serves.

The government's aims for the Futurebuilders program are to overcome obstacles to efficient service delivery; modernize the third sector for the long-term, and increase both the scope and scale of voluntary and community sector service delivery.

c. The Social Investment Business

The Social Investment Business is the trading name for Futurebuilders England Fund Management Limited. Set up in 2009, it also has responsibility for the £100m Social Enterprise Investment Fund. It manages government funds totaling over £400 million, available to third-sector organizations—charities, social enterprises, and community groups—and proclaims that "we exist to transform the sector." Its services range from interim management, business consultancy, and business support to commissioning and procurement services for local authority commissioners to deliver public services through local nonprofits.

[62] Communitybuilders was an outcome of a commitment made in the government White Paper *Communities in Control: Real People, Real Power* (Cm 7427), Stationery Office, July 2008.

[63] Futurebuilders was an outcome of recommendations made in the Treasury's Cross Cutting Review into the role of the voluntary and community sector in public service delivery, September 2002.

2. From Grants to Contracts

Statutory grants to charities were reduced from £4.6 billion in 2001 to £4.2 billion in 2006–2007 to £3.7 billion in 2007/2008.[64] It has been estimated that three-quarters of charities no longer receive any government funds.[65] However, of the some 38,000 charities (22 percent) that do, approximately 25,000 receive three-quarters of their funding tied to contracts: Government funding is now sharply focused. Recent figures published by the National Council for Voluntary Organizations reveal that in the U.K. the level of contract income earned by charities rose from £3.8 billion in 2001 to £7.8 billion in 2006, reaching £9.1 billion in 2007; an increase of 128 percent since 2000/01. In 2006–2007 alone, earned income from contracts and sales of goods and services rose from 39 percent of total revenue to 51 percent.[66] This continues a long-term trend, driven largely by the provision of greater levels of public services under contract.

3. The National Lottery

Although undoubtedly the effect of the national lottery has been to increase the resources broadly available for charitable purposes, this has favored designated charities at the expense of all others and, increasingly, lottery proceeds are being channeled toward subsidizing the running costs of mainstream government services.[67] It was intended that projects funded by lottery proceeds would be supplementary to government services but in practice a significant proportion of lottery funds are being diverted to ease the pressure on health care, and other public service provision. Moreover, following the National Lottery Act 1998 and the introduction of the New Opportunities Fund in 2006, the distributing bodies for lottery funds in the U.K. are now required to construct strategic plans in line with government policies, and have become "de facto delivery arms of government policy, funded through the lottery."[68]

[64] NCVO, *UK Voluntary Sector Almanac* (2009).

[65] NCVO, *UK Voluntary Sector Almanac* (2009).

[66] NCVO, *UK Voluntary Sector Almanac* (2009). See also, Brindle, D., "The Worst Is Yet to Come," *The Guardian*, February 18, 2009.

[67] In the U.K., the creation of the New Opportunities Fund as a separate and more directly controlled body than the Community Fund, working to government priorities, is seen by some as further evidence of takeover by stealth (Anheier, H. and Leat, D., *From Charity to Creativity: Philanthropic Foundations in the 21st Century*, Comedia, Stroud, U.K., 2002).

[68] Seddon, N., *Who Cares?*, Civitas, London, 2007, at p. 125, citing Lea, R. and Lewis, D., *The Larceny of the Lottery Fund*, Centre for Policy Studies, London, 2006, at p. 2.

4. Effect of Government Funding

The nature and extent of the above funding arrangements would seem to be in defiance of the Charity Commission's warning that "charities must be independent of government and other funders."[69] In relation to some of Britain's leading charities, Seddon has noted that "Barnardo's now receives 78%, the Shaftesbury Society gets 93%, Rainier 82%, NCH 88%, Leonard Cheshire 88%, the National Family Parenting Institute 97% and the ironically named West Sussex Independent Living Association 99.65% of their income from statutory sources."[70] He further comments that:[71] "In the mid-1980s, about 10% of overall charitable revenue came from government sources.[72] By 1991, government funding accounted for 27% of the sector's income,[73] and that figure is now at least 38%."[74]

The National Survey of Third Sector Organizations, which closed in December 2008, estimated that nearly a third of nonprofits receive funding from local government, and that this provides the largest source of statutory income (47 percent) to the U.K. sector.[75] The scale of funding to charities is such that in some circumstances the latter's service delivery is now little more than government provision by proxy. This places charity in the position of being seen as a public benefit service provider and as being accountable for service deficiencies whereas government in fact exercises control through funding and by regulating standards.[76]

C. Public Benefit Service Provision: The Practice

Government has in the main relied upon public finance initiatives (PFI) to finance the growing need for capital investment in social infrastructure that could no longer be paid for out of government capital finance. Launched in 1992 by the then-Conservative government, and lauded by Labour in "PFI: Meeting the Investment

[69] Charity Commission, "Policy Statement on Charities and Public Service Delivery," June 2005. See also Smerdon, M., *Rights with Meaning*, Baring Foundation (Working Paper No. 4), October 2009, which states that this relationship poses a "formidable threat to independence" because it increases the state's control over service providers, silences dissent, and reduces the ability of charities to set their own priorities.

[70] Seddon, Who Cares?, at p. 4. Note also the Charity Commission, RS 15, *Stand and Deliver: The Future for Charities Delivering Public Services*, London, 2007, at para. 2.3, which indicates that 38 percent of the sector's income comes from statutory sources.

[71] Seddon, Who Cares?, at p. 28.

[72] *The Times*, December 17, 1984.

[73] NCVO, *Voluntary Sector Almanac 2004*.

[74] *UK Voluntary Sector Almanac 2006*.

[75] See Cabinet Office, *Office of the Third Sector's National Survey of Third Sector Organizations*, London, 2009. See also NCVO, *UK Civil Society Almanac*, 2010.

[76] In this context, note that the introduction of Social Impact Bonds may offer the opportunity for a systemic change in the financial relationship between government and sector.

Challenge,"[77] it has become the principal means for government to inject private capital into public private partnerships designed to further the development of social infrastructure previously considered to be the government's exclusive responsibility. Resort to this procurement instrument is likely to intensify in view of the coalition government's Comprehensive Spending Review, presented in October 2010.[78] This included a reference to a set percentage of services to be transferred out of the public sector to other providers and an aspiration for the state to no longer be seen as the default provider of services.

1. Public Benefit Services and PFI

By November 2010, a total of 103 hospitals had been built using PFI funding[79] and some 845 schools had been involved in 107 PFI projects in England. It is currently planned that roughly half the government's flagship scheme "Building Schools for the Future" will be funded in this way. At the end of 2010 the U.K. government released spending figures showing that the current total payment obligation for PFI contracts in the U.K. is £267 billion.[80] It remains the U.K. government's preferred method for public sector procurement.

2. Charities and PFI

PFI is a form of financing that is not directly available to charities for various reasons mostly associated with the restrictions it would impose upon their independence. However, PFI does impact upon charities individually and collectively: in the latter

[77] See HM Treasury, *PFI: Meeting the Investment Challenge*, London, July 2003. See also the Local Improvement Finance Trust (LIFT) initiative, a scheme whereby public, private, and community sectors have formed a joint venture to build and maintain primary health care centers over a 25-year period provides a example of such a legal arrangement. The joint venture companies provide multiple facilities in a geographic area, and parties may include GPs, chemists, dentists, and other allied health professionals as well as local authorities, primary health care trusts (hospitals), and the Department of Health and Treasury. The private sector has a 60 percent holding; local stakeholders and the government departments have a 20 percent holding each, and a shared governance structure. The LIFT owns and manages the premises using rentals, government start-up finance, and commercial debt to finance its operations. The government has also established a separate corporation to provide technical support and capacity building to LIFTs known as Partnerships UK. See further http://www.haltonandsthelenspct.nhs.uk/pages/YourServices.aspx?iPageId=440.

[78] See HM Treasury, *Spending Review 2010*, Cm 7942, October 2010. See further at: http://www.google.co.uk/search?q=comprehensive+spending+review+2010+summary&ie=utf-8&oe=utf-8&aq=t&rls=org.mozilla:en-US:official&client=firefox-a.

[79] Government figures reveal that although the build cost of these hospitals came to £11.3 billion, the repayment costs will eventually total £65 billion.

[80] See the Commons Public Accounts Committee, *Lessons from PFI and Other Projects*, London, September 2011.

sense, because of its use as a government tool to leverage private finance and channel public infrastructure projects to for-profit enterprises rather than to charity; and in the former because a charity may find itself in a consortium in which one or more parties are in receipt of PFI funding. There are restrictions on involvement with PFI for any organization wishing to gain or retain charitable status because of the need to take measures to ensure that it does not place its charitable assets at risk; that it retains independence; that it furthers its charitable purpose; that restrictions of locality, service type or fees do not unduly narrow beneficiary access; and that the organization remains compliant with the public benefit test.[81]

D. Service Transfer: From Government to Charity

In England and Wales, the migration of service provision from government to charity is evident, for example, in the many newly created foundation hospitals, and education foundations, and the conversion of local council facilities to charities. This process was greatly facilitated by the Charity Commission ruling that government is entitled to establish charities that will give effect to a recognized government function, conditional upon that function being compatible with that charity's charitable purpose.[82] Much of the recent growth in schools, day care facilities for children, and nursing home provision in this jurisdiction has occurred outside the public sector, often involving charities. In the long-term, however, it is probable that by changing the way that services are funded and delivered, through initiatives such as introducing "free schools" and the practice-based commissioning of health care services, the government will succeed in strategically undoing some of the mechanisms central to the welfare state and thereby engineer its deconstruction.

1. Education

The government policy to transfer services from the public sector has had particularly important consequences for what hitherto had been the state monopoly of education. At a cost of disrupting holistic local authority planning for community-based education, and probably exacerbating local social divisions, schooling is becoming more diversified, with most independent schools now being granted charitable status (82 percent in 2010) and more parents and community representatives having some control over them. PFI has played a considerable role in facilitating this breakup of the monolithic state education system.

[81] See Charity Commission report, *Consortia for the Delivery of Public Services: The Issues for Small and Medium-Sized Charities*, London, July 18, 2011.

[82] See Charity Commission, *Applications for Registration of (i) Trafford Community Leisure Trust and (ii) Wigan Leisure and Culture Trust*, April 21, 2004.

a. Foundation and Trust Schools

Foundation schools are run by their own governing body, which employs the staff and sets the admissions criteria. Land and buildings are usually owned by the governing body or a charitable foundation. A trust school is a type of foundation school that forms a charitable trust with an outside partner—for example, a business or educational charity—aiming to raise standards and explore new ways of working. Established by the School Standards and Framework Act 1998 to replace grant-maintained schools, as the name suggests these schools have charitable status but often also allow for private investment.

b. Academies

These are schools judged to be "outstanding," which, with official encouragement, have been allowed to break away from local authority control to seek independence with charitable status, sponsored by commerce or charity. These schools have more freedom over the curriculum but continue to be funded by the state. As the Academies Act 2010 has given all grant-maintained schools the right to unilaterally opt out of local authority control and become academies, it would seem that it has now become government policy to expedite the migration of state schools to charitable status. By the end of January 2011 there were some 1580 schools registered as academies, and many more applications are pending. Under the Academies Act 2010, the schools were due to become exempt charities on January 1, 2011, meaning they would not need to register with the Charity Commission but would be subject to charity regulation by the Young People's Learning Agency. Then in Spring 2011, the Church of England announced that 70 percent (3360) of its 4800 schools were planning to apply for academy status within the next five years. For some, the introduction of academies is more evidence of government reluctance in this jurisdiction to discourage "elitist schools," a view that will be strengthened by a mass exodus of faith-based schools from state to academy status.[83] There has also been some controversy regarding the wisdom of expanding the number of exempt charities when one of the objectives of the 2006 Act was to reduce this category.

c. Free Schools

These are new-build, all-ability, independent but state-funded schools, set up in response to parental demand, which like academies are to have charitable status. In accordance with coalition government policy, charities, universities, businesses,

[83] See, e.g., Judt, T., *The Memory Chalet*, Penguin Press, London, 2010, at p. 144, where he comments: "Successive education ministers have authorised and encouraged 'academies'—furtively introducing (with the help of private money) the very process of selection of whose abolition on egalitarian grounds they once so proudly boasted."

educational groups, teachers, and groups of parents can get involved and set up free schools; by early 2011 some 323 free school applications were awaiting government approval. These schools have the same legal requirements as academies and are "free" to: set their own pay and conditions for staff, exercise greater control of their budget, deviate from the National Curriculum, and change the length of terms and school days; they are free from local authority control.[84] However, and perhaps unsurprisingly, a large proportion of such schools have a "faith ethos" which, in their case, casts some doubt on the interpretation of "free." The "free school policy" has been criticized on the grounds that it is likely to provide more opportunities in the long run for business than for charity.[85]

d. Universities

Cutbacks in government spending have had unexpected consequences for U.K. universities. The government announcement that it would introduce tuition fees for future students in England and Wales triggered not only the worst rioting experienced in London for some years, but also a warning from the Charity Commission that universities risk jeopardizing their current charitable status if they raise fees to the extent that in so doing the public benefit of their charitable purpose is restricted to a class of potential beneficiaries.

2. Social Housing

The large-scale transfer of housing stock from government to charity dates from the Thatcher government, when rules were introduced that prevented councils subsidizing their housing from local taxes, channeled grants for construction of new social housing to housing associations, and allowed council tenants to buy their homes at a large discount. This, combined with cost-cutting initiatives in local government and a housing benefit scheme that was more generous to housing associations than local authorities, led to many councils transferring their housing stock to housing associations.[86] In 1979, 32 percent of England's overall housing stock was state subsidized, but by 2005 this had fallen to 18 percent.

[84] See further Department of Education at: http://www.education.gov.uk/schools/leadership/typesofschools/freeschools/a0061428/what-are-free-schools. See also Benn, M., *School Wars: The Battle for Britain's s Education*, Verso Books, London, 2011.

[85] Edison, for example, a profit-making U.S. education provider company established in 1992, opened in the U.K. a decade later and is now involved in free schools.

[86] See further Handy, C., "The Privatisation of Social Housing: Capture and Commercialisation of the Voluntary Sector," in Dunn, A. (ed.), *The Voluntary Sector, the State and the Law*, Hart Publishing, Oxford, at pp.107–19.

a. Registered Social Landlords (RSLs)

Also known as housing associations,[87] RSLs include charitable trusts and cooperatives and must be registered and approved by the Tenant Services Authority to provide social housing for rent.[88] Although not part of the public sector, many housing associations receive government funding (e.g., for specialized housing or for regenerating neighborhoods), and they are able to borrow against equity on the private market. In addition, some RSLs build affordable housing, often in partnership with commercial developers, for sale on a shared ownership basis.

3. Justice

Although the court system and processes for administration of justice will remain in the public sector, several prisons, parts of the probation service, and community (reparation) service have been transferred to nonprofit management.

a. Prisoner Rehabilitation

Early professional intervention, which prevents later and much more expensive treatment, is viewed by government as a key element in reducing public sector costs. Although this approach is one with general application, it attracted particular interest in the context of criminal justice where prison overcrowding had become a serious issue. Given the probability that of the 40,200 adults on short-term sentences, some 60 percent would go on to re-offend within a year of release, it was decided to pilot such an approach, with charity playing a crucial role, in an attempt to reduce recidivism.

b. Social Impact Bond (SIB)

This is a form of contract between a public sector body and investors, in which the former commits to pay for an improved social outcome, the latter provides funds that are used to pay for a range of interventions to improve the social outcome, and a third party such as a charity delivers the service (see chapter 13). In March 2010, the Ministry of Justice launched the first use of an SIB in England and Wales.[89] The Ministry will fund social organizations, working to reduce the re-offending rates of short- sentence male prisoners leaving Peterborough Prison by providing payments tied to a rate of recidivism reduced below an agreed threshold. A charity, St. Giles Trust, will provide intensive support to 3000 short-term prisoners over a six-year

[87] The Housing Association Act 1985, s.1. See also, the Housing and Regeneration Act 2008.

[88] The YMCA, for example, is an RSL.

[89] Following publication of the government White Paper *Putting the Frontline First: Smarter Government*, December 2009.

period, both inside prison and after release, and help them resettle in the community. The third party is Social Finance, which will offer commercial investors and others the opportunity to invest in SIBs calculated to provide a financial return on investment that will increase in proportion to improved rates of re-offending.

It is anticipated that SIBs will be introduced across government departments including, for example, to leverage additional resources in support of early intervention approaches with children and young people.

4. Health Care

Privatization, which had already impacted upon the NHS under the Blair-led Labour government, is expected to make considerable further inroads as the coalition government's policies, as revealed in its 2010 White Paper *Equity and Excellence—Liberating the NHS*,[90] get fully underway. The government, although denying any real danger of fragmentation to health care provision, expects the NHS to make some £20 billion of savings by 2014 as it simultaneously subjects the NHS to its most fundamental post-war restructuring and intensifies its privatization program. As Marmot has pointed out, the government approach does give rise to a crunch issue: "while the real and potential contribution of the third sector to reducing health inequalities is recognised, there remains concerns about how the sector is supported, both to deliver its services and to effectively engage (with government) as a strategic partner."[91]

In practice, however, the privatization of health care is gathering momentum. Many private sector firms are well established within NHS hospitals, providing services such as cleaning and catering. Others outside the NHS offer a wide range of alternatives to treatments normally offered by those hospitals, including surgery for knee, elbow, hip and shoulder replacement and a wide range of elective procedures. In the spring of 2012 this trend experienced a step change when, amid considerable

[90] Department of Health, White Paper *Equity and Excellence: Liberating the NHS* (Cm 7881), July 12, 2010.

[91] See Marmot, M., *Fair Society, Healthy Lives: Strategic Review of Health Inequalities in England Post-2010* (The Marmot review), February 2010. See further at: http://www.marmotreview.org. Note that the health action zone (HAZ) initiative launched in 1997, which saw 26 HAZs set up in England as seven-year pilot projects "to explore mechanisms for breaking through current organizational boundaries to tackle inequalities and deliver better services," pioneered public benefit partnerships involving public and private agencies together with charities and other non-profits. HAZs have now been incorporated into the development of primary care trusts. See further, Unwin, J. and Westland, P., *Health Action Zones: The Engagement of the Voluntary Sector*, the Baring Foundation, 2000. Note also the Employment Zones, which directly incentivized contractors to achieve outcomes in helping long-term unemployed people back to work. Both the HAZ and the Employment Zone initiatives would seem to owe a lot to the Empowerment Zone/Enterprise Community (EZ/EC) program launched in the United States under the Clinton administration in 1993. See further Mulgan, G., *The Art of Public Strategy*, Oxford University Press, Oxford, 2009.

controversy, Circle Holdings, Europe's largest private health-care company, concluded a 10 year, £1 billion contract with government to manage Hinchingbrooke, a failing general hospital. For the first time since the NHS was founded in 1948, a private company will now run a NHS hospital and provide the full range of services, including an accident and emergency unit and maternity ward. It is estimated that some 20 other hospitals are in similar difficult circumstances. This precedent is one that positions shareholding, hedge funds, and venture capitalism at the heart of NHS provision and carries profound implications for the future of the NHS.

a. Foundation Hospitals

These are independent, not-for-profit public benefit corporations accountable to their local communities rather than to Central Government, with the legal status of "public benefit corporations." First introduced by the Labour government in 2002,[92] by the end of 2010 there were 130 NHS foundation hospitals (also known as Foundation Trusts) in operation across England. They remain firmly part of the NHS and exist to provide and develop health care services for NHS patients in a way that is consistent with NHS standards and principles—free care, based on need not ability to pay. Clinical activity for private patients, in theory, is strictly limited. Foundation status allows hospital managers more autonomy: They will not be line-managed by the Department of Health, they will undergo less inspection and monitoring, they will be able to borrow money from banks to finance capital programs, they will be allowed to retain the proceeds from land sales for reinvestment in local services (rather than returning the cash to a central pot), they will get access to central development budgets without having to submit formal bids, they will be able to establish private companies, and they will have the ability to pay staff over and above nationally agreed terms and conditions. Not only are they inspected by the Healthcare Commission, for compliance with health care standards and targets in the same way as all other NHS Trusts, but they are also subject to the supervision of Monitor, an independent regulator. Government is committed to transferring the delivery of all NHS services to the Foundation Trust model by 2013.

The extra powers earmarked for Foundation Trusts are powers to borrow money and decide on capital investment, powers to enter into contracts, and powers to diverge from national pay settlements, accompanied by permission to select their own local clinical priorities and a new "payment by results" funding system. The cap on private patient income is to be lifted, allowing Foundation Trusts to compete with private firms in a host of areas. Critics claim that the extra powers will lead to the new Foundations prospering at the expense of other Trusts. They argue that the policy will widen the gap between the best NHS bodies and the worst, by rewarding the best-performing Trusts, and particularly by giving them the power to pay staff more than their counterparts elsewhere in the NHS.

[92] See the Health and Social Care (Community Health and Standards) Act 2003.

b. GP Commissioning Consortiums

The coalition government's 2010 White Paper envisages the abolition of England's 152 primary care trusts to be replaced, by 2013, with consortiums of General Practitioners (GPs); this was amended in June 2011 to provide mandated places for hospital doctors and nurses on GP commissioning consortium boards. These will assume responsibility for the commissioning of services for patients under the guidance of a new Statutory NHS Commissioning Board. The first wave of GP commissioning "pathfinder" consortia commenced in January 2011 to provide services for 12.9 million people, around a quarter of England's population. This switch to GP commissioning will allow the new consortia of GPs to refer their patients to "any willing provider,"[93] thereby introducing an "open market" mechanism into the heart of the NHS. In addition to licensing competition among hospitals and other health care facilities, this clause makes space for private companies that will in the future have a much wider involvement with the NHS as the expected three to five hundred new consortiums of GPs emerge to become key purchasers of treatment for patients.

c. Social Enterprises

The right to request to be a provider of services in the NHS, instituted by the last Labour government, has seen a total of 38 social enterprises spun off from the NHS, which now provide services worth £900 million (see further below). The policy of the coalition government is to build on this provision, and currently a further 32 spin-off projects are in the pipeline. One such social enterprise is the City Health Care Partnership, launched in June 2010 with a budget of £50 million and 1200 staff, which is responsible for providing NHS services throughout the Hull and East Riding of Yorkshire region. This staff-owned nonprofit organization delivers services, including community nursing, sexual health and family planning, community dentistry, and prison health care.

Critics say that social enterprises cannot replace a well-established and joined-up public sector, and are just a route to privatization. They are private businesses, and as such will not provide unprofitable services; they are also open to being taken over or merged.[94]

[93] See NHS White Paper, *Equity and Excellence—Liberating the NHS*, which introduced the "any willing provider" as a principle for future service procurement. See also Department of Health, *Procurement Guide for Commissioners of NHS-Funded Services*, updated version, August 2010.

[94] See, e.g., Housing21, a housing association and social enterprise that recently purchased another social enterprise, Claimar Care, which, among its other services, provided social care through a company called The Complete Group. Housing21 said that The Complete Group did not fit in with its "business strategy" and so sold The Complete Group to a private equity firm, Sovereign Capital.

5. Council Services

The government has also recently been experimenting with shedding statutory responsibility for public provision by transferring council services such as leisure centers to charities.[95] Other services, including libraries, waste disposal, and museums may well follow.

V. NEW LEGAL STRUCTURES AND DONOR INCENTIVES

The rapid shift in England and Wales from a government policy of propping up its welfare state legacy to one of shedding or sharing the cost of public benefit service provision, while retaining regulatory control of standards, has been accompanied by a willingness to experiment with innovative legal structures. The process of refining the models and tools best suited to conduct effective cross-sector operations has been particularly challenging for orthodox trust-based charities. Here, more so than anywhere else in the common law world, the trust and the unincorporated association have always provided the main legal structures for charity, and continue to do so. The advance of new legal structures as detailed below must be seen against the background of a sector still dominated by large institutionalized charitable trusts. These now have to prepare for a much more adversarial market environment in which they will join in partnership[96] or compete for contracts alongside new forms of incorporated charities, rising numbers of wholly for-profit entities, and a potentially new range of mutuals, cooperatives, and social enterprises all vying to become public benefit service providers.

A. Mutuals

In 2010 the coalition government greatly expanded the "rights to provide" for public sector workers, first introduced by Labour, to enable such staff to take over the running of public benefit services. In the future every department must provide a right for civil servants directly employed by it to form mutuals. This gives effect to the commitment in *Our Programme for Government*[97] and the Spending Review 2010 to allow public sector workers the right to form employee-owned cooperatives.

[95] See the Commission's 2004 decision in relation to the Trafford Community Leisure Centre and Wigan Leisure and Culture Trust. Previously, charities had been able to deliver discretionary responsibilities—museums, parks, community centers and the like—for councils, but this ruling meant statutory responsibilities (management of cemeteries, libraries, and so on) could also be transferred.

[96] See Charity Commission CC34, *Collaborative Working and Mergers: An Introduction.*

[97] *The Programme for Government* in November 2010, announced a series of measures to make it easier for small firms and organizations to do business with government. These measures progress the government's aspiration to award 25 percent of government contracts to small- and medium-sized enterprises.

The new mutuals will negotiate contracts with the applicable departments or local commissioning bodies on the basis that they will provide improved services at lower cost by minimizing spending on administration and overheads.

1. Mutuals and Public Services

It is envisaged that mutuals will develop within NHS trusts, Sure Start centers, children's services, welfare provision, the civil service, and conceivably even in the Inland Revenue. Some could be independent of the state, or could form joint ventures with it, whereas others would include service users. There are already service hubs emerging where support services are delivered through flexible partnerships. Some Sure Start children's centers, for example, provide a focal point around which communities can organize a whole range of services to meet a variety of needs. This type of development is likely to open up new areas of public service delivery to competition and accelerate the involvement of a diversity of providers.[98]

Arguably, however, unless the forming of such mutuals is made conditional upon the inclusion of some form of mandatory asset lock, then there is a danger that they could be demutualized and sold off to the private sector, which is what occurred to British building societies in the 1980s.

B. Incorporated Charities

In recent years there have been many signs of a broad willingness to embrace incorporation, and most charities that do so become companies limited by guarantee. There has also been some experimentation with new few forms of incorporation designed specifically to bridge the gap between public and private interests. For present purposes, the most interesting aspect of the increased activity in this area is that it clearly reveals converging initiatives from charity, government, and commerce to provide new cross-sectoral legal structures.

1. Public Benefit Corporations

These are nonprofit organizations, owned by government, which carry out services or functions for the benefit of the public as laid down in statute. They are usually "charitable institutions." In this jurisdiction they had no history until introduced by the Health and Social Care (Community Health and Standards) Act 2003, which established NHS Foundation Trusts as public-benefit corporations. Schedule 1 of that Act sets out the requirements for this particular legal structure, which include a membership made up of individuals living in a specific area, employees of the

[98] See, e.g., GLL, one of the U.K.'s longest established employee mutuals, which spun off in 1993 from Greenwich council in south London and now runs over 90 leisure center in the southeast of England; see further at: http://www.gll.org/.

corporation, and service users, and a board of governors, some of whom are elected by the members based on "constituencies" such as staff, users, or the general public. It can be no coincidence that the first use of this structure is in relation to the services that lie at the heart of the welfare state.

2. Charitable Incorporated Organization (CIO)

The U.K. government used the Charities Act 2006 to introduce the charitable incorporated organization into England and Wales, the first legal structure in that jurisdiction created specifically to meet the needs of charities and available exclusively to charities.[99] This legislation contains provisions to enable charitable companies and charitable industrial and provident societies to convert to CIOs. The new CIO will not be a new corporate body to which the undertaking of the company or industrial and provident society is transferred. The existing corporate body is simply reregistered as a CIO, and the conversion process does not affect the legal personality of the organization or its business relationships. Initially expected to be available from summer 2008, and then in late 2010, implementation of the necessary statutory provisions is now anticipated to occur in early 2012, which should allow the CIO to be an available option for charities later that year.

The legislative intent is to address the situation where currently most charities, opting for a corporate structure and so becoming established as a company limited by guarantee under company law, thereby fall subject to dual regulation by the Charity Commission and by Companies House. The CIO offers all the benefits of incorporation, the creation of a "legal personality" for the charity and limited liability for trustees, but it needs neither separate registration with the company regulator nor regulation under company law. It is a corporate body with a constitution, registered with and regulated by the Charity Commission. This new legal structure enables charities to obtain the benefits of incorporation without having to undergo dual registration and regulation.[100] It provides a more appropriate alternative to the company limited by guarantee; allows members and managers to be insulated from the financial liabilities of the company; permits it to agree to contracts, hold land titles, sue and be sued; and provides for simple registration and reporting requirements. Like the CIC, described below, the CIO will have its assets locked in for the benefit of the community: It will not be able to distribute profits or assets to its members.

[99] Provisions for the establishment of CIOs, which would allow charities to incorporate without registering with both the Charity Commission and Companies House, were included in the Charities Act 2006 and expected to be available from summer 2008 but their introduction has been deferred to 2011.

[100] See further NCVS Information Sheet at: http://www.cvsnewcastle.org.uk/supporting developing/information-sheets.

3. Community Interest Company (CIC)

The Charity Commission has defined a CIC to be "a type of social enterprise company for those who want to use their profits and assets for the public good rather than being driven by the need to maximise profits for shareholders and owners."[101] This limited-liability company, designed to use its profits and assets to achieve social missions, was introduced by the U.K. government.[102] Although not itself a charity, a CIC is designed to provide a bridge between charity and commerce. By acting as a charity's subsidiary trading arm, it can join in commercial enterprises with other for-profit entities.[103] It combines the flexibility of the familiar company form with access to a range of financing options, and although it is not eligible for charitable tax exemption, it also escapes the more strict regulatory requirements of a charity. A charity can convert to a CIC with the consent of the Charity Commission but will then lose its charitable tax exemption. A charity may own a CIC, in which case the CIC would be permitted to pass assets to the charity.

A CIC may be a public limited company, a private company limited by guarantee, or a private company limited by shares. It is intended to be a tailor-made vehicle for social entrepreneurs and has several distinguishing features: It must pass a "community interest test" that ensures it operates in the public interest; it must file an annual report detailing payments to directors, dividends paid on shares, interest paid on loans, and the ways it has fostered involvement of stakeholders in the company's activities; and it also must operate under an "asset lock," which prohibits it from distributing its assets or profits to its members (this applies equally to directors' remuneration and company profits), except in cases where shareholders have an equity stake in the company.[104] In those cases, returns to shareholders must be modest, and they are capped so that most of the profits are distributed to the broader community.

By summer 2007, some five hundred Community Interest Companies had been registered.

C. Charitable Foundations

This venerable institution has long provided the traditional legal structure for charitable resources and activity. In recent years, charitable foundations have received a new lease on life as new forms of foundation have come on stream, and their

[101] See Charity Commission, *What are Community Interest Companies (CICs)?*, at http://www.charity-commission.gov.uk/faqs/starting_a_charity/285.aspx.

[102] See the Companies (Audit, Investigations and Community Enterprise) Act 2004, s.26. See also the Community Interest Company Regulations 2005.

[103] It is in a sense a "half-way house" between a commercial company and a charitable company, and some former charities have converted to CICs. Some council leisure centers have been set up as CICs rather than charities. See further at: http://www.cicreg.gov.uk/.

[104] See further the Community Interest Company Regulations 2005 at: www.legislation.gov.uk/uksi/2005/1788/pdfs/uksi_20051788_en.pdf.

relevance is likely to increase when the Charity Commission issues its revised rules on investment by charitable trusts and foundations, which will allow for social as well as a financial return. This approach, intended to free up some of the enormous assets held by trusts, in some cases for hundreds of years, is very much in keeping with government policy where it is viewed as a potentially radical step toward enhancing sector capacity. However, the traditionally cautious approach of trustees regarding any possible risk to trust funds may subvert government expectations.[105]

1. Community Foundations

Since the introduction of community foundations in England and Wales in the 1980s, some 57 of these independent charities have been established to provide professional advice and grant-making services to clients interested in addressing community issues. They serve as a platform for business, nonprofits, statutory bodies, and citizens to pool resources and tackle local issues. Although of recent origin in this jurisdiction, their growth rate is significant: total endowments stood at £224.5 million in March 2010, an increase of 48 percent over the previous year (£151 million); 649 new funds were set up in the year, up 50 percent on the previous year and almost 100 percent up in 2008; the value of this new giving was £37 million, and the average fund size was £50,000. Grants were made to the value of £74 million in 2009–2010, compared with £56 million the previous year, an increase of 32 percent. Across the network of foundations, over 26,000 grants were made. Interestingly, 45 percent of the grants were made from the private sector, compared with 40 percent in 2008–2009.[106]

2. Corporate Foundations

This form of ethical investment has become mainstreamed over the past 15 years with the number of charitable foundations established by for-profit companies in the U.K. increasing to more than one hundred.[107] As the Commission has noted:[108]

> Corporate foundations can provide: a structure and focus for corporate giving; a means of engaging with the voluntary sector; and the opportunity to share and

[105] See Charity Commission, *Investment of Charitable Funds: Basic Principles* (CC14), December 2004. Revised version to be issued in 2011. Note also the announcement by Francis Maude, the Cabinet Office minister, "I'm happy that the Charity Commission is looking at this urgently now," carrying an implication that the Commission will respect the priority given by government to this matter (November 8, 2010).

[106] See further Community Foundation Network at http://www.communityfoundations.org.uk/.

[107] See Charity Commission, *A Guide to Corporate Foundations*, February 2010. See also Smart Co. (2007), The Changing Nature of Corporate Responsibility: What Role for Corporate Foundations (CAF).

[108] Charity Commission, *A Guide to Corporate Foundations*, February 2010 at para. A1.

> apply expertise in an effort to tackle challenging social issues... Many corporate foundations are high-profile, sharing the name of the company that set them up, and can have a significant amount of media exposure. There can be reputational benefits for the company and the corporate foundation from their association.

Charitable corporate foundations, however, must be independent of the companies that set them up. Although the foundation may be wholly dependent on funding from its founding company, and use all or part of that company's name and logo, it cannot allow itself to be used merely as a public relations exercise and must ensure that it exists only to further charitable purposes for the public benefit and not for those of the founding company. It would need to be able to demonstrate that any private benefit to that company is a necessary result or by-product of carrying out the charity's purposes.

Governance questions have arisen regarding the level of corporation control over foundation boards and the influence such control may have on the charity's program activities. One recent study for the U.K. Cabinet Office and CAF found that 10 out of 29 foundations surveyed admitted that they were either completely or nearly completely controlled by their establishing corporate parents, despite the legal requirement for corporate foundations to be independent.[109]

It has been estimated that there are now approximately 126 corporate foundations in England and Wales[110] representing a 25 percent rise over 2003 when Business in the Community identified 101. Their total income was just over £208 million in 2004/2005—about 0.6 percent of overall charitable income. This ranged from under £10,000 to more than £30 million. These foundations donated some £148 million to charitable causes in 2005/2006.

D. Social Enterprises

The Department of Trade and Industry (DTI) defined social enterprise as "businesses with primarily social objectives whose surpluses are principally reinvested for that purpose in the business or in the community, rather than being driven by the need to maximize profit for shareholders and owners."[111] The introduction of the CIC (see above) was an initiative intended to represent government policy to drive forward the social enterprise movement, a goal shared with the Community Action Network, a membership association for social entrepreneurs created in 1998.

[109] Smart Co., Revealing the Foundations—A Guide to Corporate Foundations in England and Wales (Cabinet Office & CAF, 2006).

[110] Smart Co., Revealing the Foundations.

[111] See Department of Trade and Industry (DTI) (2004) at http://www.google.co.uk/search?q=%2C+Department+of+Trade+and+Industry+%28DTI%29&ie=utf-8&oe=utf-8&aq=t&rls=org.mozilla:en-US:official&client=firefox-a.

E. Donor Incentives

This jurisdiction has a range of donor incentive schemes, including payroll deduction, but the most significant is Gift Aid,[112] which was introduced in 1990, extended in 2000 and considerably bolstered by measures introduced in the 2008 Budget. In comparison with the United States (see chapter 7), the most distinctive characteristic of this donor incentive scheme is that the tax benefit goes to the recipient charity rather than to the donor: the tax dividend, in effect, adding 25 percent to the value of the donation; the charity concerned therefore benefiting twice, from the donor and from the government (see chapter 12).[113] The Income Tax Act 2007, Chapter 2 of Part 8, then introduced tax relief measures for individuals who make charitable donations, and this served to incentivize donors.

Recently, however, heated debate has been generated by a government initiative predicted to function as a donor disincentive: the Chancellor of the Exchequer's announcement in the Spring Budget of a £50,000 cap on tax relief, or 25 percent of income if that is higher; effective from April 2013. The NCVO warns that as nearly half the money donated to charities by individuals comes from just 7 percent of all donors, most of whom are higher-rate taxpayers, charities are thus likely to be seriously affected by the cap.[114] That umbrella organization, along with many leading charities, is consequently campaigning to persuade the government to drop the cap while others argue that government rather than donor discretion should determine the targeting of social need. A point made by those defending the cap is that the discretion of high rate taxpayer donors, bringing with it a government subsidy, is more likely to divert tax revenue toward maintaining opera houses than hospitals, constituting both a doubtful expression of altruism and a lesser contribution to the total quotient of public benefit than might be expected from government utilizing the same tax revenue.

VI. CHARITIES, TRADING, AND CONTEMPORARY CASE LAW

In the teeth of economic recession, the already well-established involvement of charities in trading has been steadily increasing as they struggle to augment depleted resources and substitute for decreasing government grant aid. The nature of that engagement has already undergone considerable change and is clearly set to change yet further. From a position of having become accustomed to the contract culture,

[112] Gift Aid is a scheme for gifts of money by individuals who pay U.K. tax. Gift Aid donations are regarded as having the basic rate tax deducted by the donor, which as the result of increasing the value of a declared charitable donation by 25 percent.

[113] See further Income Tax Act 2007 c 3, ss.521–23.

[114] See National Council for Voluntary Organisations (NCVO) "Treasury 'Buries Bad News' on Charity Tax," at: http://www.ncvo-vol.org.uk/news/civil-society/treasury-%E2%80%98buries-bad-news%E2%80%99-charity-tax.

charities have recently had to accommodate the complexities of public finance initiatives, and now await the imminent challenges of joint ventures and competition with commercial entities for the public benefit service provision opportunities promised by government. Additional opportunities and constraints on the freedom of the charities to avail themselves of the opportunities provided by the above-coalition government policies emanate from legislation, the common law, and recent rulings of the Charity Commission and courts.

A. Legal Framework

The law governing charities and commerce is currently to be found in provisions of the Charities Act 2011 and eligibility for tax exemption is provided for largely in the Corporations Tax Act 2010, s.478, s.479(2) and (3) and s.480, together with the Income Tax Act 2007, s.524 and s.525. Guidance to the law and practice is available in the Charity Commission leaflet CC35 (replacing CC37).[115]

The fact that the Charity Commission rather than the Revenue is the lead regulatory body, together with the complex institutional links that now link government and the nonprofit sector, provide a quite distinctive environment for the operation of charity law.

1. Charity Law

For a charity to engage in trading, the requisite powers must be provided for in its governing documents. In primary purpose trading, a charity must ensure that any commerce corresponds and gives effect to formal objects in its constitution; the nature of the trading must be an appropriate way of furthering its charitable purpose.

The Charities Act 2011, which came into effect on March 14, 2012 (replacing most of the Charities Acts 1992, 1993 and 2006 all of the Recreational Charities Act 1958), provides the current relevant statutory framework and is of particular relevance because it introduced changes to established common law definitions and rules that have set this jurisdiction apart from all others presently being considered in some fundamental respects. The reversal of the public benefit presumption and its replacement with a mandatory statutory public benefit requirement, even in respect of the advancement of religion, constitutes a step change in charity law and a challenge to all other common law jurisdictions. In particular, the reversal of the presumption in favor of the poverty head, which has long benefited from benign interpretation by the judiciary and the Commission, can only lead to a growing rift between this (the U.K. and Irish jurisdictions) and all other common law jurisdictions. The extension to the *Pemsel* heads of charitable purposes, combined with

[115] Other legislation may also be relevant: e.g., the Trustee Act 2000 or the Companies Act 2006.

their transfer from a common law to a statutory context making them amenable to government amendment, is itself a fundamental change to the workings of charity law, giving it a contemporaneous political edge that it has not had until now and does not have elsewhere in the common law world.

2. Charity, the Law and Taxation

Tax exemption or tax relief is available on most of the income and gains received by charities provided the money is only used for charitable purposes. So, to give some examples, tax relief is available on: income received from individuals through "Gift Aid" donations;[116] most types of investment income; certain types of regular sources of income including bank or building society interest, royalties, and stocks; income received from renting out land or property (whether in the U.K. or overseas) that the charity holds for charitable purposes; and capital gains on the proceeds of a disposal. Tax concessions may also extend to entities that are not charitable but altruistic in their purpose, such as amateur sports clubs.

3. Activities Test

In this jurisdiction, the courts have long considered an activities test to be justifiable. For example, in *Inland Revenue Commissioners v. City of Glasgow Police Athletic Association*[117] it was explained that:

> in order to ascertain what the purposes of an association are, the court is not limited to consideration of its rules or its constituent documents...I begin with the rules...But it will not do to stop there...The question is what are the purposes for which the association is established, as shown by the rules, its activities and its relation to the police force and the public.

Again, the *Oldham*[118] decision indicated that:

> To ascertain the objects of an institution...where the objects are comprehensively set out in a document, it is necessary to refer to that document...It is irrelevant to inquire into the motives of the founders or how they contemplated or intended that [entity] should operate or how it has in fact operated. To determine whether the object, the scope of which has been ascertained by due process of construction, is a charitable purpose, it may be necessary to have regard to evidence to discover the consequences of pursuing that object...What the body has done in pursuance

[116] Such donations to a specified charity are only eligible for the additional tax dividend if they are accompanied by a signed declaration indicating donor intent.

[117] [1953] 1 All ER 747, per Lord Normand, at pp. 751–52.

[118] Inland Revenue Commissioners v. Oldham Training and Enterprise Council (1996) STC 1218.

of its objects may afford graphic evidence of the potential consequences of the pursuit of its objects.

In more recent years, the Commission has come more firmly to the view that this additional test is necessary in circumstances where there is doubt regarding the alignment between a charity's purpose and its practice.[119] Take, for example, the charity formerly known as the Knotty Ash Special School Trust, which owned land and buildings; it was established with the purpose of providing services and facilities to schools in Liverpool for special educational needs, and its sole corporate trustee was Liverpool City Council. The recently completed Charity Commission investigation found that: the land to be transferred had not been used for significant charitable purposes for many years; a Council employee had been permitted to live rent-free on the premises; and the Council had breached its trustee duty to act in the best interests of the charity. As the Commission noted:[120] "Many charities have a local authority as a sole trustee. Where this is the case, a local authority must make sure that when it is acting as a trustee it acts in the best interests of the charity and does not permit its interests as a local authority to interfere with its decisions as a charity trustee."

B. Charitable Trading, the Law, and Tax

In England and Wales, the line drawn between entities established for charitable purposes and for trading purposes remains at least visible: An entity with a trading purpose cannot be a charity.[121] In practice, a charity will set up a subsidiary company to undertake trading activity: The subsidiary is not a charitable entity and is free to conduct its trading outside the constraints of charity law; if it then gift aids all its profits to the parent charity it will not pay tax. However, there are risks in that relationship, as the Charity Commission inquiry into War on Want Trading illustrates.[122] In that investigation, the Commission found that the interest-free advances extended by the charity to its subsidiary trading company constituted an application of charitable funds for non-charitable purposes.

[119] See, e.g., Charity Commission, RR2 *Promotion of Urban and Rural Regeneration,* (Version—March 1999), "Tests for Charitable Status". To be charitable, an organization will need to demonstrate that "the public benefit from its activities outweighs any private benefit" (at para. 4).

[120] See Charity Commission report into Knotty Ash Charity (March 23, 2012) at: http://www.charitycommission.gov.uk/RSS/News/pr_knotty_ash.aspx.

[121] See Breen, O., "Holding the Line: Regulatory Challenges in Ireland and England when Business and Charity Collide," in McGregor-Lowndes, M. and O'Halloran, K. (eds.), *Modernising Charity Law,* Elgar, Cheltenham, 2010, pp. 136–63.

[122] See Charity Commission, War on Want Inquiry (1991), and the reference to the inquiry in Picarda, H., *The Law and Practice Relating to Charities* (3rd ed), Butterworths, London, 1999, at p. 1138.

In recognition of the gap between charitable status and trading activity, the charitable interest company (CIC) has now been introduced (see above).

1. Charity Trading and Tax

The government has long sought to guard against the possibility of some charities exploiting their status to gain an unfair commercial advantage: "conducting trading activities within the tax exempt structure of charities would offend the principle of a level playing field with the private sector business."[123] However, in reality, part of the attraction for government in having charities as public benefit service providers lies in the probability that the true market costs of such provision will be reduced (by use of charity resources, volunteers donations, etc.), which in turn places the for-profit competition at a disadvantage. Squaring this particular circle is not easy, and in practice it falls to the Revenue, through its tax administration powers, to make such adjustments in terms of tax liability as are possible to minimize the unfair consequences of market distortion.

The Finance Act 2006 amended the Income and Corporations Taxes Act 1988 to permit a differentiation between primary purpose and non-primary purpose parts of trade for tax purposes: the former being tax exempt as long as its profits are used for charitable purposes; the latter being taxable, although the exemption for small-scale trading may apply.[124] Subsequently, the Corporation Tax Act 2010, s.479, provided the following definition of charitable trade:

1) For the purposes of this Part a trade carried on by a charitable company is a charitable trade if—
   (a) the trade is exercised in the course of carrying out a primary purpose of the charitable company, or
   (b) the work in connection with the trade is mainly carried out by beneficiaries of the charitable company.

Where charities engage in trading it is almost always "primary purpose," "ancillary," or "non-primary purpose" in nature. The first two, but not the third, are normally tax-exempt; there is also a statutory exemption for small-scale trading activity. In many cases a charity will engage in a mix of trading, which should be accounted for separately, although the recent introduction of an apportionment rule

[123] Home Office (2003) response to Cabinet Office report *Private Action, Public Benefit*, 2002.

[124] Income and Corporations Taxes Act 1988, s.505(1B), introduced by Finance Act, 2006, s.56 and Income Tax Act, 2007, ss.525(2) & (3). Provision for the "small scale exemption" is to be found in the Finance Act 2000, s.46, which provides exemption from income and corporation tax provided the trading turnover, together with the other relevant income, does not exceed a specified threshold; the Corporation Tax Act 2010, s.480; and the Income Tax Act 2007, s.526.

now allows for a reasonable overall assessment to be made of tax liability.[125] This is a significant development for trading charities and is in keeping with the Cabinet Office's 2002 proposal to allow charitable organizations to carry out commercial activities directly without the need for a subsidiary trading organization.[126]

In this jurisdiction, the list of possible charitable purposes has been significantly extended by the 2011 Act, thus providing charities with a correspondingly longer list of primary purpose trading opportunities.

a. Primary Purpose

Trading is "primary purpose" when it is conducted by a charity in the course of actually carrying out its primary charitable purpose, and any profits are exempt from tax as long as they are used exclusively for the purposes of the charity.[127] In *Grove v. Young Men's Christian Association*,[128] the YMCA was denied tax exemption for its restaurant, which was open to the general public and run on a commercial basis, because this form of trading did not correspond to its charitable purpose. Where the trading is carried on mainly by the charity's beneficiaries, then it may qualify for exemption, under this heading, but only if "more than half" of the work is done by the beneficiaries.[129]

In this jurisdiction, the list of possible charitable purposes has been significantly extended by the 2011 Act, thus providing charities with a correspondingly longer list of primary purpose trading opportunities.

b. Ancillary and Incidental

Trading is "ancillary" when it is merely incidental to the carrying out of a charitable purpose. The benchmark case for determining when a purpose cannot be defined as "ancillary and incidental" is *Oxford Group v. Inland Revenue Commissioners.*[130] In this case, a charity declared its primary charitable purpose to be "the advancement of the Christian religion," with a secondary purpose for "the maintenance, support, development and assistance of the Oxford Group Movement in every way." The

[125] See further HM Revenue & Customs, "Charities—Trading and Business Opportunities," at: http://www.hmrc.gov.uk/charities/guidance-notes/annex4/sectiona.htm.

[126] Cabinet Office, Strategy Unit (2002), *Private Action, Public Benefit: A Review of Charities and the Wider Not-for-Profit Sector*, London: HMSO, para. 4.46. Breen, "Holding the Line," at p. 144 questions whether this in effect "amounts to a surreptitious introduction of an American UBIT equivalent into U.K. law."

[127] Income Tax Act 2007, s.525; Income and Corporation Taxes Act 1988 (c. 1), s.505(1)(e).

[128] (1903) 4 TC 613.

[129] See, Fawcett Properties v. Buckingham [1960] 3 All ER 503 per Morton L.J., at p. 512. See also Brighton Convent of the Blessed Sacrament v. Inland Revenue Commissioners (1933) 18 TC 76 below at fn 114.

[130] (1949) 2 All E.R. 537 and In re Harpur's Will Trusts (1962) 1 Ch. 78, at p. 87.

court held the secondary purpose to extend well beyond the bounds of the religious purpose, and potentially licensed the Oxford Group to engage in all forms of secular activity. It was neither ancillary, nor was it incidental and secondary; instead the purpose was substantial and independent of the main purpose, and had therefore fatally undermined the latter's claim to be exclusively charitable. In England and Wales there is no fixed mathematical or proportionate calculation for determining the relativity of "ancillary."[131]

c. Non-Primary Purpose

Trading is "non-primary purpose" when it is not directly related to the achievement of a charitable purpose. In this jurisdiction it is the scale of the unrelated trade relative to all other (trading) activity that is crucial. Small-scale trading occurs where the annual total turnover does not exceed £5000, or 25 percent of the charity's total incoming resources, subject to a limit of £50,000. It applies only where all the relevant profits or income are applied for a charity's purposes.

Where unrelated trading may involve a significant risk to a charity's assets, then, under the Corporations Tax Act 2010, ss.479(2) and the Income Tax Act 2007, ss.525(2), it must be undertaken by a trading subsidiary.

C. Charitable Trading: The Case Law in a Public Services Context

Given the abrupt and radical changes implemented in this jurisdiction, which has seen public benefit services dislodged from their welfare state silos and exposed to the harsh competitive dynamics of the market, it is perhaps surprising that so few trading-related cases have appeared before the Charity Commission and the courts. However, service provision by charities under contract to government departments is most likely to take the form of primary purpose trading: for example, charities with the charitable purpose of relieving those in need will most often be engaged in running care homes, sheltered accommodation, and so forth. In legal terms this is really quite straightforward. Where issues have emerged they have, unsurprisingly, tended to concern aspects of the public benefit test, particularly in relation to the imposition of fees as a barrier to services. Besides, privatization was largely a missed opportunity for charities. It was private sector entrepreneurs rather than charities that crossed the accepted public/private divide and laid claim to the new opportunities for public benefit service provision afforded by government withdrawal. As the public sector was slowly dismantled, commercial companies made considerable inroads into the health, social care, and education sectors. For charities this was an uncertain time. They had become accustomed to their prescribed role as contracted service providers. Constrained by limited charitable purposes and inflexible legal

[131] Unlike the situation in the United States and Canada.

structures, they were poorly equipped to compete or collaborate with the new generation of social enterprises and venture philanthropists.

The 2006 Act, now the 2011 Act, introduced a new *Pemsel*–plus list of statutory charitable purposes offering many opportunities for charities, and for organizations seeking charitable status, to direct their resources toward public service provision: the advancement of health or the saving of lives; the advancement of citizenship and community development; the advancement of the arts, culture, heritage, or science; the advancement of environmental protection or improvement; and the relief of those in need by reason of youth, age, ill-health, disability, financial hardship, or other disadvantage. There is no equivalent, outside the U.K., to such an explicit public service agenda of areas legislatively tabled for charitable intervention. Nor has such a statutory listing been necessary for the past four hundred years. It is an initiative that effectively calls time on an established approach to charity law that had allowed all common law nations to dip into and contribute to a shared pool of jurisprudence and continue the collective cultivation of their common law legacy. It is perhaps not inappropriate that it should fall to England and Wales, the progenitor jurisdiction, to uproot charity law from its historical common law context and place it onto the statute books, a move subsequently replicated in all U.K. jurisdictions. In so doing, the U.K. is making a decisive break from the approach of other nations (even though common law rules, principles, and precedents will remain in effect). By confining future developments to legislative parameters rather than leaving them open to judicial discretion, this in time will produce precedents that other jurisdictions will be unable to follow, and will result in the U.K. having its own indigenous and contained body of case law. On the plus side, the extended and explicit list accompanied by a newly defined public benefit test will allow the law to catch up with practice and will likely generate a short-term surge in charity registrations. On the minus side, any system of statutory classification can quickly become restrictive as emerging unforeseen social needs fail to find a fit with defined charitable purposes with organizations then, perhaps, choosing not to address such needs as the attached price tag of being denied charitable status is too high. Most obviously, this initiative places the management of charity, particularly the definition of what constitutes charitable activity, firmly within the grasp of the government of the day as it is now able to use legislative amendment and regulatory procedures to tailor charitable purposes to meet its public benefit service provision requirements.

Many new charities have now been established to pursue these statutory purposes and are entitled to do so by means of delivering services under government contract: they may not, however, be set up solely as service providers. Together with the new legal structures that have been introduced, charities are now better positioned to compete with the private sector, and this is likely to generate more case law in the future.

1. Fees

The requirement that services be accessible to the public, or a sufficient section of it, is a condition of charitable status. The Charity Commission advises that "charities can charge for the services or facilities they provide... can also charge fees that more than cover the cost of those services or facilities" but that the opportunity to benefit must not be unreasonably restricted by ability to pay any fees charged, and people in poverty must not be excluded from the opportunity to benefit.[132] The issue for a fee-charging charity is the effect that charging fees has on those who have the opportunity to benefit from its services or facilities and, where relevant, whether there is sufficient opportunity to benefit for people who cannot afford to pay the full fees charged. This is likely to be a public benefit issue where the service or facility for which there is a charge forms a significant part of the charity's aims, or the way it carries out those aims, and/or when the fees being charged for that service or facility are high. The higher the level of fees, the greater the number of people who will be denied access to the service and, therefore, the more the charity will have to do to provide those people with sufficient opportunity to also derive some benefit; the benefit must be one that in nature is meaningfully related to the charity's aims, and in quantity is reasonable in proportion to the service (both would most obviously be achieved by providing access on a free, subsidized, or concessional basis to those who cannot afford the fees). If the charity cannot demonstrate that it is addressing that correlation, then it will be in breach of the public benefit test. The priority that the charity must give to this issue will vary according to whether the charged-for service or facility is a major or minor aspect of its aims.

It should also be borne in mind that "trading" is a slippery concept in public benefit service provision where there may not be any "profit," or it is not taken out but rather recycled.[133]

2. Private Education

Since the introduction of the 2006 Act, now the 2011 Act, independent fee-paying schools with charitable status have had to show that their objects, aims, and activities are in keeping with the purpose of advancing education and compatible with the public benefit test. Each is required to produce evidence that admission fees do not impose an absolute restriction on public access to their educational services as the fee-paying inhibition is balanced by other means of accessing that service. The provision of a charitable service cannot be restricted to a "public" defined solely by their fee-paying ability. To acquire or retain charitable status, a school cannot deny access to the poor.[134]

[132] See Charity Commission, *Charities and Public Benefit*, "Restrictions Based on Ability to Pay Any Fees Charged," in *Charities and Public Benefit* (January 2008).

[133] In Religious Tract and Book Society of Scotland v. Forbes (1896) 3 TC 415, it was held that as its transactions produced no profit, the charity was not engaged in trading.

[134] See Re Resch [1969] 1 AC 514 (PC). Note also the bearing of Article 2, Protocol 1 of the European Convention, as incorporated into national law by the Human Rights Act 1998, which provides that no person shall be denied the right to education. Arguably, where fees are such as to bar access to school for those without the means to pay, then this provision may well be engaged. See, e.g., *Belgian Linguistic* (1968) 1 EHRR 252.

a. "Public" Schools

In England and Wales, a public school is still defined according to the characteristics ascribed to it more than a century ago by Fry L.J.:[135]

> a perpetual foundation; a portion of its income is derived from charity; it is managed by a public body; no private person has any interest in the school; no profit was or is in the contemplation of its founders or managers; and lastly the object of the school is the benefit of a large class of persons.

If an institution is too exclusive, it may fail the public benefit test, but exclusivity is not to be determined by fees alone.[136]

The courts have consistently held to the view that "public schools" in England and Wales are charitable. In *Abbey Malvern Wells Ltd. v. Ministry of Local Government and Planning,*[137] for example, the argument that a school that charged full fees could not be a charity was met with the judicial response that this was "a rather startling proposition," which was "several centuries out of date." However, the tacit assumption that such schools provided a public benefit service did not survive the reversal of the public benefit presumption in the 2006 Act, now the 2011 Act, which had the effect of imposing a new requirement on such schools that they demonstrate their compliance with this test; two of which had failed to do so.[138] The Charity Commission stated the principle that private schools must offer educational benefits to families that are unable to pay fees and, in response, the Attorney General referred to the Charity Tribunal the matter of how an assessment of the public benefit is applied to fee-charging schools.[139] This was a key issue not only for the existing 2500 private schools, but one with implications for the broader government policy

[135] Blake v. London Corpn (1887) 19 QBD 79.

[136] See, e.g., Ackworth School General Committee v. Betts (1915) 6 TC 642, where a Quaker school was held not to be a "public school" because its curriculum was so different from that provided by mainstream schools. Although denominational schools, or those that are "faith based," will not per se fail this test, they may if their interpretation of "schooling" deviates so far from the norm that they fall into the *Ackworth* category. Note also Brighton Convent of the Blessed Sacrament v. Inland Revenue Commissioners (1933) 18 TC 76, where a convent school that charged admission fees was held to be trading but, as the tuition was provided by the nuns who could therefore be construed as "beneficiaries," the income earned was tax-exempt.

[137] [1951] Ch. 728.

[138] In 2009, two private schools were told by the Charity Commission that they had failed the public benefit test. St Anselm's preparatory school in Derbyshire and Highfield Priory in Lancashire were criticized for failing to give any full bursaries. They were each given 12 months to overhaul their bursaries or risk losing charitable status. Two other private schools were told to make more efforts to publicize their bursaries.

[139] Subsequently this referral was joined by a judicial review application submitted by the Independent Schools Council, and both were scheduled to be heard by the Upper Tribunal (Tax and Chancery Chamber).

in respect of taking schools, health care facilities, and council amenities out of the public sector, and with regard to the compatibility of university tuition fees and university charitable status. In court, neither party brought much weight to bear on the two central questions: what a school's objective needs to express in order for it to be entitled to charitable status, and what a school actually needs to do to be seen as operating for the public benefit.

In October 2011, the Tribunal delivered its judgment.[140] It ruled that it was not for the Charity Commission or the courts to impose on the trustees of a school a prescribed interpretation of what constitutes the "public benefit" for the purpose of determining charitable status. The tribunal indicated that the new legislation did not introduce any new legal requirement in that regard. Provided a charity ensures that the poor are able to benefit in a way that is more than minimal or tokenistic, it is free to make its own assessment of how it will ensure that the public benefit requirement is satisfied.

The full implications of a ruling that would seem to establish the viability of a subjective interpretation of what constitutes "public benefit" are still being analyzed. It certainly leaves the Charity Commission, which applies the public benefit test to determine charitable status, in an awkward spot. However, even before the ruling there was evidence that fee-charging charitable schools are already changing their practices. An annual benchmarking survey showed that in 2007, for the first time, such schools allocated more money to means-tested bursaries for poor pupils than to scholarships awarded to the most able.[141]

3. Private Health Care

Much the same issues have surfaced in a health care context. Again the threshold at which the level of fees filters access, to the point where the public benefit is compromised, is contentious.

a. Private Hospitals

The statutory exemption from tax "must be restricted to hospitals supported wholly or in part by charity,"[142] but "if it is a hospital which is, as a whole, maintained by the payments of patients, whether some pay less than their costs and others more"[143] then it will not qualify for that exemption.

[140] See Independent Schools Council and the Charity Commission for England and Wales (Defendant), National Council for Voluntary Organizations and the Education Review Group (Interveners); Attorney General v Charity Commissioner for England and Wales (Referrer) and the Independent Schools Council (Respondents) [2011] UKUT 421 (TCC).

[141] See National Independent Schools' Benchmarking Survey (2008), Guidance for Independent Schools. Benchmarking Financial Performance in Independent Schools, London, Horwath Clark Whitehill, 2008.

[142] Needham v. Bowers (1888) 21 QBD 436, per Charles, J.

[143] Royal Antediluvian Order of Buffaloes v. Owens (1928) 13 TC 176, per Rowlatt, J. at p. 182.

In the *Odstock* case,[144] the imposition of high fees was open to the challenge that this breached the "public" requirement of the test. Odstock Private Care Limited was proposed for registration with objects to relieve sickness and preserve the health of patients by providing health care facilities and ancillary services at Salisbury District Hospital. There was a statutory limit on the capacity of Salisbury NHS Foundation Trust to benefit from private health care work. Clinicians wished to bring private work in and the hospital would then benefit from the extra income. Odstock was formed for such a purpose by means of a loan from the NHS Foundation Trust. It would (1) enter into agreements with patients and insurance companies for the provision of private care, and (2) contract with the NHS Foundation Trust for the provision of staffed facilities to enable that work to be carried out by clinicians at the hospital. A general referral system to Odstock involving GPs over a very wide area was in place. The Commission's concern was that people in poverty would be precluded from benefit for lack of ability to meet the high cost.

Odstock had few overheads and was committed to keeping the charges as low as possible. It was claimed that people on low incomes in Salisbury could access treatment; there was a wider public benefit because "any surpluses" would be ploughed back into additional NHS facilities available generally at the hospital, treating some patients privately will have knock-on effects on the efficiency of the hospital for NHS patients, and insurance was available to poorer patients.

The scales of charges indicated in the private care tariffs were not affordable and accessible by everyone: Illustrative sums ranged from £661 for a colonoscopy to £8063 for a knee replacement.

People living in poverty (even the poor of Salisbury) could not afford to pay sums of that order and would therefore not have access to those particular services. The Commission found that Odstock's scheme was not available to the public at large but only to those with the ability to pay the fees. The Commission needed evidence that the opportunity to benefit was in principle available to the public generally, including those of the public who were well-off. In particular, the Commission ruled, people in poverty must not be excluded from benefit.

Surpluses for application more generally for NHS work were likely to be minimal because the organization was said to be operating, as a matter of practice and policy, on very low margins. The indirect benefit inferred from the fact of private work undertaken freeing up NHS time and accelerating NHS waiting lists would not, of itself (and failing the demonstration of more direct benefits), be sufficient to establish that Odstock's purposes may so be operated as to benefit the public generally. Failing direct provision of financial assistance by Odstock to poor people who were sick, they would need to fall back on insurance. It had not been shown that relevant insurance was affordable by people on low incomes. Thus those in poverty

[144] See Charity Commission and "Decision on an application for registration as a Charity by a company limited by guarantee called "Odstock Private Care Limited" ("Odstock")," September 25, 2007.

had not been shown to be capable of benefiting in a real sense, either directly or indirectly. Consequently, the public benefit test was not satisfied and charitable status was refused. This decision is in keeping with the ruling in *Re Resch,*[145] the earlier ruling holding that a school cannot deny access to the poor.

4. Social Housing

In the U.K., the assumption by housing associations of service responsibilities previously borne by local authority has provided an interesting example of how the policy of shifting public benefit provision from government to the nonprofit and for-profit sectors has worked in practice. There is now a considerable history of cases concerning the charitable status of housing schemes for the elderly or disabled and the compatibility of such status with an element of private profit and the level of rents payable by tenants.[146] Problems have also occurred where the possibility of charitable status being compromised arises from issues regarding the independence of the entity concerned. This has been central to a number of cases that focused on whether a nongovernment housing body could be construed as truly independent when performing service provision duties on behalf of a government body or whether in fact it was functioning as a public authority.

In *Poplar Housing and Regeneration Community Association Ltd v. Donoghue,*[147] for example, the Court of Appeal ruled that the Association was acting as a public authority for the purposes of the Human Rights Act 1998, s.6(3)(b), partly because the Association had agreed that the tenant in question "would be treated no better and no worse than if she remained a tenant of Tower Hamlets."[148] Also, the Association had been established by the London Borough of Tower Hamlets: Five members of its board were also members of the authority, and the Association remained subject to the authority's control in the manner with which it dealt with its tenants. Such a close relationship indicated that the Association's activities amounted to public functions. The absence of such a close relationship was equally determinative in *R (Heather) v. Leonard Cheshire Foundation*[149] when the Foundation was found not to be exercising functions of a public nature when providing care under contract to Surrey County Council, which was charged with a public duty to make available such provision under the National Assistance Act 1948. As Woolf L.J. then explained:[150]

> If the authority itself provides accommodation, it is providing a public function. It is also providing a public function if it makes arrangements for the accommodation

[145] [1969] 1 AC 514.

[146] See, e.g., Garfield Poverty Trust [1990] 1 AC 514 (PC).

[147] [2001] EWCA Civ 595, [2002] QB 48.

[148] 2001] EWCA Civ 595, [2002] QB 48, per Woolf, L.J., at p. 70.

[149] [2002] EWCA Civ 366, [2002] 2 All ER 936.

[150] R (Heather) v. Leonard Cheshire Foundation 2002] EWCA Civ 366, [2002] 2 All ER 936, per Woolf, L.J., at p. 15.

> to be provided by LCF. However, if a body which is a charity, like LCF, provides accommodation to those to whom the authority owes a duty... it does not follow that the charity is performing a public function.

Again, in *YL v. Birmingham City Council,*[151] it was decided that a private body providing publicly funded residential care was not engaged in "functions of a public nature" under the Human Rights Act 1998. In this case the court was influenced by the for-profit nature of the body concerned and that it was acting under a series of contracts, all more indicative of private law rather than public functions. It was noted, however, that the level of public funding and the nature of the duties undertaken were also relevant and could indicate "functions of a public nature." The distinction made by the Council in regard to its duty under the National Assistance Act 1948, to arrange rather than to provide, was viewed as insignificant as Parliament had determined that the service should be provided, but the means of doing so was unimportant.

More recently, the finding in *Weaver v. London and Quadrant Housing Trust*[152] may be seen as having considerable significance in terms of its implications for government policy and for the independence of charities. The Trust in question was a registered social landlord under the Housing Act 1996 and, despite the fact that only 10 percent of its housing stock had been transferred from the public sector, with the remaining 90 percent of its properties having either been built or purchased from the private sector, the court held that it could nonetheless be classified as a public body. The court stated that the Housing Association sector was "permeated by state control and influence with a view to meeting the government's aims for affordable housing, and in which RSLs work side by side with, and can in a very real sense be said to take the place of, local authorities." The logic of the court's decision,[153] that the management and allocation of housing stock by London & Quadrant was a function of a public nature, and it was therefore to be regarded as a public authority when performing those functions, may well transfer to other areas of public benefit service provision. Arguably, in many instances the setting up of education and health care service providers outside the public sector is no less a part of government policy, is similarly subject to its regulation, and remains permeated by state control, funding, and influence. The observation then made by Richards L.J. may well cause many government-funded service provider charities to reflect on their position:

> Of particular importance is the nature and extent of public subsidy of the activities of [London & Quadrant], in common with other RSLs... [London & Quadrant's] business as a whole is heavily subsidized by the State and that this funding was

[151] [2007] UKHL 27. Note that subsequently the Health and Social Care Act 2008, s.145, was introduced, which provides that care homes are to be taken as exercising a function of a public nature when providing accommodation that is publicly funded.

[152] [2008] EWHC 1377 (Admin); [2008] WLR (D) 207.

[153] In November 2009 the Supreme Court refused leave to appeal to the House of Lords.

> attributable to the role that it, like other registered social landlord's, played in the implementation of government policy.

If, as suggested by Lord Nicholls LJ in *Aston Cantlow and Wilmcote with Billesley Parochial Church Council v. Wallbank*,[154] the courts should give "a generously wide scope to the expression 'public function,'" then a considerable swath of current public benefit service provision by charities could be construed as "functions of a public nature." Such a recognition that the charities concerned had chosen to compromise their independence to the point where they operated as a de facto arm of government would, arguably, have implications for their entitlement to charitable status.

5. Council Services

Of considerable strategic significance for government policy was the Charity Commission decision in the *Trafford and Wigan* case,[155] which granted charitable status to entities established by government to provide what until then had been local authority public services, with almost total government funding. The Charity Commission has advised that:[156]

> it is not a bar to charitable status that a new body has been created with a view to discharging a function of central or local government, provided that the new body was established for exclusively charitable purposes (which may coincide with a governmental authority's function) and not for furthering the non charitable purposes of securing and implementing the policies of any governmental authority.

Provided it is established exclusively for charitable purposes in the public benefit, not simply and solely as a means of carrying out a public authority's duties or policy, it would seem there is nothing preventing government from setting up a charity to deliver, either exclusively or as part of a wider range of activities, a particular public service or services for which until then it had borne full responsibility. In such circumstances the line to be drawn between an entity that is in fact a creature of government and one entitled to charitable status can be difficult to draw. This was clearly demonstrated in *Weaver* but the issue also surfaced in a VAT case[157] concerning a trust that had taken over the provision of services that had previously been the responsibility of the local authority. The VAT Tribunal held that where this

[154] [2003] UKHL 37; [2004] 1 AC 546 at para.11.

[155] See Charity Commission, *Applications for registration of (i) Trafford Community Leisure Trust and (ii) Wigan Leisure and Culture Trust*, April 21, 2004 where "it was accepted as a good charitable purpose to relieve the community from general or local taxation provided that such purpose was applied for the benefit of a sufficient section of the community." See further at: http://www.charity-commission.gov.uk/library/start/traffordecision.pdf.

[156] Charity Commission RR7, *The Independence of Charities from the State*, London, 2001.

[157] Bath Festivals Trust Ltd v. Revenue and Customs [2008] UKVA V20840.

activity fell within the scope of the council's strategy relating to the promotion or improvement of social well-being, then the trust is acting as a public authority.

Government funding has frequently been found insufficient in itself to indicate an inappropriate level of control over the recipient charity's affairs. The fact that an entity is largely or even wholly funded by government would not necessarily prevent it from being a charity.[158] However, there is a fine balance to be struck here, with each case turning on its own set of facts. Where in reality the level of funding, the degree of government control, and the extent to which the entity is linked to government policy in total indicates that it is performing functions of a public nature, and is merely acting in an agency capacity to carry out government functions, then for such purposes that entity must in law be regarded as a public body. In that situation, where the entity in question is seeking to acquire or retain charitable status, it would find it difficult if not impossible to demonstrate that the necessary independence, powers, and discretionary capacity of its trustees were not severely restricted or curtailed. This would be fatal for charitable status. It is not impossible that this area of law may need revisiting in the light of the Court of Appeal ruling in the *Weaver* case.

D. Charitable Trading: The Case Law in a Commercial Context

There is a distinct lack of recent case law in England and Wales concerning the involvement of charities in mainstream commercial activity. To some extent this is a consequence of the established charity law requirement that trading activity be primary purpose or ancillary in nature; within those parameters there is less scope for the adventurism that can lead to legal issues. It is also the natural outcome of close working relationships between government and charity resulting in the fact that the bulk of charitable trading is occurring in the context of public benefit services. Perhaps, also, the shedding of public utilities and the engineering of privatization through PFI, a process of commercializing aspects of public benefit provision, has largely bypassed charities, leaving them truer to their roots in health, social care, housing, and education. Although private sector entrepreneurs have for some decades been invited to carve out new roles in the public sector, charities and other nonprofits such as mutuals and social enterprises have only comparatively recently begun to develop similar initiatives. Mostly this is attributable to the legacy of the welfare state: Charities are less accustomed, in this jurisdiction than some others in the common law world, to competition or partnership with for-profit entities, and, therefore, there have been fewer opportunities for the clash of interests that require arbitration by court or Commission. This situation is rapidly changing as the fall in income from traditional sources forces more charities to bolster dwindling funds

[158] Direct Ministerial control, as in the case of Construction Industry Training Board v. A-G [1973] Ch 173, has been held to be not incompatible with charity status.

by developing trading ventures that are often totally unrelated to their charitable purposes.

1. Private Benefit

The principle that no undue private benefit should result from charitable trading is well established.[159]

In the *Oldham* case,[160] the promotion of trade, commerce, or enterprise with the ancillary object of providing support services and advice to new businesses was considered too permissive and allowed a private profit element that negated charitable status. The court decided that these objects allowed the organization to promote the private interests of individuals regardless of whether there would be any consequential benefits to the wider community. Lightman J. held that the Council was not charitable, as it was mainly concerned with promoting the private benefit of individuals engaging in commercial enterprises and that any public benefit accruing to the Oldham community would be remote. It has been shown that a degree of private benefit is in fact permissible, as illustrated by the *Royal British Legion Attendants* case.[161] This case concerned a charity established to promote the employment of ex-servicemen, to which end they ran a car park staffed by an ex-soldier and an ex-merchant seaman. Notwithstanding the element of private benefit, the Court of Appeal found this commercial venture charitable because it would "encourage a person to join the Forces, raise his moral and efficiency while he is serving and help him…when he returns to civilian life."[162] Where the level of private profit appears inordinate, then the Charity Commission will investigate.[163]

2. Public Benefit

The issue of benefits being unduly restrictive and therefore not available to a sufficient section of the public has often arisen in the context of charities established for educational purposes, for leisure pursuits, or for community development that

159 See, e.g., Re Smith's Will Trusts [1962] 1 WLR 763 (CA).

160 Inland Revenue Commissioners v. Oldham Training and Enterprise Council (1996) STC 1218.

161 Royal British Legion Attendants Company v. Commissioner of Valuation [1979] NI 138.

162 Royal British Legion Attendants Company v. Commissioner of Valuation [1979] NI 138, at p. 146.

163 Currently, the Commission is investigating the relationship between the Salvation Army and Kettering Textiles Ltd., which manages the charity's 4500 clothes recycling banks across the country, in the light of reports that the commercial company gained £10 million in profits from the sche me over the past five years compared with profits to the Salvation Army of £16.3 million over the last three years. See further Ribeiro, C., "FRSB Refers Salvation Army Clothing Collection Bank Complaint to Charity," Civil Society Fundraising, February 1, 2011, at: http://www.civilsociety.co.uk/fundraising/news/content/8201/frsb_refers_salvation_army_clothing_collection_bank_complaint_to_charity.

decides to raise funds to further their purpose by attaching a licensed social outlet to an existing facility. Where the evidence shows that such a trading arm is ancillary to the charitable purpose, then it will not breach the charitable status of the parent body. For example, the student union of a medical college was accepted as a charity, as its objects were "to promote, encourage and co-ordinate social, cultural and athletic activities amongst the members and to add to the comfort and enjoyment of the students." Although a "club which provides athletic and social activities for its members is not, per se, charitable," the integration of the union in the educational purposes of the medical college gave it a charitable character. In light of all the facts, the union was found to be dedicated solely to further the educational purposes of the medical college, and the benefits it provided to students were merely incidental to that purpose.[164] Where the social element is merely incidental it will not fatally compromise a charitable purpose.[165]

E. Jurisdictional Characteristics of Charitable Trading

In England and Wales, charitable trading has largely remained very much concentrated on public benefit service provision undertaken on the basis of government contracts. In recent years there has been evidence of increased cross-sectoral activity with charities using social enterprises and CICs to engage with government and business in consortiums to develop new approaches to public service provision. Although charities are certainly becoming more willing to set up business ventures unrelated to their primary charitable purpose, so far the scale of such activity bears little resemblance to that undertaken by their U.S. counterparts (see chapter 7).

1. Profits

All profits from trading must be applied exclusively to the purposes of the charity, although transfer of money from one charity to another would constitute "applying."[166]

The "destination of income" test is not crucial. However, in *Inland Revenue Commissioners v. Helen Slater Charitable Trust Ltd*[167] it was established that where one charitable company made a donation from its income to another, the act of donating could be interpreted as the first charity having "applied (its income) for

[164] London Hospital Medical College v. Inland Revenue Commissioners and another [1976] 2 All E.R. 113.

[165] See, e.g., Barralet and others v. Attorney-General and others [1980] 3 All E.R. 918 and Re Mariette; Mariette v. Aldenham School Governing Body [1914–15] All E.R. Rep 794. See also Royal Choral Society v. IRC [1943] 2 All ER 101.

[166] See IRC v. Helen Slater Charitable Trust Ltd [1982] Ch. 49. There are clear resonances with the ruling in the Australian case Commissioner of Taxation v. Word Investments Limited (2008) 236 CLR 204.

[167] [1982] Ch 49.

charitable purposes only."[168] The fact that the receiving charity did not apply the donation in ways that would specifically further its charitable purpose, but instead merely added the sum to its reserves, was beside the point.

VII. CONCLUSION

England and Wales, the progenitor of charity law in a common law context, has since guided the development of that law in the many nations that constitute the common law world, and in all probability, now that it is statutorily reconfigured, will continue to do so. The changes introduced by the Charities Act 2006, as further consolidated under the Charities Act 2011, will have significance far beyond their immediate impact on charity law in England and Wales.

In addition to its leadership in charity law reform, there are other important ways in which this jurisdiction has, in recent years, taken an innovative initiative. Of these none is as important as the fact that it pioneered the construction of a sophisticated institutional infrastructure to enhance the capacity of the nonprofit sector and to bridge the gap between it and government. There is now more central control of intersectoral traffic than is possible elsewhere. Further, it has largely moved the resolving of charity law disputes from adjudication to administration: Ongoing Commission monitoring and advice has reduced the probability of litigation and the need for recourse to the courts. There is also less scope for contention between government and charity, as the latter becomes steadily more dependant upon the funds and policies of the former.

For present purposes it is the scale and range of service decanting from the public to the business and nonprofit sectors, and the prominent role played by charities in this process, which is of particular interest. The creative experimentation with a mix of public and private funding, together with new legal vehicles to facilitate intersectoral collaboration, has been of considerable importance. Among the more significant innovations to emerge from this intensive period of trial and error have been the CIC and the SIB, both of which demonstrate the possibilities of releasing equity capital for use by charities. Hitherto, the inability of charities to realize capital from the equity locked up in assets they were entrusted to preserve has been a serious problem. Coming as it does at a time when the security of funding streams is at best precarious, such developments could be of considerable long-term significance.

[168] Thereby meeting the terms as stated in the Income and Corporation Taxes Act 1988, s.505(1)(c)(1–3).

6

EUROPE: RECENT DEVELOPMENTS

I. INTRODUCTION

Freedom of movement, of people and goods, is the raison d'être of the European Union and the central plank of the EC Treaty. The issues associated with opening up the market, and extending to nonprofits the freedoms and responsibilities enjoyed by their for-profit counterparts, made it inevitable that the sector in continental Europe would eventually attract focused political and academic attention. Nonetheless, examination of the sector as a collective entity is still in its infancy. There is a long way to go before the European sector can be said to be receiving anything like the level of scrutiny that has long been directed toward its counterparts in the developed common law countries.[1] Currently, little exists in the way of pan-European nonprofit sector information, let alone data analysis. Many of the developments that have come to characterize the sector and its dilemmas elsewhere are as yet unformed in this region, or are perhaps just not as visible due to lack of information.

In recent years, it has been evident that some momentum is gradually building in the direction of recognizing and delineating the complex dimensions of continental Europe's nonprofit sector.[2] The sector has become of increasing salience due to the

[1] See, e.g., the series of studies conducted by Salamon, L., et al, as part of the John Hopkins Comparative Nonprofit Sector Project. For continental Europe, see, e.g., the International Center for Not-for-Profit Law, *Survey of Tax Laws Affecting NGOs in Central and Eastern Europe*, Washington, D.C., ICNL, 2002.

[2] Signaled, perhaps, by the 2003 publication of the draft *Fundamental Legal and Fiscal Principles for Public Benefit Foundations* by the European Foundation Centre and the interdisciplinary conference in Hamburg that year on the nonprofit sector, followed by the conference on *Comparative Corporate Governance of Nonprofit Organizations*, sponsored by the Max Planck Institute for Private International Law and the University of Heidelberg, July 6–9, 2006.

EC need to introduce a framework, first of principles, then of law, that would nudge its 27 Member States toward an agreed conformity of practice such as would facilitate, or at least not continue to obstruct, the free movement of money and goods. Such a framework must marry or bridge the different traditions of common law and civil code countries, and the heritages of welfare state and communism. It would also have to be wholly compliant with human rights and other Convention requirements. In part the challenge has been to formulate rules and mechanisms that will permit reciprocal recognition, and facilitate the pan-European work, of nonprofit entities, including charities.

This chapter examines the principles, policies, and emerging body of law that reveal how the EC is coping with trans-jurisdictional trading charities. Of necessity it differs considerably from the other jurisdiction-specific chapters: the loose template, deemed appropriate for present purposes to outline and compare the developed common law nonprofit sectors, does not as readily fit or accommodate the more distinctive aspects of its European counterpart. For example, whereas on the one hand there is little as yet to be said on the incipient relationship between the Commission and the collective sector, on the other there is equally little to be gained (for present purposes) in examining and comparing the history of government/sector relationships among the 27 very different Member States (though to ignore that history would be a serious mistake). Nor is there very much that can be usefully achieved by evaluating the European law reform process. The case law relating to and illustrative of the commercial activity of nonprofits generally, and charities in particular, is also virtually nonexistent, or perhaps simply not readily identifiable. Nonetheless, the differences between sector progress in Europe and elsewhere are instructive and throw an interesting light on the relative importance of profits for contemporary charitable organizations.

The chapter begins with an overview of the nonprofit sector in continental Europe, taking into account such information as is available to outline its size and socioeconomic characteristics. It then briefly considers the political context for a developing government/sector relationship, as framed by the EC Treaty and Conventions, before focusing on the pressures causing a readjustment from state to sector of responsibility for provision of public benefit services. Some attention is given to the gradually unfolding process whereby new legal structures are emerging to facilitate nonprofit activity on a pan-European basis. This leads into an examination of the principles and case law now governing cross-jurisdiction trading by charities and other nonprofits; the objective is to examine the implications for charity, at the interface between civil and common law jurisprudence, as articulated in Convention principles and EC policy and arbitrated by the European Court of Justice (ECJ).[3]

[3] The European Court of Justice is the highest court in the European Union in matters of European Union law. As a part of the Court of Justice of the European Union it is tasked with interpreting EU law and ensuring its equal application across all Member States. The Court was established in 1952, is based in Luxembourg, and is composed of one judge per member state—currently 27—although it normally hears cases in panels of 3, 5, or 13. The court has been led by President Vassilios Skouris since 2003.

II. SECTOR PROFILE

There is no agreed and common definition of the nonprofit sector in Europe. It is often referred to as the third sector, as opposed to the public or business sectors. In the Scandinavian countries, it is known as the independent sector; in Central and Eastern Europe as the civil society; in the United Kingdom, it is the charitable sector or voluntary sector; and in France and Belgium it is the "économie sociale." However, these all refer to an aggregate of various types of organizations—such as cooperatives, mutual societies, associations, and foundations—that neither belong to government nor operate solely for financial gain.

A. The Nonprofit Sector

In terms of its asset base, expenditure, and employment rates, the foundation sector has acquired considerable economic weight, as was revealed in a recent study by the European Foundation Centre.[4] A sample of 55,552 foundations in 15 countries found combined assets of some €237 billion, an average of €4 million per foundation, based on 2005 data.[5] The 58,588 public benefit foundations surveyed in 14 EU countries reported total spending of €46 billion, an average of €1 million per foundation.[6]

1. Employment and Volunteers

The foundation sector plays an important role in the labor market for both salaried and voluntary workers. Foundations act directly as employers themselves and, by funding organizations and individuals in the nonprofit sector, they indirectly support employment and voluntary engagement in their areas of interest. In 10 EU countries (Belgium, the Czech Republic, Estonia, Finland, France, Germany, Hungary, Italy, the Netherlands, and Spain), according to figures mostly from 2005, some 34,400 foundations employ a total of 311,600 staff, an average of nine employees per foundation,[7] excluding employment created or sustained by foundations. In 2007, two-thirds of European Foundation Centre members were working across borders and were active outside their country of origin.

Volunteering remains an important feature of the foundation sector. The 31,800 foundations sampled in seven EU countries (Belgium, Finland, France, Germany,

[4] See European Foundation Centre, "Foundations in the European Union: Facts and Figures," May 2008, at pp. 6–7.

[5] European Foundation Center, "Foundations in the European Union," at p. 5.

[6] European Foundation Center, "Foundations in the European Union," at p. 6. Also based mostly on 2005 figures.

[7] European Foundation Center, "Foundations in the European Union," at p. 7.

Hungary, Italy, and Spain) have 231,600 volunteers, an average of seven volunteers each.[8]

B. Nonprofit Organizations

Recent research suggests that there are currently no fewer than 95,000 public benefit foundations in 24 EU Member States;[9] in Germany alone there are an estimated 600,000 associations and 15,000 foundations.[10] As entities serving public purposes, nonprofits qualify for tax exemption in much the same way as in the common law countries.

Foundations in particular have seen dramatic growth over the past 15 years. In nine countries (Belgium, Estonia, France, Germany, Italy, Luxembourg, Slovakia, Spain, and Sweden), 43 percent of foundations were established during the last decade.

1. Charities

"Charity" has a much broader legal definition in the common law nations than in continental Europe, where it is often limited to basic public welfare service provision and poverty relief.[11]

2. Range of Legal Structures

In Europe, it has been observed that "the nonprofit sector is diverse and multifunctional; nonprofit organizations appear in different organizational forms with different legal traditions in common law and civil law."[12] The bare fact that legal structures for charitable activity are necessary was established some decades ago by the

[8] European Foundation Center, "Foundations in the European Union," at p. 7.

[9] There are currently are around 55,000 charitable organizations qualifying for tax exemption in the Netherlands, and this number increases by about 3000 a year. Research conducted by Mariani in April 2011 showed that of the 2.604 qualifying organizations, 1952 were foundations, 36 associations, and the remainder were indeterminate.

[10] As Ingerfurth, S., advises, most of these are the so-called "eingetragener Verein" ("e.V.") a specific legal form of German nonprofit organization of which there are approximately 550,000 (note to author, November 8, 2011). See also Von Hippel, T., "Nonprofit Organizations in Germany," in Hopt, K. J. and Von Hippel, T. (eds), *Comparative Corporate Governance of Non-Profit Organizations*, Cambridge, Cambridge University Press, 2010, at p. 200. See also Anheier, H. and Seibel, W., *Defining the Nonprofit Sector: Germany*, The Johns Hopkins Comparative Nonprofit Sector Project, 1993, at: http://www.google.co.uk/search?q=Defining+the+Nonprofit+Sector%3A+Germany%2C+The+Johns+Hopkins+Comparative+Nonprofit+Sector+Project%2C+1993&ie=utf-8&oe=utf-8&aq=t&rls=org.mozilla:en-US:official&client=firefox-a.

[11] As noted by Picarda, H., in "Harmonising Nonprofit Law in the EU," in Hopt, K. J. and Von Hippel, T. (eds.), *Comparative Corporate Governance of Non-Profit Organizations*, at p. 175.

[12] Picarda, "Harmonising Nonprofit Law in the EU," at p. xxix.

European Court of Human Rights (ECtHR) in *McFeeley v. United Kingdom*,[13] where it was held that an NGO that is membership-based must not simply be a gathering formed with the object of pursuing certain aims, but must also have a degree of stability with regard to its existence and thus have some kind of institutional structure to which the persons comprising it can be regarded as belonging. Theoretically, the primary legal structures are readily recognizable—associations, trusts, nonprofit corporations, and foundations—whereas the traditional legal forms of association and foundation continue to dominate (particularly in France), and "the trust is nearly unknown."[14] Continental Europe has also relied heavily upon cooperatives.

In practice, legal structures of the same type can vary greatly. The "foundation," for example, is open to widely different interpretations across Europe and tends to serve quite different functions in central and eastern Europe than it does in western Europe, though there are signs of convergence. Until the early 1990s, foundations in central and eastern Europe were primarily concerned with economic reform, and were often prohibited from engaging in trading activity. By the mid-1990s, however, new legislation was beginning to introduce a more balanced approach, though it has often severely curtailed the scope of foundations to manage and invest charitable assets; in Hungary it remains the case that not more than 50 percent of a foundation's total income may be derived from commercial activities. By the end of the 1990s, foundations across Europe were financing a broader range of activities than before, moving from simple assistance in the economic reform process to more complex grant-making and operating programs and assuming a central role in building an awareness of sector identity.

In Europe generally, the lack of an agreed system for mutual recognition of foundations has been an obstacle for cross-border philanthropic activity. Although in principle a foundation's legal personality and public benefit status are ordinarily accepted by most EU countries, in practice there have been problems. As a general rule, a domestic registration is required, but some countries, such as Estonia and Italy, require a special recognition.[15] In Poland and Bulgaria, foreign foundations need to go through special recognition procedures and establish representative offices. In some countries, such as Hungary, branches of foreign foundations may not be set up. In those countries where foundations are defined as pursuing certain public benefit purposes only, foreign foundations that pursue different purposes may face difficulties.

The European Foundation Centre has developed a functional definition of foundations. These structures are seen as independent, separately constituted nonprofit bodies with their own established and reliable sources of income, usually but not exclusively funded by an endowment, with their own governing boards; they have

[13] (App. No. 8317/7820), D.R. 44 (1980).

[14] Picarda, "Harmonising Nonprofit Law in the EU," at n, 10, p. xli.

[15] In April 2011, for example, the EC referred The Netherlands to the ECJ because of its failure to provide a registration system obliging charities to register with the tax authority. The author is grateful to Mariani, E., for this information.

been given goods, rights, and resources to perform work and provide support for public benefit purposes, either by supporting organizations or individuals, or by operating their own programs. In addition, they do not have members, but associate private resources for public interest purposes.

When comparing the nonprofit sectors of the common law world and continental Europe, a significant differentiating factor to be borne in mind is the low reliance on corporate legal structures relative to the use made of foundations and associations throughout the 27 EC jurisdictions.

3. Range of Activities

The vast range of European nonprofit organizations, from small local groups to large international organizations, have in common their aim to serve public or mutual benefit purposes. They provide programs and services to the community in different fields such as the arts, culture, humanities, education, protection of the environment, health, social services, disaster relief, or international and foreign affairs. In relation to foundations, the most significant vehicle for charitable activity in Europe, Leat points out that:[16]

> the 21-country study of 'Visions and Roles of Foundations in Europe', coordinated by the Centre for Civil society at the London school of Economics,[17] found that in general foundations in Europe most commonly described their roles in terms of innovation and complementing other sectors, including government. The majority of foundations did not see themselves as having much, if any, influence on social policy change. In part, this was attributed to politicians' lack of understanding and knowledge of foundations.

C. Financing the Sector

In Europe, the main sources of income for nonprofit organizations are: grants from private institutions; contracts from public authorities such as the European Commission (the executive arm of the European Union), national governments, regional or local authorities; individual donations, such as charitable gifts or legacies; and fees for services, sales of products, or earned interest on investments. Funding sources for each nonprofit vary with much income being derived from private donations.

16 Leat, D., "Foundations and Policy Influence in Europe," in MacDonald, N. and de Borms, L. T. (eds), *Philanthropy in Europe: A Rich Past, a Promising Future,* Alliance Publishing Trust, London, 2008, at p. 259.

17 Anheier, H. K. and Daly, S., *The Politics of Foundations: A Comparative Analysis,* Routledge, London and New York, 2007.

1. EU Funding

In 2000, the Commission estimated that over €1000 million a year is allocated directly by its services to NGO projects[18] that meet the requirement of the Financial Regulation (the Commission's financial manual) that "grants may not have the purpose or effect of producing a profit for the beneficiary" (Article 109(2) of the Regulation).[19] The largest part of EU funding is not paid directly by the European Commission, but is channeled through the national and regional authorities of the Member States. This is the case for payments under the Common Agricultural Policy and most payments under the structural funds (e.g., the European Regional Development Fund or the European Social Fund) that make up, in money terms, the great bulk of EU funding. The Commission pays direct grants in pursuance of other common policies in such fields as research and development, education, training, environment, health, and consumer protection, information, and EU external relations. In particular it directs considerable funds toward research and innovation (more than €4 billion in 2005).

2. Self-Financing

The well-endowed foundations that constitute the heartland of the sector have sufficient financial security to maintain a level of independence from government. In 2006, it was estimated that the top 50 European foundations had assets of €147.2 billion.[20]

It is also worthy of note that in Germany the churches maintain their own tax administration, and are constitutionally empowered to collect "church tax," a portion of income tax that is levied by the state through employee payroll deductions and transferred to the churches. The church tax provides churches with a stable, inflation-proof income. The church tax is only voluntary in the sense that taxpayers can opt out by denouncing their church membership and formally registering that fact. Both the Protestant and the Catholic churches, for example, each acquire approximately €10 billion annually from this source. Church members benefit considerably from the

[18] See Commission discussion paper, "The Commission and Non-Governmental Organizations: Building a Stronger Partnership," January 2000.

[19] Note that in Spring 2010 the European Commission published a *Synthesis Report on Submissions to the Public Consultation on the Review of the Financial Regulation*, which included a recommendation for greater flexibility in interpretation of the nonprofit rule.

[20] Capgemini/Merrill Lynch, *World Wealth Report*, Global Wealth Management, 2007, at p. 21 (http://www.capgemini.com/insights-and-resources/by-publication/world_wealth_report_2007/). See also Foundation Center, *Foundation Yearbook*, 2006, at: http://www.google.co.uk/search?q=Foundation+Center%2C+Foundation+Yearbook%2C+2006&ie=utf-8&oe=utf-8&aq=t&rls=org.mozilla:en-US:official&client=firefox-a.

social services provided, and consequently a large proportion of nonprofit organizations operating in the social sector are religious.[21]

3. Sector Cohesion

EU Member States come from a very mixed political background that has left some of their respective nonprofit sectors ill-equipped to cope with the challenge of building a civil society.

The eastern European countries, most notably Romania and Slovakia, recently emerged from under their blanket of Communist rule, are still familiarizing themselves with the idea of a layer of civil society organizations that might fill the newly created public space between state, market, and citizen. Poland only began to revive its sector in 1989. In other states, there has been no history of private institutions created for the public benefit. In France, not until 1987 did foundations gain (or regain, following their suppression in the post-revolutionary period) statutory recognition, whereas in Turkey more than 35,000 foundations were thriving throughout the Ottoman period before being drastically reduced from the mid-to-late 19th century into the early 20th century. The current mix of Member States, some with a strong tradition of independent public benefit organizations and others with none, is not conducive to fostering cross-border sector activity. Consequently, there is little sense of a continental European nonprofit sector as a coherent entity in which its 27 very different participants have acquired anything like a collective identity, common purpose, and agreed agenda.

4. Umbrella Bodies

Understandably, pan-European nonprofits with a collective sector advocacy role are few in number and recent in origin. A handful, however, can be seen as aspiring to that role, including the following.

The European Cultural Foundation founded in 1954, is probably the oldest, if not the only, pan-European foundation. With its origins in Geneva, it is an independent nonprofit organization that promotes cultural cooperation in Europe. It has sought to address the cultural ramifications of EU enlargement and has focused on easing the tensions resulting from the increasing diversity that resulted from enlargement and global migration within the European Union.

The European Foundation Centre (EFC),[22] established in 1989, is self-described as "an independent association dedicated to creating an enabling environment for foundations, strengthening the infrastructure of the sector, and promoting collaboration, both among foundations and between foundations and other actors, to advance the public good in Europe and beyond." An independent, international, nonprofit

[21] The author is grateful to Ingerfurth, S., for this information.

[22] See The European Foundation Centre, http://www.efc.be/Pages/EfcWelcomePage.aspx.

association established under Belgian law, in 2011 it had a core membership of more than 230 members in some 30 countries.

The Donors and Foundations' Networks in Europe,[23] established in 2006, is a pan-European formal network of national donors and foundations' networks that supports charitable foundations and other grantmakers at the national level. It represents 22 member organizations from across Europe, has a collective membership of over 5000 foundations, and "sets out to underpin the individual activities of its members and to strengthen their collaboration to contribute to a fruitful environment for philanthropy and especially for public benefit foundations in Europe."

The Network of European Foundations for Innovative Co-operation[24] is a prominent force for European foundation collaboration around key policy issues. It is not a membership organization but a "platform" to enable joint projects to get off the ground, involving 62 foundations (in 2007) participating in one or more projects, including work on integration and migration, deliberative democracy, and the European Fund for the Balkans.

The European Citizen Action Service[25] was created in 1991 as an international nonprofit organization, independent of political parties, commercial interests, and the EU Institutions. It describes its mission as "to enable NGOs and individuals to make their voice heard with the EU by providing advice on how to lobby, fundraise, and defend European citizenship rights."

III. GOVERNMENT AND THE SECTOR

The legal framework within which the Commission together with the governments and sectors of Member States must develop a working relationship is dominated principally by two binding instruments: the EC Treaty; and the European Convention for the Protection of Human Rights and Fundamental Freedoms 1950. The first, signed in Rome in 1957, brought together France, Germany, Italy, and the Benelux countries in a community, subsequently enlarged to its present 27 members, dedicated to achieving integration via trade with a view to economic expansion. It became the European Community (EC) after the Treaty of Maastricht in 1992. The second, preceding and underpinning the EC Treaty and indeed the whole EC enterprise, requires the compliance of all 27 Member States, many of which have legislated to incorporate the Convention or most of its rights into national law. These rights are now being employed to gradually leverage developments in the nonprofit sector, not least to challenge as discriminatory the obstacles preventing the law reform process from achieving parity between for-profits and nonprofits in choice of legal structures for pan-European economic activity.

[23] Details of DAFNE are available at Donors and Foundations' Networks Europe, European Foundation Centre, http://www.efc.be/Networking/Pages/Dafne.aspx.

[24] See further at www.nefic.org.

[25] See The European Citizen Action Service, http://www.ecas-citizens.eu/.

A. Government Bodies and the Sector

The considerable variety of cultural baggage that accompanied the 27 Member States constituting the European Union is not readily amenable to integration within one coherent model. In particular, the historical variance in political ideology or "style" of government has direct implications for the development of any future relationship between the European Commission (the executive body for the EU), national governments, and the nonprofit sector.

1. Government/Sector Relations: Historical Background

There remain deep-seated differences between the strong welfare state background of the U.K. and Scandinavian countries, where government has assumed lead responsibility for public benefit service provision with sector bodies left to support and fill in the gaps, as well as the corporatist and institutionalized arrangements in Germany, France, Belgium, and the Netherlands, where government has tended to contract with well-established institutions, in "a form of societal corporatism,"[26] to deliver core public benefit services, and the more Catholic countries of southern Europe, where government control and provision of public services tends to be the norm, with religious charities left to play their traditional caring role for the more socially disadvantaged.

Because of this disparity, and the accompanying "margin of appreciation" rule,[27] the European Commission has naturally tended to be very hesitant before resorting to legislation, preferring to make progress slowly and cautiously by first securing a broad commitment to basic principles and standards. An indication of the difficulties in collectively managing the disparate interests of its members surfaced with the 2007 decision to defer the planned substitution of the present Treaty with a Constitution for Europe.

2. Harmonization

Initially conceived as a framework for facilitating economic activity between Member States, the EC has only in recent years begun to acknowledge a need to address economic and other issues as they relate to the nonprofit sector. Under Articles 2 and 3 of the EC Treaty, Member States are committed to work together to create, inter alia, a "common market and an economic and monetary union," including the establishment of an "internal market characterised by the abolition,

[26] See De Borms, L.T., *Foundations: Creating Impact in a Globalized World*, John Wiley, New York, 2005, at pp. 41–45.

[27] The term "margin of appreciation" refers to the space for maneuver that the Strasbourg organs are willing to grant national authorities in fulfilling their obligations under the European Convention on Human Rights.

as between Member States, of obstacles to the free movement of goods, persons, services and capital."[28] They are jointly dedicated to removing all obstacles to the establishment of the internal market, in particular any obstacles that may impinge on the fundamental freedoms enshrined in the EC Treaty. The journey toward harmonization of economic activity has been guided by principles established as a consequence of human rights litigation. Indeed, as an experiment in managing cultural tensions—not least those between Christians and Islam—by applying a rights template across borders, races, and political ideologies, the EC has established a valuable precedent. Some of these rights have a particular significance for the nonprofit entities that exist in the variable space between state and market that has long been such a characteristic feature of the countries comprising continental Europe.

B. The Human Rights Convention

The rights embodied in the European Convention for the Protection of Human Rights and Fundamental Freedoms 1950 are enforced by the European Court of Human Rights (ECtHR), the Convention's dedicated court, and by the European Court of Justice. Certain rights that are of central importance to the nonprofit sector are likely to be at least influential in ensuring future parity of opportunity for nonprofits and for-profits within the EC and will shape the terms of reference for a future government/sector relationship.

1. Freedom of Association

The Convention provides in Article 11 that:

1. Everyone has the right to freedom of peaceful assembly and to freedom of association with others, including the right to form and to join trade unions for the protection of his interests.

The right of citizens to form, join, or not to join associations constitutes a hallmark of democracy.[29] Indeed the very existence of nonprofit organizations is conditional upon this right. Its significance has been recognized by the legislatures of democratic states for centuries, and the constitutions of most countries in the world contain

[28] See Treaty Establishing the European Community, Articles 2 and 3, at http://eur-lex.europa.eu/en/treaties/dat/12002E/htm/C_2002325EN.003301.html.

[29] The International Covenant on Civil and Political Rights (ICCPR) and the Universal Declaration of Human Rights both guarantee freedom of association internationally, as does the Helsinki Accords of the Organization (former Conference) on Security and Cooperation in Europe (OSCE). See also the Freedom of Association and Protection of the Right to Organise Convention, 1948 (No. 87) and the Right to Organise and Collective Bargaining Convention, 1949 (No. 98).

articles protecting freedoms of association and assembly.[30] The Convention requires all laws and practice not only to be compliant with this right, which is a precondition for "civil society," but that governments also ensure they positively promote it;[31] they must "both permit and make possible"[32] opportunities for its enjoyment.

The ECtHR in *Sidiropoulos and Others v. Greece*[33] held that the ability of citizens to form a legal entity in order to act collectively in a field of mutual interest is "one of the most important aspects of the right to freedom of association, without which that right would be deprived of any meaning."[34] The ruling of the court is important because of its emphasis on the existence of minorities and different cultures in a country as a historical fact that a "democratic society" has to tolerate, and even protect and support. This principle has clear application both to indigenous minority culture groups (e.g., the Roma) and to the more prevalent socially disadvantaged groups requiring public benefit provision (e.g., the aged, disabled, mentally ill, etc.).[35] In the latter context, it will be central to determining the potential role of the sector as service provider.

2. Freedom of Expression

Article 10 of the Convention states that:[36]

> 1. Everyone has the right to freedom of expression. This right shall include freedom to hold opinions and to receive and impart information and ideas without interference by public authority and regardless of frontiers.

Again, this right is one of the hallmarks of a democratic society and is particularly important for those who need to present their case and argue for the public benefit services necessary to improve their circumstances. The promotion of human rights

[30] See, e.g., Canada and the Canadian Charter of Rights and Freedoms where the freedom of association has become an entrenched right; the United States and the First Amendment to the U.S. Constitution, which reads:

> Congress shall make no law respecting an establishment of religion, or prohibiting the free exercise thereof; or abridging the freedom of speech, or of the press; or the right of the people peaceably to assemble, and to petition the government for a redress of grievances.

[31] Wilson and Palmer v. United Kingdom (2002) 35 EHRR 20.

[32] See National Union of Belgian Police v. Belgium (1975) 1 EHRR 578, at para. 39.

[33] Sidiropoulos and Others v. Greece (26695/95) 27 EHRR (1998).

[34] Sidiropoulos and Others v. Greece (26695/95) 27 EHRR (1998), at para. 40.

[35] See also The Socialist Party of Turkey and Others v. Turkey (1998) 27 EHRR 51, Partidul Communistilor (Nepeceristi) and Ungureanu v. Romania (App. No. 46626/99), (2005), Refah Partisi v. Turkey, App. Nos 41340/98 and 41342/98, February 13, 2003, and RSPCA v. Attorney General and Others [2002] 1 WLR 448.

[36] See also Article 19 of the International Covenant on Civil and Political Rights.

is now a charitable purpose: a fusion of public law rights and private law principles with powerful potential for any future government/sector relationship.

The ECtHR in *Steel and Morris v. the United Kingdom*[37] (generally referred to as the "McLibel Case") ruled that two environmental activists (members of London Greenpeace) convicted of defaming the McDonald's Corporation in 1997 were denied freedom of expression (Article 10) by the British government and did not receive a fair trial (Article 6). The court expressed the view that in a democratic society even small and informal campaign groups, such as London Greenpeace, had to be able to carry on their activities effectively. There existed a strong public interest in enabling such groups and individuals outside the mainstream to contribute to the public debate by disseminating information and ideas on matters of general public interest such as health and the environment. The free circulation of information and ideas about the activities of powerful commercial entities, and the possible "chilling" effect on others, were also important factors to be considered in this context. This case is an important benchmark for the rights of individuals and small groups to actively campaign for peaceful change and to disseminate their views through the media. It gives permission and encouragement for small local nonprofits to challenge the market-dominating, global, for-profit companies where public benefit matters are at issue.

3. Freedom from Discrimination

Article 14 of the European Convention provides that:[38]

> The enjoyment of the rights and freedoms set forth in this Convention shall be secured without discrimination on any ground such as sex, race, colour, language, religion, political or other opinion, national or social origin, association with a national minority, property, birth or other status.

The right not to be discriminated against, traditionally associated with religious differences, is a most important aspect of life in a democratic society. Its wide social policy significance is demonstrated by its general extension to afford protection from discrimination on the grounds of gender, age, and race, and from differences arising from other such status designations.[39] For a successful claim, it must be

[37] (App. No. 68416/01) (2005).

[38] See also Article 26 of the International Covenant on Civil and Political Rights and the Convention on the Elimination of All Forms of Racial Discrimination and the Convention on the Elimination of All Forms of Discrimination Against Women.

[39] See, e.g., the ongoing case of *D. H. and Others v. the Czech Republic* in which the applicants, 18 Roma children forced to attend racially segregated schools in the Czech Republic, challenged the practice of educational discrimination—widespread throughout Central and South East Europe—in which Roma children are routinely placed in schools for the mentally disabled, regardless of their actual intellectual abilities.

shown that an applicant: is subject to a difference in treatment from others in a similar situation; is in the enjoyment of one of the rights protected by the Convention; and suffers from a difference that cannot be objectively and reasonably justified, having regard to the concepts of legitimate aim, proportionality, and margin of appreciation.[40]

The ECtHR in *Thlimmenos v. Greece*[41] considered the effects of indirect discrimination where a blanket ban was imposed by a professional body on the employment of anyone with a criminal record, and ruled that it had a disproportionate effect on the applicant that could not be justified. For minority groups, including those socially disadvantaged who are dependant upon public benefits and their related nonprofit service providers, this is an important decision as it recognizes that Article 14 also operates to afford protection from legal provisions that, although applied equally to all, have an adverse effect and discriminatory consequences for a few.

a. Religion

Within the common law tradition, the advancement of religion has long been a most important charitable purpose, carrying at least an implicit presumption (and explicit in the statute law of some countries such as Ireland) that gifts to and the activities of religious organizations are for the public benefit and therefore, ipso facto, are charitable. The interpretation of "religion" within this tradition has suffered from being construed in narrow terms, has often been applied inconsistently and has tended to exclude nontheistic religions. The Convention now requires that any interpretation of "religion" be applied objectively, have reasonable justification[42] and be nondiscriminatory; any differential treatment must comply with strict standards.[43] This legal benchmark for nondiscrimination in matters of religion is underpinned by Article 14 and supported by Article 9 (the right to freedom of thought, conscience, and religion) and by Article 1 of the First Protocol (the right

[40] See, e.g., Lithgow v. United Kingdom (1986) 8 EHRR 329, Fredin v. Sweden (1991) 13 EHRR 784, Abdulaziz, Cabales and Balkandali v. United Kingdom (1985) 7 EHRR 471.

[41] Application no. 34369/97), 6th Apr 2000.

[42] See, e.g., Tsirlis and Kouloumpas v. Greece (1997) 25 EHRR 198. See also the Belgian Linguistic Case (1968)(No 2) 1 EHRR 252 where the ECHR held that there must be an objective and reasonable justification for differential treatment, and this will only exist where there is a "legitimate aim" for the action, and where the action taken is "proportionate" to that aim.

[43] For a fuller discussion, see Quint, F. and Spring, T., "Religion, Charity Law & Human Rights," in *Charity Law & Practice Review*, Vol. 5, No. 3, 1999, at pp. 153–86. Note also the recent decision of the ECtHR in Mustafa Kamal Mustafa (Abu Hamza) (No. 1) v. the United Kingdom, 31411/07 [2011] ECHR 211 when the Charity Commission's suspension of Mustapha Kamal Mustapha as Imam of Finsbury Park Mosque on grounds of his alleged terrorist connections was upheld.

to peaceful enjoyment of property).[44] It has the effect of requiring governments and other public bodies to give parity of recognition to Christian and non-Christian religions such as Buddhism and Hinduism, and serves to reinforce the principle that "religion," as known to charity law in a common law context, must accommodate at least non-Christian faiths.

The corollary, that religious and nonreligious organizations should also enjoy parity of treatment, is likely to become as much an area of contention for the sector in continental Europe as it has over recent years in the United States and the U.K. Issues such as those relating to government funding of religiously affiliated charities, the application of nondiscrimination laws to such charities, and the preferencing of faith-based organizations in the delivery of public benefit services have potential to be at least as equally contentious in Europe. So also are the accompanying difficulties that arise in the preferential treatment exercised by such organizations in whom they employ and to whom they direct their services, and in the services they choose not to make available.

4. Freedom of Thought, Conscience, and Religion

Article 9 of the European Convention states:[45]

> 1. Everyone has the right to freedom of thought, conscience and religion.

The first time this Article was invoked to limit state action with regard to freedom of religion was in 1993[46] and, except for two cases, until 1995 the European Commission on Human Rights has always denied applications from religions that could be called "new," "minority," or "nontraditional."[47]

The ECtHR in *Kokkinakis v. Greece*[48] and *Manoussakis v. Greece*[49] ruled, respectively, that the Greek anti-proselytism law impermissibly interfered with freedom of religion and "the right to freedom of religion . . . excludes any discretion on the part of the state to determine whether religious beliefs or the means used to express such

[44] Article 1 of Protocol 1 of the European Convention on Human Rights provides:

> (1) Every natural or legal person is entitled to the peaceful enjoyment of his possessions. No one shall be deprived of his possessions except in the public interest and subject to the conditions provided for by law and by the general principles of international law.
> (2) The preceding provisions shall not, however, in any way impair the right of a state to enforce such laws as it deems necessary to control the use of property in accordance with the general interest or to secure the payment of taxes or other contributions or penalties.

[45] See also Article 18 of the International Covenant on Civil and Political Rights.

[46] See Gunn, T. J., "Adjudicating Rights of Conscience under the European Convention on Human Rights," in Van der Vyver, J. D., & Witte, J. D. (eds.), *Religious Human Rights in Global Perspective: Legal Perspectives*, Martinus Nijhoff, The Hague, 1996.

[47] Gunn, "Adjudicating Rights of Conscience," at p. 311.

[48] (A/260-A) (1994) 17 EHRR 397.

[49] (18748/91) (1996) 21 EHRR CD3.

beliefs are legitimate." These cases affirm the significance of freedom of religion for modern democratic states and indicate the nature and extent of its implications for future social policy. Given that many contemporary socially disadvantaged groups (e.g., some faith-based schools), communities (e.g., in Northern Ireland) and cultures (e.g., Islam) coalesce around a set of religious beliefs, it is clearly a matter of considerable importance that all public bodies are required to impartially facilitate the right to practice in accordance with religious beliefs.[50] Again, any government policy that implied, or produced the effect of, a differentiation between service users or between providers, on the basis of their religious beliefs or any analogous set of philosophical beliefs, would be at risk of breaching this Article.

5. Convention Benchmarks

Certain social justice benchmarks are emerging from Convention case law as key building blocks for international human rights jurisprudence. These are being absorbed into the practice and procedures of public bodies and are becoming an influence on the law relating to charity, as in relation to other matters, in all Member States. In addition, the Convention gives permission not just to challenge state institutions but also to access and use those institutions in order to increase the effectiveness of that challenge.

Convention benchmarks include, for example, the key standards of "necessity," "proportionality," "subsidiarity,"[51] and "equality of arms" against which relevant national legislative provisions and decision-making processes of all Member States can be tested. They inject standards to qualify the traditional roles of parties in the "gift relationship," and, in their general application they also serve to guide entitlement to public benefit services. By identifying a body of specific rights, the weighting of corresponding charitable purposes are reinforced in law. By establishing a clear rights framework and processes for access, the option of reliance on rights rather than on charity becomes available for some as an appropriate route to secure a remedy for social need. The main impact of such a body of rights, however, remains largely undetected: By modifying the decision-making processes of national public bodies, particularly the courts, the rulings of the relevant court operate to embed conduct that is human rights–compliant and, hopefully, obviate the need for it to hear further applications on that subject.

The above benchmarks interpose standards to qualify the traditional roles of parties in the "gift relationship." For all concerned, the encoding of specific fundamental human rights imposes parameters on charity by demarcating between a rights entitlement and a discretionary gift. By establishing a clear rights framework and processes for access, the option of reliance on rights rather than on charity becomes available for some as an appropriate route to secure a remedy for social need.

[50] Note also Tsirlis and Kouloumpas v. Greece (1997); the Belgian Linguistic Case (1968); the International Covenant on Civil and Political Rights, Art. 18; and the prohibition against organizations such as the Church of Scientology and Refah Partisi.

[51] According to which, as mentioned in Article 5.2 of the Treaty, the Community can only act if a certain objective cannot be achieved by a Member State and can be better achieved by the Union.

C. Nonprofit Law Reform

Nonprofit law reform has trailed behind the slow progress made in the for-profit sector. A long, drawn-out process of negotiation eventually resulted in the EC overcoming, to a large extent, the challenge presented by the disparity in the laws of an ever-growing number of Member States, and new agreed legal structures are now in place to facilitate cross-border for-profit activity. However, the difficulties in relation to the autonomous right of Member States, under Articles 43 and 48 of the EC Treaty, to enjoy a right to freedom of establishment within the territory of another Member State continue to trouble the EC Commission and generate a steady flow of cases toward the ECJ.

1. Drivers of Reform

Article 10 imposes an obligation on Member States to ensure the fulfillment of obligations arising out of the EC Treaty and to "abstain from any measure which could jeopardise the attainment of the objectives of this Treaty." Member States must not, therefore, impose restrictive or discriminatory tax measures that would be contrary to their obligations under Article 10. They must ensure that national tax measures neither discriminate on the basis of nationality nor restrict the exercise of free movement rights guaranteed by the EC Treaty, and thereby impede the attainment of the single-market objective.

In practice, however, although the number of Member States has steadily increased, the problems involving capital-asset movement and the variation in tax treatment of donations have remained to obstruct the cross-border activity of nonprofits. Member States have each been free to continue applying their particular legal criteria for defining public benefit for tax purposes, to determine the ancillary legal requirements placed on a nonprofit seeking tax relief, and to further develop their laws on such matters.

The "freedom of establishment rule" in particular has long been a cause of contention.[52] In a succession of cases concerning for-profit companies,[53] the ECJ has upheld the principle that entities in Member States enjoy a freedom to be permanently

[52] Beginning, perhaps, with Commission v. France ("Avoir Fiscal") [1986] ECR 273, which found that Article 43 of the EC Treaty prohibits "as a restriction on the freedom of establishment, any discrimination on grounds of nationality resulting from the legislation of the Member State."

[53] In particular, see Marks & Spencer v. Halsey (HM Inspector of Taxes) (C-446/03), in which the ECJ then determined that a group relief scheme that does not allow a parent company to deduct the losses of its subsidiaries established abroad under any circumstances is incompatible with Community law; in OY AA (C-231/05), the ECJ ruled that Finnish rules concerning intragroup financial transfers were compatible with the Community's freedom of establishment; and Lidl Belgium GmbH & Co. KG v. Finanzamt Heilbronn (C-414/06), where the ECJ found that Germany did not violate Article 43 of the EC Treaty by denying loss relief for the losses of a German company's permanent establishment in Luxembourg. See also the German cases concerning online gambling: Markus Stoss (C-316/07) and Carmen Media Group (C-46/08); C-316/07 (*Stoss*) is joined with the cases C-358/07 (*Kulpa*), C-359/07 (SOBO), C-360/07 (*Kunert*), C-409/07(*Avalon*), and C-410/07 (*Happel*).

established either within that state or in another Member State; this right falls within Article 43 of the EC Treaty. A second and separate rule, prohibiting any restriction on the free movement of capital, comes into play as an unavoidable consequence of any restriction on the freedom of establishment. The first is applicable to the residence of charities, and the second concerns the flow of donations to those charities.

This freedom of establishment also prohibits the "Member State of origin from hindering the establishment in another Member State of one of its nationals or of a company incorporated under its legislation." As Salole argues:[54] "foundations are obliged to set up multiple branches in different countries in order to carry out their transnational work, and are met with a considerable extra administrative burden and unnecessary increased costs, which together erode the sum of money available to spend on their target beneficiaries—Europe's citizens."

For nonprofits, a constant difficulty arising from this rule has been the consequent restriction on tax exemption eligibility to those established within the territory of the Member State. A requirement that discriminated against organizations based outside the Member State in which exemption was being claimed discouraged cross-border activity, and any such restriction on exemption eligibility would be promptly challenged by the European Commission. Of the 27 Member States, only the Netherlands, Poland, and Slovenia allowed a resident's donations to a foreign-based public benefit organization to be income-tax deductible; 16 did not allow deductibility under any circumstances for such donations, despite allowing deductions for donations to similar domestic organizations.[55] The discriminatory treatment of nonresident foundations eventually resulted in the *Stauffer*[56] and *Persche*[57] cases heard before the European Court of Justice (see below).

Foundations may also face a nonrefundable withholding tax on cross-border investments, as well as national gift and inheritance tax. Unlike resident foundations, foreign foundations in most countries are unable to receive tax-deductible individual or corporate donations.

2. The Law Reform Process

In 2001, after some 30 years of wrangling and following in the wake of company law changes finally achieved in the for-profit sector, it seemed probable that equivalent nonprofit reform was attainable. In particular, it was hoped to secure the introduction of new legal forms equivalent to the European Company Statute adopted in 2001, the European Economic Interest Grouping and the European Co-operative Society adopted in 2003, and the more recent European Private Company Statute (Societas

[54] Salole, G., "The Importance of There Being a European Foundation Statute," in MacDonald, N. and de Borms, L.T. (eds.), *Philanthropy in Europe: A Rich Past, a Promising Future,* Alliance Publishing Trust, London, 2007, at p. 293.

[55] See further, IJNL, Vol 10, Issue 3.

[56] [2006] ECJ C-386/04.

[57] [2008] ECJ C-318/07.

Privata Europaea). The advocacy work of the European Foundation Centre,[58] campaigning for a specific pan-Europe legal form for public benefit entities, began at this time with the translation of its *Fundamental Legal and Fiscal Principles*[59] into a draft *Model Law for Public Benefit Foundations*. The possible need for a European Foundations Statute was identified as a medium-term priority in the EU Company Law and Corporate Governance Action Plan adopted in 2003. Since then the EFC finalized its draft recommendations on a European Statute for Foundations in 2005 and has persistently lobbied for such a statute and for a European Statute for Associations, enacted by way of European Council Regulation, to be directly applicable to all Member States.

However, all efforts to progress nonprofit law reform have so far been unsuccessful. In 2006 the Commission withdrew its proposals for Regulations on the Statute for a European Association and the statute for a European Mutual Society, introduced in 1991, on the overarching grounds that they "were not found to be consistent with the Lisbon and Better Regulation criteria, unlikely to make further progress in the legislative process or found to be no longer topical for objective reasons."[60]

In November 2007, a fresh initiative was launched when a feasibility study was initiated by the Max Planck Institute for Comparative and International Private Law in Hamburg and the University of Heidelberg. In 2008, following submission of the feasibility study, the Commission then commenced a process of public consultation on the difficulties foundations face when operating across borders, on the content of a possible European Foundation Statute, and on how such a statute might affect donors' and founders' attitudes. If a European Foundation Statute were to be proposed, the objective would be to make possible the use of a single legal form instead of up to 27 national ones. However, it would be an additional rather than a replacement structure, existing alongside current national legal forms, and its use would be optional.[61] In 2009, the European Commission launched its public consultation on the difficulties foundations face in their cross-border activities and on the content and likely effect of a possible European Foundation Statute. As the Commissioner then explained:[62]

> Foundations play an important role in Europe, especially in supporting public benefit causes. We need to ensure that we have appropriate structures in place in Europe to support their activities which are increasingly cross-border in nature.

[58] Building on the European Parliament's adoption of the Committee on Legal Affairs and Citizens' Rights *Report on Nonprofit Making Associations in the European Community*, Working Documents, Series A 2-196/86, January 8, 1987.

[59] See further at: http://www.google.co.uk/search?q=Fundamental+EFC+Legal+and+Fiscal+Principles&ie=utf-8&oe=utf-8&aq=t&rls=org.mozilla:en-US:official&client=firefox-a.

[60] OJ C 64, March 17, 2006, at p. 3.

[61] See further DG MARKT, Unit F2, European Commission, B-1049 Brussels or contact markt-consultation-ef@ec.europa.eu.

[62] See Internal Market and Services Commissioner Charlie McCreevy, The European business network for CSR press release, "Commission Consults on a Possible European Foundation Statute," at: http://www.csreurope.org/news.php?type=&action=show_news&news_id=2300.

In March 2011, the process was taken a step further when the European Parliament issued a written declaration calling upon the European Commission to introduce proposals for European statutes for associations, mutual societies, and foundations.[63]

In the meantime the Commission is steadily making progress in reducing cross-border difficulties by bringing infringement procedures against countries that tax foreign foundations in a discriminatory way, requiring national rules to be changed so that they are compliant with the EC Treaty. Such procedures have been brought against Belgium, Ireland, and the U.K. So far, only Poland, Finland, Slovenia, and the Netherlands (which is still not wholly compliant) have opted to align their laws with the EC Treaty regarding cross-border giving to public benefit foundations.

IV. READJUSTING PUBLIC BENEFIT SERVICE PROVISION

Readjusting from state to sector, the sharing of responsibility for providing future public benefit services, is the challenge facing all modern developed nations. The same inverse correlation between tax revenues and health and social care costs—driven by a mix of inexorable demographic trends, outsourced manufacturing, population displacement, and a growing propensity for global market failure—is sharpening a general political awareness. The fact that "the maths don't work" is a common theme in all the countries studied, and testimony that this is as much a problem for continental Europe as for the U.K., the United States, and elsewhere is provided by Hopt, who comments:[64]

> There are well-founded doubts that the traditional European welfare state will still be able to cope with the ever-increasing welfare, environmental and developmental problems of modern society in the future. Nonprofit organizations may step in and create a rapidly growing zone between the state and the market. There they can take over tasks that the state can no longer fulfil because of scarcity of financial resources, and that for-profit organizations in the market will not be able and willing to take over because these tasks do not yield enough of the necessary profits.

[63] As announced in the Single Market Act, the European Commission is committed to put forward a proposal on a European Foundation Statute before the end of 2011 and is currently working on the impact assessment.

[64] Hopt, K. J., "The Board of Nonprofit Organizations: Europe," in Hopt, K. J. and Von Hippel, T. (eds.), *Comparative Corporate Governance of Non-Profit Organizations*, Cambridge, Cambridge University Press, 2010, at p. 534.

A. Public Benefit Service Provision: The Policy

Bode is of the view that: "regarding core fields of social welfare provision, continental European countries have witnessed an increasing institutionalization of the corporatist governance regime during the 20th century…these fields became based on highly formalized partnerships between service-providing charities and public bodies (social insurance and welfare bureaucracies) which are expected to subsidize their activities."[65] This was quite evident, for example, in Germany where the doctrine of "subsidiarity" (which requires decision making to be distributed to the most appropriate level) has heavily influenced government policy with the result that public benefit service provision has customarily been provided or managed by non-statutory organizations, with the majority of social (and medical care) services being delivered by independent service providers, mostly nonprofits,[66] under contracts set by government departments. Such a corporatist arrangement between state and nonprofit sector has also characterized service provision in other countries, such as France and Belgium, and been accompanied by considerable nonprofit leverage on related political and policy matters. In recent years, beginning in the 1990s, social insurance policies have enabled those in need to purchase services from for-profit providers, which has led to considerable expansion in the volume of services provided on that basis in certain areas, notably elderly care, disability, and youth work. This trend began to progressively weaken the long-standing corporatist arrangement between state and nonprofits (the latter being often faith-based). In other countries, although the subsidiarity doctrine has not been so influential, the same trend toward increased exposure of public benefit services to market forces is steadily becoming more evident.

By the end of the 1970s, across continental Europe, the trends of falling economic growth, rising unemployment, and consequent depleted tax revenues had began to erode government capacity to maintain customary levels of public benefit service provision and to test its corporatist underpinnings. By the 1990s, with unemployment at 10 percent in many European countries, a continuation of the "welfare state" approach was clearly no longer tenable, or not at traditional levels. The welfare state became gradually more compromised as government reined in public spending while increasing regulatory control. The New Public Management model erased sectoral differences, and corporatism made room for more pragmatic market considerations. Consequently, in continental Europe perhaps more so than

[65] Bode, I., "Creeping Marketization and Post-Corporatist Governance: The Transformation of State-Nonprofit Relations in Continental Europe," in Phillips, S. D. and Rathgeb Smith, S. (eds.), *Governance and Regulation in the Third Sector*, London, Routledge, 2011, at pp. 115–41.

[66] Evers, A. and Sachße, C., "Social Care Services for Children and Older People in Germany: Distinct and Separate Histories," in Anttonen, A., Baldock, J., and Sipilä, J. (eds.), *The Young, the Old and the State: Social Care Systems in Five Industrial Nations*, Cheltenham, Edward Elgar, 2003, at pp. 55–70.

in the "developed" common law countries, there has been a growing concern that the nonprofit sector is losing its traditional "place" and "voice" in political and social terms, and is in danger of slipping into a neutered and dependent role in relation to government.

1. Welfare Benefit Cuts

Trends in demography and unemployment, with their drastic implications for tax revenues, dictated that government cuts and nonprofit initiatives would have to be in related areas such as housing, childcare, facilities for the elderly, and skills training.

B. Sector Capacity Building

The European Commission contributes to building sector capacity by allocating part of its budget to companies and organizations, including nonprofits, in the form of calls for tender, grants, or funds, and other financing programs. The INTERREG program, for example, has focused on developing infrastructure and sustainable urban environments, and on addressing cross-border problems, whereas the PROGRESS program has tackled employment, social inclusion, antidiscrimination, and gender inequality.

The Commission can directly grant funds to projects or organizations that further the interests of the EU or contribute to the implementation of an EU program or policy.[67]

1. Nonprofits and Government Funding

The governments of Member States, with Commission support, have tended to look to social enterprises as the means for filling in the widening gaps in public service provision—particularly to offset the myriad of social problems accompanying the rise in numbers of unemployed. However, in the more welfare state countries of northern Europe and Scandinavia, the tradition of government core funding to many nonprofits engaged in public benefit activity has continued, whereas in others, as Rutzen et al. have noted, it is becoming the norm:[68]

> Increasingly, governments are providing direct funding to NPOs and seeking to facilitate privatization of state resources to private actors, including NPOs. The trend is to facilitate this process and ensure that the shift of government resources to the NPO sector is performed in a transparent manner.

[67] See further Public Contracts and Funding, European Commission, http://ec.europa.eu/contracts_grants/index_en.htm.

[68] See Rutzen, D., Moore, D., and Durham, M., "The Legal Framework for Not-for-Profit Organizations in Central and Eastern Europe," in *IJNL*, Vol 11, No. 2, 2009. See further at: http://www.icnl.org/research/journal/vol11iss2/art_1.htm.

C. Public Benefit Service Provision: The Practice

The nonprofit sectors in continental Europe, as elsewhere, have come under considerable government pressure to make good the shortfall in traditional public service provision; unlike the common law jurisdictions, this pressure is one that falls mainly on foundations. Leat has rightly expressed concern at this development:[69]

> Foundations in a number of countries were facing increasing pressures to substitute for state services and the issue of substitution and relationships with statutory funding was for many foundations the most difficult current issue. The dilemmas and trends some foundations identify regarding foundations being reluctantly cajoled into assuming roles that are not their key priorities somewhat compromise assertions about independence and autonomy. The signs are that this will continue in the broader scenario of the restructuring of European welfare states.[70]

The spending priorities of foundations in central and eastern Europe have been toward strengthening local civil society and assisting the transition to a more transparent and democratic society, with many of the foundations coming from outside the region, often from the United States. Indeed, throughout the 1990s, foreign foundations provided a major source of funding for education infrastructure and other basic civil society activities. The agenda of U.S. foundations such as the Charles Stewart Mott, George Soros's Open Society, and the Andrew W. Mellon was to assist the shift to democracy and to a market economy.

A more recent brief survey of EFC members, with an admittedly low response rate, provides some indication of the type of provision attracting foundation support.[71] Just over three-quarters (33) of those that responded said that they make grants to "civil society organizations," whereas 36 said they make grants to other entities. Universities were singled out for special mention as grant recipients, and this was so across the geographic spread. Indeed, an outstanding example can be seen in the Central European University of Budapest, which is the first[72] foundation-based, fully endowed private university in Europe, able to run its core operations on the basis of its own regular

[69] Leat, D., "Foundations and Policy Influence in Europe," in MacDonald and de Borms, *Philanthropy in Europe*, at p. 261.

[70] Citing, Anheier, H. K., and Daly, S., *The Politics of Foundations: A Comparative Analysis*, Routledge, London and New York, 2007.

[71] Hartnell, C., "European Foundations' Support for Civil Society: A Means to an End or an End in Itself?," in MacDonald and de Borms, *Philanthropy in Europe*, at p. 246 (citing a survey carried out in December 2007 when 44 out of 210 responded, a 21 percent response rate, with responses coming from 18 different countries—including two from Russia, three from Turkey, one from Jordan, and two from the United States).

[72] Contrary advice from Mariani, E. indicates that the Yrje Universiteit, a privately funded university established in Amsterdam in 1880, has a better claim to the accolade of being the first such university in Europe.

income resulting from the investments of some €420 million. Other entities supported were government, municipalities, museums, health-related organizations, and think tanks.

1. State/Sector Collaboration

Although there is great variation among its 27 Member States, there is nonetheless a sense that a legacy of corporatism remains prominent within parts of the EU, and that this may constitute a significant factor differentiating its state/sector relations from those characteristic of the developed common law countries.[73] Bode's observation seems broadly on target:[74]

> the core fields of social welfare provision... became based on highly formalized partnerships between service providing charities and public bodies (social insurance and welfare bureaucracies) that are expected to subsidise their activities. Importantly, these archetypes of 'partners in public service'[75] also engaged with the very design of welfare programs which enabled nonprofit organizations to end up as major *political* stakeholders of the overall system. This model of intersectoral collaboration was (and still is) deeply entrenched in the welfare culture of mainland Europe.

Intersectoral collaboration, with government essentially controlling the contribution of large institutional nonprofits, is probably still a feature of state/sector relations, and not necessarily confined to those countries where the welfare state is winding down. However, Bode has also drawn attention to what is seen as a creeping "marketization and commercialization" in state–nonprofit relations and nonprofit activity now evident in both France and Germany.

2. Public Procurement

The public procurement process no longer refers mainly to services to be provided by government but has expanded to accommodate the ever-growing contribution made directly by nonprofit and for-profit providers in areas such as welfare-to-work, further education, social care, and health. Although its sector role varies from country to country, there is a general acknowledgement that public procurement is a key government mechanism for managing nonprofit public benefit provision. In

[73] See, e.g., Salamon, L. M. and Anheier, H. K., "Social Origins of Civil Society: Explaining the Nonprofit Sector Cross-Nationally," *Voluntas*, Vol. 9, 1998, at pp. 213–48.

[74] Bode, I., "Creeping Marketization and Post-Corporatist Governance," at p. 118.

[75] Citing, Salamon, L. M., *Partners in Public Service: Government-Nonprofit Relations in the Modern Welfare State*, John Hopkins University Press, Baltimore, MD, 1995.

Europe, this process has been regulated and gradually harmonized since the 1970s[76] and has produced a great deal of ECJ case law on issues such as the distinction between works contracts and land deals;[77] the exemption for "in-house" awards;[78] the material changes to contract that give rise to a new award;[79] the content and disclosure of award criteria,[80] and the duty to advertise.[81]

V. NEW LEGAL STRUCTURES AND DONOR INCENTIVES

The EC Treaty, virtually by definition, favored for-profit activity. Consequently, the new legal structures necessary to facilitate pan-European associational activity were pioneered by the for-profit sector. The introduction of the European Company (Societas Europaea), followed by the European Private Company (Societas Privata Europaea), showed the way and generated a momentum of demand for equivalent nonprofit structures. However, as nonprofit organizations are "highly path-dependent with little or no chance of harmonization in the European Union,"[82] any modernization of their legal structures would have to take the form of new agreed alternatives. In the absence of any legislative initiative to provide for the nonprofit sector any equivalent to the new structures now available for its for-profit counterpart, it remains the case that the burden of meeting new demands continues to fall largely on that workhorse of public benefit provision throughout continental Europe—the foundation.

A. Foundations

The foundation sector in Europe is growing dynamically and is gradually achieving a significant economic footprint. There are 110,000 public-benefit foundations

[76] See EU Directive 2004/18, which applies to the State, regional, and local authorities, plus other "contracting authorities" including "bodies governed by public law" (i.e., a body:

(i) established to meet "needs in the general interest, not having an industrial or commercial character"; and
(ii) financed, supervised or appointed, for the most part, by the State or other public authorities).

[77] See European Court of Justice cases: C-220/05 Auroux v. Roanne; C-536/07, Commission v. Germany; and C-351/08, Helmut Muller.

[78] See European Court of Justice cases: C-107/98, Teckal; C-573/03, Sea Srl; and C-480/09, Com. v. Germany.

[79] See, European Court of Justice cases: C-454/06, Pressetext; C-160/08, Com. v. Germany; C-91/08, Wall v. Frankfurt; and C-423/07, Commission v. Spain.

[80] See European Court of Justice cases: C-532/06, Lianakis; C-199/07, Commission v. Greece; and C-299/08, Commission v. France.

[81] See European Court of Justice cases: C-324/98, Teleaustria; C-507/03, Com. v. Ireland; and C-147/06, SECAP.

[82] Hopt, K. J. and Von Hippel, T. (eds.), *Comparative Corporate Governance of Non-Profit Organizations*, Cambridge, Cambridge University Press, 2010, at p. xliv.

(almost four foundations per 10,000 people) located in the European Union. Some 43 percent of these foundations were set up as recently as the early 1990s. In 2006, it was estimated that one public benefit foundation was created per day in Spain and two per day in Germany. Foundations spend between €83 and €150 billion annually, over twice as much as the U.S. foundation sector: The giving of the top 50 foundations rose from €4.4 billion in 2006 to virtually €6.3 billion in 2008 (according to *Philanthropy in Europe*).

Foundations are also big employers, providing direct full-time employment to between 750,000 to 1 million people in the EU. Foundations, for example, play a prominent role in funding research, and yet:[83]

> Given the billions of euros spent by public authorities and businesses, one might ask what impact comparatively small-scale foundations can achieve in this area. It is indeed not the overall amount of money spent but rather the approach taken by foundations that makes the difference. Their autonomy, alertness and flexibility enable them to operate effectively as facilitators of change, to establish islands of success, and thereby to achieve considerable impact on policymakers and decision-makers. By fostering risky projects, encouraging networking across disciplinary, institutional and national borders, and helping some of the most creative researchers to break new ground, foundations are able to prove that even on a European scale, small things matter.[84]

Insofar as there is a problem, it lies, as noted by Martin, in the inherent conservatism that pervades European foundations:[85] "[T]he investment policies of European foundations are typically far less aggressive than those of their North American counterparts" and "compared to their U.S. counterparts, European foundations hold much lower percentages of alternative asset classes such as hedge funds and private equity, and greater percentages of stock in affiliated companies." This, he suggests, is partly due to "an ultra-conservative approach to investment management motivated by the correct and honorable desires to preserve assets"; it may also be interpreted as a disinclination to adopt the adventurism indulged in by their American counterparts. By way of illustration, he refers to a recent study of foundations[86] involved in mission investing that lists only a few European foundations, for example the Canopus Foundation (40 percent of assets, mainly in wind parks), the Esmee Fairbairn Foundation (loans to

[83] See Krull, W., "Encouraging Change: European Foundations Funding Research" in MacDonald and de Borms, *Philanthropy in Europe*, at p. 237.

[84] Citing Krull, W., "Encouraging Change, the Role of Private Foundations in Innovation Processes,", in Albers, Sönke (ed.), *Cross-Functional Innovation Management: Perspectives from Different Disciplines*, Springer-Verlag, New York, 2004.

[85] Martin, M., "Engaged Philanthropy and Market-Based Solutions," in MacDonald and de Borms, *Philanthropy in Europe*, at pp. 279–81.

[86] Martin, "Engaged Philanthropy and Market-Based Solutions," at p .282.

nonprofits, under 1 percent of the endowment), and the Shell Foundation (socially targeted, venture capital–type investments in East Africa).[87]

1. Community Foundations

The fastest growing type of public benefit organization in Europe are community foundations, which exist or are under consideration in at least 19 countries or regions including Bulgaria (11), Germany (100), Italy (17), Poland (21), Portugal (1), Slovakia (12), Slovenia (4) Estonia (3), Lithuania (8), Latvia (4), and Russia (20). Developments in this field can also be observed in countries such as Bosnia and Herzegovina, and Turkey.[88] Community Philanthropy Watch reports that much of this growth, which has taken place in the past 15 years, has been fuelled by a number of trends affecting local communities. These include: decentralization and reduced spending by national governments (e.g., welfare cuts); changing roles for local government; failure of conventional approaches in solving local problems; desire by local residents to have a direct voice in helping to set community priorities and identifying potential solutions; and increasing interest in strengthening grassroots groups and community-based nonprofits to tackle local problems.

2. The European Foundation

The European Commission's decision to present a regulation on a European Foundation Statute by the end of 2011[89] would seem to signal that the long drawn-out law reform process is finally coming to a close, with the likelihood of a new model foundation being introduced by statute law for pan-European use.[90] The necessity for such a new legal structure has never been more evident. If the foundation sector, now consisting of more than 110,000 public benefit foundations and contributing over €100 billion annually, is to continue to grow, then the current restraints on the foundations' cross-border activities, amply illustrated by the *Stauffer*[91] and *Persche*[92] cases, will clearly have to be removed. A European Statute, as has been said, "would enable simpler management, more efficient administration, and increased mobility and responsiveness, while facilitating the pooling of expertise and resources

[87] Citing Kramer, M. and Cooch, S., *Investing for Impact*, Foundation Strategy Group, Boston, 2006. See Center for Social Philanthropy, Boston, MA at: http://socialphilanthropy.org/knowledge.php.

[88] See Community Philanthropy Initiative, *Community Philanthropy Watch* research results 2007, further at: http://www.efc.be/NewsKnowledge/Pages/CommunityPhilanthropy/CPIResearch.aspx.

[89] See European Commission press release "Towards a Single Market Act—For a Highly Competitive Social Market Economy" released on October 27, 2010.

[90] Details of the European Foundation Statute are available on its dedicated webpage, http://www.efc.be/EuropeanFoundationStatute.

[91] [2006] ECJ C-386/04.

[92] [2008] ECJ C-318/07.

in those areas that require increased scaling-up of funds and help Europe to meet global challenges."[93]

B. Social Enterprises and Other Innovative Developments

Since the 1990s, European nonprofit cooperatives or associations have been steadily increasing their use of social enterprises with support from the Enterprise Directorate-General of the European Commission. The governments of Member States have also been active, and a number have introduced laws and specific legal structures (such as the CIC in the U.K.), which, as the Commission has explained, aim to "encourage the entrepreneurial and commercial provision of social and welfare services and to increase the participation of women in labor markets, whilst involving various stakeholders (workers, voluntary workers, target groups, and municipalities) in the production process."[94] Much of the accompanying government policy and funding has been somewhat narrowly focused, tending to be concentrated on promoting and supporting enterprises directed toward assisting the unemployed into employment or on providing social care services.

As noted by Kerlin, "social enterprise in Europe is viewed as belonging to the 'social economy' where social benefit is the main driving force. Indeed, main organizations in the social economy include cooperatives, mutual organizations, associations, and foundations."[95] She is undoubtedly right to comment that "the kinds of services supported by social enterprise are fewer in Europe (when compared to the wide range supported by social enterprise activity in the United States) because European social enterprises tended to address those particular areas the welfare state had retreated from or had not been able to meet demand for (i.e., employment programs for the long-termed unemployed, personal social services, etc.)."[96]

European social enterprises are also distinctive in terms of governance and legal form. As Young and Salamon observe, "in Europe, the notion of social enterprise focuses more heavily on the way an organization is governed and what its purpose is rather than on whether it strictly adheres to the nondistribution constraint of a formal

[93] See joint statement from the European Foundation Centre (EFC) and the Donors and Foundations' Networks in Europe (DAFNE), Brussels, March 10, 2011.

[94] Commission of the European Communities, "Co-operatives in Enterprise Europe," a consultation paper, 2001, at p. 25. Also note the EMES (Emergence of Social Enterprise in Europe) publications. This organization, launched in 1996, is funded by the European Commission to conduct research on social enterprise in EU countries.

[95] See Kerlin, J. A., "Social Enterprise in the United States and Europe: Understanding and Learning from the Differences," *Voluntas*, Vol. 17, 2006, at pp. 247–63.

[96] Kerlin, "Social Enterprise in the United States and Europe," at p.253.

nonprofit organization,"[97] whereas Kerlin argues that in continental Europe, "social enterprise has generally come to mean a social cooperative or association formed to provide employment or specific care services in a participatory framework."[98] Indeed, multi-stakeholder cooperatives, as a distinct form of cooperative, are becoming increasingly popular in Europe.

1. Venture Philanthropy

The European Venture Philanthropy Association (EVPA) defines venture philanthropy as a "field of philanthropic activity where private equity/venture capital models are applied in the nonprofit and charitable sectors." As has been pointed out:[99]

> Venture philanthropy in Europe has strong links to the private equity and venture capital community, giving it opportunities to influence the corporate social responsibility of a set of major players in Europe's financial services industry. Several new venture philanthropy funds have been established by philanthropists with successful careers in private equity. Europe's transitional countries, in Central and Eastern Europe, the Baltic States and former Soviet Union, have under-capacitated social sectors and widespread, unmet social needs. Venture philanthropy may have a particularly valuable role to play in helping build stronger civil society institutions in these countries.

Europeans began taking an interest in venture philanthropy around 2000. The Impetus Trust, launched in the U.K. in 2002, was the first fund to overtly describe itself as a venture philanthropy organization and was greatly influenced by U.S. models. In 2003, EVPA was founded; it opened to membership in 2005 and now boasts some 124 organizations as members across 20 countries.[100] Although venture philanthropy in Europe is becoming increasingly popular, to-date in many European countries there are still only a few venture philanthropy organizations, and these are small compared to the more traditional charitable foundations.

2. Donor Incentives

Crucial to encouraging private philanthropy to support public benefit activity are tax incentives to individuals and corporations donating to public benefit

[97] Young, D., & Salamon, L., "Commercialization, Social Ventures, and For-Profit Competition," in Salamon, L. (ed.), *The State of Nonprofit America*, Brookings Institution Press, Washington, DC, 2002, at p. 433.

[98] Kerlin, *Voluntas*, at p. 250.

[99] John, R., *Venture Philanthropy: The Evolution of High Engagement Philanthropy in Europe*, Skoll Centre for Social Entrepreneurship, Saïd Business School, Oxford University, 2006, at p. 5.

[100] In 2003, five private equity professionals came together to found the European Venture Philanthropy Association (EVPA). It comprises a network of venture philanthropy funds aiming "to create a new market for philanthropy in Europe."

organizations.[101] Such tax incentives may take the form of tax credits, or more typically, tax deductions: Several countries in Central and Eastern Europe, including Slovakia, allow taxpayers to allocate 1 or 2 percent of their payable income tax to a charitable organization. Almost invariably, donor incentives are linked to either the public benefit status of the recipient or to enumerated public benefit activities in which the recipient is engaged. For example, Hungary, France, and Germany allow only public benefit organizations to receive tax-deductible donations. In France, only general interest associations, public utility associations, and public utility foundations are entitled to receive tax-deductible donations. In Germany, only certain public benefit organizations—those pursuing general public benefit purposes, benevolent or church-related purposes, or especially support-worthy general purposes—may receive tax-deductible contributions.

VI. NONPROFITS, TRADING, AND CONTEMPORARY CASE LAW

Although a considerable amount of the ever-growing body of ECJ case law has a bearing on nonprofits as much as on any other European entity engaged in economic activity, very little of its caseload is instigated by nonprofits, the outcomes are seldom nonprofit-specific, and only a fraction touches on the trading activities of charities.

A. Legal Framework

The EC Treaty, ancillary EU directives, and a rapidly expanding body of ECJ case law now form a broad legal framework for the activities of Europe's nonprofits. In addition, each Member State, to a greater or lesser extent, has its own sector supervisory regime in which nonprofits are subject to the rules and regulations of their respective organizing bodies (health care, education, etc.). Since the 1990s, the legal framework for nonprofits in central and eastern Europe has undergone dramatic change[102] from a position where that framework was either incomplete, out-of-date, or unduly burdensome, to one where, as Lester Salamon and Helmut Anheier noted in 1999, "in many ways, the new legal frameworks emerging in the region appear to be superior to those in the West, which developed in a far more haphazard fashion."[103]

[101] See Moore, D., Hadzi-Miceva, K., and Bullain, N., "A Comparative Overview of Public Benefit Status in Europe," in *The International Journal of Not-for-Profit Law*, Vol. 11, No. 1, November 2008. See further at: http://www.icnl.org/research/journal/.

[102] See Rutzen et al., "The Legal Framework for Not-for-Profit Organizations in Central and Eastern Europe."

[103] See Salamon, L., Anheier, H., and Assoc., "Civil Society in Comparative Perspective," in *Global Civil Society: Dimensions of the Nonprofit Sector*, The Johns Hopkins Center for Civil Society Studies, Baltimore, 1999, at p. 34.

1. Regulatory Bodies

There is no tradition of nonprofit-specific, or charity-specific, state regulatory control in continental Europe, although a form of general public control is exercised by bodies such as the French Cour des Comptes, or the Spanish patrocinado. In some countries,[104] the authority to determine whether an entity should have public benefit status and qualify for tax exemption is vested in the tax authorities (e.g., Germany). In other countries, the courts (e.g., Hungary) or a governmental entity, such as the Ministry of Justice, confers public benefit status (e.g., Bulgaria). Others have empowered independent commissions to decide the question (e.g., Moldova). In some countries, a state body grants the status, based on a recommendation of an independent commission (e.g., Poland, Latvia). In Estonia, the status is approved by the Government of the Republic after obtaining a recommendation from a Committee of Experts. In Greece and Hungary it falls to the courts to certify or recognize public benefit organizations. In France, the Conseil d'État has authority to decide whether associations and foundations qualify for "public utility" status. Further, as Hopt points out, "enforcement by the founder or donor is limited and by the beneficiaries is nonexistent."[105] Such supervision as exists is undertaken by national tax authorities as an incidental aspect of raising taxes, which is the case in Denmark, Finland, Germany, Greece, the Netherlands, Portugal, and Sweden.

2. Activities Test

Article 13(A)(1)(m) of the EC Sixth VAT Directive[106] indicates that the categorization of an organization as nonprofit-making must be based on all of the organization's activities. Any other interpretation would imply that commercial undertakings, normally acting with a view to profit, could, in principle, request a VAT exemption when exceptionally providing nonprofit-making services.[107] In the *Kennemer Golf Club*[108] case, the ECJ ruled that Article 13(A)(1)(m) and 13A(2)(a)[109] of the

[104] See Moore, Hadzi-Miceva, and Bullain, N., "A Comparative Overview of Public Benefit Status in Europe"; see further at: www.icnl.org/research/journal/vol11iss1/vol11iss1.pdf.

[105] Hopt, "The Board of Nonprofit Organizations," at p. 561.

[106] The Sixth VAT Directive providing a uniform basis of assessment for liability to value added tax was issued in 1977. On January 1, 2007, Directive 2006/112/EC was issued to consolidate all the amendments made to the Sixth VAT Directive. See further at Sixth VAT Directive: Uniform Basis for Assessment, http://europa.eu/legislation_summaries/other/l31006_en.htm.

[107] See European Court of Justice: Case C-174/00; Kennemer Golf & Country Club v. Staatssecretaris van Financiën, March 21, 2002.

[108] Kennemer Golf & Country Club v. Staatssecretaris van Financiën, March 21, 2002.

[109] Article 13(A)(2)(a) of the 6th VAT Directive, since redrafted into Article 133 of the Principal VAT Directive 2006/112/EC, allows exemption for the supply of certain cultural services, and the supply of goods closely linked thereto, by bodies governed by public law or by other cultural bodies recognized by the Member State concerned.

Directive must be interpreted as meaning that an organization may be categorized as nonprofit-making even if it systematically seeks to achieve surpluses that it then uses for the purposes of the provision of its services.

B. Charitable Trading, the Law, and Tax

Nonprofit economic activity is an established practice in Europe where "the trend is to allow NPOs to engage in a broad range of income-generating activities, treating economic activities as a tax issue and not as an NPO status issue."[110] An entity engages in economic activity when it indulges in "any activity consisting in offering goods and services on a given market"[111] and the nonprofit-making nature of the organization is irrelevant for the purpose of qualifying as an undertaking.[112] Income from economic activity related to a statutorily defined public benefit purpose is tax exempt, whereas income from unrelated EA is taxed on the same basis as the income of businesses. The ECJ considers that "in the context of Community competition law the concept of an undertaking covers any entity engaged in any economic activity, regardless of the legal status of the entity or the way in which it is financed."[113]

1. Economic Activity

Under Article 2(1) of the Sixth VAT Directive, every purchase of goods or services within the territory of a Member State by a taxable person acting as such is subject to VAT. Article 4(1) of the Directive defines a taxable person to be "any person who independently carries out any economic activity." As Kleis and Nicolaides point out, the decisive factor is engagement in an "economic activity" and "it is irrelevant that it may concern a private or public[114] entity, a nonprofit or for-profit entity or even only one individual who is engaged in the activity in question."[115] Under Article 4(2) of the Directive, the term "economic activity" is held to include all the activities of producers, traders, and persons supplying services, and also the exploitation of tangible or intangible property for the purpose of obtaining income

[110] See Rutzen et al. "The Legal Framework for Not-for-Profit Organizations in Central and Eastern Europe."

[111] See European Court of Justice: Case C-180/98 to C-184/98—Pavel Pavlov and Others v. Stichting Pensioenfonds Medische Specialisten, para.75 with reference to cases Commission v. Italy C-118/85 and Commission v. Italy C-35/96.

[112] See European Court of Justice: Case C-244/94, at p. 21; and Case C-355/01, at p. 25.

[113] See European Court of Justice: Case C-180/98 to C-184/98—Pavel Pavlov and Others v. Stichting Pensioenfonds Medische Specialisten, para.108. See also European Court of Justice, Case C-41/90, Klaus Hofner, at para. 21.

[114] Citing Commission v. Italy (Case C-118/85, [1987] ECR, 1-02599, para.7), where the ECJ held that the state can also engage in economic activities.

[115] See Kleis, M. and Nicolaides, P., "The Concept of Undertaking in Education and Public Health Systems," European Institute of Public Administration, Maastricht, The Netherlands, June 9, 2006.

from the property on a continuing basis. Article 4(5) and Article 13(A)(1)(i) of the Directive provide exemptions in favor, respectively, of states, regional and local government authorities, and other bodies governed by public law (in respect of activities or transactions in which they engage as public authorities); and of children's or young people's education, school, or university education, and vocational training or retraining, including the supply of closely related services and goods, provided by bodies governed by public law.

The need and opportunities for charitable organizations to engage in such economic activity are much the same in continental Europe as in the common law nations; indeed as Hopt and Hippel point out "a regulatory problem in its own right is the *economic activities of nonprofit organizations and foundations*."[116] As they go on to observe, "practice and legal reactions differ considerably in the various countries. In Sweden and Denmark one can find especially interesting examples of well-run 'commercial foundations.'"[117] In Scandanavian countries generally, foundations are free to establish tax-exempt for-profit businesses.[118] In Germany, a foundation is free to engage in commercial activity but a nonprofit association is prohibited from having as its purpose "the object of commercial business":[119] A German foundation will lose its tax-exempt status if it allows unrelated business activity to become dominant, as the tax law recognizes a need to protect "charitable identity."[120]

The ECJ ruling in *Humber and Edel*[121] would seem to have made an important distinction between non-remunerative public benefit service provision (in this case, the education system as delivered by the state) and "economic activity," exclusion from the latter definition being attributed partly to the fact that performance is in accordance with a statutory duty but also to the absence of any intent to "engage in gainful activity." The second component is clearly one with general applicability to the sector: Where a nonprofit is engaged in mission-related, public benefit provision on a non-gainful basis then it would seem to be safely within the rule; the corollary being that where it is in fact overtly trading to generate profit, through any commercially expedient venture, then (as with the UBIT regime in the United States) it probably is not.

[116] Hopt and Von Hippel (eds), *Comparative Corporate Governance of Non-Profit Organizations*, at pp. xlii–xliii.

[117] Hopt and Von Hippel (eds), *Comparative Corporate Governance of Non-Profit Organizations*, at pp. xlii–xliii.

[118] See Hemstrom, C., "Nonprofit Organizations and Economic Activities/Enterprises," in Hopt and Von Hippel, (eds), *Comparative Corporate Governance of Non-Profit Organizations*, 740–770.

[119] See German Civil Code, s.21, dealing with noncommercial associations.

[120] Note, tax exemption is not based on the Civil Code but on articles 51 and further of the Abgabenordnung. German charities must exclusively (*ausschlie-lich*) and directly (*unmittelbar*) pursue favored goals. The author gratefully acknowledges the advice of Mariani, E., on this matter.

[121] See European Court of Justice, Case C-263/86, at para. 18.

2. Related Business

The ruling in the above *Humber and Edel* case would seem to indicate that where a nonprofit is trading to generate profit in an area directly related to its public benefit mission, it will not be jeopardizing its tax-exempt status.

3. Constraints on Nonprofit Trading

The EC Treaty, designed primarily to promote freedom of trade within EC borders, provides the governing legal framework within which nonprofits have had to seek authority for cross-border trading activity. Article 43 of the Treaty guarantees the freedom of establishment. Articles 39 and 48 guarantee freedom of movement and freedom from establishment, whereas Article 12 guarantees freedom from discrimination. However, although statute law eventually introduced tailor-made incorporated vehicles—the European Company (Societas Europaea) and the European Private Company (Societas Privata Europaea)—to facilitate pan-European for-profit trade, there was no equivalent in the nonprofit sector. It was inevitable that the lack of any European legal vehicle or mechanism, allowing nonprofits reciprocal recognition when their activities transcended their country of origin, would present problems in an EC context premised on the free movement of people and goods between Member States. In due course, cases illustrative of these constraints were brought before the ECJ.

The first such case was *Centro di Musicologia Walter Stauffer v. Finanzamt München fürKörperschaften,*[122] which concerned a tax-exempt Italian charitable foundation that received rental income from property in Germany. The German authorities sought to impose German tax on the rental income. Had the charity been established in Germany rather than in Italy, it would have been exempt from the tax under German law. The case was brought on the questions of freedom of establishment and of movement of capital.

The ECJ held that freedom of establishment was not relevant because the investment property in Germany was not actively managed by the Italian charity. The issue that remained, therefore, was whether the domestic law constituted an obstacle to the free movement of capital and, if so, whether a restriction could be justified under Article 58(1)(a). This article states that:

> The provisions of Article 56 shall be without prejudice to the right of Member States to apply the relevant provisions of their tax law which distinguish between taxpayers who are not in the same situation with regard to their place of residence or with regard to the place where their capital is invested.

The court determined that this derogation must be strictly interpreted. The application of Article 58 "must concern situations which are not objectively comparable

[122] (C386/04).

or to be justified by overriding reasons in the general interest." The court then held that in this particular case, there were no reasons for derogating because the objects of the Stauffer foundation would have been recognized as charitable in Germany had it been established there. Following this decision, the Commission issued a press release[123] formally requesting that several named jurisdictions end their discrimination against foreign charities,[124] on the basis that allowing tax relief for gifts to charities, but only if they are established within the jurisdiction, is discriminatory in respect of charities in other Member States that are excluded from the relief and contrary to the EC Treaty. "The rules of the Internal Market forbid discrimination of charities in other Member States," asserted EU Taxation and Customs Commissioner László Kovács. "Gifts to bona fide charities in other Member States should get the same tax treatment as gifts made to domestic charities." This decision held that discriminatory German tax law breached the EC Treaty, thereby providing a precedent for infringement procedures to be taken against other EU countries with discriminatory tax laws. It could also have a favorable impact on inheritance or gift taxes on cross-border giving to charities located in other Member States as these are explicitly defined as capital movements in Annex I of the Council Directive 88/361/EEC, of June 24, 1988.

The second case, *Hein Persche v. Finanzamt Ludenscheid*,[125] concerned a German tax advisor, Mr. Persche, and the deductibility for German tax purposes of a gift he had made to a retirement home and children's center in Portugal after the German tax authorities refused to grant him a tax deduction as the recipient was not a German charity. According to the applicable German income tax law, cash gifts as well as gifts in-kind can be tax deductible if the recipient has philanthropic aims, but only if the chosen organization operates on German soil under the appropriate German company law. The matter eventually came before the European Union's Advocate General Mengozzi. Apart from Mr. Persche's concerns, he focused on whether a gift by a German national to a charitable organization in another Member State, namely, Portugal, was covered by the European Convention's Article 56, which espoused the free movement of capital between Member States.

With the backing of the European Free Trade association, the ECJ decided that gifts in-kind effected through an exchange of current consumer goods did constitute a movement of capital between Member States. Therefore, such capital movement must not be constrained.

Next, the Advocate General's attention turned to Article 58 of the EC, which seeks to ensure that the various national taxation measures do not impede this freedom of capital movement within the European Union through discriminatory operation against charities resident in other Member States. It was concluded that Germany's taxation law did constitute such an impediment. Despite all Member

[123] Reference: IP/06/964, (July 10, 2006).

[124] The request being in the form of a "reasoned opinion" under Article 226 of the EC Treaty.

[125] [2008] ECJ C318/07. This account is taken from a case note prepared at QUT; see further at https://wiki.qut.edu.au/display/CPnS/Hein+Persche+v+Finanzamt+Ludenscheid.

States' legislative commitment to supporting philanthropy, a charitable gift made in Portugal by a German citizen was being treated differently by the German taxation authority than a similar one given in his homeland. Persche's gift in-kind was considered to be a movement in capital, which could be tax deductible in a fellow Member State.

The European Court of Justice, following the opinion of the Advocate General, held that:

1. Donations by individuals resident in one Member State to organizations based in and recognised as charitable by another Member State concern a movement of capital within the meaning of Article 56 of the EC Treaty;
2. For Member States (such as the UK and Ireland) which give tax reliefs on donations to organizations recognised as charitable and located in their own Member State, it is contrary to Articles 56 and 58(3) not to allow a taxpayer the opportunity to prove that charitable organizations based in other Member States also fulfil the requirements for tax relief; and
3. Fiscal authorities should not have to liaise directly with the authorities in the recipient body's Member State to determine whether the criteria for relief exist and may put the burden of proving that a deduction should be given onto the donor taxpayer.

More recently, the ECJ again considered the issue of tax discrimination in *Missionswerk Werner Heukelbach v. Belgium*,[126] which concerned Missionswerk, a registered charity in Germany. In 2004, a Belgian resident died and nominated Missionswerk as her residuary legatee. The charity duly filed a "succession statement" with the Belgian authority responsible for inheritance (more properly, succession) taxes. The tax authority imposed an 80 percent marginal rate on the legacy, and demanded a total of €60,000. Missionswerk then formally applied to have the duty reduced from 80 percent to the 7 percent to which charitable and other nonprofit organizations are entitled under the Belgian Tax Code. The Belgian tax authority refused, citing Article 60(1) of the Code, which limits the 7 percent concession to bodies that are based either in Belgium or in the deceased's country of domicile, stating that there was insufficient evidence that the deceased had resided or worked in Germany. Missionswerk challenged this ruling through various courts, maintaining that the Belgian code discriminates against European charities and individuals merely on the fact of their country of residence. Ultimately the ECJ found against Belgium, ruling that Belgium's legislation impedes the free movement of capital between EU states and thus violates Article 45 of the EU Treaty.

The implications arising from these decisions are of profound significance for the future of all pan-European trading nonprofits in the 27 constituent jurisdictions. The offending discriminatory approach embodied in the interpretation of

[126] (2011 EUECJ C-25/10).

"establishment" will have to be addressed. The compatibility of the legal structures for charity in all these jurisdictions will also require attention.

C. Nonprofit Trading: The Case Law in a Public Services Context

The ECJ defined an "undertaking" in the *Klaus Hofner* case[127] as "every entity engaged in an economic activity, regardless of the legal status of the entity and the way in which it is financed," and this definition has proved to be seminal in terms of demarcating between state public service provision and for-profit entities. This was reaffirmed in *Poucet and Pistre*,[128] when the ECJ ruled that organizations involved in the management of the public social security system—which fulfills an exclusively social function, performs an activity based on the principle of national solidarity, and is entirely nonprofit-making—are not "undertakings" within the competition rules of the EC Treaty; indeed, in a number of cases, the ECJ can be seen to be interpreting "undertaking" in an expansive sense.[129] As Kleis and Nicolaides comment:[130]

> The case law as well as the Commission decisions demonstrates that entities which operate within the public and education and public health system are normally not considered to be undertakings. Nevertheless, a Member State can create a market for activities which traditionally fall within the boundaries of these systems thereby transforming them into 'economic' activities.

Much the same type of public benefit services has generated nonprofit and for-profit activity across continental Europe: core provision being in the areas of training for employment, care facilities for the elderly, disabled, and children.

1. Education

In the *Humber and Edel* case,[131] the ECJ determined that in providing a public education, the state is "not seeking to engage in gainful activity" but rather is merely giving

[127] See European Court of Justice, Case C-41/90, at para. 21.

[128] February 17, 93, Joined Cases C-159/91 and C-160/91.

[129] See C-41/90—Höfner and Elser; Joined Cases C-159/91 and C-160/91- Poucet and Pistre; C-244/94 - Federation Francaise des Soietes d' Assurance; C-67/96—Albany International BV v. Stichting Bedrijfspensioenfonds Textielindustrie; Joined Cases C-115/97, C-116/97 and C-117/97—Brentjens' Handelsonderneming BV v. Stichting Bedrijfspensioenfonds voor de Handel in Bouwmaterialen; and C-219/97—BV Maatschappij Drijvende Bokken v. Stichting Pensioenfonds voor de Vervoer- en Havenbedrijven.

[130] See Kleis and Nicolaides, , "The Concept of Undertaking in Education and Public Health Systems," at p. 7.

[131] See European Court of Justice, Case C-263/86, at para. 18.

effect to its statutory public benefit duties. The Commission's[132] subsequent decision to construe state aid to universities enabling them to establish online teaching facilities as not being within the definition of "economic activity" would seem wholly congruent with the ECJ view. Again, when the Commission took the view that state subsidies to private R&D contractors were analogous to those given to a public body—because of factors such as the particular status of the organizations concerned, their public benefit obligations and the absence of any private special interests—this would also conform to established governing principles.[133] However, the corollary also holds true: Where the research establishments or private schools are not analogous to a public body by being for-profit entities in status and purpose, offering an alternative to an available public service, then this would fall within the definition and normal tax rules would apply. For example, in *Commission of the European Communities v. Federal Republic of Germany*,[134] the Commission found that the research activities contracted out by German universities to private companies were subject to VAT and that the German exemption for such activities was incompatible with Article 2 of the Sixth VAT Directive. The ECJ held that Article 2 defines the activities subject to VAT[135] and that only the activities referred to in Article 13 of the Directive may be exempt. In respect of the interpretation of an exemption, the ECJ referred to earlier case law in which it was decided that the terms used to specify the exemptions referred to in Article 13(A) of the Directive must be interpreted strictly.[136] The ECJ indicated that Article 13(A)(1)(i) of the Directive does not make any reference to the research activities of state universities, and that this exemption covers only the supply of goods and services necessary for education, such as teaching materials. The fact that research activities for the benefit of private persons may be of assistance to education is not sufficient to establish the existence of a sufficiently close legal relationship between education and the activities concerned. Access to university education is not hindered by increased costs resulting from the fact that the closely related supply of goods and services is subject to VAT: The fact that research is subject to VAT does not increase the costs of education.

2. Health and Social Care Provision

The *Poucet and Pistre*[137] case is a long-standing landmark in the law relating to the commercial activities of European nonprofits. Its importance is not only in its establishing

[132] Commission Decision of January 15, 2002, NN 152/2001, Netherlands—Digitale Universiteit.

[133] See Commission Decision of February 19, 2003, NN 76/02 Denmark—Contract Research and Technology Organizations.

[134] Case C-287/00, June 12, 2002.

[135] Citing Commission v. Italy, C-203/87.

[136] Citing Stichting Uitvoering Financiële Acties, C-348/87 and Institute of the Motor Industry, C-149/97 and D., C-384/98. However, see the new Community Framework relating to state aid for research and development.

[137] February 17, 1993, Joined Cases C-159/91 and C-160/91.

that a nonprofit may nonetheless be operating as a commercial entity, but also that it may in fact be operating a mix of for-profit and nonprofit activities and thereby incurring a differentiated tax liability. The case concerned a nonprofit organization that managed an optional old-age insurance scheme intended to supplement a basic compulsory scheme, and operated it in accordance with the normal principles; rules of capitalization; and conditions relating to membership, contributions, and benefits. The court concluded that this was an "undertaking" for the purposes of Article 85 et seq. of the Treaty, as the nonprofit was carrying on an economic activity in competition with life assurance companies, and explained:

> the mere fact that (it) is a non-profit-making body does not deprive the activity which it carries on of its economic character, since...that activity may give rise to conduct which the competition rules are intended to penalize.

However, the *Bettercare II*[138] case, which involved the conduct of a local authority in Northern Ireland that procured nursing home places from private companies while also providing some places itself, raised some fundamental questions that still await answers. The case was initially heard and settled, under fair trade legislation, in favor of the local authority. BetterCare appealed on the grounds that the ECJ defines the purchasing of care as an economic activity, and the UK Commission was obliged to follow the ECJ ruling. The appellants had alleged that the authority was abusing its dominant market position by setting the service cost too low, and this constituted a violation of the competition rules. The authority responded by claiming that the competition rules did not apply, as the provision of social services was not an economic activity. In a decision that poses a challenge to the U.K. government's "contracting out" policy, the Competition (Commission) Appeal Tribunal found that the local authority was acting as an undertaking in purchasing care, and that when it contracted out the care services it was engaging in "economic activity"—and this was also the case when a local authority forms partnerships with the private sector. The tribunal rejected earlier theories by the Office of Fair Trade, the relevant competition authority whose decision was being appealed, which amounted to splitting the activities in question between "economic activities" and "non economic activities" on the basis of a distinction between provision and purchasing, or according to the source of funding used by each resident. It has been claimed that this decision is of fundamental importance for government's policy of contracting out public benefit services:[139]

> Firstly, it challenges the whole rationale of government policy, which is that contracting and commissioning will encourage the NHS and local authorities to use

[138] See BetterCare Group Limited v. Director General of Fair Trading. Competition Appeal Tribunal: case no. 1006/2/1/01; neutral citation, [2002] CAT 7.

[139] See Pollock, A.M., "The BetterCare Judgment: A Challenge to Health Care; European Competition Law May Cover Publicly Funded, Privately Provided Care," *British Medical Journal*, London, February 2003.

> their purchasing power as bulk buyers to drive down prices... Secondly, the ruling puts in question policy statements by the government on user charges in the NHS. The government maintains that it does not matter who provides the services so long as they are publicly funded. The appeal tribunal's ruling opens the way for a legal challenge to a public pricing policy that could force the trust to pay higher prices for nursing home care if it were found to be abusing its dominant position as a purchaser... Thirdly, the tribunal's decision has relevance for the planned expansion of acute care purchasing by primary care trusts. It gives commercial hospitals and foreign investors a mechanism for challenging the prices paid for secondary and tertiary inpatient care.

Subsequently, in the *Fenin*[140] case, the Court of First Instance upheld a decision by the European Commission to reject a complaint alleging abuse of a dominant position by 26 bodies or organizations (including three ministries of the Spanish government) responsible for the Spanish national health system. In determining whether an activity could be construed as the act of an undertaking, the court examined the purpose of that activity, specifically whether it was connected with offering goods or services in a market (as opposed to, in this case, implementing a health care "solidarity" scheme). The Commission rejected the complaint on the grounds that these bodies were not acting as undertakings in their dealings with suppliers, and were not therefore subject to the Article 82 prohibition irrespective of the existence or otherwise of competitive constraints and anticompetitive effects of their conduct. The complainants appealed to the ECJ, which dismissed the appeal[141] and confirmed that a purchasing activity is only subject to competition law if it is undertaken for an economic purpose, such as a supply of goods or services on a market, rather than for a purely social purpose. The ECJ accepted the Commission's argument put concisely at paragraph 24 of the ECJ judgment that "[it is] the act of placing goods or services on a given market which characterises the concept of economic activity and not purchasing activity as such."

In the *Smits/Stitchting Ziekenfonds*[142] case, the court rejected the argument that hospital services could not constitute economic activities, and pointed out that medical services are covered by Article 60 of the Treaty: There was no difference "between care provided in a hospital environment and care provided outside such

[140] Federación Nacional de Empresas de Instrumentación Científica, Médica, Técnica y Dental (FENIN) v. Commission of the European Communities. See European Court of Justice, Case C-205/03.

[141] On July 11, 2006, the European Court of Justice (ECJ) dismissed an appeal by FENIN against a judgment of the court of first instance, which held that Article 82 of the EC Treaty did not apply to the purchasing activities of the organizations in charge of the Spanish health system on the basis that they were not acting as undertakings for the purposes of competition law. The ECJ held that the appeal was partly inadmissible and partly unfounded.

[142] See European Court of Justice, Case C-157/99, Smits and Others. See also European Court of Justice, Case C-475/99, Ambulanz Glockner.

an environment."[143] Also, in the *Henning Veedfald*[144] case, the court held that "the fact that products are manufactured for a specific medical service for which the patient does not pay directly but (is) financed from public funds maintained out of taxpayers' contributions cannot detract from the economic and business character of that manufacture."

3. Occupational Pension Funds

Pension funds play an important role in meeting the costs of national public benefit service provision. Increasingly, they are being viewed by governments as an essential part of the costing infrastructure that maintains a nation's health and social care services: a resource that in social function terms has become more public than private.

In several cases, the ECJ has addressed issues relating to pension funds in the context of the competition articles of the Treaty.[145] Of central importance has been the implications arising from a public authority decision to grant a pension fund the exclusive right to manage a supplementary pension scheme for the membership (compulsorily required by the public authority) of a professional body. This was at issue in the *Pavel Pavlov*[146] case where, in preliminary findings, the ECJ found that the Fund in question: was carrying out an economic activity because it managed contributions, benefits, and functions on the basis of capitalization and was therefore an undertaking within the meaning of the competition articles of the Treaty; should be regarded as "contributing to the management of the public social security service";[147] was non-profit-making, as the profits were being distributed to pensioners and affiliated members alike by increasing their pension entitlements; continued to be generally supervised by the public authorities; and was operated on the basis of the principle of solidarity, which was evident from the grant of retroactive pension rights to members already practicing when the scheme came into effect and the

[143] Smits/Stitchting Ziekenfonds. See European Court of Justice, Case C-157/99, Smits and Others at paras. 52–53.

[144] See European Court of Justice, Case C-203/99, Veedfald.

[145] See European Court of Justice, Case C-67/96—Albany International BV v. Stichting Bedrijfspensioenfonds Textielindustrie; Joined Cases C-115/97, C-116/97 and C-117/97—Brentjens' Handelsonderneming BV v. Stichting Bedrijfspensioenfonds voor de Handel in Bouwmaterialen; and C-219/97—BV Maatschappij Drijvende Bokken v. Stichting Pensioenfonds voor de Vervoer- en Havenbedrijven.

[146] See European Court of Justice, Case C-180/98 to C-184/98, Pavel Pavlov and Others v. Stichting Pensioenfonds Medische Specialisten.

[147] As testimony to the important role it played in that service, the Netherlands government was quoted as explaining:

> As in the case of a sectoral pension fund, an occupational pension fund will not be set up as a commercial venture but as an institution with a social purpose which will work in the best way possible for its members in their reciprocal social relations.

index-linking of pension payments so as to maintain their value, etc. The *Albany*[148] case included the same three elements—social function, nonprofit-making character, and the principle of solidarity—but there, the management of a supplementary pension scheme was established by a collective agreement (not by the profession's representative body as in *Pavel Pavlov*) concluded between organizations representing employers and workers in a given sector. In three cases, *Albany, Brentjen's,*[149] and *Drijvende Bokken*[150], the ECJ ruled that the decision of an organization representing employers and workers to establish a sectoral pension fund, and their request to the public authorities to make membership of that fund compulsory, was not contrary to Article 85 of the Treaty.[151] The Court took the view that: the decision by members of a profession to establish a pension fund entrusted with the management of a supplementary pension scheme did not appreciably restrict competition within the common market, and that Articles 5 and 85 of the EC Treaty were not infringed when public authorities made compulsory the affiliation to a professional pension fund at the request of a representative professional organization.

Further, the ECJ ruled in *Pavel Pavlov* that despite the compulsory requirement to become a member of the professional body, coupled with the exclusive rights granted to the Fund by the public authorities, which together placed the Fund in a dominant position in the market (indeed, allowing it to exercise a legal monopoly in that sector), the Fund could not be said to be in breach of Articles 90(1) and 86 (now Articles 86 and 82) of the EC Treaty.[152] This resonates with its finding in *Höfner and Elser*[153] that the creation of a dominant position by the granting of an exclusive right does not itself infringe Article 86; infringement can only occur where the undertaking cannot avoid abusing its dominant position and where "the undertaking in question is manifestly not in position to satisfy the demand prevailing in the market for the activities of that kind."[154] Articles 86 and 90 of the EC Treaty do not preclude the public authorities from granting to a pension fund the exclusive right to manage a supplementary pension scheme for the members of a profession.

[148] See European Court of Justice, Case C-67/96, Albany International BV v. Stichting Bedrijfspensioenfonds Textielindustrie.

[149] See, European Court of Justice, joined cases C-115/97, C-116/97 and C-117/97—Brentjens' Handelsonderneming BV v. Stichting Bedrijfspensioenfonds voor de Handel in Bouwmaterialen.

[150] See European Court of Justice, Case C-219/97, BV Maatschappij Drijvende Bokken v. Stichting Pensioenfonds voor de Vervoer- en Havenbedrijven.

[151] Article 81, para.1 (ex Article 85) prohibits all agreements between undertakings, decisions by associations of undertakings, and concerted practices that may affect trade between Member States and that have as their object or effect the prevention, restriction, or distortion of competition within the common market.

[152] Article 90(1) refers to undertakings that enjoy exclusive rights by the Member States and provides that in case of such undertakings the Member States shall neither enact nor maintain in force any measure contrary to the competition rules of the Treaty.

[153] See European Court of Justice, Case C-41/90—Höfner and Elser.

[154] European Court of Justice, Case C-41/90—Höfner and Elser, at para. 31.

More recently, in the *Hans Oymanns*[155] case, the ECJ can be seen again to hold resolutely to the consistent approach followed in the aforementioned cases. In *Hans Oymanns*, the ECJ ruled that German statutory sickness insurance funds are "bodies governed by public law," as they meet general interest needs relating to public health; are financed mostly by members' compulsory contributions, plus some direct funding from federal authorities; have their members' contributions fixed by German law and approved by a supervisory public body; and have funds that are nonprofit-making as contributions must match expenditures.

Whether social policy is shaping the law, or vice versa, it would seem that these cases disclose an important recognition that an area of commerce is becoming integral to government public benefit provision. For that reason, it would seem, pension funds are to be excused from the constraints that normally apply to ensure an open, competitive marketplace. The ECJ would seem to be indicating that the "level playing field" principle does not necessarily apply in such circumstances.

D. Charitable Trading: The Case Law in a Commercial Context

Although there is naturally a great deal of ECJ case law on issues relating to trading within the EU, much of which is also relevant to nonprofits, very few of these cases are nonprofit-specific.

1. Shareholding as Economic Activity

In *Wellcome Trust Ltd. v. Commissioners of Customs and Excise,*[156] the U.K.'s biggest charity raised £2 billion from the sale of shares in order to diversify its investments, and then sought to recoup the tax paid. The ECJ ruled that Wellcome was not so entitled because the mere exercise of rights of ownership could not by itself be regarded as constituting "economic activity" within Article 4(2) of the Sixth Council Directive on VAT. But, in early 2006, the European Court ruled that substantial shareholding in companies by foundations could be seen as economic activity, and therefore tax breaks received by these foundations could be regarded as unlawful "state aid" in terms of the EC Treaty.

2. Trading and Fundamental Human Rights

In the recent case of *Association Belge des Consommateurs Test-Achats ASBL and others,*[157] the ECJ declared Article 5(2) of the Gender Directive[158] to be invalid as it had to be assessed in the light of the fundamental rights guaranteed by the European

155 See European Court of Justice, Case C-300/07, Hans Oymanns.
156 [1996] STC 945 (ECJ).
157 Case C-236/09.
158 2004/1213/EC.

Convention for the protection of Human Rights and Fundamental Freedoms and incorporated into Articles 21 and 23 of the EU Charter of Fundamental Rights (the Charter). These provisions prohibit discrimination based on gender and therefore prohibit sex-specific differences in premiums and benefits based on risk assessed by actuarial and statistical data. The decision thereby ensures that future insurance policies and annuities will be unable to use gender as a determinant of risk and a basis for differentiating between policies. In so ruling, the court unequivocally endorsed the earlier opinion of the Attorney General that "like race and ethnic origin, gender is also a characteristic which is inseparably linked to the insured person as an individual and over which he has no influence,"[159] concluding that EU law provided no less protection by a prohibition on race discrimination as it does on gender discrimination and that it is therefore inappropriate to link risk to an individual's sex.

E. Jurisdictional Characteristics of Charitable Trading

In the EU's 27 constituent Member States, the foundation continues to be the main legal structure for furthering nonprofit public benefit purposes. In some countries, the tradition of corporatism continues to be a distinctive feature of the relationship between state and sector; in many, the trading activity of foundations is well established, and a broad range of commercial ventures are tolerated leading to treatment as a tax rather than a status issue. Perhaps in all, however, a "creeping marketization"[160] can now be detected.

1. The Leading Role of the ECJ

The case law of the ECJ reveals that it continues to focus on defining the twin key concepts of "undertaking" and "economic activity" and using them to drive forward a distinction between core "welfare" work and other activity. This distinction essentially turns on an "activities test," and the outcome is determinative regardless of whether the entity concerned is a nonprofit, government, or for-profit body.

VII. CONCLUSION

Foundations form the heartland of the nonprofit sector in continental Europe, and constitute the main repository for its assets, although associations are, of course, far more numerous. Although it is dangerous to generalize when referring to a community of 27 countries, it can perhaps be safely said that charities and the sector as a whole in continental European are more conservative than their counterparts in the other jurisdictions studied: This is evident in the risk-averse approach to investment

[159] See Opinion of Advocate General Kokott, delivered on September 30, 2010. See further at: http://eur-lex.europa.eu/LexUriServ/LexUriServ.do?uri=CELEX:62009C0236:EN:HTML.

[160] See Bode, "Creeping Marketization and Post-Corporatist Governance."

and commercial opportunities, and is also apparent in the restrained recourse to new legal structures and in the limited spread of social enterprises. On the other hand, the wealth of case law produced by the ECJ and the ECtHR is illuminating for all jurisdictions, even those outside the EC.

There is every indication that legislation to launch the long-anticipated European foundation statute may soon be prepared. When that statute finally comes into force, it is likely to trigger a surge in pan-European philanthropic activity. In the meantime, the countries that constitute the EU lack the basic building blocks of mutually agreed definitions for charities and public benefit organizations. Until these are settled, and the European foundation statute with related regulatory processes are in place and operational, any consideration of the effect of nonprofit law in marking out sector boundaries on a pan-European basis would be at best speculative.

7

THE UNITED STATES OF AMERICA

I. INTRODUCTION

Because of its more market-led approach to public benefit service provision, its strong tradition of associations[1] and community-based services, with a long-standing history of government respect for devolved administration,[2] a concern to keep separate matters of church and state,[3] and a resistance to the welfare state ethos,[4] the United States is a particularly interesting jurisdiction for the purposes of this study. Moreover, whereas the United States shares with the U.K. and other jurisdictions some of the same pattern of trends that are pushing government and sector into new collaborative arrangements, it differs from them in at least one important respect: The demographic trends reveal stronger fertility rates.[5] This, alongside sustained levels of immigration, allows the United States to look to the future with relatively greater confidence that its tax revenues may be better able to cope with the task of providing for an aging population. However, as with other common law countries,

[1] As testified to in the writings of Alexis de Tocqueville: see, e.g., *Democracy in America* (1835). trans. George Lawrence, New York, Harper Collins, 1988.

[2] The U.S. Constitution of 1789 (as amended); the Fourteenth Amendment.

[3] The Establishment Clause; the First Amendment.

[4] See, e.g., Alesina, A., Glaeser, E., and Sacerdote, B., "Why Doesn't the United States Have a European-Style Welfare State?," *Brookings Papers on Economic Activity,* 2:2001; see further at: www.wcfia.harvard.edu/sites/default/files/423__0332-Alesina11.pdf.

[5] The U.S. fertility rate, at 2.03, is dramatically higher than almost all other developed countries. Europe's aggregate fertility varies between approximately 1.3 and 1.5, depending upon region, and Japan is at 1.3. Global fertility rates are in general decline, with this trend being most pronounced in industrialized countries, especially Western Europe, where populations are projected to decline dramatically over the next 50 years. See further at: http://www.indexmundi.com/united_states/total_fertility_rate.html.

the rising costs of health and social care will require the United States to supplement existing means of providing for public benefit services as the cumulative attrition of long-term pensions and health care issues continue to erode the nation's tax revenue base. Addressing this asymmetric financial equation will require much the same boundary adjustment between government, nonprofits, and for-profits in the United States as is occurring elsewhere, if future levels of public benefit provision are to be safely maintained.

This chapter begins with a brief sector profile: It analyzes contemporary statistics and trends, identifies the different funding arrangements for the sector, considers the changes affecting the role of charities within the broader nonprofit world, and assesses the difficulties in achieving sector cohesion within a federated jurisdiction. This leads into an outline of the steps so far taken to build a relationship between government and the sector, including a review of the charity law reform process; it is followed by an examination of recent policy and practice initiatives launched to readjust public benefit provision. The emergence of new legal nonprofit structures and donor incentive schemes designed to facilitate such provision is also examined. The bulk of the chapter then focuses on the case law that illustrates the issues associated with charities and trading in this, the most open market of all common law jurisdictions.

II. SECTOR PROFILE

In the United States, the term "nonprofit sector" is arguably a misnomer: The commonality for many of its constituent entities is no longer the absence of profit but the principled basis for its distribution; although the term "sector" implies a coherence, a shared sense of direction, and an agreed voice on an agenda of issues, that has yet to be achieved. Moreover, the overall incoherence is exacerbated by the sheer unwieldiness of a system that formally allows nonprofits to be organized under the different state laws while their operations are largely shaped by the requirements of the federal Internal Revenue Code (IRC). There is, arguably, a significant disconnect between embedded federal presumptions of law and policy, which are particularly influential in the case of nonprofits, and the decision-making processes of local elected state officials, which can often be idiosyncratic.

A. The Nonprofit Sector

Since the early 1980s, when President Reagan began dismantling government public benefit services at much the same time that Prime Minister Thatcher was similarly engaged in the U.K., the nonprofit sector has become a steadily more potent socioeconomic force. It is now large, wealthy, and growing. It employs more people, draws in more revenue, and contributes more to the gross domestic product than it did a decade ago. Whereas in 1940 there were only approximately 14,000 federally tax-exempt organizations, by 2008 over 1.7 million were registered on the Internal Revenue Service (IRS) business master file (excluding most churches) in

30 different categories. The largest single category—§ 501(c)(3) public charities—included over 950,000 organizations and accounted for three-fourths of nonprofit revenue and six-tenths of nonprofit assets.[6]

According to *The Nonprofit Almanac 2010*, the number of registered exempt organizations grew 31 percent from 1998 to 2008.[7] The National Center for Charitable Statistics (NCCS) estimates that in 2008 there were 1,536,134 nonprofits including: 974,337 public charities; 115,340 private foundations; and 446,457 other types of nonprofit organizations, including chambers of commerce, fraternal organizations, and civic leagues. This represented a 32.7 percent growth in all nonprofits since 1998.[8] The relative strength of the U.S. sector is as explained in the 2007 research published by the Johns Hopkins Center for Civil Society Studies:[9]

> The nonprofit institutions sector that comes into focus in the NPI satellite accounts is a significant economic force. Including the value added by volunteers, these institutions account for an average of 5% of Gross Domestic Product in the eight countries for which satellite account data are available. This varies from a high of 7.3% in Canada to a low of 1.3% in the Czech Republic. The United States is at 7.2%.

Religious organizations receive by far and away the biggest segment of donations provided to the sector.[10]

1. Employment and Volunteers

Employment in the nonprofit sector in America continues to grow faster (2.5 percent) than business (1.8 percent) or government (1.6 percent). According to the latest edition of the Nonprofit Almanac,[11] the number of Americans employed in the nonprofit sector has doubled in the last 25 years. Nonprofit employment represents

[6] Wing, K. T., Roeger, K. L. and Pollak, T. H., *The Nonprofit Almanac 2010*, Urban Institute Press, Washington, September 2010. See also National Council of Nonprofit Associations, *United States Nonprofit Sector*, Washington, DC, 2005. Note that "§" signifies a Treasury (Tax) Regulation.

[7] Wing et al., *The Nonprofit Almanac*.

[8] National Center for Charitable Statistics, citing as source: NCCS *Business Master File* 10/09.

[9] See Salamon, L. M., Haddock, M. A., Wojciech Sokolowski, S., and Tice, H. S., *Measuring Civil Society and Volunteering: Initial Findings from Implementation of the UN Handbook on Nonprofit Institutions* Working Paper No. 23. Johns Hopkins Center for Civil Society Studies, Baltimore, 2007.

[10] Lester Salamon's statistics for 1977–1997 show that religious organizations' absolute percentage of the share of total revenue from philanthropy for various segments of the nonprofit sector decreased from 86 percent to 84 percent during that time, a figure that seems high; Brody, E., estimates that churches attract a bit over 50 percent of total annual philanthropic donations (note to author; September 18, 2011). Salamon et al., *Measuring Civil Society and Volunteering*, at p. 37.

[11] See Independent Sector, *Nonprofit Almanac*, September 2010, as posted by the Center for Community-Based and Nonprofit Organizations, Austin Community College, at www.austincc.edu/npo/library/documents/NPOemploymentnatl.pdf.

9.5 percent of all employed persons, with total employees numbering 12.5 million. The Almanac estimates that in 2001: 42 percent of all workers were employed in health services, specifically in nonprofit hospitals; education was second, employing 22 percent of all workers in the sector; in combination, health services and education employed 64 percent of all workers in the sector. The largest percentage increase in employment between 1997 and 2001 among the major nonprofit industries was recorded in social services, with a growth rate of over 17 percent.

The residential care component of social services grew the most, with an employment gain of nearly 19 percent.

B. Nonprofit Organizations

The contribution of nonprofits to the collective public benefit of the community has a well-established history in the United States. Indeed, Alex de Tocqueville in the 1830s "noted with special interest the prominent place of voluntary associations in American society... Churches, community groups, fraternal associations and civil organizations... did for themselves through these voluntary efforts what people in other societies expected governments and elites to do to them."[12]

A range of nonprofit entities and religious organizations are known to the IRS and governed by § 501(c) of the IRC. Over 1.5 million were registered with the IRS in 2008, not including those organizations with less than $5000 annual revenue,[13] and the many religious congregations that are not required by law to register with the IRS and choose not to do so. There are hundreds of thousands of organizations, including literary clubs, sporting organizations, unions, trade associations, political organizations, churches, hospitals, and condominium and neighborhood associations that are exempt from income tax but fall outside charity law, as it is known elsewhere in the common law world, as their exempt status is not linked explicitly to pursuing a *Pemsel* charitable purpose.[14] Because of this broad coverage, the IRS consistently refers to "exempt purposes" (i.e., those specified in the statute) rather than using the undefined term "charitable," and indeed has named its bureau that has been assigned supervisory responsibility as the Tax-Exempt and Government Entities (TEGE) division.

[12] As cited in Wuthnow, R., "The Voluntary Sector: Legacy of the Past, Hope for the Future," in Wuthnow, R. (ed), *Between States and Markets: The Voluntary Sector in Comparative Perspective*, Princeton, NJ, Princeton University Press, 1991, at p. 3.

[13] Note that all values in this chapter are expressed in U.S. dollars.

[14] It was the Tariff Act of 1913 that initially excluded public benefit nonprofits such as churches from paying federal income tax. Specifically this act exempted organizations in which "no part of the net income of which inures to the benefit of any private shareholder or individual" was exempt from the federal income tax; see further Hopkins, B. R., *The Law of Tax-Exempt Organizations*, Wiley, New York, 1998, at p. 32.

1. Charities

For federal tax purposes, under § 501(c)(3), the IRS makes a distinction between "public charities" and "private foundations," distinguished (loosely) by the "public support test" that requires many organizations to demonstrate a comparatively broad base of support to qualify for the status of "public charity." Both will meet the IRS definition of "charity" if they are exempt from federal income tax and eligible to receive tax deductible contributions under federal law.[15] This will be the case where the entity is appropriately organized, and operated for purposes that are beneficial to the public interest, and its organizing document (for example, articles of incorporation, trust documents, or articles of association) limits its purposes to being charitable, and permanently dedicates its assets to charitable purposes. The organization must refrain from undertaking a number of other activities such as participating in the political campaigns of candidates for local, state, or federal office, and must ensure that its earnings do not benefit any individual.[16]

In general, the charity law distinction between charities and all other nonprofits is not so clear-cut as in other common law jurisdictions for a number of reasons: Charitable "purpose" for the IRS has long been as listed below rather than as classified by *Pemsel*. The distinct legal status of "charity" is recognized in accordance with common law principles, but other classes of organizations are also held to have charitable characteristics, and the nonprofit sector as a whole is classified in a graduated scheme, encompassing in separate blocks "public benefit" and "mutual benefit" nonprofit corporations. Many states, however, make no formal statutory distinction between "mutual benefit" corporations and "public benefit" organizations.[17]

Congress has defined what constitutes charitable "exempt purposes" in the Internal Revenue Code, moving somewhat beyond the charitable purposes approach set by the Preamble/*Pemsel* parameters to define the equivalent of a "charitable organization" as an entity whose public benefit activities are organized for the:[18]

1. Relief of the poor, the distressed, or the underprivileged,
2. Advancement of religion,
3. Advancement of education or science,

[15] See I.R.C. §§ 170(c)(2), 501(c)(3), 2055(a)(2), 2106(a)(2)(A)(ii), 2522(a)(2) (West. Supp. 2008).

[16] Fremont-Smith, M. R., *Governing Nonprofit Organizations*, Cambridge, MA, Harvard University Press, 2004.

[17] This distinction has been adopted by the California Nonprofit Corporations Code and by the American Bar Association's Revised Model Nonprofit Corporation Act 1988, and is now enacted in about half the states. Putnam Barber advises that the Model Nonprofit Corporation Act, Third Edition 2010, enacted, as of September 2011, only in the District of Columbia, and deprecated by some scholars (notably Fremont-Smith and Evelyn Brody)—abandons this distinction (note to author, September 9, 2011).

[18] I.R.C. § 501(c)(3).

4. Erection or maintenance of public buildings, monuments, or works,
5. Lessening the burdens of government,
6. Lessening of neighborhood tensions,
7. Elimination of prejudice and discrimination,
8. Defense of human and civil rights secured by law, and
9. Combating community deterioration and juvenile delinquency.

Charitable exempt organizations, as noted above, are of two types: public charities[19] and private foundations.[20]

A public charity is an organization that receives at least one-third of its finances from a broad segment of the general public, such as a school, hospital, church, or any other charity that receives its financial support from a broad group of donors or patrons. Section 509 of the IRC and associated regulations also identify two other types of public charities termed "publicly supported" organizations, because the funding requirements stipulated in the Code and regulations are aimed at ensuring that only organizations with widespread financial support from the general public will qualify. One type qualifies as publicly supported because it normally receives at least one-third of its basic financial support in the form of contributions and grants from the general public, from governmental entities, from certain other organizations that themselves qualify as publicly supported organizations, or from any combination of the foregoing. The other qualifies under § 509 (a)(3) if it satisfies two tests: not more than one-third of its basic financial support may be investment income or certain income from commercial activities unrelated to the organization's charitable purposes, and at least one-third of its basic financial support must come in the form of a combination of contributions, membership dues, and income generated from the performance of the organization's charitable purposes. As Fishman has succinctly observed, "Churches, schools and hospitals fall into the charmed public charities circle as they are the most venerable and influential members of the charitable sector."[21]

Public charities constitute the largest part of the nonprofit sector. In 2008, public charities accounted for 63 percent of registered nonprofits and 59 percent of reporting nonprofits. The number of registered public charities grew 61 percent from 1998 to 2008, whereas the number of reporting public charities grew 56 percent. In addition to the 1.186 million registered charities, the charitable sector also includes thousands of churches and small charities that are not required to register with the IRS. The total number of exempt organizations known to the IRS has recently fallen by over 300,000 as the IRS, in the summer of 2011, began to enforce the requirement to file the Form

[19] A public charity is defined in § 170(b)(1)(A)(i)–(vi).

[20] See I.R.C. §§ 509, 501(c)(3). A private foundation is neither a public charity nor a supporting organization.

[21] See Fishman, J., "Nonprofit Organizations in the United States," in Hopt, K. J. and Von Hippel, T. (eds.), *Comparative Corporate Governance of Non-Profit Organizations*, Cambridge, Cambridge University Press, 2010, at p. 145.

990-N notice and began to revoke the exempt status of small charities that had failed to do so within the three previous years.[22]

2. Range of Legal Structures

It has been noted that "charities are usually created in one of two legal forms, corporations or trusts, with the corporation being the most common form utilized in the United States since the mid-twentieth century."[23] Certainly, for some time now it has been the case that most charities in the United States and almost all the large ones are in corporate form.

To begin with, in order for an organization to qualify for exempt—or charitable—status under § 501(c)(3) of the Internal Revenue Code, it must be organized as a corporation, trust, or unincorporated association.[24] The most popular form chosen by organizations is the nonprofit corporation.[25] Every U.S. and foreign charity that qualifies as tax-exempt under this section is considered a "private foundation" by default unless it demonstrates to the IRS that it falls into another category.[26] When organizations register in another category other than a private foundation, the clear majority file as public charities as defined in § 509(a) of the Internal Revenue Code.

The private foundation, deeply rooted in the common law, has evolved to become a distinctive phenomenon and a significant feature on the U.S. charity landscape.[27] For the regulatory framework relating to charitable organizations, the distinction between public charities and private foundations is of fundamental importance[28] and one which the IRS has been at pains to police in order to copper-fasten the requirement that the purposes and activities of a public charity are absolutely committed to public benefit

[22] See Automatic Revocation of Exemption at: http://www.irs.gov/charities/article/0,,id=239696,00.html. See also Internal Revenue Service, *Data Books*, available at www.irs.gov/taxstats/article/0,,id=102174,00.html.

[23] See Fremont-Smith, M. R., *Governing Nonprofit Organizations: Federal and State Law and Regulation*, Belknap Press of Harvard University Press, Cambridge, MA 2004, at p. 116.

[24] The Unincorporated Nonprofit Association Act 1992, adopted by the Commissioners on Uniform State Laws, has only been accepted by a minority of states.

[25] The Model Nonprofit Corporation Act 1952, revised in 1957 and 1964, was redrafted in 2008 by the American Bar Associations Committee on Nonprofit Law, which removed the distinction between public benefit, mutual benefit, and religious corporation, and published it for consultation as the Model Nonprofit Corporation Act (3rd Edition).

[26] The National Council of Nonprofit Associations, in its *United States Nonprofit Sector*, 2003 report, estimated that private foundations represented 11 percent (103,021) of registered § 503(c)(3) organizations, and 19 percent (66,398) of reporting § 503(c)(3) organizations.

[27] The private foundation, in its present form, was largely defined by the Tax Reform Act of 1969.

[28] Note that although public charities may engage in limited lobbying activity, private foundations are prohibited from engaging in any: I.R.C. § 4945.

and to focus on possible donor control in private foundations.[29] Where there is doubt, the latter is the default designation.[30]

A private foundation[31] usually derives its principal fund from an individual, family, corporation, or some other single source, more often than not a grantmaker; it does not solicit funds from the public, and its investments were traditionally subject to "the prudent man" rule.[32] They are subject to substantially more restrictions than public charities (e.g., they are not permitted to engage in any political activities or lobbying whatsoever, either directly or indirectly) and are also required to distribute a specific amount of their income each year, defined as 5 percent of the aggregate fair market value of the foundation's assets in excess of indebtedness incurred with respect to the assets ("distributive amount"), whereas their donors receive less favorable tax treatment for contributions. A foundation or public charity[33] generally receives grants from individuals, government, and private foundations, and although some public charities engage in grantmaking activities, most conduct direct service or other tax-exempt activities.

a. Endowed Private Foundation

An endowed private foundation is a powerful and independent form of charity, often with considerable wealth and unique social and political leverage; it is able to take the long-term view and act strategically on behalf of the sector. It is a corporate form of charity modeled on the Rockefeller Foundation, which was established in 1913 to

[29] A useful description of what private charities do and the current issues with regard to them can be found in Lenkowsky, L., "Foundations and Corporate Philanthropy," in Salamon et al., *Measuring Civil Society and Volunteering,* at pp. 355–86. Fremont-Smith, M. also discusses the developments leading up to the 1969 Tax Reform Act and the outcomes in terms of greater regulation of private foundations. See Fremont-Smith, M., *Governing Nonprofit Organizations,* at pp. 71–84.

[30] As a result, 48 states have passed laws adopting the distinction between private foundations and public charities and prohibiting private foundations from being controlled by substantial donors, holding certain investments, dealing with insiders, etc.

[31] Examples of a private foundation would be the Rockefeller Foundation and the Bill & Melinda Gates Foundation.

[32] See Harvard College v. Amory, 26 Mass. (9 Pick.) 446, 460 (Mass. 1830). This case provides authority for the rule that that a person entrusted with fiduciary responsibility is only required to exercise an average standard of discretion and average intelligence when making investments. It is sufficient that the person acts as any reasonable individual interested in receiving a good return of income while preserving his or her capital would do; the person is not expected to possess exceptional or uncanny investment skills.

[33] Examples of operating foundations or public charities include the Elizabeth Glaser Pediatric AIDS Foundation, American Cancer Society, Inc., and the World Wildlife Fund.

exist in perpetuity as an entity[34] with a mission to "promote the well-being of mankind throughout the world."[35] The subsequent proliferation of private foundations and community foundations[36] as vehicles for "donor-advised funds"[37] has relied on the use of the same foundation structure. Despite, however, being "created and governed by the country's elite... deeply embedded in its political systems,"[38] such entities have not been at the fore in exercising sector leadership. Some, however, have a record of experimentation in entrepreneurial ventures, and for pioneering a mix of public benefit mission with profit-making zeal that has pushed the traditional sector boundaries. Haag and Richter have drawn attention to this:[39]

> A few decades ago, charitable organizations in the U.S. discovered hedge funds as an attractive investment opportunity and began to increasingly invest in hedge funds... For instance, in 1987 Yale University still had over 85 percent of its core assets

[34] The term "benevolent trusts" was coined by Rockefeller, J. D., in his *Random Reminiscences of Men and Events*, Doubleday, Page and Company, New York, 1909, pp. 186–88. He used it to indicate that combinations were occurring in philanthropy as in business. See also Dobkin Hall, P., "An Historical Overview of the Private Nonprofit Sector," in Powell, W. W. (ed.), *The Nonprofit Sector—A Research Handbook*, Yale University Press, New Haven, CT, 1987, at p. 12. See generally Karl, B. D. and Katz, S. N. "The American Private Philanthropic Foundation and the Public Sphere, 1890–1930," in *Minerva*, Vol. 19, 1981, at pp. 236–70.

[35] See Rockefeller Foundation, http://www.rockfound.org/about_us/about_us.shtml. Interestingly, after sustained efforts to secure a federal charter from Congress had been frustrated, the Rockefeller Foundation was incorporated by special charter from the New York legislature. See Freund, E., "Legal Aspects of Philanthropy," in E. Faris, F. Laune and Aodd (eds.), *Intelligent Philanthropy*, Patterson Smith, Chicago, 1930, at p. 160.

[36] The Cleveland Foundation is the oldest of these foundations dedicated to supporting local communities. See the Cleveland Foundation website, http://www.clevelandfoundation.org/Home.asp. Peter Dobkin Hall points out that local boards of trade and civic federations helped to support the development of such foundations, which he calls "a rationalization and centralization of the charitable resources of communities" (see Dobkin Hall, P., "An Historical Overview," at p. 13). Note that community foundations in IRS terms are public charities precisely because they receive broad public support.

[37] A donor-advised fund (DAF) is any separately identified fund or account owned and controlled by a sponsoring organization such as a community foundation or other public charity if the donor has or expects to have advisory privileges over distributions of amounts from the fund. DAFs have come under increasing scrutiny and were the subject of legislation under the Pension Protection Act 2006 (PPA), PL 109–280, August 2006, available at http://waysandmeans.house.gov/media/pdf/taxdocs/pensiontextpt1.pdf.

[38] See Anheier, H. and Leat, D., *From Charity to Creativity: Philanthropic Foundations in the 21st Century*, Comedia, Stroud, U.K., 2002, at p. 67.

[39] See Haag, M. and Richter, A., "Legal Standards for Capital Investments by Foundations in Hedge Funds According to German and American Law," in Hopt and Von Hippel (eds.), *Comparative Corporate Governance of Non-Profit Organizations*, at p. 712, citing Fishman, J. J. and Schwarz, S., *Nonprofit Organizations* (2nd ed.), Foundation Press, New York, 2001, at pp. 602–04. They note (at p. 714) that Harvard University lost US$1.3 billion in hedge funds in 1998.

invested in stocks and fixed-interest bonds: in 1998, this percentage had declined to 30 percent, with the rest invested in alternative investment strategies including hedge funds.

The size, capacity, durability, and prominent social profile of private foundations makes them difficult to ignore when they adopt an advocacy role, and they are attractive partners for government bodies and commercial enterprises engaged in the provision of health, social care, and education services. In the latter context, such foundations have acted as brokers and financial contributors to pioneer the public/private partnerships that have driven sector involvement with business, resulting in the rapid expansion of domestic public benefit provision and international aid in recent years.

b. Community Foundation

This is a tax-exempt organization that generally holds a number of permanent funds created by many separate donors, all dedicated to the long-term charitable benefit of a specific community or region. Community foundations are generally recognized as public charities, are not subject to the more stringent rules that apply to private foundations, and have been a prominent feature on the charity landscape in the United States since the forming of the Cleveland Trust Company in 1914. Typically, a community foundation provides grants and other services to assist other charitable organizations in meeting local needs, while also offering services to help donors establish endowed funds for specific charitable purposes. They may be incorporated.

c. Corporate Foundation

Also known as a company-sponsored foundation, a corporate foundation is a private foundation that receives its primary funding from a profit-making business. The foundation is a separate, legal charitable organization even though it often maintains close ties with the founding company, and it must abide by the same rules and regulations as other private foundations.

d. Charitable Remainder Trusts

This type of trust is established by a donor to provide an income stream to a specified beneficiary, and when that trust ends (usually upon the death of the beneficiary), it allows the remaining value to be diverted to a named public charity or private foundation. These "split interest" trusts are defined in § 664 of the IRC and are normally tax-exempt. They hold in balance both private and public benefit sets of interests.

3. Range of Activities

Public charities are mostly active in the arts, education, health care, human services, and other areas to which donors can make tax-deductible contributions. Human services, the most numerous type of organization, accounts for a third of reporting public charities, with education a distant second at 18.2 percent.[40] Other subsections of 501(c) exempt the income of advocacy organizations, labor unions, business and professional associations, and social and recreational clubs, as well as a variety of more obscure types. Generally, § 170 provides charitable deductions from the donor's income only for gifts to § 501(c)(3) organizations.

From 1998 to 2008, one of the fastest-growing categories of nonprofits was concerned with international development and relief, and those organizations nearly doubled in number. Another fast-growing sector was the environment and animals, where the number of nonprofits did more than double. Church organizations and health are numerically the largest categories, with health-related nonprofits the fastest growing subgroup in recent years.[41]

C. Financing the Sector

According to *The Nonprofit Almanac 2010*,[42] from 1998 to 2008 the revenues of reporting nonprofits grew 40 percent, expenses grew 49 percent, and assets grew 44 percent, after adjusting for inflation. In 2008, 597,307 nonprofits reported over $1.9 trillion in revenue and $4.3 trillion in assets.

1. Public Charities

In 2008, public charities reported $1.4 trillion in revenue and $2.6 trillion in assets. Hospitals and primary care facilities accounted for the largest percentage of total revenue and total assets, 47.7 and 30.6 percent, respectively. Higher education followed with 11.7 percent of total revenue and 21.5 percent of total assets. In that year, those reporting annual expenses of $10 million or more accounted for just 3.9 percent of charities, but 84.8 percent of all reporting public charity spending.

The largest source of revenue across all reporting public charities is fees from the sale of goods and services, such as patient care (including Medicare and Medicaid), tuition, or admission tickets. Overall, such fees accounted for 69.8 percent of

[40] See further at: nccsdataweb.urban.org. See also National Center for Charitable Statistics, IRS Business Master File 04/2010, at: http://nccsdataweb.urban.org/PubApps/profileDrillDown.php?state=US&rpt=PC.

[41] nccsdataweb.urban.org.

[42] See Independent Sector, *The Nonprofit Almanac 2010*, at: www.austincc.edu/npo/library/documents/NPOemploymentnatl.pdf. The following statistical data is also largely drawn from that source.

revenue in 2008. Of this, 45.5 percent came from private sources and 24.3 percent from government sources. Contributions and grants accounted for 20.4 percent of revenue, of which private sources account for 12.4 percent and government sources for 8.0 percent.[43] Considering both fees and grants, government accounts for 32.3 percent of revenue of reporting public charities. Compared with 2007, the share from contributions dropped 6 percent, reflecting the beginning of the recession. The share of support from government increased 12 percent from 2007 to 2008.

2. Government Funding

The most striking change in the relationship between state and sector since the middle of the 20th century has been the increase in available public funding for charities, in all subsectors, including health, social services, culture, and education. Indeed, Chapter IV of the Filer Commission report[44] is entitled "The State as a Major Philanthropist."[45] A very large proportion of sector funding now comes from the federal or state governments.[46] Writing in 2002, Lester Salamon notes that between 1977 and 1997, government funding for the sector grew by 195 percent, "proportionally more than any other source."[47] NCCS's findings indicate that in 2007, of the $1.4 trillion in total revenues reported by public charities, 67 percent came from program service revenues, which include government fees and contracts.[48]

However, in recent years a very distinct trend has emerged: the growing proportion of sector funding, including funds flowing into charities, that comes from earned income. Fees for services are now set to become a major, if not the major, source of revenue; commercial activity is displacing decades of reliance upon government funds.[49] Although this development is far from being confined to the United States, it is more advanced there than in other common law jurisdictions. The combination of an entrepreneurial culture and "open market" capitalism has encouraged the proliferation of commercial ventures and unlikely alliances between charities and business. As the economic recession has caused funding streams from government and the general public to flow more sluggishly, it is clear that, for charity and the nonprofit sector more generally, notwithstanding the current influx of

[43] National Center for Charitable Statistics, Core Files 2008.

[44] The Commission on Private Philanthropy and Public Needs (the Filer Commission) from 1973 to 1975 conducted the most far-reaching and detailed examination of American philanthropy, concluding with its final report *Giving in America: Toward a Stronger Voluntary Sector.*

[45] Commission on Private Philanthropy and Public Needs, *Giving in America*. For a historical perspective, see Cutlip, S. M., *Fund Raising in the United States*, first published (by Rutgers University Press) in 1965, Transaction Publishers, New Brunswick, NJ, 1990.

[46] See Salamon, L. M. (ed.), Chapter 1, "The Resilient Sector," in *The State of Nonprofit America*, Washington, DC, 2002, at pp. 32–34.

[47] Salamon, "The Resilient Sector," at p. 33.

[48] The Urban Institute, National Center for Charitable Statistics, *Core Files* 2004.

[49] See Freemont-Smith, *Governing Nonprofit Organizations*, at p. 8.

contributions from high worth donors, future income will have to be largely generated by fees for services.

3. Charitable Giving and Volunteering

In 2009, according to *Giving USA 2010*,[50] private charitable contributions stood at $303.8 billion, down 3.6 percent from the revised estimate for 2008. It reports that faith-based charities, including churches, received the most in 2009, amounting to $100.95 billion or 33 percent of total U.S. contributions in that year. Education organizations received 13.2 percent, the second-largest share.

Foundation giving, a component of private charitable contributions, was $42.9 billion in 2009. This was an 84 percent increase from 10 years earlier, but an 8 percent decrease from 2008. There were 75,595 grantmaking foundations in the United States in 2008, a 61 percent increase from 10 years earlier, though it needs to be borne in mind that there are complications with funding in respect of foundations as they both receive and make contributions. Corporations as well as individuals made their contribution to society, with corporate giving increasing by 5.5 percent to $14.1 billion.[51]

In 2009, 26.8 percent of U.S. adults said they volunteered through an organization. Volunteers contributed a total of 15 billion hours during the year, worth $279 billion at average wages.[52] The second largest use of volunteers was for social service and care activities, accounting for 22 percent of total volunteer time, the same as in 2008.

D. Sector Cohesion

The nonprofit sector in the United States is not a well-defined, coherent entity. The open market economy, where entrepreneurial innovation, a frontier spirit, and a cavalier approach to boundaries have always been greatly prized, has generated so much cross-sector activity that nonprofit frontiers are increasingly hard to find. Many of the key markers pegging out public from private that would be readily recognized in welfare state jurisdictions, such as hospitals and universities, could in the United States be housed by government, business, or the nonprofit sector, and could be rehoused tomorrow. The indistinct shape is compounded by the disparate entities within it: many with not enough in common to motivate a willingness to coordinate resources for the collective good of the sector; some with much stronger

[50] See Giving USA Foundation, *Giving USA 2010: The Annual Report on Philanthropy for the Year 2009*, Giving USA Foundation, Indianapolis, at http://www.givingusa2010.org/products/GivingUSA_2010_ExecSummary_ Print.pdf.

[51] See Giving USA Foundation, *Giving USA 2010*. The 2010 report can be found at: www.givingusa.org and www.philanthropy.iupui.edu.

[52] Wing, K., Roeger, K. L., and Pollak, T. H., *The Nonprofit Sector in Brief: Public Charities, Giving and Volunteering, 2010*, Urban Institute Press, Washington, DC, September 2010.

lateral ties to similar enterprises in another sector. Moreover, the weight and complexity of intersectoral links militate against initiatives to separate out any set of interests that could be said to be both singularly nonprofit and worth risking cross-sector investment to campaign for.

1. Umbrella Bodies

The U.S. sector has sought to develop a self-regulating regime, and in that context some umbrella bodies have emerged. This can probably be traced back to 1918 when a coalition of nonprofits established the National Charities Information Bureau (which recently merged with the Better Business Bureau Philanthropic Advisory Service of the BBB Wise Giving Alliance) to help the public learn about the ethical and stewardship practices of fund-raising organizations. Since then, associations have encouraged their members to meet standards, and strengthen their systems of governance, ethical conduct, and accountability, whereas organizations have developed mandatory standards for their members and training programs to improve ethics throughout the charitable community. Subsequently the Filer Commission provided the incentive to found Independent Sector,[53] a national umbrella organization that has brought together for the first time nonprofit organizations with philanthropic foundations and business corporations. More recently, the Independent Sector adopted a Statement of Values and Code of Ethics for Nonprofit and Philanthropic Organizations intended as guidance for nonprofits and foundations nationwide. As noted in a Johns Hopkins report:[54]

> The evidence at hand thus suggests that a substantial majority of nonprofit organizations, and certainly those belonging to the major national umbrella organizations, already have in place many of the ethics and accountability controls that the Senate Finance Committee staff has proposed to mandate by law.

Umbrella bodies, such as the Council on Foundations, also tend to be set up to provide support and represent the interests of a segment of the sector. There are a myriad of such special interest support bodies, including the Foundation Center, the National Center for Charitable Statistics (affiliated with the Urban Institute), the Aspen Institute's Nonprofit Sector Research Fund, Boardsource, etc. What is missing is any equivalent to the NCVO in England and Wales, which is able to

[53] The Independent Sector—self-described as a "nonprofit, nonpartisan coalition of charities, foundations, and corporate philanthropy programs, collectively represents tens of thousands of charitable groups in every state across the nation"—is the leadership forum for charities, foundations, and corporate giving programs. It leads, strengthens, and mobilizes the charitable community. See further at http://www.independentsector.org.

[54] See Salamon, L. M. and Geller, S. L., *Nonprofit Governance and Accountability,* the Johns Hopkins Nonprofit Listening Post Project Communique No. 4, 2005, at p. 13.

rally and coordinate all manner of entities and negotiate with government on issues representing the collective interests of the sector.

There is also the National Council of Nonprofits, a membership-based organization of state and regional associations that represents thousands of nonprofits throughout the country. It works at the national level to coordinate and support the activities of state associations and similar groups and, through them, individual nonprofits, ensuring the provision of training and technical assistance to improve the operations and effectiveness of organizations. It is interesting to note that the predominant approach in the United States is to focus on infrastructure organizations within the sector itself to enhance the sector's policy capacity and to coordinate its policy voice.

III. CHARITIES AND GOVERNMENT: BUILDING A RELATIONSHIP

The political frame of reference that set the parameters for a relationship between government and the nonprofit sector in the other common law countries currently being considered is largely absent in the United States. If anything, the reverse is the case. The independence of associations, in particular the right to establish such entities and to manage them free from government interference, has been an enduring hallmark of society in this jurisdiction.[55] The framing of the U.S. Constitution and its Bill of Rights sought to ensure, among other things, that federal powers would not interfere with the independence of law-abiding individuals, communities, and their associational activity. This has not proved conducive to building a formal relationship between government and sector. That relationship continues to be conducted, virtually exclusively, through the medium of taxation as administered and moderated via the IRS.

In recent years, however, the context for such a relationship has changed. In the wake of the global war against terrorism there has been a government concern, shared by many in the sector, to track the flow and use of nonprofit funds. The collapse of major financial institutions, and with them much of the credibility of the business sector, has raised the profile of altruistic entities, and the relative social utility of a values-led sector has become more attractive. The economic recession has triggered an increase in demand for public benefit services that government, faced with the draining effect of conducting its war efforts and coping with falling revenues, cannot hope to fully fund. In this climate, there is growing awareness of the need for a government/sector dialogue.

[55] See, e.g., de Tocqueville, *Democracy in America,* at p. 513 ("In every case, at the head of a great new undertaking, where in France you would find the government or in England some territorial magnate, in the U.S. you are sure to find an association").

A. Government Bodies and the Sector

Historically, it has not been found necessary to have government bodies or formal structures to bridge the gap between government and sector. The many hundreds of thousands of organizations that constitute the sector, ranging from churches and hospitals to trade associations and political organizations, and including sports clubs and neighborhood associations, are linked neither to each other nor to government by any body of legal principles. The framework of charity law, providing in other common law jurisdictions a web of principles and charitable purposes for government and sector to recognize their separate sets of interests, and forming a policy agenda for negotiating a relationship, has not had a similar role in the United States. Aside from dealing with regulatory concerns and responding to emergency situations, government and sector have only relatively recently shown an interest in developing boundary-crossing strategies, and this has largely been through the medium of "charitable choice" as developed during the G.W. Bush administration.

1. Absence of Sector-Specific Government Bodies

The only operational framework linking sector entities and sector to government has been the regulatory regime for determining income tax exemption through the Department of Treasury and its IRS. In this most exemplary model of an open-market social economy, government has chosen to rely on its executive powers to constrain or channel particular sector activity, rather than formulate any broad policy for developing government/sector relationships, whereas the differentiating effect of the tax regime has served to perpetuate a lack of sector cohesion. The traditional roles and responsibilities of the revenue department and the office of state attorneys general, reinforced by the customary range of regulatory bodies, have by and large been seen as sufficient to mediate between the interests of government and sector.

2. Government/Sector Relationships

There is an established tradition in the United States of associational activity pursued for locality-based goals: one involving volunteers working for the collective benefit of their community, and in which both charities and government would have complementary roles to assist in the provision of public welfare services. A number of national programs and foundations have been created by government to promote voluntary action, such as AmeriCorps (and more generally the Corporation for National and Community Service, of which AmeriCorps is a program), and the Points of Light Foundation (though this is actually a private nonprofit entity that merged with the Hands On Network in 2007).[56] At the state level, more than 40 councils and associations of nonprofit organizations have spearheaded efforts to engage government in policy dialogue. However, as yet there have been no initiatives comparable with those undertaken in countries such as the U.K. and Australia to build a formal strategic relationship between the nonprofit sector and national government. The significance of this is evident in the lack of any equivalent drivers to reform the legal framework for government/sector relations. When, in the early years of this century, government began a process of reviewing the law relating to nonprofits, this was a precursor to rather than a product of a negotiated government/sector relationship. Government tardiness in this regard is at least partially attributable to its relatively weaker sense of responsibility for providing, as opposed to regulating, public benefit services.

3. Faith-Based Initiatives

Arguably, the infrastructure of government bodies constructed to facilitate permeability along the government/sector boundary in other common law countries (most notably in the U.K., but also in Ireland, Australia, and New Zealand) exists in a faith-based form in the United States. Beginning in 1996, under President Bill Clinton, a body of legislation accompanied by a network of government offices, funding bodies, and a good deal of controversy has come into existence around the government/sector boundary. In January 2001, President George W. Bush created the White House Office of Faith-Based and Community Initiatives within the Executive Office of the President by an executive order.[57] Later, executive orders created centers for the Office within the Departments of Justice, Labor, Health and Human Services, Housing and Urban Development, Education, and Agriculture, as well as at the Agency for International Development. Since then some 22 states have created state Offices of Faith-Based and Community Initiatives, 39 have appointed persons into Faith-Based Liaison positions, and 41 have passed legislation or enacted administrative policy changes to give effect to faith-based initiatives.

Overall, it would seem that this jurisdiction has in fact acknowledged a need for formal government/sector linking structures, but has chosen a faith-based route for achieving this. It is possible that this may be a political shift in cultural clothing, one

[56] See George H. W. Bush, 41st President of the United States, "Inaugural Address," January 20, 1989, when he referred to "a thousand points of light, of all the community organizations that are spread like stars throughout the Nation, doing good." See further at: http://www.pointsoflight.org/faq. It is, however, clear that many of these community organizations addressing social policy issues can do so only because they receive large grants or contracts with state (and federal) agencies, which are outsourcing work in the fields for which they are responsible.

[57] The White House Office of Faith-Based and Community Initiatives was rechristened by the Obama Administration as the White House Office of Faith-based and Neighborhood Partnerships. See Office of Faith-based and Neighborhood Partnerships, Office of the White House, www.whitehouse.gov/administration/eop/ofbnp/about.

that sidesteps the explicit political recognition of sector importance that governments in other common law jurisdictions have found to be necessary.

B. Charity Law Reform

It is a misnomer to refer to the U.S. review, undertaken at federal level in the middle of the first decade of this century, as a process of "charity law reform." It was not particularly concerned with charity law as that regime is understood elsewhere in the common law world: "Charity" is treated in law and for tax purposes very largely as just another nonprofit. Nor was law itself necessarily the focus of attention; it was rules and regulations, and the roles of the bodies involved in determining tax liability, that preoccupied most of the process. This was a review of the legal framework for nonprofits, driven primarily by the customary government urge to prevent abuse and financial irregularities, intended to result in greater transparency and accountability, with more rigorous measures for increasing the efficiency and effectiveness of regulatory agencies. Launched in 2004, it was and continues to be in the main a review of tax administration, and as such is the most comprehensive review of the governance, regulations, and operations of the charitable community undertaken for at least three decades.

The federal review of the tax system did not dwell unduly on the definitional matters crucial to charity law in a common law context. Whether the public benefit test should or should not be statutorily defined, how this test might accommodate fee-paying access to charitable services, and the continuation of existing presumptions in respect of it and its potential application to religious organizations—did not seem to warrant much attention. Neither did the need for and the feasibility of extending the *Pemsel* heads of charity to better address contemporary areas of social disadvantage attract prolonged debate. Whereas these cornerstones of the common law legacy were elsewhere revised and then embedded in legislation, they were not seen as being matters around which a reformed U.S. regulatory framework could, or perhaps should, be organized.

The question as to whether determining charitable status should be decoupled from determining tax liability, and whether the IRS should be displaced by a new charity-specific body as the lead regulatory agency with responsibility for matters relating to charitable status, did not delay the U.S. process. At the federal level, the IRS sought reform to increase broad compliance with tax-exemption requirements, with greater transparency, accountability, and better surveillance of nonprofit funds. At the state level, the authorities were concerned about nonprofit governance, fund-raising, and clarification of the responsibilities of the Attorney General. The sector, in the meanwhile, was focused mostly on the need to reduce the onerous burdens of reporting requirements, adjust taxes to favor nonprofits, and improve fundraising capacity.

1. The Process

In June and July of 2004, the U.S. Senate Finance Committee conducted hearings on *Charity Oversight and Reform: Keeping Bad Things from Happening to Good*

Charities[58] and convened a roundtable discussion on oversight and reform. It then released a discussion draft of possible solutions.[59] The Senate Finance Committee then prepared a document that listed several potential reforms, including a five-year review of tax-exempt status, reforms for DAFs, a revised reporting Form 990, etc. The Committee later held hearings on the proposed reforms in June 2004[60] and April 2005.[61] The Chair of the Committee and the Ranking Member followed up with additional suggestions to the IRS.[62] Because the focus of the Senate Committee was on issues related to accountability, transparency, and ultimately governance, its proposals had implications for the federal government as the regulator of good governance.

Early in autumn 2004, the Senate Finance Committee invited the Independent Sector to assemble a group of leaders from the charitable sector to consider and recommend actions to strengthen governance, ethical conduct, and accountability within public charities and private foundations. The Independent Sector responded in October 2004 by announcing the creation of the Panel on the Nonprofit Sector,[63] which then created two advisory groups: the Expert Advisory Group, drawn from academia, law, and nonprofit oversight; and the Citizens Advisory Group, comprising leaders of America's business, educational, media, political, cultural, and religious institutions. It also formed five Work Groups to examine key issues in governance and accountability.

The House Committee on Ways and Means also began an examination of the charitable community in 2004. It examined the legal history of the tax-exempt sector; its size, scope, and impact on the economy; the need for congressional oversight; and the role of the IRS in improving compliance with the law. It commissioned the staff of the Joint Committee on Taxation to issue a report in 2005 dealing

[58] This contained proposals to tighten the definition of public charity, or simply to force all public benefit organizations to abide by the same strict self-dealing rules that currently apply only to private foundations. See further, 108th Cong. (2004), available at http://finance.senate.gov/sitepages/hearing062204.html.

[59] Senate Finance Committee staff discussion draft, 108th Cong., *Tax-Exempt Governance Proposals* 7 (2004).

[60] The written statements of those invited to testify are available at http://www.senate.gov/~finance/sitepages/hearing062204.htm.

[61] The written statements from these hearings are available at http://finance.senate.gov/sitepages/hearing030505.htm.

[62] One of the most significant issues concerned the Form 990 reforms, which were eventually made in order to make the information easier to understand and hence IRS audits easier to conduct. See statement of Senators Baucus and Grassley at Charity Reform Update, June 2007: Senate Finance Committee Leaders Advocate Form 990 Revision, GuideStar, http://www.guidestar.org/DisplayArticle.do?articleId=1134.

[63] The panel consisted of 24 members who were distinguished leaders from public charities and private foundations from around the country.

with issues of reform for the tax legislation related to charities.[64] The Committee also held hearings,[65] the focus of which was far broader than the issues raised in the Senate.

Throughout 2005 and early 2006, the Senate Finance Committee and Joint Committee on Taxation considered a number of proposals to expand IRS oversight of exempt organizations, particularly charitable organizations. One outcome of this process was the preparation by the National Conference of Commissioners of Uniform State Laws of a Model Protection of Charitable Assets Act, adopted in July 2011: The legislative intent was to strengthen the capacity of the state attorneys general to protect the assets of charities.[66]

C. Implications for Government/Sector Relations

There is no comparison between the U.S. law reform process and that of other common law nations. In particular, there was no suggestion that the process should be used to review the respective interests of government and sector in relation to public benefit provision. It was not seen by either party as an opportunity to revisit the core principles and mechanics of charity law, to ensure that it became a framework that better represented their interests, and to reset the terms of their relationship for the 21st century. As Rosenman has rightly pointed out, government did not need to go down that road, as more discrete ways were available to it:[67]

> Governments are increasingly aware of their power to influence the programmes and operation of these groups by addressing their preferential tax treatment and conditioning exemption and deductibility. By altering the definition of what is or is not a legitimate charitable purpose, by establishing terms of reference for what is or is not an appropriate programmatic approach to achieving that purpose, and by identifying who is and who is not a legitimate recipient of charitable services, government has the power to render the nonprofit sector its subjugated creature.

Charity law was not the focus of reform because it was not as relevant to the management of the tax administration system in the United States as it was elsewhere.

[64] See Joint Committee on Taxation, "Historical Development and Present Law of the Federal Tax Exemption for Charities and Other Tax-Exempt Organizations" (JCX-29–05), April 19, 2005, available at www.house.gov/jct/x-29-05.pdf.

[65] The written statements are available at: http://waysandmeans.house.gov/News/Document Single.aspx?DocumentID.

[66] See, Model Protection of Charitable Assets Act, National Conference of Commissioners on Uniform State Laws (Uniform Law Commission), http://www.law.upenn.edu/bll/archives/ulc/ocaa/MPOCAA_Final_2011.pdf.

[67] See Rosenman, M., "Independence: A Matter of Definition—The Charitable Sector in the United States," in Smerdon, M. (ed.), *The First Principle of Voluntary Action*, Baring Foundation, London, October 2009, at pp. 99–120, at p. 112.

However, running alongside the latter stages of the tax administration reform process a study group launched by the American Law Institute[68] has been taking slow and tentative steps to formulate and agree on "Nonprofit Principles" (see Tentative Drafts adopted in 2007–2008, 2009, and 2011 to assist practicing lawyers, regulators, and judges dealing with charitable legal issues).[69] As Brody, the ALI reporter, has explained: "the two-decades-long Restatement (Third) of Trusts (completed in 2011) and the decade-long Principles of the Law of Corporate Governance (completed in 1992) serve as two—sometimes difficult to reconcile—models for the Principles of the Law of Nonprofit Organizations."[70] In addition, as she notes, two other nonprofit law reform projects have also been in process simultaneously, led by different nonprofit institutions: the American Bar Association (whose membership is voluntary), and the Uniform Law Commission (created and funded by the states).

IV. READJUSTING PUBLIC BENEFIT SERVICE PROVISION

In 2007, the United States began to lapse into its worst economic recession since the 1930s, reaching its lowest point in late 2008 with the collapse of the Lehman Brothers investment bank, from which it is now staging a slow and still uncertain recovery. The economy shrank 4.1 percent from the fourth quarter of 2007 to the second quarter of 2009, compared with its previous worst 3.7 percent fall. The rate of unemployment doubled to reach a 26-year high of 10.1 percent in October 2009. Additionally, an early feature of the U.S. economic recession was the bankruptcy of some of the nation's leading public benefit service providers such as Freddie Mac and Fanny Mae. Against such a background, government has struggled to fund social services and has had a greater need to rely on the nonprofit sector to make up some of the shortfall.

A. Public Benefit Service Provision: The Policy

During the 1980s, there was a widespread withdrawal of federal government spending in areas of general health and social care, community development, and

[68] The American Law Institute (ALI) is described on its website as "the leading independent organization in the United States producing scholarly work to clarify, modernize, and otherwise improve the law…The Institute (made up of 4000 lawyers, judges, and law professors of the highest qualifications) drafts, discusses, revises, and publishes Restatements of the Law, model statutes, and principles of law." It is currently examining the law relating to non-charitable nonprofits. See further at: www.ali.org/.

[69] See further American Law Institute, http://www.ali.org/index.cfm?fuseaction=meetings.detail&meetingid=126.

[70] See Brody, E., "The Ambitions and Limitations of U.S. Nonprofit Law Reform Projects," *NVSQ*, September 2011, at p. 5.

family support services. This occurred against a background of ideological conservatism that flowered during the Reagan era, which sought to shrink the size and expense of government and was presented as government deliberately stepping aside to allow more room for the engagement of the armies of volunteers, organized by reputable nonprofit bodies, who could thereby make a vital contribution to building more responsible and caring communities. Accordingly, the government shed much of its social service responsibilities, either by way of contracting with charitable organizations for service delivery or by simply privatizing services, resulting in nonprofits becoming major providers of various social welfare functions while also becoming increasingly dependent on the government for financial support. It has been estimated that the scale of welfare retrenchment in the 1980s resulted in the loss of some $38 billion for nonprofits outside the health care field.[71] Legislative and financial underpinning for this policy can be dated to the introduction of Title XX of the Social Security Amendments 1974, which gave states discretion to use federal money to fund public benefit service provision and generated a rapid expansion in the number of charities.

In due course, religious organizations emerged as the government's partners of choice for sharing the burden of public benefit service provision. Faith-based initiatives fit well with the more conservative approach of recent administrations in which fiscal rectitude and civic responsibility have been policy keynotes. Closer ties between church and state also served to confer greater legitimacy on government while shifting accountability to religious organizations as successive administrations sought to retain popular support and simultaneously cut service provision.

1. Religious Organizations

Religious corporations have a long history in the United States, and their exemption from taxes has been held not to violate the Constitution.[72] In all 50 states, religious organizations have an established track record of providing social services. Many larger religious organizations have been a part of the traditional provision of social services through separate nonprofit agencies such as the Catholic Charities and Lutheran Social Services. These agencies are religiously influenced, but maintain separate nonprofit organizations registered with the IRS under § 501(c)(3) and thereby separate their social service functions from their purely religious functions: a bright line that

[71] See Salamon, L., *Holding the Center: America's Nonprofit Sector at a Crossroads*, Nathan Cummings Foundation, New York, 1997. Consequently, as Putnam Barber puts it, "the principal effect of the narrowing of federal support for addressing poverty has been to increase the burdens faced by community and social service nonprofits at the local level" (note to author, November 9, 2011).

[72] See, e.g., Walz v. Tax Commission of the City of New York, 397 U.S. 664 (1970).

represents the separation of church and state.[73] Religious corporations constitute a strong and growing segment of the U.S. nonprofit sector with, as has been said, "the largest piece of America's charitable pie going to the sustenance of religious groups—for their facilities, their operating costs, and their clergy salaries."[74] There is no definitive legal requirement placed upon religious organizations to demonstrate how their activities satisfy the public benefit test, and their relative autonomy has been considerably strengthened by a recent Supreme Court decision vindicating their right to hire and fire ministry personnel in accordance with the organization's religious beliefs even where such action may conflict with the human rights of the personnel concerned.[75]

2. Welfare Benefit Cuts

Wealth redistribution is not part of American culture and has no role to play in the national tax system as administered by the IRS. For example, there are no national welfare benefit systems to assist the unemployed or low-income families with children as the national program of Aid to Families with Dependent Children (AFDC) and the JOBS Act for the nonworking poor were both abolished. The Personal Responsibility and Work Opportunity Reconciliation Act (PRWROA)[76] (also known as the Welfare Reform Act) initiated the Temporary Assistance to Needy Families (TANF) program,[77] but access to benefits was conditional upon recipients actively seeking employment. A social security program, funded by employer and employee contributions, provides some support for the elderly and the disabled. The federal government's "Earned Income Tax Credit" (EITC), as its name implies, is only relevant to the working poor.[78] In 2000, Congress repealed the charitable exemption of the retirement savings organization TIAA-CREF.

[73] Proselytization with federal funds would violate the First Amendment to the Constitution. See Hein v. Freedom From Religion Foundation, 551 U.S. 587 (2007) in which the Supreme Court ruled that taxpayers do not have the right to challenge the constitutionality of expenditures by the executive branch of the government. See also Flast v. Cohen, 392 U.S. 83 (1968); Bowen v. Kendrick, 487 U.S. 589 (1988); and Valley Forge Christian College v. Americans United for Separation of Church & State, 454 U.S. 464 (1982).

[74] See Brown, M., *Giving USA 2005, the Annual Report on Philanthropy for the Year 2004,* (50th ed.), Giving USA Foundation, AAFRC Trust for Philanthropy, New York, 2005.

[75] See Hosanna-Tabor Evangelical Lutheran Church & School v. EEOC, 132 S. Ct. 694 (2012).

[76] Public Law 104–93 (August 1996), available at http://wdr.doleta.gov/readroom/legislation/pdf/104-193.pdf.

[77] The reauthorization of PRWORA in the Deficit Reduction Act of 2005 (S. 1932) maintains the original law's requirement that 50 percent of states' welfare caseloads fulfill statutory work requirements. To fulfill work requirements, TANF recipients must be participating for 20 hours per week (or 30 hours in cases where the youngest child is six years old or older) in one or more of the 12 work activities named in the statute.

[78] The EITC is a refundable tax credit that reduces or eliminates the taxes that low-income married or single working people pay (such as payroll taxes); it also frequently operates as a wage subsidy for low-income workers.

Health-related welfare programs are available on a strictly limited basis for the poor (Medicaid), the elderly (Medicare), and children (SCHIP).[79] Generally it is up to individuals to obtain health insurance: Most get coverage through their employers; others sign up for private insurance schemes. President Obama fulfilled his election pledge to make health care more affordable and health insurers more accountable, and to provide mandatory health insurance for all citizens;[80] he succeeded in securing the support of the 111th Congress for a major U.S. health care bill, America's Healthy Future Act 2009.[81] This, among other important reforms, imposed significant requirements on § 501(c)(3) hospitals in order to ensure that they specify their community benefit contribution sufficiently to justify tax exemption. At an estimated cost of $848 billion over 10 years, its most controversial element is the creation of a government insurance program to compete with private firms.

B. Sector Capacity Building

The downsizing of government commitment to antipoverty programs, accompanied by a conspicuous effort to shift some of the cost of service provision to faith-based organizations, has necessitated channeling new funds into the sector. Thus, Charitable Choice supplemented a general move by nonprofits to develop social enterprise activities as a way to finance the provision of services already in place.[82] Legislation extended the Charitable Choice concept beyond welfare programs to such areas as job training, juvenile delinquency prevention initiatives, and drug rehabilitation programs, where for-profit providers may also compete for government funding.

1. Charitable Choice

This refers to a policy of providing direct government funding to religious organizations for the provision of social services. Charitable Choice was launched as part of a government welfare reform strategy intended to replace public welfare

[79] However, in 2008, the U.S. Census Bureau estimated that 46.3 million people in America, out of a population of 300 million, were uninsured. The passing of the health care bill in March 2010 added approximately 32 million people to the total insured population, 16 million via Medicaid.

[80] It is said that the health reform legislation signed into law by President Obama in March 2010 will make health care more affordable, make health insurers more accountable, expand health coverage to all Americans, and make the health system sustainable, stabilizing family budgets, the federal budget, and the economy. See further at www.whitehouse.gov/health-care-meeting/reform-means-you.

[81] S. 1796, § 6007. Note that on March 21, 2010, the U.S. House of Representatives passed H.R. 4872, the Patient Protection and Affordable Care Act (PPACA). This bill, signed into law by President Obama on March 23, provides most U.S. citizens with the right, duty, and means to acquire health insurance.

[82] See Kerlin, J. A., "Social Enterprise in the United States and Europe: Understanding and Learning from the Differences," in *Voluntas*, Vol. 17, 2006, at pp. 251–52.

benefit entitlement with nonprofit and privatized service provision by s.104 of the Personal Responsibility and Work Opportunity Reconciliation Act 1996. This states that those jurisdictions that contract with nonprofit organizations for delivery of social services must include religious organizations as eligible contractees; it also allows government officials to purchase those services from religious providers using Temporary Assistance for Needy Families (TANF), Welfare-to-Work, and Community Services Block Grant (CSBG) funds. Implemented primarily through a variety of executive orders issued by President Clinton, it was incorporated into the Community Services Block Grant Act of 1998, included in the Substance Abuse and Mental Health Services Administration's (SAMHSA) block grant in October 2000, and made part of the Children's Health Act of 2003 by President George W. Bush. Most recently, the Obama administration has announced an expansion of government funding for "faith-based initiatives."[83] In each of these programs, government funds are placed directly into the hands of private social service providers via grants and purchase of service contracts.

In programs subject to Charitable Choice, when funding goes directly to the social service providers, the ultimate beneficiaries are empowered with a choice. Beneficiaries who want to receive services from a faith-based organization (FBO) may do so. On the other hand, if a beneficiary objects on religious grounds to receiving services at an FBO, then the state is the alternative provider. If a beneficiary selects an FBO that receives funding, the provider cannot discriminate against beneficiaries on account of their religion or their refusal to participate actively in a religious practice. FBOs retain their exemption from federal employment discrimination laws, which enables them to select staff on a religious basis. According to the Department of Health and Human Services, Charitable Choice rests on four major principles:[84]

1. *A level playing field*—Faith-based providers are eligible to compete for funds on the same basis as any other providers, neither excluded nor included because they are religious, too religious or of a different religion.
2. *Respect for allies*—The religious character of faith-based providers is protected by allowing them to retain control over the definition, development, practice, and expression of their religious beliefs. Neither federal nor state government can require a religious provider to alter its form of internal governance or remove religious art, icons, scripture or other symbols in order to be a program participant.
3. *Protecting clients*—In regard to rendering assistance, religious organization shall not discriminate against an individual on the basis of religion, a religious belief,

[83] President Obama's White House Office of Faith-based and Neighborhood Partnerships has developed a comprehensive partnership guide, *Partnerships for the Common Good.*

[84] See Department of Health and Human Services, *Charitable Choice Provisions and Regulations; Final Rules*, 2003. See further at: www.twc.state.tx.us/svcs/charchoice/chchoice.html.

or refusal to actively participate in a religious practice. If an individual objects to the religious character of a program, a secular alternative must be provided.

4. *Church-state separation*—All government funds must be used to fulfill the public social service goals, and no direct government funding can be diverted to inherently religious activities such as worship, sectarian instruction, and proselytization.

However, in several cases the judiciary have criticized the operation of Charitable Choice program both because they have been offered to participants who lack true freedom of choice (children and prisoners in particular[85]) and because they can in practice allow government funds to flow along channels that discriminate between recipients and non-recipients on religious grounds, contrary to the constitutional imperative that church and state remain separate (see below).

C. Nonprofits and Government Funding

The Compassion Capital Fund, established in 2001 through the Department of Health and Human Services, distributed almost $200 million to various faith- and community-based organizations, in itself a comparatively trivial amount relative to the overall financing needs of nonprofits. Legislative appropriations processes in 16 states have offered some type of funding to FBOs or OFBCIs, leading to 42 separate appropriation bills that have allocated approximately $70 million. In 2007 alone, a total of 10 appropriation laws were passed in 10 states, thus greatly increasing the overall funding for faith-based initiatives.

1. Government Funding of Nonprofits: The Principal/Agent Relationship

In this jurisdiction, there have been indications of judicial recognition that the public benefit functions of government and charity are inherently congruent. In 1959,

[85] In recent years, several judges have concluded that children and teenagers, like prisoners, have too few options and too little power to make the voluntary choices the Supreme Court requires when public money flows to programs involving religious instruction or indoctrination. That was the conclusion of a federal judge in Michigan in Teen Ranch v. UDOW, 389 F. Supp. 2d 827 (W.D. Mich. 2005), a case filed by Teen Ranch, a nonprofit Christian facility that provides residential care for troubled or abused children ages 11 to 17. In 2003, state officials imposed a moratorium on placements of children there, primarily because of the facility's intensively religious programming. In another case, Freedom From Religion Foundation v. Towey, No. 04-C-381-S, 2005 U.S. Dist. LEXIS 39444 (W.D. Wis. January 11, 2005), a federal judge struck down a federal grant in 2003 to MentorKids USA, a ministry based in Phoenix, to provide mentors for the children of prisoners. In this case, filed by the Freedom From Religion Foundation in Madison, Wisconsin, the judge noted that the exclusively Christian mentors had to regularly assess whether the young people in their care seemed "to be progressing in relationship with God."

for example, the Court of Appeals of Kentucky concluded in *Ferguson v. Gardner*[86] that the Attorney General lacked standing to defend against the contestation of a will containing a charitable bequest as that official would be conflicted in such cases because the state has a financial interest in the invalidity of charitable bequests due to the tax privileges available for charities. Such an acceptance of congruity of function can quite naturally lead to circumstances where charity actively engages in government public benefit service delivery programs compatible with its charitable purpose. The power imbalance in this relationship may then effectively result in a charity acting as a government agent. This jurisdiction has seen some judicial examination of the perennial dilemma as to whether, or to what extent, government funding may enduce a principal/agent relationship with the recipient nonprofit.

In *Blum v. Yaretsky*,[87] for example, the court held that pervasive regulation and receipt of government funding at private nursing homes does not make nursing home decisions state action. In *Rendell-Baker v. Kohn*,[88] it was found that although a private school's being heavily funded by the state did not make the school a state actor. Again, in *Flagg Bros., Inc. v. Brooks*,[89] it was stated that mere acquiescence by the law in the private actions of a warehouse did not convert those acts into those of the state. Finally, in *Young v. Shawnee Mission Med. Ctr.*,[90] the court determined that a religious hospital did not lose its Title VII exemption merely because it received thousands of dollars in federal Medicare payments because such payments did not "transform [the hospital] into a federally funded institution." In these cases, the judiciary was clear in holding that funding in itself did not transform a relationship to the extent that the resulting actions of the recipient could be imputed to the funder, on the principal/agent rule. However, it remains unclear whether this would still be the position where the funding strand of that relationship is accompanied by a constraining policy and procedure strand to the effect that the aims and objectives of the funder, together with the wherewithal for achieving them, are wholly controlled by the funder.

2. Government Funding of Charities

Religious organizations, along with many other government-funded nonprofits, often have charitable status. As charities, such organizations are required under charity law principles to retain independence and autonomy. The scale of government funding, however, together with accompanying policy constraints, may well

86 327 S.W.2d 947 (Ky. Ct. App. 1959). See further, Parachin, A., "The Definition of Charity and Public Law Equality Norms," paper presented at the conference *Private and Public Law—Intersections in Law and Method*, the T C Beirne Law School at the University of Queensland, Brisbane, July 2011, at p. 38, where he cites Brody, E. as his source.

87 457 U.S. 991, 1002–12 (1982).

88 457 U.S. 830, (1982).

89 436 U.S. 149, 164 (1978).

90 No. 88-2321-S, 1988 U.S. Dist. LEXIS 12248 (D. Kan. Oct. 21, 1988).

unduly impact upon the independence of a recipient charity. Although the *Mitchell* and *Bowen* cases serve as reminders that there is a continuum along which a nonprofit must proceed with some caution if it is to avoid falling into an agency role in relation to government, there is also an additional hazard for a charity that allows its independence to be compromised by the swamping effect of accepting government funds and delivering on government policies.

D. Public Benefit Service Provision: The Practice

In the United States, certain services or utilities of a public benefit nature—such as universities, hospitals, and community social services—have never been viewed as necessarily the responsibility of government, and are often provided by nonprofit organizations. Since 1996, this distribution of responsibility has been extended to a series of faith-based initiatives involving partnerships between religious organizations and government to deliver the social services that can no longer be paid for by federal funds. One measure of the importance of the nonprofit contribution to the nation's health care and education is that currently nearly 75 percent of the charitable sector's annual income flows to health care and educational organizations.

1. Health Care

The sharp distinction between public and private, or between the responsibilities of state and charity for the health and well-being of citizens, associated with the welfare state experience, is missing in the United States. Instead there is and has long been an acceptance that service users get what they pay for, and providers—whether government, business, or charity—will compete in an open market to deliver accordingly. For some academics, the distinction between health care enterprises run by commerce or by charity has become barely discernible.[91] The following comment, offered in testimony to Congress nearly 50 years ago, is equally true today:[92]

> The image of a voluntary institution as a charitable organization, financing its care of patients to a substantial degree through philanthropy... is largely anachronistic.

[91] See Brown, E. and Silvinski, A., "Nonprofit Organizations and the Market," in Powell, W. W. and Steinberg, R. (eds.) *The Nonprofit Sector: A Research Handbook* (2nd ed.), Yale University Press, New Haven, CT, 2006, at 140–159; see also Tuckman, H. P. and Chang, C. F., "Commercial Activity, Technological Change and Nonprofit Mission," in Powell and Steinberg (eds.), *The Nonprofit Sector,* at 629–645. See also Colombo, J. D., "Private Benefit, Joint Ventures and the Death of Health Care as an Exempt Purpose," in 34 *Journal of Health Law,* Vol. 34, 2001, at pp. 505, 521.

[92] Hearings on Conditions and Problems of the Nation's Nursing Homes, Subcommittee on Long Term Care, Special Committee on Aging, U.S. Senate, 89th Cong., 1st Sess., Pt. 2 (February 15, 1965), at p. 559.

> Philanthropy, though increasing, has not been able to match the redoubled demands for health care.

The provision of health care and related facilities, particularly hospitals, has long been recognized by the IRS as charitable.[93] This has resulted in health service organizations, such as hospitals and nursing homes, accounting for nearly 60 percent of total nonprofit spending.[94] In fact until very recently the presumption that hospitals should qualify for charitable tax exemption had become a routine expectation, not dissimilar to the approach taken toward churches. In all states, the booming health care industry has produced innumerable examples of hospitals, nursing homes, day care facilities, etc., offering much the same type and standard of service whether owned or operated by charity, business, or a combination of both.

The recently enacted America's Healthy Future Act 2009,[95] almost certainly initiated in response to judicial concerns, has set out a basis for differentiating between tax-exempt hospitals and their for-profit counterparts. It requires the former to complete a community needs assessment every three years; adopt and publicize a financial assistance policy; refrain from billing at its highest rates patients who qualify for financial assistance; and to refrain from pursuing aggressive debt collection actions against patients.

2. Education

Along with health care, education is at the center of current dense intersectoral fiscal linkages. Universities, colleges of higher education, schools, and preschool facilities may all be provided by government, business, or nonprofits, and are frequently the subject of financial investment or management by cross-sectoral consortia.

The requirements of charity law as it applies to the advancement of education are to be found in the regulations under § 501(c)(3), which define "educational" as (1) the instruction or training of individuals for the purpose of improving or developing their capabilities, or (2) the instruction of the public on subjects useful to individuals and beneficial to the community. The first class of organizations has been treated quite expansively by the IRS, which has extended tax-exempt status, for example, to college bookstores[96] and alumni associations.[97] Educational organizations account for some 17 percent of total nonprofit spending.

[93] Rev. Rul. 69–545, 1969–2 C.B. 117.

[94] See Arnsberger, P., "Charities, Social Welfare, and Other Tax-Exempt Organizations, 2004," in *Stat. Income Bull.*, Fall 2007, at pp. 210, 213.

[95] S. 1796, § 6007.

[96] Rev. Rul. 69–538, 1969–2 C.B. 116.

[97] Rev. Rul. 60–143, 1960–1C.B. 192.

3. Community Development

In 1993, in order to address the complex, interrelated social issues associated with deprived rural and urban communities, the Clinton administration launched the Empowerment Zone/Enterprise Community (EZ/EC) program. Consisting of three U.S. congressional designations—the Renewal Communities (RCs), Empowerment Zones (EZs), and Enterprise Communities (ECs)—the program allows the federal government to channel a combination of grants, tax credits for businesses, bonding authority, and other benefits into impoverished communities across the nation. This initiative was subsequently replicated in the U.K. In December 2010, President Obama signed the Tax Relief, Unemployment Insurance Reauthorization, and Job Creation Act of 2010 (Public Law 111-312) to extend tax incentives worth billions of dollars for all Federal Empowerment Zones and the District of Columbia Enterprise Zone, retroactively, through to December 2011. In the Empowerment Zones and Renewal Communities, the most widely used Community Renewal tax incentive is the employment credit, which provides tax benefits to businesses that employ residents from the designated areas.

V. NEW LEGAL STRUCTURES AND DONOR INCENTIVES

In the United States, the entanglement of nonprofits with commerce is now so dense and well-established that any attempt to neatly disaggregate their commercial activities from those of for-profits, in accordance with legal structures and status, would be futile and misleading. It has been said that:[98] "in recent times, as the trends towards social entrepreneurship and venture philanthropy have accelerated and as the bounds between for-profit and nonprofit have blurred our vague, ill-discussed, ill-defined legal definition of charity has been too amorphous to lend structure to the difficult task of sorting out what is and is not charitable in the eyes of the law." Moreover, the impact of the MBA approach to organizational management across all sectors has been so pervasive for so long that nonprofits, including charities, have come to resemble in form if not function their for-profit and government counterparts. Perhaps as a reaction to this rather closed world, the United States has, in recent years, led the way in developing innovative cross-sectoral legal structures.[99] Open market experimentation in methods of delivering public benefit services

[98] See Kelley, T., "Rediscovering Vulgar Charity: An Historical Analysis of America's Tangled Nonprofit Law," in *Fordham Law Review*, Vol. 73, No. 6, 2005, at pp. 2437–499.

[99] The Aspen Institute, for example, has explored the question of whether there should be a new legal form in the United States for "Fourth Sector" ventures. (A summary of Aspen's September 2006 roundtable on "Mixing Mission and Business: Does Social Enterprise Need a New Legal Approach?" is available at: http://www.nonprofitresearch.org/usr_doc/New_Legal_Forms_report_FInAL.pdf).

has incubated a rich variety of arrangements and hybrid legal structures, such as the LC3, which may involve microfinance schemes, leading for-profit companies, or hedge funds working with charities in collaborative philanthropic ventures. As Kelley has commented:[100]

> During the 1990s, the trend toward commercialization of charity strengthened as technology boom millionaires entered the charitable realm and insisted on the adoption of business methods, and as private foundations increasingly adopted the rhetoric and practices of 'venture philanthropy.' By the end of the 1990s, it was becoming difficult to distinguish between business and charity.

The general desire to do things differently, competitively, and remuneratively, has seen an explosion in the number and variety of social enterprises. The indications are that legislative change is also in the offing.[101]

A. Foundations

Foundations are defined by the Foundation Center as independent foundations, corporate foundations, community foundations, and operating foundations.[102] According to *Giving USA 2010*,[103] corporations and foundations in 2009 contributed 4 percent and 13 percent respectively to total U.S. philanthropic funds, and together their contribution constituted 17 percent of funds for that year. In 2009, foundations decreased their giving by 8.4 percent from 2008 to $42.9 billion, of which 72 percent came from independent foundations, 10 percent from community foundations, and 10 percent from corporate foundations, while 8 percent came from operating foundations.[104]

1. Private Foundations

In 2010, according to the NCCS, there were almost 121,000 private foundations in the United States, with their assets totaling $562 billion.[105] The duty of care on the director or trustee of a private foundation requires them to invest the foundation

[100] Kelley, "Rediscovering Vulgar Charity", at p. 2441,

[101] This may follow from a 2011 study issued by the Congressional Budget Office, "Options for Changing the Tax Treatment of Charitable Giving," which examines and evaluates 11 ways that changes in the tax code could impact individual charitable giving and the consequences of each for federal tax revenue.

[102] See further at Foundation Center, http://foundationcenter.org/getstarted/.

[103] *Giving USA 2010*, a report compiled annually by the American Association of Fundraising Counsel.

[104] NCS, *Quick Facts about Nonprofits*, citing as its source the Foundation Center; see further at: http://nccs.urban.org/statistics/quickfacts.cfm.

[105] See IRS Business Master File 04/2010, at http://nccsdataweb.urban.org/PubApps/profile DrillDown.php?state=US&rpt=PF.

capital in such a way as to secure reasonable revenues.[106] The Tax Reform Act 1969, permitting private foundations to merge their investing and program functions to make Program Related Investments, has become a significant contributor to modern philanthropy. A PRI, combining a grant and an investment, allows a private foundation to invest in a for-profit company provided the foundation follows stringent "expenditure responsibility" rules. For example, the IRS has permitted the Gates Foundation to invest in for-profit pharmaceutical companies to help reach its goal of reducing disease in developing countries.[107]

2. Community Foundations

In the 1970s and 1980s, large private foundations such as the Ford Foundation and the Charles Stewart Mott Foundation began to champion and support community foundations as a means of responding to local community needs and serving as catalysts and resources within communities. Their growth picked up speed again in the 1990s, as community foundations began actively promoting donor-advised funds, which attracted some money that may otherwise have gone into private foundations. A new and proliferating form of foundation is the "pooled funds or mutual foundation," which is a commercial community foundation that provides more flexibility than a private family foundation. The past two decades have seen substantial growth in community development corporations that concentrate all grantmaking on community development projects. In 2000, there were estimated to be 664 community foundations in the United States, a 150 percent increase since 1990: the top 20 percent then controlled more than 88 percent of the sector's assets; the top 5 percent held 60 percent of assets.[108]

The Council on Foundations recently launched the Community Foundations National Standards Board, a new organization that will administer the National Standards for the U.S. Community Foundations accreditation process. To date, more than 450 community foundations are in compliance with the standards, which have been updated in 2008.

3. Corporate Foundations

The practice whereby some for-profit companies donate a portion of their profits, staff time, or resources to charity, often referred to as "corporate philanthropy," can be achieved by using a corporate foundation as an intermediary. Under IRC § 170(c)

[106] Lynch v. John M. Redfield Foundation, 88 Cal. Rptr. 86, 89 (Cal. Ct. App. 1970).

[107] In a Private Letter Ruling, the IRS permitted the foundation to make program-related investments in private, for-profit industry to accelerate the discovery, development, and adoption of health interventions to reduce disease in developing countries. I.R.S. Priv. Ltr. Rul. 200603031 (January 20, 2006). As cited in Hines, J. R., Horwitz J. R., and Nichols, A., "The Attack on Nonprofit Status: A Charitable Assessment," in *Michigan Law Review*, Vol. 108, 2010, at p. 1188.

[108] See further at www.communityfoundations.net/.

a corporation may obtain a charitable deduction if it makes a donation to a qualified donee, such as a qualified charitable organization or a governmental unit for public purposes, although this is qualified by § 170(b)(2), which restricts the amount a corporation can deduct from its tax liability in lieu of its charitable donations to a ceiling of 10 percent of taxable income in any given tax year.

There is a long tradition of government incentives to induce corporate support for nonprofits in the United States,[109] and consequently, as Silk has pointed out, "corporate philanthropy has become a permanent feature of the legal landscape."[110] This was facilitated by the introduction of the Uniform Management of Institutional Funds Act 1972 (extended to trusts by the Uniform Prudent Investor Act 1994), subsequently replaced in 48 states by the Uniform Prudent Management of Institutional Funds Act (2008), which significantly simplified entrepreneurial investments by incorporated charitable organizations and has led to the present situation where charitable organizations often invest in hedge funds.

However, according to the Committee Encouraging Corporate Philanthropy, an international forum focused exclusively on corporate philanthropy: "60 percent of companies cut their philanthropic donations from 2008 to 2009, and most of those trimmed them by more than 10 percent."[111] Nonetheless, corporate giving, which is tied to corporate profits, is reported by the Committee Encouraging Corporate Philanthropy to have increased in 2009 to $14.1 billion, or 5 percent of all charitable giving, reflecting an increase in corporate in-kind donations.[112] An example of corporate giving is the practice adopted by Microsoft in matching any donation of up to $10,000 per year that any employee in North America makes to any nonprofit. As a result, Microsoft donates to between 16,000 and 20,000 different organizations annually, and in 2010 raised more than $96 million for 16,000-plus community organizations.[113] This initiative was adopted by Apple, on the same terms, in late 2011.

Corporate philanthropy makes good business sense whether or not there is also an altruistic motive: Showcasing a company and polishing its image in the marketplace by supporting and publishing its support for good causes raises its market profile. Indeed,

[109] Dating at least from the Tax Act of 1936, which allowed corporations to deduct charitable gifts up to 5 percent of federal taxable income, following the Supreme Court decision in Old Mission Portland Cement Co. v. Helvering, 293 U.S. 289, 293 (1934).

[110] See Silk, T., "Corporate Philanthropy and Law in the United States: A Practical Guide to Tax Choices and an Introduction to Compliance with Anti-Terrorism Laws," in *The International Journal of Not-for-Profit Law*, Vol. 6, No. 3, June 2004.

[111] See further Corporate Citizenship: Awards, Microsoft, http://www.microsoft.com/about/corporatecitizenship/en-us/about/awards/.

[112] There is some doubt regarding this statistic. The number of respondent companies was considerably down on previous annual polls; large companies, each with a sizeable philanthropic commitment (e.g., Chrysler, Lehman Brothers, Freddie Mac, and Fannie May) had disappeared into bankruptcy; and the uplift may have been largely an aberration attributable to the valuation reported by pharmaceutical companies on the drugs they dispensed with at a loss.

[113] See further at: www.microsoft.com/about/corporatecitizenship/us/ . . . /default.mspx.

most companies with any profile, if only for commercial reasons, can no longer afford not to be seen to be engaged in community benefit activity.

4. Social Enterprises

As Young has pointed out, there is a "convergence around social enterprise between the nonprofit and for-profit sectors: more businesses are becoming socially conscious and active along philanthropic fronts while nonprofits are coming to rely more heavily on commercial sources of revenue and business methods."[114] As the convergence may take many different forms, social enterprise is consequently an uncertain entity though it has been defined by the Social Enterprises Alliance as "an organization or venture that advances its primary social or environmental mission using business methods."[115] The number and variety of social enterprises are increasing rapidly in this jurisdiction as nonprofits and for-profits collaborate to find new ways of operating in the open market to address social goals while also providing for some profit distribution.[116] Kerlin adds that social enterprise is open to wider interpretation in the United States than elsewhere and, when pursued by nonprofits, "may take on a number of different organizational forms including internal commercial ventures, for-profit and nonprofit subsidiaries, and partnerships with business including cause-related marketing."[117] She makes the point that in practice much social enterprise remains focused simply on revenue generation by nonprofit organizations. Unlike in Europe, "the U.S. nonprofit definition does not allow any profit distribution" and, rather than belonging to the "social economy" where social benefit is the main driving force, "in the United States, the concept of a social economy is not used and nonprofit social enterprises are often discussed as operating in the market economy."

5. Low-Profit Limited Liability Companies (L3C)

L3Cs can accept program-related investments—loans, equity investments, etc.—from foundations with the expectation of below-market (or zero) returns. As opposed to grants, if such investments return to the foundation, the grantor must

[114] See Young, D., "Social Enterprise in the United States: Alternate Identities and Forms," paper presented at The EMES Conference, The Social Enterprise: A Comparative Perspective, Trento, Italy, December 13–15, 2001, at p. 4.

[115] Self-described as "the membership organization leading the creation of a social enterprise movement" with a purpose to "mobilize communities of nonprofit organizations and funders to advance earned income strategies." It is run by and for social enterprise practitioners. See further at https://se-alliance.org/.

[116] Google.org is unique in that although its mission—addressing climate change, poverty, and emerging disease—is typical of a charity, it also retains the right to distribute profits to its shareholders and to engage in the unlimited lobbying of public officials.

[117] Kerlin, "Social Enterprise in the United States and Europe," at pp. 247–63.

reinvest the amount into a similar enterprise within one year. Essentially, this is a risk management device that permits foundations to invest as the anchor tenant in a social enterprise and, by bearing the greatest burden of risk, thereby encouraging other investors to commit funds in furtherance of an agreed collaborative social venture. Taxed according to the tax rates of partners at the table, L3Cs offer tranched investments: Different stakeholders invest in the social enterprise with different rates of return, and this mix offers greater security for mainstream private investors than would other nonprofit ventures.

The first limited liability company statute was passed in Vermont in 2008 (see chapter 13), and at least five other American states have since passed similar legislation, in a development viewed by some as "a step in the direction of facilitating the creation of for-profit charities."[118] However, so far, complementary recognition has not been given to the L3C in the Internal Revenue Code. Thus, it has no special tax-exempt status.

6. Donor Incentives

In the United States, tax incentives for charitable giving date back to the colonial era.[119] The culture of donor incentive schemes is so well ingrained here that it is often quite candidly acknowledged that many philanthropists are motivated as much by tax gains as altruism. This view was corroborated more recently in a report published by the Independent Sector, which suggests that the decisions of U.S. donors regarding the size of their gifts to charity are influenced by their ability to claim a tax deduction for the donation.[120] A study by The Center on Philanthropy at Indiana University shows that over half of all dollars given to charity are donated by individuals with a household income of $200,000 or more, which again suggests that there is a strong link between high earners and charity donations that is likely to be prompted by the higher rate of tax offset.[121] Furthermore, wealthy donors who create charitable remainder trusts (large gifts, typically $100,000 or more), are favored with a generous tax offset of at least five figures; sufficient to allow the donor to derive a substantial income tax benefit from the gift.

[118] Hines, Horwitz, and Nichols, "The Attack on Nonprofit Status," at p. 1189.

[119] See Howard, C., *The Hidden Welfare State: Tax Expenditures and Social Policy in the United States*, Princeton University Press, Princeton, NJ, 1997. As cited by Wright, K., in "Generosity vs. Altruism: Philanthropy and Charity in the United States and United Kingdom," *Voluntas: International Journal of Voluntary and Nonprofit Organizations*, Vol. 12, No. 4, 2002, at p. 410.

[120] See Independent Sector, "Deducting Generously: The Effect of Charitable Tax Incentives on Giving," April 16, 2003. See further at: http://www.independentsector.org/giving_volunteering.

[121] See The Center on Philanthropy at Indiana University, *Patterns of Household Charitable Giving by Income Group, 2005*, Summer 2007, http://www.philanthropy.iupui.edu/research/giving%20focused%20on%20meeting%20needs%20of%20the%20poor%20july%202007.pdf.

This culture has proven very resistant to change. President Obama, in his first budget in February 2009, sought to impose change with a proposal that taxpayers earning more than $250,000 would have their ability to deduct contributions to charities reduced to a rate of 28 percent from a rate of 35 percent. By Summer 2011 this law remained unchanged. The Tax Relief, Unemployment Reauthorization, and Job Creation Act 2010 extended the income tax rate reductions enacted during the Bush administration through December 31, 2012 so that income and capital gains tax savings from lifetime charitable gifts of cash or other assets will remain unchanged at least until the year following the next presidential election.

The fact that the United States has "the world's most generous tax concessions"[122] for philanthropy and that "no other nation grants subsidies at such a high level or across so many types of activities"[123] must go some way toward explaining why private and corporate philanthropic foundations have long been such a conspicuous feature on the U.S. charity landscape. It is far from coincidental that such foundations flourish when set in the context of the world's most free-market economy; often the same entrepreneurs and organizations are the market leaders in both capitalist and philanthropic enterprises. Such foundations have attracted criticism on the grounds that they are more likely to serve the private interests of the rich rather than the stated intended charitable purpose: Private individuals may create private foundations as a vehicle to protect their assets from taxation; such foundations may hold almost any type of asset (real estate, jewelry, stock, options, etc.) and follow almost any investment strategy, allowing their descendants to assert control over such assets almost in perpetuity. From the perspective of the profits of charity, the phenomenon of U.S. philanthropic foundations would seem to have a particular significance.[124]

7. Donor-Advised Funds

A donor-advised fund (DAF) is a fund created in a public charity by or for a corporation or other donor. It may be offered by community foundations as well as by DAFs affiliated with commercial organizations, such as mutual funds. All donations, together with complete legal control over the fund, pass from the donor to the donee, but the donor may offer advice to the donee with regard to charitable distributions from the fund, subject to mutually agreed terms and conditions. The recognition of commercially created DAFs initially met with resistance from the

[122] See Clotfelter, C., "Tax-Induced Distortions in the Voluntary Sector," in *Case Western Law Review*, Vol. 39, 1988/1989, at pp. 663–94.

[123] See Weisbrod, B., "The Pitfalls of Profits," in *Stanford Social Innovation Review*, Winter 2004, at pp. 40–47.

[124] See Anheier and Leat, *From Charity to Creativity*. However, it must be acknowledged that the Gates/Buffet initiative has been on a scale that does exhibit definite altruistic characteristics without an accompanying concern about maximizing personal tax advantages.

IRS[125] and remained undefined in law until the federal Pension Protection Act of 2006. It was only with the establishment of several national funds, set up by financial services companies in the 1990s, that they became available and known to many Americans. By 2006, the country's 99 largest funds had more than $19.2 billion in assets and had donated more than $3.5 billion to charity each year according to the National Philanthropic Trust.[126]

Philanthropists are increasingly unwinding their private foundations into donor-advised funds, which invest assets and make grants to charities from individual accounts based largely on donors' recommendations. The funds, which operate as independent charities, have other advantages besides allowing donors to take an immediate tax deduction after making contributions. Donors advise the fund on where the grants should go, but the funds do not have to make distributions as often as a foundation would. Donors can also give many types of assets—including cash, securities, and even art—depending on the fund's specific rules. Unlike foundations, donor-advised funds are not subject to annual disbursement requirements, and they benefit from more generous tax deductions than foundations.

VI. CHARITIES, TRADING, AND CONTEMPORARY CASE LAW

As Kerlin has noted, "in the U.S., the use of commercial activities by nonprofits to support mission-related activities has been in practice from the very foundation of the country."[127] The shift of charities towards the commercial profit-making world came early, has been decisive, and is now well established. Caught up in the maelstrom of market forces that have contorted the sector since the early 1980s, charities have often found themselves in court as they struggled to plot a way through a landscape previously dominated by government or commerce. The difficulties involved in abiding by the rules governing charitable status while simultaneously trying to take advantage of new service provision opportunities has been and continues to be fraught. For the IRS, the task of policing the fuzzy line separating charitable and commercial activity has become a responsibility to be more frequently shared with the judiciary as the many variants of nonprofits experiment with ever-more innovative structures and schemes to acquire the funds no longer readily available from government or the general public. The resulting relatively high level of nonprofit litigation in the United States, unlike in other common law jurisdictions, clearly reveal the issues appearing before the court and the changing social role of charity.

[125] See National Foundation, Inc. v. United States, 87–2 U.S.T.C.¶ 9602 (Ct. Cl. 1987), in which the IRS was unsuccessful in its initial attempt to persuade courts to outlaw donor-advised funds. See also Fund for Anonymous Gifts v. United States, 99–1 U.S.T.C. ¶ 50,440 (D.C. Cir. 1999).

[126] See further at http://www.nptrust.org/.

[127] See Kerlin, "Social Enterprise in the United States and Europe," at p. 251.

A. Legal Framework

As Fishman points out:[128]

> There is no single law of charities in the United States.[129] Instead there are several statutes that apply, depending on the form of organization—trust or corporation; the focus of the regulator—state or federal, and even local; and the purpose of the regulation.[130]

However, some legislation with federal application has emerged: for example, the Model Protection of Charitable Assets Act 2011 was passed by the Uniform Laws Commission in Summer 2011. The unifying influence of the IRS, as it applies the IRC to all the nation's nonprofits, brings some administrative coherence to the sector. The higher incidence of litigation concerning charities, a feature of charity law in this jurisdiction, demonstrates that the traditional common law system and its reliance upon the judiciary for development of charitable purposes remains relatively potent.

1. Regulatory Bodies

The usual tax-driven regulatory framework that has long typified all common law jurisdictions, other than England and Wales, also governs charities in the United States. The courts, the customs and excise, and the state attorneys general have their customary roles in respect of charities, albeit this is somewhat complicated by operating within a federated jurisdiction. The exercise of the traditional *parens patriae* authority of the Attorney General is seldom utilized and, although the right to intervene in the public interest subsists, in many states this official exercises little oversight over charities, leaving regulation of the sector to the IRS.[131] Indeed, in some cases, the Attorney General has been held to lack standing in charity cases. This occurred in *Ferguson v. Gardner*[132] where it was ruled that because the state stood to gain financially if a charitable bequest in a will was found to be invalid, the appointment of the Attorney General to defend the will would place that official in a compromised position. Public benefit organizations (both charitable organizations and social welfare organizations), like numerous other kinds of nonprofit organization, are generally exempt from federal income tax, with certain limited exceptions; churches generally are presumed tax-exempt even without registering with the IRS.

[128] Fishman, J. J., "Nonprofit Organizations in the United States," at p. 130.

[129] One effort toward creating unified fiduciary standards for charities is the American Law Institute's project on the Principles of the Law of Nonprofit Organizations.

[130] For example, protecting charitable assets is covered under certain statutes, protecting the public is covered under others.

[131] See further Fishman, J. L., "The Development of Nonprofit Corporation Law and an Agenda for Reform," in *Emory Law Journal*, Vol. 34, 1985, at pp. 619–83.

[132] 327 S.W.2d 947 (Ky. Ct. App. 1959).

One of the principal features of this regulatory framework is the predominance of the Treasury Department and the Internal Revenue Service in making decisions with regard to what is charitable.[133] Although state courts continue to play a role in this regard,[134] it is the Tax Exempt and Government Entities (TEGE) Division of the IRS that is most involved in determining charitable status.

2. Internal Revenue Service (IRS)

Constitutional arrangements, specifically the powers reserved to the federal government under the Tenth Amendment, allow the Internal Revenue Service (IRS) to administer a uniform tax regime across all states, including assessing eligibility for tax exemption on charitable grounds. The IRS maintains a register of all tax-exempt or nonprofit organizations, of which public benefit organizations (the term usually used to describe "charities" or "charitable organizations" in the United States) receive the highest level of tax benefits (including tax-preferred donations).[135] It provides a level of supervision and accountability through a system of annual returns, audits, penalties, and fines. Charitable organizations are required to make available their annual business income returns for public inspection, which includes disclosure of unrelated business income.

3. Internal Revenue Code

The IRS applies the Internal Revenue Code to categories of organizations exempt from federal income tax. The IRC does not, however, simply differentiate between charities and other nonprofits as in the U.K. Instead it provides for charitable organizations together with other classes of nonprofits, which are also tax-exempt and of which there were some 455,693 registered with the IRS in 2010, with total assets estimated at $961.4 billion in 2008.[136] Not all nonprofits are necessarily tax-exempt: a

[133] Both the Treasury Department and the IRS are involved with setting tax policy regarding charities. The Treasury issues regulations, which are more general, whereas the IRS issues Revenue Rulings, which are pubic documents describing how the IRS will treat various types of organizations or transactions.

[134] In addition to hearing cases involving fiduciary duties, state courts become involved in determining whether bequests qualify as charitable, and whether the organization qualifies for a state charitable property tax exemption (state law tends to be more generous for bequests than property tax exemption).

[135] *See* I.R.S., *Search for Charities, Online Version of Publication 78*, at: www.irs.gov/charities/article/0,,id=96136,00.html.

It might be added that an organization is perfectly free to set itself up as a charity and undertake charitable activities and need never be known to the IRS unless it also chooses to seek tax exemption status and/or becomes incorporated.

[136] See, National Center for Charitable Statistics (NCCS) at http://nccs.urban.org/statistics/quickfacts.cfm

purpose may not fit within the list of purposes described in § 170(c) of the Internal Revenue Code.

a. § 501(c)(3)

Charitable organizations are registered under § 501(c)(3). This states that charitable organizations must be both organized and operated exclusively for "religious, charitable, scientific, testing for public safety, literary, or educational purposes, or to foster national or international amateur sports competition... or for the prevention of cruelty to children or animals." The Treasury Department defines the term "charitable," for the purposes of this list, to include giving relief to the poor, the distressed, or the underprivileged; advancing religion; advancing education or science; erecting or maintaining public buildings, monuments, or works; lessening the burdens of government; lessening neighborhood tensions; eliminating prejudice and discrimination; defending human and civil rights secured by law; and combating community deterioration and juvenile delinquency.[137] The usual common law rules govern charity's legal characteristics, and the "primary purpose" test applies to profit distribution. The benefits of § 501(c)(3) status include exemption from federal income tax as well as eligibility to receive tax-deductible charitable contributions.

For the regulatory framework relating to charitable organizations in the United States, the distinction between public charities and private foundations is of fundamental importance.[138] Since 1975, 48 states and the District of Columbia have passed laws imposing the restrictions on private foundations as stated in Chapter 42 of the Internal Revenue Code.[139] The IRS reports that there were 115,340 private foundations in 2008, of which 110,099 were grantmaking (non-operating), and 5241 were operating foundations. The Bill & Melinda Gates Foundation[140] is the largest with over $38 billion in assets but most are much smaller, with 93 percent having less than $10 million. In aggregate, private foundations in the United States control over $628 billion in assets.

b. § 501(c)(4)

Social welfare organizations, provided for under § 501(c)(4), include certain managed health plans and a mix of advocacy groups, civic clubs, etc. Income is generally exempt from tax and is subject to the rules on private inurement and excessive payments to insiders; however contributions to it are not deductible as charitable contributions. As the IRS advises, to be tax-exempt as a social welfare organization, an entity must not be organized for-profit and must be operated exclusively to promote social welfare. Pursuant to changes enacted as part of the Taxpayer Bill of Rights 2, the earnings

137 § 1.501(c)(3)-1(d)(2).

138 Note that although public charities may engage in limited lobbying activity, private foundations are prohibited from engaging in any: I.R.C. § 4945.

139 See Fremont-Smith, *Governing Nonprofit Organizations*, at p.26.

140 See further at http://www.gatesfoundation.org/about/Pages/overview.aspx.

of such an organization may not inure to the benefit of any private shareholder or individual. If the organization engages in an excess benefit transaction with a person having substantial influence over the organization, an excise tax may be imposed on the person and any managers agreeing to the transaction. It must operate primarily to further the common good and general welfare of the people of the community (such as by bringing about civic betterment and social improvements). Such an organization may further its exempt purposes through lobbying as its primary activity without jeopardizing its exempt status, but it may be required to either provide notice to its members regarding the percentage of dues paid that are applicable to lobbying activities or pay a proxy tax. The promotion of social welfare does not include direct or indirect participation or intervention in political campaigns on behalf of or in opposition to any candidate for public office, although an organization may engage in some political activities, so long as that is not its primary activity.[141]

c. § 501(c)(5), (6), and (7)

Labor unions, farm bureaus, and others are registered under § 501(c)(5), business leagues under § 501(c)(6), and social and recreational clubs under § 501(c)(7). All pay tax on their nonmember income.

d. § 4942

This section requires private foundations to annually distribute for charitable purposes at least 5 percent of the value of their investment assets. Problems can arise in defining investment assets and what constitutes a program-related purpose; mission-related investments do not count. This provision is expressly aimed at preventing private foundations from hoarding their assets, and the derived investment income, to build the wealth of the foundation rather than pursue the purposes for which they were established.

4. Charity Law

The distinct legal status of "charity" is recognized in accordance with the usual common law principles governing "exclusivity,"[142] public benefit,[143] private benefit,[144]

[141] See further, IRS, *Social Welfare Organizations,* http://www.irs.gov/charities/nonprofits/article/0,,id=96178,00.html.

[142] A charity's activities must be restricted to furthering its purpose or purposes as identified at registration.

[143] Both the "public" and the "benefit" requirements must be satisfied: § 1.501(c)(3)-1(d)(1)(ii). In a state case construing a bequest, see the influential decision in Jackson v. Phillips, 14 Allen (Mass.) 539, 556 (1867). The Supreme Court of Massachusetts then made it clear that "a charity in the legal sense, may be more fully defined as a gift, to be applied consistently with existing laws, for the benefit of an indefinite number of persons..."

[144] A charity must ensure that no private benefit inures to any individual. See United Cancer Council v. Commissioner, 165 F.3d 1173 (7th Cir. 1999) and Ginsberg v. Commissioner, 46 TC 47 (1966).

political activity,[145] and public policy[146] (see chapter 1). However, some caveats must be added; for example, charitable intent has never been a necessary legal constituent of charitable status in this jurisdiction; the utility of a gift may compensate for an absence of altruism;[147] the exclusivity requirement has been interpreted more flexibly; the operational test applied by the IRS interprets "exclusively" to mean "primarily" or "substantially";[148] and charity has developed a considerable and distinctive "private" dimension alongside the common law public benefit benchmark.

5. Activities Test

In the United States, as in some other common law jurisdictions, the Treasury Department regulations require a charity to satisfy both an organizational test and an operational test,[149] which operate as a check on whether the organization's current operations actually conform to its stated purpose. In recent years the IRS has developed a practice of examining the activities of § 501(c)(3) nonprofits in order to determine whether their tax-exempt status is justified. Schedule H of the Form 990, for example, specifically requires hospitals to report on their activities.

B. Charitable Trading, the Law, and Tax

Subject to the usual common law caveats, charities are clearly permitted to engage in commercial activities. Indeed, in this open market economy there has always been a higher level of charity entanglement with commerce than in other jurisdictions. This more pragmatic approach, where utility trumps altruism, was demonstrated at an early stage when, as Kelley explains:[150]

> In an oft-cited case from 1899,[151] the Supreme Court of New Jersey was asked to decide whether a home for aged and disabled men qualified for property tax purposes as charitable where it paid for its operations—including a mortgage note and superintendents' salaries—by purchasing firewood, requiring residents to turn it

[145] IRC Section 4911 imposes an "excise tax" on excess lobbying expenses. See Christian Echoes National Ministry, Inc. v. United States, 470 F.2d 849 (10th Cir. 1972).

[146] A charity must not violate fundamental public policy: Rev. Rul. 75–384, 1975–2C.B. 204. See, e.g., Bob Jones University v. United States, 461 U.S. 574 (1983).

[147] See, e.g., Fire Insurance Patrol v. Boyd, 120 Pa. 624, 643 (1888).

[148] Treas. Reg. § 1.501 (c)(3)-1(c)(1).

[149] See B.S.W. Group, Inc. v. Commissioner, 70 T.C. 352, 356–57 (1978) where the Commissioner explained that it is the "purpose towards which an organization's activities are directed, and not the nature of the activities themselves, [that are] ultimately dispositive of the organization's right to be classified as a section 501(c)(3) organization."

[150] Kelley, "Rediscovering Vulgar Charity," at p. 26.

[151] Patterson Rescue Mission v. High, 64 NJL 116, 118–19, 44 A. 974, 975, 1899. See also Read v. Tidewater Coal Exchange, Inc., 13 Del. Ch. 195, 116 A. 898 (1922), finding a trade association formed to move coal efficiently through tidewater ports is charitable.

> into kindling, and then selling it for a profit. The court had no trouble finding that "where the objects and purposes of the institution are wholly charitable, with no element of private gain, the receipt of compensation from those who enjoy the benefits do not affect its charitable nature."

Determining the circumstances in which "compensation" is distinguishable from "profit" can, however, prove difficult.

1. Charity Trading and Tax

The Unrelated Business Income Tax (UBIT) legislation,[152] together with § 1.501(c)(3)-1(e) of the tax code, as amended in 1990, form the tax boundaries for charitable trading. The relationship among charities, trading, and UBIT has been explained as follows:[153]

> Unrelated business income is produced from an activity that is conducted on a regular basis and is not directly related to an organization's tax-exempt mission. Income earned by an organization is treated as unrelated business income if it meets two basic requirements. First, the income is derived from a trade or business that is regularly carried on by the organization. Second, the income is earned from a trade or business that is not substantially related to the performance of the organization's exempt purpose or function. Even if profits from such activities are used by tax-exempt organizations to finance their exempt purposes, income that meets these two requirements generally is treated as unrelated business income.

In practice, however, "it has proved administratively difficult for federal, state, and local taxing authorities to differentiate taxable and nontaxable commercial activities."[154]

In the ensuing discussion it should be borne in mind that whereas exemption from income tax is most usually the form of exemption referred to, and assumed to be of most importance to charities, in practice exemption from property tax is also of increasing importance, particularly where the property in question is large and located

[152] The Unrelated Business Income Tax Act 1950, added to the IRS Code, removed the "destination of income" test under which charities could claim tax exemption on commercial activities that were unrelated to their charitable purpose if they could show that the profits generated went to further those purposes.

[153] Ludlum, M., "Unrelated Business Income Tax Returns, 2005," *Statistics of Income Bulletin*, Department of the Treasury, Internal Revenue Service, Winter 2009, at p. 1.

[154] See Cordes, J. and Weisbrod, B., "Differential Taxation of Nonprofits and the Commercialization of Nonprofit Revenues," in Weisbrod, B. (ed.), *To Profit or Not to Profit: The Commercial Transformation of the Nonprofit Sector*, Cambridge, Cambridge University Press, 1998, at p. 85. See also Brody, E., "Business Activities of Nonprofit Organizations," in Cordes, J. and Steuerle, E. (eds.), *Nonprofits and Business*, Urban Institute Press, Washington, DC, 2009, at p. 91.

in a high-rated city area; this is often the case with older charitable institutions such as hospitals. It has been estimated that in total such property tax exemption may be worth as much as between $8 and $13 billion annually to the nation's charities.[155]

2. Related Business

To the extent that the income-producing activity of a nonprofit is "substantially related" to the organization's tax-exempt purpose, the income derived from that activity is tax-free. I.R.C. § 513(a). The Department of the Treasury has elaborated that "[t]rade or business is related to exempt purposes, in the relevant sense, only where the conduct of the business activities has a causal relationship to the achievement of exempt purposes (other than through the production of income)."[156] The problem in practice is that an exempt purpose, according to Treasury Regulation § 1.501(c)(3)-1(d)(2), encompasses such uncertain activities as "lessening of the burdens of government," and the "promotion of social welfare," which as Kelley points out makes it "extremely difficult for judges and regulators and for charities themselves to make meaningful, legally recognizable distinctions between commercial activity that is and is not in furtherance of a charitable purpose."[157]

3. Unrelated Business Income Tax (UBIT)

A business activity is considered unrelated to the organization's charitable purpose if that activity does not contribute in any significant way to accomplishing the purpose that provides the grounds for that organization's tax exemption,[158] and income derived therefrom is subject to §§ 511–14 of the IRC,[159] which applies the UBIT regime to the unrelated business income of all § 501(c) tax-exempt organizations as well as to charitable trusts.[160] As a general rule, § 512 defines "unrelated business taxable income"

[155] See Cordes and and Steurerle, *Nonprofits and Business*, at p. 91, citing Cordes, J., Gantz, M., and Pollack, T., "What Is the Property-Tax Exemption Worth," in Brody, E., (ed.), *Property-Tax Exemption for Charities: Mapping the Battlefield*, Urban Institute Press, Washington, DC, 2002, at pp. 81–112. See also Brody, E., "All Charities Are Property-Tax Exempt, but Some Charities Are More Exempt than Others," in *New England Law Review*, Vol. 44, 2010, at pp. 621–732.

[156] 26 C.F.R (Treas. Reg.) § 1.513-1(d)(2).

[157] Kelley, T., "Rediscovering Vulgar Charity," at p. 53.

[158] See further Hansmann, H., "Unfair Competition and the Unrelated Business Income Tax," in *Virginia Law Review*, Vol. 75, 1989, at pp. 605–35; Atkinson, R., "Altruism in Nonprofit Organizations," in *Boston College Law Review*, Vol. 31, 1990, at p. 501; Colombo, J. and Hall, M., *The Charitable Tax Exemption*, Westview Press, Boulder, CO, 1995; and Stone, E. G., "Adhering to the Old Line: Uncovering the History and Political Function of the Unrelated Business Income Tax," in *Emory Law Journal*, Vol. 54, 2005, at p. 1475.

[159] 26 U.S.C. §§ 511–14.

[160] See § 511(a) (imposing the corporate tax rate on the unrelated business income of 501(c)-exempt organizations) and § 511(b) (applying estate and trust tax rates to the unrelated business income of charitable trusts).

as "the gross income derived by any organization from any unrelated trade or business (as defined in § 513[161]) regularly carried on by it, less the deductions allowed which are directly connected with the carrying on of such trade or business," subject to specific modifications elsewhere in the statute.[162] The carve-outs exempting income from UBIT include when income is derived from infrequent transactions, rather than regular business; generated substantially by volunteers, the sale of donated items, or the conduct of certain nonprofit gaming (e.g., bingo); arises from passive investments such as dividends, interest, annuities, payments with respect to securities loans, royalties, and property rentals; or comes from research.

Some believe that UBIT was intended to prevent tax-exempt organizations from using their tax exemption to unfairly compete with for-profit companies, whether directly or by acquiring for-profit companies. However, neither then nor later has this been underpinned by statute provision or judicial precedent explicitly requiring evidence of unfair competition. Indeed, the courts have repeatedly noted the absence of any requirement to justify the imposition of UBIT by first showing that a tax-exempt entity is engaging in unfair competition.[163] Moreover, the wording of the UBIT provisions and their subsequent IRS interpretation extends beyond giving effect to the congressional intent to level the playing field between tax-exempt nonprofits and others. The sweeping definition of gross income under § 61(a) and the application of UBIT to "debt financed property" reflect Congress's "obvious purpose to tax income comprehensively"[164] using "'the full measure of its taxing power'...to bring within the definition of income 'any accessio[n] to wealth.'"[165]

Over the 60-year period since its introduction, several exceptions[166] have been made to the scope of UBIT, along with one serious but failed attempt to completely

[161] Section 513 provides a general (albeit somewhat circular) definition for an unrelated trade or business:

> [I]n the case of any organization subject to the tax imposed by section 511, any trade or business the conduct of which is not substantially related (aside from the need of such organization for income or funds or the use it makes of the profits derived) to the exercise or performance by such organization of its charitable, educational, or other purpose or function constituting the basis for its exemption under section 501...

See Treas. Reg. § 1.513-1(a).

[162] See § 512(a)(1).

[163] See Disabled Am. Veterans v. United States, 650 F.2d 1178, 1184 (Ct. Cl. 1981) and American Bar Endowment v. United States, 4 Cl. Ct. 404, 409 (1984).

[164] See Commissioner v. Jacobson, 336 U.S. 28, 49 (1949).

[165] See Helvering v. Clifford, 309 U.S. 331, 334 (1940) and Commissioner v. Glenshaw Glass Co., 348 U.S. 426, 431 (1955).

[166] See I.R.C., § 513 setting out the "convenience doctrine" that exempts from UBIT any business activities operated by a tax-exempt organization or college or university for the convenience of its members, patients, students, officers or employees. See also I.R.C. § 512 setting out "modifications" to UBIT, which largely exclude certain types of income from the scope of UBIT.

reform it.[167] However, an argument can be made that UBIT is now mostly irrelevant. An IRS special statistical report on UBIT in 2007 established that little unrelated income of nonprofits was in fact taxed. About 4 percent of nonprofit charitable organizations reported unrelated business income, which was less than one-half of 1 percent of their aggregate revenue, which was $US 1072.2 billion. This resulted in $US 63.3 million in paid tax. This small amount of tax is attributed to a number of drivers such as the width of exemptions, sophisticated tax planning, errors, and ignorance of the specific provisions.

C. Charitable Trading: The Case Law in a Public Services Context

The United States is exceptional among the developed common law countries as regards the extent to which service providers in health, education, and other fields are drawn from both for-profit and nonprofit sectors to supplement government provision.[168] This open market economy has generated dense intersectoral financial and management linkages with many instances of networks in which charities or other nonprofits work collaboratively alongside for-profit companies, assisted by government grants. This is particularly evident in areas of public benefit provision such as family services, job training, child day care, and facilities for the aged, and in social amenities such as museums, radio and television broadcasting, botanical gardens, and zoos. The volume of collaborative and competitive enterprises also produces a high level of litigation, and consequently the United States has amassed a considerable body of case law on the issues key to intersectoral boundary disputes in all common law jurisdictions.

1. Health and Social Care Provision

Contests involving charity law principles have been nowhere more evident than in the health and social care field, as hospital and other health organizations have never been expressly categorized as tax-exempt organizations and have achieved that status only by qualifying as "charitable" organizations. Exemption that may be won under the Internal Revenue Code might be unattainable at the state level where property tax requirements are stricter. In *Methodist Old Peoples Home v. Korzen*,[169] one of the earlier state cases, the foundations were laid for subsequent judgments. The court had to determine whether the plaintiff's property was exempt from taxation on the grounds that the property was used for charitable purposes, specifically as a home for

[167] The Tax Reform Act of 1969 extended UBIT to all tax-exempt organizations (including churches), except government entities.

[168] See Stevens, R., "'A Poor Sort of Memory': Voluntary Hospitals and Government before the Depression," in *The Milbank Memorial Fund Quarterly. Health and Society*, Vol. 60, No. 4, 1982, at pp. 551–84.

[169] 39 Ill.2d 149, 233 N.E. 2d 537 (1968).

the aged.[170] Drawing from past decisions, the court suggested the following principles constituted a frame of reference that should be generally applied:

> It has been stated that a charity is a gift to be applied consistently with existing laws, for the benefit of an indefinite number of persons, persuading them to an educational or religious conviction, for their general welfare—or in some way reducing the burdens of government;[171] that the distinctive characteristics of a charitable institution are that it has no capital, capital stock or shareholders, earns no profits or dividends, but rather derives its funds mainly from public and private charity and holds them in trust for the objects and purposes expressed in its charter;[172] that a charitable and beneficent institution is one which dispenses charity to all who need and apply for it, does not provide gain or profit in a private sense to any person connected with it, and does not appear to place obstacles of any character in the way of those who need and would avail themselves of the charitable benefits it dispenses;[173] that the statements of the agents of an institution and the wording of its governing legal documents evidencing an intention to use its property exclusively for charitable purposes do not relieve such institution of the burden of proving that its property actually and factually is so used;[174] and that the term "exclusively used" means the primary purpose for which property is used and not any secondary or incidental purpose.

Applying this framework of principles, the court found the Methodist Old Peoples Home to be non-charitable. In coming to this decision, the court explained that "the fact that it allocates living space from the standpoint of desirability of location and size on the basis of the amount of the Founder's Fee and monthly charges paid by a resident seems to us lacking in the warmth and spontaneity indicative of charitable impulse . . . rather, it seems more related to the bargaining of the commercial market place." This approach illustrates the bearing of the "commerciality test" (see below) while the principles have subsequently formed the basis for other decisions, most recently that taken by the Illinois Supreme Court in *Provena*[175] where the court disagreed with the argument that the organization was charitable because it provided the community with the invaluable service of health care. The riposte of the appellate court draws a bright red line with important policy implications: "[b]y holding

170 Pursuant to the provisions of § 19.7 of the Revenue Act of 1939. Ill. Rev. Stat. 1965, chap. 120, par. 500.7, as amended by H.B. 1328, passed by the 1967 General Assembly.

171 Citing Crerar v. Williams, 145 Ill. 625 (1893).

172 Citing People ex rel. Cannon v. Southern Illinois Hospital Corp., 404 Ill. 66 (1949); People ex rel. Hellyer v. Morton, 373 Ill. 72 (1940); Congregational Sunday School and Publishing Society v. Board of Review, 290 Ill. 108 (1919).

173 Citing Sisters of Third Order of St. Francis v. Board of Review, 231 Ill. 317 (1907).

174 Citing Skil Corp. v. Korzen, 32 Ill.2d 249 (1965) and People ex rel. Pearsall v. The Catholic Bishop of Chicago, 311 Ill. 11 (1924).

175 Provena Covenant Medical Centre v. Department of Revenue, Docket No. 107328 (Ill. March 18, 2010).

medical care to be, in and of itself, charity, we effectively would excuse charitable hospitals from their ongoing mission of giving."

2. Hospitals

Nonprofits[176] constitute nearly 60 percent of all U.S. hospitals and, prior to the enactment of Medicaid in the 1960s, IRS policy made exempt status under § 501(c)(3) conditional upon providing free or below-cost service to those unable to pay to the extent of their resources.[177] The IRS replaced this standard with a "community benefit" test, which Congress recently bolstered with additional reporting requirements. Nonprofit hospitals, as Colombo has noted, "are essentially fee-for-service businesses that may or may not differ operationally from for-profit counterparts, but their exemption today is largely the result of historical forces, rather than a considered policy judgement that hospitals deserve exempt status."[178] Nonetheless, their present relative market dominance is at least in part due to the significant tax exemptions they receive. The Congressional Budget Office reported in 2006 that nonprofit hospitals receive an estimated $12.6 billion in annual tax exemptions on top of the $32 billion in federal, state, and local subsidies the hospital industry receives each year.[179]

In 1956, the IRS articulated an approach in Revenue Ruling 56-185, which held that a hospital could qualify for tax-exempt status only if it was "operated to the extent of its financial ability for those not able to pay for the services rendered and not exclusively for those who are able and expected to pay," the so-called "charity care standard." Revenue Ruling 69-545[180] modified the policy by introducing the "community benefit" standard, permitting a hospital to maintain its exempt status by operating for the benefit of the community "as a whole."[181] Further modification came with Revenue Ruling 83-157, which removed accident and emergency care from the community benefit standard (thereby preventing hospitals from relying on the standard open-door policy of their A&E unit as evidence of charitable service contribution to the community). This untidy federal framework, with all its subjectivity and exceptions, sits uneasily alongside state legislation that often employs quite different terms and definitions for state tax purposes.

[176] See Carreyrou, J., "Nonprofit Hospitals, Once for the Poor, Strike It Rich," *Wall St Journal*, April 4, 2008.

[177] Note that some nonprofit hospitals may also be able to qualify for exemption as s.501(c)(4) social welfare organizations.

[178] Colombo, J., "The Role of Tax Exemption in a Competitive Health Care Market," in *Journal of Health, Politics, Policy & Law*, Vol. 31, 2006, at pp. 621, 625.

[179] Carreyrou, J., "Nonprofit Hospitals".

[180] Arguably, Revenue Ruling 69–545 substantially changed the availability of hospital services for the poor by providing that "Revenue Ruling 56–185 is hereby modified to remove therefrom the requirements relating to caring for patients without charge or at rates below cost."

[181] See further Lunder, E. K. and Liu, E. C., *501(c)(3) Hospitals and the Community Benefit Standard*, Congressional Research Service, Washington, DC, November 2009.

In *Eastern Kentucky Welfare Rights Org. v. Schultz*,[182] a decision that the IRS had "acted unlawfully in approving tax exemptions for hospitals without regard to their provision of care for the indigent" was reversed by the D.C. Circuit Court of Appeals and ultimately dismissed by the Supreme Court for lack of standing. The Sixth Circuit also rejected a similar claim in *Lugo v. Miller*.[183] These and other cases commenced in 2004 and thereafter failed not on the merits of their arguments, but because the courts have held that § 501(c)(3) does not permit a private right of action against organizations for failure to fulfill their charitable mandates. Most recently, the *Provena* case,[184] in which the Illinois Supreme Court finally determined in 2010 litigation commenced in 2004 (relating to tax year 2002), has again brought into focus the principles that entitle a charitable health service provider to avoid paying tax on its property. The case concerned Provena, a nonprofit corporation with § 501(c)(3) status and exemption under federal law, which owned and operated six hospitals in Urbana, Illinois. Claiming that, as a health care ministry of the Roman Catholic Church, its purposes were charitable, it protested against a bill of $1.1 million in property taxes imposed by Champaign County. The court emphasized that the onus lay on Provena to prove "clearly and conclusively" that its property was entitled to the tax exemption.

Applying standards from *Methodist Old Peoples Home v. Korzen*,[185] the court established six distinctive characteristics of a charitable institution: (1) the institution provides benefits to an indefinite number of people for their welfare, or reduces said individuals dependence on the government; (2) the organization has no shareholders or capital structure; (3) the funds come from charitable gifts; (4) charity is dispensed to all who need it and apply for it; (5) the institution puts no obstacles to those seeking the charity; and (6) the primary use of the property is for charity. It found that Provena had failed to meet the second, third, and fifth of these requirements for the tax year in question: Virtually all of Provena's income came from noncharitable sources, its provision of charity care did not reach all who needed it, and its charity care policies were by no means obstacle free. It also found that the land in question was not used exclusively for charitable purposes, that Provena did not advertise charitable care, and that its services did not significantly alleviate government provision because the amount of free and discounted care offered to uninsured patients was "de minimis," "with very limited exception, the property was devoted to the care and treatment of patients in exchange for compensation through private insurance, Medicare, and Medicaid, or direct payment from the patient or

[182] D.D.C., 370 F. Supp. 325 (1973).

[183] 640 F. 2d 823 (6th Cir. 1981).

[184] Provena Covenant Medical Center v. Department of Revenue, Docket No. 107328 (Ill. March 3, 2010). As Evelyn Brody rightly comments, the eventual decision in this case provides little guidance for any future interpretation of the law: "the specific precedential value, remains uncertain; two of the seven justices did not participate, and the plurality opinion attracted three votes, with two justices writing a narrow concurrence" (note to author, September 18, 2011).

[185] 39 Ill.2d 149, 233 N.E. 2d 537 (1968).

the patient's family." The court noted that Provena devoted only 0.7 percent of its total revenue to charity, with some judges referring to its charity care as "often illusory" as the discounts given to uninsured patients (50 percent and 25 percent in certain cases) frequently resulted in the patient being billed at an amount in excess of actual care costs, and unpaid bills were automatically referred to a debt collection agency. In the year in question, only 302 of Provena's 110,000 hospital admissions were granted any reduction in their bills. The *Provena* decision would seem to signify a tougher judicial stance on the issue as to whether specific charitable acts should be required of organizations that enjoy tax benefits.[186]

3. Access for the Poor

Initially, the IRS took a stand on the principle that if a charity was to operate a hospital or offer other forms of health care provision, then it should allow for a poverty component (i.e. it must provide free or below-cost treatment to individuals unable to pay for such services).[187] Such an approach commonly applies at the state level. So, for example, in *Sisters of Third Order of St. Francis v. Board of Review,*[188] the hospital operated by the Sisters of St. Francis charged for accommodation in accordance with location and desirability, and admitted all who applied without prior screening as to health and ability to pay, and without an admission committee approval based on such screening. Nor did it require any payment to the general funds of the institution over and above its regular charges. Also, insofar as the hospital was concerned, many persons who could not and did not pay anything were admitted without question. Furthermore, the property it used was provided, in main, by gifts, bequests, and donation, rather than from the proceeds of any lump sum payment such as a Founder's Fee. The hospital was thus found to be a charity. In this respect it met all requirements of serving an indefinite number of people, placing no obstacles in their way, and complying generally with its charitable purposes.

[186] As noted in Hines, Horwitz, and Nichols, A., "The Attack on Nonprofit Status," at p. 1181, there has been academic debate on this issue for some time, citing (at f/n 6) the following: Bloche, M. G., "PERSPECTIVE: Tax Preferences for Nonprofits: From Per Se Exemption to Pay-for-Performance," in *Health Affairs,* Vol. 25, 2006 (arguing that tax benefits for hospitals and health plans should be tied to certain accomplishment), Hyman, D. A., and Sage, W. S., "PERSPECTIVE: Subsidizing Health Care Providers through the Tax Code: Status or Conduct?," in *Health Affairs,* Vol. 25, 2006 (advocating linking tax exemption to conduct), and Frank, R. G. and Salkever, D. S., "Nonprofit Organizations in the Health Sector," in *Journal of Economic Perspectives,* Vol. 8, at pp. 129, 130 (1994) (noting that, in the health care sector, "the subsidy is generally tied to the nonprofit "title" rather than specific performance criteria"), with Horwitz, J., "PERSPECTIVE: Nonprofit Ownership, Private Property, and Public Accountability," in *Health Affairs,* Vol. 25, 2006 (advocating linking tax exemption to status).

[187] Rev. Rul. 56–185, 1956–1 C. B. 202. See also *Eastern Kentucky Welfare Rights Organization v. E. Simon,* 506 F. 2d 1278 (D.C. Cir. 1974).

[188] 231 Ill. 317, 321 (1907). See also People v. Y.M.C.A., 365 Ill. 118 (1937).

However, at the federal level, this approach changed in 1969 when the IRS ruled that a hospital could, by meeting the community benefit standard (lessening the burdens of government), qualify for tax-exempt status. The states continue to wrestle with the standards for property tax exemption for hospitals, retirement homes, and other fee-for-service facilities.[189] For an approach contrary to that taken in Illinois, see the Michigan Supreme Court decision in *Wexford Medical Group v. City of Cadillac*[190] where, despite the total amount of pure charity care in one year being only $2400 (out of a total budget of $10 million), the court found this to be sufficient as the legislature had not quantified a necessary amount of charity care. Thus, in recent years, considerable controversy has been generated by the policy that a hospital or other such facility treating patients regardless of their ability to pay without providing profits to private individuals, is charitable and merits an exemption from property taxes, notwithstanding that it does not specify the amount of free care available.[191] In *Eden Retirement Center v. Dept. of Revenue*,[192] for example, the Illinois court stated that charity is something that is dispensed to all who need and apply for it, and no obstacles should be placed in the way of those seeking its benefits. In this case, the benefits of the duplex units were available only to those able to pay the substantial entrance fees. Although Eden's bylaws provided that the entrance fees may be waived or reduced, in the last 15 years this simply had not happened. The court found that the entrance fee was an obstacle placed in the way of those seeking the benefits of Eden's independent living units, and held that the units were thus not used primarily for charitable purposes.

The IRS has sought to enforce the community benefit standard by requiring hospitals to declare the extent to which their services address this objective. The introduction of Schedule H to Form 990 in December 2007 was designed to specify how this is achieved by requiring information on matters such as extent of free care, unreimbursed Medicaid, unreimbursed costs from other means-tested government programs, community health improvement services, health professions education, subsidized health services, research, and contributions to other community groups. The disclosure approach is often echoed at the state level for regulatory purposes and state property tax exemption. At a substantive level, the issue from a government perspective is whether such facilities are sufficiently compensating the state for its lost tax revenues by treating those who are too poor to pay the market cost

[189] See Eastern Kentucky Welfare Rights Org. v. Schultz, 370 F. Supp. 325, *rev'd*, 506 F. 2d 1278 (D.C. Cir. 1974), *vacated on other grounds*, 426 U.S. 26, 96 S. Ct. 1917 (1976).

[190] 474 Mich. 192, 713 N.W.2d 734 (2006).

[191] See, e.g., Carreyrou, J. and Martinez, B., "Nonprofit Hospitals, Once for the Poor, Strike it Rich; With Tax Breaks They Outperform For-Profit Rivals," *Wall St Journal*, April 4, 2008, at p. A.1.

[192] 213 Ill. 2d 273, 821 NE 2d 240 (2004).

for services.[193] In times of economic recession and public service retrenchment, this financial equation is likely to become a significant driver of government policy in an open market environment.

4. Conversion

For the IRS, the difficulties in policing the extent to which charities may engage in commercial activity took an alarming turn when a number of charities opted to abandon their hitherto much-coveted charitable status and convert to for-profit companies. Although this Damascus conversion to capitalism had the merit of simplifying future status and tax liability issues, it did so at the price of raising immediate difficult issues regarding ownership of assets. Clearly, when the contribution of untold numbers of taxpayers, volunteers, and the fund-raising general public, perhaps over many generations, has protected and nurtured a charity, licensing it to build up its market share and niche, then there needs to be a means of ensuring that it makes some form of restitution if it is to cash in its public benefit credits for opportunities to enrich its owners.

In the *Empire Blue Cross Blue Shield* case, the payback mechanism came in the form of legislation introduced to place the organization's assets in two specially created funds: the Public Asset Fund (95 percent) and the Charitable Asset Fund (5 percent).[194] The legislation prescribed the specific health care services to which the funds are to be put, a three-year period of expenditure, and the model of governance. Recourse to such a process in New York and other states where there have been hospital conversions illustrates the willingness in the United States to experiment with new methods, but it also raises questions as to the grounds on which government will in the future intervene in such conversion cases.[195] During the 1990s, there were a considerable number of other such instances when nonprofit organizations (mainly hospitals and other health/social care facilities) were taken over or bought out by commercial businesses or where they simply converted from nonprofit to for-profit status.[196]

[193] At the federal level, see new paragraph (r) of I.R.S. Code § 501. Earlier, a bill in the 109th Congress, the Tax Exempt Hospitals Responsibility Act 2006 (H.R. 6420), would have imposed a tax on § 501(c)(3) hospitals that failed to treat low-income uninsured patients; in the 110th Congress, the Charity Care for the Uninsured Act 2007 (H.R.973), was intended to create a new tax credit for physicians who provide charity care.

[194] See Corbet, C., "Stewardship of Public Assets under Nonprofit Conversion Models: New York's Empire Blue Cross Blue Shield Case Study," in *Nonprofit Management & Leadership*, Vol. 16, No. 2, 2005, at p. 153.

[195] The use of conversion foundations, as they are called, has created a sizable literature. See, e.g., the resources available on the Foundation Center website at http://foundationcenter.org/getstarted/topical/healthco.html.

[196] See further Goddeeris, J. H. and Weisbrod, B. A., "Conversion from Nonprofit to For-Profit Legal Status: Why Does It Happen and Should We Care?," Institute for Policy Research at Northwestern University, 1998, available at ideas.repec.org/d/ipnwuus.html.

5. Education

From child care centers[197] to universities, educational facilities have attracted IRS and judicial recognition as charitable organizations. Some 50 years ago, the courts took a firm stand in *Scripture Press Foundation v. United States*[198] when it was found that the plaintiff was not a charity: Although only spending a consistent 3–5 percent of its annual profit on religious education, it was nonetheless held to be primarily engaged in the sale of religious literature; its purpose of stimulating Sunday school growth was incidental to its commercial activity. Twenty years later, in *Presbyterian Reformed Publishing Co. v. Commissioner*,[199] the court adopted a more flexible approach when it found in favor of the plaintiff's charitable status, reversing and admonishing the Tax Court for the weight it had given to indicia of nonexempt business activity "it is doubtful that any small-scale exempt operation could ever increase its economic activity without forfeiting its tax-exempt status under such a definition of non-exempt commercial character."

The well-established practice of corporate gifts to universities, and some of the hazards of doing so while ensuring compliance with IRS rules, as illustrated in the *Mueller* case (see above), was also evident more recently in *LB Research and Education Foundation v. The UCLA Foundation*,[200] which concerned a conditional gift made to a university foundation to establish a chair in cardiothoracic surgery. The tax-exempt status of a trust established to support a university was also at issue in the *Cornell Trust* case.[201] During the 1999 and 2000 tax years, the trustees invested some of the Cornell Trust's funds in stocks "on margin," that is, using funds borrowed from their broker to purchase the stocks. Following an audit of its 1999 tax return, pursuant to the UBIT provisions tax was paid on the income derived from selling those margin-purchased securities for both the 1999 and 2000 tax years. Cornell Trust then sought a tax refund, which the IRS refused. At issue was whether securities purchased on margin for a trust established on behalf of one of the nation's great universities constituted "debt-financed property" such that income derived therefrom was subject to UBIT. In addition to the Cornell Trust, a "substantially similar" instrument had been used to create a trust for the benefit of the University of New Haven. The UNH Trust also bought securities on margin,

[197] See San Francisco Infant School, Inc. v. Commissioner, 69 T.C. 957 (1978). See also § 501(k).

[198] 285 F.2d 800 (Ct. Cl. 1961).

[199] 743 F.2d 148 (3d Cir. 1982).

[200] California Court of Appeal, 130 Cal. App. 4th 171, 29 Cal. Rptr. 3d 710, Cal. App. Dist., (June 14, 2005). The court found that the gift did not constitute a charitable trust, and therefore the donor could sue to enforce the conditions of the agreement.

[201] Henry E. and Nancy Horton Bartels Trust for the Benefit of Cornell University et al. v. United States; No. 1:03-cv-02526, June 30, 2009. It also offers an interesting variation on the "feeder" role of an income-generating organization such as the one featured in C. F. Mueller Co. v. Commissioner of Internal Revenue, 190 F.2d 120 (3rd Cir. 1951).

subsequently paid income tax (including interest and penalties) on the securities pursuant to the UBIT, and then sought a refund for those taxes.

The court found that it was of no consequence whether such a securities investment constituted an "unrelated trade or business," because § 512(b)(4) treats all income derived from debt-financed property as taxable and as deriving from an unrelated trade or business. It also noted that the Cornell Trust incorrectly conflated the purpose of producing income to support Cornell with the mechanism of using debt-financed or margin-purchased securities for that purpose.[202] The Trust could not avoid tax liability because I.R.C. § 61(a) applied to "all income from whatever source derived," which includes both periodic income (e.g., rents, royalties, dividends, annuities, pensions, interest) and nonperiodic income (e.g., compensation for services, gains from dealings in property, distributed shares of partnership gross income, etc.).[203] It had not established that it must purchase securities on margin to support Cornell University, or that its use of margin-purchased securities was substantially related to its support of Cornell University aside from the Cornell Trust's need for funds to contribute.[204]

The fact that a tax-exempt nonprofit must still pay income tax on commercial transactions unrelated to its tax-exempt purpose was also evident in *United States v. Am. College of Physicians*[205] when a tax-exempt medical organization was required to pay income taxes on funds generated by the sale of advertisements in its journal, because the sale of advertisements was not "substantially related" to the educational purpose of the journal and was thus taxable unrelated business income. This was further underlined in 2010 when the IRS embarked on an audit of 40 tax-exempt colleges, including Harvard, to establish, among other things, whether their business activities (unrelated to their educational mission) should be subject to UBIT.

6. Public Benefit Services and Public Policy

The charitable purpose of advancing education must be pursued in a manner that does not breach fundamental public policy. The danger and penalties for failure to do so were memorably illustrated in the *Bob Jones University* case.[206] In 1970, after a court issued an injunction prohibiting the IRS from awarding tax-exempt status to racially discriminatory schools,[207] the IRS released a revenue ruling indicating that

[202] Citing as authority Ricci v. DeStefano, 129 S. Ct. 2658, 2671, 174 L. Ed. 2d 490 (2009).

[203] Citing as authority United States v. Burke, 504 U.S. 229, 233 (1992).

[204] See also Elliot Knitwear Profit Sharing Plan v. Commissioner, 71 TC 765 (1979), *aff'd*, 614 F.2d 347 (3d Cir. 1980), at p. 350 (purchase of securities on margin does not appear to create unfair competition, but is nevertheless subject to the UBIT).

[205] 475 U.S. 834, 848–50 (1986).

[206] See Bob Jones University v. United States, 461 U.S. 574, 103 S. Ct. 2017 (1983), when the charitable status of two schools with racially discriminatory policies was revoked.

[207] See Green v. Kennedy, 309 F. Supp. 1127 (D.D.C. 1970).

such schools could no longer qualify as charities under U.S. tax law.[208] Consistent with this revenue ruling, the IRS concluded on the ground that they were discriminatory that two religious schools (Bob Jones University and Goldsboro Christian Schools) could not qualify as educational charities under federal income tax law. These schools engaged in racially discriminatory practices to further religious beliefs against interracial dating and marriage.[209]

The matter wound up before the U.S. Supreme Court, which agreed that neither of these educational institutions could qualify as charities for tax purposes. Writing for the majority, Justice Burger adopted what is essentially a tax expenditure–based view of the tax treatment of charities. He observed that "[w]hen the Government grants exemptions or allows deductions all taxpayers are affected; the very fact of the exemption or deduction for the donor means that other taxpayers can be said to be indirect and vicarious 'donors'."[210] He did not, however, conclude that the government is constitutionally prohibited from subsidizing discriminatory charities through tax concessions. Instead, Justice Burger reasoned that, given the income tax privileges of charitable status, charities "must serve a public purpose and not be contrary to established public policy."[211] While emphasizing that the public policy doctrine should be applied "only where there can be no doubt that the activity involved is contrary to a fundamental public policy,"[212] he concluded that this test was met, because there was "no doubt" that a public policy against racial discrimination existed.[213] There are, he observed, "few social or political issues" that have "been more vigorously debated and more extensively ventilated than the issue of racial discrimination."[214] He cited, as evidence of this public policy, constitutional equal protection jurisprudence, civil rights legislation, and executive orders. Because the Goldsboro Christian Schools and Bob Jones University discriminated on the basis of race, it was clear that they contravened an established public policy against discrimination. Neither the sincerity with which the underlying religious beliefs were held, nor the fact that education is itself a qualifying purpose made any difference. This case, although purportedly based on the Court's statutory interpretation of the IRC rather than constitutional law, remains controversial, and has not been extended to other areas of asserted discrimination such as gender discrimination.

208 Rev. rul. 71–447, 1971–2 CB 230.

209 The Goldsboro Christian Schools enforced a racially discriminatory admissions policy. Bob Jones University initially declined to admit any African-American students. This policy was changed in the 1970s, when the university began to admit African-Americans, but it nonetheless maintained a disciplinary rule that made interracial dating and marriage grounds for expulsion.

210 *Bob Jones*, 461 U.S. at 591.

211 *Bob Jones*, 461 U.S. at 586.

212 *Bob Jones*, 461 U.S at p. 592.

213 *Bob Jones*, 461 U.S at p. 588.

214 *Bob Jones*, 461 U.S at p. 596.

7. Public Benefit Services, Government Funding, and Religious Organizations

In *Mitchell v. Helms*,[215] Justice O'Connor advised that religious organizations should monitor and "compartmentalize" government funding received in the form of aid for education program. Where the aid is used for secular educational functions, then there would be no problem. If, however, the aid flowed into the entirety of an educational activity, and some "religious indoctrination [is] taking place therein," then that indoctrination "would be directly attributable to the government."[216] In relation to the facts of that case, she noted that the educational aid in question would supplement rather than supplant monies from private sources, that the nature of the aid was such that it could not reach the coffers of a religious school, and that the use of the aid was statutorily restricted to "secular, neutral, and non-ideological" purposes. This approach is consistent with that adopted in *Bowen v. Kendrick*,[217] when the court approved cash grants to religious organizations, even in the particularly "sensitive" area of teenage sexual behavior, as long as there is no "use of public funds to promote religious doctrines." Both decisions would seem to infer that there are circumstances in which a consequence of government funding could entail an imputing of functional responsibility from nonprofit service deliverer to government funder in accordance with the agent/principal rule.

This issue came to prominence again more recently in a number of cases involving vulnerable groups such as prisoners and children. In 2007 the civil rights group Freedom From Religion Foundation filed a lawsuit challenging the legality of the White House Office of Faith-Based and Community Initiatives, alleging that any such preferencing of religious organizations breached the Establishment Clause and violated the constitutional imperative that church and state remain separate.[218] The resulting decision of the Supreme Court in *Hein v. Freedom From Religion Foundation*[219] ruled that taxpayers do not have the right to challenge the constitutionality of expenditures by the executive branch of the government, a decision that in effect gave the green light to further government faith-based initiatives. *Americans United For Separation of Church and State v. Prison Fellowship Ministries*[220] concerned the Iowa InnerChange Freedom Initiative (IFI), a faith-based pre-release program for prisoners, which had a record of successfully rehabilitating criminals. This was part of the Prison Fellowship Ministries, launched in 1976, which operated the InnerChange Freedom Initiative in states such as Texas,

215 530 U.S.793, 120 S. Ct. 2530 (2000).

216 See also *School District v. Ball*, 473 U.S. 373, 398–400 (1985).

217 487 U.S. 589, 623 (1988).

218 The plaintiffs relied on the authority of precedents established by the Supreme Court in Flast v. Cohen, 392 U.S. 83 (1968), Bowen v. Kendrick, 487 U.S. 589 (1988), and Valley Forge Christian College v. Americans United for Separation of Church & State, 454 U.S. 464 (1982).

219 551 U.S. 587 (2007).

220 432 F. Supp. 2d 862 (S.D. Iowa 2006).

Minnesota, Kansas, Arkansas, and Missouri with federal funding of $56 million per year. The IFI, an intensely religious rehabilitation program, required an enrolled prisoner to constantly satisfy the evangelical Christian program organizers that he or she was making acceptable spiritual progress. It aimed to reduce recidivism by inspiring prisoners to live a more Christian way of life. In return for enrolling in the program, prisoners were rewarded with access to better facilities within the prison. The program had been a matter of concern to Roman Catholic inmates who found their faith being criticized by staff members and volunteers from local evangelical churches whereas Jews and Muslim participants would have been required to participate in Christian worship services even if that deeply offended their own religious beliefs. In June 2006, the district court held that the program violated the Establishment Clause, expelled the program from the prison, and directed IFI to repay the Department of Corrections the $1.5 million that it had been paid by the state. The defendants appealed to the U.S. Court of Appeals for the Eighth Circuit, which, in December 2007, largely upheld the district court's decision. It held that Iowa's involvement with IFI violated the Establishment Clause by supporting the indoctrination of inmates, that IFI's discriminated against non-Christian inmates, and that IFI was "pervasively sectarian." In March 2008, Iowa terminated the IFI program.

D. Charitable Trading: The Case Law in a Commercial Context

Any attempt to draw a distinction between charities and commercial entities is somewhat fraught as more charities have been engaged in providing fee-based services, and for longer, than has been the case in other common law jurisdictions. Their commercial and public service activities are also often entangled as charities involved in education and health care take advantage of open market opportunities to diversify into income-generating ventures.

1. Subsidiary and Incidental

The level of turnover is a factor in determining whether trade qualifies as ancillary; there is no specific level of annual turnover that decides this question. This principled, as opposed to mathematical, approach to the issue of ancillary trading is the professed approach of the IRS.[221]

[221] See General Counsel Memorandum 32689 (1963) and GCM 32689 (1964) stating:

> [The test is] essentially a test of proof. As such, it becomes a test of whether there is a real, bona fide, or genuine charitable purpose, as manifested by the charitable accomplishments of the organization, and not a mathematical measuring of business purpose as opposed to charitable purpose.

2. Private Benefit

Violation of the private inurement restrictions, as applied by § 501(c)(3) and (2) and by the private benefit rules under Treasury regulations,[222] will breach charitable status.[223]

In the Scientology cases,[224] the IRS determined that elements of mutual benefit and private profit in the practices of that organization debarred it from charitable status, though the church subsequently recovered its exempt status. More recently, it has vigorously pursued schemes in which the role of charity is little more than to provide a shelter for tax avoidance purposes.[225] Private benefit was also found to be fatal to the plaintiff's case in *Rameses School of San Antonio, Texas v. Commissioner*[226] and in *Redlands Surgical Services v. Commissioner.*[227] At the state level, where property tax exemption is more difficult to obtain, a practice associated with private benefit and equally fatal to tax-exemption might be to engage in unfair competition. This provided the grounds in *Selfspot Inc. v. The Butler County Family YMCA*[228] for a commercial health club to stop a nearby YMCA's "plans to build a new 35,000 square foot, full-service fitness center... which will feature a state-of-the-art health club and will operate as a tax-exempt charity." As charities increasingly resort to hiring professional fundraisers[229] and engage in joint ventures with businesses, the

[222] Treas. Reg. § 1.501(c)(3)-1(d)(1)(ii) (as amended in 2008). Note that § 501(c)(3) contains the specific requirement that no part of the net earnings of [the exempt organization] inures to the benefit of any private shareholder or individual. In addition, under the regulations, an organization is not treated as organized and operated for exclusively exempt purposes "unless it serves a public rather than a private interest." Tax-exempt status is thus not available to any organization if its net earnings inure to the benefit of private individuals "in whole or in part."

[223] See, e.g., Dale, H. P., "The Crux of Charity: Inurement, Private Benefit, and Excess Benefit Transactions," October 28, 2004.

[224] See Church of Scientology of California v. Commissioner, 823 F.2d 1310, 1313 (9th Cir. 1987), cert. denied, 486 U.S. 1015 (1988); Founding Church of Scientology v. United States, 133 U.S. App. D.C. 229, 409 F.2d 1146 (1969).

[225] See New Dynamics Foundation v. United States, 70 Fed. Cl. 782 (Fed. Cl. 2006).

[226] T.C. Memo. 2007–85 (April 10, 2007), where the school's tax-exempt status was revoked because its founder and executive director received private benefit from the school by using school funds for personal expenses and drawing a salary in excess of the amount approved by the board.

[227] 242 F.3d 904 (9th Cir. 2001), where ceding effective control of partnership activities was found to impermissibly serve private interests. See also Vision Service Plan v. United States, 2008 U.S. App. LEXIS 2388 (9th Cir. 2008), construing § 501(c)(4).

[228] 818 A.2d 58a7 (Pa. Commw. 2003).

[229] See, e.g., United Cancer Council v. Commissioner (7th Cir., February 10, 1999). The Seventh Circuit then held that the Internal Revenue Service had improperly revoked an organization's charitable tax exemption on the grounds that the organization's net earnings had inured to the benefit of a professional fund-raising company it hired despite the fact that only $2.3 million from a total of $28.8 million raised by the company ever reached the organization.

potential for a degree of private profit to infiltrate the practice and negate the charitable tax exemption—at the state level, if not at the federal level—is becoming a more common hazard.

3. Public Benefit

The public benefit requirement for tax exemption has been assiduously policed by the IRS. Federal legislation dating from 1969 requires that hospitals, for example, must meet a "community benefit" standard. In practice this is open to abuse, with claimants pointing to costs such as the training of medical students, the presence of an A&E unit, and the conducting of research as satisfying the standard and justifying tax exemption.

In *Fire Insurance Patrol v. Boyd*,[230] the fact that the provision of a fire patrol by an insurance company was commercially motivated did not negate its benefit to the public and its eligibility for charitable status.

4. Profits

When a charity engages in income-producing activities related to its charitable purpose, the problem is not the fee-charging per se. As was noted in the *Methodist Old Peoples Home* case,[231] "charging fees would not necessarily remove plaintiff from the category of a charitable institution"[232] and "charging fees and dispensing benefits to persons who are not necessarily poverty stricken would not destroy its charitable character."[233] However, where for-profit and nonprofit entities collaborate, then the profit motive of the former can color the joint enterprise, and in so doing undermine the nonprofit's status as a charitable organization.[234]

In practice, where problems have arisen, this has been in the relationship, if any, between the nature and scale[235] of the activity relative to the purpose, coupled with the issue of whether the activity of such a tax-exempt organization constitutes unfair competition for other for-profit traders. Those that engage in such activities run certain risks: If the trade or business is not in furtherance of its exempt purpose and becomes predominant, the organization can lose its charitable status

230 120 Pa. 624, 643 (1888).

231 Methodist Old Peoples Home v. Korzen, 39 Ill. 2d 149, 233 NE 2d 537 (1968).

232 Citing American College of Surgeons v. Korzen, 36 Ill. 2d 340, 348; People v. Y.M.C.A., 365 Ill. 118 (1936).

233 Citing People v. Y.M.C.A., 365 Ill. 118 (1936); Sisters of Third Order of St. Francis v. Board of Review, 231 Ill. 317 (1907)

234 See, e.g., St. David's Health Care System v. United States, 349 F.3d 232, 237 (5th Cir. 2003).

235 Some cases from the 1970s, such as People ex rel. Gorman v. Sinai Temple, 20 Cal. App. 3d 614 (Cal. Ct. App.1971), have dealt with the question of whether a nonprofit organization was engaged in too much business activity. These issues may also arise in the context of a state property tax exemption, as they did in State v. North Star Research and Development Institute, 294 Minn. 56, 200 N.W. 2d 410 (1972).

and entitlement to tax exemption.[236] In addition, it is "the purpose towards which an organization's activities are directed, and not the nature of the activities themselves, [that are] ultimately dispositive of the organization's right to be classified as a section 501(c)(3) organization."[237] The IRS and the state courts have devised certain tests, which overlap and are applied inconsistently, that add to the general incoherence of the law governing trading by charities. Importantly, even a charity exempt under federal law might find that its real estate fails to qualify for state property tax exemption.

a. The "Primary Purpose" Test

From time to time, the IRS has refused tax exemption status to organizations engaged in activities (e.g., adoption) because the business is being conducted in ways indistinguishable from commercial entities. The IRS rule governing this area permits charities to "operate a trade or business as a substantial part of its activities, if the operation of such trade or business is in furtherance of the organization's exempt purpose or purposes and if the organization is not *organized or operated* for the primary purpose of carrying on an unrelated trade or business."[238] The importance of this requirement was emphasized in the *Provena* case[239] where the appellant claimed that its nonprofit hospital, owned by three Roman Catholic religious orders, should be charitably exempt from property tax on the grounds that its property was used exclusively for the pursuit of its charitable purpose. The court found that, on the contrary:

> the primary purpose for which the [Provena] property was used was providing medical care to patients for a fee. Although the provision of such medical services may have provided an opportunity for various individuals affiliated with the hospital to express and to share their Catholic principles and beliefs, medical care, while potentially miraculous, is not intrinsically, necessarily, or even normally religious in nature.

b. The Commerciality Test

This examines the services provided, looking at whether they are performed for a profit. Largely fact-specific, it is based upon the profitable nature of the activity, the magnitude of the activity in relation to the organization's other exempt activities, and the way the activity supports or furthers the exempt purpose(s) of the organization, as well as whether the activity is one that is ordinarily conducted by for-profit

[236] Treas. Reg. § 1.501(c)(3)-1(d)(e)(1).

[237] B.S.W. Group Inc. v. Commissioner, 70 TC 352, 356–57 (1978).

[238] Treas. Reg. § 1.501(c)(3)-1(e)(1).

[239] Provena Covenant Medical Centre v. Department of Revenue, Docket No. 107328 (Ill. March 18, 2010).

entities and what business and marketing practices employed in conducting the activity. Inconsistent in its application and outcome, it was utilized in *Trinidad v. Sagrada Orden de Predicadores*[240] and gave rise to the destination of income test.

The commerciality test, as currently applied,[241] disregards the final resting place of funds and instead takes a broad look at the overall activities of an organization. It considers the commercial hue of an organization,[242] an approach illustrated in *Living Faith Inc. v. Commissioner*[243] when the court considered that the plaintiff's religious purpose of health promotion was outweighed by its commercial purpose: "[I]t's difficult to see how the experience of dining or shopping at Living Faith's restaurant and health food stores differs, if it does, from the same experience one might have while dining or shopping at other vegetarian restaurants and health food stores." An organization that does not engage "primarily in activities which accomplish one or more of such exempt purposes specified in § 501(c)(3)" will not qualify for federal income tax exemption. Some academics have questioned the premise of this test, arguing that in practice resorting to commerce does not necessarily help organizations to carry out their missions or deliver services.[244]

c. The Destination of Income Test

The Supreme Court in *Trinidad v. Sagrada Orden de Predicadores*[245] interpreted the income tax exemption as applying to income earned on both investments and business activities of a religious order, stating quite clearly what came to be known as the destination of income test:[246]

> [Charitable] activities cannot be carried on without money; and it is common knowledge that they are largely carried on with income received from properties dedicated to their pursuit. This is particularly true of many charitable, scientific and educational corporations and is measurably true of some religious corporations. Making such properties productive to the end that the income may be thus used does not alter or enlarge the purposes for which the corporation is created and conducted.

[240] 263 U.S. 578 (1924).

[241] See, e.g., the cases involving credit counseling organizations.

[242] See Better Business Bureau v. United States, 326 U.S. 279 (1945).

[243] 950 F.2d 365 (7th Cir. 1991). See also Presbyterian Reformed Publishing v. Commissioner, 70 TC, 1070, *rev'd*, 743 F.2d 148 (3rd Cir. 1982).

[244] Guo, B., "Charity for Profit? Exploring Factors Associated with the Commercialization of Human Service Nonprofits," in *Nonprofit and Voluntary Sector Quarterly*, Vol. 35, No. 123, 2006, at p. 135.

[245] 263 U.S. 578, 44 S. Ct. 204, 68 L. Ed. 458 (1924).

[246] *Trinidad*, 263 U.S. 578.

From that time onward, the tax laws permitted charities to engage in income-seeking activities for their support. Not until the *Mueller Macaroni* case[247] did pressure come for change. Mueller, which sold pasta and allied products and channeled the profits to the NYU Law School, successfully established that it was exempt from tax on the basis of being *organized and operated* exclusively for charitable purposes in accordance with the § 501(c)(3)-1(e)(1) rule. This decision, following the *Trinidad* case and *Roche's Beach, Inc. v. Commissioner*,[248] confirmed the "destination of income" test as the determinant of charitable status for such "feeder" entities as *Mueller*. In response, the U.S. Congress enacted legislation denying tax exemption to feeder organizations, even if they donated their entire profits to charitable organizations,[249] and introduced the "unrelated business income tax" ("UBIT") now codified in § 511-514 of the Code (see above). As a result, the "destination of income" ceased to be a determinant of charitable tax exempt status.

d. The Commensurate Test

Essentially, this test requires § 501(c)(3) organizations to conduct charitable activities commensurate in scale with their resources: Asset-rich tax-exempt nonprofits are expected to undertake significant and costly projects in pursuing their charitable purposes. Intended to prevent charities from hoarding their assets, it has been in evidence from time to time,[250] but acquired fresh prominence in 2008 when the IRS indicated an intention to develop a policy for applying the test. More recent IRS applications of the test indicate that it has begun to compare gross and net revenues and the relative proportion of business and charitable activities in order to determine tax-exempt status.[251]

E. Jurisdictional Characteristics of Charitable Trading

Altruism, the hallmark of charity in other common law jurisdictions, has never had a comparable defining role in the United States. From an early stage it was accepted

247 C. F. Mueller Co. v Commissioner of Internal Revenue, 190 F.2d 120 (3rd Cir. 1951).

248 96 F.2d 776 (2nd Cir. 1938).

249 IRC § 502 (1954), codified by Revenue Act of 1950, § 301(b) ("An organization operated for the primary purpose of carrying on a trade or business for profit shall not be exempt under section 501 on the ground that all of its profits are payable to one or more organizations exempt under section 501 from taxation.")

250 See the 1964 IRS ruling (64–182, 1964–1 CB 186).

251 See further, Ellis Carter, "Nonprofit Law Jargon Buster: The Commensurate Test," in *Charity Lawyer*, August 16, 2010, http://charitylawyerblog.com/2010/08/16/nonprofit-law-jargon-buster-the-commensurate-test/#ixzz18lqfWpkb[AQ: Please include this Note details to the Bibliography list.]

that the utility of a gift could compensate for an absence of altruism.[252] But then in the United States, charity and charity law have not been as central to defining the nonprofit sector. In a resolutely open market economy, where an overtly tax-driven administration provides the only nationwide system for demarcating and policing sector boundaries, attention has tended to focus more on the utility or "public good" of an organization's activities and of gifts to them, rather than on charitable purposes. "Charity" as a concept, as the basis for a body of sector-defining law, and as a social policy agenda for government/sector relations, has not carried the same weight in this jurisdiction as elsewhere.

The diluted requirement for altruism would seem to have as a corollary a greater tolerance for a private benefit dimension to coexist alongside the public benefit requirement in constituting a "charitable organization" or a charitable gift. Private foundations,[253] charitable remainder trusts, DAFs, and the tax deductible provisions of the IRC together occupy a large part of the philanthropic world, and all make room for a greater degree of private control over resources entrusted for the public benefit than is customary in other jurisdictions. Charity, or philanthropy, accommodates a close affinity between private and public benefit in the United States, which, again, is attributable to its distinctive open market economy and related underpinning political ideology. The latter may also help explain the high profile of religious organizations, particularly as channeled through Charitable Choice, in delivering public benefit services in the United States.

1. Profits

In the United States, the related activity test as applied through the UBIT regime rather than destination of income prevails while, more simply, the test of the commercial hue of an organization will often be determinative.

[252] See, e.g., Fire Insurance Patrol v. Boyd, 120 Pa. 624, 643 (1888) where the fact that the provision of a fire patrol by an insurance company was commercially motivated did not negate its benefit to the public and its eligibility for charitable status. Other cases where charitable status was similarly upheld, as cited by Kelley, T., "Rediscovering Vulgar Charity"; Patterson Rescue Mission v. High, 64 N.J.L. 116, 118–19, 44 A. 974, 975, 1899 (home for aged and disabled men that paid for its running costs by requiring residents to manufacture and sell firewood); House of Refuge v. Smith, 140 Pa. 387, 1891 (juvenile correction home where employed residents contributed to running costs); Trustees of Academy of Protestant Episcopal Church v. Taylor, 150 Pa. 565, 1892 (school, open to the public, charging students to cover running costs); Contributors to Pennsylvania Hospital v. Delaware County, 169 Pa. 305, 1895 (profit from sale of convalescent farm produce used to maintain hospital); and Trustees of Kentucky Female Orphan School v. City of Louisville, 36 S.W. 921 (Ky. Ct. of App. 1896) (revenue from service users paid for upkeep of school).

[253] Note, e.g., the involvement of the Gates and Ford foundations in the R&D departments of pharmaceutical companies.

VII. CONCLUSION

As the rate of national poverty increases in the United States, from 12 percent in 2005 to its present level of 15.7 percent, with 47.8 million of Americans now living in poverty,[254] the resources of charities and the nonprofit sector more generally are under correspondingly increased pressure. Although it is clear that charities, other nonprofits, and the sector as a whole do not hold the answer to poverty in the United States, it is evident that the demands on their resources are greater than before, and their need to access additional funding is now also that much greater.

One way of generating the necessary additional cash flow is through the taxation system, and undoubtedly the world's largest concentration of billionaires is using the generous tax offset privileges to channel funds in that direction. Relying on public donations for funding is not, however, a promising option, both because the level of giving is falling[255] due to economic circumstances and because such donor choice does not favor the socially disadvantaged; less than one-third of the money individuals gave to nonprofits in 2005 was focused on the needs of this group.[256] Relying on prospective grant aid from a government burdened with massive public debt is also unrealistic. The need for more funding is instead pushing charities and the sector generally toward increased earned income activity, both in terms of public benefit service provision and in terms of commercial ventures, mission-related or otherwise. As charity inevitably steps up its recourse to profit-making activity, the sufficiency of the UBIT framework is likely to face further challenges, and the above-mentioned judicial tests will be honed yet further. More troubling is the perhaps prescient alarm bell sounded by Justice O'Connor to the effect that when charities step wholly into the shoes of government in their delivery of core public benefit services (such as education), then they are acting as agents of government. This may give rise to serious accountability issues for both parties.[257]

[254] According to statistics released by the U.S. Census Bureau in January 2011. See further at: www.census.gov/.

[255] According to The Center on Philanthropy, Indiana University, U.S. charitable giving fell 3.6 percent in 2009 to $303.75 billion.

[256] See The Center on Philanthropy, Indiana University, *Patterns of Household Charitable Giving by Income Group 2005* (Summer 2007), available at http://www.philanthropy.iupui.edu/Research/Giving%20focused%20on%20meeting%20needs%20of%20the%20poor%20July%202007.pdf.

[257] Mitchell v. Helms, 530 U.S. 793, 120 S. Ct. 2530 (2000).

8

CANADA

I. INTRODUCTION

Canada's status as a federated jurisdiction results in individual provinces and territories that each have their own legislative and judicial areas of competence, control over local public services, and related spending. The administration of charity law and the regulatory framework for nonprofits in general are also devolved matters,[1] whereas the overstretched Canadian Revenue Authority (CRA)[2] and the Supreme Court exercise jurisdiction at the federal level. There is a general absence of the nationwide government bureaucracy and sector organizations necessary for implementing coherent and systemic change. Further complications arise from bijural constitutional arrangements that seek to marry Canada's common law and civil code heritages, legacies from the respective colonial rule of England and France.

The chapter begins with a socioeconomic overview of the nonprofit sector, its development, current issues and trends, and the role of charities within it. This leads into a section that traces and reflects on the building of the sector/government relationship. The crucial part played by the Voluntary Sector Initiative in advancing a common sector/government agenda is considered, as are the faltering steps so far taken toward achieving charity law reform. Attention is then given to

[1] See the Constitution Act 1867, which expressly reserves the regulation of charities to the provinces, subject to s.91(3), which designates the raising of taxes to the federal jurisdiction. Constitution Act, 1867, 30 & 31 Vict. Ch. 3 (U.K.).

[2] The Federal Court of Appeal, in International Pentecostal Ministry Fellowship of Toronto v. M.N.R., 2010 FCA 51.1, upheld the federal regulatory jurisdiction of the CRA over all Canadian charities, rejecting the assertion that the agency's constitutional jurisdiction was void from the outset because exclusive legislative authority with respect to the regulation of charities lay with the provinces.

the Canadian experience of shifting levels of responsibility for public benefit service provision from government to the nonprofit and for-profit sectors, with a focus on government use of funding and sector capacity building. This is followed with a brief review of the limited impact made by new legal structures for charity on the nonprofit sector. The case law section deals with contemporary trading activities of charities, and occupies a good portion of the last half of the chapter. In particular, the rulings of court and the CRA on what constitutes a "related business," and the significance of the "activities test" and the "destination of income test" are examined. The remarkably few cases concerned with the role of charities in mainstream commercial ventures are noted, but the primary focus is on the public benefit role of charities as illustrated in the case law relating to service provision in areas such as education, social and health care, and community development.

II. SECTOR PROFILE

Canada's geographic size, combined with very uneven population distribution containing a significant indigenous component,[3] all governed by a federated administration, encouraged the development of what has become a localized spread of nonprofit organizations with a distinct emphasis on public benefit service provision. The nonprofit sector reflects Canada's multilayered system of governance by being fragmented and regionally different in accordance with the cultural environment and the role expectations set by local government. There is no matrix available (other than aggregate economic indicators) that can bring cohesion to what is a patchy nonprofit sector.

A. The Nonprofit Sector

According to Imagine Canada, a national charitable organization formed by the union of two of the state's leading charitable umbrella organizations, Canada has proportionately the second largest nonprofit and voluntary sector in the world: The Netherlands is the largest, and the United States is fifth.[4] Recent estimates suggest that the nonprofit and voluntary sector contribute to between 2.4 percent to 6.8 percent of Canada's GDP, depending on the definition used.[5] The smaller provinces

[3] The Constitution Act of 1982 recognized the First Nations people, Inuits, and the Métis as three distinct indigenous groups and granted them special status.

[4] Presumably on a proportionate basis. The Imagine Canada website is available at http://www.imaginecanada.ca/?q=en/node/32.

[5] See further Statistics Canada, "The Social Economy across the Rural to Urban Gradient: Evidence from Registered Charities," 2008, at http://www.statcan.gc.ca/pub/21-601-m/21-601-m2010092-eng.htm.

have a higher number of organizations relative to their populations and the top 1 percent of organizations command 60 percent of all revenues.[6]

1. Employment and Volunteers

Nonprofits employ some 2 million people, representing 12 percent of Canada's economically active population and providing 13 percent of its nonagricultural employment. Roughly half (54 percent) of all nonprofits and charities are run entirely by volunteers. The Minister of Industry[7] published a report in 2006 that described the results of a 2004 study conducted by Imagine Canada and Statistics Canada, the national statistical agency, on the giving and volunteering habits of Canadians, and revealed that "the bulk of the charitable dollars and volunteer hours are provided by a relatively small percentage of the population."[8] As noted in its 2009 report (based on a 2007 study): Although the donation rate is virtually the same as that reported in 2004 (85 percent), the number of donors increased by approximately 2.9 percent, in part due to a 3.7 percent increase in the population of Canadians aged 15 and older; the rate of volunteering also remained largely unchanged from the 45 percent reported in 2004.

B. Nonprofit Organizations

The Income Tax Act defines a nonprofit organization in Canada as a club, society, or association that is not a charity and that is organized and operated exclusively for social welfare, civic improvement, pleasure, or recreation, or for any other purpose except profit. To be an NPO, no part of the income of the organization can be payable to, or be available for, the personal benefit of any member, unless the member is a Canadian amateur athletics association.

[6] See further, Imagine Canada, "Charities & Nonprofit Organizations," http://www.imaginecanada.ca/node/32.

[7] The Minister of Industry is responsible for promoting Canada's economic development, and also manages Statistics Canada, which is a federal agency that produces statistics for a better understanding of the lives, society, and commerce of the country. See Statistics Canada, http://www.statcan.gc.ca/start-debut-eng.html.

[8] National Survey of Nonprofit and Voluntary Organizations (NSNVO), *Highlights from the 2004 Canada Survey of Giving, Volunteering and Participating (GSGVP)*, Statistics Canada, Ottawa, 2006, at p. 7, available at http://www.givingandvolunteering.ca/pdf/CSGVP_Highlights_2004_en.pdf. See also Canada Survey of Giving, Volunteering and Participating (CSGVP), *Caring Canadians, Involved Canadians: Highlights from the 2007 Canada Survey of Giving, Volunteering and Participating*, Statistics Canada, Ottawa, 2009.

The National Survey of Nonprofit and Voluntary Organizations revealed the first national portrait of the nonprofit sector.[9] It estimated that in 2003 there were 161,000 nonprofit and voluntary organizations, including a wide variety of organizations such as "day-care centres, sports clubs, arts organizations, social clubs, private schools, hospitals, food banks, environmental groups, trade associations, places of worship, advocates for social justice, and groups that raised funds to cure diseases."[10] The nonprofits tended to be focused on providing services within their own neighborhood, city, town, or rural municipality with a variable nationwide distribution: More organizations were located in Quebec (29 percent) and Ontario (28 percent) than in any other province or territory.[11]

The Johns Hopkins University Comparative Nonprofit Sector Project, which resulted in the 2005 report *The Canadian Nonprofit and Voluntary Sector in Comparative Perspective*, notes that:

> the sector contributes importantly to Canada's GDP; when service organizations in the fields of health and education are excluded from the statistics, it contributes 4 percent of GDP; much of the sector is involved with social service provision and is highly dependent on government sources of revenue; and that government support is also important for civic organizations and advocacy organizations.[12]

1. Charities

In Canada, charities and government social service agencies have coexisted alongside each other for generations. By 2003, it was estimated that of the 161,000 entities comprising the nonprofit sector, approximately 85,300 were registered as charities,[13] employing over 2 million people and accounting for about 7 percent of the Canadian GDP.[14] Charities are registered under the Income Tax Act[15] as a "charitable organization," "public foundation," or "private foundation." They carry

[9] National Survey of Nonprofit and Voluntary Organizations (NSNVO), *Cornerstones of Community: Highlights of the National Survey of Nonprofit and Voluntary Organizations*, Statistics Canada, Ottawa, 2003 (revised 2005). The National Survey was carried out by Statistics Canada and eight not-for-profit organizations, with the Canadian Centre for Philanthropy as the lead organization.

[10] NSNVO, *Cornerstones of Community*, at p. 8.

[11] NSNVO, *Cornerstones of Community*, at p. 12.

[12] Hall, M. H., Barr, C. W., Easwaramoorthy, M., Sokolowski, M. S. W. and Salamon, L., *Canada's Nonprofit Sector in Comparative Perspective* (the John Hopkins report), the John Hopkins Comparative Nonprofit Sector Project, John Hopkins University, Baltimore, MD, 2005 at III–IV ("Johns Hopkins Report").

[13] According to the database maintained by the Charities Directorate of the Canada Revenue Agency, located at http://www.cra-arc.gc.ca/ebci/haip/srch/advancedsearch-eng.action.

[14] See further Bourgeois, D. J., *The Law of Charitable and Not-for-Profit Organizations* (3rd ed), Butterworths, Toronto, 2002, at p. 1, where it is mentioned that in 2000 "these charities have assets of over $100 billion and annual revenues of $90 billion."

[15] Income Tax Act (R.S.C., 1985, c. 1 (5th Supp.)).

out charitable activities by either gifting funds to a qualified donee or by undertaking activities through employees, volunteers, or intermediaries. They differ from other nonprofits in that the latter are unable to issue tax receipts for donations but are free to direct their resources toward non-charitable purposes, and can do so without restrictions on political lobbying.[16] Canadian charities can also, within certain limitations, conduct fund-raising activities,[17] business activities,[18] political activities,[19] and social activities.

Religious organizations constitute a significant proportion of total Canadian charities: 94 percent of such organizations have charitable status (the highest proportion in the sector); places of worship represent about 40 percent of all registered charities and receive about 60 percent of all receipted donations.

2. Range of Legal Structures

Trusts did not become the preferred legal structure for charity and neither, therefore, did the considerable body of equity-based principles that governed trustees acquire any significant regulatory significance. Instead, Canada gave an early preference to corporate structures matched by a corresponding reliance upon models of governance built around corporate boards rather than on the powers and duties of trustees. The charitable resulting trust has played a not-insignificant role as a legal structure for making charitable gifts.

3. Range of Activities

Nonprofits in Canada are mostly service providers and are primarily involved in: sports and recreation (21 percent of all organizations); religion (19 percent); social services (12 percent); grantmaking, fund-raising, and voluntarism promotion (10 percent); arts and culture (9 percent), and development and housing (8 percent).[20]

C. Financing the Sector

With revenues totaling $112 billion, nonprofits play a substantial role in the Canadian economy.[21] Gross domestic product in the sector grew 6.0 percent to $35.4 billion in

[16] See Scarborough Community Legal Services v. The Queen (1985) 17 DLR (4th) 308 (FCA) for an instance where a nonprofit was denied charitable status because of its political activities.

[17] See CRA's recent *Guidance on Fundraising.*

[18] See CRA's CPS-019 *What is a Related Business?*

[19] See CPS-022. See also Gilbert, N. and Bridge, R., "Helping Charities Speak Out: What Funders Can Do," in *The Philanthropist*, Vol. 20, No 2. (2005), at pp. 153–157.

[20] Canada Survey of Giving, Volunteering and Participating (CSGVP), *Caring Canadians, Involved Canadians: Highlights from the 2007 Canada Survey of Giving, Volunteering and Participating,* Statistics Canada, Ottawa, 2009.

[21] Note that all values in this chapter are expressed in Canadian dollars.

2008: accounting for 2.4 percent of the nation's GDP, up from 2.3 percent in 2007, a share that has remained stable since 2002; this rate of growth was faster than the 5.2 percent increase in GDP for the nation as a whole.[22]

Hospitals (including residential care facilities), universities, and colleges account for the bulk of nonprofit economic activity. Together these institutions command 33 percent of all revenues, employ 34 percent of all paid staff, and engage 2 percent of volunteers. During the 12-year period 1997–2009, they represented an average of 66.2 percent of total GDP in the nonprofit sector. In 2008 alone, their GDP totaled $71.0 billion. Sports and recreation and religious organizations are also economically significant, accounting for 11 percent of revenues, 11 percent of paid staff, and 39 percent of all volunteers.

Nonprofit institutions serving households accounted for 21.2 percent on average, whereas nonprofit institutions classified in the corporate sector accounted for 12.6 percent.

The core nonprofit sector received $80.0 billion in revenues in 2008, either earned from market activity or received from government, businesses, or households. Other important sources of revenue in that year were membership fees (17.1 percent) and donations from households (11.2 percent), together accounting for over one-quarter of sector revenue. Income in the core nonprofit sector rose 4.7 percent in 2008, compared with a 6.5 percent increase in 2007. The slowing in growth in 2008 stemmed from a decline in donations from households, principally charitable donations.

1. Government Funding

Forty-nine percent of all revenues reported by nonprofit and voluntary organizations came from government, with 39 percent coming from provincial sources. This has resulted in funding shortages for a sector accustomed to relying on government for 60 percent of its funding.[23] As has been noted: "hospitals, universities and colleges, and social service organizations tend to depend more on government funding,"[24] the first three receiving 74 percent of their revenue from government. Setting aside hospitals, universities, and colleges, 36 percent of the remaining organizations' revenues come

[22] Statistics Canada, *Satellite Account of Non-Profit Institutions and Volunteering 1997–2008*, Statistics Canada, Ottawa, December 2010.

[23] See Canadian Centre for Philanthropy, Non-Profit Sector Research Initiative, Volunteer Canada, Canadian Heritage, Health Canada, Human Resources Development Canada, and Statistics Canada, *Caring Canadians, Involved Canadians: Highlights from the 1997 National Survey of Giving, Volunteering and Participating.* Ministry of Industry, Ottawa, 1998.

[24] See Statistics Canada, *Cornerstones of Community: Highlights of the National Survey of Nonprofit and Voluntary Organizations*, Statistics Canada, Ottawa, 2004.

from government. In recent years, as Scott has pointed out, serious funding problems have arisen for nonprofits:[25]

> The erosion of the financial capacity of nonprofit and voluntary organizations has prompted particular interest and reflection on the part of the sector and its funders.
>
> Nonprofit and voluntary organizations receive funding from a variety of private and public sources—such as donors, foundations, governments, corporations, individuals, earned income—and through a variety of mechanisms—such as tax assistance, grants, contracts, and contributions. Divergent funding policies, regulations and practices work singly or in combination to facilitate, or hinder, nonprofit and voluntary organizations in pursuit of their missions. Recent trends in funding, however, appear to threaten the continued viability of the sector. The shift away from core funding that is evident across Canada, to name just one example, has heightened competition among nonprofit and voluntary organizations for increasingly scarce resources. Much organizational time is now devoted to chasing short-term sources of funding, often at the expense of the organizations' mission and core activities.

2. Self-Financing

Earned income from nongovernment sources accounts for 35 percent of nonprofit revenues; gifts and donations account for 13 percent. Apart from hospitals, universities, and colleges, 43 percent of the remaining organizations' revenues come from earned income from nongovernment sources, 17 percent from gifts and donations, and 4 percent from other sources.

Business and professional associations and unions, sports and recreation, arts and culture, and development and housing organizations rely more on earned income from nongovernment sources.

3. Charitable Giving

The 2006 report by Statistics Canada[26] revealed that in 2004 some 22 million Canadians (85 percent of the total population) donated to charities; donations totaled $8.9 billion, an average of $400 per individual; religious charities received the largest percentage of the amounts donated (45 percent), followed by health

[25] Scott, K., *Funding Matters: The Impact of Canada's Funding Regime on Nonprofit and Voluntary Organizations*, Canadian Council on Social Development, Ottawa, 2003, at p. ix, available at http://www.ccsd.ca/pubs/pubcat/fm.htm.

[26] Statistics Canada, *Canada Survey of Giving, Volunteering and Participating* (GSGVP), 2007, available at http://www.givingandvolunteering.ca/pdf/CSGVP_Highlights_2004_en.pdf.

organizations (14 percent), and social services organizations (10 percent).[27] Almost 12 million Canadians (45 percent of the total population) volunteered their time,[28] amounting to almost 2 billion hours, the equivalent of 1 million full-time jobs, and volunteers contributed an average of 168 hours over the course of a year. The 2009 report revealed a 12 percent increase in the total amount of donations, from $8.9 billion in 2004 to $10.0 billion in 2007 but otherwise noted that the above figures remained essentially unchanged.

D. Sector Cohesion

The Canadian nonprofit sector has traditionally lacked overall cohesion. Much of Canadian nonprofit activity sprang from religious organizations, which were naturally oriented toward their local parishes. Social service providers in general were inevitably more attuned to the needs and trends within their respective communities. The urban/rural divide, cultural differences, lack of population homogeneity, and geographical complications all combined to promote the growth of a fragmentary sector comprised of special interest groups and a disparate range of nonprofit entities. Moreover, the funding of nonprofits has been such as to militate against the emergence of any one organization with the leadership, resources, and independence necessary to develop a mandate and mission that could unite the sector. There has also been a difficulty in conceptualizing what it is that nonprofits have in common that would constitute a "sector." Only relatively recently have government and nonprofits moved beyond a tacit recognition that "volunteerism" was the main unifying thread to acknowledge the existence of other dimensions.

The Voluntary Sector Initiative, launched in 1995, provided funding that facilitated the emergence of nonprofit coalitions in several provinces. In 2002, a further step was taken with the creation of the Canadian Federation of Non-Profit and Voluntary Sector Networks, which in August 2011 merged with the Carleton Centre for Community Innovation (3ci).[29]

1. Sector Umbrella Bodies

Community Chests, the predecessors of today's United Way agencies, were federations of welfare agencies that engaged in united fund-raising appeals to their local communities. Leaders of the Chests tended to also be representatives on state and federal government panels and advisors to the welfare agency. These forerunners of

[27] Statistics Canada, *Canada Survey of Giving, Volunteering and Participating* Giving statistics are found at p. 9.

[28] Statistics Canada, *Canada Survey of Giving, Volunteering and Participating*, at p. 10. This includes mandatory community service. All the volunteering statistics are found on p. 10.

[29] See further Carleton Centre for Community Innovation, "Non-Profit & Philanthropic Management," http://www3.carleton.ca/3ci/3ci_files/NPPM%20Main.html.

contemporary Canadian umbrella bodies served as coordinators of local nonprofits, while networking with businesses and facilitating contact between sector and government bodies, but only within their immediate locality and for the purpose of generating funds and support for local charitable causes. They neither sought nor, in all probability, saw any need for a role as advocates on behalf of sector issues. In fact their existence and limited focus may well have hindered recognition of the need for sector-wide bodies that could speak for and to the sector on matters of strategic importance.

Currently, Canada has a number of nonprofit umbrella or apex organizations.[30] They do much to contribute to sector cohesion, though their capacity to cultivate a strategic role was for many years compromised by a requirement that they also perform as a charity. As CRA now makes clear in its 2008 Guidelines, "an organization does not have to work directly with individual charitable beneficiaries in order to be considered to be advancing a charitable purpose." Instead CRA "accepts that umbrella organizations can advance a charitable purpose by directing their activities at improving and enhancing the charitable activities of other generally community-level organizations." The 2008 Guidelines note that the work of such umbrella organizations is charitable "in so far as it contributes to an improvement in the quality of service to the public, as well as increasing the level of service available to the public."[31] The Guidelines identify three types of umbrella organizations considered to be charitable: charities established to improve the efficiency and effectiveness of other registered charities, umbrella organizations that work with and through constituent groups that may or may not be registered charities in order to achieve a recognized charitable purpose, and charities that may or may not be an umbrella organization but that hold property for other registered charities.

However, as Elson has noted: "when collective representation has been made by national nonprofit and voluntary sector apex organizations, the advocacy focus has been on tax rather than social policy."[32]

[30] E.g., the Centre for Voluntary Sector Research and Development, the Health Charities Coalition, and the Canadian Federation of Voluntary Sector Networks.

[31] Note: The rules related to umbrella organizations changed in May 2008. "CRA, Guidelines for the Registration of Umbrella Organizations and Title Holding Organizations," at http://www.cra-arc.gc.ca/chrts-gvng/chrts/plcy/cps/cps-026-eng.html.

The Guidelines replace CRA's earlier policy statements on similar issues, namely CPS-00818 and CPS-00919, in their entirety.

[32] See Elson, P. R., "Independence in a Cold Climate: A Profile of the Nonprofit and Voluntary Sector in Canada," in Smerdon, M. (ed.), *The First Principle of Voluntary Action*, Baring Foundation, London, October 2009, at p. 28. He adds "It's a cold climate for advocacy in Canada and while this current political environment is difficult, it is also exacerbated by the lack of a collective sectoral representational infrastructure, policy agenda and collective vision for the future."

III. CHARITIES AND GOVERNMENT: BUILDING A RELATIONSHIP

Unlike contemporary developments in other leading common law nations (notably, the U.K. jurisdictions, Australia, and New Zealand), there have been no equivalent initiatives in Canada to bridge the gap between government and the nonprofit sector by establishing institutional or ministerial departments with specific responsibilities for nonprofit issues. The absence of structural links is in all probability connected, whether as cause or effect, to the failure at federal and province level to create and sustain formal working forums in which government and sector representatives can negotiate strategic policy issues. In the main, the government's relationship with the sector continues to rest on the traditional tax-driven model with primary orientation and regulatory oversight directed by the CRA toward issues of charitable tax exemption.

A. Government Bodies and the Sector

It has been asserted that "In order to meet the policy challenges, new relations must be forged among state, civil society and the economy, and with different branches and levels of government."[33] Many issues ranging from urban poverty to economic development and homelessness do not align with governmental structures. It has been pointed out that these "wicked problems" resist solutions by one agency and can only be tackled by crossing departmental and governmental boundaries with other players, including the voluntary sector from the local level upwards.[34] However, in Canada the multilayered systems of governance together with the added challenges of cultural, bijural, rural/urban, rates of immigration, and other complications, present serious obstacles to any such efforts to realign the resources of government and sector. Perhaps the first steps in this direction were taken with the framing of Urban Development Agreements,[35] which laid out very concretely the relationship between government and the nonprofit/voluntary sector in urban communities.

[33] Bradford, N., "Place-Based Public Policy: Towards a New Urban and Community Agenda for Canada," Research Report F/51, Family Network, *CPRN* March 2005, p. 10.

[34] Torjman, S., "No Small Answers to Big Problems," OpEd, *Toronto Star*, September 17, 2007.

[35] Urban development agreements involved all three levels of government and civil society organizations jointly forming social policy to deal with issues such as homelessness and economic development. They were terminated in 2010. Doberstein, C., "Institutional Creation and Death: Urban Development Agreements in Canada," *Journal of Urban Affairs*, Vol. 33, No. 5, December 2011, at pp. 529–548; at: http://onlinelibrary.wiley.com/journal/10.1111/%28ISSN%291467-9906/homepage/Contact.html.

1. The Voluntary Sector Initiative

In 1995, 12 national umbrella organizations covering most parts of the voluntary sector came together as the Voluntary Sector Roundtable to enhance the relationship between government and sector, to strengthen the latter's capacity, and to improve its legal and regulatory framework. When this was promptly followed by the publication of the first of many charity law reviews[36] to be conducted by common law jurisdictions, it seemed as though in Canada the seeds for a government/sector partnership had been well sown.

In 1999, having examined the environment for nonprofit organizations, the Voluntary Sector Roundtable issued two reports,[37] the first of which in particular laid essential groundwork in shaping a new relationship between sector and government. In June 2000, the Voluntary Sector Initiative (VSI) was launched, and the Joint Regulatory Table was then formed to address the issue of improving the legislative and regulatory environment in which the sector operates. In the following year, the Government of Canada and the voluntary sector signed the *Accord Between the Government of Canada and the Voluntary Sector*, designed to enhance the relationship between both parties and strengthen the capacity of the voluntary sector.[38] As Prime Minister Jean Chrétien then explained:[39]

> Today, more than ever before, Canada depends on the combined strength of its private, public and voluntary sectors. While each of these contributes to our quality of life and deserves recognition, we are showcasing today the special value of the voluntary sector. A sector that engages Canadians across the country in the life of their communities, providing services and giving voice to shared concerns. A sector that is, in short, essential to our collective well being.

[36] See Ontario Law Reform Commission, *Report on the Law of Charities*, 1996.

[37] The first was from the Panel on Accountability and Governance in the Voluntary Sector, *Building on Strength: Improving Governance and Accountability in Canada's Voluntary Sector*, chaired by Ed Broadbent (the "Broadbent Panel"). The second was the Report of the Joint Tables, *Working Together—A Government of Canada/Voluntary Sector Joint Initiative*, which made recommendations to improve the regulatory framework. This group consisted of leaders from the sector and key federal government (the "Joint Tables Report"). Following the release of the Broadbent Panel report, voluntary sector members and federal officials met in three groups, called "joint tables," to make recommendations on sector/government relationships, to strengthen the voluntary sector's capacity, and to improve regulations and legislation. The Joint Tables issued their combined report in August 1999. See further http://www.vsi-isbc.org/eng/products/reports.cfm.

[38] The Joint Accord Table developed two Codes of Good Practice: the *Code of Good Practice on Policy Dialogue*, intended to encourage voluntary sector participation in the public policy process; and the *Code of Good Practice on Funding*, intended to guide the funding aspect of the relationship between the voluntary sector and the Government of Canada and reinforce reciprocal accountability. See further http://www.vsi-isbc.org/eng/policy/policy_code.cfm.

[39] Jean Chrétien, "Introduction," *An Accord between the Government of Canada and the Voluntary Sector*, Voluntary Sector Task Force, Ottawa, December 2001.

However, as it worked out, the Accord failed to live up to expectations, and government quietly ceased to view it as representing a policy commitment to build a partnership with the sector.[40] The Joint Regulatory Table continued the work on regulatory issues that had begun with its *Working Together* report, and in 2003 issued its recommendations for an improved regulatory system in *Strengthening Canada's Charitable Sector: Regulatory Reform*, but the work done by the Ontario Law Reform Commission was lost en route; indeed, the Joint Table mandate conspicuously prevented any enquiry into most of the issues addressed by the Commission. Although there is little in the way of legislative or institutional change to show for the many years of government/sector negotiations, the legacy of the VSI remains evident in such developments as the system of Satellite Accounts that measure the economic output of the sector, the National Survey of Nonprofit and Voluntary Organizations, the organizations strengthened through the VSI's Sectoral Involvement in Departmental Policy Development (SIDPD), the Human Resources Council on the Voluntary Sector, and the Canada Volunteerism Initiative.

B. Government/Nonprofit Sector Relationships

Although the political momentum has faded on a federal basis, recent years have seen significant developments in a number of Canadian provinces and territories, with the emergence of task forces, ministerial appointments, policies, and special initiatives dedicated to strengthening the relationship between the nonprofit sector and government.

1. Charity Law Reform

Canada was the first to launch a charity law reform process[41] (ambitious in scope and watched with optimism and envy across the common law world) in response to much the same pressures emanating from the inadequacies in the common law approach and the regulatory framework as triggered reform in other jurisdictions. It was also the first to fail. The reasons for failure, that the reform process was perhaps too large a step at that time, and the long haul back to the negotiating table, illustrate problems of political context that have a direct bearing on achieving the balanced government/charity relationship necessary for managing the devolving of public benefit service provision.

The reforms ultimately introduced by government were based on the recommendations made in the 2003 report *Strengthening Canada's Charitable Sector: Regulatory Reform*, all but six of which were accepted and subsequently incorporated into the Tax Act.[42] The accepted recommendations included regulatory

[40] See Elson, P. R., "Independence in a Cold Climate: A Profile of the Nonprofit and Voluntary Sector in Canada," in Smerdon (ed.), *The First Principle of Voluntary Action*, at p. 18.

[41] See the Ontario Law Reform Commission Report 1996.

[42] Income Tax Act (R.S.C., 1985, c. 1 (5th Supp.)).

adjustments to the appeal process in respect of decisions taken by the regulator, and changes to the penalties for abuse of charitable status and to fund-raising matters. Although the internal revision of CRA policies that ensued as a result of the report were viewed favorably by the sector, there is much truth in the observation that "Canada's attempts at modernising the law of charities have constituted little more than tinkering at the edges."[43] Unlike other common law jurisdictions, no legislative steps have been taken in Canada to transfer lead regulatory responsibility from the CRA to a charity or sector specific federal agency, to place the key common law concepts onto the statute books, and thereby equip government with the future capacity to amend charity law as required by changing social circumstances or political expediency, to broaden the traditional *Pemsel* list of charitable purposes, or to alter the public benefit presumption. The absence of any alteration to the substance of the definition, or to the categories, of purposes to be recognized as charitable means that the traditional interpretation of "charity," "charitable purpose," and "public benefit," together with accompanying common law rules, continue to form the basis of charity law in this jurisdiction.

2. Implications for Future Government/Sector Relations

Although the gestation period of Canadian charity law reform has so far stretched to 16 years with little in the way of substantive change, the process itself has proved conducive to strengthening government/sector relationships. It was a unique experiment for Canada. Establishing seven joint tables, each comprising equal numbers of senior government officials and senior sector representatives, and each charged with examining an aspect of the government/sector relationship, was a significant step toward building greater mutual understanding. That this was underwritten by the *Accord Between the Government of Canada and the Voluntary Sector* 2001 was sustained for several years, and produced outcomes almost all of which translated into legislative provisions, testifies to the willingness and trust established. It is noteworthy that this was accomplished without either the driving force of umbrella organizations or the tier of intermediary government bodies that seemed to play such important roles in the reform processes of other jurisdictions. Whether having done the groundwork, the process will be able to move on without such components and eventually conclude with the introduction of meaningful legislative and institutional change at federal level, or whether it will remain stalled, is uncertain. For now, it would seem that there are no drivers for government to proceed in that direction, and no sector bodies pushing for partnership that the government could negotiate with to achieve such an objective.

[43] See Wyatt, B. and Hunter, L., "Charity Law Reforms: Overview of Progress since 2001," in *Modernising Charity Law*, Elgar, Cheltenham, U.K., 2010.

IV. READJUSTING PUBLIC BENEFIT SERVICE PROVISION

Canada, like Australia, has traditionally relied upon government-funded nonprofits to deliver public benefit services rather than establish, as in the U.K., a centralized bureaucracy of government departments to ensure nationwide provision. Also, in keeping with Australia, and in marked contrast to the U.K., Canada has not been over-exposed to the effects of the 2008 economic recession, and consequently is not in the position of having to take drastic measures to rein in public service expenditure. Nonetheless, the changes being implemented to the delivery of such services are very similar to those introduced in other leading common law nations.

A. Public Benefit Service Provision: The Policy

Canadian government, at the federal and provincial levels, has for some years pursued a policy of increasing the involvement of nonprofits in public benefit service provision. This was a source of concern to McMullen and Schellenberg in 2002, when they noted that "[g]overnments and public sector organizations have been restructured over the past decade and have withdrawn from the provision of some goods and services. At the same time, nonprofit and for-profit organizations have taken on activities that were previously 'public sector' responsibilities."[44]

The consequent erosion of the boundary between government and nonprofit bodies, as the latter become transformed into a service arm of the state, was described by Forder and Knapp as a process of "coercive isomorphism."[45] The transfer of responsibility, however, has not been exclusively to the nonprofit sector: Commerce has also taken advantage of the market opportunities presented by government withdrawal. As Scott has pointed out:[46]

> governments have shed many of their long-standing service roles and replaced direct provision of services with contracting out, notably with the nonprofit and voluntary sector. At the same time, private sector firms have begun to enter "markets" once occupied almost exclusively by nonprofit and voluntary organizations, and they are increasingly marketing their products through identification with causes and organizations in the nonprofit and voluntary sector.

[44] McMullen, K. and Schellenberg, G., CPRN Research Series on Human Resources in the Non-Profit Sector, "Mapping the Non-Profit Sector," Appendix 2, Canadian Policy Research Networks, Ottawa, December 2002, at p. 53.

[45] Forder, J. and Knapp, M., "Social Care Markets: The Voluntary Sector and Residential Care for Elderly People in England," in Saxon-Harrold, S. and Kendall, J. (eds.), *Researching the Voluntary Sector*, Charities Aid Foundation, Tonbridge, U.K., 1993. See also Scott, *Funding Matters*, at p. 151.

[46] Scott, *Funding Matters*, at p. 151.

1. Religious Organizations

According to the CRA, religious organizations constitute the largest proportion of Canadian registered charities. However, their share of the sector is steadily shrinking: in 1967, when charities were first registered, it was calculated that 4 out of every 5 were religious bodies; by 1991 they comprised 45.2 percent of the total, declining to some 41 percent in 1999. By the time that the National Survey of Nonprofit and Voluntary Organizations had published its 2003 report,[47] the proportion had fallen to 19 percent of the nation's 161,000 nonprofit and voluntary organizations, or almost 31,000 religious organizations. They were then considered to be the second-most common type of nonprofit and voluntary organization in the country, with total annual revenues of $6.8 billion—6 percent of the $112 billion total annual revenues for all organizations.

The long-established common law rule that the advancement of religion is prima facie charitable and assumed to be for the public benefit,[48] although now statutorily repealed in its jurisdiction of origin, continues in effect in Canada.[49] The CRA holds to the traditional conservative definition of religion:[50] "there has to be an element of theistic worship... to foster a belief in proper morals or ethics alone is not enough."[51] Similarly, the courts have upheld the traditional interpretation and have leaned toward a generously inclusive approach.[52] In *Fletcher* v. *A.G. Alta.*, for example, the Supreme Court of Canada expressed the view that:[53]

> [r]eligion, as the subject matter of legislation, wherever the jurisdiction may lie, must mean religion in the sense that it is generally understood in Canada. It involves matters

[47] See Statistics Canada, *Cornerstones of Community: Highlights of the National Survey of Nonprofit and Voluntary Organizations*, Statistics Canada, Ottawa, September 2004.

[48] See, e.g., Re Watson [1973] 1 W.L.R. 1472, in which the court, accepting as charitable a gift to publish and disseminate religious tracts that were judged to be without any merit, stated that "a religious charity can only be shown not to be for the public benefit if its doctrines are adverse to the foundations of all religion and subversive of all morality...."

[49] See Re Caus [1934] Ch. 162, Gilmour v. Coats (1949), 1 All E.R. 848, Neville Estates Ltd. v. Madden [1962] Ch. 832, Re Watson, [1973] 3 All E.R. 678 and Holmes v. Attorney General, The Times [1981] Ch. Comm. Rep., and U.K. Charity Commission, Application for Registration as a Charity by the Church of Scientology (England and Wales), November 17, 1999.

[50] See, e.g., in Re Russell (1977) 1 ETR 285 (Alta. SCTD), which held that theosophy was not a religion.

[51] See CRA, "Registering a Charity for Income Tax Purposes," Form T2050, accompanying explanatory note.

[52] In Re Armstrong (1969) 7 D.L.R. (3d) 36 (N.S. S.C.), the Nova Scotia Supreme Court decided that a direction in a will to an estate trustee to make payments to a church for ancillary projects fell within the definition of advancement of religion as a head of charity, where such projects were connected to the church's main activities.

[53] Fletcher v. A.G. Alta., [1969] 66 W.W.R. 513, at p. 521.

> of faith and worship, and freedom of religion involves freedom in connection with the profession and dissemination of religious faith and the exercise of worship.

However, more recently in *Syndicat Northcrest v. Amselem*,[54] the Supreme Court, in a majority opinion delivered by Iacobucci J., moved away from the traditional institutional interpretation of "religion" to embrace a view that respected an individual's human right to adhere to religious beliefs without the necessity of those beliefs having to be endorsed by a religious authority.[55] The decision is important in that it recognizes the significance of freedom of religious belief and freedom of religious practice by making clear that the state and the courts must not inquire into the validity of an individual's religious beliefs or practices. As such this decision may influence future CRA policy in determining applications for charitable status by organizations whose activities, believed by their members as advancing religion, are not necessarily endorsed by the doctrines of a religious authority.

2. Sector Capacity Building

For the Canadian government, at all levels, an incentive to increase sector capacity came from the pressing need to ensure that nonprofits were equipped to undertake new service delivery responsibilities to standards of efficiency and effectiveness that would satisfy regulatory controls and meet user expectations. The VSI can be seen as a joint effort by the federal government and sector representatives to further this objective, and one which succeeded at least in generating throughout the sector a new awareness of matters that needed to be addressed. For example, the Panel on Accountability in the Voluntary Sector, established in 1997, broadly consulted the sector and the general public. Its 1998 discussion paper, *Helping Canadians Help Canadians: Improving Governance and Accountability in the Voluntary Sector*, and its final report, *Building on Strength: Improving Governance and Accountability in Canada's Voluntary Sector*,[56] focused attention on the importance of governance and accountability.

There have been some recent adjustments to the fiscal environment that have significantly enhanced sector capacity. In Ontario, for example, the repeal of the Charitable Gifts Act 1949 on the introduction of the Good Government Act 2009 removed provisions that had restricted charities from owning businesses and from undertaking business activities, such as preventing an Ontario charity from owning more than 10 percent of an interest in any business. As a result of the Ontario changes, a charitable organization, but not public or private foundations, may now own 100 percent of a "related business." This development greatly enhances the ability of charities in Ontario to engage in commercial activity.

[54] [2004] 2 S.C.R. 551.

[55] See also R. v. Big M Drug Mart Ltd (1985) 1 SCR 2.9.5.

[56] See Panel on Accountability in the Voluntary Sector, Ottawa, February 1999.

At the federal level, the disbursement quota reform in the 2010 Budget removed the 80/20 expenditure requirement for Canadian registered charities that had been in place since 1977. That mandatory disbursement quota, requiring every registered charity to divest itself of at least 80 percent of the total amount for which it had issued donation receipts in the previous financial year, had the effect of preventing charities from setting aside income and saving toward a planned capital investment. The change will make it easier for donors and charities to more flexibly endow charities or create a reserve for either a foundation or a charitable organization. Charities will be able to accumulate a reserve or have some investments, and can now accumulate the capital needed to invest in or set up a "related business." They may instead, of course, simply choose to hoard their assets.

B. Nonprofits and Government Funding

From the early 1990s, in keeping with the experience in other leading common law countries, government funding of nonprofits in Canada shifted from grant aiding to contracting for specified service provision. The main features of this development conform to much the same pattern as practiced elsewhere:[57]

- Funders are adopting an increasingly targeted approach to funding.
- There has been a marked shift away from a core funding model, which funds organizations so they may pursue their missions. The new model is project-based and is characterized by contracts that give funders increased control over what the organization does and how it does it.
- Funders are reluctant to fund administrative costs that cannot be directly tied to a project or program.
- Funding is being provided for shorter periods of time, and is increasingly unpredictable.
- Reporting requirements have increased.
- Funders are increasingly requiring organizations to make joint submissions with other project partners and to demonstrate that they have secured funding from other sources—either financial or in-kind contributions—before the funders extend their support.

As more succinctly expressed in the Johns Hopkins report: "[C] urrent government funding practices appear to be turning many nonprofit and voluntary organizations into cost-efficient extensions of government."[58] Such government "capture"

[57] See Scott, K. & Pike, D., "Funding Matters…for Our Communities: Challenges and Opportunities for Funding Innovation in Canada's Non-Profit and Voluntary Sector," Canadian Council on Social Development, Ottawa, 2005. Cited by Eakin, A., in "We Can't Afford to Do Business This Way: A Study of the Administrative Burden Resulting from Funder Accountability and Compliance Practices," *Wellesley Institute*, 2007. See further at www.wellesleyinstitute.com.
[58] Hall et al., The Johns Hopkins Report, at p. 33.

of a large section of the sector is a matter of growing concern to many observers who fear that a loss of independence and erosion of any capacity to negotiate for sector interests is the price being paid by the nonprofits involved.

1. Underfunding

The harnessing of nonprofit public benefit service provision to serve government policy objectives has been furthered by the latter's practice of underfunding the service providers: Short-term, unpredictable, project-based funding frequently fails to cover the actual costs of project delivery, and typically falls short of covering organizations' administrative costs. Moreover, this unstable funding environment is overlaid with regulation designed to eliminate risk by imposing rigid and controlling accountability and reporting requirements on grant recipients.[59] Research has found that most government grants are funded at rates below cost recovery[60] and that multiyear grants are uncommon—only one in five of the 66 grants in the Eakin 2007 study were multiyear. As well as ensuring their dependency, such practices also severely restrict nonprofits from exercising the flexibility and discretion necessary to innovate or adjust services, or to partner or develop new ways of responding to the complex challenges facing communities. Scott and Struthers, in their introduction to the study *Pan-Canadian Funding Practices in Communities,*[61] cite numerous studies that raise serious concerns about the current effectiveness of community investments, the sustainability of the nonprofit sector, and its capacity to address the complex problems facing Canadian communities. Scott has warned that "the capacity of the nonprofit and voluntary sector to fulfill its important role in Canadian society is being undermined and eroded by new funding strategies that are intended to increase accountability, self-sufficiency and competition."[62]

C. Public Benefit Service Provision: The Practice

The above mentioned government policy of withdrawing from some areas of public benefit service provision is matched by a corresponding steady growth of such activity in the nonprofit sector. From 1997 to 2009, more than three-quarters of sector economic activity in every year derived from nonprofits in social services, development and housing, culture and recreation, education and research, religion, and business and professional groups. In particular, between 1997 and 2008 the output attributable to charity services, social services, and development and housing rose while the share

[59] Eakin, A., "We Can't Afford to Do Business," at Sec 2:2.

[60] Eakin, L. "Community Capacity Draining: The Impact of Funding Practices on Community Organizations," *Community Social Planning Council of Toronto*, Toronto, 2004.

[61] Scott, K., & Struthers, M., "Pan-Canadian Funding Practice in Communities: Challenges and Opportunities for the Government of Canada," Canadian Council on Social Development, Ottawa, 2006.

[62] Scott, *Funding Matters*, at p. xiii.

of religion, other health, business and professional associations, and culture and recreation declined. The increased community dependence on these nonprofits can be seen in the observation that for the 2009–2010 period, "on average, total revenues have decreased slightly while expenditures increased by almost 5 percent."[63]

1. Nonprofit Institutions Serving Households (NPISH)

Statistics Canada collates data in respect of this group of providers,[64] which includes social services, housing, health, education, culture, and religious nonprofits that deliver support and services to people and neighborhoods. In 2007, the data revealed this particular constellation of nonprofit public benefit service providers to be of considerable economic significance: valued at $22.1 billion (up from $12.1 billion in 1997), or about 22 percent of the overall nonprofit sector; and employing 488,000 paid workers; relying on earned income for 38 percent of revenue, followed by 24 percent from government grants, and 21 percent from donations. Further, in both 2007 and 2008, almost one-third of economic activity produced by NPISH was social services, which mostly comprised child and youth services, individual and family services, and community food and housing services. Together, health and social services made up 43 percent of GDP produced by NPISH in 2007, and this share has remained virtually unchanged since 1997.[65]

V. NEW LEGAL STRUCTURES AND DONOR INCENTIVES

Charitable organizations, for the purposes of the Income Tax Act, s.149(1)(L), may be either incorporated or unincorporated, and therefore can be legally structured as corporations, unincorporated associations established by constitution, or charitable trusts.[66] During the period 1991–2009, the CRA recorded an extraordinarily strong growth rate for charitable trusts and charitable corporations: Welfare charitable corporations increased by 62.8 percent, health charitable corporations by 54.8 percent, health charitable trusts by 61.8 percent, and community charitable trusts by 106.1

[63] Imagine Canada, *Sector Monitor*, No. 3, 2010, at p. 3.

[64] Statistics Canada explains that the following are part of the "nonprofit institutions serving households" universe: Child and Youth Services; Other Individual and Family Services; Community Food Services; Community Housing Services; Emergency and Other Relief Services; Religious Organizations; Grant Making and Giving Services; Social Advocacy Organizations; Civic and Social Organizations; Labour Organizations; and Political Organizations.

[65] Statistics Canada at http://www.statcan.gc.ca/pub/13-015-x/2009000/sect08-eng.htm.

[66] The definition of "charitable foundation" indicates that public and private foundations must either be corporations or trusts: s.149(1)(L) of the Act.

percent.[67] The corollary to such a resurgence of interest in traditional structures has been the markedly cautious approach to innovative models. With the introduction of the 1999 amendments to the Competition Act, a federal statute with a legislative intent to maintain and encourage competition throughout Canada, this resistance may weaken and allow increased recourse to new legal structures. The Act contains, in s.2(1), a definition of "business" that specifically includes "the raising of funds for charitable or other non-profit purposes."[68] Together with the NotforProfit Corporations Act 2009, a different statutory framework has now been created, one which may trigger a new era for innovation in the structuring of Canadian charities.

A. Corporate Subsidiaries

Charitable organizations are permitted to acquire control of a corporation. As such, the CRA suggests that a charitable organization may operate a business through a taxable share capital corporation with the charitable organization retaining control over that corporation "through share holdings or a power to nominate the board of directors,"[69] and goes on to explain that if a charity establishes a separate taxable corporation, it can invest in the corporation on the same basis that it can invest in any other for-profit business. The charity's directors/trustees would need to satisfy themselves that the investment represents a prudent use of the charity's assets. They also need to be alert to ensure no benefit of a private nature is conferred on the corporation. As long as its own governing documents and provincial legislation allow it to do so, the charity (if it is a charitable organization) can retain control over the taxable corporation through share holdings or a power to nominate the board of directors.

As regards the implications of a charitable organization holding shares of a subsidiary corporation that operates a business involving the rental and sale of real estate: The charity must abide by the requirement in the Income Tax Act, s.149(1)(L), to devote all of its resources to charitable activities carried on by the organization itself. The now-revised disbursement quota recognizes that a charity will, within limits, incur administrative costs, including the costs of making and monitoring investments that are of a passive nature. The CRA advises that it is a question

[67] As cited in Phillips, J., Chapman, B. and Stevens, D. (eds.), *Between State and Market: Essays on Charities Law and Policy in Canada*, McGill-Queen's University Press, Montreal, 2002, at p. 15.

[68] Competition Act (R.S.C., 1985, c. C-34).

[69] CRA Policy Statement CPS—019, "What Is a Related Business?," March 31, 2003, at paragraphs 47 and 48. As a result of the application of the Charitable Gifts Act, this option is not available to charities in Ontario.

of fact whether the relationship between the charitable organization and the subsidiary corporation is suggestive of activities that are other than passive in nature.[70]

B. Foundations

The establishment of foundations has a considerable history in Canada, and now a wide range of different types exist, including those set up by service groups, by special interest groups, by government, and by families. Indeed, 11 of the top 20 foundations by assets are family or private foundations. Although usually associated with the more cautious and conservative tendencies of the nonprofit sector, in recent years certain types of foundations have experienced a surge in growth.

1. Community Foundations

Created in the communities whose names they bear, these foundations usually receive their funds from the bequests of their citizens. In 1921, Canada's oldest community foundation, the Winnipeg Foundation, was established, and by the end of 2001 it had made grants of more than $100 million.

In the past, many community foundations achieved only modest growth, with the notable exceptions of the Vancouver Foundation, established in 1943, and the Winnipeg Foundation, whose accumulated assets exceeded $608 million and $564 million, respectively. According to the Community Foundations of Canada, the number of such foundations has more than quadrupled over the past decade—from 32 in 1990 to almost 140 in 2004. These foundations have granted more than $95 million to local charitable causes and hold more than $1.8 billion in assets.

2. Corporate Foundations

Research in the 1970s found that only a handful of companies were giving 1 percent or more of their pretax income to charities, but by 2001 over 550 companies had joined the list of Caring Companies through the IMAGINE program. In 1988, however, the Canadian Centre for Philanthropy established the IMAGINE program to encourage and recognize giving and volunteering. The program recognizes companies that have committed a minimum of 1 percent of their pretax profits to charitable activity. By 1999, corporate donations as a percentage of corporate pretax profits were 0.93 percent. Since the launch in 1988, corporate donations increased from $64,891,000 to more than $1.2 billion in 2001, and over 550 companies had

[70] Blumberg, M., "Canadian Charity Law," CRA letter in response to query (August 18, 2009) at http://www.canadiancharitylaw.ca/index.php/blog/comments/canadian_charities_and_holding_shares_of_subsidiary.

joined the IMAGINE list of "Caring Companies."[71] For many years corporations generally separated their philanthropic giving from their core business activity. This has changed significantly in recent years, as there has been a trend for companies to support charitable organizations that align more closely with their business and strategic plans. In addition, companies are using their marketing budgets to align with charities and develop partnerships.

In 2000, the National Survey of Giving, Volunteering and Participating reported that 67 percent of Canada's 6.5 million volunteers were employed, and of those volunteers almost one-half (47 percent) had an employer that provided the employees with some type of support for their volunteer work. In 1990, the top 10 corporate foundations had assets of $35 million and granted $2.2 million. Subsequent surveys conducted in 2004 and 2007 revealed little change in this pattern. The 15th edition of the Canadian Directory to Foundations & Grants contained entries on 59 Canadian corporate foundations; the largest 10 reported assets of $520 million, with $61 million awarded in grants.[72]

C. Social Enterprises

Canada has not experienced the same rapid growth rate in social enterprises as has occurred in the United States and the U.K. Approximately one-third were started in just the last two years, according to Social Innovation Generation,[73] whereas about 20 percent have been in existence for 20 years or more. This, to some degree, may be attributable to the lack of legislation to provide new forms of corporate structure, similar to the CIC in the United Kingdom or the L3C in the United States, which have done much to accelerate development in those jurisdictions. The fact that neither the federal Not-for-Profit Corporations Act 2009 nor Ontario's Not-for-Profit Corporations Act 2010 made any explicit provision for new corporate structures to facilitate social enterprise will not assist further change. There would also need to be an amendment to the Income Tax Act to treat any such new entity as tax-exempt and/or to permit it to be considered a "qualified donee"; the latter would be necessary to access investment from charitable foundations registered in Canada.

Social enterprises in Canada are often structured through a non-share capital organization so that it might qualify for tax-exempt status under the ITA definition of "non-profit organization." The definition of a non-profit organization under the ITA clearly contemplates that the entity will have a social benefit purpose (as

[71] See further Imagine Canada, "Caring Company Program," http://www.imaginecanada.ca/en/node/18.

[72] Taniguchi, Jason, *Canadian Directory to Foundations and Grants* (15th ed.), Center for Canadian Philanthropy, Toronto, 2001.

[73] Social Innovation Generation (SiG), a national project partnered with the MaRS Discovery District in Toronto. See further Waterloo Institute for Social Innovation and Resilience, http://sig.uwaterloo.ca.

distinct from a charitable purpose). Such entities are generally (although not always) established as non-share capital entities so that there is not a concern about owners and shareholders accumulating wealth. As such, these entities can earn revenues on a tax-exempt basis, but it is not possible for third parties (whether individuals, for-profit entities, or charities) to invest in the way that would be possible with a share-capital corporation. Many social enterprises in Canada have been operated successfully using this structure. However, concerns have been raised as to whether commercial activities for social purposes can be pursued on a tax-exempt basis by non-share capital organizations that purport to qualify as nonprofit organizations under the ITA. This concern is being raised by the CRA (in a series of technical interpretations issued by it) on the basis that one of the elements in the definition of a nonprofit is that such an entity must be established for purposes other than to make a profit.

1. Donor Incentives

The core charitable tax incentives in Canada are tax deductions and tax credits. It has been claimed that "the shift in tax policy since 1996 to encourage donations of assets (typically capital property), rather than income, has made the Canadian incentive system the most generous in the world."[74]

This policy shift has prompted unprecedented large gifts and increased overall giving by 140 percent, from $3.6 billion in 1995 to $8.65 billion in 2007. By contrast, growth in the previous 10 years was 24 percent, from $2.7 billion in 1985 to $3.6 billion in 1995.[75] Government policy has been to promote taxpayer choice matched with individualized rewards: tax credits and incentives for fitness programs for children, education savings, public transit, and, most recently, home renovations. The most important donor incentive lies in the entitlement to a 100 percent reduction of the donation from the donor's tax liability. In this way, the ITA gives effect to a clear policy that charities are as important as the state in terms of delivering public benefit. As Burrows points out, this can provide a very tangible incentive for middle-income donors who may, for example:[76]

> pay an average tax rate of 32 percent, but they could receive a combined federal and provincial tax credit of between 40 percent and 50 percent depending on their province of residence. Rather than a mere tax offset that high income donors receive with their tax credits, middle- and low-income donors can receive a bonus incentive for giving, if they give more than $200 annually.

[74] See Burrows, M. D., "Charitable Tax Incentives in Canada: Overview and Opportunities for Expansion," *The Philanthropist*, Vol. 22, 2009, at p. 3.

[75] Burrows, "Charitable Tax Incentives in Canada," citing Statistic Canada.

[76] Burrows, "Charitable Tax Incentives in Canada," at p. 9. In Alberta donors who give more than $200 annually receive a 50 percent tax credit—even though the provincial highest marginal rate is 39 percent. In some cases it has became cheaper to make donations than to pay taxes.

In short, this Canadian donor incentive strategy bypasses altruism to ensure that for such donors there is profit in charity but, and in marked contrast to the U.S. system, the benefit comes in the form of tax credits rather than a straightforward tax reduction. Also, as he goes on to point out, "surveys show that between 78 percent and 81 percent of Canadians make cash donations to charity each year...most of these donations by volume are not claimed on tax returns."[77]

An important aspect of the post-1996 incentives is that they enable the federal and provincial governments to influence donor choices through targeted matching fund programs. Major gifts are matched or leveraged through a variety of programs. Federal matching programs such as the Canada Innovation Foundation, Genome Canada, and the Natural Areas Conservation Program are influential in aligning significant donor dollars with government priorities. Direct funding of hospitals, universities, the arts, social service agencies, and international development organizations (through CIDA, the Canadian International Development Agency) help create the capacity and confidence that supports successful fund-raising. As Burrows comments, "[t]his is the unseen hand of government in the Canadian system. It guides many (but not all) charitable donations to the priorities supported by government."[78] His concluding observation that "the bigger issue is getting the right balance between altruism and tax benefit" would seem wholly accurate.[79]

VI. CHARITIES, TRADING, AND CONTEMPORARY CASE LAW

As Donald J. Bourgeois has observed:[80]

> Charities and not-for-profit organizations need money. That basic principle is inescapable. Money is necessary to pay rent, purchase supplies, hire employees, run programs, and support volunteers. But charities are not supposed to be in the business of making money. This dichotomy raises an ongoing issue, especially for charities, one for which there is no easy resolution.

A. Legal Framework

There are no comprehensive legislative provisions governing Canadian charities. The Income Tax Act, the sole related statute with federal application, fails to define "charity": under s.248(1), a "registered charity" is defined to include "a charitable organization, private foundation or public foundation, within the meanings assigned by s.149(1)(L)"; this section defines a "charitable organization" as an

[77] Burrows, "Charitable Tax Incentives in Canada," at p. 15.

[78] Burrows, "Charitable Tax Incentives in Canada," at p. 8.

[79] Burrows, "Charitable Tax Incentives in Canada," at p. 22.

[80] See Bourgeois, D. J., "Business Activities—Raising Revenue through Business Activities without Violating Legal Principles," *Charity Law Bulletin*, No. 196, February 25, 2010.

organization "all the resources of which are devoted to charitable activities carried on by the organization itself." "Charitable activities" itself is not defined.

Currently, "there is no overarching Canadian statutory regime for charities but rather a mix of common law and taxation law combined with some special or sector specific legislation that governs certain charitable activities, such as health care or education."[81] Only Ontario has legislated to regulate certain aspects of charitable organizations,[82] though other provinces have introduced statutes to regulate fund-raising.[83] The *Pemsel* heads of charitable purposes,[84] together with associated common law concepts, rules, and case law precedents, form the legal context for determination of charity issues by court and regulator. In addition some legislation applying to sectoral interests may also have application to charities, in particular, the Not-for-Profit Corporations Act 2010—which replaces the Corporations Act 1917.

1. Regulatory Bodies

All charities must be registered[85] as such with the CRA.[86] To be registered, s.149(1)(L) of the Income Tax Act requires that an organization must devote all of its resources to "charitable activities carried on by the organization itself." The advantages of being a registered charity under the Income Tax Act[87] include: the organization is able to issue "official donation receipts" for gifts to the registered charity, which may assist a Canadian donor in reducing the amount of federal and provincial tax payable (this can result in a reduction in taxes of between 40–60 percent of the donation depending on the province of the taxpayer and type of property donated); it is easier to receive funds from certain entities such as other Canadian registered charities (e.g., foundations), or being a registered charity may be a condition of applying for grants from business or government, etc.; there are reputational advantages; and other advantages exist including reductions in property tax,

[81] Bourgeois, D. J., "Business Activities."

[82] The Charitable Gifts Act 1949 (now repealed), the Charitable Institutions Act, and the Charities Accounting Act.

[83] See, e.g.: the Charitable Fund-Raising Act of Alberta; the Charities Endorsement Act of Manitoba; the Religious Organizations Lands Act of Ontario; the Charities Act of Prince Edward Island; the Charitable Fund-Raising Businesses Act of Saskatchewan; and the Taxation Act of Québec.

[84] See Guaranty Trust Company of Canada v. Minister of National Revenue [1967] SCR 133 and Vancouver Society of Immigrant & Visible Minority Women v Minister of National Revenue [1999] 1 SCR 10.

[85] For an organization to qualify for registration under s.248(1) of the Income Tax Act: (1) the purposes of the organization must be charitable, and must define the scope of the activities engaged in by the organization; and (2) all of the organization's resources must be devoted to these activities unless the organization falls within the specific exemptions of s.149.1(6.1) or (6.2).

[86] http://www.cra-arc.gc.ca/chrts-gvng/menu-eng.html.

[87] Income Tax Act, Income Tax Act (R.S.C., 1985, c. 1 (5th Supp.)).

exemptions, and rebates under the Goods and Services Tax/Harmonized Sales Tax (GST/HST) system.

There is, it should be added, an argument that the Canadian tax credit system has a considerable downside. Because the donor contribution is matched by a rebate of approximately 50 percent, in effect the government (and the taxpayer) is being forced to endorse and subsidize donor-selected charitable causes (wealthy donors at that, as the 40 percent of Canadians on low incomes either do not donate or do not seek tax credits for their more modest donations); there is no way of ensuring that donor choice corresponds to any objective prioritization of social need, nor is there any possibility of ensuring transparency and accountability in respect of the flow of funds. Although this is in essence the legal point of charity (donor discretion, operational within the charitable purposes framework), wealthy donor choice should not also dictate a corresponding diversion of government resources, nor should it require taxpayers to support causes they have not been consulted about and with which they may not be in agreement.[88]

Registered charities are subject to a regulatory regime maintained by the CRA. It supervises charities, offers guidance, provides for deductibility of charitable donations, and adjudicates on charitable status. Charities are required to file an annual information return with this agency and must meet certain requirements of the Income Tax Act concerning their expenditures and activities. The CRA maintains a list of charities that makes the following information publicly available: a determination whether a charity is registered under the tax legislation and is therefore eligible to issue official donation receipts for income tax purposes; a charity's information return; a charity's financial information (assets, liabilities, income, and expenditures); the activities of a registered charity; and a charity's contact details. Although this is the only government agency that holds a federal regulatory brief for charities, for most purposes the supervision of their activities falls to the provincial governments. The role and responsibilities of the CRA conform to the traditional tax-oriented, non-differentiating model, which is simply concerned with establishing the tax liability of charities and other nonprofits in accordance with the statutory tax provisions. It is not in a position to give preference to charities by enlarging its interpretation of charitable purposes to meet emerging areas of social need where to do so would be to the detriment of other taxable entities and further erode the tax revenue base.

[88] See further, Brooks, N., "The Tax Credit for Charitable Contributions: Giving Credit Where None Is Due," in Phillips, Chapman, and Stevens (eds.), *Between State and Market*, at pp. 457–81. The contrast with the Australian approach (also, Singapore and South Africa) is interesting: Although the Deductible Gift Recipient scheme is similar, the donor incentive system focused on public benevolent institutions ensures that government-selected area of social need determines the flow of donor and taxpayers' contributions.

As pointed out in the *A.Y.S.A.* case:[89] "the scheme of the *ITA* does not support a wide expansion of the definition of charity, and it is imperative to preserve the distinction that the *ITA* makes between charitable and non-profit organizations." Indeed, s.149(1)(L) of the Income Tax Act clearly sets out the rules that make such a distinction, and the CRA has stated its intention to police the interpretation of the phrase "organized and operated exclusively for... any other purpose except profit," which defines a nonprofit in the Income Tax Act. In 2009, it released two "Technical Interpretations" indicating that profits may in fact be earned by a nonprofit but these must generally be unanticipated and incidental.

The Charities Directorate, a structurally separate area of the CRA, is responsible for administering the law in relation to registered charities and certain other "qualified donees." The role of the Charities Directorate includes: reviewing applications for registration; providing guidance on maintaining registered status; ensuring that organizations comply with requirements; and providing information and education programs for the charitable sector and for donors.

Other government departments may also be involved with regulating charities; an incorporated charity is subject to the rules of the incorporating statute in the relevant province, whereas a federal non-share capital corporation is governed under the Canada Corporations Act. Different types of charities are subject to sectoral regulation—for example universities, hospitals, daycare centers, etc.

2. Charity Law

The traditional common law rules govern the definition of charity in this jurisdiction: To be a charity an entity must be confined exclusively to charitable purposes;[90] be for the public benefit; be independent, non–profit distributing. and nonpolitical; and it must be established within the jurisdiction. The *Pemsel* categories of charitable purposes, as enlarged through case law, continue to constitute the legal definition of charity;[91] the interpretation of "poverty," for example, has been expanded to reflect changing social conditions.[92] The Supreme Court has ruled that the courts should develop the common law "in a manner consistent with the fundamental values

[89] A.Y.S.A. Amateur Youth Soccer Association v. Canada (Revenue Agency) [2007] 3 S.C.R. 217, 2007 SCC 42, at para. 151.

[90] See R v. The Assessors of the Town of Sunny Brae [1952] 2 SCR 76 ("Sunny Brae"), where the Canadian Supreme Court found on the facts that the relevant entity had mixed charitable and non-charitable objectives.

[91] Scarborough Community Legal Services v. M.N.R. [1985] 2 F.C. 555, at 577 (C.A.); Guaranty Trust Co. of Can. v. M.N.R., [1967] S.C.R. 133. The Supreme Court implicitly adopted the *Pemsel* classification in The King v. Assessors of the Town of Sunny Brae, [1952] 2 S.C.R. 76 and explicitly in Guaranty Trust Co. of Canada v. Minister of National Revenue [1967] SCR 133.

[92] See Minister of Municipal Affairs of New Brunswick v. (Maria F.) Ganong Old Folks Home (1981), 129 D.L.R. (3d) 655 (N.B. C.A.) and Re St. Catharine's House (1977), 2 A.R. 337 (C.A.).

enshrined in the Constitution."[93] The presumption that purposes for the prevention of poverty, the advancement of education, and advancement of religion are for the public benefit continues to underpin charity law. Judicial decisions with the effect of broadening the interpretation of charitable purposes to conform more appropriately to contemporary manifestations of social need have been infrequent. This lack of judicial input to the contemporary regulatory regime constitutes a structural flaw in the operation of the common law system and suggests that Canada will need to seek federal solutions to address current failings in its charity law regime. Iacobucci J. acknowledged as much when he emphasized, in a majority opinion for the Supreme Court of Canada, that there are limits to the law reform that may be undertaken by the courts:[94]

> Judges can and should adapt the common law to reflect the changing social, moral and economic fabric of the country. Judges should not be quick to perpetuate rules whose social foundation has long since disappeared. Nonetheless, there are significant constraints on the power of the judiciary to change the law. As McLachlin J. indicated in *Watkins, supra,* in a constitutional democracy such as ours it is the legislature and not the courts which has the major responsibility for law reform; and for any changes to the law which may have complex ramifications, however necessary or desirable such changes may be, they should be left to the legislature. The judiciary should confine itself to those incremental changes which are necessary to keep the common law in step with the dynamic and evolving fabric of our society.

3. Activities Test

As in other common law jurisdictions, there has been a degree of judicial[95] and academic[96] contention in Canada regarding the standing of an activities test and its relative weighting, if any, in relation to charitable purpose. The relevance of the test for charity law in Canada, however, is accentuated by the fact that the definition of "charitable organization" in s.149(1)(L) of the Income Tax Act focuses on "charitable activities" rather than on purposes. Iacobucci J., writing for the majority in the *Vancouver Society* case, indicated that a nexus should exist between activities and a

[93] See Retail, Wholesale and Department Store Union, Local 580 v. Dolphin Delivery [1986] 2 S.C.R. 573 (S.C.C.), per McIntyre J., at para. 39.

[94] Vancouver Society of Immigrant & Visible Minority Women v Minister of National Revenue [1999] 1 SCR 10, at para. 150, citing R. v. Salituro, [1991] 3 S.C.R. 654, at p. 670.

[95] See, e.g., the views expressed by Iacobucci J. in Vancouver Society of Immigrant & Visible Minority Women v. Minister of National Revenue [1999] 1 SCR 10 and Sharlow J. in The Challenge Team v. Revenue Canada FCA 2000.

[96] See, e.g., Lewis, D. J., "Principled Approach to the Law of Charities in the Face of Analogies, Activities and the Advancement of Education," *Queen's L.J.* Vol. 25, 1999–2000, at p. 679.

purpose to demonstrate that the activities are "in direct furtherance of a charitable purpose."[97] As he put it:

> Another [problem with the standard in s.149(1)(L)] is its focus on "charitable activities" rather than purposes. The difficulty is that the character of an activity is at best ambiguous... it is really the purpose in furtherance of which an activity is carried out, and not the character of the activity itself, that determines whether or not it is of a charitable nature.

The difference between "purposes" and "activities" was also given some consideration by Marceau J. in *Toronto Volgograd Committee v. M.N.R.*[98]

B. Charitable Trading, the Law, and Tax

Charitable trading is well established in Canada, where it is governed by the provisions of the Income Tax Act[99] and the principles of common law. A distinction is made between tax privileges accorded to nonprofits (exemption from income tax) and accorded to charities (income tax exemption plus the deductibility of donations). The 1999 amendments to the Competition Act[100] were passed to maintain and encourage competition throughout Canada, and created increased exposure to liability for charities and nonprofits involved in fund-raising programs. In the new amendments, the definition of "business" under s.2(1) of the Act was extended to explicitly include "the raising of funds for charitable or other non-profit purposes." The amendments removed the exemption previously enjoyed by charities and nonprofit organizations. In 2009, the NotforProfit Corporations Act was introduced to promote accountability, transparency, and good corporate governance for the nonprofit sector, thereby extending to the sector the statutory application of standards now required from commercial entities. Its introduction marks the first substantive change to the law governing federal nonprofit corporations in over 90 years.

1. Charity Trading and Tax

In July 2010, the provincial sales tax (PST) was replaced by the harmonized sales tax (HST) in Ontario and British Columbia (though it has since been repealed in

[97] Vancouver Society of Immigrant & Visible Minority Women v Minister of National Revenue [1999] 1 SCR 10, at para. 158. The reference to "direct" is somewhat misleading as Iacobucci J. at para. 152 provided the following example of a direct activity: writing a letter to solicit donations.

[98] See Toronto Volgograd Committee v. M.N.R. [1988] F.C. 251, at p. 255 (C.A.).

[99] The Income Tax Act (R.S.C. 1985 c.1 (5th supp.)) ss. 149.1(1), 188.1(1), (2) and para. 188.2(1)(a).

[100] R.S.C. 1985, c. C-34.

the latter). Administered by the CRA, the HST combines the federal goods and services tax (GST) with the PST in participating provinces. Newfoundland, New Brunswick, and Nova Scotia adopted the HST in April 1997. A "charity" for GST/HST purposes includes most registered charities for income tax exemption, but does not include those that are a school authority, a public college, a university, a hospital authority, or a local authority determined to be a municipality. For the purposes of both charity law and the Income Tax Act, a trading charity is required to have exclusively charitable purposes and cannot, therefore, allow any commercial venture to become a purpose in its own right. A trading charity's eligibility for tax exemption is dependent upon the trading remaining subordinate to charitable purpose, and on it being a business that is related to that purpose.

2. Related Business

In the Income Tax Act, s.149.1, the concept of a related business is defined as follows: "[a] "related business," in relation to a charity, includes a business that is unrelated to the objects of the charity if substantially all persons employed by the charity in the carrying on of that business are not remunerated for that employment."

Charitable organizations[101] and public foundations[102] can carry on a related business[103] that accomplishes or promotes their charitable objects, but only if this does not become a substantial commercial endeavor. If either carry on an unrelated business, that organization's charitable status may be revoked.[104] They can both carry on any other business activity if substantially all (i.e., at least 90 percent) of the staff involved in these activities are volunteers. Private foundations cannot carry on any business activities.[105]

The CRA identifies two kinds of related businesses: those run substantially by volunteers, and those that are linked to a charity's purpose and are subordinate to it. The fact that the profits from a business are applied to a charitable purpose is not sufficient to constitute the necessary linkage[106] as charities are always required to apply their resources to charitable purposes whether or not they are carrying on a business. This point, which forms the basis for the "destination of income test," found support

[101] Paragraph 149.1(6)(a) of the Income Tax Act.

[102] Private foundations, however, may not carry on any business activity, otherwise their charitable status may be revoked: para 149.1(4)(a) of the Income Tax Act.

[103] See Canada Revenue Agency Policy Statement CPS—019 entitled "What Is a Related Business?," March 31, 2003.

[104] Paragraphs 149.1(2)(a) and 149.1(3)(a) of the Income Tax Act.

[105] CRA, CSP-B02. See also the Income Tax Act, para. 149.1(2)(a) for charities designated as charitable organizations, and para. 149.1(3)(a) for charities designated as public foundations.

[106] See Earth Fund/Fond pour la Terre v Minister of National Revenue, 2002 FCA 498, 2003 D.T.C. 5016 (Eng.), 298 N.R. 391, [2003] 2 C.T.C. 10.

from the Federal Court of Appeal when it ruled in the *Alberta Institute* case[107] that the Institute was not carrying on a wholesale business and that its objects were sufficient to make the activity a related business. But in the *Earth Fund* case,[108] the Federal Court of Appeal repudiated that *ratio decedendi* and clearly stated that the decision in *Alberta Institute* does not stand for the proposition that any business is a related business. Instead, it is the nature of the business, and whether it has some direct connection to a charity's purpose, that determines whether it is a related business.

The CRA considers a business to be linked to a charity's purpose if it is: a usual and necessary concomitant of charitable programs; an offshoot of a charitable program; or a use of excess capacity; or if it involves the sale of items that promote the charity or its objects. It considers a business to be subordinate to a charity's purpose if it remains subservient to a dominant charitable purpose, as opposed to becoming a non-charitable purpose in its own right, and will be guided by the usual "ancillary and incidental" rules[109] when making that determination.

C. Charitable Trading: The Case Law in a Public Services Context

According to the CRA, during the period 1991–2009 the register of charities recorded the strongest rate of growth for charities concerned with welfare (45.7 percent), closely followed by benefits to the community (38 percent). This corresponds with Brooks's observation that "although contracting out social services to voluntary bodies has a long history in Canadian public administration, over the past two decades it has increased dramatically."[110] Such charity case law as there has been in recent years would seem to be similarly aligned, thereby reinforcing the impression that more charities and more charitable activity are becoming focused on public benefit service provision of a core "welfare" nature.

1. Health and Social Care Provision

In Canada, as in other common law jurisdictions, organizations established to promote and maintain high standards of health care, to conduct research designed to improve drugs, or to innovate other forms of treatment, will be eligible for charitable status. Gifts intended to promote good health, thereby avoiding the need to treat sickness, may also be deemed to be charitable. The range of service provision

[107] Alberta Institute on Mental Retardation v. The Queen [1987] 2 C.T.C. 70, 87 D.T.C. 5306 (F.C.A.).

[108] Earth Fund/Fond pour la Terre v Minister of National Revenue 2002 FCA 498, 2003 D.T.C. 5016 (Eng.), 298 N.R. 391, [2003] 2 C.T.C. 10.

[109] See Scarborough Community Legal Services v. The Queen (1985) 17 DLR (4th) 308 (FCA).

[110] See Brooks, N., "The Role of the Voluntary Sector in a Modern Welfare State," in Phillips, Chapman, and Stevens, (eds.), *Between State and Market*, at p. 193.

recognized by the Canadian courts as charitable includes those relating to mental illness,[111] blindness,[112] and the neglect of children.[113] In the latter context, the sweep of the court's judgment in ruling as charitable a gift that established a home for children in need is notable as it was justified on grounds that ranged from "the relief of poverty in general, for the relief of suffering and distress of children, a gift to the destitute, and, in part, a gift to help accomplish governmental purposes, all of which, alone or together, have been held charitable."[114]

There has been no specific "public aspect" requirement to be satisfied for a trust to qualify under this category of charity[115] nor has entitlement to government assistance debarred a recipient from receiving benefits under a charitable bequest.[116] Further, charity need not be restricted to those suffering from poverty as the rich may also be entitled to benefit from charitable services.[117]

On the relatively few occasions where the opportunity to do so has arisen, the Canadian judiciary have tended to take a broad view of matters that could be construed as contributing to promoting health and social care and therefore falling within the definition of charity. This approach has its roots in the persuasive precedent established by the ruling in *Re Laidlaw*,[118] where the Ontario Supreme Court decided that it was apt to distinguish a gift in the year 1895 from one made in 1981 for the encouragement of sports that promote health and physical fitness. However, a more recent attempt to rely upon this ruling in a claim that an Ontario amateur youth soccer association should be registered as a charity within the meaning of subsection 248(1) of the Income Tax Act failed as the court held that its purposes and activities were not charitable.[119] The court noted the submission made on behalf of the government that 21 percent of all Canadian nonprofits were sports and recreation organizations, and to concede charitable status in the present case would have a significant impact on the income tax system. As Justice Rothstein stated, "this would seem to be closer to wholesale reform than incremental change, and is best left to Parliament... substantial change in the definition of charity must come from the legislature rather than the courts."[120] In addition he drew attention to a wider point, also made by Justice Iacobucci in *Vancouver Society*, that as regards the general scheme of the Income Tax Act, the distinction drawn in the Act between registered charities and nonprofit organizations is

[111] Moorcroft v. Simpson (1921), 64 D.L.R. 231 (Ont. H.C.).

[112] Re McDonald (1980), 105 D.L.R. (3d) 681 (B.C. S.C.).

[113] Re Kinny (1903), 6 O.L.R. 459 (In Chambers).

[114] See Re Forgan Estate (1961) 34 WWR 485 (Alta QB), at p. 499.

[115] Jones v. T. Eaton Co., [1973] S.C.R. 635.

[116] Re Forgan (1961), 29 D.L.R. (2d) 585 (Alta. S.C.).

[117] Re Bethel (1971) 2 O.R. 316 aff'd [1973] S.C.R. 635.

[118] Re Laidlaw Foundation (1984) 13 DLR 491.

[119] A.Y.S.A. Amateur Youth Soccer Association v. Canada (Revenue Agency) 2007 SCC 42.

[120] A.Y.S.A. Amateur Youth Soccer Association v. Canada (Revenue Agency) 2007 SCC at pp. 28–29.

intended to give effect to the principle that not all nonprofit social welfare activities should be considered charitable.

The ruling in *Laidlaw* reflects the contemporary concern of both the government to protect its revenue base from any further erosion by charitable exemption and of the judiciary to sidestep issues of policy on the grounds that to venture into that arena would be to trespass on matters deemed to be the prerogative of Parliament.[121] This cautious and guarded approach was also evident in the *Vancouver Society* case,[122] which, again, revealed the futility of relying on the contemporary workings of the common law system as the means for modernizing charity law.

A more assertive judicial approach was, perhaps, evident in *Everywoman's Health Centre Society v. Canada*,[123] which concerned a society established to provide "necessary medical services for women for the benefit of the community as a whole" (an abortion clinic) and "educational activities incidental to the above." The Federal Court of Appeals for British Columbia focused on the provision of health care: As the organization operated a clinic like other health clinics, then, in the words of Decary J. "the controversy that surrounds abortion should not deter us from seeking the true purpose of the clinic, which is to benefit women receiving a legally recognized health care service in a legally constituted clinic." As it provided a "legally recognized health care service," it was entitled to charitable status. In *Minister of Municipal Affairs of New Brunswick v. (Maria F.) Ganong Old Folks Home*,[124] which considered the definition of relief of poverty for purposes of the meaning of charity, the court decided that the home could be considered to be a charity even though some of the persons served by it were not poor. Again, in *Northern NSW Football Limited v. Chief Commissioner of State Revenue*,[125] a nonprofit organization established for the objectives of promoting football and certain related matters, was found to be a charity, as its dominant purpose was to benefit the community, with the benefit being the improvement in the health and general well-being of participants by providing through the medium of football education about healthy lifestyles and nondiscrimination. Promoting the general good of the community also provided

[121] An argument played out most recently in the Australian courts during the prolonged Aid/Watch appeal process, which culminated in Aid/Watch Inc. v. Commissioner of Taxation [2010] HCA 42 with the judiciary taking a quite different approach to that adopted by their Canadian counterparts.

[122] Vancouver Society of Immigrant & Visible Minority Women v. Minister of National Revenue [1991] 1 SCR 10 (1999) 169 D.l.R. (4th) 34, SC.

[123] Everywoman's Health Centre Society v. Canada, [1991] 92 D.T.C. 6001 (operation of an abortion clinic viewed as being analogous to a hospital).

[124] (1981), 129 D.L.R. (3d) 655, at 663–64 (B.C.S.C.).

[125] [2009] NSW ADT 113.

the rationale for the judicial confirmation of an organization's charitable status in *Vancouver Regional FreeNet Association v. M.N.R.*[126] and other cases.[127]

However, that there are limits to the accommodating approach of the Canadian judiciary was demonstrated in *Nanaimo Community Bingo Assn. v. British Columbia (Attorney General).*[128] In this case, the British Columbia court dealt with the distinction between charity and government in the context of the use of proceeds from lottery licenses. The Attorney General argued that the use of proceeds by government for education and health care were charitable purposes. Justice Owen-Flood disagreed, commenting:

> I see no merit in this contention. While it may be true that the *Criminal Code* does not require that the same charitable or religious aim must exist between the licensee of the bingo event and the end to which the proceeds from that event are eventually put, it goes without saying that Government responsibility for health care and education is not a matter of charity but rather one of duty. It is a novel proposition of the respondent that government funds directed to health care and education constitutes an act of charity. In any event, just as it would have ill behooved Robin Hood to have robbed from charity to give to other charities, likewise, it ill serves Government, even with the best of motives, to in effect expropriate charitable and religious funds.

This is a rare and interesting judicial attempt to draw a line between the legal role of government and charity in respect of responsibility for the more core components of public welfare. Funding for education and health care service provision is set aside as being among the duties of government: There are certain aspects of public benefit service provision for which charity may choose to assume a role, but for which government cannot avoid responsibility.

2. Education

The issue of how broadly the courts should interpret "education"[129] was featured in *Re Vancouver Regional Freenet Association v. Minister of National Revenue,*[130]

[126] [1996] 3 F.C. 880. The court then utilized the "spirit and intendment" rule to confirm the charitable status of an organization established to provide free community access to the Internet.
[127] See, e.g., Notre Dame de Grâce Neighbourhood Assn. v. M.N.R., 85 N.R. 73, at 77 [1988] 3 F.C. D-39 (C.A.). See also Native Communications Society v. M.N.R. [1986] 3 F.C. 471, which concerned the development of radio and television productions relevant to native peoples. The Society, which had objectives that included making the community aware of cultural activities and attempting to foster language and cultures, was held to be charitable.
[128] (1998) 52 B.C.L.R. (3d) 284 (S.C.). For a view that echoed an earlier ruling of the Alberta Court of Appeal to the effect that courts must maintain currency with social conditions and realities, see Re St. Catharine's House, 80 (1977), 2 A.R. 337 (C.A.).
[129] See Canada Trust Co. v. Ontario (Human Rights Commission) (1990) 20 A.C.W.S. (3d) 736 (Ont. C.A.); revg. (1987), 61 O.R. (2d) 75, 42 D.L.R. (4th) 263 (H.C.).
[130] (1996) 137 D.l.R. (4th) 206.

where the court viewed the provision of free community access to the Internet as a contemporary equivalent to the "highways" declared charitable in the Preamble. This was followed by the ruling in *Interfaith Development Education Association v. Minister of National Revenue*,[131] in which Stone J. noted that the "advancement of education" had a restricted meaning in Canadian charity law.[132] In keeping with the test established by Robertson J. in *Briarpatch*,[133] Stone J. upheld the decision to refuse charitable status on the ground that the appellant had failed to demonstrate the "formal training of the mind" or "improvement of a useful branch of human knowledge" necessary to meet that restricted meaning. A similar decision was also reached in *Human Life International*,[134] where again the *Briarpatch* test was not satisfied. Then came *Vancouver Society*,[135] which concerned a society with objectives to provide educational forums and workshops for immigrant women to help them find employment, carry on incidental and ancillary political activities, and raise funds for these purposes. Ultimately, the organization was held not to be eligible for registration as a charity on the basis that the objects of the organization were not exclusively charitable. However, the ruling is important because of the judicial finding that the advancement of education is not restricted to teaching, but includes research, provided that this is of educational value to the person conducting the research or advances knowledge, which may in turn be taught; and could also encompass as advancing education the workshops, seminars, etc. that the society made available, and the provision of information and advice for a narrowly defined purpose, such as attaining employment.[136]

The decision in *Adler v.* Ontario[137] is important because of the Supreme Court's finding that the provision of state funding for Catholic schools violated neither the human rights principle of freedom of religion nor the equality rights of other religions. Iacobucci J.'s judgment on behalf of the court makes it clear that government funding of Catholic schools is protected.[138] The future of this crucial source of funding, for the considerable proportion of educational services delivered by such religious organizations, is thus similarly protected. The issue of whether such practice

[131] [1997] 97 DTC 6096 (FCA).

[132] Citing a consistent line of recent cases including Briarpatch Incorporated v. Her Majesty the Queen (1996), 96 DTC 6294 (F.C.A.); Positive Action against Pornography v. Minister of National Revenue [1988] 2 F.C. 340, and Maclean Hunter v. The Deputy Minister of National Revenue for Customs and Excise [1988] 88 DTC 6096.

[133] Briarpatch Incorporated v. Her Majesty the Queen (1996), 96 DTC 6294 (F.C.A.).

[134] Human Life International in Canada v. M.N.R. [1998] 3 F.C. 202.

[135] Vancouver Society of Immigrant & Visible Minority Women v Minister of National Revenue [1991] 1 SCR 10 (1999) 169 D.l.R. (4th) 34, SC.

[136] See Wood v. R. [1977] 6 W.W.R. 273 (Alta. T.D.) and Seafarers Training Institute v. Williamsburg (1982), 39 O.R. (2d) 370 (T.D.).

[137] [1996] SCR 609.

[138] Protected by s.93 of the Constitution Act 1867, which was deemed by Iacobucci J. to be "immune from Charter scrutiny." See further Philips J., "Religion, Charity, and the Charter of Rights," in Phillips, Chapman, Stevens (eds.), *Between State and Market*, at p. 327.

constitutes government tax preference of some religious bodies to the detriment of others, and to the detriment of nonreligious education providers and, if so, whether this amounts to discriminatory practice in violation of human rights principles, is a matter that remains to be directly examined by Canadian legislators and judiciary.

D. Charitable Trading: The Case Law in a Commercial Context

Canadian regulators, whether courts or the CRA, share with their counterparts in other leading common law jurisdictions in recognizing that charities increasingly must look toward commerce as a means of acquiring the funds that are no longer as readily available from government or from the general public if they are to step up their contribution to community, social, and health services. If charities and other nonprofits are to make up the shortfall in government public service provision, their recourse to commercial activity should not be unnecessarily obstructed. Therefore, a broad view tends to be taken when determining whether or not an activity can be construed as a business with an organization's activities seen as a whole rather than isolating the commercial component from its context. In general, the concern of courts, the CRA, and other regulators has focused on determining what activities constitute a "business" and the type and scale of such activities undertaken by charitable organizations relative to their charitable purposes.[139]

1. Subsidiary and Incidental

In *McGovern et al. v. A.G. et al.*,[140] the court stressed that:

> The distinction is thus one between (a) those non-charitable activities authorised by the trust instrument which are merely subsidiary or incidental to a charitable purpose, and (b) those non-charitable activities so authorised which in themselves form part of the trust purpose. In the latter but not the former case, the reference to non-charitable activities will deprive the trust of its charitable status. The distinction is perhaps easier to state than to apply in practice.

As Anderson J. commented in *Re Public Trustee and Toronto Humane Society et al*, "the final statement is a classic understatement."[141] In Ontario, under the Charitable Gifts Act[142] (since repealed), the term "business" was interpreted by the courts to construe a medical arts building owned by a public hospital to be an investment

[139] The CRA has articulated the underlying policy relating to commercial charity activity in a number of documents, including "Summary Policy CSP-B02" (revised June 14, 2007).

[140] [1982] Ch. 321, at 341, [1981] 3 All E.R. 493 (C.A.).

[141] (1987) 60 O.R. (2d) 236, at 254 (H.C.).

[142] R.S.O. 1990, c. C.8.

rather than a business undertaking.[143] The courts also ruled that an "exceptional and sporadic" activity is probably insufficient to deprive an organization of charitable status,[144] and that in situations where business activity is ancillary or incidental to the objects, and is not statutorily prohibited or restricted, any profits earned must be used exclusively for the charitable objects of that charitable corporation.

In practice, the CRA and the courts will consider business activity that is not a substantial commercial endeavor to be a "related business" activity and therefore compatible with charitable status when: the activity is related to the charity's objectives or ancillary to them; there is no private profit motive, because any net revenues will be used for charitable activities; the business operation does not compete directly with other for-profit businesses; and the business has been in operation for some time and is accepted by the community. The CRA also notes that in some circumstances, a business activity may not meet all four factors, but will still be considered as "related." For example, a hospital may compete with privately operated parking lots in providing a parking lot for patients and visitors to use. The business activity must not have become an end in itself.[145] It must be borne in mind that:[146]

> The fact that an activity or purpose happens to have a beneficial by-product is not enough to make it charitable. If every organization that might have beneficial by-products, regardless of its purposes, were found to be charitable, the definition of charity would be much broader than what has heretofore been recognized in the common law.

2. Private Benefit

If the underlying purpose of a nonprofit is not exclusively charitable, then it will forfeit any entitlement to charitable status. For example, in *Co-op College of Can. v. Sask. Human Rights Comm.*,[147] the Saskatchewan Court of Appeal held that the college had educational purposes, but that these were primarily to educate members of the cooperative and credit union movement. The educational purposes provided a private and not a public benefit. Again, if the activities are too member-oriented and not oriented toward the public, it will lack the requisite public character.[148]

[143] See Re Centenary Hospital Assn. (1989), 69 O.R. (2d) 1 (H.C.).

[144] See Scarborough Community Legal Services v. M.N.R. [1985] 2 F.C. 555 (C.A.), where the judgment in relation to political activities was equally applicable to business activities.

[145] Alberta Institute on Mental Retardation v. Canada, [1987] 3 F.C. 286, (1987) 76 N.R. 366, [1987] 2 C.T.C. 70, (1987) 87 DTC 5306 (F.C.A.), leave to appeal dismissed, [1988] S.C.C.A. No. 32.

[146] A.Y.S.A. Amateur Youth Soccer Association v. Canada (Revenue Agency), 2007 SCC 42 at para. 41.

[147] (1975) 64 D. L. R. (3d) 531, 538.

[148] National Model Railroad Assn. v. Seventh Division, Pacific Northwest Region M.N.R. [1989] 2 F.C. D-1, 31 E.T.R. 268 (C.A.).

3. Public Benefit

As Iacobucci J. explained in the *Vancouver Society* case:[149] "[r]ather than laying claim to public benefit only in a loose or popular sense, it is incumbent upon the Society to explain just how its purposes are beneficial in a way the law regards as charitable."

A trust established by a trade union and an employer in order to retrain employees would not be a charitable trust because it does not provide a sufficient degree of public benefit.[150] Any private benefits must arise only as a means of achieving an ultimate public benefit and, therefore, must be ancillary or incidental to it. If the benefit is in fact private, an end in itself, then this cannot be construed as satisfying the public benefit test.[151]

4. Profits

Charitable status requires an organization's governing document to include a non-profit clause forbidding the distribution of profits to its proprietors, members, shareholders, trustees, or settlors, both during its lifetime and on its dissolution.

In Canada, the authorities have wrestled with the difficulties in accommodating a profit dimension within charitable status. The CRA advises that the presence of fees does not necessarily mean that a program is non-charitable,[152] or that the charity is engaging in a business activity, provided the profits are devoted to its charitable purposes. Programs remain charitable as long as they manifest the two essential characteristics of charity—altruism and public benefit.[153] They can cease to be charitable programs and become businesses if these elements are lost.

In the *Gull Bay* case,[154] for example, where the income from a logging company was directed toward the economic and social welfare of residents in the Gull

149 Vancouver Society of Immigrant & Visible Minority Women v. Minister of National Revenue [1991] 1 SCR 10 (1999) 169 D.l.R. (4th) 34, SC at para. 176.

150 L.I.U.N.A., Local 527, Members' Training Trust v. R. (1992), 47 E.T.R. 29.

151 Travel Just v. Canada Revenue Agency, 2006 FCA 343 [2007] 1 CTC 294.

152 Re Cottam's Will Trusts [1955] 3 All E.R. 704, at 705: "The fact that persons have to pay something under a trust of a charitable nature does not necessarily render that trust one that is not charitable..." See also Everywoman's Health Centre Society v. Canada, [1991] 92 D.T.C. 6001: "The Society is to be carried on an exclusively charitable basis with no intention to make a profit...Any surplus or charitable donations are to be used to reduce charges to patients." As cited by the CRA in CPS-019.

153 See further the CRA guidance in CPS-019.

> Two central principles have long been embedded in the case law.... These two principles, namely, (1) voluntariness (or what I shall refer to as altruism, that is, giving to third parties without receiving anything in return other than the pleasure of giving); and (2) public welfare or benefit in an objectively measurable sense, underlie the existing categories of charitable purposes, and should be the touchstones guiding their further development.

Vancouver Society of Immigrant and Visible Minority Women v. M.N.R. [1999] 1 S.C.R. 10.

154 Development Corp. v. The Queen [1984] Ex. C.R. 159, 62 DTC 1099.

Bay Indian Reserve, the court found that such activity was compatible with the company's tax-exempt status under s.149(1)(L) of the Income Tax Act. However, in *Hutterian Brethren of Wilson v. R*,[155] the organization was held to have both a charitable purpose (advancement of religion) and a business purpose (operation of a commercial farm). The latter had in actuality become the organization's main area of activity. The court took the view that a commercial farming operation run for profit does not become a charitable activity for the sole reason that it is being carried out by a charitable organization to raise funds for its charitable activities.[156] In this case, the motivation of the individuals may have been for religious purposes, but the corporate entity carried out those activities for business purposes. The courts have taken a similar view in relation to investments. Where this is more than simply channeling some surplus funds toward a safe investment to earn income to be spent on pursuing its charitable purpose, but becomes instead a major focus of the organization's activity, conducted to maximize profit, then as in *Church of Christ Development Co. v. M.N.R.*,[157] it will be considered to have lost its "charitable" character and become a commercial or business enterprise even if the "profits" are subsequently used for charitable purposes.

In *Alberta Institute of Mental Retardation v. The Queen*[158] a hospital that operated a paid parking lot for its patients and their visitors was found to be engaged in charitable activity despite the fact it competed with commercial lots. This decision provided authority for the view that a charity does not compromise its status as such by making a profit providing that the profit does not accrue to individuals or shareholders but is directed solely toward furthering its tax-exempt purpose—the so-called "destination of funds" test—a test that has since been repudiated.

E. Jurisdictional Characteristics of Charitable Trading

1. Profits

An important aspect of Canadian charity law when applied in a commercial context is the judicial rejection, in the *Earth Fund* case,[159] of the "destination of funds" test.

> I do not accept the argument of counsel for the appellant that the Alberta Institute case is authority for the proposition that any business is a "related business" of a charitable foundation if all of the profits of the business are dedicated to the foundation's

[155] [1980] 1 F.C. 757.

[156] Hutterian Brethren Church of Wilson v. R. [1980] 1 F.C. 757, at 759 (C.A.). Citing Hofer v. Hofer [1970] S.C.R. 958.

[157] [1982] C.T.C. 2467, 82 D.T.C. 1461 (T.R.B.).

[158] [1987] 2 C.T.C. 70, 87 D.T.C. 5306 (F.C.A.)

[159] Earth Fund/Fond pour la Terre v. Minister of National Revenue, 2002 FCA 498, 2003 D.T.C. 5016 (Eng.), 298 N.R. 391, [2003] 2 C.T.C. 10.

> charitable objects... the appellant proposes to do nothing except market and sell lottery tickets in a manifestly commercial arrangement that will, if all goes as planned, result in a profit that will be donated, I assume, to qualified donees. The appellant is in exactly the same position as any commercial enterprise that commits itself to apply its profits to charitable causes. Such a commitment, by itself, does not derogate from the commercial nature of the activity that generates the profit... the appellant's proposed lottery operation would be a business of the appellant that is not a "related business", and thus would not qualify as a charitable activity.

This ruling is in keeping with the approach adopted by regulators in most other common law jurisdictions but is in sharp contrast to the judicial stance currently adopted in Australia.[160]

Recently, the CRA introduced new practice requirements for nonprofits following the decision in *BBM Canada v. The Queen*.[161] Two "Technical Interpretations" now establish a higher threshold to be met by nonprofits, as opposed to charities, if they are to avoid taxation on profits. Essentially, it would appear that CRA now views any profit accrued by a nonprofit as being problematic unless the profit or surplus was incidental and not intended. It advises that:[162]

> Paragraph 149(1)(L) requires that an organization be organized and operated "exclusively" for "any other purpose except profit" in order to be exempt from tax under that provision. In our view, the use of the word "exclusively" indicates that while an organization may have many purposes, none of those purposes may be to earn a profit. Thus, where an organization intends, at any time, to earn a profit, it will not be exempt from tax under paragraph 149(1)(L) even if it expects to use or actually uses that profit to support its not-for-profit objectives.

VII. CONCLUSION

Canada maintains the traditional common law tax-driven approach to charity. In this jurisdiction, charities and government both have a long-established track record of public benefit service provision. There is an accepted policy that government and the sector have joint responsibility for maintaining such provision, and in the last few years sector activity has greatly increased in areas such as social services, development and housing, culture and recreation, education and research, religion, and business. This is reinforced by judicious use of tax incentives. Some incentives directly assist donor-preferenced charitable activity and are open to the criticism that this allows wealthy donors to choose their favorite causes and have

[160] Commissioner of Taxation v. Word Investments Limited [2007] FCAFC 171 and (2008) 236 CLR 204.

[161] 2008 D.T.C. 4129 (Tax Court of Canada).

[162] Technical Interpretation 2009–0337311E5, November 5, 2009.

them supported by matching government funds, with or without the approval of the average taxpayer. Moreover, the generous tax offset allowances could be seen as substituting profit for altruism as the primary incentive for donations.

The orthodox rules of primary purpose and "incidental and ancillary" continue to provide the main parameters for charity involvement in commerce, which is undoubtedly hampered by the lack of legislative structures equivalent to the CIC in the U.K. or the L3C in the United States. The few recent judicial rulings on such matters reject the "destination of income" test as having any relevance for trading charities in Canada.

9

AUSTRALIA

I. INTRODUCTION

The recent federal changes of government in this jurisdiction, from Liberal[1] to Labor[2] to the present Labor/Green coalition,[3] have brought with them a distinct change in the government/sector relationship. As this millennium's second decade gets underway, all indications point toward an unparalleled rapprochement that may finally culminate in the long promised new legal framework for the sector that will put nonprofits, including charities, center stage as future public benefit service providers.

This chapter examines the implications of the changing political climate for government/sector relations in Australia. It begins with a broad sector profile highlighting the importance of service delivery as the traditional core of the government/charity relationship. It then explores further the nature of present arrangements between government and the sector as regards public benefit service provision, and traces the laborious steps taken to construct a partnership framework. Consideration is given in particular to the difficulties that have been such a feature of the charity law reform process in Australia. This is followed by a brief account of the legal structures that now house charitable activity. The final section considers the part played by the judiciary in arbitrating on the issues that have affected the capacity of charities to engage in trading, both in the context of public benefit services and more broadly in the open market.

[1] The conservative Liberal Party's term of office closed under Premier John Howard (1996–2007).

[2] In 2007, the center-left Australian Labor Party was elected to form the federal government under Premier Kevin Rudd.

[3] In 2010, in a general election following an internal Labor Party upheaval, a coalition government led by Premier Julia Gillard took office.

II. SECTOR PROFILE

The federated Commonwealth of Australia is the world's thirteenth-largest economy: ranked third in the Index of Economic Freedom in 2010, with the 11th highest per capita GDP, higher than the United Kingdom and Canada, and on par with that of the United States. Of considerable importance is the fact that Australia largely avoided the worst effects of the 2008 economic downturn triggered by a banking crisis that had such drastic consequences for public sector spending in England and Wales and other leading common law nations.

A. The Nonprofit Sector

The sector:[4]

> broadly consists of organizations which seek to achieve a community, altruistic or philanthropic purpose, and who are involved in the supply of goods and services that have a social value greater than the price that a consumer could or would otherwise pay. The NFP sector can also be defined in broad terms, as encompassing all those in the economy who are not households, government or businesses that operate for-profit.

The Productivity Commission[5] reported that in 2006–2007 the sector was making a considerable contribution to the Australian economy: some 59,000 nonprofits were "economically significant" with an active tax role. In 2006–2007, the sector contributed $43 billion to Australia's GDP or 4.3 percent to total gross value added.[6] This figure is comparable to the contribution of the wholesale trade sector ($48 billion), transport and storage ($48 billion), and government administration and defense ($40 billion). It is larger than the gross value added of the communications sector ($25 billion), but smaller than that of finance and insurance ($77 billion). Although the sector experienced strong growth from 1999–2000 to 2006–07, it did so with considerable variations across activity areas: contribution to GDP grew at an annual average rate of 7.7 percent in real terms, to $42.9 billion; sector value added grew to $41 billion in 2006–2007; a real annual average growth rate of 7.8 percent. The corollary to the growth of the sector is the corresponding growth in tax concessions that it absorbs: the tax concessions granted to the 52,775

[4] See the Treasury, *Scoping Study for a National Notforprofit Regulator: Consultation Paper*, Commonwealth of Australia, Jan. 2011, at para. 8.

[5] The Productivity Commission is the Australian Government's principal review and advisory body on microeconomic policy and regulation. It is an independent statutory authority in the Treasury Portfolio and responds to references from the Treasurer. See further at Productivity Commission, Australian Government, http://www.pc.gov.au.

[6] Note that all values in this chapter are expressed in the Australian dollar.

charitable organizations known to the Australian Taxation Office (ATO) at the end of October 2009[7] will have made a considerable dent in Australia's tax revenues.

1. Employment and Volunteers

Sector employment grew from 6.8 percent of total employment in 1999–2000 to 8.5 percent in 2006–07 with all activity areas (except culture and recreation) reporting positive growth in the number of employees. At the end of June 2007, according to the Productivity Commission, nonprofit organizations employed 889,919 people, accounting for approximately 8 percent of employment nationally. The value of volunteer time rose from $8.9 billion in 1999–2000 to $14.6 billion in 2006–2007, with 2.2 percent annual growth in total hours.[8] In 2006, 5.2 million people, or 34 percent of the Australian population aged 18 years and over, participated in voluntary work.

B. Nonprofit Organizations

In 2010, the Productivity Commission estimated that the nonprofit sector comprised approximately 600,000 entities[9] compared with around 520,000 in 1995–1996.[10] A considerable portion of these organizations belonged to or were associated with religious organizations, and were therefore charities. Religious bodies have always played a significant role in Australia's nonprofit sector and, although not numerous, they tend to be the largest, wealthiest, and longest-established entities in the sector.

1. Charities

There is no register of charities in Australia. However, of the 600,000 nonprofits that constitute the sector, it is estimated that by October 2011 some 55,039 were "charitable" institutions or funds, a 2.4 percent increase since October 2010.[11] An unknown, but probably fairly small number are in the legal form of a charitable

[7] Australian Taxation Office, Taxation Statistics 2007–08 (2009), at p. 104.

[8] Australian Bureau of Statistics, *Non-Profit Institutions Satellite Account,* Cat No. 526.0, Canberra, 2002.

[9] See Productivity Commission Discussion Paper *Contribution of the Not for Profit Sector,* released on February 11, 2010, at p. 53. See also the Australian Bureau of Statistics (ABS) surveys measuring the sector's direct contribution to economic activity (ABS 2002, 2009c). According to the ABS 2008 data, in June 2007 there were some 41,000 not-for-profit organizations listed with an ABILLION. By way of comparison, in England and Wales there are some 167,000 registered charities for a population of some 54 million.

[10] See Lyons, M., and Hocking, S., *Dimensions of Australia's Third Sector,* Centre for Australian Community Organizations and Management, University of Technology, Sydney, 2000. Note that as at end June 2009, there were 177,109 organizations with an active tax status classified as nonprofit by the ATO.

[11] See further Australian Taxation Office, 'Taxation Statistics 2010-11: Charities and Deductible Gifts', at: http://www.ato.gov.au/corporate/content.aspx?menuid=0&doc=/content/00305922.htm&page=35&H35..

trust, with the vast bulk being corporations with charitable objects. Many of the older, wealthier, and more established nonprofits—such as universities, church bodies, hospitals etc—tend to have charitable status together with the social and political leverage that goes with their institutional role. An indication of their aggregate wealth and sector weight was revealed in the Productivity Commission note that nine trustee companies, managing about 2000 charitable trusts and foundations with assets of about $3.9 billion, distributed $280 million in 2006–2007. A considerable constraint on charitable activity is the restriction of gift deductibility to a small subset of approximately 27,028 charitable bodies (half of which are Public Benefit Institutions[12]) that focus on directing assistance to the poor.

2. Range of Legal Structures

Of the sector's 600,000 nonprofits the Commission estimates that the bulk, some 440,000, were unincorporated and approximately 160,000 were incorporated in some form or another. The most common form of incorporation was the incorporated association of which, in 2008–2009, there were 136,000. All incorporated entities have grown in number, with the exception of cooperatives, which have fallen significantly over the 12 years to 2007–2008. Each state and territory has legislation enabling groups to incorporate as associations. Other common forms of incorporation available to nonprofits include a company limited by guarantee and as a cooperative, of which there are about 10,000 of the former and 3500 of the latter. In October 2011, 27,783 organizations had Deductible Gift Recipient status,[13] most of which are nonprofits.

3. Range of Activities

Measured by organization numbers, the largest sector is religion. The broad category encompassing environment, development and housing, law, advocacy, philanthropic and international organizations is also significant, as is the category of culture and recreation services. Measured by activity levels, education and research make up 27 percent of the sector's activity, with the other categories constituting some 16 to 19 percent. Measured by employment, the largest categories are social services and education and research.

C. Financing the Sector

The majority of public funding for nonprofits is no longer provided in the form of grants or discretionary funds; nonetheless funds distributed via grants to the third

[12] See The Perpetual Trustee Co. Ltd. v. Federal Commissioner of Taxation [1931] 45 CLR 224. Although a charity is eligible for tax exemption, only a public benefit institution (PBI) is, in addition, eligible for a donation deduction.

[13] A deductible gift recipient (DGR) is an organization that is entitled to receive income tax–deductible gifts and deductible contributions. Charities can receive tax deductible gifts provided the organization is a deductible gift recipient.

sector directly from central government totaled $1754 million in 2003/2004.[14] The Productivity Commission reported that in 2006–2007, nonprofits received $76.6 billion in income of which 33.2 percent or $25.5 billion[15] came in the form of government grants, 30.5 percent was income from services, and 9 percent or $7.2 billion came through donations, fund-raising, and sponsorship. Self-generated income, excluding government-contracted services, fell from almost 58 percent in 1999–2000 to 50 percent of the total in 2006–2007. It noted that the pattern of sector funding sources in Australia is similar to that in other leading common law nations:[16]

> Self-generated income represents 55 per cent of sector income in New Zealand, 45 per cent in the United States and 43 per cent in the United Kingdom. Government funding represents 25 per cent of the of sector income in New Zealand, 40 per cent in the United States and 45 per cent in the United Kingdom. Philanthropic funding represents 20 per cent of the of sector income in New Zealand, 15 per cent in the United States and 11 per cent in the United Kingdom.

An important finding in the Productivity Commission report was that of the 600,000 organizations that constitute the sector, only about 10 percent are in a funding relationship with government.[17]

In addition, government estimates show that in 2010–2011 the sector benefited by approximately $3.3 billion in terms of foregone taxes.[18] This figure was hotly disputed by the sector.

1. Government Funding

In Australia, direct funding by government of the sector has been substantial, has grown considerably (from $8.3 billion in 1995/1996 rising to $25.5 billion in 2006–2007), and is now becoming more focused.[19] As pointed out in the 2011 Scoping Study for a National Notforprofit Regulator (see below), the sector's annual growth

[14] Treasury 2005, *Final Budget Outcome 2003–04, Part 3 Australian Accounting Standards Financial Statements*, Australian Government. See further, at: http://www.budget.gov.au/2003-04/fbo/html/fbo-04.htm.

[15] Productivity Commission Discussion Paper *Contribution of the Not for Profit Sector*, released on February 11, 2010, at p. 275.

[16] Productivity Commission Discussion Paper *Contribution of the Not for Profit Sector*, released on February 11, 2010, at p. 73.

[17] Productivity Commission Discussion Paper *Contribution of the Not for Profit Sector*, at chap. 11 "Direct Government Funding," at pp. 275–96, released on February 11, 2010.

[18] See Commonwealth of Australia, "2010 Tax Expenditures Statement," January 2011.

[19] See Lyons, M., *Third Sector: The Contribution of Nonprofit and Cooperative Enterprises in Australia*, Allen & Unwin, Crows Nest, Australia, 2001, at p. 36, where it is explained that "it was government funding, particularly from the Commonwealth government, that generated the growth of the sector, starting in the 1950s but especially from the late 1960s." This continued, if at a reducing rate, through to the 1990s. Most of the increased funding went to the older traditional charities to boost their levels of service provision.

rate of 7.7 percent "is partly due to the growing trend for governments to contract with NFP entities to undertake service delivery. This has significantly changed the way the sector is funded."[20] Government funding has grown strongly, rising from 30.2 percent of sector income in 1999–2000 to 33.2 percent in 2006–2007.

2. The Social Enterprise Development and Investment Fund

This Fund was launched in July 2010, with up to $20 million invested by government, to provide financial support for starting or expanding social enterprises. Subsequently, the government called for banks, financial institutions, and other entities to submit proposals to match its investment and grow the investment pool to $40 million. This is intended to be an entirely new approach that will build new partnerships among the finance, social, and corporate sectors, and represents a new way for government to work with the sector. It complements the government's Jobs Fund and Innovation Fund, which has already invested over $74 million in more than 100 social enterprises. The Department of Education, Employment and Workplace Relations (DEEWR) has released guidelines to coordinate the efforts of government, social enterprises, and the investment sector.

3. Charitable Giving

Total giving to nonprofit organizations by individuals and businesses was $11 billion in 2004, made up of: $7.7 billion from individuals (13.4 million people, or 87 percent of adult Australians), in the year to January 2005, and $3.2 billion from 525,900 businesses (or 67 percent of all businesses), in the 2003–2004 financial year.[21] Personal giving has grown strongly, notably since the introduction of Private Ancillary Funds[22] in 2001. There are 879 of these now in existence, an increase of 6.9 percent during 2009–2010, with a total value in 2008–2009 of $2016 million, and with distributions increasing by 28.8 percent during 2009–2010, reaching a total of some $197 million in that year. Corporate philanthropy has also become an increasingly important source of support and, for some nonprofits, a more predictable source of income.

[20] See the Treasury, *Scoping Study for a National Notforprofit Regulator: Consultation Paper,* Commonwealth of Australia, January 2011, at para. 11.

[21] The 2010 issue of the CAF *World Giving Index* identified Australia and New Zealand as topping the Index for charitable giving and other philanthropic behavior; see further at http://www.apo.org.au/research/world-giving-index-2010.

[22] A Private Ancillary Fund (PAF) is a fund established by trust instrument to which businesses, families, and individuals can make tax-deductible donations. They were introduced by special legislation and guidelines in June 2009 and came into effect in October. See further Australian Taxation Office, "Taxation Statistics 2009–10: Charities and Deductible Gifts," at: http://www.ato.gov.au/corporate/content.aspx?menuid=0&doc=/content/00305922.htm&page=35&H35.

D. Sector Cohesion

The nonprofit sector in Australia is very much a product of its environment and history: Community and geographic links are attenuated, and social cohesion is complicated by disparate patterns of immigration and the presence of Indigenous People with their own distinct culture, while organizational capacity is fragmented by a federated administration. The lack of population homogeneity, coupled with a tradition of local communities being strongly self-reliant relative to the more distant and less intrusive government, perhaps resulted in citizens becoming accustomed to looking inward to their communities when it came to volunteering, donating, and in other ways engaging in capacity-building activity. Charities and voluntary organizations in general, including church bodies, were also very much locally based. Some, by virtue of size and longevity, have managed to remain true to their roots as local service providers while also acquiring a nationwide brief as sector advocates; the Brotherhood of St Laurence, based in Melbourne, is a good example of such a charity.

Arguably, the result has been the growth of a sector considerably more dessicated than its U.K. counterpart, being very largely comprised of an eclectic array of nonprofits established to address the specific needs and issues of local communities and provide services for their disadvantaged members. Consequently, it has been pointed out that "there is a limited capacity for internal dialogue across the whole of the sector as to an 'agreed position' and there are relatively strong pockets of special interest groups: specific industry umbrella groups, large religious coalitions, and professional associations."[23]

1. Umbrella Bodies

Peak bodies are Australia-wide sector organizations, generally established for the purposes of developing standards and processes, or to act on behalf of members when lobbying government or promoting the interests of their members. Their emergence in recent years has allowed the sector to begin generating and disseminating a range of data on its activities, to initiate innovative approaches for measuring and applying standards, and to generally improve efficiency and effectiveness. ACOSS, the Australian Council of Social Service, for example, produces an annual survey of member organizations in the community sector whereas the Fundraising Institute of Australia and Philanthropy Australia[24] compiles and publishes information on

[23] See McGregor-Lowndes, M. and O'Halloran, K. (eds.), *Modernising Charity Law*, Elgar, Cheltenham, U.K., 2010, at p. 42.

[24] Philanthropy Australia, launched in 1977 is the peak body for charitable trusts. It took some time to establish itself and until the late 1990s concentrated largely on serving existing members.

philanthropy.[25] More recently, the Community Council for Australia (CCA), launched in March 2010 expressly to provide sector leadership, is an independent, nonpolitical member-based organization with the professed aim of bringing the nonprofit community together and making representations to government on common broad-sector issues. It remains to be seen whether it can achieve the necessary span of leadership needed to bring sector coherence. There has, however, been a problem for peak bodies in this jurisdiction as they are usually denied charitable status and donation deductibility status on the grounds that they do not themselves, necessarily, actually perform charitable services,[26] although most are tax-exempt under other provisions.

These bodies are now emerging from an extended period in the wilderness when, under the recent Liberal administration, some academics had expressed the view that "advocacy organizations, such as peak bodies, are systematically being excluded from policy making and defunded because of their advocacy work."[27] However the sector still has some way to go before it has in place bodies with a mandate to speak for, and negotiate authoritatively with government on behalf of, an agreed agenda of sector-wide issues. Although peak bodies are being courted by the present Labor administration with as much energy and conviction as they were disdained by its Liberal predecessor, there is no reason to suppose that in the meantime they have become any better equipped to deal with government. It is not improbable that peak bodies could find themselves recruited to further the agenda of government before they have had the opportunity to nurture into being a coherent sector with a distinct and authentic identity and a clear sense of direction, let alone have earned the right to negotiate on its behalf.

[25] See further Melville, R. "The State and Community Sector Peak Bodies: Theoretical and Policy Challenges," in *Third Sector Review*, Vol. 3, 1999, at pp. 41–65; Melville, R. "Australian Peak Bodies and the Market Policy Culture," in *Social Policy for the 21st Century: Justice and Responsibility*, Proceedings of the National Social Policy Conference, Sydney, July 21–23, 1999, Vol. 1. (eds: Shaver, S. & Saunders, P.), Social Policy Research Centre, Reports and Proceedings No. 141, December, 1999; Melville, R., "Nonprofit Umbrella Organizations in a Contracting Regime: A Comparative Review of Australian, British and North American Literature and Experience," in *International Journal of NotforProfit Law*, Vol. 1, at p. 4,; Melville, R., "Voice and the Role of Community Sector Peak Bodies," *Third Sector Review*, special issue, Vol. 7, No. 2, 2001, pp. 89–110; and Melville, R. and Perkins, R., "Changing Roles of Community Sector Peak Bodies in a Neo-Liberal Policy Environment in Australia," NCOSS Conference Paper, University of Wollongong. NSW March 12, 2003. See also Dalton, B. and Lyons, M., "Advocacy Organizations in Australian Politics: Governance and Democratic Effects," in University of Technology Sydney, *Third Sector Review*, Vol. 11 No. 2, 2006, 59–78.

[26] See ATO, TR 2005/21 and Ziliani and Another v. Sydney City Council (1985) 56 LGRA 58. Note that in the *AidWatch* case, this restriction was given a good deal of judicial attention, and it may be safely deduced that one of its side effects was to quash that particular ATO rule.

[27] Melville, R., Perkins, R. "Changing Roles of Community Sector Peak Bodies in a Neo-Liberal Policy Environment in Australia."

III. GOVERNMENT AND THE SECTOR: THE ROAD TO PARTNERSHIP

The pace of social change and its effects on public spending has impacted upon Australia in much the same way as it has on other developed common law nations. Australia is experiencing a demographic shift toward an older population, with more retirees and fewer people of working age resulting in a weaker tax base and less revenue for funding public services. Particularly since the 1990s, the consequences have been evident in the erosion of the welfare state and the move to New Public Management styles, and in a much greater reliance on "open market" mechanisms. In general, the history of government/sector relationships during this period was not conducive to building any form of partnership. Evidence of mutual commitment toward such a strategy, either in terms of the sector putting forward the representative bodies able to negotiate on issues identified as being of strategic importance to it, or in terms of government putting in place institutions and processes to bridge the gap with the sector, was virtually non-existent. In fact such evidence as existed indicated a government concern to keep the sector at arm's length coupled with a desire to stifle any voices of dissent from that quarter.

A. Contraction of Public Benefit Services

The partial deregulation of the labor market accompanied by the privatization of public sector businesses, most notably in telecommunications,[28] was well underway by the latter half of the 1990s. Public sector utilities fully or partly privatized included ports, airlines, ships, banks, and power plants. In 1999, the federal government established the Reference Group on Welfare Reform (RGWR) to develop a new welfare reform blueprint to address welfare dependency.[29] The RGWR approach was that "the nation's social support system must be judged by its capacity to help people participate economically and socially, as well as by the adequacy of its income support arrangements."[30] This led to a tightening of eligibility requirements for unemployment benefits whereas the 2005 budget announced further reforms to pensions for sole mothers and persons with a disability. During the same period, individual states were forced to rationalize their health and welfare services through the imposition of conditional federal funding and a requirement to adopt New Public Management processes (see chapter 11). The combined effect of these measures prompted Mission Australia to protest that "the for-profit, not-for-profit and public sectors are now becoming more closely merged through outsourcing of

[28] Parham, D., "Microeconomic Reforms and the Revival in Australia's Growth in Productivity and Living Standards," Conference of Economists, Adelaide, October 1, 2002.

[29] Reference Group on Welfare Reform, *Participation Support for a More Equitable Society*. Final Report, Department of Family and Community Services, Canberra, 2000.

[30] Reference Group on Welfare Reform, *Participation Support for a More Equitable Society*, at p. 3.

public activity, and it is difficult to distinguish between the sectors on the basis of activities."[31]

Additionally, there was every reason to believe that government was developing a new, tougher approach to charities and to the sector generally, moving away from any possible partnership discourse and toward imposed control through funding streams, a muting of dissent, and an unwillingness to engage with special interest groups.[32] In the closing years of the 20th century government/sector relations did not augur well for any move toward partnership.

1. Government Funding and Sector Accountability

As part of its strategy to regain control of public sector finances, government sought to tighten its regulatory supervision of nonprofit public benefit service provision. Indeed, each government in turn has increased auditing and accountability measures to accompany its funding. In the health and community services sector the funding relationship has moved toward a procurement model with imposed quality frameworks and competitive tendering. Agreements for state funding under the Liberal government often contained harsh conditions such as transfer of liability, appropriation of all intellectual property, refunding of any surpluses, and invasive auditing. In some extreme cases, acceptance of funding was conditional on foregoing the right to publicly comment on relevant policy matters or on any press release by the funding agency.

B. Drivers of Charity Law Reform

In Australia, as elsewhere among the developed common law nations, the principal drivers of charity law reform conformed to a familiar pattern. In addition, the introduction of the New Tax System legislation[33] providing Goods and Service Tax (GST) concessions for nonprofits also created a fiscal imperative to identify and classify those organizations entitled to the concession, which gave added impetus to the drive for law reform.

1. Weaknesses in the Common Law Approach

Government, prompted by demographic and economic pressures, had a pressing need to share the costs of public service provision and therefore had to negotiate with the sector where charities in particular had an entrenched involvement in the

[31] See Castles, F. G., *The Wage Earners' Welfare State Revisited*, Australian National University, Graduate Program in Public Policy, 1994.

[32] See, e.g., Melville, R., "The State and Community Sector Peak Bodies: Theoretical and Policy Challenges," at pp. 41–65, and Melville, R., "Voice and the Role of Community Sector Peak Bodies," at pp. 89–110.

[33] A New Tax System (Goods and Services Tax) Act 1999 (Cth).

provision of health, education, and social care services. This necessarily involved loosening the constraints on charitable activity, broadening the existing range of charitable purposes, reviewing the application of the public benefit test, enabling charities to engage more freely in trading, and removing anomalous rules that favored employers relations, etc.

Moreover, for charity law to function effectively, the common law required a continuous case flow that would permit judicial review of principles in the light of practice. In Australia as in most other developed common law nations, this flow had become at best an intermittent trickle for the same reasons of high cost, lengthy procedures, and inhibiting effect of media exposure. As the ATO had no brief to be proactive in giving recognition to charities engaging in new forms of public benefit activity, and the courts seldom had the opportunity to do so, the common law basis for charity law was grinding to a halt.[34]

2. Weaknesses in the Regulatory Framework

The fact that no mechanism existed to permit ongoing review and adjustment of the law and ensure an appropriate fit with contemporary patterns of social need brought into question the tax-driven basis for regulating charity and raised again the abiding issue of whether a charity-specific (or even sector-specific) regulator might not be more appropriate. This structural fault was accompanied by the lack of a central register and the absence of any mandatory and uniform financial reporting requirements that could enable the ATO to maintain an informed overview of the sector; there were concerns also about how best to ensure good governance arrangements. At the state and territory level, the disparity between jurisdictions in relation to registration and supervision requirements, the role of the attorneys general, fundraising laws etc., was confusing and resulted in some forum shopping by nonprofits. Confusion also pervaded the legal distinction between the status of charity, Public Benevolent Institution, and Deductible Gift Recipient, with few laypersons understanding the difference and grasping the resulting significance for tax exemption privileges. It was a situation not helped by legal provisions that failed to harmonize the requirements for charities structured as companies or trusts.

As always there was also a perceived need to tighten regulatory controls, at least for the customary reasons of preventing abuse, but, in the post-9/11 era, the new global imperative of preventing any possible flow of funds through the nonprofit sector to terrorists imposed new strictures on all governments.

[34] Before the decision in Central Bayside Division of General Practice Ltd v. Commissioner of State Revenue [2005] VSCA 168, the last major charity law case was Commissioner of Land Tax (NSW) v. Joyce (1974) 132 CLR 22, some 30 years earlier.

C. Government/Sector Relationship and the Liberal Government

It seemed to some that although the Liberal government espoused a belief in partnership, the legal relationship it developed with the sector was in practice closer to one of master and servant.[35]

1. Charity Law Reform

At the end of the 1990s, the government announced its willingness to respond to sector concerns and consider the prospect of charity law reform. This was not because it had become convinced that building a new relationship with the sector would be a sound strategy but, more prosaically, it was simply making a forced party political concession as the price for support to ensure the timely passage of its new consumer tax (GST). This did not deter the prime minister from introducing the charity law reform process,[36] in September 2000, with an acknowledgment conveying the prospect of better relationships and that the government shared responsibility for community care with the sector:[37]

> Charitable, religious and community service not-for-profit organizations play a vital role in our community and are pivotal members of the social coalition. The Government has recognised their importance in a range of policy areas, including the business and community partnership, illicit drugs policy, welfare reform and the Job Network.

The Inquiry into the Definition of Charities and Related Organizations was launched amid political rhetoric regarding the need to strengthen regulatory processes, update common law concepts, and improve sector capacity. The pace of reform began promisingly with the submission of a report in 2001[38] that made 27

[35] McGregor-Lowndes, M. and Turnour, M., 2003, "Recent Developments in Government Community Service Relations: Are you really my partner?," in *The Journal of Contemporary Issues in Business and Government*, 9(1), pp. 31–42. See also "Revenue Ruling Pay-Roll Tax –3.2" (QLD), which states:

> The key determinant in establishing whether a master/servant relationship exists is "control." If the principal party to the contract controls the incidental manner by which the contractor to the contract performs his or her duties, a master/servant relationship exists (citing Narich Pty Ltd v. Commissioner of Pay-Roll 84 ATC 4035 at 4036 and 4039).

[36] Note that the earlier charity law reform process, which resulted in the 428-page Australian Industry Commission Report, *Charitable Organizations in Australia*, 1995, was subsequently ignored.

[37] See The Hon John Howard MP, Prime Minister, September 18, 2000, *Inquiry into Charitable and Related Organizations*, Press Release.

[38] Sheppard, I., Fitzgerald, R. and Gonski, D., *Inquiry into the Definition of Charities and Related Organizations*, CanPrint Communications Pty Ltd, Canberra, June 2001.

recommendations. Among the more important of these were calls for the introduction of: an independent administrative body for federal law and a statutory definition of "charity" that extended the four *Pemsel* heads of charity to seven (the advancement of health, education, social or community welfare (including care of young people), religion, culture, the natural environment, and any other purpose beneficial to the community).[39]

However, following considerable lobbying from a sector that was dissatisfied with the report, the ensuing protracted stop-and-start reform process ended with the government eventually withdrawing the draft Charities Bill in May 2004.

2. Consequences for the Government/Sector Relationship

The collapse of the charity law reform process, leaving behind only the bare remnants to be salvaged by the 2004 Act, was a serious rebuff to the sector. It represented a lack of government commitment to charities and to the nonprofit sector as a whole. This outcome served only to widen the gap between government and sector, increasing government readiness to impose controls and stifle the "voice of the sector."[40]

IV. GOVERNMENT AND THE SECTOR: RAPPROCHEMENT

The transition from a Liberal to a Labor government in 2007 saw a transition also in government/sector relations. The incoming government immediately embarked on a series of steps to demonstrate its commitment to building a new working relationship with the sector. This began with the appointment in December 2007 of Senator Ursula Stephens to the newly created post of Parliamentary Secretary for Social Inclusion and the Voluntary Sector, and this was quickly followed by a number of related initiatives. Other steps toward repairing government/sector relations came with the compact, the reports of the Productivity Commission,[41] and the Henry tax review.[42] These were followed by a private bill, the Economics Legislation Committee report into the Tax Laws Amendment (Public Benefit Test) Bill 2010,[43] all of which played their part in ensuring that the charity law reform process was revisited.

[39] The Report is available at http://www.cdi.gov.au/html/report.htm.

[40] See Dalton and Lyons, "Advocacy Organizations in Australian Politics," at pp. 59–78.

[41] Australian Government, Productivity Commission, *Contribution of the Not-for-Profit Sector* (October 2009) at: www.pc.gov.au.

[42] Henry, K., *Australia's Future Tax System Review*, released on May 2, 2010.

[43] The Economics Legislation Committee, *Tax Laws Amendment (Public Benefit Test) Bill 2010 Report*, Canberra, 2010, see further at http://www.aph.gov.au/Senate/committee/economics_ctte/public_benefit_test_10/report/index.htm.

A. Labor Government and the Sector: Building Structural Links

Initiatives so far taken to build a new working relationship with the sector indicate a Labor government enthusiasm for learning from the U.K. experience and a drive to emulate that by putting in place, rapidly, much the same institutions and processes to bridge the government/sector gap.[44] Although it is too soon to assess the differences made by the new infrastructure, there is no doubt that the process of creating it has galvanized and focused the sector, bringing to bear a sense of collective purpose and generating a willingness to cooperate that it had previously lacked. It has also in itself brought government and sector into a closer working relationship.

1. The Social Inclusion Unit

Located within the Department of Prime Minister and Cabinet (since transferred to the Office for the Not-for-Profit Sector within that department), the Social Inclusion Unit was established in December 2007 to perform a strategic policy advisory and coordination function across government, advising on third sector reform for strengthening local communities, including the National Compact. The government has since published an exposition of its social inclusion agenda,[45] which, with its focus on redressing inequality, increasing participation and social connectedness, and providing better services and support to citizens, has the potential to make significant inroads into inequalities in the social determinants of health.

2. National Compact

In July 2009 a workshop in Canberra, consisting of over 70 sector leaders and government representatives, drafted the principles for a National Compact and disseminated them for nationwide consultation with representative groups and organizations across the sector.[46] The process culminated in March 2010 with the government launch of the *National Compact: Working Together.*[47] Bearing more than a passing resemblance to its U.K. counterpart, the compact is both a statement of governing principles and a framework for new ways of governing, including through forming innovative partnerships

[44] See, e.g., the government's policy document *An Australian Social Inclusion Agenda* (2007). As it then stated, "rebuilding trust and reciprocity will form the foundation of a new relationship between Federal Government and the community sector" (p. 11).

[45] See Government of Australia, *A Stronger, Fairer Australia: National Statement on Social Inclusion*, Canberra, 2009. See further at www.socialinclusion.gov.au.

[46] See National Compact, Government of Australia, http://www.nationalcompact.gov.au/.

[47] Department of Families, Housing, Community Services and Indigenous Affairs, *A New Relationship between the Australian Government and the Third Sector—National Compact between the Australian Government and the Third Sector*, February 2010.

with the sector. As the then Prime Minister of Australia explained when launching the National Compact between the Australian Government and the Third Sector:

> The Compact will provide a framework for building the capacity of non-profit and other non-government community organizations to improve community well-being. The Compact will be supported by an overarching Commonwealth action plan focused on the eight priority action areas identified during consultation and joint portfolio-sector action plans will be developed over the next twelve months.

This important step was underpinned, in February 2010, by the National Compact Sector Advisory Group established to work collaboratively with the government in support of the Compact's shared vision that "the Australian government and the third sector will work together to improve social, cultural, civic, economic and environmental outcomes, building on the strengths of individuals and communities."[48] Unfortunately, this group was disbanded prior to the election.

3. Not-for-Profit Sector Reform Council

In December 2010, following the general election, the Labor government launched the Council to help drive forward its plans to reform the sector. The Council will examine the scope of a national one-stop-shop sector regulator; provide advice on streamlining tendering and contracting processes for government-funded nonprofits; consider harmonization of federal, state, and territory laws on fund-raising; and support the implementation of the National Compact. It is established for a three-year period and is intended to provide support for the planned Office for the Not-for-Profit Sector, to be located within the Department of Prime Minister and Cabinet, which will drive and coordinate the policy reform agenda for the sector in the light of the Productivity Commission report.

B. Law Reform and the Henry and Productivity Commission Reports

Given the evident government commitment to creating a new working relationship with the sector, coupled with its need to review the basis for future of public benefit service provision, it was inevitable that the charity law reform project would be revived.

1. The Productivity Commission

Early in 2009, the Productivity Commission was issued with terms of reference requiring it to examine how government could engage the sector efficiently and

[48] See further the Sector Advisory Group, terms of reference at http://www.nationalcompact.gov.au.

effectively in providing public benefit services, and to assess the related regulatory framework. Among its primary conclusions were: an endorsement of the findings of the Industry Commission in 1995,[49] a recommendation that government should accept and implement the 2001 report,[50] a recommendation that a central sector regulator should be established,[51] a suggestion that new legal structures be made available for nonprofit public benefit service provision, and a determination that nonprofit income tax exemptions should remain and include unrelated business income.[52]

2. The Henry Report

The Henry report outlined a platform for comprehensive tax reform and recommended that the existing tax exemption be extended beyond charities to all nonprofits and that unrelated business income should continue to be exempt.[53] It recommended that a national charities commission be established to monitor, regulate, and provide advice to all nonprofits, and that the commission should also be tasked with streamlining the nonprofit tax concessions (including the application process for gift deductibility) and modernizing and codifying the definition of a charity. It also recommended, as had the Productivity Commission, that changes be made to reduce Fringe Benefit Tax concessions for the sector. The Henry Review, although widely welcomed, attracted a more cautious academic response.[54]

[49] Industry Commission, *Charitable Organizations in Australia*, Melbourne, Australian Government Publishing Service, 1995.

[50] Inquiry into the Definition of Charities and Related Organizations, *Report of the Inquiry into the Definition of Charities and Related Organizations*, Canberra, the Treasury, 2001.

[51] The 2008 Senate Economics Committee inquiry into *Disclosure Regimes for Charities and NFP Organizations* also recommended the establishment of a single independent national regulator for NFP organizations as did the 2010 Senate Economic Legislation Committee inquiry into the Tax Laws Amendment (Public Benefit Test) Bill 2010.

[52] The Productivity Commission is the Australian Government's independent research and advisory body on a range of economic, social, and environmental issues affecting the welfare of Australians. See, Productivity Commission report *Contribution of the Not-for-Profit Sector*, February 2010, at: http://www.pc.gov.au/projects/study/not-for-profit.

[53] The Australian Treasury, *Australia's Future Tax System Review* (the Henry Review), Terms of Reference, no. 9, at http://taxreview.treasury.gov.au/content/Content.aspx?doc=html/reference.htm.

See also *Australia as a Financial Centre—Building on Our Strengths* (the Johnson Report), released in November 2009.

[54] See McGregor-Lowndes, M., Turnour, M., and Turnour, E., "Not for Profit Income Tax Exemption: Is There a Hole in the Bucket, Dear Henry?," in *Australian Tax Forum*, Vol. 26, 2011, at pp. 601–631.

3. Implications for Charity Law Reform

As the nonprofit sector has frequently pointed out, there have been five different major reviews of the sector in the last 15 years. The indications are that this time, having accepted all Commission recommendations, including those in the reinstated 2001 report and some made by Henry, the government will now press forward with an implementation program, the core elements of which are well known.

The Scoping Study for a National Notforprofit Regulator[55] recommended, and provided the government with a blueprint for, a national regulator (the NFP Regulator): a one-stop shop for the sector as a whole, not just for charities. It recommended that a principles-based regulatory framework be established where the principles of regulation would apply broadly across the NFP sector, regardless of entity type or industry, and the introduction of a single regulator, with the removal of the present requirement that reports be made to other regulators, such as the Australian Securities and Investments Commission (ASIC) It further recommended that the regulator should determine the NFP status of entities, including charities and PBIs, with the determination being accepted by every Commonwealth agency.[56] The regulator is to be separately structured, branded, and identified. It will apply a public benefit test, require greater transparency and accountability, and bring more coherence throughout the sector. It will maintain a mandatory registration system and provide supervision and support for all nonprofits whether incorporated or otherwise. The Scoping Study recommended that the role of the regulator be to assist in educating the sector about governance and reporting standards and to support understanding of the new regulatory arrangements.

The government, having accepted these proposals, has announced its intention to launch a new statutory regulatory agency the Australian Charities and Not-For-Profits Commission (ACNC) by July 1, 2012 (now extended to October 2012) to be followed by a public information portal by July 1, 2013. The ACNC will determine the status of all nonprofit entities, including charities and PBIs, by reference to a new statutory definition of "charity" that the government will introduce in 2013. It remains to be seen how the ACNC will relate to the others that presently constitute the legal framework: the boundaries with other functions of the ATO and the responsibilities of the state attorneys general; the differentiation between its regulatory powers and those of the companies regulator, and the remit of the High Court. The fact that the government has decided that the Commissioner of Taxation will

[55] See the Treasury, *Final Report—Scoping Study for a National Notforprofit Regulator*, Commonwealth of Australia, April 2011.

[56] The Productivity Commission recommended that such a regulator should be established as a statutory body or organ within ASIC as it already registers and regulates a number of NFP entities, and is the national portal for the collection of corporate and financial public record information entities under the *Corporations Act 2001*, and that there would be synergies associated with ASIC IT services, corporate governance education support, and national presence.

retain responsibility for administering tax concessions for the nonprofit sector does clearly raise the issue of how the functions of the Commissioner and the ACNC will interface and, critically, the circumstances in which one agency will defer to the other.

As the Scoping Study recommended that the definition of "charity" be based on the 2001 Charities Definition Inquiry, this will see new charity legislation encode an extended list of seven heads of charity as the advancement of: health, education, social or community welfare (including care of young people), religion, culture, the natural environment, and any other purpose beneficial to the community. However, it also recommended that the final content of the statutory definition of charity should be the subject of further consultation; which, again, the government has accepted. As in the U.K., a statutory definition will give the government more scope when planning the basis for future public benefit provision. In the words of the Scoping Study, "a statutory definition of charity has the advantage that it can be altered by Parliament over time to ensure it remains appropriate and reflects modern society and community needs."[57] Although it is certain that the public benefit test will be legislatively incorporated as a determinant of charitable status, along with other common law definitional criteria (exclusive, nongovernmental, non–profit distributing, nonpolitical, etc.), and it is clear that the test will have a mandatory and uniform application to all charitable purposes, the test itself has yet to be defined. In response to recommendations made by the Senate Economics Legislation Committee Inquiry into the Tax Laws Amendment (Public Benefit Test) Bill 2010, the government stated that it "considers that religious observance should not be regarded as a shield behind which breaches of the law can be hidden,"[58] which might imply that it intends the public benefit test to also have a statutory application to religious organizations.

V. READJUSTING PUBLIC BENEFIT SERVICE PROVISION

The steady growth rate of the Australian economy, sustained for some years, has recently slowed down in the face of global economic recession, but Australia has otherwise largely escaped the impact suffered by most other developed nations. This is evident in the current approach to public sector expenditure. There is no equivalent to the U.K. government policies designed to address crippling balance

[57] See, the Treasury, *Final Report—Scoping Study for a National Notforprofit Regulator*, Commonwealth of Australia, April 2011, at p. 35. See also the Senate Economics Legislation Committee, *Inquiry into Tax Laws Amendment (Public Benefit Test) Bill 2010: Government Response*, Australian Senate, Canberra, Feb. 2011, at: aph.gov.au. See also McGregor-Lowndes, M. (ed.), *The Australian Nonprofit Sector Legal and Accounting Almanac 2011*, Australian Centre for Philanthropy and Nonprofit Studies, Brisbane, March 2012, for further information on recent Treasury papers relating to preparations for the new regulatory regime.

[58] See Senate Economics Legislation Committee Inquiry into Tax Laws Amendment (Public Benefit Test) Bill 2010: Government Response, http://www.openaustralia.org/senate/?id=2011-02-28.77.2.

of payment problems by drastically reducing the scale of public spending, privatizing or hiving off public utilities and services, radically cutting welfare benefits, or rethinking the basis of public service provision. Indeed, the introduction of paid maternity leave will cause a considerable increase in public expenditure. Although some initiatives are being taken on all these fronts, they are being introduced cautiously as modest adjustments rather than as prescriptive and draconian measures driven by government urgency to regain control of national finances. The indications are that the Labor government is intent on a partnership-building strategy and is unlikely to risk antagonizing its prospective partner by introducing controversial policies in respect of public services or welfare benefits. Adjustments rather than radical change would seem, at this stage, to be the preferred way forward.

A. Public Benefit Service Provision: The Policy

It has been observed that "the growth of the (community) sector in Australia, unlike in some other countries such as the United Kingdom, has not been as a result of privatisation or contracting-out."[59] A good deal of public benefit service provision has always been in the hands of nonprofits, even if many have been and remain in effect government providers by proxy. That said, it must be conceded that the public finance initiative (PFI) applied so enthusiastically in the U.K. was pioneered in Australia where it was originally applied to toll road and railway projects (though probably in fact derived from the U.S. example of toll roads). Moreover, the range of quasi-governmental "public service" bodies that inhabit a no man's land between government and other sectors is growing at an increasing rate. Several cases have come before the Australian courts in relation to bodies such as ambulance, fire brigade, and mine rescue authorities that have pushed back the boundaries of what constitutes a public benevolent institution.[60]

For the future, as Barraket argues, because Australia is now exposed to much the same pressures as other countries, it should prepare for a similar range of responses from the sector, including: "new approaches to mobilising resources, through commercial activity; the formation of new partnerships within and across sectors; and the establishment of new forms of 'hybrid' organizations that combine the logic of business with a not-for profit mission."[61]

1. Religious Organizations

In Australia, more so than in most other common law nations (with the exception of Ireland), it would be difficult to overstate the "importance of religion as the midwife

[59] Lyons, M. *Third Sector,* at p. 37.

[60] Metropolitan Fire Brigade Board v. The Commissioner of Taxation (1990) 27 FCR 279; Mines Rescue Board (NSW) v. The Commissioner of Taxation (2000) 101 FCR 91; Ambulance Service of New South Wales v. Deputy The Commissioner of Taxation (2003) 130 FCR 477.

[61] See, Barraket, J. (ed.), *Strategic Issues for the Not-For-Profit Sector,* UNSW Press, Sydney, 2008, at p. 3.

to many prominent third sector endeavours in the community services industry."[62] Indeed, "prior to the Second World War, social services were almost entirely delivered by charities and most of them were religious–based."[63] As Lucas and Robinson have explained, public benefit service provision developed quite differently here in comparison to equivalent provision in countries such as the U.K. and the United States:[64]

> In Australia, government largely took the view that there were already existing charities delivering these services and that it would be more effective and efficient if the increased government funding of these areas occurred through government subsidy of those existing services rather than by a replication of them through the creation or growth of government departments. This decision has had a profound impact on the character, nature and size of charities and nonprofit organizations in Australia compared to the United Kingdom, or, indeed, the USA. Christian charities dominate in Australia in a way that they do not elsewhere.

However, although government has largely continued to work through the established network of religious service providers, this approach has been diluted in recent years due to factors such as the declining resources and staff of religious orders available to maintain levels of such provision, the need to extend services to new rural communities, and the inroads on market share made by entrepreneurial business ventures. Nonetheless, an indicator of the enduring importance of religious organizations to Australian society is that one of the very few measures salvaged from the charity law reform debacle and incorporated in the Extension of Charitable Purposes Act 2004 (Cth), s.5, was the assigning of charitable status to closed or contemplative religious orders that regularly undertake prayerful intervention at the request of members of the public.

2. Welfare Benefit Cuts

Arguably, the Australian system of welfare benefits redistributes tax revenue from rich to poor more efficiently than the equivalent systems of most other developed nations.[65] Although access may be protected by rigorous means testing (income and assets), the flat rate benefits (usually not linked to past earnings) then available are targeted toward the poor (the poorest 20 percent of households receives 42 percent of all benefits). During the period 1980–2001, total Australian social spending increased from 11.3 percent to

[62] Lyons, *Third Sector*, at p. 35.

[63] Lucas, B. and Robinson, A., "Religion as a Head of Charity," in McGregor-Lowndes and O'Halloran (eds.), *Modernising Charity Law*, at pp. 188–89.

[64] Lucas and Robinson, "Religion as a Head of Charity," at p. 190 ("there are also more charities per capita in Australia than in England and Wales or Ireland").

[65] See Whiteford, P., "Pulling Our Welfare Weight," University of NSW, Social Policy Research Centre, *Uniken*, August 2009, at http://www.apo.org.au/commentary/pulling-our-welfare-weight.

18 percent of GDP, higher than most OECD countries. However, in 2006 the Howard government's new "welfare to work" system, coupled with substitution of Newstart Allowances (unemployment benefits) instead of Parenting Payments or Disability Support Pensions, introduced a welfare benefits regime designed to reduce public sector costs. The eligibility criteria for unemployment benefits were relaxed somewhat when the Labor government took office in 2008 but otherwise, as inflation creeps upward and with public debt estimated to be in the region of $50 billion in 2011, the Howard regime has so far remained largely in place. In the 2011 budget, for example, government announced its plans to save $1.1 billion (over four years) with increased public service efficiency, $1.9 billion (over four years) by means testing the private health insurance rebate, and $3.1 billion (over four years) by closing some dental services.

B. Nonprofits and Government Funding

The ACOSS Community Sector Survey (2010) found that 69.6 percent of sector funding was from government, 8.5 percent from client fees, and the remaining 21.9 percent from own source income (including donations, sponsorships, and sales to the public). The Productivity Commission advises that government funding for nonprofit activities falls into three broad categories:[66]

- citizen entitlements—for example, primary and secondary health care, primary and secondary education;
- social safety net—unemployment, disability, and age pensions are examples of government committing to provide for minimum basic needs; and
- activities that government assesses as having significant community benefit—in relation to nonprofits these cover the activities of a myriad of organizations such as sporting clubs, environmental organizations, national cultural institutions, and universities. Government may also fund peak bodies as a mechanism for engaging with the sector on policy and other issues, such as the development of standards.

The first two categories are activities that government sees as essential and feels obliged to ensure, although what belongs in these categories can change over time and with governments. The third category covers activities that are desirable, at least to some in the population.

1. Direct Funding

Direct funding of the nonprofit sector is substantial and growing. Government funds nonprofits to deliver public benefit services viewed as citizen entitlements or part of the social safety net. It also contributes financially to nonprofit activities that

[66] Productivity Commission Discussion Paper *Contribution of the Not for Profit Sector*, at pp. 275–76.

have significant community benefit. Direct funding constitutes the largest share of income for those nonprofits involved in health, social services, and education and research: Some obtain all their income from this source; mostly in support of service delivery.

The 2010 ACOSS survey of 518 agencies involved in the provision of welfare services found that three-quarters of their income was received from government. Given that only a small proportion of the sector is in receipt of government funding, this finding highlights that funds are very carefully targeted, most usually for the purchase of services. Indeed, as the Productivity Commission comments, the picture is one of "government engagement with the sector primarily as a vehicle for service delivery."[67] The announcement that the government intends to give charities at least an extra $500 million to ease the transition into a new regulatory regime has been welcomed by the sector.[68]

2. Underfunding

It has been accepted practice among many government bodies to make a contribution to the cost of nonprofit service provision rather than to pay the full market price. Indeed, the ACOSS survey found that around 85 percent of providers disagreed with the statement "Government funding covers the true cost of delivering contracted services." From a government perspective, this practice may to some extent be justified by the fact that nonprofit provider costs are defrayed by donations and volunteer input, but also by a perception that, by granting tax exemption if not also grant aiding the nonprofit, government has already made a down payment on such services. From the nonprofit perspective underfunding is seen as having a range of effects on the efficiency and effectiveness of the sector: on the reach of services and their quality, on access to services in rural and remote areas, and on the scope for services to innovate. From a for-profit perspective, such underfunding simply constitutes unfair competition. The Productivity Commission has proposed[69] that Australian governments should fully fund those services and activities that they would otherwise provide directly, having regard to whether the funded activity is considered essential, as part of the social safety net or an entitlement for eligible Australians.

[67] Productivity Commission Discussion Paper *Contribution of the Not for Profit Sector*, at p. 76.

[68] Australian Government, Office of Assistant Treasurer, press release: The Hon Tanya Plibersek MP, Minister for Human Services and Social Inclusion—"Making It Easier for Charities to Help Those Who Need It," May 10, 2011.

[69] Australian Government, Office of Assistant Treasurer, "Making It Easier for Charities to Help Those Who Need It," at p. 289. See also pp. 280–01 where it is recorded that government only defrays 70 percent of actual service delivery costs. It is worth noting that such underfunding would in other countries be construed as an unfair practice on the grounds that it distorts free open market competition.

In the meantime other fora may force the pace of change as the deliberations on the claims of health and community sector employees for equal pay runs its course. In *Australian Municipal Administrative, Clerical and Services Union and Ors*,[70] Fair Work Australia (FWA), the regulator on industrial relations, found that employees in the social and community services (SACS) sector are "predominantly women and are generally remunerated at a level below that of employees of state and local governments who perform similar work."[71] Consequently, it issued an order for equal remuneration. In so doing the regulator has significantly ratcheted up the cost to government of contracting for care services to be provided by charities and other nonprofit sector entities and prepared the ground for greater market neutrality between the for-profit and nonprofit sectors as service providers. As has been said: "The challenge now is for Australian governments and the nonprofit sector to implement the award increase without diminishing services to the community, particularly the vulnerable who rely most on assistance from skilled workers in the sector."[72]

C. Public Benefit Service Provision: The Practice

The level of government funding for nonprofit public benefit services differs according to the type of the service provided. In 1995–1996, this was distributed in the following proportions: for education, nonprofits received 53 percent of their revenue in the form of government grants; for community services, the proportion was 50 percent; for arts and culture, 25 percent; with nonprofits in sport and recreation receiving only 2 percent of their revenue from this source.[73] This, of course, is more complex in reality and can give rise to issues as to the proportion of true service cost actually borne by the nonprofit provider and by the user. The money flow—in terms of tax revenue, charitable donations, value of volunteer input, national social insurance contributions, and often access fees—is to a degree somewhat circular. At point of delivery, the cost of core public benefit services (education, health, social care, etc.) has inevitably been partially prepaid by the user regardless of provider status.

In the past, government has largely left market forces to determine provision of these core services. It has confined its role to a possible block grant to help establish a facility, then to subsidizing service users through the issue of means-tested vouchers while also imposing regulatory controls to monitor standards and cap fees. The voucher form of subsidy has been particularly prevalent in relation to child care, nursing homes, and disability services. For the future, government has undertaken to facilitate nonprofit service provision by developing a new, common form contract or "master agreement" for use between government and nonprofits, and it will

[70] [2011] FWAFB 2700 (16 May 2011); [2012] FWAFB 1000 (1 February 2012).

[71] [2011] FWAFB 2700 at 276.

[72] See Lavarch, L., "Equal Pay and Pay Equity," in McGregor-Lowndes, M. (ed), *The Australian Nonprofit Sector Legal and Accounting Almanac 2011*, at p. 147.

[73] See Lyons, *Third Sector*, at p. 182, citing the Australian Nonprofit Data Project.

consider the possibility of expanding Standard Business Reporting to include reporting requirements by such organizations.

1. Education

Government expenditure on education is considerable, with $14.9 billion spent on nongovernment schools in 2008, and $11.4 billion going to Higher Education in 2009. Private schools, run by religious organizations and therefore with charitable status, have always played a prominent role in Australia's education system: Some 30 percent of Australian children are educated in non–public sector schools; many of these are nonprofits. The private and nonprofit share of the nation's schooling became more firmly established in the mid-20th century with the commencement of government funding, which provides 55 percent of their revenue, with 35 percent being contributed by parents in the form of tuition fees. The removal in 1996, of government restrictions on private schools being located in the catchment area of government schools has increased non–public sector provision.

The higher education sector is an even more complicated mix of public, private, and nonprofit. Some universities such as the Australian Catholic University are charities whereas others such as Notre Dame Australia are nonprofits. Most are nominally government institutions, with the facility and education being funded by government, but with large private or nonprofit ancillary components that provide accommodation, catering, shops, etc. Medical research, consultancies, and other revenue-generating university services involving university staff are often established with funding from business interests.

2. Social Housing

Nonprofit involvement in housing provision was fairly insignificant until the 1970s, when federal funding became available for community groups to build specialized housing units (e.g., for Indigenous People). Under current government policy for affordable housing, the role of nonprofit providers is widening significantly, from small organizations catering to a niche market and managing a modest proportion of the overall social housing stock, to "growth providers" with substantial functions in property procurement and disposal and in housing development. In some states, government is pursuing a policy of divesting itself of housing stock to nonprofits.[74]

[74] For more information on the Australian Government's efforts regarding housing and the nonprofit sector, see National Rental Affordability Scheme, Department of Sustainability, Environment, Water, Population and Communities, http://www.environment.gov.au/housing/nras/index.html.

3. Health Care

In Australia, health care is fragmentary and patchy with an uneven and changing mix of provision by government, business, and nonprofits, which varies across the federation of states and territories.

Some hospitals have traditionally been charitable institutions as they have been largely owned, if not always managed, by religious bodies. In recent years this area of health provision has become more complex, and its traditional characteristics are fading as charity hospitals accommodate more public sector–funded beds, and some lose government funding and become privatized. Although new rural hospitals tend to be public sector provision, they often also accommodate a charitable dimension.

As elsewhere, nursing homes have steadily become privatized. Services for the mentally ill and community health centers tend to be public sector provision.

National health care is provided through Medicare, which came into existence in 1984, and is now nominally funded by the "Medicare levy" through an income tax surcharge currently set at 1.5 percent. The management of public health has been split between the state and federal governments: The states manage hospitals and attached outpatient services, while the commonwealth funds the cost of medicines through the Pharmaceutical Benefits Scheme and general practice. The Labor government had proposed a health reform plan that would have allowed the federal government to take "full responsibility for primary health care," essentially taking control of hospitals and outpatient services from the states. This proposal has since been modified to permit responsibility to continue to lie at state level but with federal funding.

4. Family Services

Government provides funding to the sector to pay for the sector's delivery of programs and services on behalf of government. For example, the Australian Government provides $444 million through the Family Relationship Services Program to NFPs to provide family services such as counseling.

5. Child Care

The provision of child care by nonprofits became a statutory charitable purpose with the introduction of the 2004 Act. Child care services include those of day care, long day care (full-time and part-time), casual care, before– and after–school hours care, vacation care, occasional care, and similar sorts of care. These services are not limited to preschool-aged children. The provision of child care services includes matters that are merely incidental or ancillary to those services.

This legislative initiative did not prevent the collapse of Australia's biggest child care provider, ABC Learning, in 2008. The Australian Government then stepped in to provide financial support, totaling $56 million, to ensure the continued operation of hundreds of child care centers. It also provided an opportunity for one of the more significant recent examples of government/charity/business partnership as GoodStart, a consortium consisting of Mission Australia, the Benevolent Society, the Brotherhood of St Laurence, and Social Ventures Australia, was then able to buy 570 of the childcare centers with the assistance of a $15 million federal government loan. This particular type of public benefit provision also illustrates an aspect of such service provision that is very typical: Whether the provider is from the public, private, or nonprofit sector (and often it would be a collaborative enterprise), some proportion of the cost will be paid by the service user in the form of a fee.

VI. NEW LEGAL STRUCTURES AND DONOR INCENTIVES

In Australia, the sharp distinction between the trust form for charity, with its distinctive set of governing principles but without any matching regulatory regime, and the incorporated form, which is subject to the usual rules and regulatory machinery of company law, has long been recognized as a problematic anomaly. Unlike the U.K., there are no corporate law provisions linking the charitable objects of a corporate body to the supervision of a charity regulator or to charity law. The lack of a charity-specific regulator, able to bridge the gap between common law and company law regimes, has been indirectly addressed in the Australia courts.[75] It also attracted attention in the 2004 *Reforming Not-for-Profit Regulation* report,[76] which recommended the establishment of a single regulatory regime; modification of the role of the Australian Securities and Investment Commission, the current nonprofit sector regulator; and founding of a nonprofit advisory body. More recently, the Productivity Commission has added its weight to the call for a new regulator.

This enduring lacuna in the law has probably contributed to the development of a conservative and fragmentary sector dominated by a number of large, often religious, charities engaged in fairly traditional activity. There has yet to be an emergence of new charity-specific corporate structures equivalent to the charitable incorporated organization in the U.K. In recent years, this well-established pattern has been disrupted to some extent by the appearance of new nonprofits able to respond more flexibly to cross-sectoral opportunities and to contemporary manifestations of social need.

[75] Re Inman [1965] V.R. 258; Sir Moses Montefiore Jewish Home v. Howell and Co, (No.7) Pty Ltd [1984] 2 N.S.W.L.R. 406 and Victoria, "Report on Charitable Trusts," Chief Justice's Law Reform Committee, Melbourne, 1965, at p. 26; Ford, H. A. J., "Dispositions for Purposes," in P. Finn (ed.), *Essays in Equity*, Law Book Company Limited, Sydney, 1985, at p. 168.

[76] Woodward, S. and Marshall, S., *A Better Framework: Reforming Not-for-Profit Regulation*, Centre for Corporate Law and Securities Regulation, University of Melbourne, 2004. See Recommendation 6:

> We recommend the Australian Government further investigate establishment of a corporate form for not-for-profit organizations, which will require accountability and stewardship, but that is less onerous on directors than the liabilities that apply to corporate boards.

A. Traditional Types of Structure

Of the small proportion of nonprofits with charitable status, only a minority are charitable trusts. The vast majority of charities are incorporated associations or companies limited by guarantee. There are now approximately 11,500 companies limited by guarantee, and these are almost identical to their U.K. counterparts. There are special statutory provisions for cooperatives and indigenous associations, and private acts of parliament provide for large associations such as religious organizations.

1. Associations

The bulk of nonprofits in Australia are small, unincorporated associations.[77] This structure is valued because it is inexpensive to establish, flexible to operate, and free of statutory requirements regarding transparency, accountability, and governance arrangements. During the 1980s, all states and territories either reformed or introduced a simple form of incorporation designed specifically for small community associations and sporting bodies: the "incorporated association."[78] These are administered through the Fair Trading Offices of states and territories. There are now over 138,000 incorporated associations in existence, many with charitable purposes.[79]

2. Charitable Trusts

A charitable trust is a public trust made with a charitable intention, for a purpose that complies with one of the categories specified in *Pemsel* as extended by the 2004 Act, and which satisfies the public benefit test. Its governing instrument is a deed of trust. It provides the legal structure for the more traditional institutional charities: Many nonprofit hospitals, schools, universities and the older public benefit service providers are structured entirely or partially in this form. The absence of any charity-specific regulatory body or registration process means that it is difficult to estimate numbers, duration, and developmental trends in relation to this important but numerically small part of the nonprofit sector. Like the unincorporated association, it lacks legal capacity and is similarly limited in the extent to which it can engage in any form of contractual activity. Again, like that entity, it may become incorporated, and most religious bodies have done so, which is of importance because many service provider charities are owned by such bodies.

[77] Lyons, *Third Sector.*

[78] Associations Incorporation Act 1984 (NSW); Associations Incorporation Act 1981 (Vic); Associations Incorporation Act 1981 (Qld); Associations Incorporation Act 1985 (SA); Associations Incorporation Act 1987 (WA); Associations Incorporation Act 1964 (Tas); Associations Incorporation Act 1991 (ACT); Associations Act 2003 (NT).

[79] See Fair Trading Offices at http://www.bus.qut.edu.au/research/cpns/whatweresearch/usefullinks.jsp#stats.

For many charitable trusts, the safer alternative to engaging in commerce has traditionally been to rely on trustee companies. These were created in the late 19th century and offer a risk averse, passive investment approach to the management of trust funds.

3. Foundations

The term "foundation" refers to a body established by an initial endowment, which may or may not be dedicated to charitable purposes; they are often established for private or family purposes. A charitable trust holds money or property endowed to it for charitable purposes and, most usually, uses the income from the endowment for grant disbursements. Currently there are about 5665 charitable funds and 858 PAFs in Australia. A foundation acquires legal personality on incorporation. Where there is a charitable purpose, to which the endowment is addressed, this will on incorporation remain as stated by the founder in the governing instrument. As Lyons has quite accurately pointed out, "endowed foundations have been relatively unimportant in the development of Australia's nonprofit sector."[80]

4. Cooperatives

Since the first known cooperative was formed in Queensland in 1859, they have become widely prevalent. There are now more than 1700 operating in Australia covering a diverse range of activities—from financial services, community enterprises, and business services, to agriculture, consumer groups, and social enterprises. Unlike Friendly societies and Industrial and Provident societies, the cooperatives (together with Credit Unions and mutuals) have retained a relatively strong and viable presence within the Australian nonprofit sector.[81]

B. Modern Types of Structure

The endowed foundation has spawned some modern variants.[82] For present purposes the community and the corporate foundations are most relevant. Although Lyon's reflections on the past contributions of the endowed foundation to the growth of the sector remain accurate, the indications are that the community and corporate foundations, which derived from that initial model, will be of growing

[80] Lyons, M., "Defining the Nonprofit Sector: Australia," in Salamon, M. and Anheier, H., *The Johns Hopkins Comparative Nonprofit Sector Project*, The Johns Hopkins University Institute for Policy Studies, Baltimore, MD, 1998, at p. 9.

[81] However, Lyons records a total of 3600 cooperatives in Australia in 1996: A 50 percent fall in 15 years would indicate a downward trend if not a collapse in the cooperative movement. See, Lyons, "Defining the Nonprofit Sector: Australia," at p. 9.

[82] See, e.g., The Benton Foundation, which is a private foundation, an institutional hybrid, bridging the worlds of philanthropy, public policy, and community action: see further at www.benton.org.

significance in the future. Venture philanthropy initiatives are also beginning to make their presence felt.

1. Community Foundations

A community foundation is an incorporated nonprofit company or association, which is endorsed by the ATO as an income tax– exempt charity; it is also the trustee of a trust (Public Fund) endorsed as an income tax exempt–charity and as a deductible gift recipient.[83] The first Australian community foundations were the Victorian Community Foundation, established in 1983, followed by the Queensland Community Foundation in 1986. In 1999, Philanthropy Australia developed a plan to support the development of community foundations, particularly as a means of encouraging the renewal of rural communities. This triggered a growth spurt from five community foundations in 2000 to over 20 in various stages of development by 2003, largely due to the Foundation for Rural and Regional Renewal[84] working in conjunction with Philanthropy Australia, the Sidney Myer Fund, and other supporters. It has been estimated that currently there are 26 established community foundations with Public Fund and DGR status, 2 incorporated community foundations, 1 in the process of incorporating, and at least 10 more communities that are conducting feasibility studies.[85]

2. Corporate Foundations

Unlike the traditional form of endowed foundation, with its financial independence secured by an endowment, the corporate version has its asset base secured by its parent company, usually topped up by an annual donation. Despite the requirement for demonstrable independence, the governance arrangements of corporate foundations are often routinely compromised by the company appointment of trustees who are most usually company employees. Again, unlike the endowed foundation, the Australian corporate foundation is relatively strong, and would seem to be growing vigorously in comparison with those of other developed common law nations.

[83] See further Community Foundations reform paper at: http://www.treasury.gov.au/contentitem.asp?NavId=037&ContentID=1907.

[84] The Foundation for Rural and Regional Renewal was launched at the Regional Australia Summit in October 1999; its role is to promote, for the public benefit rural and regional renewal, regeneration, and development in Australia in social, economic, environmental, and cultural areas. It has been a catalyst for the development of foundations by giving financial support for feasibility studies and providing ongoing support to established foundations.

[85] See further Community Foundations Gateway at http://communityfoundations.philanthropy.org.au/.

It has been estimated that total business giving to the sector amounted to $3.2 billion in 2004,[86] a marked increase from the 1996 estimate of $1.65 billion.[87] Not all of this was channeled through corporate foundations. Instead, some companies provide in-house fund-raising schemes for staff-designated charities, or they may offer mentoring, partnership, or volunteer programs to specific nonprofits, or perhaps enter into a sharing arrangement with regard to office space, equipment, or skilled staff. In total, around one-fifth of businesses now have what they see as a partnership with nonprofits.[88] Collaboration between business and nonprofits is now very much "part of the landscape."[89]

3. Venture Philanthropy

Venture philanthropy assists nonprofit organizations in the planning, launch, and management of new programs or social purpose enterprises. It draws on networks of entrepreneurs to combine financial contributions and professional skill to achieve philanthropic goals. It may provide seed money for a project, for its expansion, for professional guidance, for training support, for capacity building, and even for counseling on productivity and efficiency enhancement. It emerged in the 1990s in the United States, and there are now a handful of venture philanthropy funds in Australia.

The SVA Boost Fund is Australia's first venture philanthropy fund.[90] It was established in 2002 by the Benevolent Society, the Smith Family, WorkVentures, and the AMP Foundation in order to integrate the Australian public, corporate, and social sectors to create entrepreneurial, innovative, and results-driven solutions to Australia's social problems. It supports social ventures focused on bringing their organization to scale with clear, accountable, and measurable programs and a capacity to produce long-term community benefits. The bulk of the funding to social ventures is aimed at developing management and organization depth so as to enable program growth.

[86] See Department of Family and Community Services, *Giving Australia: Research on Philanthropy in Australia*, Department of Family and Community Services, Canberra, 2005.

[87] Lyons, M., "What Do We Know of Corporate Support for Australian Nonprofits? A Research Note," *Third Sector Review*, Vol. 5, No. 2, 1999, at pp. 71–80.

[88] Zappalà, G. and Lyons, M., "Non-Profit Organizations and Business: Mapping the Extent and Scope of Community-Business Partnerships in Australia," in Barraket (ed.), *Strategic Issues for the Not-For-Profit Sector*, at pp. 16–44.

[89] Zappalà and Lyons, "Non-Profit Organizations and Business," at p. 42. See also Centre for Corporate Public Affairs, *Relationship Matters: Not-for-Profit Community Organizations and Corporate Community Investment*, Centre for Corporate Public Affairs, Sydney, 2008; see also previous reports *Corporate Community Involvement: Establishing a Business Case* (Centre for Corporate Public Affairs 2000) and *Corporate Community Investment in Australia* (Centre for Corporate Public Affairs 2007), completed by the Centre in conjunction with the Business Council of Australia.

[90] See further Social Ventures Australia, www.socialventures.com.au.

4. Social Enterprises

Again this is an aspect of nonprofit activity that is not readily amenable to definition. Barraket has suggested that social enterprises are organizations that: are led by an economic, social, cultural, or environmental mission consistent with a public or community benefit; trade to fulfill their mission; derive a substantial portion of their income from trade; and reinvest the majority of their profit/surplus in the fulfillment of their mission.[91] They will always have a business element, but may be given effect through any of the above legal structures (or any combination of them). The growing numbers of social enterprises received significant government support in July 2010 when the Professional Partnership Project was launched. This initiative represents a partnership between the government and four key professional services firms, which are investing a collective $1 million worth of pro bono services to assist around 30 social enterprises. The assistance will take the form of consulting services to strengthen financial and business practices as well as governance structures. As Senator Stephens explained when launching the project: "This initiative is an important step in developing long-term partnerships between government and the private sector to support highly disadvantaged Australians."[92]

5. Donor Incentives

The donor incentive of gift deductibility is limited to a small subset of charitable bodies (mainly Public Benefit Institutions), which in effect focus on directing relief to the poor.[93] The restrictions imposed by the courts in their interpretation of organizational activity deserving of PBI status have not been conducive to boosting the DGR pool.[94] In recent years, tax-deductible giving in Australia increased by an average of nearly 15 percent per annum, due in part to the incentives to encourage philanthropy such as Prescribed Private Funds (now Private Ancillary Funds) and a strong Australian economy. In 2008–2009, during the midst of the global economic financial instability, the number of taxpayers claiming tax-deductible donations

[91] Barraket, J., *Finding Australia's Social Enterprise Sector,* Australian Centre for Philanthropy and Nonprofit Studies (ACPNS), June 2010; see further at http://www.socialtraders.com.au/finding-australias-social-enterprise-sector-fases.

[92] Senator Stephens, the Parliamentary Secretary for Social Inclusion and the Voluntary Sector, expressed this view on July 10, 2010, when launching the Professional Partnership Project. See further the Barraket survey of Australian Social enterprises at Finding Australia's Social Enterprise Sector, Queensland University of Technology, http://www.socialeconomy.net.au.

[93] See the Income Tax Assessment Act 1997 (Cth), Division 30.

[94] See, e.g., Metropolitan Fire Brigades Board v. Commissioner of Taxation (1990) 27 FCR 279, Mines Rescue Board (NSW) v. Commissioner of Taxation (2000) 101 FCR 91 and the Ambulance Service of New South Wales v. Commissioner of Taxation (2003) 130 FCR 477, in all of which the emergency services were found not to be PBIs because essentially they were organized or controlled by government.

increased, but the amount of these donations decreased for the first year in well over a decade (down 10.79 percent from 2007–2008).[95]

VII. CHARITIES, TRADING, AND CONTEMPORARY CASE LAW

Essentially, the law governing contemporary charities and their activities is derived from the English Charitable Uses Act 1601,[96] has remained true to its common law origins, and in general adopts and follows U.K. case law developments.[97] The main point of difference is that in Australia the determination of both charitable status and eligibility for tax exemption falls to the Revenue agency, the ATO.

A. The Legal Framework

As was pointed out in the recent Scoping Study, "there are more than 178 pieces of Commonwealth, state or territory legislation that involve 19 separate agencies regularly determining the charitable purpose or status of an entity."[98] However, for all practical purposes the legal framework for the sector essentially consists of the common law, which governs charities; the Income Tax Assessment Act 1997[99] (as amended), which applies to charities and all other nonprofits; and sundry specialized legislation such as the Corporations Act 2001, which applies to companies limited by guarantee and is supplemented in each state by an association incorporation statute.

1. Regulatory Bodies

The ATO, by default the nonprofit regulator at the Commonwealth level, currently provides a traditional and typically tax-oriented regulatory environment for charities as for all other income-earning nonprofits. It also maintains a level of engagement with the sector through its Charities Consultative Committee, and provides information and guidance in relation to governance and compliance obligations through its website, news service, and dedicated information phone service. However, the government is now committed to establishing a new, sector-wide, independent statutory

95 McGregor-Lowndes, M. and Pelling, E., "An Examination of Tax-Deductible Donations Made by Individual Australian Taxpayers in 2008-09," ACPNS Working Paper 54, 2011, http://eprints.qut.edu.au/43323/.

96 43 Elizabeth 1 c. 4.

97 Not always: the ruling in Gilmore v. Coates [1949] AC 426 (HL) to the effect that a "closed" religious order could not be charitable was not followed in Australia, and neither did McGovern v. Attorney General [1982] 1 Ch 321 nor Bowman v. Secular Society Ltd [1907] SALR 190 ever find specific approval in Australia.

98 See the Treasury, *Scoping Study for a National Notforprofit Regulator: Consultation Paper*, Commonwealth of Australia, January 2011, at para. 33.

99 In conjunction with the Tax Laws Amendment (2005 Measures No. 3) Act 2005.

agency—the Australian Charities and Not-for-profits Commission (ACNC)—by July 1, 2012. The Commissioner, who will be appointed by the government and report to parliament through the Assistant Treasurer, is to have sole responsibility for determining charitable, PBI, and nonprofit status. As a first step, on July 2011 the ATO shed its role of determining charitable status.

Agencies that provide direct grants and have service delivery contracts with nonprofits take on a guidance role in relation to governance and compliance obligations, as do bodies such as Philanthropy Australia and the Australian Institute of Company Directors. ASIC is the regulatory authority for the 11,500 nonprofits constituted as companies limited by guarantee. The 440,000 small, unincorporated entities, comprising three-quarters of the sector, largely fall outside the current regulatory system. Some entities, such as churches and religious organizations, incorporated by special statutes, by Royal Charter, or as branches of international organizations, are also unregulated.

In addition, the state attorneys general provide a degree of regulatory oversight in relation to charitable trusts. With the exception of a small but important number of recent cases, the courts have not played a significant role in issues affecting the sector.

2. Charity Law

The courts in Australia, following the *Pemsel* classification, have generally come to recognize the following categories of charity: the relief of poverty; the relief of the needs of the aged; the relief of sickness or distress; the advancement of religion; and the advancement of education. The law continues the public benefit presumption in relation to the first three *Pemsel* heads and, at all levels of jurisdiction, it applies the common law definitional matters as they were applied in England and Wales before charity law reform.[100] The limited reforms introduced by the Extension of Charitable Purpose Act 2004 did no more than extend the *Pemsel* list to include child care, self-help groups,[101] and contemplative religious orders. As a result of the revived, and only just concluded, charity law reform process, it is now anticipated that a new national definition of "charity" will be introduced in forthcoming legislation to take effect on July 1, 2013.

Although Australia also inherited the trust, and associated principles requiring the trustee to apply the donor's gift exclusively for charitable purposes, it has never relied on the trust form as the primary legal structure for charity, incorporated structures being preferred from an early stage. The principles of trust law now sit alongside the legislative provisions of company law and tax law to form the legal framework for philanthropy in Australia.

[100] See, e.g., Navy Health Ltd v. DFC of T 2007 ATC 4568.

[101] Under s.5, provision is made for self-help groups to acquire charitable status provided that they are "open and non-discriminatory."

In the 1930s, in an important deviation from that legacy, a distinction was made between institutions and funds when the concept of a "public benevolent institution" (PBI) was introduced. This is an "institution organized for the relief of poverty, sickness, destitution or helplessness"[102] and qualifies for donation deductions. Although all PBIs are charities, only about one-third of charities meet this narrower definition; judicial principles relating to PBI cases do not necessarily have equal application to charity cases as a whole.

3. Charity, Nonprofits, the Law, and Taxation

The ATO has long applied a conservative interpretation of "charity": "[a] charitable purpose must be for the benefit of the community. Charity is altruistic and intends social value or utility. The benefit need not be for the whole community; it may be for an appreciable section of the public."[103]

More generally, tax concessions are afforded only to those nonprofits providing welfare, education, worship, sport, art, and other community services. For example, subdivision 50-A of the Income Tax Assessment Act 1997 provides an exemption from income tax for the income of a number of altruistic entity types, including: charitable institutions, religious institutions, scientific institutions, public educational institutions, charitable funds,[104] and community service organizations.[105] It also makes provision for societies and associations established for the purpose of promoting the development of certain primary and secondary resources, including aviation and tourism,[106] and for clubs, societies, and associations established for the encouragement of animal racing, art, a game or sport, literature, or music, or for musical purposes.[107]

This approach has been employed to restrict entitlement to charitable tax exemption and is destined to change when the new legislation takes effect in July 2013.

4. Activities Test

As in other jurisdictions, there has been considerable debate in Australia on the issue as to whether, or in what circumstances, it is permissible to look beyond the statement of purpose in an organization's governing instruments and examine its activities in order to determine charitable status. In *Royal Australasian College of Surgeons v. FCT*[108] and in *Glebe Administration Board v. Commissioner of Pay-roll Tax*,[109] the court took the view that the question whether an entity is charitable is to be resolved by determining

[102] See The Perpetual Trustee Co. Ltd. v. Federal Commissioner of Taxation [1931] 45 CLR 224 per Starke J., at p. 232.

[103] See ATO, *Draft Taxation Ruling* TR 1999/D21, at para. 43.

[104] See Items 1.1 to 1.5B in the table in subsection 50-5 of the ITAA 1997.

[105] See Item 2.1 in the table in subsection 50-1 of the ITAA.

[106] See items 8.1 and 8.2 in the table in subsection 50-40 of the ITAA 1997.

[107] See Items 9.1 and 9.2 in the table in subsection 50-45 of the ITAA 1997.

[108] (1943) 68 CLR 436.

[109] NSW (1987) 10 NSWLR 352 87 ATC 4825.

the entity's essential character by having regard to both the purpose for which it was formed and maintained and the activities it carried on. This was firmed up by Gummo J. in the recent *AidWatch* hearing during which, with no equivocation, he used the test to challenge counsel for the respondent: "It is one thing to have objectives. Another question is what you are actually doing."[110]

B. Charitable Trading, the Law, and Tax

Any nonprofit may undertake commercial activities in carrying out its purposes, but any profit must be used to carry out the entity's purposes and not distributed to its owners, members, or other private people. Nonprofit engagement in commerce is well established in Australia, with some large organizations operating significant business ventures, either as an extension of their charitable purpose[111] or with little or no relation to it: the Smith Family, for example, has the largest non–woven goods manufacturing plant in the country (recycling donated clothing);[112] the Hillsong church has links with the Gloria Jean's coffee shop franchise;[113] whereas the Wesley Mission in Sydney operates profitably a large orchard bequeathed to it.[114] In particular, the association between religious bodies and unrelated commercial activity is noticeable and probably more extensive than commonly realized. For example, the court noted in *Re Smith (dec'd): Executor Trustee and Agency Co of South Australia Ltd v. Australasian Conference Association Ltd*[115] that the "natural and probable consequence" of the business activities of the deceased was the furtherance of the Sydney Sanitarium and Benevolent Association Ltd.'s ("Sydney Sanitarium") religious purposes.[116] This history of charity

[110] Aid/Watch Incorporated v. Commissioner of Taxation [2010] HCA 42; [2009] FCAFC 128. See also ATO, TR2005/21 paras. 165–77; Royal Australasian College of Surgeons v. FC of T (1943) 68 CLR 436; and Navy Health Ltd v. DFC of T [2007] FCA 931 per Jessup J. at para. 25.

[111] See McGarvie Smith Institute v. Campbelltown Corp. (1965) 83 NSWWN (Pt. 1) 191 where an institute conducting veterinary research also manufactured and sold vaccines. See also Dart, R., "Charities in Business, Business in Charities, Charities and Business—Mapping and Understanding the Complex Non-Profit/Business Interface," in *The Philanthropist*, Vol. 18, No. 3, 2004, at pp. 181–98.

[112] See further The Smith Family, www.thesmithfamily.com.au.

[113] Gloria Jeans' is a major coffee house franchise operating in Australia, widely known for its association with Hillsong Church. See further at http://www.smh.com.au/national/charities-face-profits-being-taxed-in-budget-20110506-1ec2u.html.

[114] Lyons, *Third Sector*, at p. 36.

[115] [1954] SASR 151.

[116] Particularly as Ligertwood J found that "[t]he motive behind the establishment of the Health Food Company was no doubt religious, and its profits were no doubt used exclusively in aid of the teachings, activities and purposes of the religious body," at pp. 159–60. The same comment could be made in relation to Glebe Administration Board v. Commissioner of Pay-Roll Tax (1987) 10 NSWLR 352. See also Sydney Homeopathic Hospital v. Turner (1959) 102 CLR 188 at p. 221, per Kitto J.; Sir Moses Montefiore Jewish Home v. Howell & Co (No 7) Pty Ltd [1984] 2 NSWLR 406 at p.416, per Kearney J.; and Australian Executor Trustees Ltd v. Ceduna District Health Services Inc. [2006] SASC 286 at p.23, per Vanstone J.

involvement in business activity, unrelated to charitable purpose but tax–exempt, is interesting and provides a backdrop to the *Word* decision.

The rate of such involvement, whether through primary purpose service delivery funded by contract or through for-profit engagement for funding purposes, has definitely increased in recent years and, until the recent government announcement, showed every sign of continuing to do so.[117] This fact and the reasons for it have been judicially noted:[118]

> With the decline of the welfare state, charitable organizations are expected to do more with the same resources. Reliance on donations alone will, in many cases, be insufficient. Hence many charitable organizations have established business ventures to generate the income necessary to support their activities.

The resulting central issue "where commercial activities are undertaken by charitable organizations: other organizations engaging in similar commercial activities are placed in a competitive disadvantage"[119] has also been noted.

It needs to be borne in mind, however, that charitable organizations are not the only form of nonprofits engaged in tax-exempt business ventures.

1. Charity Trading

The law governing trading by charities has been very similar to that in England and Wales. Essentially, although trading itself is not a charitable purpose, charities may trade where this is ancillary to and in furtherance of their exclusively charitable purposes, provided no profits inure to private individuals.

In the *Word* case,[120] the ATO refused to endorse Word as an income tax–exempt charity on the grounds that commercial enterprise entities are not charities, irrespective of whether the enterprise gives its income to charitable institutions.[121] This

[117] According to the National Roundtable of Nonprofit Organizations, *The Nonprofit Sector in Australia: A Fact Sheet*, in 1999/2000, 58 percent of the nonprofit sector's income came from sale of goods or services as compared with only 30 percent from government grants and contracts.

[118] Commissioner of Taxation v. Word Investments Ltd [2007] FCAFC 171 and (2008) 236 CLR 204, per Sundberg J.

[119] See the Commonwealth of Australia, *Report of the Taxation Review Committee* (the "Asprey Report"), 1975, at p. 667. See also: Industry Commission, *Charitable Organizations in Australia* (1995); Commonwealth of Australia, *Inquiry into the Definition of Charities and Related Organizations* (2001); and the Productivity Commission, *Contribution of the Not-for-Profit Sector* (2010).

[120] Commissioner of Taxation v. Word Investments Limited [2007] FCAFC 171 and (2008) 236 CLR 204.

[121] Authority for such an approach may be found in such cases as: Glebe Administration Board v. Commissioner of Pay-roll Tax NSW (1987) 10 NSWLR 352; Theosophical Foundation Pty Ltd v. Commissioner of Land Tax (NSW) (1966) 67 SR (NSW) 70; and Re Smith, Deceased; Executor Trustee and Agency Co. of South Australia Ltd v. Australasian Conference Association Ltd [1954] SASR 151 at p. 159.

firm and clear stand against the "destination of income" test was ultimately negated by the decision of the High Court that set Australian law on a diverging trajectory from that in the U.K. This decision was taken despite the misgivings of Kirby J. that permitting charities to conduct commercial enterprises might affect "competitive neutrality," as charities would have a tax advantage over for-profit businesses; it might erode the income tax base; and many taxpayers might "disagree" with the objectives of religious institutions, which they would be indirectly subsidizing as a result of the award of income tax exemption.

However, in Budget Paper No. 2[122] the government announced its intention to address the effects of that decision. Consequently from July 1, 2011, the government's initiative to reverse the effect of *Word* and tighten the tax concessions for charities that run unrelated profit-making businesses has required such charities to pay income tax on any earnings from any newly created businesses that are not ploughed back into their core charity work. A charity will pay tax on profits from its unrelated commercial activities that are not directed back to its altruistic purpose (the earnings retained in its commercial undertaking), but this will not interfere with the tax concessions available to nonprofits to further their altruistic purposes "even where the charitable operation is conducted commercially." As the minister explained, "the government believes it is important that charities use their tax concessions only to assist disadvantaged people and not for unrelated commercial activities . . . the government's reforms encourage charities to direct profits generated by unrelated commercial activities back to altruistic purposes."[123] Although the new rules on the unrelated commercial activities of charities will at first apply only to new commercial ventures begun after a future date yet to be determined, they are also to be retrospective in effect, and it is anticipated that in due course they will be brought to bear on established commercial enterprises including those run by religious organizations such as those mentioned above.

C. Charity Trading and Tax

"As one of the few remaining jurisdictions where income derived by charitable organizations from carrying on commercial activities is not subject to limitations on the taxation concessions afforded," in the words of Sadiq and Richardson,[124] "it is not surprising that Australia has been described as a tax haven for charitable organizations."[125]

[122] See, 2011–12 *Australian Government Budget—Budget Paper No. 2*, (May 10, 2011).

[123] Australian Government, Office of Assistant Treasurer, "Making It Easier for Charities to Help Those Who Need It." See further Commonwealth of Australia, The Treasury, *Consultation Paper: Better Targeting of Not-for-Profit Tax Concessions*, Canberra, May 2011.

[124] See Sadiq, K. and Richardson, C., "Tax Concessions for Charities: Competitive Neutrality, the Tax Base and "Public Goods" Choice," *Australian Tax Forum*, Vol. 25, No. 4, 2010, at p. 600.

[125] Sadiq and Richardson, "Tax Concessions for Charities," at p. 600, citing United Nations, *Handbook on Non-Profit Institutions in the System of National Accounts* (2003).

Division 50 of the Income Tax Assessment Act 1997[126] provides the relevant income tax exemption regime for Australia's nonprofits, which may claim, at the Commonwealth level, relief from income tax, GST concessions, fringe benefits tax, and DGR status tax concessions. The Fringe Benefits Tax Assessment Act 1986 (Cth) is also relevant, as s.65J(1)(j) provides for income tax exemption for nonprofit bodies established for community service purposes:[127]

> The words "for community service purposes" are not defined but are to be given a wide interpretation. The words are not limited to those purposes beneficial to the community which are also charitable. They extend to a range of altruistic purposes. The words would extend to promoting, providing or carrying out activities, facilities or projects for the benefit or welfare of the community, or of any members of the community who have particular need of those activities, facilities or projects by reason of their youth, age, infirmity or disablement, poverty or social or economic circumstances.

The states and territories each have their own tax concessions for nonprofits, such as payroll tax and land tax concessions. In 1999, the New Tax System legislation was introduced,[128] which provides GST concessions for nonprofits. The classification of charitable trading follows the customary distinction among "primary purpose," "ancillary," or "non-primary purpose."

1. Primary Purpose

This is trading conducted by a charity in the course of carrying out its primary purpose[129] and includes trading in which the related work is mainly undertaken by beneficiaries of the charity.[130]

[126] See further Australian Taxation Office, *Income Tax Guide for Non-Profit Organizations* (2007). As both the Henry Review and Productivity Commission rightly indicate, other forms of taxes may need to be dealt with on a different basis from income tax, e.g., Fringe Benefits Tax concessions. Deductibility issues may also arise under Division 30 of the Income Tax Assessment Act 1997 (Cth), Fringe Benefit Tax, GST or other tax concessions.

[127] See Navy Health Ltd v. DFC of T 2007 ATC 4568, per Jessup J. at para. 82:

> When purposes are directed to the benefit or welfare of members of the community in particular need, that need must arise by reason of youth, age, infirmity or disablement, poverty or social or economic circumstances. These causes of need are intended to be read broadly. Infirmity or disablement, for example, could be intellectual or physical, and could be congenital or the product of disease or of injury. Similarly, social or economic circumstances could include such varied matters as sex, living in a remote area, or inability to speak English.

[128] A New Tax System (Goods and Services Tax) Act 1999 (Cth).

[129] See, e.g., The Incorporated Council of Law Reporting of the State of Queensland v. FC of T (1971) 125 CLR 659 (the preparation and sale of law reports), and McGarvie Smith Institute v. Campbelltown Municipal Council (1965) 11 LGRA 321 (the manufacture and sale of animal vaccines).

[130] Salvation Army (Victoria) Property Trust v. Fern Tree Gully Corporation (1952) 85 CLR 159.

2. Ancillary and Incidental

Australian common law holds to the general principle that a trust expressed for both charitable and non-charitable purposes is invalid, but a charitable institution can have non-charitable purposes that are merely incidental or ancillary to its charitable purposes. As Lockhart J. explained in *Cronulla Sutherland Leagues Club Limited v. FC of T*:[131] "it [the club] may have other objects or purposes which are merely incidental or ancillary thereto or which are secondary and even unrelated to the main object or purpose without disqualifying the body from the exemption."

This issue arose in *Congregational Union of New South Wales v. Thistlethwayte*[132] where a religious association had objectives that were a mix of charitable and non-charitable. The non-charitable objectives were maintaining philanthropic agencies and preserving civil and religious liberty. However, when viewed in the context of the constitution as a whole, the court found that the offending objects were ancillary to the appellant's main objective of advancing religion.[133] Until the High Court ruling in *Word*, the ATO view prevailed that when an institution's profit-generating activity goes beyond what is incidental or ancillary to the exempt purposes, that institution loses its charitable character.

3. Non-Primary Purpose

Trading is "non-primary purpose" when it is not directly related to the achievement of a charitable purpose. In practice this means trading carried on with the main or sole aim of raising funds for a charity. In this jurisdiction, until the decision in *Word*, it was the scale of the non-primary purpose trade relative to all other trading activity, rather than the "destination of income" test, that was crucial.

D. Charitable Trading: The Case Law in a Public Services Context

Prior to the present government taking office, when charity law reform had failed and initiatives to either construct institutional arrangements or equip umbrella organizations to bridge the gap between government and the sector had yet to be attempted, it was largely left to the courts to arbitrate on issues in which the interests of both parties had become entangled. Against a background of political volatility, an absence of legislative initiative, and a cowed sector, there were some cases that illustrated

[131] 90 ATC 4215 at 4225; (1990) 21 ATR 300 at p. 312.

[132] (1952) 87 CLR 375.

[133] See also Court, Salvation Army (Vic) Property Trust v. Fern Tree Gully Corporation (1952) 85 CLR 159 (home for neglected boys that also provided training through its farm), and Trustees of the Dean Leigh Temperance Canteen v. Commissioners of Inland Revenue (1958) 38 TC 315 (the promotion of temperance through the running of a canteen).

the difficulties facing government and sector when it came to public benefit service provision.

1. Health and Social Care Provision

The principle that charges could be raised by a charity for the services it provides, even if the charges produce a profit, was established in the leading common law case of *Re Resch,*[134] a Privy Council case from New South Wales concerning a gift to a private hospital that charged fees. The hospital was established to relieve demand for admission to an adjacent public hospital by providing medical and nursing care for which there was a need. It was open to contributors under medical benefit schemes and was not conducted for profit. Although the charitable status of the hospital was confirmed, Lord Wilberforce added an important caveat that would thereafter be a reference point for judiciary and regulators across many common law jurisdictions: An organization that wholly excluded "the poor" from any benefits, direct or indirect, would not be for the benefit of the public and therefore could not be a charity.[135] Subsequent case law revealed a benign judicial approach prepared to grant charitable status to organizations despite their services being limited to local communities.[136]

Central Bayside,[137] the first charity law case to reach the High Court of Australia in 30 years,[138] focused on a dispute regarding the charitable status of a government health care scheme. It concerned a company limited by guarantee, established to deliver such a scheme within a small geographic area in accordance with a national plan. Its members were general medical practitioners in the Central Bayside area of Melbourne, and the directors were appointed by the members, but its funding was almost entirely provided by government. The court at first instance upheld the ruling of the ATO that Central Bayside was not a "charitable body" because its main purpose was to protect and advance the interests of its members, and it was merely a government conduit executing government policy. On appeal this decision was overturned when all five judges of the High Court, in three separate judgments giving varying reasons, concluded that Central Bayside was a "charitable body." A majority determined that the funding agreements did not take independence away from Central Bayside: It could decide whether to accept or reject the funding, as

[134] [1969] 1 AC 514 (PC).

[135] [1969] 1 AC 514 (PC), per Wilberforce L.J. at p. 544. See also Queensland Trustees Limited v. Green [1911] St R Qd 1005 at p. 110 per Real A.C.J., and Re Sutherland (deceased) [1954] St R Qd 99 at p. 103 per Macrossan C.J. (as cited by Dal Pont, G., *Charity Law in Australia and New Zealand,* Oxford University Press, Melbourne, 2003, at p. 26, n.198).

[136] See, e.g., West Australian Baptist Hospital & Homes Trust Inc v. City of South Perth [1978] WAR 65.

[137] Central Bayside Division of General Practice Ltd v. Commissioner of State Revenue [2005] VSCA 168.

[138] Bathurst City Council v. PWC Properties (1998) 195 CLR 566 concerned a church car park; the previous case was Commissioner of Land Tax (NSW) v. Joyce (1974) 132 CLR 22.

it had an independently formed board that made its own decisions; and whether partially or wholly funded by government, this was insufficient to deny a body charitable status.[139]

The ruling determined that just because a charity may have the same goals as government, it does not mean, without more, that it is not independent of government. This significant decision has broadened the interpretation of "charitable purpose" to permit closer partnership arrangements between government and charities.[140] It is, however, open to question whether the decisions in *Central Bayside* and *Metro West*[141] (see below) are wholly compatible.

More recently, in *Kay v. South Eastern Sydney Area Health Service*,[142] a fund for the treatment of white babies was upheld as charitable. The court relied in part upon the dubious ground that "the receipt of a fund to benefit white babies would just mean that more of the general funds of the hospital would be available to treat non-white babies so that, in due course, despite the testatrix's intention things will even up."[143]

2. Education

In *Royal North Shore Hospital of Sydney v. Attorney-General (NSW)*,[144] it was held that encouraging the teaching of technical education in state schools was a valid charitable object, and that a bequest for that purpose was not void as a trust for the attainment of a political object. The interpretation of matters constituting "education" was broadened by the court decision in *Lloyd v. Federal Commissioner of Education*[145] where a trust for a sea cadets corps, which gave young people the basic training necessary for a seafaring career, was found to be charitable. More to the point, an institution set up to train young people in agriculture was found to be an educational charity despite its reliance to some extent on the income raised from selling its surplus farm produce.[146] The ratio decendi for such an approach was, as subsequently expressed in *Bathurst City Council v. PWC City Properties Pty Ltd.*,[147]

[139] Robson v. Stuart (1891) 12 LR (NSW) Eq 47 at pp. 49–50; Re Sutherland (deceased) [1954] St R Qd 99 at p. 105 per Macrossan CJ; Alice Springs v. Mqwetererre Aboriginal Corporation (1997) 139 FLR 236 at 254 per Thomas J. (as cited by Dal Pont, *Charity Law in Australia and New Zealand*, at p. 25, n.189).

[140] The importance of health care provision to charity and government had become apparent in the earlier case of Re Resch [1969] 1 AC 514 (PC), which although decided by the Privy Council in London, in fact originated in New South Wales and established that a hospital could charge fees for its services without compromising its charitable status.

[141] Metro West v. Sudi (Residential Tenancies) [2009] VCAT 2025.

[142] [2003] NSWSC 292.

[143] [2003] NSWSC 292 at para. 19.

[144] (1938) 60 CLR 396.

[145] (1955) 93 CLR 645 at p. 670 per Kitto J.

[146] Salvation Army (Victoria) Property Trust v. Fern Tree Gully Corporation (1952) 85 CLR 159.

[147] (1998) 72 ALJR 1470 at p. 1478.

explained in terms of "the fact that some non-charitable purposes may coincidentally be served does not itself destroy the legal character of a legal trust."

3. Social Housing

This area of provision most usually falls under the fourth *Pemsel* head, which attracts the full rigors of the public benefit test. If it can be fitted under the poverty head, which in Australia carries a presumption of compliance, this will more readily allow a conferring of charitable status.[148]

In the case of *Metro West v. Sudi (Residential Tenancies)*,[149] the logic of *Bayside* seemed to resurface but led to a different outcome. In *Metro*, the level of government funding, the existence of statutory provisions authorizing the transfer of what had been public service responsibilities, and the nature of the functions being performed by a private body, were sufficient to indicate that the body was in reality exercising public functions and should in law be treated as a public authority. It was then pointed out that the question turns upon the nature of the functions and whether they are being exercised in the public interest, rather than the nature of the entity exercising those functions. In finding the functions to be of a public nature, the court held that it was relevant to consider the responsibility that government has for the care and protection of vulnerable and disadvantaged people. Basically, where government can be shown to have set up a situation where an ostensibly independent body is in actuality acting in an agency capacity, then the legal relationship is one of principal and agent, with the subordinate body being in effect a public authority.[150]

This case, which closely followed the earlier English decision in *Weaver v. London and Quadrant Housing Trust*,[151] would seem to suggest that where a body is subject to

[148] See, e.g., *In re Hilditch (deceased)* (1985) 39 SASR 469 where a trust to provide a home for poor and distressed past or current members of a particular South Australia Freemasons Lodge was held to be a charitable trust.

[149] Metro West v. Sudi (Residential Tenancies) [2009] VCAT 2025. Bell J. then held that Metro West exercised the relevant functions on behalf of the state because: there was a service agreement between Metro West and the government where the government contracted out the performance of its obligations, that service agreement included performance standards and obligations upon Metro West to comply with the government's standards and policies in providing the services, Metro West received "block" funding from the government to perform these services, and Metro West exercised delegated statutory functions. For these reasons, Bell J made a declaration that when exercising the function of providing transitional housing (including the management of tenancies) under the service agreement with the government, Metro West is a public authority. See also Attorney-General v. M'Carthy (1886) 12 VLR 535.

[150] Control is only one of the factors and is never the sole determinant. As Lockhart J. pointed out in Cronulla Sutherland Leagues Club Ltd v. Federal Commissioner of Taxation, 89 ATC 4936 (1989) 20 ATR 1404, relevant features "include its constitution, its activities, its history and its control."

[151] [2008] EWHC 1377 (Admin); [2008] WLR (D) 207.

detailed regulation and permeated by state control and influence, and is in receipt of extensive public subsidy including capital grants because of the role it plays in implementing government policy, then, regardless of the fact that it is constituted and governed by its own rules, has its own assets, and is free to enter into private law contracts, the courts may find that it is so inextricably linked to government policy that in actuality it is performing functions of a public nature and must in law be regarded as a public authority.[152] In that situation, where the body in question is seeking to acquire or retain charitable status, it would find it difficult if not impossible to demonstrate that the necessary independence, powers and discretionary capacity of its trustees were not severely restricted or curtailed. This would be fatal to charitable status. Any such providers could be exposed to the agency challenge and revealed as public authorities in disguise unless they can demonstrate that their trustees retain a real capacity for independent decision making.

4. Community Services

In *Commissioner of Taxation v. Wentworth District Capital Limited*,[153] the court considered whether a nonprofit entity, established to facilitate face-to-face banking services in a rural town without such services, could be construed as being established for "community service purposes" and thus be entitled to tax exemption status under ss.50-1 and 50-10 of the Income Tax Assessment Act 1997 (Cth). The court found that the provision of banking services to customers of a commercial bank could not be viewed as the provision of a community service as it amounted to the provision of an ordinary retail service, for reward, to customers. However, the facilitation of the commercial supply of some services would be a community service, if this could be characterized as a real or tangible benefit to the community. In a town with no face-to-face banking services, the facilitation of such services provided a substantial benefit to the community. As in this instance the entity was not established to provide banking services, but merely to facilitate the provision of face-to-face banking

[152] Note that the Inquiry Report agreed with the judiciary in Metropolitan Fire Brigade Board v. The Commissioner of Taxation (1990) 27 FCR 279 and Mines Rescue Board of New South Wales v. Commissioner of Taxation (Cth) (2000) 44 ATR 107 at p. 30 (both state government–formed bodies) that the test for determining whether an entity is a government body and therefore not tax deductible is that it be constituted, funded, and controlled by government.

[153] [2011] FCAFC 42. See further the ATO Decision Impact Statement where the ATO accepts that the facilitation of certain commercial services in certain circumstances is capable of amounting to community service purposes within the meaning of Item 2.1 of section 50–10 of ITAA 1997 as determined by the Full Federal Court. However, whether that will be so in the particular case is a question of fact and circumstances. Further at: http://law.ato.gov.au/atolaw/view.htm?DocID=LIT/ICD/NSD1144of2010/00001.

services, its main or dominant purpose for which it was established was therefore a community service and it was entitled to tax exemption.[154]

E. Charitable Trading: The Case Law in a Commercial Context

The guarded stance adopted by the ATO toward organizations that sought to combine charitable status with commerce,[155] together with its concern to protect tax-paying businesses from unfair nonprofit competition, has occasionally been challenged in the courts.

1. Private Benefit

Necessarily, the involvement of charity in commerce gives rise to a concern that entrepreneurial initiatives might result in undue private benefit being received, in breach of charitable status. In *Navy Health Ltd v. DFC of T*[156] Jessup J. held that due to membership criteria and level of contributions, the applicant was neither a "charitable institution" within the meaning of s 65J(1)(b) of the Fringe Benefits Tax Assessment Act 1986 (Cth) Act nor a "non-profit association,... established for community service purposes" within the meaning of s 65J(1)(j). In fact, it operated as a competitive commercial business in a manner not unlike any other private health insurance fund.

Even where there is no financial reward the court has been prepared to find that the presence of benefit is sufficient to negate charitable status. It has, for example, found that the preparation and sale of law reports in Australia,[157] unlike the same activity in England and Wales,[158] did exactly that, and it therefore denied charitable status to the body concerned, the benefit being construed in Australia in terms of information and being limited to a narrow class of the "public." The thorny dilemma of whether in substance there exists an underlying element of self-interest, whereby a professional group is seeking to secure benefits restricted to its members, resurfaced with a contrary outcome in *Victorian Women Lawyers' Association v. Federal Commissioner of Taxation*.[159] This case concerned an association with the principal purpose "to remove barriers and increase opportunities for participation by and

[154] Citing Cronulla Sutherland Leagues Club Limited v. Commissioner of Taxation (1990) 23 FCR 82; Navy Health Ltd v. Federal Commissioner of Taxation [2007] FCA 931, (2007) 163 FCR 1; Royal Australasian College of Surgeons v. The Federal Commissioner of Taxation [1943] HCA 34, (1943) 68 CLR 436; Spencer v. The Commonwealth of Australia [2010] HCA 28, (2010) 241 CLR 118; and Victorian Women Lawyers' Association Inc v. Federal Commissioner of Taxation [2008] FCA 983; (2008) 170 FCR 318.

[155] See ATO, Taxation Ruling 2005/21.

[156] 2007 ATC 4568.

[157] Incorporated Council of Law Reporting of the State of Queensland v. FC of T (1971) 125 CLR 659.

[158] Incorporated Council of Law Reporting for England and Wales v. Attorney-General [1972] 1 Ch 73.

[159] (2008) 170 FCR 318.

advancement of women in the legal profession in Victoria." The court held that any such "social or professional" activities or any element of "political advocacy" were incidental or ancillary to its main purpose, which was itself charitable.[160]

2. Public Benefit

The legal requirement that the benefits of charity must be made available to a sufficiently broad section of the public[161] can be constrained in a commercial environment where the market may impose its own limitations.[162]

The case of *FC of T v. The Triton Foundation*[163] concerned a foundation whose main objective was "the promotion of a culture of innovation and entrepreneurship." As well as broader programs (in schools, publicity and media exposure, self-assessment tools for inventors, and seminars), it was also "visibly assisting innovators to commercialise their ideas." Particular applicants selected by the foundation could receive "resource-intensive help" with commercialization. The court was satisfied that the services were available to the public without discrimination, and the selection of inventors "who were likely to be the best exemplars of innovation" was rational and in keeping with the foundation's main object of promoting an innovative and entrepreneurial culture "to the public at large." In *Tasmanian Electronic Commerce Centre Pty Ltd v. FC of T*[164] the court found a company that adopted a form of electronic commerce qualified for charitable status.

The *Social Ventures* case[165] was one in a similar vein. It concerned Social Ventures Australian Limited (SVA), a company limited by guarantee, which had public charities as its founding members and a constitution that restricted the operations of the company to pursuing charitable purposes only and to applying its income to those purposes. The main constitutional objective was "to improve the management of operational performance and to enhance the long-term financial viability of charitable organizations by, without limitation, providing educational, mentoring and support services to charitable organizations." In 2008, SVA was assisting 15 charitable organizations and had received $6.15 million in donations in the year ending June 30, 2007. The court found that SVA was charitable under the fourth

[160] A decision in keeping with the principle established in Incorporated Council of Law Reporting for England and Wales v. Attorney-General [1972] Ch 73.

[161] See, e.g., Re Income Tax Acts (No 1) [1930] VLR 211; Thompson v. Federal Commissioner of Taxation (1959) 102 CLR 315; Strathalbyn Show Jumping Club Inc v. Mayes (2001) 79 SASR 54; and Victorian Women Lawyers' Association (2008) 170 FCR 318.

[162] In Hobart Savings Bank v. Federal Commissioner of Taxation (1930) 43 CLR 364, savings banks were found not to be charitable. Similarly, in Re Davis [1965] WAR 25, when a gift "for the expansion of co-operation and the work of the co-operative movement in Western Australia" was not charitable because it would benefit only existing commercial firms.

[163] 2005 A.T.C. 4891; (2005) 60 A.T.R. 451.

[164] (2005) 142 FCR 371; 2005 ATC 4219; (2005) 59 ATR 10.

[165] Social Ventures Australia Limited v. Chief Commissioner of State Revenue, 2008 NSW ADT 331 (December 12, 2008).

head of charity as the activity of assisting "public charities" by way of management, education, advice, and funding was charitable.

3. Profits

The U.K. decisions in *Incorporated Council of Law Reporting* (where the Council charged a fee for the production of the law reports)[166] and *Scottish Burial Society* (where the society charged fees for cremation services)[167] provide good authority in Australia for the proposition expressed by Sundberg J. that:[168]

> the making of a profit through trade or business is not necessarily inconsistent with a charitable purpose and that the true question to be asked is the purpose of the making of the profit. If the purpose is commercial then the exclusive purpose of the organization is not charitable; if the purpose is selfless then it may be.

Further, the fact that profits may result from an activity that is incidental to furthering a charitable purpose, as in the *Fern Tree Gully* case,[169] does not breach the charitable status of the entity concerned. If, however, the profit "is not merely incidental to a charitable purpose but is collateral to that purpose" then, as the court found in *Nunawading Shire v. Adult Deaf & Dumb Society of Victoria*,[170] a breach will result as the purposes of the entity will no longer be exclusively charitable.[171]

F. Jurisdictional Characteristics of Charitable Trading

The law in this context is currently under review, with government engaged in a process of public consultation before committing to legislative change.

1. Profits

The destination of income test had not been determinative of charitable status for trading entities in Australia,[172] but became so after the ruling in *Word*.

[166] Incorporated Council of Law Reporting for England and Wales v. A-G [1972] Ch 73 (CA).

[167] Scottish Burial Reform and Cremation Society Ltd v. Glasgow Corp. [1968] AC 138 (HL).

[168] Commissioner of Taxation v. Word Investments Limited (2008) 236 CLR 204 at para. 37.

[169] (1952) 85 CLR 1259.

[170] (1921) 29 CLR 98.

[171] See Ong, D. S. K., *Trusts Law in Australia*, Federation Press, Annandale, N.S.W., 2007, at p. 346.

[172] See TR 2005/22. Note the resonance with Re Smith (dec'd): Executor Trustee and Agency Co of South Australia Ltd v. Australasian Conference Association Ltd [1954] SASR 151. See also Roman Catholic Archbishop of Melbourne v. Lawlor [1934] HCA 14, which until *Word* had been relied upon by the ATO as authority that for the proposition that a company that is bound by its objects to apply its profits to charitable purposes, but which earns those profits by activities that are not charitable, may not be a charitable institution; and Glebe Administration Board v. Commissioner of Pay-Roll Tax (1987) 10 NSWLR 352. The role of "feeder" bodies in relation to the destination of income test is a matter that has attracted interest in other jurisdictions.

The *Word* case[173] concerned a nonprofit company of that name, limited by guarantee, which was founded by members closely associated with Wycliffe (a religious charity). In the period 1996 to 2002, Word operated a business of conducting funerals, not all Christian, for profit. The profits generated from the investment business and the funeral business were used to support Christian activities in the form of Bible translation and missionary work largely carried out by Wycliffe and other bodies. Basically, Word was solely engaged in commercial activity, the proceeds from which it donated to Wycliffe and other bodies to further charitable purposes that they pursued almost entirely outside the jurisdiction of Australia.

The ATO challenged the charitable status of Word because it raised its funds through various activities such as investing money borrowed at noncommercial rates from supporters, offering financial planning for a fee, and operating a funeral business. In rejecting the application for charitable tax exemption, the ATO explained that "[c]ommercial enterprise entities are not considered to be charities. This is the case irrespective of whether charitable consequences flow from the entity's activities."

The court at first instance noted that with the decline of the welfare state, charitable organizations are expected to do more with the same resources, and reliance on donations in many cases will be insufficient. It further noted that many charitable organizations have established business ventures to generate the income necessary to support their activities and, as it could see no reason for distinguishing Word, it held its activities to be charitable.[174] As explained by Sundberg J. in the Federal court, "There may appear to be a vast difference between selling lamingtons at a church fete and selling funeral services, but where the object of raising funds is the same, I can see no reason to draw a legal distinction between the two."

Although the activities of Word in raising funds by commercial means were not intrinsically charitable, they were still charitable in character because they were carried out in furtherance of a charitable purpose. This finding was upheld on appeal to the High Court where the emphasis was placed on "purpose" as the determining element in characterizing organizations as "charitable."[175] The majority then found that Word had objectives in its memorandum indicating that its own purpose was the advancement of religion. Allsop J. drew a "fine, but real" distinction between a company formed for commercial purposes applying its profits to charity, and a company formed for charitable purposes applying its profits to charity. The latter may be properly characterized as charitable, the former not. The majority also found that Word was not prevented from being a "charitable institution" by reason of the fact that the institutions to which it gave its profits "were not confined as to the use

[173] Commissioner of Taxation v. Word Investments Limited [2007] FCAFC 171 and (2008) 236 CLR 204.

[174] Note that in the Full Federal Court, Jessup J. commented (obiter): "I do not say anything about the large question whether a trading company, regardless of the nature of the activities which it undertakes, would necessarily be a charitable institution merely because, as a matter of practice, it distributes all its profits to charities."

[175] Citing Inland Revenue Commissioners v. Helen Slater Charitable Trust Ltd [1982] Ch 49 at p. 52.

to which they may put the funds distributed to them,"[176] stating that "Wycliffe was at liberty to select any method it chose for the purpose of effectuating translations of the Christian Scriptures." Finally, the Income Tax Assessment Act 1997, s50-50(a), required Word to have both a physical presence in Australia and incur its expenditure and pursue its objectives in Australia. The majority concluded that these conditions were satisfied. This decision that an organization devoted solely to business activities could still be pursuing charitable purposes and thus be entitled to exemption[177] significantly if briefly increased the capacity of charities to engage in commercial activity without endangering their tax-exempt status.

a. The Destination of Income Test and the "Look through" Approach

As the practice of setting up trading entities to provide funds for charities (subsidiary companies, corporate foundations, etc.) becomes more prevalent, the ATO and its regulatory counterparts elsewhere have been paying closer attention to the status of the trading entity. The argument that the charitable purpose of the parent company is determinative, and the legal standing of a controlled fund-raising entity can be simply imputed to its controller (as in an agency or "master and servant" relationship) has not found favor with the ATO. The suggestion that the regulatory focus should be wholly on the controlling entity, as its purposes provide the destination for the controlled entity's funds, would be to wholly disregard the latter's legal standing. Such a "look through" approach would be sidestepping the "ancillary and incidental" rule. Consequently, the ATO and other common law regulators have been at pains to establish the status of "feeder" entities and the nature and extent of the controls exercised over them by their parent bodies, whether the latter are government or charity. This jurisdiction has quite a history of dealing with such matters.

In *Commissioner for ACT Revenue Collections v. Council of the Dominican Sisters of Australia,*[178] for example, although the ultimate aim of the Corporate Council was to serve the religious ends of its founders, the Council itself sought exemption from payroll tax as a religious institution. The Full Federal Court, overturning the tribunal hearing, ruled that the crucial issue was whether the promotion or advancement of religion was the primary and dominant object of the Council, not its founders. Similarly in *Glebe Administration Board v. Commissioner of Pay-roll Tax (NSW)*[179]

[176] This followed the rationale of the *Slater* case (see chapter 5). The court endorsed the approach then taken, stating that: "[I]t is likely that the position in Australia is similar."

[177] Allsop J. in the Full Federal Court stated that Christian Enterprises Ltd v. Commissioner of Land Tax (1968) 72 SR (NSW) 90 offered authority for the view that a body that conducts only commercial activity and directs the profits from that activity by donation solely in accordance with the charitable objects of the body is capable of being characterized as being itself charitable (in that case as a "religious society").

[178] 91 ATC 2010; (1991) 22 ATR 3021.

[179] (1987) 10 NSWLR 352; 87 ATC 4825; 19 ATR 297.

the relationship between the Board and a religious institution was one in which the latter created a non-religious board controlled by, but distinct from, the institution, to raise money in a commercial way for its religious purposes. It was held that the Board was "a statutory corporation doing commercial work within limitations fixed by reference to religious principles." Although the Board was controlled by the religious institution, that was insufficient to invest it with a religious purpose. Again, in *Theosophical Foundation Pty Ltd v. Commissioner of Land Tax (NSW)*,[180] all shares in the Foundation were held by two companies limited by guarantee, one holding assets for an unincorporated national society promoting theosophical doctrines, and the other a lodge having the same theosophical objects. The Foundation mainly managed the commercial letting of a building, operated a bookshop and library in the building, and published a magazine and pamphlets. The issue was whether the Foundation was a religious society. It was found to be a member of a group of affiliated bodies, corporate and unincorporated, of which one, at least, was a religious society. The respondent company was called into existence as a member of that group for the purpose of acquiring and commercially managing a particular piece of property for the benefit of other members of the group. This did not make the respondent a "religious society."[181] In these and other instances, where the primary purpose is clearly commercial, the entity cannot be charitable.[182]

Although the above cases demonstrate a well-established resistance to employing a "look through" approach in both charity law and tax law contexts, and are congruent with the *Bayside* decision,[183] it is not immediately apparent how they can be reconciled with the finding in *Metro West*.[184]

VIII. CONCLUSION

The revival of Australia's protracted period of charity law reform that, following a flurry of activity in recent years, would now seem to be close to completion, stands as testimony to the difference that can be made by a change in political climate. However, as the reform process gained momentum, it suffered an unexpected setback with the verdict in *Word*, which carried implications for further distorting the

[180] (1966) 67 SR (NSW) 70.

[181] See also Cremation Society of Australia Ltd v. Commissioner of Land Tax (NSW) (1973) 2 NSWLR 704; 4 ATR 194; Cronulla Sutherland Leagues Club Ltd v. Federal Commissioner of Taxation, 90 ATC 4215; (1990) 21 ATR 300.

[182] See Re Smith (deceased); Executor Trustee and Agency Co. of South Australia Ltd v. Australasian Conference Association Limited [1954] SASR 151 (the purpose being carrying on the manufacture and sale of vegetarian foods).

[183] Central Bayside Division of General Practice Ltd v. Commissioner of State Revenue [2005] VSCA 168.

[184] Metro West v. Sudi (Residential Tenancies) [2009] VCAT 2025.

"level playing field" between nonprofits and commerce,[185] and was conspicuously out of step with current international practice. As predicted, "the implications for the revenue of the decision in *Word Investments* may incline the Australian Government to intervene in the wake of the Henry review of the Australian taxation system,"[186] and indeed steps have now been taken to reverse that decision.[187] Other steps have followed, and Australia is on the verge of finalizing its charity law process with an extensive program of legislative reform that has come as somewhat of a surprise to the sector.

Although it had seemed that Australia was intent on painstakingly replicating the full U.K. structural model for bridging the gap in government/nonprofit relations, with a Charity Commission as its centerpiece, it is now apparent that a significant adjustment is to be made. The new regulatory body, instead of being charity-specific as is the case in the U.K. (and in Ireland, New Zealand, Singapore, and Hong Kong), is to have a sector-wide brief. Given that of the estimated 600,000 nonprofits that constitute the sector, only 55,039 have charitable status, and many of the sector's socioeconomic initiatives are increasingly being generated by a new wave of social enterprises and other hybrid organizations, it perhaps makes good sense not to restrict such an important institutional government/sector bridge to the work of charities. On the other hand, however, of the sector's 600,000 constituent bodies, some 440,000 are small, unincorporated entities, whereas charities will undoubtedly continue to be the main players in terms of resources and socioeconomic significance, and as potential partners with government in future public benefit service provision. Bearing in mind the size, expense, and workload of the Charity Commission in England and Wales, it is at present hard to see how the ACNC can hope to effectively regulate the entire nonprofit sector. There is a possibility that charity could be shortchanged.

[185] Note that the Productivity Commission's terms of reference (pp. iv–v of the Research Report) include to "examine the extent to which tax exemptions assessed by the commercial operations of not-for-profit organizations may affect the competitive neutrality of the market."

[186] Dal Pont, G., *Law of Charity*, LexisNexis Butterworths, 2010, at p. 63.

[187] Australian Government, Office of Assistant Treasurer, "Making it Easier for Charities to Help Those Who Need it." Also, see further Commonwealth of Australia, The Treasury, *Better Targeting of Not-for-Profit Tax Concessions*, Canberra, May 2011.

10

NEW ZEALAND

I. INTRODUCTION

This small nation has achieved an impressive reputation, disproportionate to its size among modern developed nations, for successfully translating into law some of the more complex relationships that link the public and private, the citizen and the state. Centuries of negotiations between the institutions of government and the *tangata whenua*[1] have proved instructive in preparing the government for undertaking the broader task of bridging the gap between it and the nonprofit sector. Its recent initiatives may seem slow and guarded, with results that are often a compromise, but they are taken for the most part in step with the sector as part of a process that may in the long-term prove more sustainable, embodying a reasonable working balance between the interests of sector and government, than some "off-the-shelf" prescriptions relied upon in other jurisdictions.

This chapter explores the route taken in New Zealand toward formalizing government/sector relations, including its charity law reform outcomes, and the resulting consequences for trading charities. Beginning with an overview of the sector, consideration is given to the relative significance of charities within the array of other nonprofits. It examines the distorting effect of the contract culture on the government/sector relationship, the measures subsequently taken to retrieve the situation, and the building of the infrastructure now gradually materializing to represent a more collaborative endeavor. This is followed by a brief account of the contemporary legal structures housing charitable activity. The bulk of the chapter, dealing with the current charity law framework and related case law, then follows. This includes a focus on judicial analysis of parameters for trading by charities in

[1] This Maori term loosely translates as "people of the land" and refers to the indigenous people of Aotearoa/New Zealand.

New Zealand. The chapter concludes with a summary of the more distinctive characteristics of charitable trading in this jurisdiction.

II. SECTOR PROFILE

The Auckland Ladies' Benevolent Society, formed in 1857 to help destitute women and children, was probably the first charitable association in New Zealand, and it was closely followed by benevolent societies in Dunedin in 1862, Christchurch in 1865, and Wellington in 1867. The subsequent slow development of the nonprofit sector in a country that until well into the 20th century consisted largely of widely dispersed village-based communities has been thoroughly documented by others.[2]

A. The Nonprofit Sector

This is a significant sector by international standards, being proportionately 25 percent bigger than Australia's, and larger than that of the United States and of the average of all Anglo-Saxon countries. The following information on sector dimensions is largely drawn from statistics published by the Office for the Community & Voluntary Sector.[3]

1. Employment and Volunteers

It has been recently estimated that the sector contributes 2.6 percent to GDP. This increases to $6.95 billion (or 4.9 percent of GDP) when taking into account the volunteer labor contribution.[4] (This is similar to the contribution of the entire construction industry.)[5] The sector contains more than 1.2 million volunteers and has over 105,000 paid employees—but only 10 percent of all nonprofit organizations employ paid staff, as the other 90 percent rely entirely on volunteers.[6]

[2] See, e.g., Tennant, M., Sanders, J., O'Brien, M. and Castle, C., *Defining the Nonprofit Sector: New Zealand*, Working Papers of the Johns Hopkins Comparative Nonprofit Sector Project, No. 45, Baltimore, MD, The Johns Hopkins Center for Civil Society Studies, 2006, at pp. 3–15.

[3] See Office for the Community & Voluntary Sector, citing: Statistics NZ's "NZ Non-Profit Institutions Satellite Account: 2004" and the "How Do New Zealanders Give?" report, which was sourced from Nielsen Media Research Panorama (January–December 2007 database)/Nick Jones & Associates "Consumer Who Cares" service. See further at http://www.ocvs.govt.nz/work-programme/building-knowledge/subsector-facts.html.

[4] Note that all values expressed in this chapter are in New Zealand dollars.

[5] See also Nowland-Foreman, G., "No Longer Overlooked and Undervalued," at the launch of *The New Zealand Non-Profit Sector in Comparative Perspective*, Wellington (August 12, 2008).

[6] See further Office for the Community and Voluntary Sector, *Government Support for Volunteering 2002–2008* (2008), which includes references to legislative and policy changes, research, and promotion of volunteering.

B. Nonprofit Organizations

The sector consists of some 97,000 nonprofits, most of which are to be found in the "culture, sports and recreation" and in the "social services" subsectors. Charities, though numerically not necessarily dominant, generally tend to be the oldest and often the wealthiest organizations in the sector.

1. Sector Groups

The first of these consists of a mixture of cultural, arts, and sports organizations, social clubs, and other recreational clubs such as film societies, community theaters, garden societies, operatic societies, pipe bands, Maori performing arts groups, tramping clubs, and vintage car clubs. It is by far the largest (44.6 percent) in terms of numbers of nonprofits (43,220), but is only the third largest (16 percent) by number of employees (16,820), almost all of which (94.5 percent) rely entirely on volunteers to maintain their operations. Its income is mostly derived from sales of goods and services (61 percent) and from donations, memberships, and grants (29 percent).

"Social services," the second largest group (11.6 percent) in terms of numbers of nonprofits (11,280) but the largest group (29.9 percent) by number of employees (31,480) includes welfare organizations, emergency and relief services, and income support providers. Most of these nonprofits (84.4 percent) rely entirely on volunteers to maintain their operations. Their income is mainly derived from sales of goods and services (72.7 percent) and from donations, memberships, and grants (18.2 percent). Many social services are provided by religious institutions—sometimes as stand-alone entities, and sometimes as part of an ecclesiastical structure. Iwi-related social services are an important part of this group.[7] Well over half the group revolves around community care services, such as accommodation for the aged, and residential and nonresidential facilities.

The development and housing group of nonprofits includes tangata whenua governance entities, organizations involved in employment or employment-related training, tourism boards, and neighborhood institutions. It comprises 7580 nonprofits, is the fourth largest sector group in terms of numbers (7.8 percent) and, with 3730 employees, is the sixth largest sector employer (3.5 percent). A total of 92.61 percent of these nonprofits rely entirely on volunteers to maintain their operations. The economic contribution is the eighth largest of the various sector groups (2.9

[7] The indigenous people of New Zealand have a well-developed communal culture. The critical organizational construct is the tribe, an extended kinship organization comprising subtribes and extended family groups. The tribal identity was and is the iwi. The tribal institutions of whanua (extended family or kin group), hapu (subtribe), hui (meeting of the iwi), and marae (ceremonial center) remain key features of contemporary Maori culture. Maori belong to diverse communities: some identify with a particular iwi, hapu, and whanau irrespective of where they reside; others identify with their tribal connections but do not know their ancestry or whakapapa; whereas others prefer to identify simply as Maori.

percent), and its income is derived mainly from sales of goods and services (43.3 percent) and from government grants (27.2 percent).

The education and research group includes kindergartens, playcenters, kohanga reo (Maori language immersion programs), private primary and secondary schools, private tertiary providers, other education providers such as English for nonnative speakers, and research institutions. It comprises 7400 nonprofits, is the sixth largest sector group in terms of numbers (7.6 percent) and, with 20,140 employees, is the second largest sector employer (19.1 percent). A total of 77.4 percent of these nonprofits rely entirely on volunteers to maintain their operations. The economic contribution is the second largest of the various sector groups (16 percent), and its income is derived mainly from sales of goods and services (48.3 percent) and from government grants (38.5 percent).

The health services group of nonprofits comprises 2210 organizations, is the ninth largest sector group in terms of numbers (2.3 percent) and, with 15,090 employees, is the fourth largest sector employer (14.3 percent). A total of 80.1 percent of these nonprofits rely entirely on volunteers to maintain their operations. The economic contribution is the fourth largest of the various sector groups (12.8 percent), and its income is derived mainly from sales of goods and services (81.5 percent) and from membership, donations, and grants (12.2 percent). This group is set to expand considerably if clause 7 of the Statutes Amendment Bill (No 2),[8] introduced on February 22, 2011 to amend the definition of "charitable purpose" in the Charities Act, receives parliamentary approval. The proposed amendment will specifically include as charitable the purpose of an entity that promotes sport, if the purpose is "expressed to be, and is in fact, the means by which a charitable purpose (such as the promotion of health or education) will be achieved."

Other subgroups constitute the remainder of the sector and are classified in accordance with the United Nations International Classification of Nonprofit Organizations (ICNPO), including: "environmental/animal protection," "civic and advocacy groups," "philanthropic and other intermediaries," and "international organizations, aid and relief."[9]

2. Charities

As of July 30, 2011, there were 25,620 charities registered with the Charities Commission, with the largest single grouping comprised of education/training/research, followed by those involved in religious activities.[10] In that year charities generated a total income of $14.2 billion, a considerable increase from the $6.1 billion recorded in 2009. Education and health are the dominant sectors (55 percent)

[8] 271–72 (2011), see further at www.legislation.govt.nz/bill/government/2011/.../DLM3560693.html www.legislation.govt.nz/bill/government/2011/.../DLM3560693.html.

[9] See further Tennant et al., *Defining the Nonprofit Sector*, at pp. 24–32.

[10] Charities Commission, *A Snapshot of New Zealand's Charitable Sector*, Wellington, 2011.

in terms of income flowing into the sector. Religious activities and health are the two areas that attract the highest volunteer contribution.

Some charities are designated "donee organizations" by the Inland Revenue. This entity is defined as a society, institution, association, organization, or trust, the activities of which are not carried on for the private pecuniary profit of any individual and the funds of which are, in the opinion of the Commissioner, applied wholly or principally to any charitable, benevolent, philanthropic, or cultural purposes within New Zealand. Donors can claim tax concessions for donations made to such organizations.

3. Range of Legal Structures

In a deliberate attempt to boost voluntary effort, the Hospitals and Charitable Institutions Act 1885 provided a formal mechanism for government to subsidize charities that agreed to incorporate under the Act. This early illustration of government intent to build a formal relationship with the nonprofit sector,[11] fittingly applied in the area of health care, failed as the so-called "separate institutions" mostly ended up absorbed into the public sector hospital and charitable aid boards.[12]

The contemporary rate of incorporation among nonprofits is higher compared, for example, to that in Australia. If, however, as has been estimated, around one in every two nonprofits are not legally incorporated,[13] this would mean that there are approximately 50,000 unincorporated nonprofits in New Zealand.[14] In comparison, those that are incorporated constitute perhaps as much as 60 percent of all 97,000 nonprofit organizations: Membership-based organizations frequently incorporate under the Incorporated Societies Act 1908, charitable societies under the Charitable Trusts Act 1957, and trading operations with a charitable purpose under the Companies Act, whereas many religious and other organizations are also incorporated by specific legislation. All incorporated entities must be registered as such with the Registrar of Incorporated Societies.

Charitable trusts and societies are the second most common form of nonprofit incorporation: About 15 percent of nonprofits are incorporated as charitable trusts and 22 percent as incorporated societies. Nonprofits can also assume the legal structure of a

[11] As cited in Tennant et al., *Defining the Nonprofit Sector,* at pp. 8–9.

[12] See Tennant, M., *Paupers and Providers: Charitable Aid in New Zealand,* Allen and Unwin/ Bridget Williams Books, Wellington, 1989.

[13] Bradford, S. and Nowland-Foreman, G., *Mahi Tahi Working Together: Civil Society in Aotearoa/ New Zealand,* Association of Non-Governmental Organizations of Aotearoa, Wellington, 1999, at p. 87.

[14] Tennant et al, *Defining the Nonprofit Sector,* at p. 17 and Sharp, A., "The History of the Taxation of Maori Authorities in New Zealand: A Unique Reflection of Law and Public Policy Working Together?." in Maples, A. and Sawyer A. (eds.), *Taxation Issues: Existing and Emerging,* The Centre for Commercial & Corporate Law Inc., University of Canterbury, 2011, at p. 163. See also Maples and Sawyer, *Taxation Issues;* Statistics New Zealand, 2007.

company, as facilitated by the Companies Act 1993, though this is relatively uncommon, or that of a friendly society, industrial and provident society, cooperative, credit union, or other form of mutual benefit organization. In addition, Maori nonprofits may be unincorporated or incorporated or may take the form of a Maori-specific legal structure.

C. Financing the Sector

Traditionally, the nonprofit sector as a whole has been very dependent upon government funding, either directly or through funding streams overseen by government, such as the state-controlled lotteries system, state-regulated gaming machine proceeds, and statutory community trusts. From the 1970s the scale of government financial support increased, and by 1986, at a very conservative estimate, government funding had reached $75.4 million. Most of this was in the form of direct grants and subsidies to aid the delivery of services in areas of need identified by the agencies concerned, and 68 percent of it was allocated as a fixed recurring annual budget item.[15]

It has been estimated[16] that by 2002, in addition to central government and lottery grants funding, other sources of income for the sector included: local government ($28.2 million, 1 percent); gaming machine trusts ($131.2 million, 4 percent); other philanthropic and community trusts ($142.8 million, 5 percent); personal donations ($281.9 million, 10 percent); bequests ($37.7 million, 1 percent); corporate giving ($80.0 million, 3 percent); and payments and fees for services ($1, 250.0 million, 42 percent). Since 2002, the increase in funding from nongovernment sources has significantly increased: In 2005, for example, funding from gaming machine trusts had reached $382 million.[17]

1. Government Funding

The 1980s and 1990s saw the emergence of a market-driven ethos that began to shape the relationship between government and the nonprofit sector: The purchase of services through contracts became the preferred mechanism for transferring resources from the state to nonprofit organizations. The shift from largely untied grants to contracts signaled a fundamental change in the way in which nonprofit

[15] Maples and Sawyer, *Taxation Issues,* at p. 13; citing Driver, S. and David Robinson, C., *Voluntary Social Services: A Review of Funding,* Planning Paper No. 28, New Zealand Planning Council, Wellington, 1986.

[16] Maples and Sawyer, *Taxation Issues,* at p. 13, citing Robinson, D. and Hanley, P., *Funding New Zealand 2002: Resource Flows to the Community Nonprofit Sector in New Zealand,* Philanthropy New Zealand, Wellington, 2002, at pp. 35–36. Caution is especially required with the estimates for corporate giving and for payments and fees for service, as these are based on international comparisons rather than specific information from Aotearoa/New Zealand.

[17] Maples and Sawyer, *Taxation Issues,* at p. 13, citing Department of Internal Affairs, Gambling Expenditure Statistics 1981–2005. See also Gousmett, M. J., "Economic Development Corporations as Charitable Trusts," in Maples and Sawyer, *Taxation Issues,* at p. 177.

organizations engaged in their activities: pushing them into delivering services and activities identified by the state, instead of determining their own priorities.

By 2002, central government funding to nonprofits more generally (including, as well as health and welfare, those in the areas of sport and recreation, art and culture, religion, the environment, and employment and economic development) were estimated at $920.6 million. A further $91.3 million came from the Lottery Grants Board.[18] Funding for the sector currently comes, not only from purchase of services, but also from a range of small special schemes, such as the Community Organization Grants Schemes and the Community Initiative Fund. Many of these smaller schemes are significant for their encouragement of new initiatives, or for promoting employment in the nonprofit sector. Central government and lottery grants funding have been estimated as representing 31 percent and 3 percent respectively of total nonprofit income. The most recent and most comprehensive, albeit still conservative, estimate of government funding of nonprofit activity suggests it accounts for around 25 percent of their total revenues, or equating to at least $2 billion in 2004.[19]

In addition, the concept of "donee organizations" has allowed government to manipulate tax concessions and donation incentives and so extend real support to selected charities.

2. Self-Financing

It has been reported that the sector generates most of its own income.[20] Although the estimated 25 percent contribution from government is probably an underestimate, it is still likely to be below the Australian level and that of the average common law country.

D. Sector Cohesion

There is no history of sector cohesion in New Zealand. The linkages among the Maori-related organizations always gave cohesion to part of the sector, but otherwise the nonprofit subsets functioned quite independently of each other: Sport and recreation, for example, found little in common with the service silos of health and social care, and sector divisions tended to sharpen when government elected to relate to nonprofits primarily through the hard and fast boundaries of service contracts. Only comparatively recently has there been a coming together of Maori organizations with other local broad-based community and specialized nonprofits.

[18] Maples and Sawyer, *Taxation Issues*, at p. 13; citing Driver and David Robinson, *Voluntary Social Services*, at p. 10.

[19] See Sanders, J., O'Brien, M, Tennant, M, Sokolowski J, Wojciech, and Salamon, L., *The New Zealand Non-Profit Sector in Comparative Perspective,* Office for the Community and Voluntary Sector, Wellington, 2008, as cited in O'Brien, M., Sanders, J. and Tennant, M., *The New Zealand Non-Profit Sector and Government Policy,* Office for the Community and Voluntary Sector, Wellington, 2009, at p. 13.

[20] See Nowland-Foreman, "No Longer Overlooked and Undervalued."

1. Sector Umbrella Bodies

There has been a marked lack of powerful umbrella bodies representing community, voluntary, and iwi/Maori organizations. The nation-wide peak body, Philanthropy New Zealand, was only established in 1990.

In New Zealand, a number of umbrella groups now provide coordination and representation within specific fields as does, for example, the New Zealand Federation of Voluntary Welfare Organizations for social services. Others act as umbrella groups in a more task- or topic-specific sense, drawing together and representing a range of local activities on a particular issue at a national level. Commentators have noted the absence of entities sufficiently representative of the sector as a whole, with the resources and maturity to engage with government on behalf of the sector.[21] In recent years, both the Association of Non-Governmental Organizations of Aotearoa (ANGOA) and the Community Sector Taskforce have sought, with limited success, to provide a sector-wide mechanism to bring nonprofits together to coordinate, advocate, and develop the sector's own capacity to engage with government in policy framing processes.

III. CHARITIES AND GOVERNMENT: BUILDING A RELATIONSHIP

In New Zealand, the government has had a long-standing formal policy, embedded in law, of working in partnership with the Maori.[22] This experience colored the slowly evolving government/sector relationship and has given it a distinctive dimension. Not until the late 1990s did the government adopt a broader approach when, following political developments in the U.K., it also pursued the "third way" democratic pluralist approach to social development. This has drawn Maori charities, other ethnic organizations, and the sector more generally toward assuming a growing share of responsibility for community social service and health needs as an alternative to continued dependence on state provision.[23] Eventually, in 2001, the government extended this to create a formal partnership with the community, voluntary, and iwi/Maori organizations,[24]

[21] See, e.g., Baxter, K., "Community-Government Relationships: Issues in Establishing Formal Linkages between Central Government and the Community Sector," paper for presentation at the *Strengthening Communities through Local Partnerships Symposium,* University of Auckland, April 12, 2002.

[22] Embodied in the principles of the Treaty of Waitangi.

[23] See Walker, P., "Exploring Trans-Cultural Partnerships within Third Sector Organizations in New Zealand," in *International Journal of Interdisciplinary Social Sciences,* Vol. 5, No. 3, at pp. 423–34.

[24] See Ministry of Social Policy, *Communities and Government—Potential for Partnership Whakatopu Whakaaro,* 2001. The Office of Ethnic Affairs, launched in 2001, works by engaging with communities in order to provide advice, increase the development of networks, and enhance the development of social capital within the sector.

and then in 2003 consolidated it by putting in place new structures, policies, and procedures to formally link government and the sector.

A. Maori Governance, the Sector and Government

The Treaty of Waitangi established a partnership relationship between the Crown and iwi/Maori as tangata whenua. Within that framework, there has long been a system of governance whereby designated entities exercise stewardship over the interests and affairs of hapu, marae, and other specific aspects of Maori life. Although many of these are mandated by the Crown, they do not have sovereign authority of a nature sufficient for them to be defined as part of government. The Maori/government partnership provided a model for an evolving government/sector relationship and has operated in tandem with it.

B. Government Bodies and the Sector: Formulating Policy

In the 1980s–1990s, the switch in government funding tactics from grant aiding the sector to service contracts with targeted nonprofit providers marked a significant change in its policy and a period of deterioration in government/sector relations. Smith noted "the new relationship which gives Government considerably greater control of that voluntary sector activity which it funds,"[25] whereas Wilson argued that government funding redefined the nature of the relationship between the state and nonprofit organizations as "government has moved from investment in voluntary organizations to purchase of core government services, with voluntary organizations becoming alternative rather than complementary service providers."[26] This was a period of well-recorded dissatisfaction with the contract culture[27] and consequent soul searching for the sector:[28]

> During this time debates occurred about the nature and role of sector organisations—was their primary purpose to be a vehicle for the achievement of government policy objectives or did they also have an independent role that they defined? Was there accountability of sector organisations to Government, to the wider public (however defined), to clients or to donors and other supporters? Was it right that government

[25] Smith, V., "Contracting for Social and Welfare Services: The Changing Relationship between Government and the Voluntary Sector in New Zealand," research paper presented at the Australian and New Zealand Third Sector Research Conference, Wellington, July 2–5, 1996; citing O'Brien et al., *The New Zealand Non-Profit Sector and Government Policy,* at p. 13.

[26] Wilson, C., *The Changing Face of Social Service Volunteering: A Literature Review,* Ministry of Social Development, Wellington, 2001, at p. 132. See also Baxter, "Community-Government Relationships."

[27] See, e.g., Nowland-Foreman, G., "Can Voluntary Organizations Survive the Bear Hug of Government Funding under a Contracting Regime? A View from Aotearoa/New Zealand," in *Third Sector Review,* Vol. 3, 1997, at pp. 5–39; Cribb, J., "Accounting for Something: Voluntary Organizations, Accountability and the Implications for Government Funders," in *Social Policy Journal of New Zealand,* Vol. 26, 2005, at pp. 43–51.

[28] O'Brien et al. *The New Zealand Non-Profit Sector and Government Policy,* at p. 13.

agencies should specify the priorities of organisations from which it purchased services, rather than supporting their causes of origin?

The new Labor government elected in 1999 brought with it, as in the U.K. and as would later be the case in Australia, a new approach toward the sector. Government began to place greater emphasis on ways in which "community-government partnerships... help create social capital and social cohesion."[29]

1. The Community and Voluntary Sector Working Party

This body of experts and community representatives was established by the government in 2000 to take a whole-of-government approach and consider a possible formal agreement between the government and the sector, though, ultimately, a formal compact such as in the U.K. was not pursued. The working party's report[30] provided a powerful acknowledgement of the poor state of the government-sector relationship and expressed a shared commitment to developing a better way of working together. In 2001, the government responded by issuing a "Statement of Government Intentions for an Improved Government-Community Sector Relationship" indicating that it would implement changes in the culture of government to facilitate respect for the sector, progress cooperation, and develop the institutions of civil society. In June of that year, it issued its discussion document *Tax and Charities*,[31] and in October the Minister for Finance announced a decision in principle to introduce registration, reporting, and monitoring requirements for charities claiming tax-free status. The government agreed that a second phase of relationship building would occur throughout 2001–2002. This involved further collaboration between community representatives and government officials to the Community-Government Relationship Steering Group, which decided on three work streams: participatory processes, resourcing and accountability, and strengthening of the community sector. This resulted in the document *He Waka Kotuia—Joining Together on a Shared Journey*[32] and other actions documented in *A Community-Government Relationship: The Road to a Cross-Sectoral Forum*.[33] Together with the appointment in 1999 of

[29] Ministry of Social Policy, *Models of Community-Government Partnerships and their Effectiveness in Achieving Welfare Goals: A Review of the Literature*, Ministry of Social Policy, Wellington, 2000.

[30] Community and Voluntary Sector Working Party, *Communities and Government: Potential for Partnership* report, Ministry of Social Policy, Wellington, 2001.

[31] See Inland Revenue Department, Policy Advice Division, *Tax and Charities*, Wellington, 2001.

[32] See Community-Government Relationship Steering Group, *He Waka Kotuia—Joining Together on a Shared Journey*, Community Policy team, Ministry of Social Policy, Wellington, 2002.

[33] See Office for the Community and Voluntary Sector, *A Community-Government Relationship: The Road to a Cross-Sectoral Forum*, Office for the Community and Voluntary Sector, Wellington, 2007.

a minister with specific responsibility for the sector, these initiatives indicated a preparedness to positively engage in a new phase of relationship-building.

2. "Statement of Government Intentions for an Improved Community-Government Relationship" (SOGI)

An early indicator of the government's willingness to work with nonprofits differently came in 2000 when the Ministry of Health launched its own policy initiative, entitled "Framework for Relations between the Ministry of Health and Health and Disability Non-Government Organizations," which provided for regular policy meetings to be convened at which government and sector representatives could negotiate matters of funding, policy, and practice.

On a broader front, the "Statement of Government Intentions for an Improved Community-Government Relationship" (SOGI), outlined a new government policy to strengthen its relationship with, and build the capacity of, the sector. This was to include "streamlining and restructuring its NPO-funding procedures, supports to build NPO organizational capacity, and new consultation processes between government and the community and NPO sector."[34] This formal document, with its vision for "strong and respectful relationships between government and community, voluntary and iwi/Maori organizations," marked a significant turning point in government policy.[35] The 2002 report, *He Waka Kotuia*, provided advice to be implemented through three work streams:

- **Participatory processes**: work to assist public servants to effectively engage community, voluntary, and Maori organizations in decision making and policy development;
- **Resourcing and accountability**: improvements to government's funding mechanisms, including contracting, reporting, and use of grant funding; and
- **Strengthening the community sector**: finding ways to overcome the fragility of community, voluntary, and Maori organizations and build their capability.[36]

It also recommended the establishment of a Community Forum Taskforce and Action Group Maori (established as Te Wero) to build the capacity of the sector.

During 2008, the government funded the Association of Non-Governmental Organizations of Aotearoa (ANGOA) to undertake an assessment of government responsiveness to the SOGI. The review reported in 2009 that: "from the perspective of the tangata whenua, community and voluntary sector, the SOGI has continued

[34] Ministry of Social Development, *Statement of Government Intentions for an Improved Community—Government Relationship,* Ministry of Social Development, Wellington, December 2001.

[35] Ministry of Social Development, *Statement of Government Intentions for an Improved Community—Government Relationship.*

[36] Community-Government Relationship Steering Group, *He Waka Kotuia,* at n. 32.

value as an affirmation of Government's trust and respect as the essential underpinning of its relationship with the community and voluntary sector."[37]

3. The Community Sector Taskforce

Established in 2003 by the Community-Government Relationship Steering Group, and initially called the Community Forum Taskforce, this body was seen as a way of progressing recommendations made by *He Waka Kotuia*. The taskforce changed its name to the Community Sector Taskforce shortly after it was established, and extended its mandate to include providing an independent perspective, to assist in decision making about issues concerning the sector, and to develop strategies that would assist in government-sector communications including organizing forums around the country and supporting a range of initiatives within the sector.[38]

The taskforce became involved in a number of sector initiatives such as development of a Tangata Whenua, Community and Voluntary Sector Research Centre (which has since become separately established and funded from public and private sources).[39] In 2009, the government provided funding to a re-emergent taskforce to strengthen local community networks to engage with each other, and to assist community organizations to work within the Treaty of Waitangi framework.

4. Pathway to Partnership

The four-year Pathway to Partnership government funding strategy was introduced in 2008 to "build stronger, sustainable and more effective community-based social services for families, children and young people."[40] The strategy details how the government intends to work with community groups to deliver "high quality" services and early support to families, children, and young people. For present purposes, two aspects of this strategy indicate significant progress in government/sector relationships.

First, members of the Pathway to Partnership steering group were recruited from a range of medium-sized to large social service organizations. This process would seem to have legitimized the sector representatives as strategic brokers for the development

[37] Cook, L., *"Good Intentions": An Assessment of the Statement of Government Intentions for an Improved Community-Government Relationship*, Association of Non-Governmental Organizations of Aotearoa (ANGOA), January 2009, available at: http://www.angoa.org.nz/angoa_docs/SOGI-Full-Review.pdf.

[38] See further Community Sector Taskforce, *A New Way of Working for the Tangata Whenua, Community and Voluntary Sector in Aotearoa/New Zealand* (Version 2), Community Sector Taskforce, Wellington, 2006.

[39] See Tangata Whenua, Community and Voluntary Sector Research Centre, www.communityresearch.org.nz.

[40] Ministry of Social Development, at www.msd.govt.nz/.

and implementation of government funding policies and priorities.[41] Second, one of the key features of the Pathway to Partnership strategy was a new funding model for community third sector organizations that provide "essential services" to vulnerable families. Under this funding model, the government introduced an outcomes- rather than output-based partnership model of contracting, together with other impact measures, that fully funds essential contracted services to 100 percent of their service costs. This "funding for outcomes" approach is said to reconfigure contract processes and accountability in an attempt to reduce compliance costs, offer a "holistic" service under bilateral contract arrangements, and report program achievements outside of contracted services.[42] In short, this new model marks a significant step away from the previous, bare, and underfunded competitive-tendering, government approach to funding nonprofit service provision, which had emasculated the sector and skewed the balance in the government/sector relationship.

C. Government Bodies and the Sector: Structural Links

The installation of a new Labor government in 1999 triggered a series of measures, replicating those taken in the U.K. and foreshadowing those to come in Australia, to put in place mediatory structures that would give institutional recognition to the new government policy of rapprochement with the nonprofit sector. The appointment of a minister with specific responsibility for the sector was followed with the creation of the Office for the Community and Voluntary Sector and establishment of the Charities Commission, following completion of the charity law reform process. Other initiatives were also instigated, including increased tax relief for donations to nonprofit organizations.[43]

1. Minister Responsible for the Community and Voluntary Sector

In recognition of the value of building strong government-sector relationships, this new ministerial portfolio was established in 1999. Among the initiatives taken by the minister was the appointment of the Kia Tutahi-Standing Together steering group of community members and government officials. This group was established to develop the Community-Government Relationship Agreement. It has set out a vision and principles for how government and communities can work together in the "Draft Relationship Agreement between Communities of Aotearoa New Zealand and the Government of New Zealand." However, it needs to be borne in mind that

[41] See Aimers, J. and Walker, P., "Alternative Models of Accountability for Third Sector Organizations in New Zealand," paper presented at International Society for Third Sector Research, Barcelona, 2008, at p. 4.

[42] See Pomeroy, A., "Changing the Culture of Contracting: Funding for Outcomes," *Social Policy Journal of New Zealand*, No. 31, 2007, at pp. 158–169.

[43] O'Brien et al., *The New Zealand Non-Profit Sector and Government Policy*, at pp. 13–23.

this ministerial post is not part of the Cabinet, which, arguably, reflects the lesser degree of importance the government attaches to the sector.

2. Office for the Community and Voluntary Sector

This office was created within the Ministry of Social Development in 2003 "to address overarching issues affecting the community and voluntary sector and to raise the profile of the sector within government."[44] Acting as the central hub for coordinating the government's engagement with the sector, the mission of the Office was to work across government to build strong and respectful relationships between government and the sector.[45] The Office has led a number of initiatives across the sector, and works to provide leadership on issues of importance to the sector. Activities include organizational development support; research about the scope, nature, and impact of the sector, and promotion of policies in other departments that facilitate and support the work of community organizations. It has been responsible for leading the "Building Better Government Engagement" project and for producing "Managing Well" and the "Community Resource Kit." In February 2011, the office was transferred from the Ministry of Social Development to the Department of Internal Affairs.

3. Charity Law Reform

Following on from its largely tax-centered attempts at reform in 1979,[46] 1989,[47] and 1998,[48] government in New Zealand completed its charity law reform process with the launch of the Charities Act 2005, which is seen as a cornerstone of its partnership policy. As a government minister then declared, "[t]his legislation is a symbol of this government's commitment to growing the relationship between government and the charitable sector."[49]

The outcome, however, is remarkably anodyne, leaving in place many of the constraints removed by equivalent legislation in the U.K. and Irish jurisdictions, but the government has taken some cautious legislative steps toward modernizing charity law by making changes to the regulatory framework that should strengthen the sector. This

[44] As stated on the website of OCVS, see further at http://www.ocvs.govt.nz/about-us/index.html#Ourrole1.

[45] Office for the Community and Voluntary Sector, *Briefing for the Incoming Minister,* Ministry of Social Development, Wellington, 2005.

[46] Property Law and Equity Reform Committee, *Report on the Charitable Trusts Act,* Wellington, 1979.

[47] Working Party on Charities and Sporting Bodies, *Report to the Minister of Finance and the Minister of Social Welfare by the Working Party on Charities and Sporting Bodies,* Treasury, Wellington, 1989.

[48] Committee of Experts on Tax Compliance, *Tax Compliance: Report to the Treasurer and Minister of Revenue,* Inland Revenue Department, Wellington, 1998.

[49] From media statement made by the Hon. Judith Tizard, Associate Minister of Commerce announcing the new legislation on April 14, 2005.

has mainly consisted of decoupling the institutional responsibility for determining charitable status and tax exemption, with the former now being vested in the Charities Commission. The Charities Act 2005 together with the Income Tax Act 2007 (in conjunction with the Incorporated Societies Act 1908 and the Charitable Trusts Act 1957) provide the new legislative framework for charities, albeit one that is primarily focused on registering and regulating to improve accountability and transparency standards. It also provides for donor incentive schemes and simplifies charity-related fiscal matters.

The legislative product of charity law reform in New Zealand was a quite restrained statute. Possibly this indicates that government and sector are content to make progress cautiously, given the need to consult with many local Maori communities, and constantly check that reform achievements do not overstep the broadest level of attained consensus. New Zealand is a jurisdiction in which government strives to ensure that social policy and legislation are formed on an inclusive basis.

4. Charities Commission

The reform outcomes included the creation of a Charities Commission—a new lead, charity-specific regulatory body that loosely resembled its U.K. counterparts[50]—with responsibility for determining charitable status. This government body, with little if any independence from government control, was required to establish and manage systems for the registration, supervision, and support of charities. Establishing such a Commission indicated a government willingness to move away from the traditional tax-driven approach toward charities and their activities. In theory, this was a move with considerable strategic significance for the future balance of legal functions within the regulatory framework for charities in New Zealand, and in practice the Commission did function with considerable drive and autonomy.

However, in May 2011, as part of sweeping cost-cutting measures, the government announced a review of state agencies, and then in August in the light of review findings it proposed the transfer of the functions of the Charities Commission to the Department of Internal Affairs (DIA). In Spring 2012, the government introduced a composite Crown Entities Reform Bill that included an outline for a Charities Amendment Bill providing for: the disestablishment of the Commission and a statutory board of three people to oversee independent registration and related functions, whereas the DIA is vested with monitoring, investigating, and prosecuting functions. Although viewed by many in the nonprofit sector as a retrograde step, and one in sharp contrast with that currently being taken by New Zealand's neighbor, Australia, this development may at least serve to consolidate the functions of the Charities Commission and the Office for the Community and Voluntary Sector under the roof of the Ministry of Internal Affairs. It may be that the review of the Charities Act, which is scheduled to take place once the ongoing review of the

[50] That is: the Charity Commission for England and Wales; the Office of the Scottish Charity Regulator established by the Charities and Trustee Investment (Scotland) Act 2005; and the Charity Commission for Northern Ireland, established by the Charities Act (Northern Ireland) 2008.

Incorporated Societies Act 1908 is completed, will provide a fresh context within which to reconsider a future role for an independent Charities Commission.

D. Implications for Future Government/Sector Relations

The modest outcomes of charity law reform culminating in the aborted attempt to establish a Charities Commission will probably prove to be of less significance in the long-term than the process of government/sector engagement by which they were achieved. The reform process was conducted with ongoing input from the sector, and the outcomes must be viewed in the context of other evidence of government goodwill such as: the creation of an Office for the Community and Voluntary Sector, accountable to the Minister for the Community and Voluntary Sector; the revised contract funding arrangements; and the inclusion, in Clause 45 of the proposed Charities Amendment Bill, of a new requirement that each board member act independently in exercising his or her judgment without direction from the Minister. It may be that government intends to gradually build a more coherent and structured partnership with the sector, but to do so it will have to rebuild the setback in relations caused by its cursory approach to the importance the sector placed on the role of a Charity Commission, and move forward at a pace set by progress made in negotiations with the sector.

1. The 2007 Tax Reforms

In his Budget 2007, the Revenue Minister announced the removal of the cap on rebates for charitable donations (and the 5 percent deduction limit on donations made by companies and Maori authorities). Donations of any amount, up to an individual's total net income, are now eligible for a 33.3 percent rebate. This initiative has done much to support charitable giving in New Zealand.[51] Subsequent legislative changes allowed unlisted companies with five or fewer shareholders to have access to company deductions for donations.[52]

IV. READJUSTING PUBLIC BENEFIT SERVICE PROVISION

In New Zealand, the migration from a welfare state to a mixed economy of service provision has followed much the same route as in the U.K. As Tennant has noted:[53]

> the increasing use of various forms of contractual arrangements between government and sector organizations make the notion of "institutional separation" more porous.

[51] See further http://www.ourcommunity.com.au/files/OCMILLIONATIONALJUNE2007.pdf.
[52] In July 2006 the Inland Revenue Department released a discussion document, ED0088 Interaction of tax and charities rules, covering tax exemption and donee status. Note also that the government decision to abolish the gift duty came into effect on October 1, 2011.
[53] Tennant et al, *Defining the Nonprofit Sector,* at p. 35.

> Historically, with some important exceptions, the state has been the major provider of health, education, and social services. This has changed in the last two decades with increasing service provision through nonprofit organizations under contract to the state. In some instances new nonprofit organizations have been formed as a direct result of government funding decisions. These changes continue to alter the nature of the government-nonprofit relationship.

The authors follow this observation by raising the dilemma that is now intrinsic to the government/sector relationship, in the context of public benefit service provision, in all the jurisdictions currently being considered: the extent to which government control, through contracts and related audit mechanisms, compromises the independence of the sector.

A. Public Benefit Service Provision: The Policy

Although welfare state policies largely followed the example set in the U.K. in the early and mid-20th century by displacing charity with government run-services, by the 1970s this had changed to a "mixed economy of welfare" with close links established between state and charity.[54] The evidence indicates that all governments, regardless of political stripe, have subsequently sought to shape sector activity in order to offset the effects of a steady reduction in spending on public services and to assist government to achieve broad social and economic goals.[55]

1. Welfare Benefit Cuts

In the late 1980s and throughout the 1990s, the welfare state underwent a radical overhaul as the government imposed cutbacks in public sector spending. In 1991, most benefits, such as the Sickness, Domestic Purposes Benefit and Unemployment Benefit, were cut by between 5 percent and 27 percent.[56] Certain health subsidies, formerly universal, were restricted to low-income families through the introduction of the Community Services Card. The move toward an ever more tightly targeted welfare state was underway.[57]

On March 17, 2010, the Cabinet Social Policy Committee agreed to establish an independent Welfare Working Group "to conduct a wide ranging and fundamental

[54] Cordery, C. and Baskerville, R., "Charity Financial Reporting Regulation: A Comparative Study of the UK and New Zealand," in *Accounting History*, February 2007, Vol. 12, No. 1, at pp. 7–27, citing Tennant, M., "Governments and Voluntary Sector Welfare: Historians' Perspectives," in *Social Policy Journal of New Zealand*, Vol. 17, December 2001, at pp. 147–60.

[55] O'Brien et al., *The New Zealand Non-Profit Sector and Government Policy*, 2009, at p. 25.

[56] See the 1991 Budget document *Welfare that Works* and Shipley, H. J., *Social Assistance: Welfare That Works*, Government Printer, Wellington, 1991.

[57] See, e.g., St John, S., "Redesigning the Welfare State in New Zealand," conference paper presented at School of Social Work and Social Policy, University of Queensland, Brisbane, October 4–5, 2001.

review of New Zealand's welfare system."[58] On February 22, 2011, the Working Group's final report was released; it contained 43 recommendations for the reform of the welfare system into a work-focused program.

2. Provision of Public Benefit Services

The ongoing policy of engaging the sector in providing public benefit services, in lieu of government bearing the cost and political burden of maintaining a fully funded welfare state, dates from this period when the sector was induced to involve itself in the provision of primary care services for vulnerable populations.[59] The increasingly close working relationship led to the Ministry of Health and health sector NGOs developing a "Framework for Relations" in 2002.[60] The framework agreement was between the Ministry and all health and disability NGOs with which it had contractual relationships. An NGO desk was also set up to improve communication between the Ministry and the NGO community, which focused on promoting sector forums for discussion, understanding, information sharing, and relationship development. The Ministry intended the desk to be an anchor to "provide continuity and a link with the NGO-related work of the MOH and other government departments."[61] More recently, the Pathway to Partnership program was launched to provide funding to those community-based organizations delivering services to families, children, and young people (see above). This is currently being maintained with some increase in funding.

3. Religious Organizations

In New Zealand, as in other common law jurisdictions, religious organizations have traditionally made a significant contribution to sector capacity, particularly as regards service provision in the areas of education and health and social care. Many of the now-established social services were originally instigated by religious organizations, and responsibility for a considerable proportion of such services continues to lie within their control. The so-called "religious and welfare sector" has long been associated with care for the elderly: Residential facilities were originally run by a mixture of public sector and religious welfare organizations, though much of this provision is now in the hands of secular nonprofit and private sector providers.

[58] Welfare Working Group, http://ips.ac.nz/WelfareWorkingGroup/Index.html.

[59] Crampton P., Dowell A., and Woodward A., "Third Sector Primary Care for Vulnerable Populations," in *Social Science and Medicine*, Vol. 53, No. 11, 2001, at pp. 1491–502.

[60] http://www.ngo.health.govt.nz/moh.nsf/indexcm/ngo-resources.

[61] Ministry of Health, *Framework for Relations between the Ministry of Health and Health/ Disability Non-Government Organizations*, Ministry of Health, Wellington, 2002.

Currently, religious organizations constitute the third-largest sector group (10.2 percent) in terms of numbers of nonprofits (9890), with the second-largest number of institutions (1910) employing staff, but only the fifth-largest number of employees (9390). A total of 80.7 percent of these organizations rely entirely on volunteers to maintain their operations. Their main source of income is from donations, memberships, and grants (71 percent). Religious charities are also strongly represented in other sector groups such as education and research, and in social services.[62]

4. Sector Capacity Building

In recent years, successive governments have signaled a commitment to address the previous two decades of difficult relationships with the nonprofit sector. For instance, there is evidence of the state seeking to work collaboratively in areas such as capacity building and capability development. These developments include projects in the information and computer technology area, the development of a range of guides and resources for nonprofits, and the development of policies concerning volunteering.[63]

5. Nonprofits and Government Funding

The public sector reforms of the 1980s and 1990s had a significant effect on the relationship between government agencies and the sector. Although this involved an increase in funding to the sector, it came at a price: the shift from grants that supported organizations to pursue their own aims to contracting generated a closer if more functionally defined relationship between government and targeted sector service providers;[64] it also marginalized all other sector entities. The effects of partial funding, which predated contracting but have been exacerbated by the tighter specification of contracts, have been particularly evident in the child, family, and community services field.

The signaling of a willingness to move from contracting toward more grant-like funding arrangements came with the Ministry's Good Practice Guide,[65] which indicated that grants should be used for low-risk activities that are not part of core

[62] See Office for the Community & Voluntary Sector at http://www.ocvs.govt.nz/work-programme/building-knowledge/subsector-facts.html.

[63] See Office of the Minister for the Community and Voluntary Sector, *Volunteers and Volunteering Policy Project- Paper One—Recognition and Valuing of Volunteering,* report to Cabinet Social Development Committee, Office for the Community and Voluntary Sector, Wellington, 2002, www.ocvs.govt.nz; and *Volunteers and Volunteering Policy Project- Paper Two—Key Issues Impacting on Volunteering,* report to Cabinet Social Development Committee, Office for the Community and Voluntary Sector, Wellington, 2002.

[64] O'Brien et al., *The New Zealand Non-Profit Sector and Government Policy,* at p. 4.

[65] Ministry of Social Development (2006) *Good Practice Funding Guide—Funding Processes;* Ministry of Social Development (2006), *Good Practice Funding Guide—Glossary.*

government activities, thereby allowing nonprofits more flexibility in deciding how to meet stated goals. This was followed by the announcement of the Pathway to Partnership program in 2008, by the then Minister for Social Development and Employment, which stated an intention to move toward fully funding organizations that provide what are described as "essential services."[66] This multiyear government strategy of investment aimed at strengthening community-based family, child, and youth focused services was introduced starting from July 1, 2008, with government increasing its investment in these services by $446 million over the following four years. This was an important policy commitment with long-term strategic implications for charities engaged in service provision, and indeed for the rest of the nonprofit sector: By freeing up such charities from the tyranny of the short-term and underfunded contract regime, it gives them security to plan for the future and to rebalance their service and mission responsibilities. It also draws them into a closer and perhaps, ultimately, a more compromising relationship with government; in so doing it will have a divisive effect on the sector, with those nonprofits not deemed to be providers of "essential services" at risk of being left outside the tent in terms of building any future government/sector relationship.

B. Public Benefit Service Provision: The Practice

The legacy of charitable and other nonprofit involvement in public benefit provision is structurally embedded in the social infrastructure of New Zealand.

1. Housing

Historically, there have been few exclusively nonprofit housing organizations, although there are indications that this is changing. In New Zealand, housing activity has historically occurred from within social service organizations, as has community development.

2. Education and Research

Most informal and small adult or community education schools and colleges are either public (government-owned) or private. The latter include church and other nonprofit schools as well as those that are run as private profit-making institutions. Many of these draw on state funding. The tertiary education field has a mixture of government-funded, nonprofit, and profit-making providers. Most of these organizations charge fees for student enrollment and also draw on government funding. It has been argued that the current application of the public benefit test, in the context of the advancement of education, permits some schools with charitable status to

[66] http://www.msd.govt.nz/about-msd-and-our-work/work-programmes/initiatives/pathway-to-partnership/key-information/key-information-background.html.

charge prohibitively expensive fees that restrict the educational opportunities for many socially disadvantaged children.[67]

3. Health

Health care is, and has long been, the crucial frontier for government/sector relations in New Zealand:[68] "The interface between the state and nonprofit organizations is primarily through primary health, mental health, and child health services. The Ministry of Health also works with the disability, personal, and public health areas within the health sector."

For over the past century, government has been wrestling with the health and social care infrastructure. The Hospitals and Charitable Institutions Act 1885 sought to organize facilities on a localized basis, listing purposes and objects deemed to be charitable and giving formal recognition to charitable institutions, whereas the Hospitals and Charitable Institutions Act 1909 brought those localized facilities into a countrywide health care scheme.

It was not until the 1980s that nonprofits providing comprehensive primary medical and related services started having a significant presence in New Zealand. In 1994, a range of union health centers, tribally based Mäori health providers, and community-based primary care providers established a formal network, the Health Care Aotearoa. Although not representing all sector primary care providers in New Zealand, Health Care Aotearoa was the best-developed example of a grouping of such primary care organizations. They served populations that were largely non-European and lived in deprived areas, and tended to adopt population approaches to funding and provision of services. The development of Health Care Aotearoa has been consistent with international experience of third sector involvement: There were perceived "failures" in government policies for funding primary care and private sector responses to these policies, resulting in lack of universal funding and provision of primary care and continuing patient co-payments.

Health care is most clearly represented by hospitals, most of which are publicly owned and provide comprehensive secondary and tertiary care. A small number are privately owned, and run on a for-profit basis providing mostly elective surgical care. Some hospitals are operated on a nonprofit basis, as incorporated societies, charitable trusts, or friendly societies. The Canterbury Charity Hospital initiative,[69] for example, was launched in 2007 and has since expanded across the islands, providing elective surgery procedures at no cost to patients. In doing so, the service frees up equivalent

[67] See *Educational Fees Protection Society Inc. v. Commissioner of Inland Revenue* [1992] 2 NZLR 115.

[68] O'Brien et al., *The New Zealand Non-Profit Sector and Government Policy*, 2009, at p. 33.

[69] See The Canterbury Charity Hospital Trust, www.charities.govt.nz CC28963. The Auckland Regional Charity Hospital Trust has since been established, using the Canterbury Charity Hospital as a model. See www.charities.govt.nz CC38587. The author is grateful to Michael Gousmett for this information.

public health provision, and for that reason is of considerable interest to government. Ironically, however, St George's Hospital in Christchurch (founded in the 1920s) has been undergoing a reverse transformation from charity to fee-charging at market rates supplemented by government-funded contracts. There is also evidence of the involvement of for-profit relationships with St George's Hospital through a complex shareholding structure involving a variety of trusts, nominee trusts, and private companies.[70]

The primary health organizations (PHOs), formed as part of the government's Primary Health Strategy (2001), are also important as they provide a good illustration of current government policy in relation to the sector. In creating a whole new group of nonprofits specifically for the purpose of implementing its strategy for health services delivery, the government has demonstrated the reliance it intends to place upon the nonprofits rather than on for-profit as its preferred partner in key policy areas. District Health Boards provide an important conduit for channeling funds and developing relationships between statutory health and nonprofit health organizations. However, the exact amount of funding that flows from statutory health funders to nonprofits is unknown. Indeed, it has been claimed that in the health sector, government does not distinguish between for-profit and nonprofit service providers and, therefore, has difficulty identifying the quantity of funding paid to nonprofit groups.[71]

Health care also includes a wide range of service providers with a remit for the aged and the disabled, and for various forms of family support. Although much of this form of provision was initially established by nonprofits, often religious organizations, there is now evidence that for-profit agencies are expanding within aged-care services and buying out nonprofit facilities. Emergency services may also be seen as constituting a part of health care, and this is an area in which nonprofits play an important role: Most ambulance services, air-rescue services, and surf patrols are nonprofits. St. John Ambulance, for example, provides ambulance and emergency services on a national basis, and volunteers, particularly in small communities, comprise a significant proportion of the workforce.

A wide range of organizations provide community-based health services and activities that include women's health, Pacific peoples' health, and mental health services. Alongside this is a significant group of organizations that provide nonhospital health services and support to the Maori. Some of these are provided out of iwi structures whereas others operate as Maori or *kaupapa*[72] Maori service providers.

[70] Perhaps there are resonances here with the United States where Brody has noted that "some nonprofit hospitals [were] testing their very entitlement to exemption by engaging in 'whole hospital' joint ventures with unrelated taxpaying partners"; see Brody, E. and Cordes, J., *The Unrelated Business Income Tax: All Bark and No Bite?* The Urban Institute (2001), at www.urban.org.

[71] O'Brien et al., *The New Zealand Non-Profit Sector and Government Policy*, 2009, at pp. 27–28.

[72] *Kaupapa* means principle, philosophy, or policy.

4. Child Care

In New Zealand, most early childhood services are provided by either nonprofit or for-profit entities rather than by government. The provision of day care typically occurs within an educational context: Providers deliver an early childhood curriculum alongside daycare. In addition to mainstream providers, there are a number of specific early childhood organizations that provide total immersion language services for Maori children (*Te Kohanga Reo*) and also for Pacific children (Pacific language nests). These are all nonprofit providers. Interestingly, however, all kindergarten staff are public sector employees working with local service providers, each of which is established either as an independent voluntary incorporated society or as a private for-profit entity. This, again, is an instance where government and nonprofits or, in some cases, for-profits, are working collaboratively within new structures designed for that purpose and erected in the usually disputed frontier between the three sectors.

V. NEW LEGAL STRUCTURES AND DONOR INCENTIVES

The introduction of incorporated societies was well ahead of its time, but now the legislation governing legal structures for charities seems very dated. The need to rely upon such charitable forms as the trust and the unincorporated association in the highly professional, flexible, and competitive modern marketplace can inhibit charities from taking advantage of opportunities for cross-sectoral collaboration and competition. In jurisdictions such as New Zealand, where some indigenous people live with their extended family in closed communities and suffer embedded deprivation, these restrictions may be particularly obstructive. The charity law reform process was a missed opportunity to introduce new legal structures for charity. However, the Law Commission is currently undertaking a program, *Review of the Law of Trusts*,[73] which will in time lead to a revision of the Charitable Trusts Act 1957. Moreover, a recent Law Commission *Issues Paper* invites comment on a review of a range of trust matters that focus primarily on ways to make it easier for beneficiaries to hold trustees accountable,[74] and the Charities Act 2005 is due for review in 2015 when the findings of the Incorporated Societies Act 1908 review should also be available.

[73] See The Law Commission at www.lawcom.govt.nz.

[74] See Law Commission, *Court Jurisdiction, Trading Trusts and Other Issues: Review of the Law of Trusts—Fifth Issues Paper*, December 2011. See further, http://business.scoop.co.nz/2011/12/19/law-commission-releases-fifth-issues-paper-on-trusts.

A. Public Benefit Service Providers

The Treaty of Waitangi[75] has provided the legal framework and a body of principles to guide and benchmark the development of formal government/Maori relationships. This process eventually broadened to accommodate contractual relationships between government and Pacific peoples[76] and prepared the way for government initiatives in the late 1990s that placed an emphasis on ways in which "community–government partnerships . . . help create social capital and social cohesion."[77]

1. Public Health Organizations

These organizations are a good example of innovatory legal structures, designed by government to facilitate cross-sectoral delivery of public benefit services. They are treated as part of the nonprofit sector because of their self-governing character. However, they are a key component of the state's primary health care strategy and are responsible for the disbursement of significant amounts of state funding of health services. Arguably they function as agencies of government being controlled by the latter's policy and funding arrangements.[78]

2. Children's Services

Some children's services, notably kindergartens, are interesting hybrids: Established by government, which provides their funding and staff, they are formally separate from government and have significant functional autonomy, but are nonetheless designed to give effect to government strategic policy. In some instances, organizations may switch between the state and nonprofit sectors over time. Children's Health Camps are such uncertain legal entities that operate as semiautonomous nonprofits closely aligned to government, which provides almost all their funding.

[75] Signed on February 6, 1840 by representatives of the British Crown, and Maori chiefs from North Island at Waitangi on the Bay of Islands in New Zealand, and eventually consolidated by the Treaty of Waitangi Act 1975.

[76] See further Sanders et al., *The New Zealand Non-Profit Sector in Comparative Perspective*, at p. 39.

[77] Ministry of Social Policy, *Models of Community-Government Partnerships and Their Effectiveness in Achieving Welfare Goals: A Review of the Literature*, Ministry of Social Policy, Wellington, 2000, at p.7.

[78] See Tennant et al., *Defining the Nonprofit Sector*, at p. 36. Note also Reid, M., "Community Councils and Public Sector Reform—A Case of Conflicting Signals," paper delivered at ANZTSR Conference, Victoria University, Wellington, 1996, in which he comments that changes to the arts sector in the 1990s blurred the distinction between the nonprofit and commercial sectors.

B. Community Trusts

Community trusts are an example of organizations that sit at the boundary between the nonprofit and statutory sectors in terms of self-governance. They were established in the 1980s, following the privatization of the community-owned regional banks across the country. Constituted by statute with their members appointed by government, they are nevertheless responsible for their own activities, including allocation of grants, and can initiate a change in their trust deed, even though the Minister of Finance makes the final decision on the content of these documents. Many larger, older, and wealthier organizations, including most major churches, have been established under their own statute, as was the case with the Royal New Zealand Foundation of the Blind. However, although they control their own operational activities, they can only change their purpose or dissolve with government permission.

Organizations can migrate over time between state control and self-governance, and at different points in a nation's history some organizations will be considered in or out of the sector, but their core purposes will not have undergone much change. Water Safety New Zealand Inc, for example, was initially called the Water Safety Council and was part of a government department. Over time it was separated out and provided with a government grant, which in due course was cut, with the responsibility of funding ultimately falling on the New Zealand Lottery Grants Board.

C. Social Enterprises

As Grant observed in 2008, "Social enterprise in New Zealand is still in its infancy, with no recognised framework to inform knowledge of current or future developments."[79] Corporate foundations and various other means of giving effect to corporate social responsibility, which may be viewed as forms of social enterprise, have yet to attain any significant scale in this jurisdiction.

1. Donor Incentives

Donor incentive schemes are fairly conservative. Since 2008 the changes made to the New Zealand Income Tax Act 2007 enable individuals to donate without limit to their charity of choice and receive one-third of the total amount as a tax credit for that tax year and to receive the same 33.33 percent tax credit through payroll giving. Companies can deduct the total amount of donations made from their yearly taxable income, as long as this is not more than the company's net income. In December 2010, the Revenue Minister Peter Dunne endorsed recommendations by the Cultural Philanthropy Taskforce on changes to the tax rules, including that

[79] Grant, S., "Contextualising Social Enterprise in New Zealand," in *Social Enterprise Journal*, Vol. 4, No. 1, 2008, at pp. 9–23.

with gift aid the benefit of charitable donations should go directly to the charitable organization rather than the donor; an important policy change indicating a clear government preference for prioritizing altruism over tax offsets.

VI. CHARITIES, TRADING, AND CONTEMPORARY CASE LAW

Although nonprofits in general continue to be governed by the provisions of the Incorporated Societies Act 1908 and the Charitable Trusts Act 1957, charities are now specifically made subject to the Charities Act 2005 and to the regulatory regime applied by the Charities Commission. In addition, the Inland Revenue Department continues to have some regulatory responsibilities alongside those of the Commission, whereas other bodies such as the Companies Office may also exercise powers of intervention.

A. Legal Framework

The Charities Act 2005 provides, together with the Income Tax Act 2007, a new legislative framework for charities (in conjunction with the Incorporated Societies Act 1908 and the Charitable Trusts Act 1957), but no legislative steps have been taken to broaden the traditional *Pemsel* list of charitable purposes or to alter the public benefit presumption, although New Zealand's Charities Commission has stated that:[80]

> all charities must have public benefit. When we look at that, we look at, firstly, whether there is a benefit, which means that we will also look at whether there are harms that are caused; and, secondly, we look at the extent to which the charity is accessible to the public.

Moreover, the tax legislation sets out the criteria for tax credit granted to individuals who donate money for public benefit purposes, and applies to a broad sweep of nonprofit activity: the Income Tax Act 2007, s.LD3, extends to "charitable, benevolent, philanthropic or cultural purposes."

Unlike the United States, Canada, or Australia,[81] this jurisdiction has now placed the key common law concepts onto the statute books, thereby, in keeping with the U.K. and Irish jurisdictions, giving the legislature the future capacity to amend and extend the *Pemsel* list and adjust the public benefit rules. The traditional interpretation of "charity," "charitable purpose," and "public benefit," together with

[80] Mr Trevor Garrett, Chief Executive, Charities Commission New Zealand, Committee Hansard, June 28, 2010, at p. 25. As cited in the Economics Legislation Committee, *Tax Laws Amendment (Public Benefit Test) Bill 2010 Report*, Canberra, 2010, at p. 18.

[81] The Extension of Charitable Purpose Act 2004 did, however, designate child care, self-help groups, and closed/contemplative religious orders as charitable.

accompanying common law rules, are as before, whereas the Charitable Trust Act 1957 continues to define the content of charitable trusts, regulates their creation and administration and, under s.61B, allows a trust with a mix of charitable and non-charitable or invalid purposes to be "saved" by permitting it to be interpreted as though the non-charitable or invalid purposes did not apply.[82] A charitable trust exists where trustees administer property, including cash, that has been given or bequeathed to the trust, and must use it for the benefit of a registered charity.

1. Regulatory Bodies

The Charities Commission, the New Zealand charities regulator, was established by the Charities Act 2005 as an Autonomous Crown Entity—and as such was required to have regard for government policy when so directed by the responsible minister. Currently its role includes: registering charities, providing education in relation to good governance, collecting annual returns, maintaining a public register, and inquiring into any misconduct. Registering with the Commission is voluntary: A charity that chooses not to register can still call itself a charity and solicit funds from the public. It may also be eligible for IRD (Inland Revenue Department) approval regarding tax concessions in the form of tax credits to donors. In many cases, these organizations also have to comply with other legal requirements relating to the rules of a body to which they are affiliated, as will be the case if they are registered under the Incorporated Societies Act 1908, the Charitable Trusts Act 1957, or the Companies Act 1993.

The Inland Revenue administers charitable tax exemptions under the terms of the Income Tax Act 2007 and is empowered, by s.91E(1) of the Tax Administration Act 1994, to issue binding rulings in that regard, unless one of the statutory exceptions applies. Donee status is awarded by the Inland Revenue to organizations established within New Zealand, the funds of which are wholly or principally applied to charitable, benevolent, philanthropic, or cultural purposes within the jurisdiction; many of the major overseas aid and development nonprofits are specifically exempted from the latter restriction. Obtaining such status is not dependent upon organizations being registered with the Commission; individuals can claim a tax rebate for a donation they make to such an organization, and societies for the promotion of an amateur game or sport are usually ineligible, unless their activity falls under one of the four heads of charity, such as the advancement of education.[83]

Eligibility for income tax exemption is a matter for the Inland Revenue not the Charities Commission but, generally, registration by the Commission is accepted

[82] The courts will require evidence of a substantial charitable content or character for s.61B to apply: see Re Beckbessinger [1993] 2 NZLR 362 and Re Ashton [1955] NZLR 192 (CA).

[83] The issue of amateur sport is the subject of the Statutes Amendment Bill (No 2) 271–72 (2011). This clarifies that amateur sport, which in itself not charitable, "may be charitable when it is the means to achieve one of the traditional four heads of charity, as set out in section 5(1) of the Charities Act 2005."

by Inland Revenue so that registration will, in most cases, lead to tax exemption.[84] However, it has been pointed out[85] that a ruling by the Inland Revenue that a society or institution is established and maintained exclusively for charitable purposes, for the purposes of section CW 41 of the Income Tax Act, is legally binding on the Commission (see section 13(2)(a) and (3) of the Charities Act). This is the opposite of the equivalent position in the U.K.

2. Charity Law

The Charities Act 2005 incorporated the established common law governing charities into legislation. The four *Pemsel* "heads of charity," together with the accompanying common law rules and concepts (which require, for example, that an organization be established and maintained exclusively for charitable purposes,[86] be for the public benefit, and that no private profits accrue to any individual), were placed onto the statute book, but otherwise no alteration was made to the long-established substance of the law.[87] The public benefit presumption prevails in regard to the first three *Pemsel* heads but "the question whether a gift is or may be operative for the public benefit is a question to be answered by the Court by forming an opinion on the evidence before it"[88] whereas it must be expressly proven in respect of the fourth.[89]

3. Activities Test

Pursuant to s.50(2) of the 2005 Act, the Commission may examine the activities and proposed activities of the charitable entity, the nature, objects, and purposes of the charitable entity, and the results and outcomes achieved by the charitable entity. Section 18(3)(a), more specifically, requires the Commission when considering charitable status to have regard for: the activities of the entity at the time the application was made, and the proposed activities of the entity. Where an entity's governing

[84] See further at: http://charities.govt.nz/.

[85] See Barker, S. and Yesberg, K, "Charities Act Review," *NZLawyer Online*, Chen Palmer, Wellington, April 8, 2011, at http://nzlawyermagazine.co.nz/Archives/Issue157/157F1/tabid/3167/Default.aspx.

[86] See MK Hunt Foundation Ltd v. Commissioner of Inland Revenue [1961] NZLR 405 where the presence of non-charitable objects was fatal to a claim for charitable status. See also Auckland Medical Aid Trust v. Commissioner of Inland Revenue [1979] 1 NZLR 382 and New Zealand Society of Accountants v. Commissioner of Inland Revenue [1986] 1 NZLR 147 at p. 157 per Somers J.

[87] Note, however, that clause 7 of the Statutes Amendment Bill (No 2), introduced on February 22, 2011, proposes to amend the definition of "charitable purpose" in the Charities Act to include an entity that promotes sport, if the purpose is "expressed to be, and is in fact, the means by which a charitable purpose (such as the promotion of health or education) will be achieved."

[88] Molloy v. Commissioner of Inland Revenue [1981] 1 NZLR 688 at p. 695.

[89] Canterbury Development Corporation v. Charities Commission [2010] 2 NZLR 707.

instruments do not identify its main object(s) with sufficient clarity, case law indicates that the objects are to be assessed in tandem with the entity's activities.

In New Zealand, both judiciary and regulators have upheld the relevance of an activities test as illustrated, for example, by the decision in *Hester v. Commissioner of Inland Revenue.*[90] This was an approach earlier adopted by Tipping J., who stated that "[i]n so far as there may be uncertainty on an examination of the relevant document or documents it is permissible to look and see what the body actually does or has been doing."[91]

The High Court in *Canterbury Development Corporation v. Charities Commission*[92] would seem to have relied on s.18(3)(a) in deciding based on an analysis of its activities that the Corporation was not charitable.

B. Charity Trading, the Law, and Tax

In its 2001 policy document *Tax and Charities,*[93] the government took the view that trading charities' competitive advantage arises "only from the ability to grow a business faster by accumulating pre-tax funds," and suggested that trading operations owned by charities should be subject to tax in the same way as other businesses, but with an unlimited deduction for distributions made to the relevant charitable purposes. In the decade that followed, trading operations owned by charities have not been made subject to income tax, although an amendment was made to section DB 41 of the Income Tax Act in 2007 allowing companies an unlimited deduction for donations made to charitable entities (capped at the level of their taxable income).[94] In this jurisdiction it remains the case that income derived directly or indirectly from a business will only be tax-exempt if it was derived "by or on behalf of or for the benefit of trustees in trust for charitable purposes within New Zealand, or derived directly or indirectly from any business carried on by or on behalf of or for the benefit of any society or institution established exclusively for such purposes and not carried on for the private pecuniary profit of any individual." If the purposes are not limited to New Zealand, the Commissioner may apportion the income between those purposes within New Zealand and those outside, and allow a partial exemption.

[90] [2005] 2 NZLR 172, which suggests a nexus based on the "natural and probable consequences" of activities. See also the Charities Commission registration decision in re the *New Zealand Computer Society* (March 18, 2010).

[91] Institute of Professional Engineers New Zealand Inc v. Commissioner of Inland Revenue [1992] 1 NZLR 570 at p. 573.

[92] [2010] 2 NZLR 707.

[93] See Inland Revenue Department, Policy Advice Division, *Tax and Charities*, Wellington, 2001.

[94] See further Barker and Yesberg, "Charities Act Review," at http://nzlawyermagazine.co.nz/Archives/Issue157/157F1/tabid/3167/Default.aspx.

1. Charity Trading

In the Charities Act 2005, sections 5(3) and (4) provide that an entity with non-charitable secondary purposes, undertaken in support of a main charitable purpose, will be allowed to register with the Commission. This provision essentially restates the common law rule that charities may trade where this is ancillary to and in furtherance of their exclusively charitable purposes, and no profits accrue to private individuals.

2. Charity Trading and Tax

Certain types of income of charitable and other tax-exempt entities are exempt from income tax. This exemption includes nonbusiness income derived by a trust, society, or institution established exclusively for charitable purposes, and business income derived by such a charitable body, subject to certain exceptions. Since July 1, 2008, charities are required by the 2005 Act to be registered with the Charities Commission in order to be eligible for the charitable income tax exemption under sections CW 41 and CW 42 of the Income Tax Act 2007. Exemption from business income tax requires a charity to provide the Department of Inland Revenue with evidence, in the form of restrictions in its governing instruments, that its business income may only be applied within the jurisdiction of New Zealand. Other nonprofits, such as clubs and societies for the promotion of any amateur game, sport, arts, cultural, and other recreational organizations, may qualify for limited exemptions from income tax as also may some Maori organizations under the provisions of the Taxation (Maori Organizations, Taxpayer Compliance, and Miscellaneous Provisions) Act 2003.[95] Incorporated societies, charitable trusts, and companies that do not qualify for any of the above concessions generally pay a tax rate of 33 percent whereas unincorporated organizations, similarly unqualified, usually pay tax at the rate set for individual taxpayers. The 2007 Budget that took effect in April 2008 altered rebates on donations to charitable organizations to enable donors to claim a 33.3 percent tax rebate for all donations to eligible organizations up to the level of their annual income. This effectively moved New Zealand from one of the least-generous rates of tax support among OECD countries to one of the highest.[96]

C. Charity Trading: The Case Law in a Public Services Context

The case law is heavily concentrated in the areas of health and social care, community development, and to some extent in education, with the issues tending to focus on traditional matters associated with the balance between public and private benefit.

[95] The Charities Act 2005 amended the common law rules to allow Maori organizations, which would otherwise be debarred from charitable status due to their blood ties, to be registered and thus be eligible for tax exemption.

[96] See further Tennant et al., *Defining the Nonprofit Sector*, at p. 22.

1. Health and Social Care Provision

In *Auckland Medical Aid Trust v. Commissioner of Inland Revenue*,[97] the court found that medical services per se were charitable. It therefore followed that the provision of "a comprehensive health and welfare service related to the human reproductive process and its control" was a charitable purpose; that the contraception, sterilization, and abortion services provided by the plaintiffs were charitable; and that the income derived from such service provision was entitled to charitable exemption from tax. This presumptive approach was later endorsed by Thomas J in *Commissioner of Inland Revenue v. Medical Council of New Zealand*[98] when he noted that a purpose that is beneficial to the public is prima facie charitable unless good reason is put forward for holding that it is not. The majority were then of the view that objects beneficial to the public or of public utility are presumed to be within the spirit and intendment of the preamble to the Statute of Elizabeth in the absence of any ground for holding otherwise. In *Re Bingham*,[99] for example, it was held that a gift for the care of aged women was for the relief of poverty and therefore charitable.

Where an organization, or a gift to it, becomes compromised by an overt political purpose, the intended promotion of a form of health provision may fail. In *Molloy v. Commissioner of Inland Revenue*,[100] for example, the Society for the Protection of the Unborn Child was denied charitable status, as its main object was to preserve the current law on the subject, which fatally compromised its charitable purpose. Similarly, in *Knowles v. Commissioner of Stamp Duties*[101] an organization ostensibly established to promote temperance in alcoholic consumption was determined to be non-charitable on the grounds that its main purpose was in fact to effect changes in the law.

2. Education

As noted in *Re Education New Zealand Trust*,[102] "the authorities suggest that any meaningful connection with the provision of education is likely to qualify a purpose as being for the advancement of education." The broad view generally taken by the New Zealand courts and regulators as to what qualifies as an educational purpose has excluded only those organizations or gifts to them that breached basic standards. In *Re Collier*,[103] for example, which concerned a bequest for the publication of a book, the court concluded that the purpose of advancing education could

[97] [1979] 1 NZLR 382.

[98] [1997] 2 NZLR 297 at p. 318.

[99] [1951] NZLR 491.

[100] [1981] 1NZLR 688.

[101] [1945] NZLR 522.

[102] HC, Wellington, CIV-2009-485-2301 (June 29, 2010), at para. 22.

[103] [1998] 1 NZLR 81. Following *Re Elmore* when the testator's manuscripts were held to be literally of no merit or educational value. See also Re Education NZ Trust HC, Wellington CIV-2009-485-2301 (June 29, 2010).

not include promoting a particular point of view. As was then explained, "[t]here is no educative value, or public utility in the 'book.' Further, it is no more than an attempt to perpetuate a private view held by Mrs Collier."[104]

In *Re Draco Foundation (NZ) Charitable Trust v. Charities Commission*,[105] the court upheld the decision of the Charities Commission[106] that the Trust did not have substantially charitable purposes. Justice Ronald Young held that material published by Draco on two websites was neither for the advancement of education nor for any other purpose beneficial to society. There was no evidence of educational or training material beyond that on the websites. Further, Draco was not exclusively charitable: Its partisan material was non-charitable, and the non-charitable purposes in its trust deed were not ancillary to any charitable purpose.

That said, the absence of education-related charity case law indicates more a general lack of contention rather than any lack of activity by charities and other nonprofits. Such entities are well established in education and research in New Zealand: From preschool to tertiary level, this is a field in which the presence of charities and other nonprofits has long been accepted, and where the market has become accustomed to the structural role of these organizations in service provision.

3. Community Development

The New Zealand courts have had little difficulty in finding a trust for the benefit of the residents of a defined area[107] and the economic development of a disadvantaged community to be charitable under the fourth *Pemsel* head.[108] They have also found the beautification[109] and preservation[110] of a locality, the maintenance of public parks and gardens,[111] the improvement of public safety, and the maintenance of public buildings and facilities[112] to be charitable. Even where the gift is to a defined locality, with no specified purpose, this has been construed as charitable on the basis that it was considered to be for the benefit of the inhabitants.[113] Where, however, the purpose is to generate economic benefits, but there is no evidence that the community in question is disadvantaged, this can fatally compromise a claim that the purpose is charitable.

104 Re Collier, [1998] 1 NZLR 81, at p. 92.

105 CIV-2010-485-1275 HC, Wellington (February 15, 2011).

106 See the Charities Commission registration decision in re the *Draco Foundation (NZ) Charitable Trust* (June 11, 2010).

107 Re Carter (deceased) (1897) 16 NZLR 431 (CA).

108 See, e.g., Re Tennant [1996] 2 NZLR 633 and Tasmanian Electronic Commerce Centre Pty Ltd v. Commissioner of Taxation (2005) FC A 439.

109 Re Pleasants (1923) 39 TLR 675.

110 Re Centrepoint Community Growth Trust [2000] 2 NZLR 325.

111 Morgan v. Wellington City Corporation [1975] 1 NZLR 416 and Re Bruce [1918] NZLR 16.

112 Re Chapman (High Court, Napier, CP89/87, October 17, 1989).

113 Lysons v. Commissioner of Stamp Duties [1945] NZLR 738.

This was evident in *North Canterbury Economic Development Trust,*[114] when the Commission deregistered the trust, which had pursued its objective of supporting local businesses in a manner judged to be compatible with charitable status for the previous 25 years. As Ronald Young J. explained in dismissing an appeal lodged by the trust, such activity "does not establish [Canterbury Development Corporation] as having the necessary focus on charitable intent."[115] The court concluded that none of Trust's activities were directly focused on the relief of poverty; its educational activities were not aimed at a sufficiently broad section of the public to be charitable; its central focus was on assisting individual businesses and the economy in general; and the hope that improvements in employment might follow from this was not the direct aim, and was too remote a hope to make the trust charitable.[116] The fact that for 25 years the Canterbury Development Trust had been receiving local authority funds for use, with a mix of its own resources and public donations, in generating the development of viable self-sustaining social infrastructure, albeit one that also benefited local private businesses, would seem to have been discounted, despite the existence, presumably, of a substantial body of evidence that had previously been sufficient to prove its effectiveness.

The Commission would now seem to have taken a position, endorsed by New Zealand courts, that places the onus on the applicants to prove public benefit, evidenced by the provision of essential services and/or the alleviation of actual social disadvantage, as benchmarked by the decisions in *Re Tennant*[117] and *Tasmanian Electronic Commerce Centre Pty Limited v. Commissioner of Taxation.*[118] This is reinforced by the following advice issued by the Commission:[119]

> Community and economic development organisations are most likely to be considered in terms of the categories of charitable purpose for relief of poverty, (for example, if they provide financial assistance or housing for those in need),

[114] See Charities Commission decision in *re North Canterbury Economic Development Trust* (November 13, 2007).

[115] Canterbury Development Corporation v. Charities Commission [2010] 2 NZLR 707 per Ronald Young J. at [44].

[116] See further Gousmett, M., "Charity and Economic Development," in *New Zealand Law Journal*, March 2011, pp. 63–68, where he contrasts the commission's approach in this case with that adopted in relation to the Pacific Business Trust, which retains its charitable status despite the fact that access is restricted to persons of certain ethnicity. A non-Maori person of European decent, for example, would be prohibited from support by the PBT.

[117] [1996] 2 NZLR 633. A decision that, apparently, is to be restricted to "providing essential services for rural, remote, or disadvantaged communities."

[118] [2005] FCA 439. A decision that supported the proposition that the development of a community is charitable where that development provides "essential services for rural, remote, or disadvantaged communities."

[119] See The Charities Commission, "Charitable Purpose and Community and Economic Development," October 2009, http://www.charities.govt.nz/news/information-sheets/charitable-purpose-community-and-economic-development.

> advancement of education (for example, if they provide training or skills development for the public), or other purposes beneficial to the community (for example, if they provide public works and services or public amenities and recreational facilities).

It has been pointed out[120] that such a defensive retreat to traditional grounds of clearly identified social need coupled with the resulting necessity to provide essential services indicates a very conservative if not minimalist approach to the social challenge of stimulating economic uplift in deprived communities.

D. Charity Trading: The Case Law in a Commercial Context

There is little by way of hard case law support to indicate that charities in New Zealand are, as yet, embarking on commercialization as a means of substituting for the depletion of other sources of revenue on anything like the scale, or with the adventurism, of their counterparts elsewhere, particularly those in the United States, U.K., and increasingly in Australia. Such case law as there is, largely emanating from recent Commission rulings, tends to lean toward an orthodox defense of well-established common law principles. This conservative approach dates at least from the Court of Appeal decision 60 years ago in *Commissioner of Inland Revenue v. Carey's (Petone and Miramar) Limited*,[121] which provides authority for the proposition that conducting business activity—not in itself charitable—does not disqualify an otherwise charitable trust from characterization as charitable. His Honour Gresson P. then stated that he could not discern a justification in point of principle for reaching a different conclusion in the case of a "free-standing company which is bound, by its memorandum, to apply its profits to charitable purposes, and in fact does so."

1. Subsidiary and Incidental

Ancillary purposes that are not charitable do not prevent registration as a charitable entity so long as they are not an independent purpose of the entity. The Charities Act 2005, s.5(3), "provides that any non-charitable purpose must be ancillary to a charitable purpose," further:

> (3) To avoid doubt, if the purposes of a trust, society, or an institution include a non-charitable purpose (for example, advocacy) that is merely ancillary to a charitable purpose of the trust, society, or institution, the presence of that non-charitable

[120] See Dadelszen, M., "Economic Development—charitable?," *NZLawyer Online*, May 7, 2011, at http://www.nzlawyermagazine.co.nz/Archives/Issue156/156F3/tabid/3129/Default.aspx.
[121] [1963] NZLR 450.

purpose does not prevent the trustees of the trust, the society, or the institution from qualifying for registration as a charitable entity.

(4) For the purposes of subsection (3), a non-charitable purpose is ancillary to a charitable purpose of the trust, society, or institution if the non-charitable purpose is
   (a) ancillary, secondary, subordinate, or incidental to a charitable purpose of the trust, society, or institution; and
   (b) not an independent purpose of the trust, society, or institution.

So, where there is a mix of purposes, some charitable and others not, then the above provisions require an assessment of whether the non-charitable purpose is more than ancillary in the sense of being more than secondary, subordinate, or incidental to, and not itself an independent purpose. This, in effect, is a statutory restating of the common law rule. These 2005 provisions must be read alongside those in s.61B of the Charitable Trusts Act 1957, which have been held to apply in two situations where a trust purporting to be charitable is imperfect in the sense that there are, either as a matter of interpretation of the express purposes of the trust, or by analysis of activities undertaken, a mixture of charitable and non-charitable purposes. The section then introduces the prospect of "blue pencilling out" (excising) those parts of a trust's purposes that are non-charitable.[122]

In *Re Education New Zealand Trust*[123] (see below), Dobson J. gave some attention to disaggregating charitable and non-charitable purposes and weighing their relative importance. It was "abundantly" clear, in his view, that although the trust was engaged in the generic promotion of educational opportunities in New Zealand for foreign potential students, it was generating interest with those prepared to sign on with various of the for-profit New Zealand institutions that constituted an important aspect of its work and was a substantial purpose of the trust. He was satisfied that the relative importance of this must reduce the remaining aspect of the purposes of the trust, namely promotion for nonprofit institutions, to less than a substantially charitable purpose that would be required to trigger the jurisdiction of s.61B. His closing remarks, having dismissed the appeal, will ring true for the many practitioners in other developed common law nations who are constantly having to deal with much the same issues and their consequences:

> With respect, it ought not to be beyond the wit of legal and accounting advisers to design bifurcated arrangements for generic promotion involving some form of joint venture between a validly charitable trust for those parts of the sector that are not-for-profit, and discrete contributions from the for-profit sector, to be presented in a unified form externally.

[122] See Re Beckbessinger [1993] 2 NZLR 362 and Re Ashton [1955] NZLR 192.

[123] HC, Wellington, CIV-2009-485-2301 (June 29, 2010).

In *Commissioner of Inland Revenue v. New Zealand Council of Law Reporting*,[124] the Court of Appeal confirmed that the New Zealand Council of Law Reporting has an exclusively charitable purpose in publishing and selling law reports. Although essentially not profit-making, the terms of the 1938 statute establishing the Council of Law Reporting provided, in s.14, for the prospect of grants to the New Zealand Law Society or any district law society. The prospect of such payments was held not to disqualify the Council from enjoying charitable status because that was merely incidental.

The New Zealand judiciary would seem more recently to hold the view that the question of whether a purpose is ancillary requires both a qualitative and a quantitative analysis[125] and a "situation-specific analysis of the relative relationship between public and private benefits."[126]

2. Private Benefit

The courts and regulators in New Zealand have often determined that professional bodies are not charitable as they tend to have as a primary purpose the protection and advancement of their members' interests.[127] This approach was illustrated by the Charities Commission decision in respect of the registration application submitted by the *New Zealand Society of Diversional Therapists Incorporated*.[128] The Commissioners then concluded, in terms equally applicable to several previous cases, that "the private benefits to the members cannot be viewed as the unsought consequences of the pursuit of public purposes and cannot be disregarded as incidental or ancillary." Similarly, and more recently, in *New Zealand Computer Society*,[129] the Commission took the view, following an audit of the Society's activities, that its main purposes were to promote the interests of the Society, its members, and the industry rather than providing protection to the public, and that many of its member benefit activities constituted separate and independent purposes that could not be considered as ancillary to any charitable purpose. Its decision to de-register the Society was upheld on appeal to the High

124 [1981] 1 NZLR 682.

125 Re The Grand Lodge of Antient Free and Accepted Masons in New Zealand, HC, Wellington, CIV-2009-485-2633 (September 23, 2010), per France J. at [49]–[52] and Re Draco Foundation (NZ) Charitable Trust, HC, Wellington CIV-2010-485-1275 (February 2, 2011), per Ronald Young J. at [14].

126 Re Education NZ Trust, HC, Wellington CIV-2009-485-2301 (June 29, 2010), per Dobson J. at [44].

127 See Re Mason [1971] NZLR 714, 721; New Zealand Society of Accountants v. Commissioner of Inland Revenue [1986] 1 NZLR 147; Institute of Professional Engineers New Zealand Inc v. Commissioner of Inland Revenue [1992] 1 NZLR 570; Commissioner of Inland Revenue v. Medical Council of New Zealand [1997] 2 NZLR 297.

128 See Charities Commission decision in *re New Zealand Society of Diversional Therapists Incorporated* (December 9, 2008).

129 See the Charities Commission registration decision in re the *New Zealand Computer Society* (March 18, 2010).

Court.[130] In these and other cases, the Commission has stated its view that advancing professional proficiency is not a charitable purpose.

However, in the leading case of *Commissioner of Inland Revenue v. Medical Council of New Zealand,*[131] the Court of Appeal overturned the Commission decision not to register the Council on the grounds that the principal function of the Council was to register medical practitioners; any benefits accruing to members were incidental, and did not prevent the Council from being an institution established exclusively for charitable purposes.

Private benefit as a determinant of charitable status was evident in *Presbyterian Church of New Zealand Beneficiary Fund v. Commissioner of Inland Revenue,*[132] when a superannuation scheme for retired ministers of the Presbyterian Church was accepted as a charity. Although recognizing the financial benefits to be provided to particular persons—the ministers—the court viewed them as incidental to the advancement of religion. The importance of the ministry to the Church and the lifelong commitment were particular features influencing the decision. However, in *Hester v. Commissioner of Inland Revenue,*[133] the Deseret Benefit Plan of the Church of Jesus Christ of Latter-Day Saints was not accepted as a charity. It covered employees of two of the Church's entities, employed in administration and education. The court distinguished the circumstances from those in the *Presbyterian Beneficiary Fund* case, in which the plan covered employees generally, whose roles were more transferable to other employment, and whose employment activities were not "essential" to the operation of the Church. The court said *Presbyterian Beneficiary Fund* was an exceptional case, and did not stand for the proposition that any church-controlled superannuation scheme for its employees would be a charity.

Again, private benefit proved to be the critical element in an application for charitable status from the *Korako Karetai Trust*.[134] The Commission then found that several of the trust's purposes did not fall under any of the charitable purposes in s.5 of the Charities Act 2005. Its main purposes appeared to be restrictive and private in nature: advocating for the return of land to the descendants of Korako Karetai, engaging in commercial tourism ventures for the benefit of the descendants of Korako Karetai, and providing other benefits for those descendants.

In *Liberty Trust v. Charities Commission*[135] the High Court considered an appeal by the trust against the Charities Commission's ruling that the trust's lending scheme essentially provided private benefits for its members, and therefore the trust was not exclusively for charitable purposes. Liberty Trust submitted that its lending

130 The New Zealand Computer Society Inc v. Charities Commission, CIV-2010-485-924 HC, Wellington (February 28, 2011).

131 Commissioner of Inland Revenue v. Medical Council of New Zealand [1997] 2 NZLR 297.

132 [1994] 3 NZLR 363.

133 (2004) 21 NZTC 18,421.

134 See the Charities Commission registration decision in re the *Korako Karetai Trust* (September 23, 2010).

135 HC WN CIV 2010-485-000831 [June 2, 2011].

scheme advanced religion by teaching, through action, financial principles derived from the Bible. The Charities Commission had taken the view that teaching financial principles derived from the Bible was at best conducive to religion but did not advance religion. The High Court allowed the appeal, explaining that for a trust that has as its purpose the advancement of religion, the starting assumption is that it has a public benefit. The activities were not contended to be subversive to morality or a sham. It was not for the court to impose its own views as to the religious beliefs that are advanced through the scheme. The benefits of the scheme were not focused too narrowly on its adherents. It was open to anyone, and the money donated was "recycled" for the benefit of others. Overall it was a scheme about "giving" in order to lead a Christian life, free of the burdens of debt.

3. Public Benefit

A trust or institution must be for the public benefit to be charitable.[136] As Gallen J. put it in the *Educational Fees* case, when evaluating the presence of the requisite public benefit, the question to be addressed was whether the Society was "substantially altruistic in character."[137] A response from Dobson J., in *Re Education New Zealand Trust*, suggests:[138]

> As to whether it is a purpose that is substantially altruistic in character, the answer depends on whether the providers of the services being promoted are undertaking them with a view to making a profit in a commercial context, or are not-for-profit institutions providing such courses as an aspect of discharge of the state's responsibility for educational services.

In *Re Tennant*,[139] the New Zealand judiciary demonstrated a capacity and willingness to broaden the law relating to activities deemed to be for the public benefit as the provision of a creamery to assist a small new rural community to become economically viable was found to be charitable. Later, the basic rule that a charitable purpose must be for the public benefit (which some would argue, at least in relation to the continuing presumption in respect of the first three *Pemsel* heads, is

[136] See Rickett, C., "A Statutory Charitable Trust," in *New Zealand Law Journal*, March 2000, pp. 59–61, which examines the statutory transformation of the New Zealand Railways Staff Welfare Society into the New Zealand Railways Staff Welfare Charitable Trust, notwithstanding its member benefit purpose.

[137] Educational Fees Protection Society Inc v. Commissioner of Inland Revenue [1992] 2 NZLR 115, at p. 125.

[138] HC, Wellington, CIV-2009-485-2301 (June 29, 2010) at para. 40.

[139] [1996] 2 NZLR 633. Following the precedent established in Crystal Palace Trustees v. Minister of Town and Country Planning [1951] Ch 132; [1950] 2 All ER 857, which concluded that the promotion of industry and commerce for the public benefit was charitable.

axiomatic[140]), received pointed endorsement in *Latimer v. Commissioner of Inland Revenue*[141] (the "Crown Forestry") case. In recent years, the judiciary and regulators would seem to have abandoned earlier developmental tendencies for a much more conservative approach.

In refusing charitable status to the *Canterbury Economic Development Trust*,[142] the Commission stressed that it was essential to show that public benefit would necessarily flow from each of the stated purposes; it was insufficient to merely state a belief that it would or may do so.[143] On appeal to the High Court[144] this view was upheld. In the course of the hearing the court placed considerable significance on the decisions made in *Tasmanian Electronic Commerce Centre*[145] and *Re Tennant*[146] as both cases held that a needs assessment should be made, identifying the disadvantage to be addressed, before any proposed economic development could be considered charitable.

In *Travis Trust v. Charities Commission*,[147] the first of many unsuccessful challenges to Commission decisions, the High Court upheld the Commission's decision to refuse to register the trust as a charitable entity, stating that, as its membership was not open to the public generally, the club was not "the community"—or a sufficient section of it—to amount to "the public" as was required to satisfy the public benefit test.

a. Re Education New Zealand Trust[148]

This case is particularly interesting as it illustrates the complexities of contemporary cross-sectoral fiscal arrangements in tertiary education that are generating the same type of charity law issues in all modern common law nations. It concerned a company initially incorporated as a subsidiary of the New Zealand Trade Development Board called New Zealand Education International Limited, in order to lead efforts to promote New Zealand as a study destination for foreign students. Membership was open to organizations that represented a significant number of providers of education and/or training in New Zealand. In 1998, it was perceived that another form of organization might better undertake the promotional activities, and a charitable trust was formed to continue the work that had been started by New Zealand Education International Limited. This trust received substantial grants from the

[140] See Luxton, P., *Making Law? Parliament v. The Charity Commission*, Politea, London, 2009.

[141] [2002] 3 NZLR 195.

[142] See Charities Commission, Registration Decision: North Canterbury Economic Development Trust (18.12.09), when the Trust's application for charitable status was rejected.

[143] See also DV Bryant Trust Board v. Hamilton City Council [1973] 3 NZLR 342.

[144] Canterbury Development Corporation v. Charities Commission [2010] 2 NZLR 707.

[145] [2005] FCA 439.

[146] [1996] 2 NZLR 633.

[147] CIV-2008-485-1689, HC, Wellington (December 3, 2008).

[148] HC, Wellington, CIV-2009-485-2301 (June 29, 2010).

government by way of a portion of all Export Education Levies imposed on the providers of educational services to overseas students. The extent of the levies is related to the level of fees paid by overseas students: At the time of the court hearing more than 30 percent of the levies were in fact generated by for-profit education providers. Not dissimilar bodies, with comparable ties to government and academia, can now be found in most developed countries.

The Commission had been satisfied that the purpose of the trust was for the advancement of education, and that promoting international education and training in New Zealand would also qualify this objective as charitable under the heading "other matter beneficial to the community," but it was not satisfied that there was the requisite public benefit. In particular it was troubled by the extent to which the promotional work of the trust would generate income for private (for-profit) education providers, and rejected the suggestion that benefits accruing to the private sector could be regarded as a merely incidental purpose: some 70 percent of total institutions represented by the trust comprised state universities, schools, etc., and the remaining 30 percent were privately owned, for-profit schools. Although New Zealand was promoted generally, in reality promotion of the 30 percent for-profit sector was crucial to the success of the trust; it constituted a substantial, independent purpose. The Commission took the view that it was not necessary to support the private education providers in order to carry out the charitable purpose of assisting nonprofit educational institutions. Therefore, the noncharitable purpose of promoting the for-profit education providers was not ancillary to the charitable purpose of promoting the nonprofit providers.

The court, recognizing as did the Commission the central importance of establishing public benefit, rejected the argument that the students could be seen as "beneficiaries" of the trust:[149]

> The students are not identified as beneficiaries of the Trust in the formal sense, and nor are they beneficiaries in the substantive sense. The Trust does not subsidise their education and nor does it exist to advance their interests. None of the trustees governing the Trust are appointed to advance beneficiaries' interests and none of the trustees are beholden to overseas students in New Zealand. Rather, all of the trustees represent and account to the institutions appointing them. Success in the promotional activities of the Trust is measured by the number of students secured to attend New Zealand institutions, and is not marked in any way by the relative success of the students' subsequent educational experience in New Zealand.

The relationship between attainment of the trust's purposes, and the students who sign on for courses at any of the institutions in New Zealand, was essentially an arm's-length one. An analogy could be made of the trust as an industry-wide promotional group treating all of the institutions represented by the various members of the trust as "the businesses," and the potential overseas students as the "customers"

[149] HC, Wellington, CIV-2009-485-2301 (June 29, 2010).

of those member "businesses." Only in that broad sense could the purpose of the trust be seen as one for the "advancement of education."

As regards the argument that the trust's primary purpose was "to promote, encourage and develop international education and training in New Zealand for the benefit of people in New Zealand and elsewhere," this was dismissed on the grounds that the trust was not materially involved in monitoring the standards of education or training provided by the institutions it promotes. The content, and relative availability, of educational and training courses in New Zealand were matters outside the control of the trust.

In considering the public benefit component, Dobson J. interjected a caveat—familiar to all involved in tertiary education (and present also in health care and research)—to the generally accepted view that the singular feature distinguishing the provision of educational services on a for-profit basis as opposed to a nonprofit basis context is altruism. Invariably, though to an extent difficult to determine, there is also in play a cross-subsidizing effect whereby the nonprofits benefit from the market stimulation activities of the for-profit bodies. In this instance, he was satisfied that although the promotional success achieved by the trust in generating fee-paying customers for nonprofit institutions was sufficient to constitute altruism, the generic promotion of courses run by for-profit education providers was not, there being little to distinguish the motivation for and consequences of such promotion by the latter from, say, generic promotion overseas of New Zealand tourism operators.

4. Profits

The Charities Act 2005, s.13(1)(b)(ii), states that a requirement for registration as a charitable entity is that it "is not carried on for the private pecuniary profit of any individual."[150] This is not to imply that profits or private benefits are wholly impermissible: but they must be merely a means of achieving an ultimate public benefit and therefore be ancillary and incidental to it; the private benefits or profits cannot be or become an end in themselves. Where a profit is made, but this is incidental to its main purpose and does not constitute private profit, then a body's charitable status may be safe.[151]

Perhaps the most important case in this context was the convoluted saga of *Crown Forestry*,[152] which concerned a trust established jointly by the Crown and

[150] The Incorporated Societies Act 1908 has long provided that members can associate for any lawful purpose but not for pecuniary gain. This allowed a society to make profits from its activities so long as they were not divided among or received by members, and providing the society did not become a trading operation or pursue profits to the exclusion of its other objectives. The latitude thus permitted was well illustrated in *Auckland Medical Aid Trust v. Commissioner of Inland Revenue* where a trust, which derived almost all its income from providing abortions at a charge and virtually on demand, was found to be charitable.

[151] See Centrepoint Community Growth Trust v. Commissioner of Inland Revenue [1985] 1 NZLR 673.

[152] The Crown Forestry Rental Trust v. CIR [2002] 1 NZLR 535.

Maori to assist Maori claimants in the preparation, presentation, and negotiation of claims before the Waitangi Tribunal.[153] The Crown received rental income from forestry assets. The income was passed on to the trust as capital. The interest earned by the investment of the rent was to be made available to assist Maori before the Waitangi Tribunal in making claims involving land. The Court of Appeal, in a decision confirmed by the Privy Council, held that the trust was not established exclusively for charitable purposes, as one of its purposes was to receive and hold the rental proceeds, which was not a charitable purpose.

In *DV Bryant Trust Board v. Hamilton City Council*[154] the central issue concerned the lack of profit. This case involved a retirement village that charged rent for units at well-below market rates so that it was available to the elderly of moderate means, but in so doing it undermined equivalent local businesses. The court found the trust that ran the project was a substantial benefactor to the people of the Waikato region and did not confer private benefits on any person. It held the trust to be established for the relief of poverty and therefore a charity. In the *Canterbury Development*[155] case, however, the Commission held that a purpose relating to promoting and attracting new investment and encouraging existing businesses to remain in the area and grow was non-charitable, because it indicated that a primary purpose was to generate increased profits for private businesses. Similarly, the Commission took the view in the *Venture Taranki Trust*[156] case that a purpose of promoting the interests of current and future business owners and commercial tourist operators in the Taranki region would be primarily aimed at providing private benefits.

a. Fees

A charity can levy fees provided that the proceeds go to charity.[157] In Educational Fees Protection Society Inc v. Commissioner of Inland Revenue[158] the court considered the charitable status of an incorporated society, the first objective of which was to maintain a fund enabling continuation of the payment of fees for children at private schools in the event of the death of a parent. It was then accepted that the incorporated society was for the advancement of education and entitled to charitable status notwithstanding that it required payments to the fund through a process that had the features of a business arrangement and could be likened to a life insurance scheme. The court had been more concerned as to whether the requisite public benefit was established than

[153] This Tribunal, known to the Maori as Te Ropu Whakamana i te Tiriti, is a permanent commission of inquiry established under the Treaty of Waitangi Act 1975 to address claims brought before it that relate to any possible acts or omissions of the Crown that may be in breach of the Treaty.

[154] [1997] 3 NZLR 342.

[155] Canterbury Development Corporation v. Charities Commission [2010] 2 NZLR 707 (HC).

[156] See the Charities Commission registration decision in re *the Venture Taranki Trust* (January 26, 2009).

[157] Re Bingham [1951] NZLR 491; Centrepoint Community Growth Trust v. Commissioner of Inland Revenue [1985] 1 NZLR 673.

[158] [1992] 2 NZLR 115.

whether the purpose was charitable. In confirming public benefit, the court acknowledged the significance of the presumption favoring educational purposes: "the nature of the charitable purpose may itself be a factor in determining whether or not the requirement of public benefit has been met."[159]

The fees issue is equally relevant in relation to those hospitals and residential care facilities that by imposing service charges can, in effect, discriminate against equal access by the socially disadvantaged. The Trust Deed of St George's Hospital, for example, requires that it "apply any profits accruing from the activities or work of the Society to the furtherance of its charitable objects *especially the altruistic nursing of the sick* or for such other purposes which accord with its charitable objects [emphasis added]." However, in the 21st century, St George's Hospital is a commercially based, market-focused entity that recently began a "medical tourism" initiative to treat overseas cancer patients in Christchurch,[160] which arguably takes advantage of the special fiscal character of a charity to claim exemption from income tax.

E. Jurisdictional Characteristics of Charitable Trading

Despite the new charities legislation and the accompanying new regulatory regime, recent cases indicate that the law governing charity in New Zealand continues to be rather inert. The defensive approach of the Commission, falling back on dated precedents to challenge the compatibility of innovatory business ventures with charitable status, is in danger of perpetuating the failure of the common law system to respond adequately to contemporary manifestations of social need—which was a prime reason for embarking on the charity law reform process. It does seem somewhat ironic that the judiciary, having seldom had the opportunity to develop the law in the years prior to the 2005 Act, should, in the years subsequent, find they have a greatly increased number of opportunities to do so but elect to use them to confine charitable purposes within established parameters. The effects of this approach are clearly evident in the decisions of court and Commission in relation to the trading activities of charities.

1. The Private Benefit Constraint

The prospective advantages to private enterprise that might result from the activities of nonprofits established for public benefit purposes would seem to be obstructing the

[159] *Educational Fees Protection Society Inc v. Commissioner of Inland Revenue* [1992] 2 NZLR 115, per Gallen J. at p. 125.

[160] The website of the PlacidWay, a leading medical tourism facilitator, states that "[w]ithout a doubt, New Zealand Christchurch has become the medical tourism capital of the modern world." The Placid Way, Heart care/Surgery in Christchurch New Zealand, http://www.placidway.com/search-by-city.php?country=New%20Zealand&treatmenttype=Heart%20Care/Surgery&city=Christchurch. The author is grateful to Michael Gousmett for this information.

latter's access to or retention of charitable status.[161] In both the *Canterbury Development* and *Education Trust* cases, neither a disaggregation of public and private interests nor any evaluation of whether there could be an acceptable level at which furthering the latter would be a justifiable means for achieving the former was considered necessary. It follows on from this approach that the destination of income test has no real traction in New Zealand.

2. The Activities Test

The equivocation as to the validity or weighting to be accorded this test, which troubles many regulators, judiciary, and academics in other jurisdictions, has been laid to rest in New Zealand with its incorporation into the 2005 Act. However, as this directive applies to the Commission but not to the Inland Revenue, there remains some scope for regulatory confusion.

VII. CONCLUSION

New Zealand is unique among the nations considered in this study due to the groundwork done by government in crafting legal forms to mediate between the formal departmental structures of government and the associational structures of Maori society. In no other country is there anything comparable to New Zealand's long history of exploring new ways of managing the joint interests of two distinct populations, each with its own cultural heritage and accompanying separate sets of organizations, processes, and systems providing for the representation and negotiation of social issues. This experience paved the way for government initiatives in the early years of the 21st century to build a closer relationship with the nonprofit sector. The creation of the Office for the Community and Voluntary Sector, the introduction of the Charities Act 2005, which established a Charities Commission and a register for charities, and the amendments made to the Income Tax Act 2007 all significantly changed the legal framework for charity and contributed to the furthering of a government/sector partnership.

However, the political willingness to explore boundaries and make new links is not matched by the judiciary. The case law reveals a judiciary defensively focused on the traditional rules (public or private benefit, exclusivity, ancillary and incidental, etc.), and there have been no groundbreaking decisions. This case law is heavily concentrated in the core public benefit areas of health and social care, community development, and education. And, correspondingly, there is little in the way of case law evidence to indicate that charities in New Zealand are, as yet, engaging significantly in trading as a means of compensating for diminishing government funding.

[161] Notwithstanding the contrary authority of Crystal Palace Trustees v. Minister of Town and Country Planning [1951] 1 Ch 132.

PART 3

New Directions

11

CHARITY IN THE MARKETPLACE

I. INTRODUCTION

Charity, in an increasingly literal sense, must ply its trade in a marketplace that would seem to have become immensely more complex when viewed from a post-2008 perspective. The impact of the financial crisis and ensuing economic recession on the relationships between government, charity, and the market sets the context for this chapter and moves the book away from Part II's concentration on law to focus more on the unfolding social policy context for charity, other nonprofits, and commerce.

Following the context-setting introduction and a reflection upon the implications of the financial crisis for altruism and civil society, this chapter undertakes a comparative jurisdictional analysis of the more prominent themes and issues arising from Part II. It assesses the outcomes of the various charity law reform processes. It maps the new areas of social need targeted by legislators, noting the emphasis on charity's traditional core areas of health and social care, education, etc.; the diversification of charitable activity into more modern manifestations of public benefit; and the jurisdictional similarities and differences in the range of new charitable purposes that now designate service provision opportunities. It then considers the view that the nonprofit sector in general is in the process of being reshaped, examining the effects of isomorphism, market distortion, separation of big and little, and marginalization of unfavored charities. Across the jurisdictions studied it assesses the evidence that government is engaged in the colonization of charities, and that it is intent on increasing their efficiency. The chapter then considers charities and trading, the effect on market dynamics of government's preferment of charities, the jurisdictional variance in extent to which governments fund charities (whether through direct grant aid or through service contracts), the resulting more competitive position of favored charities, and the consequences for unfavored charities and other nonprofits. The chapter concludes with a review of the type of trading to which charities and others in the nonprofit sector are now being drawn, and a consideration of the impact of commercial competition upon charities.

II. GLOBAL RECESSION: GOVERNMENT, CHARITY, AND THE MARKET

Charities suffered directly and vicariously from the global financial crisis as the institutions in which many had invested, or from which they had been accustomed to receiving support, slid into bankruptcy or struggled to survive. They also, not unnaturally, were overstretched in coping with the surge in demand for their services from those suddenly impoverished and unemployed as the recession set in. A more fundamental challenge for charity, however, emerged from the trauma as the dynamics governing the interface between government, charity, and the market were tested and adjusted.

A. The 2008 Financial Crisis and Market Failure

The financial crisis of 2008 brought into play the role of government as a forced donor in respect of domestic organizations and institutions that traditionally would never have been seen as appropriate public benefit beneficiaries: Banks, car manufacturers, and other bastions of capitalism and private profit became the thankful recipients of immense government handouts. Then, with the financial crisis spiraling into an uneven global economic recession, the donor role assumed a new and unsettling global dimension as the scale of national debt brought several developed countries to the brink and beyond of bankruptcy. In Europe alone, three Member States—Ireland, Greece, and Portugal—became insolvent, with a negative credit rating that prevented borrowing on the international money market forcing them instead to accept massive cash infusions while ceding considerable autonomy to their EU and IMF benefactors. Others—notably Italy, Spain, and Belgium—may follow, whereas the economies of those nations generally viewed as guarantors of the monetary system—such as the U.K., Japan, and the United States—are striving to stave off bankruptcy by borrowing, though with diminishing credit ratings, on the international markets. Private commercial losses had become transformed, on a massive and international scale, into public debt.

This new and uncertain world is bringing with it a bright light to illuminate the boundaries of the "marketplace" and the dynamics of "charity," while also exposing the realities of the power imbalance in the donor/recipient relationship, revealing the interdependency of public and private interests, and casting a somewhat harsh glare on the role of altruism.

1. Public/Private Interests

The financial crisis brought an unexpected twist to the role of government in public benefit provision, adding further complexity to the distinction between "public" and "private" interests and challenging the popular perception of matters to be construed as constituting "benefit."

Governments, which until the crisis had been focused on stemming public revenue outflow by shedding responsibility for providing services and utilities, were suddenly and forcefully thrust into taking a quite different approach. Public revenue outlay was massively increased as governments scrambled to shore up failing financial institutions, precipitately redesignating icons of capitalism as public benefit utilities and, in some cases, advocating increasing public debt by subsidizing the business sector as a means of stimulating the national economy. Admittedly, much government aid was by way of loans and stock purchases rather than unconditional gifts. Nonetheless, the fact that, particularly in the U.K. and United States, untold billions of tax revenue went toward the rescue of such private enterprise entities as Northern Rock, Chrysler, AIG, Fannie Mae, and Freddie Mac while, simultaneously, government policies requiring cutbacks on health and welfare services were defended as being necessary to prevent further erosion of their tax revenue base, raised questions as to how to reconcile such disparate interpretations of "public benefit."

The political answers to such questions would seem to lie outside our reach. Clearly government action in the public interest, even at the price of unduly privileging free riders, is most readily justified even where it also satisfies private interests, on the "rising tide lifts all boats" principle. It may also be so, despite not satisfying such interests, depending on the balance between the importance of the issue and numbers likely to be adversely affected. Emergency intervention is by its nature unrehearsed, and any rescue operation is likely to be untidy: The priority must be to prevent probable worse damage engulfing all concerned. As society becomes more exposed to global trends, public and private interests in areas of basic human need (global warming, economic recession etc) are increasingly difficult to differentiate. This also holds true for future public benefit service provision in which nonprofits, including charities, must blend their contribution with that of for-profit and government bodies if adequate and sustainable service levels are to be achieved.

2. The Public Benefit Test

The parallels between the role of the public benefit test as applied in a charity law context and as applied to guide government policy in the context of addressing the current global financial crisis are interesting. In both, it has sanctioned the diversion of tax revenues to organizations with the capacity to ameliorate and possibly halt a deteriorating set of circumstances that if allowed to continue unchecked, would result in the impoverishment of many, damage social cohesion, possibly trigger wider social trauma, and be likely to cause greater government expense in the long run. The gratuitous government deployment of public revenue to for-profit companies and the quantitative easing by injection of massive funds to financial institutions would seem to be on a par with and be as compliant with the public benefit test as grant-aiding charities, though very different in scale and in breach of the private benefit rule (and possibly other charity law requirements). In all probability such measures will prove to be as effective as charity in preventing a bad situation from getting worse, although insufficient to address the causes, and, if deployed in isolation, unlikely to prevent a relapse.

Despite national and international government monetary intervention, some national for-profit institutions are proving to be nonviable as independent entities, and are lapsing wholly or partially into government ownership to become a long-term drain on public revenues. Indeed, some countries are showing every sign of becoming similarly nonviable as economic entities within their present set of circumstances. Again, the necessary political answers to these dynamics currently lie outside the reach of contemporary political strategists.

B. Ethics and Altruism in the Marketplace

The financial crisis naturally called into question the prevailing ethics of the business sector. This had at least four consequences for nonprofits: a questioning of the business values, styles of management, and models of governance so assiduously assimilated by the sector in recent years; a reawakening of interest in altruism; a more confident assertion of the need to construct a coherent civil society narrative that demonstrates how collaboration between relevant government, nonprofit, and for-profit bodies could offer an opportunity to consolidate a more ethics compliant society; and a tighter regulatory environment as already-enacted government measures, in place to prevent terrorist access to nonprofit funds, were extended to prevent in the nonprofit sector any overspill of the reckless risk management responsible for the chaos in financial institutions (see chapter 12).

1. The Business Model

For the decade or so preceding the 2008 financial crisis, the business management model and its accompanying attention to "bottom line" criteria had spread pervasively throughout the nonprofit sector. This was largely at the behest of government bodies that encouraged the model's adoption to ensure that the regulators and the nonprofits shared the same currency of measurement tools and business-speak. Subsequently, the bureaucratization of nonprofits morphed into marketization, as nonprofits emulated their for-profit counterparts in developing an enthusiasm for "branding," outsourcing, outcome and output measures, etc. Any qualms in the sector that public benefit provision did not always sit comfortably with profit margin preoccupations were set aside by service delivery nonprofits anxious to secure future government contracts.

The financial crisis, referred to by some with perhaps undue haste as the "nemesis of market fundamentalism,"[1] forced governments worldwide to step forward as

[1] Lambie, G., "Nemesis of 'Market Fundamentalism'? The Ideology, Deregulation and Crisis of Finance," in *Contemporary Politics*, Vol. 15, 2009, at pp. 157–77.

"guardians of last resort" and intervene in the for-profit sector to secure the public interest. Having had to assume responsibility, by default, for failed for-profit institutions, some of the same governments are now showing signs of a greater preference for working with nonprofits, a willingness to respect the sector's distinctive value base, and an acceptance that it may be counterproductive to induce nonprofits to become merely a cheaper, more submissive, but as efficient version of their for-profit counterparts.

2. Altruism

In the mantra often repeated during this financial crisis—that government must intervene to rescue those for-profit institutions that are "too big to be allowed to fail"—there lies a harsh truth that is not without implications for the role of altruism in charity. The massive amounts of money shunted by government into the coffers of some of society's most rapacious for-profit businesses was, in reality, nothing more than a logical and reflexive operational response to a perceived threat to the collective good: compromises made to maintain the system, as a failure in part may weaken the whole. It was little more than prudent housekeeping to rescue a failing entity, and if possible restore it to normal functioning, but primarily it was about reaffirming the integrity of the system. Social workers do the same for dysfunctional families, the UN for failing states, and the EC for defaulting Member States. Altruism is not a factor.

That charity in the main is not about altruism is readily apparent from the nature of the extended charitable purposes recently statutorily added to the Preamble/*Pemsel* agenda of matters viewed by government as suitable for charitable intervention. It is reflected also in the reliance on the proceeds of gambling, in tax rebate incentives offered to wealthy donors, and in the tax exemption entitlement that accompanies charitable status. However, the functional emphasis on utilitarian activity, fiscally reinforced, can also obscure altruism. The act of giving, or of foregoing profit, as implied when complying with that singular distinguishing characteristic of all nonprofits, the "nondistribution constraint,"[2] which prohibits them from distributing net earnings among their executive staff, is, after all, manifestly altruistic.

3. Civil Society

Ostensibly the financial crisis has exposed the fundamental flaws of capitalism: a business-driven, open market economy is going to be vulnerable to the consequences of the competing risks run by those seeking ever-greater profit margins. For some this presents a profound challenge, not just how to better regulate business, but also how to correct the "creeping marketization" that is now everywhere seeping into the

[2] See Hansmann, H., "The Role of Nonprofit Enterprise," in *Yale Law Journal*, Vol. 89, No. 5, 1980, at pp. 835–902.

nonprofit sector and perhaps bringing with it the contamination that wreaked such havoc in markets globally. The answer, many think, perhaps wishfully, lies in growing and consolidating the institutions of civil society.

One of the lessons that may be fairly drawn from recent events, however, is the interconnectedness of the various sectors and their institutions, nationally and internationally, that comprise our sophisticated modern societies. It may no longer be possible to separate out "civil society" institutions, inoculate them with altruism, and then look to them for ethically compliant leadership. Given that in the absence of any alternative, commerce will undoubtedly remain a dominant force in society, charity and the nonprofit sector may well simply have to find ways of continuing to accommodate it and trust in better regulatory processes and carefully negotiated, mutually accountable collaborative arrangements to reduce the associated risks, rather than place their faith in civil society.

C. Charities and the Marketplace

If anything, the financial crisis demonstrated government determination to uphold the mechanisms and institutions of the open market while also providing added impetus to the policy of shrinking the provision of public benefit services by government and involving the nonprofit sector in bearing responsibility for their cost and, by implication, responsibility for anticipated shortcomings.

1. The Market

Even without the financial crisis and ensuing recession, the concept of "market" was never going to readily accommodate the realities of public benefit provision. It has been made possible by applying to human *needs* a process of commodification designed to address consumer *wants*. Only by transferring, however inadequately, the purchaser/provider relationship to fit a situation where the discretionary use of goods is rarely a matter of free choice—where market price often bears little relation to cost nor utility to value—has it been possible to transpose a market scenario onto what is in fact a quite different form of transaction. Arguably, however, the price of this artifice has been real enough, including a tendency to objectification and a fragmentary rather than holistic interpretation of "need"; a translation of "consumer choice" to infer that service users can bear responsibility for treatment decisions; and a cost-driven specification for offering help or, in market-speak, for "public benefit service provision."

Any "market" is founded on a contractual capacity to buy and sell. The presence of coercion, or undue influence, will render a contract void. In most instances of public benefit service provision there is at least an absence of voluntariness on the part of the service user: In many instances, need compels the user to avail of a specific service for which they would otherwise not be in the market. In some cases there is actual compulsion. In perhaps all jurisdictions discussed in this book, for example, the education of a child is a statutory duty placed on parents: The parent has no option not to be in the market, or to refuse service. The market typology is particularly unfortunate in the context of health (cancer treatments, etc.) where only the costing out of professional time, available resources, and alternative drug treatments are amenable to marketing.

It is not just the compromised position of the service user that brings into question the validity of the market typology in a public benefit services context. A valid "bill of sale" requires the seller to "show good title" for the goods brought to market. However, determining "ownership" of the many public benefit services on offer would be far from easy. Education and health facilities, for example, whether provided by government or charity, are almost always not wholly paid for by either but are established and maintained as a result of complex funding streams in which private finance often plays a part, and real costs are defrayed by tax revenues. Moreover, in market terms, the price paid may also be compromised, with some users having free access while others pay in full, and some revenue-generating services being used to subsidize the running costs of others.

Finally, the concept of "market" is clearly politically determined. For those countries with a strong welfare state tradition (e.g., the U.K. and Scandinavia), where a corporatist approach has been embedded (e.g., Belgium, France, and Germany), or which have been accustomed to a totalitarian regime (e.g., Romania and Slovakia), the "market" is one that has been rigged by the state. Control of market forces—the parties who may engage, the terms of trade, and the "public goods" to be traded—is the signature hallmark of government in such countries. At a considerable remove from that interpretation stands the "open market" that, in its most emblematic form, is represented by the United States and is one where government retains control over matters relating to national security but otherwise opts for minimal intervention aside from setting up the rules for the market itself. Here government chooses, very largely, to regulate standards and tax outcomes while leaving the "market" to determine traders and the nature and price of goods to be traded. Currently charity, and with it the nonprofit sector, is caught up in a process that has been gaining momentum following the 2008 crisis, whereby in all jurisdictions studied, government is beating a swift strategic retreat from inherited responsibilities as provider or controller of public goods to a position that edges ever closer to the U.S. open market model.

2. Shrinking Government

As Tanzi has pointed out, a century ago the cost to government of funding the public benefit services that constituted the average European welfare state was approximately 10–15 percent of GDP whereas now it varies between 35–55 percent in most developed countries.[3] Even if the current financial crisis had not heaped debt upon

[3] See Tanzi, V., *Government versus Markets, The Changing Economic Role of the State*, Cambridge, Cambridge University Press, 2011.

the nations studied, the economic trajectory dictated by decreasing taxpayers and increasing health and social care costs for the elderly had given advanced warning that this level of costs would be unsustainable. Now, for all countries concerned, the unavoidable government task of managing reduced government expenditure while maintaining politically acceptable levels of services has acquired an accelerated urgency. The crisis, however, has also acutely compromised government options as credit margins have become more attenuated: Domestic funding has been skewed by the rising welfare costs of unemployment, and much has had to be diverted from public services to private businesses and financial institutions. International funding streams are rapidly drying up as the market deems the risks too great to extend credit, or will only do so on a short-term basis, and at rates so prohibitively high that to avail of it further feeds the prevailing instability.

In the hope that as the market created the problem, it will also provide the answer, governments would seem determined to reduce public sector expenditure[4] by pushing through austerity programs and increasing regulatory measures (more so in the U.K., less so in Australia), while at the same time seeking to involve other parties, such as insurance companies in the case of the U.S. health service reforms, so as to maintain politically defensible service levels by spreading responsibility for their costs.

3. Government/Sector Partnerships

Clearly, at least in many of the surveyed common law countries (and others such as Ireland and, to a lesser degree, Singapore), government is now committing to collaborative or formal partnership arrangements with the sector. The strategic expediency of such a policy was nicely demonstrated in Australia where, as government changed from Liberal to Labor then to the present Labor/Green coalition, it underwent a political epiphany, converting from rejecting and bullying the nonprofit sector to following the U.K.'s lead and swiftly constructing an entire collaborative architecture as evidence of its newfound belief in the sector as partner. In continental Europe, the corporatist approach had long institutionalized the shared governance of public benefit service provision. In the United States, and to some extent in Canada, although there is no sign of government subscribing to a full partnership approach, it is showing a willingness to experiment with collaborative arrangements. However, the long-established distinctive element in the U.S. approach has been the enthusiasm with which commerce has been allowed to participate in the delivery of public benefit services. In that respect, all the countries studied, and others mentioned above, show every sign of following the U.S. example.

[4] Note, e.g., the structural changes to government departments in New Zealand announced in August 2011 (including transferring the functions of the Charities Commission to the Department of Internal Affairs), estimated to result in total savings of $92 million in the four years from 2012/2013.

Charities and other nonprofits are now needed by governments: Their assets and goodwill in the community, together with their proven capacity to attract public donations and volunteers, make them ideal partners for the purposes of public benefit provision. As sector entities will be unable to rely, as formerly, on regular government grant aid, or even, in the future, on government for full reimbursement of their service delivery costs, there is a tacit acknowledgement that the shortfall in their running expenses will have to be made up through recourse to commerce (though the important contribution now being made by "high value donors" should not be overlooked). The case law clearly reveals that the judiciary has recognized this as a settled fact, despite concern regarding the rules that should apply to ensure that tax exemption privileges are not misused (see chapter 12).

III. CHARITY LAW REFORM, PUBLIC BENEFIT, AND THE SECTOR

For charities to carry more of the public service burden, a broadening of the definition of what they were legally entitled to do without jeopardizing their charitable status and tax exemption privileges was necessary. Of the handful of common law countries to so far embark on charity law reform, however, only a minority finished with a commitment to legislatively extend the traditional *Pemsel*[5] list of charitable purposes.[6] Nonetheless, the inescapable similarity in the type of new purposes being legislatively introduced reveals the shared interest of the governments concerned to ensure that charities are able to adequately enter the market as providers for particular types of public benefit services. Moreover, whether legislated for or not, the "*Pemsel* plus" list has already largely become judicially woven into the common law fabric that forms a shared basis for charitable activity in most of the nations discussed herein.

Mapping the new areas of public benefit targeted in the various charity law reform processes and taking into account the somewhat different codification of nonprofits in the United States provides a sense of the direction taken by the governments concerned as new routes are created for charity and other nonprofits to enter the market.

A. Charity Law Reform: Public Benefit Outcomes

Following the lead provided by England and Wales in the Charities Act 2006, now the Charities Act 2011, certain key outcomes were achieved by legal reform in each of the jurisdictions that to-date have completed that process, as evidenced in their respective new charity statutes. A small minority of reforming jurisdictions went

[5] Commissioners for Special Purposes of Income Tax v. Pemsel [1891] AC 531(HL).

[6] Barbados, the first nation to do so, introduced legislation that defined "charitable purposes" in accordance with suggestions made in the Goodman report, by specifying a non-exhaustive list covering 26 main purposes and 14 amplifying subheadings; they all, however, retained their essential common law character.

further than others, and this group reset the baseline for charity law. They also established a model, or signposted the way forward, for developments in other common law nations. The key components, with variable distribution among the jurisdictions, were statutory statements of core common law concepts and a new extended list of charitable purposes.

1. Common Law Concepts

It has long been established that to be a charity, an entity must: be confined exclusively to charitable purposes, be for the public benefit, be independent, be non–profit distributing, and be nonpolitical (see chapter 1). The processes of charity law reform in England and Wales,[7] Scotland,[8] Northern Ireland,[9] and Ireland[10] concluded with—and in New Zealand,[11] Australia,[12] Canada,[13] and Singapore[14] concluded without—changes to some core definitional matters. In all, the statutory definition of "charity" simply restates the legal meaning given to it under the common law.[15] In the U.K. and Irish jurisdictions, change has taken the form of a significant redefinition of "public benefit," adjustments to the "poor relations" rule, and a statutory restatement of all other common law concepts.[16] By contrast, in Australia, Canada, New Zealand, and Singapore all common law concepts remained unchanged, and no legislative steps were taken to

[7] Concluded with the introduction of the Charities Act 2006.

[8] Concluded with the introduction of the Charities and Trustee Investment (Scotland) Act 2005.

[9] Concluded with the introduction of the Charities Act (Northern Ireland) 2008.

[10] Concluded with the introduction of the Charities Act 2009.

[11] Concluded with the introduction of the Charities Act 2005.

[12] Concluded with the withdrawal of the draft Charities Bill in May 2004 and the introduction of the Extension of Charitable Purpose Act 2004.

[13] Concluded, for the time being, with the submission of the Joint Table Report.

[14] Currently at the stage of implementing the recommendations of the Inter-Ministry. Committee on the Regulation of Charities and Institutions of Public Character established in October 2005.

[15] In England and Wales, "charity" as now defined in s.1(1) of the 2011 Act means an "institution which: (a) is established for charitable purposes only, and (b) falls to be subject to the control of the High Court in the exercise of its jurisdiction with respect to charities." This definition is replicated in the legislation for Northern Ireland (Charities Act (Northern Ireland) Order 2008, s.3(1)), is more fully stated in the Irish statute (Charities Act 2009, s.3(2)), and in Scotland is simply confined to charitable purpose and to public benefit in Scotland or elsewhere (Charities and Trustee Investment (Scotland) Act 2005, s.7(1)). In both New Zealand (Charities Act 2005, s.4(1)) and Australia (the Extension of Charitable Purpose Act 2004, s.3) "charity" is defined similarly in terms of legal structure as a charitable institution, a charitable fund, a society, or any other kind of charitable body. The definition used in Singapore combines both concept and structural approaches by defining "charity" as "any institution, corporate or not, which is established for charitable purposes and is subject to the control of the High Court in exercise of the Court's jurisdiction with respect to charities" (Charities Act 1995, s.2).

[16] Note that both s.8(2)(a) of the Charities and Trustee Investment (Scotland) Act 2005 and s.3(3)(a)(ii) of the Charities Act (Northern Ireland) 2008 insert a statutory requirement that possible negative side effects should be taken into account when applying the public benefit test.

alter the public benefit presumption. However, New Zealand and Singapore have now placed the key common law concepts onto the statute books, in keeping with the U.K. and Irish jurisdictions, which give their governments the future capacity to amend and adjust the rules relating to matters such as public benefit, exclusiveness, or profits.

Moreover, although the U.K. and Irish jurisdictions reversed the public benefit presumption traditionally granted to the first three *Pemsel* heads (excepting religion in Ireland), this initiative has not been adopted elsewhere. Consequently, the traditionally shared common law conceptual basis of charity has been left in considerable disarray.

2. Charitable Purposes: Changes to *Pemsel*

The most important outcome of the reform processes lies in the fact that all common law jurisdictions chose to retain as charitable the set of purposes first identified and listed in the 1601 statute[17] and as classified in *Pemsel*. To that extent charities in the reforming jurisdictions continue to share the same core purposes, and therefore the same associated public benefit service provision opportunities, as those where reform remains uncertain. In Canada, for example, the nature of charitable purposes has been largely left to the courts to identify and interpret.[18] In the United States the situation is somewhat different, perhaps unique among the jurisdictions studied in this book. There, § 501 (c) of the Internal Revenue Code adopts a linear progression approach to tax-exempt entities, which, by providing a codified list of nonprofit public benefit activities entitled to tax exemption, has in effect extended the range of matters defined as "charity" beyond the traditional four elements of poverty, education, religion, and general community benefit.[19]

[17] Statute of Charitable Uses 1601 (43 Eliz. 1. Cap. 4).

[18] Some states and territories have, however, introduced legislation that extends the *Pemsel* purposes: in Alberta, s.1(1)(b) of the Charitable Fund-raising Act extends the common law by defining "charitable purpose" as including "a philanthropic, benevolent, educational, health, humane, religious, cultural, artistic or recreational purpose, so long as the purpose is not part of a business"; whereas in Manitoba, s.1(1) of the Charities Endorsement Act defines "charitable purpose" as including "any charitable, benevolent, philanthropic, patriotic, athletic, artistic, or civic purpose that has as its object the promotion of a civic improvement or the provision of a public service."

[19] The Regulations state:

> The term *charitable* is used in section 501(c)(3) in its generally accepted legal sense and is, therefore, not to be construed as limited by the separate enumeration in section 501(c)(3) of other tax-exempt purposes which may fall within the broad outlines of *charity* as developed by judicial decisions. Such term includes: Relief of the poor and distressed or of the underprivileged; advancement of religion; advancement of education or science; erection or maintenance of public buildings, monuments, or works; lessening of the burdens of government; and promotion of social welfare by organisations designed to accomplish any of the above purposes; or (i) to lessen neighbourhood tensions; (ii) to eliminate prejudice and discrimination; (iii) to defend human and civil rights secured by law; or (iv) to combat community deterioration and juvenile delinquency.

The law reform processes in the U.K. and Irish jurisdictions concluded not only with a statutory requirement that the *Pemsel* heads and all additional purposes be subjected to the public benefit test, but also with certain other legislative changes to *Pemsel*. First, those jurisdictions have introduced provisions allowing charitable purposes concerned with matters of poverty[20] and health[21] to accommodate a preventative dimension. Although it might be argued that the Charity Commission has for some time recognized "prevention" at least in respect of poverty, it is clear that for most common law jurisdictions this has not been the case.[22] Exceptions include Canada, where the fairly expansive definition of the courts and CRA generally includes purposes having to do with poverty prevention through community economic development, and the United States as the IRS has held that certain community development organizations that focus their work on preventing the causes of poverty instead of simply providing traditional charitable relief are charitable in nature. Permission to shift to a preventative emphasis will necessarily bring charities firmly into the political frame as they explore and address the causes, not just the effects, of poverty.

Second, a statutory definition of "religion" now forms part of charity law in the U.K. jurisdictions and, to a lesser extent, in Ireland. In the U.K. jurisdictions, but not in Ireland or in any of the other reforming jurisdictions, there is now an express reference to faiths that do not profess belief in a god as well as to polytheistic religions. This statutory broadening of "religion" for the purposes of charity law, in all probability, will encourage further faith-based initiatives in service provision. However, although most jurisdictions have opted for judicial rather than legislative-led change, it is likely that reform will also now come more swiftly for them following in the wake of Charity Commission rulings, with their persuasive influence in all common law jurisdictions, made under the auspices of the 2006 Act as now consolidated in the Charities Act 2011.

3. Charitable Purposes: Additions to *Pemsel*

The U.K. jurisdictions and Ireland, unlike any of the other countries engaged in charity law reform, have introduced legislative provisions listing a new set of "*Pemsel* plus" charitable purposes. Although these can be viewed as simply giving statutory recognition to purposes already established as charitable by the judiciary, and some are of little significance in the context of public benefit provision (e.g., the advancement of animal welfare), many are central to government's plans for broadening charity's contribution

[20] See the Charities Act 2011, s.3, and now also in the Charities and Trustee Investment (Scotland) Act 2005, s.7(2)(a), and the Charities Act (Northern Ireland) 2008, s.2(2)(a). For Ireland, see the Charities Act 2009, s.3(1)(a).

[21] See, e.g., the Charities Act (Northern Ireland) 2008, s.2(3)(b) and the Charities and Trustee Investment (Scotland) Act 2005, s.7(3)(a). For Ireland, see the Charities Act 2009, s.3(11).

[22] This has been the case in Ireland and also in Australia; see, e.g., the advice of the ATO in *Income Tax and Fringe Benefits Tax: Charities*, T.R. 2005/21 at para. 197.

to that provision. As has been recently explained,[23] this range of legislation with remarkable consistency identifies clusters of new purposes, grouped around clear social policy themes, which reveal matters central to government's intended partnership arrangement with charity. These include:

- the advancement of human rights, conflict resolution, or reconciliation,[24] and the promotion of multiculturalism;[25]
- the advancement of civil society;[26]
- the advancement of health and related services;[27] and
- the promotion of the welfare of specific socially disadvantaged groups.[28]

This *Pemsel*-plus list creates a new statutory platform to facilitate the contribution of charity to specific, government-targeted types of public benefit provision.

[23] See McGregor-Lowndes, M. and O'Halloran, K. (eds.), *Modernising Charity Law*, Elgar, Cheltenham, 2010, and see also O'Halloran, K., *The Politics of Charity*, Routledge, London, 2011.

[24] Note that the Charity Commission had prepared the ground for statutory endorsement of "reconciliation" as charitable with its ruling in *Application for Registration of Restorative Justice Consortium Limited*, January 15, 2003 when the applicant organization with its purpose "to promote restorative justice for the public benefit as a means of resolving conflict and promoting reconciliation" was held to be a charity.

[25] The wording in the Charities Act 2011, s.3(1)(h) "the advancement of human rights, conflict resolution or reconciliation or the promotion of religious or racial harmony or equality and diversity" is exactly replicated in the Charities and Trustee Investment (Scotland) Act 2005, s.7(2)(j)(k) and (l); the Charities Act (Northern Ireland) 2008, s.4 1(h); and in the Charities Act 2009, s.3(11), except that the relevant provisions are restricted to (e) "the advancement of conflict resolution or reconciliation," and (f) "the promotion of religious or racial harmony and harmonious community relations," neither of which makes any reference to "human rights."

[26] Again, the wording in the Charities Act 2011, s.3(2)(c) "includes—(i) rural or urban regeneration, and (ii) the promotion of civic responsibility, volunteering, the voluntary sector" is exactly replicated in the Charities and Trustee Investment (Scotland) Act 2005, s.7(3); the Charities Act (Northern Ireland) 2008, s.4 3(c); and, slightly embellished, in the Charities Act 2009, s.3(11)(b) "the advancement of community development, including rural or urban regeneration, (c) the promotion of civic responsibility or voluntary work."

[27] The wording in the Charities Act 2011, s.3(1)(d) "the advancement of health or the saving of lives" is exactly replicated in the Charities and Trustee Investment (Scotland) Act 2005, s.7 (2)(d) and (e); the Charities Act (Northern Ireland) 2008, s.4(2)(d); but more fully stated in the Irish Charities Act 2009, s.3 (11)(d) "the promotion of health, including the prevention or relief of sickness, disease or human suffering."

[28] The wording in the Charities Act 2011, s.3(1)(j) "the relief of those in need by reason of youth, age, ill-health, disability, financial hardship or other disadvantage" is exactly replicated in the Charities Act (Northern Ireland) 2008, s.4 (2)(j); almost exactly replicated in the Charities and Trustee Investment (Scotland) Act 2005, s.1(2)(n) "the relief of those in need by reason of age, ill-health, disability, financial hardship or other disadvantage"; and similarly in the Charities Act 2009, s.3(11)(a) "the advancement of community welfare including the relief of those in need by reason of youth, age, ill- health, disability."

When viewed in conjunction with the retained *Pemsel* purposes, there is an unmistakable emphasis on the traditional mainstream areas of social need.

Such a significant and largely identical extension to the four *Pemsel* heads made by these jurisdictions, roughly simultaneously and after several years of careful consideration and public consultation, is an indication of the level of importance attached by government to the *Pemsel*-plus purposes. They can only be viewed as setting out the governments agenda of public benefit provision by the sector. Their importance is unlikely to remain restricted to the jurisdictions concerned, as others may well either replicate that statutory initiative or transfer its consequences by judicial proxy, as the courts elsewhere in the common law world often choose to follow new lines of precedents established in the courts of the U.K. and Ireland. To both the enacting jurisdictions and the greater common law world, the policy implications of such a clear statutory statement of the matters henceforth to be regarded by government as properly the business of charity would be hard to overstate. Not since the Preamble have governments set out, in such full and explicit terms, their expectations of charity.

B. Redefined Public Benefit and the Sector

The protracted period of charity law reform resulted in some jurisdictions taking the initiative and committing to a public benefit legislative agenda comprised of clearly identified old and new charitable purposes that now designate service provision opportunities for the sector. The agenda reveals considerable jurisdictional agreement on areas deemed appropriate for sector input, for example: in the emphasis on maximizing intervention in the traditional areas of social need, in the diversification of charitable activity into more contemporary but yet quite specific manifestations of public benefit, and in the importance of increasing sector efficiency. Some of these are areas in which charities have already well-established trading ventures, whereas others may well lend themselves to commercialization.

1. Public/Private Interests and Nonprofit Service Provision

In all countries studied herein, the trends point conclusively toward government having to redress the cost basis of future provision, particularly in a reduction of the level and range of services previously available free at point of delivery, and that users and other nongovernmental providers must contribute to costs. The shift in public service provision from government to the private and nonprofit sectors that began in the U.K. in the 1980s is now well advanced elsewhere, and has done much to accentuate the blurring of the public/private boundary in health, education, housing, and social care services. As sector boundaries are seemingly left to ebb and flow in accordance with prevailing market conditions, there are unresolved but fundamental questions to be answered as to which core "public" services, if any, taxpaying citizens are entitled to hold government accountable.

In recent years, the governments of the U.K. and others have moved more toward the approach favored in New Zealand, Canada, Australia, and the United States. This move has, arguably, been largely achieved by stealth: the incremental shedding of responsibility for the delivery of core public benefit provision to both the for-profit and the nonprofit sectors, while the government retains regulatory powers and control over policy and, to a lesser degree, funding. The accompanying experiments with public/private finance schemes and hybrid legal structures, some of which have been initiated by government and some not, have added to the uncertainty as to the responsibility and accountability for related services. Again, many court cases generated by complex liability issues have resulted in accountability for breaches of public law being extended to those private and voluntary sector bodies contracted to deliver public services (see chapter 12).

However, the retreat of government from direct public service provision in so many countries and the devolution of some of that responsibility to the private and the nonprofit sectors, particularly to charities, has brought various challenges. If governments want to use charity to deliver services, they must: put in place a regulatory regime to provide for accountability; create optimal conditions to encourage the donor public to volunteer gifts of money and time and thus reduce the need for state finance; make sure that service provision is at least adequate in relation to that which government could directly provide; make certain that citizens are content with an arrangement whereby community-based entities rather than anonymous government bodies respond to their needs, thus bringing responsibility for individual well-being closer to home; and ensure that any such arrangements also generate an ongoing entrepreneurial approach in the mold of the classic actor in an open economic marketplace The preferred approach would seem to involve: government falling back to a gatekeeper role in relation to service access, standards, and providers; the cost for new public utilities being passed to the private sector; a vast increase occurring in the contribution of charities established specifically for the purpose of generating funds for hospital facilities and other public services; and a steady mixed sector contribution being made to health and social care facilities, particularly in respect of the elderly and the disabled as well as child care. All of this would result in a generally murky sense of responsibility for public benefit service provision.

2. The Core Areas of Public Benefit Provision

The Preamble footprint, as subsequently articulated in *Pemsel*, will continue to form the broad outline of future public benefit provision by charity, and indeed more generally by the nonprofit sector. Without exception, all common law nations that embarked on charity law reform emerged from that process having at least retained as charitable, if not added to, the purposes first identified and listed in the 1601 statute and as classified in *Pemsel*. The bedrock of charity law in the future will therefore remain firmly based on the *Pemsel* classification. The core areas of public benefit provision then earmarked as appropriate for charity and judicially extended in subsequent centuries will thus continue to be: alleviation of poverty; education; health and social care services; housing, training for employment; various aspects of public utility provision; promotion of civic responsibility, and physical maintenance of social infrastructure.

However, some new purposes have amplified the importance of certain aspects of established provision and now offer obvious opportunities for further commercialization. The "advancement of health and related services," for example, acknowledges the relevance of medical research, recognizes the need to encourage continuing commercial investment in developing pharmaceuticals, and opens the door yet wider for more nonprofit involvement in core welfare state provision. "Promoting the welfare of specific socially disadvantaged groups" offers a tax exemption inducement for service providers to increase provision in social care and residential facilities for groups such as children, the disabled, the mentally ill, and the elderly. Other new purposes, such as environmental protection, indicate that government foresees the need to involve nonprofits in future efforts to combat the effects of global warming or environmental justice. And the fact that some states such as the U.K., Ireland, New Zealand, and Singapore have embedded the core *Pemsel* purposes into their statutes gives those governments the additional freedom to add to that list by statutory amendment as they see fit.

3. Efficiency and Effectiveness

In addition to broadening the range of charity activity and channeling its resource towards targeted areas of social need, the reform outcomes reveal a government concern to improve the efficiency and effectiveness of domestic charities. Indeed, management by measurement has become de rigueur for contemporary government. Media's exposure of corporate corruption and mismanagement in the business world alerted governments to the potential for similar scandals in the charitable sector, and these concerns coupled with a pressing need to ensure that nonprofits were not unwittingly used as "Trojan horses" by terrorists has stimulated awareness of the need to facilitate transparency, greater accountability, proper models of governance, and provision of appropriate legal structures for charities. In England and Wales,[29] for example, s.3(1)(l) of the Charities Act 2011 (previously s.2(1) of the 2006 Act) designates as a charitable purpose "the promotion of the efficiency of the armed forces of the Crown, or of the efficiency of the police, fire and rescue services or ambulance services."[30]

[29] There is, of course, a well-established line of cases confirming that organizations that promote the efficiency of the armed forces are eligible for charitable status, e.g.: In re Good [1905] 2 Ch 60; In re Gray [1925] Ch 362; Re Meyers (1951) Ch 534; and Downing v. Commissioner of Taxation 71 ATC 4164; (1971) 125 CLR 185.

[30] This being a statutory step that endorses the stand taken by the Charity Commission in *Application for Registration of Guidestar UK*, March 7, 2003, when it held that:

> [T]here was a substantial benefit to the public in having an effective voluntary sector and that both tangible benefits (such as engaging and directing efforts of individuals that wish to help those in need) and intangible benefits (such as encouraging altruism in society) to the public would arise. The Commission was satisfied that the promotion of the voluntary sector was of benefit to the public and that public benefit was established by this purpose.

Moreover, for government to successfully engineer the outsourcing of service provision to the nonprofit sector without unduly alarming the electorate, it was preferable that the latter did not experience any marked change in the nature of the service; therefore blurring of responsibility for service provision/delivery became an art form in some jurisdictions.[31] Government had to ensure that recipients found the new providers to be acceptable, the services familiar, and the delivery to be cost effective. In short, charity had to become more efficient and less associated with compassion and helplessness: It was required to shed its traditional role in the "gift relationship" and to make its services more like those of a government body.

Debate regarding the effectiveness of charity and charities has existed for as long as the concept itself. Subject to the responsibilities of trustees and the requirements of good governance, there is no legal duty for a charity to be effective, and many are not. For individual charities, once charitable status has been conferred, then in the absence of fraud or criminal negligence they are reasonably free to mismanage their organization and its assets.[32] Such regulatory scrutiny as exists is most usually restricted to a paper exercise to check that declared purpose and objects coincide, sometimes accompanied by an "activities test" and, where statutorily required, a rudimentary scan of annual income and expenditure accounts. Exposure to the "contract culture" of government outsourcing and grant funding arrangements has, however, brought charities into the view of government bodies. This now gives government regulators increased opportunities for making inquiries into management standards.[33]

The extent of poverty among the native peoples of Australia, Canada, and the United States is also testimony to the failure of charitable activity, which, too often, has fatally compromised the cultural integrity of vulnerable ethnic groups. Perhaps particularly in this context, where the well-being of indigenous groups has been subject to such sustained intervention, philanthropy has earned its most frequent criticism: that instead of being an effective means of promoting the recipient's independence, charity can drain one's initiative, motivation, and self–respect, and induce compliant dependency.

In England and Wales, some academic work has been undertaken to introduce and test the analytical methods necessary to assess the effectiveness of charities and

[31] In the U.K. jurisdictions, for example, many ancillary services provided in public hospitals are in fact wholly private whereas some private domestic care services are wholly funded by government.

[32] Always subject to an overriding responsibility to exercise due care. A memorable account of the dissipation of an estate due to trustee mismanagement was provided in Dickens C., *Bleak House*, Bradbury & Evans, London, 1853.

[33] As exercised, for example, by the IRS in the settlement it reached with the former trustees of Hawaii's wealthiest charity, commonly known as the Bishop Estate, following the effective intervention of the Attorney General of Hawaii to halt the widespread abuse by the trustees of the charity's assets worth between $6 and $10 billion.

their activities.[34] The Charity Commission has long had a statutory duty to promote effectiveness in the U.K., and the amount of data collected by and made available on the Commission's website undoubtedly assists such analysis.[35]

IV. RESHAPING THE SECTOR: CHARITY, SERVICE DELIVERY, AND ALTRUISM

The nonprofit sector in the countries studied appears to be caught up in conflicting tensions, sideswiped by global crisis and challenged by the emergence of new forms of philanthropic intervention. All, in varying degrees, are being forced to make adjustments as nonprofits become dependent upon public service contracts and other state sources of funding, are driven to develop trading ventures, and enter into collaboration or competition with for-profits. In the more corporatist states of continental Europe, this has taken a somewhat different turn as the established hegemony of government and nonprofits has made room for commerce and competition, leading to a more distinctive sector. In the former communist regimes of central Europe, the adjustments have been complicated by the need to become familiar with democratic processes and the application of principles of transparency and accountability. In the United States and elsewhere, high net worth individuals have begun injecting funds and expertise in an effort to revolutionize public benefit services in areas such as the treatment of AIDS, and their example has served to demonstrably affirm the importance of altruism.

A. Charities and the Effects of Partnership with Government

In all jurisdictions studied, the consequences of nonprofits having to build closer administrative working arrangements with government bodies has had a significant impact on the sector, most notably on charities. This has also been affected by the introduction of tighter regulatory controls (see chapter 12).

Government favors contracting with big charities as they have the requisite infrastructure, can employ economies of scale, and can absorb and react to change more readily. This has resulted in selected charities becoming bigger, contributing to a growing division between large and small charities and also between charities and

[34] See, e.g.: Kendall, J., "Revisiting the Loose and Baggy Monster," *Charity Finance*, November 2003, pp. 30–32; Kendall, J. and Knapp, M. R. J., "Measuring the Performance of Voluntary Organizations." *Public Management* Vol. 2, No. 1 (2000), at pp. 105–32.

[35] See the duties of the Commission as stated in Charities Act 1993: "promoting the effective use of charitable resources by encouraging the development of better methods of administration, by giving charity trustees information or advice on any matter affecting the charity and by investigating and checking abuses" (s 1(3)); and the requirement that the Commission promote and make effective the work of any charity by assisting it to meet the needs designed by its trusts (s.1(4)).

other nonprofits.[36] The need to ensure that service provision by charity conforms with that normally provided by government, both for reasons of standard setting and to satisfy recipient expectations, leads to recourse to contracts, accountability systems, service specifications, etc. Indeed there is a sense in which a great deal of government activity in the area of welfare state services (including the restatementing of charitable purposes) has been about isolating, prioritizing, and packaging such services in a manner that resets public expectations from comprehensive and cohesive health and social care to "off-the-shelf" stand-alone services for users to pick-and-mix as they wish. For charities and other nonprofits, part of the price of accepting government service delivery contracts has been the acceptance also of this fragmentary approach to health and social care, coupled with the more subtle inference that responsibility for service choice is passing from state or professional to the user.[37]

1. Isomorphism

The resulting tendency for bigger charities to converge in terms of size, structure, bureaucracy, activity, and policy with the government department that provides their funding has been termed "isomorphism."[38] There is pressure, if only indirect and in furtherance of expediency, for nonprofits to become large-scale, bureaucratic, professional organizations with an increased commitment to the service provision program of their funder, and a decreased involvement in anything that may impinge upon that role. Although this is very much welcomed by government, as it eases the interface between its departments and nonprofits and blurs any distinctiveness in services delivered by either body, it can be particularly costly for charities not only in terms of diverting their resources but also their sense of mission. There is always a risk of nonprofit activity being led by the service delivery requirements of the funder and losing touch with the wider needs of the service user.

2. Advocacy

For many nonprofits, the increased dependency upon a particular funding source, whether government or commerce, tends to be accompanied by a decreased level of advocacy on behalf of the socially disadvantaged group whose needs they have

[36] See Charity Commission, RS 15, *Stand and Deliver: The Future for Charities Delivering Public Services,* London, 2007 which notes a "predominance of regionally based charities delivering public services" at para. 2.3.

[37] See, e.g., Clarke, J. and Newman, J., *Publics, Politics and Power: Remaking the Public in Public Services,* Sage, London, 2009.

[38] See, e.g., Leiter, J., "Structural Isomorphism in Australian Nonprofit Organizations," *Voluntas: International Journal of Voluntary and Nonprofit Organizations,* Vol. 16, No. 1, March 2005, at pp. 1–31.

been accustomed to represent.[39] The need to protect if not appease their funder has become a real imperative, and consequently there has been much concern expressed about the so-called "muting of dissent," "chilling effect," or "gagging clauses" that would often seem to accompany government service contracts.[40]

3. New Public Management

The New Public Management, or New Public Financial Management, has developed from process or procedural accountability to performance measurement with predicted targets and outcomes,[41] and this approach has served to align charities more closely with government (see chapter 4). The role of government departments, described in terms of New Public Management, adopts private sector management techniques, with departments acting as facilitators of public goods rather than direct providers.[42] Ostensibly concerned with modernizing and enhancing the efficiency of public services, in reality the driving force of the approach has been government's concern to reduce costs and extend its management capacity into the sector. It has introduced the terminology of "customers" and "stakeholders," "purchasers" and "providers," in substitution for more value-loaded client-oriented language. and has been accused, perhaps fairly, of being responsible for promoting a "commodification" approach, at least to health care provision. The transfer of such a partializing, measuring, and auditing approach to the health and social care service delivery role of charities and other nonprofits has done much to further separate them from the rest of the sector and from their socially disadvantaged constituencies.

4. Government Control

As charities and the sector more generally are nudged toward adopting a service provision role on behalf of government, they may find they are simultaneously

[39] See, e.g., Seddon, N., *Who Cares?*, Civitas, London, 2007, at p. 69, where he comments: "It's difficult to find explicit cases where charity has been muzzled by contracts... but the homogeneity of the worldview of many charities is becoming increasingly difficult to ignore... they are coalescing around narrowly accepted ways of thinking which suit the state bureaucracies on which they depend for funding."

[40] See, e.g., Kennedy, H., *Report of the Advisory Group on Campaigning and the Voluntary Sector*, London, 2007 where it is stressed that "when restrictions on the ability of charities to engage in political campaigning substantially curtail their contribution to civil society, charity law and regulation is clearly in need of change."

[41] See Olsen, O., Guthrie, J., and Humphrey, C., "International Experiences with Financial Management Reforms in the World of Public Services New World," in Olsen, O., Guthrie, J., and Humphrey, C. (eds.), *Global Warning: Debating International Developments in the New Public Financial Management*, Cappelen Akademisk Forlag, Bergen, 1998, at pp. 17–48.

[42] See Hood, C., "The New Public Management in the 1980s: Variations on a Theme," in *Accounting Organizations and Society*, Vol. 20, No. 3, 1995, at pp. 93–109; see also Pollitt, C., "Partnerships, Networks, Joined-up Governance, the Information Age (and All That)," in *The Essential Public Manager*, Open University Press, Philadelphia, 2003.

being recruited as center stage actors to apply government policy. In England and Wales, for example, the Charity Commission has emphasized that charity governance must, as a matter of practice, be independent from governmental authority. However, in that jurisdiction, it has been estimated that "there are 731 charities which have a local authority as a trustee. Moreover, in 595 of these bodies, the local authority is the *sole* trustee."[43]

A strictly defined service delivery relationship with government in itself carries a degree of risk as the government may seek to sidestep accountability for any eventual fall in the level or standard of such services. The greater risk is that in allowing government "capture" of charities or the nonprofit sector, the latter becomes complicit in furthering government policy which leaves them politically compromised in the event of a change of administration, and compromised also in terms of relating to their socially disadvantaged constituencies.

Also, as they assume the bureaucratic processes and the service provision or delivery responsibilities of government bodies, nonprofits have become more like those bodies by acquiring the same service orientation. This is to the detriment of those with needs lying outside the service framework, and this is particularly adverse to the interests of groups with an advocacy brief for social justice or social disadvantage. The risk for charities and the sector as a whole is that by being subordinate and dependent upon government, they compromise their singular mandate. By becoming little more than an adjunct to government, the ability to hold focus on their traditional mission erodes as they become "swamped" by the demands of their agency role.

5. Colonization

Arguably, for many if not most of the jurisdictions studied, the above processes have amounted to an implicit government colonization of the sector: selecting and deselecting by contracts and grants, favoring those willing and able to work in the context of private finance initiatives, and introducing new legal structures to facilitate partnership arrangements. The government preference for partnership with charities—because of the latter's resources, experience, and established bonds with service users—is also divisive for the sector. Other nonprofits justifiably complain about the lack of a "level playing field" as charities, already subsidized by tax exemption privileges, attract further government support by way of service delivery contracts, lottery funds, and direct grants. Frustration with such government involvement in the sector may help explain the recent sudden explosion in the number of social enterprises in the U.K., Ireland, and other states as new outlets are sought for voluntary action.

[43] Seddon, N., *Who Cares?* Civitas, London, 2007, at p. 128, citing Smith, R., and Whittington, P., *Charity: The Spectre of Over-Regulation and State Dependency*, CPS, London, 2006 (unpublished draft, p. 20, citing research by the Charity Commission).

B. Charity, Altruism, and Public Benefit Service Provision

Public benefit is necessary and sufficient both for government delivery and for the entitlement to receive public services. It is necessary but insufficient for charities to engage in public service provision. Altruism and discretion are factors that should differentiate charities from government in this context.

1. Government, Public Benefit Services, and Taxes

There is an argument, derived, perhaps, from the view that income tax concessions can be seen as tax expenditures, that the taxpayer in a modern common law democracy is placed in double jeopardy by the current government approach to charity.[44] A widening band of tax exemption for the public benefit activities of charities increases the tax shortfall for core state services that must be made up by the taxpayer.[45] At the same time, the taxpayers must play silent witness to their taxes being redirected into the funding of charities by the state, whether directly or through disbursement of lottery funds or donor incentive schemes, many of which are already heavily dependent upon government grants or contracts.[46] The government-funded charities may well be selected on a basis with which the citizen disagrees and is powerless to challenge. For example, in the U.K., national lottery funds are being used to offset costs of the Olympic Games, whereas in the United States faith-based penitentiary rehabilitation schemes receive tax revenues to provide in-prison preferential services for those prisoners who subscribe to evangelical Christian precepts. Vivisection research, family planning clinics, private schools and hospitals, and many other controversial facilities will acquire tax-exempt charitable status regardless of citizen choice, and often in the absence of any obvious element of altruism.

Donor incentive schemes can in practice be less than wholly altruistic. Although their net effect is to channel more funds toward government-selected charities than those charities would otherwise receive, donor incentive schemes also serve to attract donors whose primary motivation is to receive a tax benefit. Arguably, there is little altruism involved in giving to charity that which would otherwise be taken in taxes, and if this allows for the donor rather than government to target spending of tax revenues, then altruism may well be further compromised.

[44] O'Halloran, K., McGregor-Lowndes, M., and Simon, K., *Charity Law and Social Policy: National and International Perspectives on the Functions of the Law Relating to Charities*, Springer, The Netherlands, 2009, at p. 511 et seq.

[45] Note, however, the NCVO report that "38% of the sector's income comes from statutory sources, but only 2% of government expenditure on public service delivery is paid to the charitable sector" (see Charity Commission, RS 15, *Stand and Deliver: The Future for Charities Delivering Public Services*, London, 2007, at para. 2.3).

[46] Charity Commission, RS 15, *Stand and Deliver*, where it is reported that "only 8% of charities that said they deliver public services receive no statutory funding" at para 2.3.

Moreover, when charities and other nonprofits step into the public benefit service provision role formerly held by government, they set aside their discretionary freedom to choose public benefit beneficiaries, within their charitable purpose remit, and the means to best address their individual or collective needs. Instead they take on the standardized terms of reference that government employs to determine type of service, eligibility, and mode of delivery. For charities this surrender of discretion is particularly problematic as trustees of charitable trusts are under an obligation to maintain their independence.

2. Charity Autonomy

In virtually all the jurisdictions addressed herein, the distinctive role of charities in the nonprofit sector would seem to be in danger of being compromised by the pressure to accept service delivery responsibilities on behalf of government. The balance in that relationship varies somewhat from its more pronounced agency nature in most common law jurisdictions (noticeably so in the U.K., driven by short-term contracts, but less so in the United States where the open market culture allows greater freedom of choice for all entities) to a more entrenched shared nature in the corporatist jurisdictions of continental Europe.

Partnership in public service provision necessarily involves the parties concerned—government, charity, donor, and recipient—colluding in an arrangement that denies the importance of maintaining a distinction between responsibilities that fall to government and those that rest elsewhere. Government, to a varying degree in all jurisdictions studied, for reasons of cost and risk management is shifting public service responsibilities onto the private shoulders of charity and other nonprofits, which they in turn, for reasons of survival in an aggressively competitive market place, are willing to accept. Consequently, drawing the line between "public" and "private" is becoming increasingly difficult, and is not helped by reluctance on the part of the major players to accept any need to do so.

C. For-profits, Public Benefit Services, and Altruism

The ever-expanding for-profit input is channeling a rapidly growing volume of funds and range of skills into the nonprofit sector through various forms of venture philanthropy, corporate foundations, and social enterprise. The impact of this relatively new flow of funds (which includes government and philanthropic contributions), professional management, network expertise, and general tactical know-how is undoubtedly making its own singular contribution to reshaping the sector. Whether collaborating or competing, for-profits and nonprofits are now in much closer contact with each other and with government bodies in all jurisdictions studied. As the interface between them becomes more complex, interwoven by shared issues and pressures, the nonprofits concerned that survive will necessarily evolve more efficiency and effectiveness.

1. Professional Expertise

In part, the for-profit impact is evident in a transference of attention to administrative matters: The sector is becoming much more concerned with auditing and measuring, with detail and process. Arguably this is at the expense of its traditional strategic and representative engagement with sector issues. There is also, of course, the input of for-profit values, the rhetoric of ethical commercialism, to encourage behavior that is happily both socially responsible and tax advantageous; this is unlikely to wholly distract corporate foundations from their more basic concerns regarding cash flow, market share, and brand protection. Not that this impact is necessarily negative: The drive for business precepts and auditing coming from private donors now requires similar levels of transparency and accountability from charities as from government and business. However, the transfer of business values and practices, honed for use in a competitive market environment where profit margins are the ultimate arbiter of service availability, into the nonprofit sector has not always worked to the latter's advantage.

2. Philanthropic Capitalists

There can be no belittling the hugely beneficial influence of contributions made by "high net worth" philanthropists. The altruism and discretionary choice, exercised by individuals such as Chuck Feeney[47] in building and staffing free-access hospitals in areas of chronic social disadvantage across the world, has done much to demonstrate the values of philanthropy while keeping the sector grounded on its core business.

The phenomenon of modern capitalism converting sizeable proportions of commercial profits to public benefit purposes is confined to neither particular companies nor countries. Entities such as hedge funds are establishing philanthropic foundations, and successful businesspeople in the U.K., Australia, continental Europe, and elsewhere are emulating the example set by Bill Gates, Warren Buffet, and others in the United States. Such global philanthropic initiatives, focused on priority public benefit objectives such as eradicating malaria, can only encourage other charities and the sector in general to be equally global in scale, outlook, and impact. The voluntary redistribution of private wealth for the public benefit, coinciding with government retreat from much public service provision, is helping to redraw the traditional balance between public/private interests in modern democratic developed nations. The direct translation of commercial profits into public benefit services as evidenced by the contribution of the above individuals, even if their altruism is offset by tax incentive considerations, although not far removed from the best traditions of philanthropy, also provides an ironic counterpoint to the

[47] See Clery, C., *The Billionaire Who Wasn't: How Chuck Feeney Made and Gave Away a Fortune without Anyone Knowing*, Public Affairs, New York, 2007.

government bailing out of Citigroup, General Motors, AIG, and other corporations, and an interesting interpretation of "the profits of charity."

V. TRADING BY CHARITIES AND OTHER NONPROFITS

By the second decade of the new millennium, the marketplace in which charity has always been called upon to operate had greatly changed, and the sector has had to adjust accordingly. The traditional model continues to be used: through donor and beneficiary transactions, often via the intervention of a charitable body; through the pockets and structures of poverty that form part of our modern Western societies; and through prescriptive and mutually reinforcing roles. In all of which altruism clearly has a part to play. Such relatively personal, at times face-to-face encounters, have for many years also been supplemented by an international but sometimes more impersonal dimension: the donor state providing long-term support to a developing nation, or for more immediate disaster relief, where again a clearly identifiable charitable organization has a mediatory role, and altruism is often still discernible. Although this familiar pattern will to some extent endure, it has been at least challenged, and may yet be eclipsed by developments in recent years.

A. Funding Charity

Funding, to state the obvious, is of fundamental importance to charity: Enough of it, evenly distributed, and charity is unnecessary; without access to it, charity cannot function. Finding other funding streams to compensate for the loss of government grant aid is a challenge for charities and other nonprofits in all developed Western nations. It has led, in recent years, to the media and the high street in all common law jurisdictions being swamped with fund-raising appeals, and has also led charity into the marketplace to earn through trading the increased level of funds it now needs to respond to the needs of the socially disadvantaged.

1. Government as "Donor"

On the domestic front, funding lies at the heart of the government/charity relationship. Traditionally, charities in many countries have been accustomed to having their public benefit role subsidized by government grant aid. In recent years, diminishing tax revenues coupled with the rapidly climbing costs of services (e.g., health care for the elderly, pharmaceuticals, etc.) have meant that government must rely on charity to assume proportionately more responsibility for public benefit service provision, but, for the same reason, it cannot afford to offset the corresponding costs by way of grant aid. As government diverts funds from public services to bail out banks and private businesses, even though this has been largely by way of short-term loans, charities and other nonprofits are being forced to seek alternative funding by engaging in fee-generating services and general trading ventures.

On the international front, funding is also of central importance: The servicing of national debt repayments has long been crippling for many developing nations, requiring reliance on the resources of international charities. Now the same problem faces many developed nations: Accessing funds through the money markets is becoming impossible for some governments, forcing them to seek handouts from international institutions, which threatens to undermine the value of other currencies. It is clear that this funding equation is set to worsen: Some nations will conceivably default on their EU/IMF loan repayments and/or on agreed housekeeping measures designed to restore economic stability, with unforeseeable consequences for the international community; others will lurch into crisis as the scale of their commitments to public pension funds and "off the balance sheet" PFI arrangements emerge. For many European and most other developed common law nations, the unremitting math of demographic trends (excluding the United States), falling tax revenues, and rising hospital and social care costs (including the United States) means that responsibility for public benefit service provision will have to shift from government to charity, and more broadly to the sector with further involvement of for-profits.

Against this background, the dynamics of the government/charity relationship would seem to clearly reveal a change in government's role as donor, which in turn is forcing charities to take measures to adapt.

2. Charity as "Supplicant"

In all countries discussed herein, though to a varying degree, the financial crisis and economic recession have adversely impacted upon charities, depleting investment funds and triggering a surge in demand for services. As Anheier has pointed out:[48]

> Philanthropic foundations have seen drops in asset values of scales not seen in decades, and continue to expect more losses, especially in the book value of stocks; they anticipate reductions in grant payouts, amidst concerns about the sustainability of current programmes and commitments, and put growing emphasis on asset protection... For foundations and philanthropies generally, the crisis means balancing increased demand for support on the one hand with reduced assets and current as well as projected grant disbursements on the other.

The timing could not be worse for charities and nonprofits generally. As new social enterprises and other hybrid entities enter the market to compete for public benefit service contracts, charities are finding it particularly difficult to raise the capital necessary to improve their effectiveness. With shrinking margins of disposable

[48] See Anheier, H. K., "The Global Economic Downturn, Philanthropy and Nonprofits: Reflections on What It Means, and What to Do," paper presented at Philanthropy and Nonprofits conference, University of Heidelberg, January 2009.

income, donor contributions to charity, in keeping with government grants, are in steep decline. The option of demutualization (the process through which a member-owned company becomes shareholder-owned) taken by many banks, insurance companies, and co-ops in the U.K., Australia, and elsewhere at the turn of the century, is not available to charities. For incorporated charities, raising funds by way of share issue is equally impractical as this would dilute their independence and control, though recent experimentation with social bonds may offer a way forward (see chapter 13).

Arguably, the concept of "ownership" is itself problematic in the context of the sector's terms of reference, perhaps constituting a structural flaw in the legal forms available to nonprofits. The basic absence of an "owner" has until recently, when charity specific banks emerged, made it impossible for charities to raise bank loans or to capitalize on the strength of their equity, even if exposing its assets to such a level of risk could be justified. This inability to attract funds has become seriously compromising for charities globally, and has produced a distinct pattern of responses.

There is evidence that some foundations are simply no longer functioning as charities, but have elected to temporarily reduce or cease giving grants—instead hoarding their assets in the hope that they can better ride out the storm. In New Zealand, for example, the ongoing investigation into Liberty Trust indicates that it is not alone in opting for such a strategy.[49] Conversion, from nonprofit to for-profit status and permanently curtailing charitable functioning would seem to be a practice that is gaining traction particularly in the United States, where it has been found that some nonprofits have actually converted to for-profit status in order to raise capital to compete for social service contracts.[50] Mostly, however, charities in all countries discussed are being driven to compete in the open market to earn rather than solicit the funds necessary to maintain charitable functioning.

3. Investment-Generated Income

Particularly for charitable trusts, safe long-term investments have been the preferred method of protecting the value of a charity's assets while also securing a modest dividend (though, admittedly, major institutions such as Harvard University have demonstrated that other strategies are possible). This form of passive investment

[49] See Liberty Trust v. Charities Commission, HC WN CIV 2010-485-000831 [June 2, 2011]. The High Court then reinstated a Christian mortgage lending scheme as a charity after it was struck off the Register of Charities by the Charities Commission. As explained on the Liberty Trust website: "Since 1989 Liberty Trust has been teaching & enabling New Zealanders to follow God's financial principles of giving, lending and borrowing without interest, in order to assist those in financial difficulty, relieve financial burdens and advance the Kingdom of God." See further at http://www.libertytrust.org.nz/.

[50] Ryan, W. P., "The New Landscape for Nonprofits," in *Harvard Business Review*, January–February 1999, at pp. 127–36, p. 128.

has traditionally been relied upon, mainly by endowed foundations, to generate an annual income for distribution in furtherance of charitable purposes. It continues to be the approach adopted by the larger, more risk-averse foundations in continental Europe. Elsewhere, particularly in the United States and the U.K., charities proved to have little more immunity than other holders of assets to the contagion of rampant capitalism, and consequently have borne their share of losses incurred in the 2008 financial crisis. If anything, many charities are now chastened as a result of bad investments, and are now much more likely to safeguard their assets and look instead to earned income as a source for additional funds.

B. Trading as a Funding Source

The steadily failing capacity of state tax revenues to cope with rising health and social care costs for demographic and other reasons, which has become a settled feature of society in most developed nations, was quite sufficient to bring about a change in the accepted interface between government, charity, and the market. However, the financial crisis and consequent recession has sharply accelerated the pace at which charities and other nonprofits in the jurisdictions studied are now turning to commerce as a means of augmenting their income.

1. Law Reform, Charities, and Trading

It might have been expected that an outcome of charity law reform, predicated as it has been on the need to facilitate a broader portfolio of service provision from charity, would be new statutory provisions to address the common law constraints on trading by charities. However, this was not the case.

In England and Wales, the Charities Act 2011 makes no reference to charities and trading,[51] nor does either the Charities Act 2005 in New Zealand, the Charities Act 1995 in Singapore (revised, 2007), or the Irish Charities Act 2009.[52] In short, governments would seem to be broadly in agreement that this sensitive interface with charities would not benefit from legislative intervention, and might be best left to develop within the existing common law framework of rules and principles. Perhaps, it may be speculated, there was more to be gained by keeping the focus firmly upon charitable activity in relation to public benefit purposes rather than distract from the legislative intent by introducing new rules to govern the charities' possible ancillary and incidental commercial activities.

C. Types of Trade

A definite trend in the commercial adventurism of charities and other nonprofits is the extent to which they are increasingly prepared to develop income-generating

[51] This, presumably, is being left to the Charity Commission to address in the form of guidance.
[52] See s.3(3) plus (7) and (8) of the Charities Act 2009.

activity in areas that are unrelated to their public benefit mission. As Sadiq and Richardson point out:[53]

> pizza chains, carpet cleaning services, turf businesses, car parks, mobile phone ring tones, as well as mortgage broking, employment agencies and insurance companies, are some of the less conventional activities being run by charitable organisations on a commercial basis.[54] As such, it is suggested that charitable organisations are increasingly deriving significant income from activities pursued with the intent of earning a profit.[55] Although the profits may cross-subsidise the provision of charitable services,[56] carrying on commercial activities potentially puts charitable organisations in direct competition with the for-profit sector. The distinguishing feature of these activities is that they are pursued with the intention of deriving a profit and are not necessarily related to the organisation's purpose.

For the sector, the core trade areas continue to be mission-related, those in which charities have acquired expertise and customer credibility and those in which nonprofits have developed because the profit margins were insufficient to attract for-profits. However, trade carries risk. For charities, obligated to protect their assets, engaging in any activity with the object of making a profit presents a degree of risk that must be carefully calibrated as charitable status may be lost if, in the judgment of the regulator, that risk leaves charitable assets unduly exposed. This is more likely to be the case where charities step outside their area of expertise and engage in trading activity unrelated to their charitable purpose.

1. Mission-Related: Public Benefit Provision; Health and Social Care

In all jurisdictions, charities maintain a strong presence in their traditional health-related public benefit provision, most typically in hospital care. The religious origins of such services are usually still very evident, but in some of the more developed Western nations the continued church ownership of some facilities has become obscured by leasing arrangements and the employment of secular professional staff. Nonprofits are prevalent in residential and day care facilities for the elderly and the disabled, but less so in facilities for those with more complex health problems such

[53] Sadiq, K. and Richardson, C., "Tax Concessions for Charities: Competitive Neutrality, the Tax Base and "Public Goods" Choice," in *Australian Tax Forum*, Vol. 25, No. 4, 2010, at p. 604.

[54] Sadiq and Richardson, "Tax Concessions for Charities," citing Ferguson, A., "Charity Cases," in *Business Review Weekly*, March 24, 2005.

[55] Sadiq, K. and Richardson, C., "Tax Concessions for Charities, citing Dalton, B. and Green, J., "Sweet Charity and Filthy Lucre: The Social Construction of Nonprofit Business Venturing in Australia, the United Kingdom and the United States of America" (Working Paper No 72, *Centre for Australian Community Organisations and Management* (CACOM), 2005), at p. 26.

[56] Sadiq, K. and Richardson, C., "Tax Concessions for Charities," citing Steinberg, R., "'Unfair' Competition by Nonprofits and Tax Policy," in *National Tax Journal*, Vol. 44, No. 3, 1991, at p. 351.

as the mentally ill. For-profits are now contesting this corner of the market in many jurisdictions, and the personal care services are rapidly becoming an area of mixed sector provision.[57]

2. Mission-Related: Public Benefit Provision; Other Employment Issues

The current background of rising unemployment has brought nonprofits into the market, most often with government subsidies, to provide services designed to create opportunities and training for employment.

3. Non–Mission-Related

There are innumerable examples of charities actively pursuing commercial ventures wholly unrelated to their charitable purpose. One interesting example is the Seventh Day Adventist Church, which has established a brand of cereals under the Sanitarium label to raise funds to advance its religion. Sanitarium is wholly owned by the Church, and has annual revenues of approximately $300 million from the production of a large range of breakfast cereals and biscuits, including Weet-Bix, a top seller in the Australian and New Zealand breakfast cereal market.

A key factor is whether or not the non–mission-related trade will be treated as tax-exempt. This regulatory matter is one toward which governments often have different views (see chapter 12).

D. Trading Charities, the Market, and Paying a Price

As charities are driven into the contract culture, they accept an ever-increasing level of government funding in return for delivering services, some of which the user pays for in whole or in part. The services are of a type customarily associated with government and thus generally believed to have been pre-paid through taxes. Consequently, there is perhaps a growing resistance among the general public to continue supporting such charities through subscriptions and volunteering. Government efforts, often aided and abetted by fund-seeking charities, to assimilate the latter into public service provision, risk compromising an organization's charitable status and the integrity of its charitable purpose.

Although the increased reliance on funding from non–mission-related trading is of importance to the sector in all jurisdictions studied, the effects of fully engaging in a competitive marketplace is of particular significance for charities. Arguably, profit and charity are antithetical in nature.

[57] See Brown, E. and Slivinski, A., "Nonprofit Organisations and the Market," in Powell, W. and Steinberg, R. (eds.), *Nonprofit Organizations and the Market, in the Non-Profit Sector* (2nd ed.), Yale University Press, New Haven and London, 2006, at pp. 140–158.

1. Charity and Commercial Competition in the Marketplace

In a competitive environment, charities have to become more like their competitors. As Woolley has noted, "when non-profit and for-profit firms operate in the same environment, producing the same services and competing for the same customers, they will tend to produce similar quality goods and services."[58] This leads to the product becoming the center of attention: sharply defined, discrete, readily replicated, and packaged to attract. To succeed in that environment, goods or services, although modeled with an eye to similar competitive products, have to also offer the consumer some added value. That added extra is often the tax-subsidized low price and social cachet attached to the charity label, which can trigger protests alleging unfair competition from for-profits. In particular, increased competition creates pressure toward increased size, economies of scale, professional management, organizational sophistication, and ability to access capital to expand services. These pressures are mounting in all jurisdictions studied, in the face of competition from the many for-profits eager to secure opportunities for public benefit service contracts created by government retraction.[59]

Moreover, as product specification and the need to successfully compete become more of a pressing concern to charities, there is a corresponding increased danger of "going off mission": losing sight of established long-term strategies in exchange for tactical improvements in trading capacity, accompanied by an erosion of the values that had previously driven the charity. There is a view that a correlation exists between increased market activity, with its focus on meeting the needs of individual clients, and a decrease in strategic vision, with its focus on meeting the needs of the neighborhood or community through the provision of public goods.[60]

2. The Contemporary Market

The Hansmann "contract failure" theory[61] is now beginning to look a bit dated. Hansmann postulated that the existence of nonprofits derives from public "trust" in the mission-driven charity or nonprofit coupled with an appreciation of the effects of the nondistribution constraint, with both serving to distinguish nonprofits from

[58] Woolley, F., "The Strengths and Limits of the Voluntary Sector," in *Isuma: Canadian Journal of Policy Research*, Vol. 2, No. 2, 2001, at pp. 21–27.

[59] Young, D., & Salamon, L., "Commercialization, Social Ventures, and For-Profit Competition," in Salamon, L. (ed.), *The State of Nonprofit America*, Brookings Institution Press, Washington, DC, 2002, at pp. 425–48.

[60] Alexander, J., Nank, R., and Stivers, C., "Implications of Welfare Reform: Do Nonprofit Survival Strategies Threaten Civil Society?," in *Nonprofit and Voluntary Sector Quarterly*, Vol. 28, No. 2, 1999, at pp. 452–75.

[61] Hansmann, H., "The Role of Nonprofit Enterprise," in *Yale Law Journal*, Vol. 89, No. 5, 1980, at pp. 835–902.

for-profits. Today, Hansmann's theory no longer seems entirely adequate. In the intervening decades, as the market has become more complex, public trust has diminished, and the distinction between "public" and "private" interests is now much more nuanced.

Perhaps the most intriguing and potentially transformative development is that the concept of "market" has broadened for charities. The traditional problem for charity has been that its presence in the marketplace was circumscribed by its role as supplicant. In this sense, trustee duties prevented any investment that posed a risk to assets, and there was no "owner" whose credit could be advanced to secure the funds needed for organizational development, which left, basically, a record of past virtuous activity to be traded or leveraged to attract future altruistic donations. A charity's capacity to use the equity of its considerable assets, secured in perpetuity, to raise capital for use within a shorter time span was virtually impossible. Uniquely, among the asset-rich entities that crowded the marketplace at the turn of 20th century, charity was more a passive participant than player.

The lessons learned from the industrialization of the equity market at that time have not been lost on charity. Its creditworthiness, based on expertise and networks, reinforced by its measurable and legally secured assets that could not be jeopardized, have come to be recognized as having an equitable value. In the U.K., early indications of a charitable organization's ability to be able to capitalize on its assets came with the launch of the Big Society Bank by Prime Minister David Cameron in July 2010, backed by initial funding of £600 million, to attract additional capital to the nonprofit sector from charitable foundations, institutional investors, companies, and private individuals. The Bank is intended to support organizations that invest in the sector, helping them to provide a greater range of financial services to charities and other nonprofit organizations and to raise more money for onward investment in the sector. This initiative was established in the context of several other social finance experiments in the U.K., Israel, Canada, and elsewhere. However, perhaps of greater long-term significance for charities and the nonprofit sector as a whole has been the launch of Social Impact Bonds in the U.K. This conceptual breakthrough in investments, known in the United States as Pay for Success Bonds, promises to radically alter the marketplace by making a connection between investors and the equity locked up in charities. Through Social Impact Bonds, charities can now be placed in the market as a player. Government costs are paid post-intervention and out of accrued savings, while private investors bear any risk of loss, thus providing a real incentive for government to work in partnership with charities and co-opted private investment funding to intervene in embedded social problems with preventative schemes. A challenge to government and charity is how to utilize the "bond tool" in a way that enables nonprofits rather than for-profits to assume responsibility for core public benefit services such as the failing NHS hospitals in the U.K.

However, market failure has been the cause of many social problems with which charities are now being left to cope. Whether charities should accept an invitation to increase their market activity is a moot point. The "capitalization of charity" may be an answer to a problem in the market but if the market is itself the problem, then charity may be best advised to maintain some distance and access it, by trading and service contracts, on its own cautious terms.

VI. CONCLUSION

The 2008 financial crisis, and the global efforts made by government to retrieve the economy, stand as a reminder that the market still rules. It may collapse periodically but is clearly considered to be such an essential component of democratic nations, differentiating them from all others, that terminal decline cannot be contemplated. The flaws, represented by the continuing presence of poverty in the most affluent nations on earth, as well as its endemic nature elsewhere, and by the failings of our financial institutions, are to be accommodated and the necessary adjustments made to restore market functioning. It would seem that poverty, charity, and the recurring economic nonviability of some people, institutions, and countries are simply the price to be paid to maintain the relatively free trade approach, based on a monetary system, that powers the developed Western economies.

However, after the checks and balances are sufficiently tweaked and business returns to something like normal, it may well be that consideration could usefully be given to how charities and the nonprofit sector can be better positioned to counterbalance some of the market's more socially detrimental effects. For example, it might be prudent in the long run if charities and their purposes were protected from the risk of becoming absorbed into the market. As the nonprofit sector in general suffers the effects of a withdrawal of government funding, charities everywhere are being driven to experiment in a wide variety of non–mission-related trading ventures. When this happens and charities compete for profit margins in the marketplace, altruism takes a backseat.

If public trust in mission-driven charities is to be restored, then, rather than experimenting with new ways of enticing charities to trade in the marketplace, it may be that government should invest in grant-aiding at least those charities with a "welfare" type mission so that for them, trading is unnecessary and, possibly, prohibited. They need to be relieved from their current state of dependency: having to constantly find ways of acquiring the funds necessary to keep functioning; in a parody of the supplicant/benefactor dynamic that has traditionally epitomized the place of charity in society. Charity should be helped to regain its independence. Arguably, given market values and their effects, as demonstrated in the 2008 financial crisis, it is not unimportant that charity values are preserved.

12

NEW REGULATORY MECHANISMS

I. INTRODUCTION

The need for an efficient regulatory regime is widely accepted. Indeed, as Hopt and Hippel assert:[1]

> enforcement is crucial. In fact, this may even be the key question regarding non-profit organizations. But what kind of enforcement? The state alone cannot do it appropriately without killing initiative and enthusiasm. But there are no shareholders, in particular institutional shareholders, and no nonprofit organization share markets. This seems to remain the "central paradox of non-profit corporation governance": so much public and private largesse and so few accountability restraints. On this central unresolved question much more work has to be done.

Recognizing the dearth of state enforcement, this chapter gives particular attention to the regulatory rules now constraining charity activity as a consequence of initiatives taken by the judiciary rather than the legislature. Although such new regulatory mechanisms have a broad effect on the sector, and charities in general, their impact on charities engaged in trading remains the main focus of attention.

The chapter begins by surveying the type and effect of new regulatory mechanisms introduced as an outcome of charity law reform in the jurisdictions studied. It details the new governance and accountability requirements; the traditional constraints and new sanctions; the introduction of charity-specific lead regulatory bodies; and the fact that charitable purposes may be verified by the "activities test" in some jurisdictions. It will assess the evidence for considering the present government/charity relationship

[1] See Hopt, K. and T. Von Hippel (eds.), *Comparative Corporate Governance of Non-Profit Organizations*, Cambridge, Cambridge University Press 2010, at p. xivii.

to be one of principal and agent, and analyzes the resulting implications. In the main, the chapter examines the effect of judicial and regulatory rules that constrain charities' capacity to trade and compete in the open market. It takes into account jurisdictional differences in tax regime reforms aimed at protecting charities and encouraging donors by way of recalibrating tax systems, donor incentives, subsidies, conditions, etc. It also considers the nature and effect on trading charities of the raft of antiterrorism legislation now introduced in all jurisdictions.

II. CHARITY LAW REFORM, REGULATORY CONSTRAINTS, CHARITIES, AND THE NONPROFIT SECTOR

In all common law jurisdictions, other than in England and Wales, charities had traditionally been subject to light regulatory control: Accountability for fiscal matters lay to the Revenue, standards of practice were largely a matter for the professional bodies involved, and the High Court together with the Attorney General exercised a degree of oversight. Typically, different areas of responsibility were distributed across different sets of statutes, and government responsibility was diffuse and spread between different departments; processes had assumed a high level of path dependency that was slow to respond to emerging contemporary issues. There was a growing awareness of the need for systems to identify, register, and regulate charities, for the consolidation of legislative provisions relating to charities and their activities, and for the coordination of the many government departments and agencies involved. For a number of the jurisdictions studied, the charity law reform processes brought similar important changes to this regulatory framework reflecting the intent of the governments concerned to equip charity to play a fuller future role in public benefit provision.

A. Charity Law Reform: New Regulatory Outcomes

Following the lead provided by England and Wales in the Charities Act 2006, now the Charities Act 2011, certain key regulatory outcomes were achieved by law reform in other U.K. jurisdictions, Ireland, Australia, New Zealand, Singapore, and Hong Kong. Equivalent changes have yet to occur in the United States, Canada, and continental Europe. The changes successfully made to the regulatory framework included: a new independent lead regulatory body; an appeals tribunal or procedure; a charity register; adjustments to the traditional roles of court and Attorney General; and an updating of the law relating to other matters such as trustees, fund-raising, cy pres, and legal structures for charitable activity.

1. Decoupling Charitable Status and Tax Exemption

An outcome of considerable importance has been the decision in Scotland, Northern Ireland, Ireland, Singapore, and to a lesser extent in New Zealand (as yet only proposed in Australia), to follow the example of England and Wales and decouple the regulatory mechanisms for charities and for determining charitable status from those traditionally used to regulate tax liability. These jurisdictions have now established relatively independent, charity-specific, lead regulatory bodies[2] empowered by statute to support the sector, maintain a register of charities, determine charitable status, provide advice and improve governance, monitor by way of annual reports and financial statements, and conduct audits and investigations. More recently, in June 2011, Hong Kong announced its intention to also introduce legislation for setting up a Charities Commission that would register and regulate charitable organizations.

Armed with an extended definition of "charitable purpose" together with access to the "spirit and intendment" rule,[3] the new regulatory bodies are now positioned to adopt a more expansive approach to charitable status than Revenue ever considered desirable. Equally, for the first time, these jurisdictions now have in place a government body that can monitor activity in the nonprofit sector and serve as a bridgehead between it and government. As has been the case with the Charity Commission, the new regulatory bodies occupy strategic ground where they can support charities and develop the sector while also advising government as to sector trends and needs and assisting in formulating sector-related policy.

Consequently, Scotland, Northern Ireland, Ireland, Singapore, New Zealand, and Hong Kong, like England and Wales, will now, for the first time, have a dedicated agency with a specific brief to regulate charities, monitor their activities, protect their assets, and ensure compliance with standards of practice enshrined in statute. Appeals will lie against agency decisions.[4] In Australia, in an interesting initiative, the equivalent newly established agency will have similar powers that will extend beyond charities to include all nonprofit entities.[5] In all those jurisdictions a tighter regulatory regime will now introduce greater transparency and accountability while also providing the means for closer government tracking of cash flows in the sector and for scrutinizing matters of governance.

[2] The new bodies vested with responsibility for determining charitable status and registering and supervising charities are: in Scotland, the Office of the Scottish Charity Regulator; in Northern Ireland, the Charity Commission for Northern Ireland; in Singapore, the Commissioner of Charities; and in New Zealand, the Charities Commission.

[3] Perhaps to the exclusion of Ireland as there is no reference to the rule in the Charities Act 2009.

[4] Australia is set to follow the U.K. example, as was apparent in the recommendation of the Senate Committee that "the establishment of a Charity Tribunal is preferable to the automatic referral of compliance issues to a court within the Australian judiciary" (see Senate Standing Committee on Economics, *Disclosure Regimes for Charities and Not-For-Profit Organisations*, 2002, at para. 1.15).

[5] See Australian Government, The Treasury, *Final Report—Scoping Study for a National Not-For-Profit Regulator*, April 2011.

B. Charity Law Reform: Retention of Traditional Regulatory Rules

Charities are different from other nonprofits. The difference lies not only in the enormous wealth of some foundations that have existed for many generations, but in the intimate links forged with their particular socially disadvantaged constituencies and the stored archives of irreplaceable data. The privilege of charitable status is accompanied by responsibilities, some strictly legal and others resembling moral obligations, that require charities to behave in ways not required of their fellow nonprofits (see chapter 3). Their entitlement to considerable tax-exemption privileges comes at the price of accepting well-established common law restrictions. Other nonprofits, denied such privileges, may have good cause for grievance as charities become progressively more uninhibited, assume the behavioral characteristics of commercial enterprises, and are tempted to use their status to gain an unfair competitive advantage.

The charity law reform processes are therefore also important because of the decision by the governments concerned to leave certain matters and long-established rules unchanged. It is clearly intended that their restraining effects should carry forward to constrain the future role of charity. They include key benchmarks that differentiate charity from other nonprofits, such as the obligations resting on its trustees to protect its fiduciary base, assert its independence, represent the socially disadvantaged, maintain an exclusive focus on furthering its charitable purpose, and prevent an improper distribution of profits. These have a general applicability to charity and therefore also impact upon charities that trade (see below).

1. Protect Assets

Anheier has drawn attention to the losses suffered by charities, perhaps on an unprecedented scale, as a consequence of the recent financial crisis.[6] Evidence is also available from other sources, for example in the U.K. and the United States, that charity assets have indeed been adversely affected at precisely the time when their resources are most needed. Although it would be quite wrong to suggest that this was directly caused by reckless trading, the evidence from the protests of many U.K. charities when the Icelandic banks defaulted on repayments does indicate that they had shared to some degree in prevailing cavalier investing practices, though many simply suffered collateral damage as the investment market collapsed. The involvement of some in the world of venture philanthropy and hedge funds also negatively impacted the assets of the charities concerned. There is now a view, perhaps emanating from government sources, that foundations should show a willingness

[6] See Anheier, H. K., "The Global Economic Downturn, Philanthropy and Nonprofits: Reflections on What It Means, and What to Do," paper presented at Philanthropy and Nonprofits conference, University of Heidelberg, January 2009.

to utilize more of their assets for current public benefit purposes. As recent events have demonstrated, any such enticement of charities to help make good the damage caused to the economy by engaging more fully in the world of commerce carries the real risk of encouraging a breach of the strict obligation to safeguard funds and ensure they accrue to the benefit of the intended beneficiaries. The reform processes left untouched this most basic duty: to protect charity assets.

2. Maintain Independence

The legislative intent underpinning the Preamble[7] rested on the assumption that both government and charity would, in partnership, address the social policy agenda then outlined. In recent years, as public/private finance initiatives proliferated, accompanied by the emergence of new hybrid vehicles for facilitating joint government, and charity ventures that permit the involvement of for-profit bodies, there was growing concern as to how the principle of independence of control could in the future be realistically assured. This principal is rooted in trust law, and has long been held to be a hallmark of charitable status. That the integrity of charity is also under threat from the predations of commerce was clearly demonstrated by the rash of "conversions" in the United States from charitable to for-profit status. In that jurisdiction during the 1990s, there were a considerable number of instances where charities and other nonprofits were taken over or bought out by commercial businesses, or simply converted from nonprofit to for-profit status as sectoral boundaries became more hotly disputed and private enterprise encroached further on public benefit frontiers. This conversion trend was a growing and potentially very significant phenomenon, particularly in the field of health care,[8] but the merger mania has slowed as the economics of health care have changed. As the *Empire Blue Cross Blue Shield* case in the United States has demonstrated (see chapter 7), the time is rapidly coming when the common law nations will need to address the issues relating to the conversion from charity to for-profit. Where a charity, such as a hospital or nursing home, that has built up its expertise and efficiency over many years with the aid of tax exemptions, public donations, and government grants, wishes to transform itself into a for-profit, then some form of reparation will need to be made to the public purse on its conversion to a commercial entity.

There has never been any legislative initiative to address the problems associated with for-profit conversion, a matter of trust and proper governance, and incorporate appropriate procedures within the body of charity law. Such statutory duties as exist are to be found expressed with varying degrees of stringency in legislation specific to the type of legal structure (company law, trusts, societies, associations, etc.). Legal reform left the law relating to conversion unchanged. In all jurisdictions

[7] Preamble to the Statute of Charitable Uses 1601.

[8] See Lipman, H. "Health-Conversion Funds Hold $16 Billion in Assets," in *Chronicle of Philanthropy*, May 4, 2000, at p. 12, and Grantmakers in Health, *A Profile of New Health Foundations*, Grantmakers in Health, 2011, Washington, D.C., 2003.

concerned, the new legislation avoided incorporating any provisions that might tend to differentiate between the remit of government and charity as regards public benefit service provision,[9] and obstruct any future transfer of responsibilities from the former to the latter.

3. Advocacy

Charities must represent and act as advocates, within established common law constraints, for the best interests of their socially disadvantaged constituencies. For those that have succumbed to "mission drift," become overly complicit in a failed government policy or service delivery programs, or compromised their position by becoming publicly associated with a for-profit company or by the need to solicit or retain customers for a local trading venture, their capacity to act as advocates is constrained. The pressures on some charities to protect funding sources and their market position threaten not just their own independence but that of the sector as a whole. There is a danger of the unique identity of charity and the integrity of charitable purposes being undermined by pressures to conform to market expectations, of the charity brand being franchised out to suit the vagaries of the marketplace.[10]

The common law rule that a voluntary organization seeking to acquire or retain charitable status and qualify for attendant tax privileges must avoid having political purposes and engaging in most forms of political activity,[11] subsists with varying degrees of stringency in many common law jurisdictions.[12] It applies equally to campaigning for such change within or outside the jurisdiction in which the charity is based.[13] The reform processes avoided the opportunity to unequivocally assert the right of charities to be established for advocacy purposes. This leaves the law as it was before: any organization intending to campaign for a change in the law as

[9] See, e.g., Charity Commission, *Applications for Registration of (i) Trafford Community Leisure Trust and (ii) Wigan Leisure and Culture Trust*, April 21, 2004, and Central Bayside Division of General Practice Ltd v. Commissioner of State Revenue [2005] VSCA 168.

[10] See, e.g., Opinion Leader Research for the Charity Commission, *Report of Findings of a Survey of Public Trust and Confidence in Charities*, London, Nov. 2005, at http://www.google.co.uk/search?q=Opinion+Leader+Research+for+the+Charity+Commission%2C+Report+of+Findings+of+a+Survey+of+Public+Trust+and+Confidence+in+Charities%2C+London%2C+Nov.+2005&ie=utf-8&oe=utf-8&aq=t&rls=org.mozilla:en-US:official&client=firefox-a.

[11] See, e.g., Bowman v. Secular Society [1917] AC 406, National Anti-vivisection Society v. Inland Revenue Commissioners [1948] AC 31 (HL), and McGovern v. Attorney General [1982] Ch. 321.

[12] Note that charities may campaign against certain laws provided their goal is to educate the public to do voluntarily that which they may otherwise be statutorily required to do. For example, the purpose in Jackson v. Phillips (1867) 96 Mass. (14 Allen) 539 was to end slavery, not by changing the law, but by changing public sentiment through education.

[13] See Baldry v. Feinbuck [1972] 1W.L.R. 552; (1971) 115 SJ 965; [1972] 2 All E.R. 81 and Webb v. O'Doherty (1991) 3 Admin. LR 731, *The Times*, February 11, 1991 respectively.

its sole or main objective will still have to forego charitable status, although this rule now has a more relaxed application in the United States and in Australia.[14] As charities are increasingly drawn into service delivery contracts on behalf of government, it is a rule that for them will become progressively more inhibiting. The resulting problems have been highlighted in a report that stressed "when restrictions on the ability of charities to engage in political campaigning substantially curtail their contribution to civil society, charity law and regulation is clearly in need of change."[15]

4. Exclusively Charitable

The common law rule, now committed to statute in some jurisdictions as an outcome of charity law reform,[16] requires that a charity be established with exclusively charitable purposes. This implies that the charity should not stray beyond the parameters of its purposes in pursuit of funding. It is a rule often more honored in the breach than compliance as charities creatively reconfigure their objects and purposes as expedience requires in order to compete for contracts or to otherwise secure a market advantage. In the United States, it has long since given way to open market considerations and a more flexible interpretation.[17]

The principles of equity, which for centuries have informed the actions of trusts and continue to underpin the modern concept of charity, require the latter to accept and respect the terms on which the charity was set up. Failure to do so not only jeopardizes the right to charitable status but also exposes the organization to "mission drift" as it constantly adapts to meet the requirements of the next government contract and loses both its mandate with stakeholders and its market niche as uncertainty comes to surround its identity. All charity law reform processes left intact this traditional requirement that for a trust to be charitable, it must be confined exclusively to a charitable purpose.[18]

5. Distribution of Profits

The common law rule that charities may make profits (or gains) or accumulate surpluses, provided these are "retained for its purposes and none can enure to the

[14] Following the decision in Aid/Watch Incorporated v. Commissioner of Taxation [2010] HCA 42; [2009] FCAFC 128.

[15] See Kennedy, H., *Report of the Advisory Group on Campaigning and the Voluntary Sector*, London, 2007.

[16] See, e.g., in Ireland the Charities Act 2009, s.2(1).

[17] See Treas. Reg. § 1.501 (c)(3)-1 (c)(1) where it is explained that the operational test applied by the IRS interprets "exclusively" to mean "primarily" or "substantially."

[18] See Commissioners of Inland Revenue v. Yorkshire Agricultural Society [1928] 1 KB 611, Inland Revenue Commissioners v. City of Glasgow Police Athletic Association [1953] AC 380, Commissioner of Inland Revenue v. Royal Naval and Royal Marine Officers' Association (1955) 36 TC 187 and Oxford Group v. Inland Revenue Commissioners (1949) 2 All ER 537; in Australia, see Salvation Army (Vic) Property Trust v. Shire of Ferntree Gully (1952) 85 CLR 159.

benefit of its individual members"[19] or for distribution to its owners or members, or to any other person, either while operating or on winding up (also known as "the nondistribution constraint") continues in effect.[20] Indeed, it is given legislative authority in New Zealand by the Charities Act 2005, s.13(1)(b)(ii), and has formal regulatory standing in the United States under § 501(c)(2) and (3) and by the private benefit rules under U.S. Department of Treasury regulations.[21] The prohibition on private benefit has been assertively upheld by the judiciary in Australia[22] and by the Canada Revenue Agency in Canada.[23] In the United States, a distinction is drawn between the private inurement rule (preventing profit distribution among those responsible for the charity) and the prohibition on private benefit (preventing profit from being distributed to anyone including outsiders). Both are enforced: the former strictly so, but there is a more relaxed approach to the latter as a reasonable amount of private benefit is permissible. A breach of either may be punished by loss of charitable status. The charging of fees for services is normally consistent with nonprofit status in all common law jurisdictions. Generally, the legal reform processes did not deal with charities and trading, and did no more than restate the profit distribution rule.[24] Governments would seem to have taken the view that this sensitive interface with charities would not benefit from legislative intervention and might be best left to develop within the existing common law framework of rules and principles.

C. Law Reform and Governance

A charity in its simplest form has no need for a sophisticated system of governance. Beyond the necessary functional division between leaders and others, all involved are united in pursuance of their collective charitable purpose. Whatever their legal structure, charities tend to conform to a common typology in that they are mission-driven (though any mission statement must be consistent with, and not wider than, the charity's purposes), pursuing a focused philanthropic endeavor that, infused throughout the organization, permits and encourages overlapping board and staff functions. This serves to distinguish the modus operandi of charities from commercial companies, which tend to be driven by profit considerations.

However, ensuring good governance, transparency, and accountability are now matters of as much concern to charity as to big business. Probity, the quality

[19] Incorporated Council of Law Reporting for England and Wales v. Attorney-General [1972] Ch 73 (CA) 90, per Sachs L.J.

[20] Hansmann, H., "Unfair Competition and the Unrelated Business Income Tax," in *Virginia Law Review*, Vol. 75, No. 2, 1989, at 605.

[21] Treas. Reg. § 1.501(c)(3)-1(d)(1)(ii) (as amended in 2008).

[22] Incorporated Council of Law Reporting of the State of Queensland v. FC of T (1971) 125 CLR 659.

[23] See CRA, CPS-019.

[24] In Ireland, e.g., see the Charities Act 2009, s.3(3).

of strategic and operational planning, together with the management of staff and resources to address organizational objectives, are among the standards to be met regardless of whether a charity is functioning within the structure of a company, trust, unincorporated association, or another legal form. These standards are likely to be matters of particular concern to those governments planning on making room for charities to share more of their public service burden. To the extent that they introduced registration requirements, new monitoring mechanisms, and tightened up on reporting obligations, the law reform outcomes have improved the governance of charities. The importance of such improvements is apparent when contrasted with the lack of transparency in some continental European countries where equivalent law reform has not occurred, and where information on the disbursement and activities of foundations (such as the Sandoz Fondation de Famille and the Fondation Hans Wilsdorf in Switzerland, and the Stichting Ingka Foundation in the Netherlands) is not as readily available.

1. The New Regulatory System

Ensuring that charities are identifiable, that they exercise honesty and accountability in the use of funds given or subsidized by the public, and that the related processes are transparent and readily amenable to public inspection, are important functions of regulatory bodies. One of the more significant outcomes of charity law reform has been the introduction of a system for the registration of charities in some jurisdictions. A charity specific register would underpin an accompanying regulatory regime, requiring all entrants to submit an annual statement of accounts and a report of their activities, and is the basis for setting and monitoring standards and promoting the effective use of the property of charitable trusts or charitable organizations. This undoubtedly facilitates transparency, permits the monitoring of effectiveness, and improves accountability in relation to the activities of charities, whatever their legal form.

D. Law Reform and the Change from Adjudication to Administration

For many jurisdictions an important outcome of charity law reform has been the transfer, for most purposes, of the traditional role as the forum for developing charitable purposes from the High Court to a Commission. The *parens patriae* remit of the Attorney General[25] in relation to charities has similarly largely passed to the Commission or, as in Ireland, has entirely passed to that body. Although an adjudicative function has been provided for in some jurisdictions by the creation

[25] See, e.g., Seymour, J., "Parens Patriae and Wardship Powers: Their Nature and Origins," in *Oxford Journal of Legal Studies*, Vol. 14, No. 2, 1994, pp. 159–88.

of charity tribunals,[26] it remains to be seen whether these will survive given their limited use. The surgical excision of charity law from its common law context, in particular the stripping out of those remnants of its feudal past that gave it such an arcane image but also guaranteed the protection of the highest court in the land, and its transplanting into a more government-controlled environment, is a matter that must give rise to some concern. It comes at a time when government in many jurisdictions has a clear intent to develop a closer relationship with charity.

1. Charity and the Common Law: An Emerging Structural Flaw

The evolution of "charity" in a common law context has always rested on successive key judicial precedents. Most common law jurisdictions, by and large, have regarded decisions established in the courts of England and Wales as being at least persuasive in shaping the development of their charity law. The fact that the direction of growth in activities defined as "charitable" was thus placed in the impartial hands of the judiciary has arguably been of considerable significance for charity, strengthening the relative autonomy of the nonprofit sector throughout the common law world for many generations. However, as charity litigation became more infrequent and expensive, and more likely to attract adverse media publicity, the opportunities have faded for the High Court to continue to influence the development of charity law. For most of the jurisdictions studied,[27] the growing inability of charity law to respond appropriately to emerging patterns of social need has come to constitute a structural flaw in the contemporary role of charity within a common law context that required legislative correction. In the future, for the U.K., Ireland, and other jurisdictions, adjusting the fit between charitable purpose and social need will be a matter resting largely in the hands of government-appointed Commissioners: Law will now be "made" more by administrative than adjudicative decisions.

2. Implications for the Sector

It is, of course, no coincidence that so many jurisdictions have taken much the same steps to adjust the regulatory framework for charitable activity, at much the same time.

In the common law jurisdictions, as the nonprofit sector grew and became a more cohesive entity, the principal means of orchestrating the relationship between

[26] For England and Wales, see the Charities Act 2006, s.57 and the Transfer of Functions of the Charity Tribunal Order 2009; for Scotland, the Charities and Trustee Investment (Scotland) Act 2005, s.75; for Northern Ireland, the Charities Act (Northern Ireland) 2008, Part 3, sections 12–15; for Ireland, the Charity Act 2009, sections 75–80.

[27] The relevance of the common law approach has, perhaps, been maintained in the United States, where the courts have had a greater frequency of engagement with charity issues if less need to be guided by U.K. precedents.

it and the state[28] continued to rest on charity law. In particular, the Preamble agenda as developed by principles and precedents established by charity law over centuries, largely pooled between the common law nations, shaped a core code for mediating responsibility between government and sector on matters of public benefit provision. Although in time charity law accommodated some legislative additions (notably in relation to sport and recreation) and a judicial broadening of definitional matters, it remained largely immune from direct legislative interference by government. By the turn of the 21st century, with uncertainty surrounding responsibility for future public benefit provision, both government and sector needed to review their relationship. The regulatory outcomes of the reform processes have now introduced new legislatively imposed frameworks for charity and some broader implications for the future relationship between government and sector.

Apart from Singapore, the governments of all reforming jurisdictions engaged in a lengthy consultation process with the sector before finalizing reform outcomes. This consultation process has itself been an affirming experience for the sector. The recognition it acquired as a political entity received further acknowledgement with the substitution of the Commission for Revenue as the lead regulatory body. Establishing such a body, with a charity-specific focus, indicates that its proven mediatory role is valued as a bridging mechanism between government and sector in the context of public benefit provision. The move toward an implied public benefit partnership between government and sector has been further advanced in the U.K, Ireland, New Zealand, and Australia by the construction of an institutional infrastructure around the central role of a Charity Commission and an extended list of specified charitable purposes to bridge the government/sector divide. Nothing could more clearly demonstrate the political importance of charity to government than the latter's efforts to strategically integrate charity regulation within a broader framework of formal links with the sector. As Kendall expresses it, "when concrete relationships and practices are examined, apparently apolitical processes turn out to be politically embedded in a way that affects their trajectory systematically."[29]

Australia has gone a step further beyond the U.K. model. Instead of restricting its new regulatory framework to a charity-specific remit, the Australian government has chosen a more expansive approach by broadening the framework to apply to all nonprofits. This would seem to bring the governments of Australia and the United States into a closer alignment as regards to treating charities the same as all nonprofit entities. This could possibly reflect a weaker tradition of reliance upon the charitable trust in these jurisdictions. Given the increasing size and diversification of the sector; the

[28] There are, of course, other means of lesser importance that also contribute to the same end: Service agreements and contractual relations rather than legislation also have a part to play.

[29] Kendall, J. and Taylor, M., "On the Interdependence between Politics and Policy in the Shaping of English Horizontal Third Sector Initiative," in Gidron, B. and Bar, M. (eds.), *Policy Initiatives towards the Third Sector in International Perspective*, Springer Publishing, The Netherlands, 2009, at p. 190.

unwieldy body of dated, restrictive, and often redundant case law; the need to allow for a commercial dimension; and the baggage and connotations associated with "charity," this step taken by Australia and the United States is, perhaps, to be commended. For those jurisdictions content to adopt the U.K. model, it would seem that the frame of reference provided by charity law, reinforced by an institutional infrastructure, constituted a package sufficient to progress a rebalanced government/sector division of responsibilities for future public benefit service provision.

III. CHARITY AND GOVERNMENT: PUBLIC BENEFIT SERVICE PROVISION, THE AGENCY CONSTRAINT, AND CASE LAW

The permission given in the Preamble for public service provision to be shared by government and charity has since been pursued with some enthusiasm in many jurisdictions. Charities, however, have always been required to demonstrate a sufficient, if uncertain, degree of independence from government. As Brody and Tyler have pointed out, "foundations and other charities are not inherently public bodies and their assets are not 'public money.'"[30] Lately there have been some indications that the judiciary are beginning to explore the circumstances in which a contract between government and charity might denote the existence of a de facto agency relationship, and if so, what implications then arise for the parties concerned. In the case law principles now being tentatively formed in a number of jurisdictions may lie the seeds of serious constraints on future public service provision by charities on behalf of government.

A. Agency

The common law principle of "agency" found early expression in the Latin maxim *qui facit per alium, facit* per se (the one who acts through another, acts in his or her own interests). It has been defined as "the relationship between a principal and an agent whereby the principal, expressly or impliedly, authorizes the agent to work under his control and on his behalf."[31] Whether an agency relationship exists turns on the facts in each case; not all delegated authority necessarily constitutes agency, and the span of control exercised is crucial.

1. The "Principal and Agent" Relationship

An agent who acts within the scope of authority conferred by the principal binds the principal in the obligations created against third parties; the authority may

[30] See Brody, E. and Tyler, J., "How Public Is Private Philanthropy? Separating Reality from Myth," in *The Philanthropy Roundtable*, June 2009, at p. 63.

[31] See, e.g., Markesinis, B. S. and Munday. R. J. C., *An Outline of the Law of Agency* (4th ed), LexisNexis, London, 1998.

be expressly conferred by the principal or may arise by implication. The acts of an agent, acting within the scope of delegated authority, are imputed to the principal; failings in service delivery are the responsibility of the principal, and in matters governed by public law, the principal can be held accountable.

B. Government, Charity, and Service Delivery Contracts

Mostly, government contracts with charities take the form of discrete, well-defined packages that are not of central importance to government or a charity. The services in question merely sit within government function and within charitable purpose; their delegation does not distort the capacity of either party. In some cases, however, the services represent an important component of government function and cannot be wholly separated out, as government must retain policy control. The services are delegated with an accompanying requirement that their policy parameters be respected, and the policy advanced and the services themselves are subject to ongoing government monitoring. For the charity concerned, the services may be crucial: of marginal significance to furthering its charitable purpose but vital to its economic survival, constituting a disproportionately high level of its total activity, and contract renewal may have become its most pressing goal. Out of such circumstances an agency relationship may emerge, if not expressly then by implication.[32]

1. Jurisdictional Case Law: Delegation of Services Compatible with Charitable Status

In England and Wales, the Charity Commission decided in the *Trafford and Wigan* case[33] to grant charitable status to entities established by the government to provide what until then had been local authority public services, with almost total government funding. Where charitable purpose coincides with government function, then, provided the nonprofit does not exist simply and solely as a means of carrying out a public authority's duties or policy, it would seem that the delegation of such services is compatible with charitable status. This ruling, that the functions of central or local government can be discharged by a body established for exclusively charitable purposes, has led to the transfer of leisure centers and other public service

[32] See Handy, C., "The Privatisation of Social Housing: Capture and Commercialisation of the Voluntary Sector," in Dunn, A. (ed.), *The Voluntary Sector, the State and the Law*, Hart Publishing, Oxford, 2000, at pp. 107–19.

[33] See Charity Commission, *Applications for Registration of (i) Trafford Community Leisure Trust and (ii) Wigan Leisure and Culture Trust*, April 21, 2004 where "it was accepted as a good charitable purpose to relieve the community from general or local taxation provided that such purpose was applied for the benefit of a sufficient section of the community." See further at http://www.google.co.uk/search?q=Charity+Commission%2C+Applications+for+Rregistration+of+%28i%29+Trafford+Community+Leisure+Trust+and+%28ii%29+Wigan+Leisure+and+Culture+Trust&ie=utf-8&oe=utf-8&aq=t&rls=org.mozilla:en-US:official&client=firefox-a.

facilities to charities.[34] More recently, many schools (free schools and academies) and ever-increasing powers of the U.K.'s national health service have similarly been transferred. This jurisdiction has also seen a reverse transfer with housing associations (exempt charities) absorbed by government.

In Australia, the advice of the Australian Tax Office that "the purposes of government in carrying out its functions are not charitable," as endorsed by the Charity Definition Inquiry Report,[35] has given way to the judicial ruling in the *Central Bayside* case.[36] The Inquiry Report had agreed with the judiciary in *Metropolitan Fire Brigade Board v. The Commissioner of Taxation*[37] and *Mines Rescue Board of New South Wales v. Commissioner of Taxation*[38] (both applicant bodies in the cases established by state government) that the test for determining whether an entity is a government body and therefore not tax deductible is that it be constituted, funded, and controlled by government. Subsequently, however, in the *Central Bayside* case, the Victorian Supreme Court of Appeal determined that a nationwide organization of general medical practitioners, formed to deliver a government health care provision and wholly funded by government, was nonetheless a charity.[39]

In the United States, the charity law rule that lessening the burdens of government is a charitable purpose has long been used as a guiding principle, and is embedded in the Treasury Department Regulations promulgated under § 501(c)(3).[40] This approach is institutionalized in some countries in continental Europe, and is evident also in New Zealand and Canada.

In short, there is an increasing trend in many jurisdictions for government to delegate its public service responsibilities and related funding to organizations it has set up as charities, or to boost its direct funding of charities so as to facilitate their delivery of public services.

[34] See Charity Commission, *Applications for Registration of (i) Trafford Community Leisure Trust and (ii) Wigan Leisure and Culture Trust*, April 21, 2004.

[35] See Sheppard, I., Fitzgerald, R., and Gonski, D., *Inquiry into the Definition of Charities and Related Organisations*, Recommendation 19, Canberra, 2001; an approach endorsed by the judiciary in Fire Brigades Board v. Commissioner of Taxation (1990) 27 FCR 279; Mines Rescue Board (NSW) v. Commissioner of Taxation (2000) 101 FCR 91; and Ambulance Service of New South Wales v. Commissioner of Taxation (2003) 130 FCR 477.

[36] [2005] VSCA 168.

[37] (1990) 27 FCR 279.

[38] (Cth) (2000) 44 ATR 107 at p. 30. See also Perpetual Trustee Co Ltd v. FC of T [1931] 45 CLR 224 per Evatt J., who described the recipients of charity as:

> Those who receive aid or comfort in this way are the poor, the sick, the aged, and the young. Their disability or distress arouses pity, and the institutions are designed to give them protection.

[39] See Central Bayside Division of General Practice Ltd v. Commissioner of State Revenue [2005] VSCA 168.

[40] See Tres. Reg. §1.501(c)(3)-d (1).

2. Jurisdictional Case Law: Delegation of Services Incompatible with Charitable Status

In some jurisdictions, notably Australia, the United States, the U.K., and continental Europe, there have been indications that the judiciary are beginning to question whether government, by contracting with charities or other nonprofits for the delivery of services that could be construed as "public," is in law wholly successful in its intention to pass responsibility for such services to that body.

In the U.K., the Court of Appeal upheld the Divisional Court's decision in *Weaver v. London and Quadrant Housing Trust*[41] that the management and allocation of housing stock by a registered social landlord (the trust was an industrial and provident society with charitable status) was a function of a public nature. It held by a majority that there were several reasons for concluding that the trust was operating as a public body, including: a "substantial public subsidy which enables it to meet its objectives"; a statutory duty to cooperate with local authorities and help the authority to achieve its objectives; and the provision of subsidized housing, which is a function that can be described as governmental. In addition, it found that the trust "makes a valuable contribution to the government's objectives of providing subsidised housing," and that the regulation applying to associations is not simply about ensuring better performance, but "regulations over such matters as rent and eviction are designed, at least in part, to ensure that the objectives of government policy . . . are achieved." Moreover, it found that the termination of a tenancy was "so bound up with the idea and principles of social housing that such acts must be seen as public functions."

In Australia, the decision in *Metro West v. Sudi (Residential Tenancies)*[42] seemed to follow that in *Weaver*. Again, the level of government funding, the existence of statutory provisions authorizing the transfer of what had been public service responsibilities, and the nature of the functions being performed by a private body, were sufficient to indicate that the body was in reality exercising public functions and should in law be treated as a public authority. In finding the functions to be of a public nature, the court held that it was relevant to consider the responsibility that government has for the care and protection of vulnerable and disadvantaged people.

[41] R (Weaver) v. London & Quadrant Housing Trust [2009] EWCA Civ 587; [2008] EWHC 1377 (Admin); [2008] WLR (D) 207. In November 2009 the Supreme Court rejected the appeal application of London & Quadrant Housing Trust to the House of Lords. See, also Poplar Housing and Regeneration Community Association Ltd v. Donoghue [2001] EWCA Civ 595, [2002] QB 48, where the decision that the Association was exercising "functions of a public nature" was largely attributable to the fact that the local council was heavily represented on the Association's board and controlled its tenancy arrangements; and Bath Festivals Trust Ltd v. Revenue and Customs [2008] UKVA V20840, where it was held that when the activities of a trust, which had taken over the provision of services previously the responsibility of the local authority, fell within the scope of the council's strategy relating to the promotion or improvement of the social wellbeing, the trust was acting as a public authority.

[42] Metro West v. Sudi (Residential Tenancies) [2009] VCAT 2025.

In the European Union, the 27 Member States are obliged to ensure that their domestic laws are compliant with the provisions of the European Convention Human Rights and Fundamental Freedoms, and many have, by constitutional amendment or by statute, made such arrangements.

One aspect of that obligation is the requirement placed on public authorities to respect the right to private family life under Article 8 of the European Convention, which has led, in countries such as the U.K.,[43] to considerable controversy as to when a nongovernment entity may be construed as a public authority on the grounds that it is exercising functions of a public nature. This issue may arise in the context of public benefit service provision by charities, other nonprofits, or for-profits. The European Court of Justice has in recent years been giving attention to this matter. It has often sought to differentiate between public benefit activities that are essential functions of the state in respect of which government retains responsibility and accountability, and such activities for which responsibility and accountability can be borne by other entities. In *Calì & Figli v. Servizi Ecologici Porto de Genova*,[44] for example, a private company engaged in antipollution surveillance was found by the court to be in fact performing a government function as it was protecting the maritime environment. Again, in *Cisal di Battistello Venanzio & C. Sas v. INAIL*,[45] it held that a private company statutorily entrusted with the management of an insurance scheme for accidents at work was similarly performing a government function.

The Canadian judiciary in *Nanaimo Community Bingo Assn. v. British Columbia (Attorney General)*[46] were at pains to distinguish the respective responsibilities of government and charity in relation to education and health care service provision. The government could not sidestep its duty to provide such services, implying that even if a charity chose to become involved, accountability would still ultimately rest with government as the duty was of a nature that could not be divested. In the United States, Justice O'Connor argued in her concurrence in *Mitchell v. Helms*[47] that when government funds are channeled into educational activity where some "religious indoctrination [is] taking place therein," that indoctrination "would be directly attributable to the government."[48] This argument is very pertinent as it clearly draws attention to the likelihood of an agency relationship existing between government and a service provider in such circumstances. Again, in *Americans United For Separation of Church and State v. Prison Fellowship Ministries*,[49] the government was found to have breached the Establishment Clause because the federally funded program InnerChange Freedom

[43] See, e.g., two decisions of the Court of Appeal: Poplar Housing and Regeneration Community Association Ltd v. Donoghue [2001] EWCA Civ 595, [2002] QB 48 and R (Heather) v. Leonard Cheshire Foundation [2002] EWCA Civ 366, [2002] 2 All ER 936.

[44] [1997] ECR I-1547.

[45] [2002] ECR I-691.

[46] (1998) 52 B.C.L.R. (3d) 284 (S.C.).

[47] 530 U.S.793, 120 S. Ct. 2530 (2000).

[48] See also Sch. Dist. v. Ball, 473 U.S. 373, 398–400 (1985).

[49] 432 F. Supp. 2d 862. (S.D. Iowa 2006).

Initiative delivered by the charity Prison Fellowship Ministries was operated in a religiously discriminatory fashion.

In general, the case law shows that in determining whether a body can be said to be exercising a function of a public nature when providing publicly funded services, it will be relevant to consider: the role and responsibility of the state in relation to the area of need; the nature and extent of any statutory power or duty in relation to the function in question; the extent to which the state, directly or indirectly, regulates, supervises, and inspects the performance of the function; and the issue of whether the function in question is one for which the state is by one means or another willing to pay, whether directly or indirectly and whether as a matter of course or as a last resort. The degree to which the state has assumed responsibility for a function, or for which it has ultimate responsibility, and the public interest in having it undertaken, strongly suggest that it is of a public nature. All other things being equal, the greater the state's involvement in making payment for the function in question, the greater is the presumption that it has assumed responsibility.

C. Charities as Government Agents

In principle, any organization that allows itself to become merely a conduit or agency for delivery of government services is no longer an independent entity and could be denied charitable status. Government control, whether exercised through appointments to the boards of nonprofits, by contracts that comprehensively bind organizations to perform in accordance with policy and on terms set by government (or, conceivably, as a consequence of the dependency incurred as a result of a recurring block funding arrangement), and often by a combination of such methods, can effectively drain the recipient of any real capacity for independent functioning.

Arguably, when such a service delivery contract amounts to an agency relationship, then three issues arise of not inconsiderable importance: Government cannot avoid responsibility and accountability for the level and standard of service delivered; the entity concerned is acting as an extension of government and is therefore, to that extent, is functioning as a public body; and the independence of any such entity is so compromised as to be incompatible with charitable status.

1. Government and Responsibility

The government funding of charities or other nonprofits to deliver public benefit services is a strategy that places the delivering body in the position of being seen as a service provider, and of being accountable for service deficiencies, while government in fact exercises control through funding and by regulating standards. However, this strategy will not always allow government to avoid responsibility, as there are circumstances in which a contractual arrangement could entail an imputing of functional responsibility from service deliverer to government funder in accordance with the agent/principal rule. The extent of government funding is now often such as to at least suggest that the latter's service delivery is government provision by proxy.[50]

2. Charity/Nonprofit as a Public Body

The rulings in *Trafford and Wigan* and the *Central Bayside* cases determined that carrying out a function of government is not acting as the latter's agent: Merely because a charity has the same goals as government does not mean, without more, that it is not independent of government. Similarly, the level of government funding alone does not indicate an inappropriate level of control over a charity. Indeed, control itself is only one of the factors, and is never the sole determinant. As Lockhart J. pointed out in *Cronulla Sutherland Leagues Club Ltd v. Federal Commissioner of Taxation,*[51] relevant features "include its constitution, its activities, its history and its control." Classification as a "public body" is thus not dependent upon any single factor, but is based on the totality of an organization's relationship with government. If, however, government can be shown to have set up a situation where an ostensibly independent organization is in fact acting in an agency capacity, then the legal relationship is one of principal and agent, with the subordinate organization being in effect a public body when it is so acting. It is interesting to note, for example, that in *National Union of Teachers v. Governing Body of St Mary's Church of England (Aided) Junior School,*[52] the Court of Appeal held that a voluntary-aided school with charitable status was an emanation of the state for the purposes of the doctrine of direct effect. As the ECJ stated in *Calì & Figli,* an entity acts a public body when it is performing "a task in the public interest which forms part of the essential functions of the state and where the activity is connected by its nature, its aims and rules to which it is subject with the exercise of powers...which are typically those of a public authority."[53]

3. Agency and Charitable Status

It would seem that the judiciary are becoming more prepared to view a funded contractual relationship between government and charity, or other nonprofit, as lying somewhere on a continuum, at one end of which it could be construed as an agency relationship. At that extreme, where the functions of the entity are wholly enveloped by government, the charity has surrendered its independence and become an agent. This would be the case where the entity was receiving most of its funding from government, its activities were mostly devoted to giving effect to government functions, and—crucially—it had bound itself to implementing government policy.

[50] See, e.g., in relation to England and Wales, Seddon, N., *Who Cares?*, Civitas, London, 2007, at p. 4, where he identifies a number of prominent charities that receive 80 percent or more of their annual income from government sources.

[51] 89 ATC 4936 (1989) 20 ATR 1404.

[52] [1997] 3 CMLR 630.

[53] Cali & Figli SrL v. SEPG [1997] ECR I-1547, [1997] 5 CMLR 484 at para 23.

If there is no evidence of it having retained a discretionary capacity to make decisions or pursue options at variance with its contractual relationship, then it is essentially a creature of government.

If that entity is in fact a charity, the consequences could, and perhaps should in some cases, be fatal for its charitable status. Trustees have a fundamental duty to protect the independence of their charity. Where they have ceded control to government, and committed the charity's purpose and functions to further government policy, the trustees will have failed to fulfill an essential condition for charitable status.

IV. CHARITY TRADING: JUDICIAL CONSTRAINTS AND JURISDICTIONAL DIFFERENCES

Charity trading is an area of law that continues to be tax-oriented and governed by judicial or regulatory rules rather than by legislation. The one exception is the unrelated business income tax (UBIT) regime in the United States, which although clearly enacted by statute was triggered by a judicial decision.[54] As charities and other nonprofits increasingly contest market opportunities with private and public sector bodies, this area of law is now generating more litigation, causing the judiciary and regulators such as Revenue bodies or the Commission to constantly review the rules governing cross-sectoral engagement in trading. Practice is setting a pace currently unmatched by policy or legislation. In a rapidly changing legal environment, the judiciary can be seen referring to the decisions of colleagues in other jurisdictions and drawing distinctions, not just between the entities engaged in trading on a domestic basis, but also differentiating between jurisdictions in relation to the trading capacity of charities. The traditional common law rules are still relevant but are being more frequently tested as, in each jurisdiction, judiciary and regulators struggle to keep up with the mutating forms and content of entities now competing in the marketplace.

A. Traditional Common Law Rules

The right to engage in commercial activity has become increasingly important for nonprofits in all the jurisdictions studied. However, for charities its importance is compromised by certain basic common law principles, some governing charity per se, and which therefore also have a bearing on those that trade (see above), and others with a particular bearing on charities engaged in trading, which tend to qualify their right of access to commercial opportunities.

1. The Primary Purpose Test

This test and its U.S. equivalent, the "related business activities test," together with their respective corollaries (the non-primary purpose test and UBIT), probably constitute

[54] *See* C.F. Mueller Co. v. Commissioner, 190 F.2d 120 (1951).

the twin axes of the common law as it relates to charity and trading. The tests mark out a main point of difference in the treatment of charities in the jurisdictions studied.

In the U.K. and Irish jurisdictions, where the primary purpose test has always prevailed, it has two distinctive effects. First, non-primary purpose trading activity is only permissible where it remains ancillary and incidental to the primary purpose, and second, a charity will be prevented from engaging in trade where, in the view of the regulator, the scale of the non-primary purpose would expose the charity's assets to undue risk to the detriment of prospective long-term beneficiaries. Neither consequence results from the UBIT regime in the United States. There, UBIT offers a compromise: Income derived from a charity's trading activity that is related in nature to its charitable purpose and wholly invested in it is permissible and tax-exempt, whereas income derived from trading activity unrelated to charitable purpose, but invested in it, is permitted and taxable. If the main purpose of the organization is inherently charitable, it can qualify as tax-exempt despite earning income from non-charitable activities. Essentially, trading by charities in the United States is an issue of tax rather than charitable status. There is as yet no UBIT equivalent outside that jurisdiction.

In Canada, the "related business" test operates in a manner very similar to primary purpose in the U.K., and in New Zealand the primary purpose test has been placed on the statute books. In Australia, however, the decision in *Word*[55] ended the primary purpose approach that it had shared with the U.K. and placed the law in a situation similar to that which prevailed in the pre-UBIT era in the United States. The removal of the prohibition on exemption for feeder organizations allows exemption for an organization that operates a business and contributes the profits to charity as its primary activity rather than having to itself conduct inherently charitable activities. In continental Europe, it is generally the case that the primary purpose test prevails: A charity is free to engage in trading provided that such economic activity is neither its primary purpose nor its main activity, but that it is related to statutory objectives and is necessary to accomplish its charitable purpose.

2. The "Incidental and Ancillary" Rule

The basic rule that "a body is a charity even if some of its incidental and ancillary objects, considered independently are non-charitable"[56] continues to be more or less unchallenged. A charity may therefore engage in commerce to make profits where this is merely incidental and ancillary to the carrying out of a purpose that is otherwise charitable.

[55] Commissioner of Taxation v. Word Investments Limited (2008) 236 CLR 204.

[56] As stated by Dixon C.J., McTiernan, Williams, and Fullagar J.J. in Congregational Union of NSW v. Thistlethwayte (1952) 87 CLR 375, at p 442. See dicta to the same effect in: Re White; White v. White [1893] 2 Ch 41; Salvation Army (Vic) Property Trust v. Fern Tree Gully Corporation (1952) 85 CLR 159.

In most of the common law jurisdictions studied this rule still holds,[57] and a breach of either arm of the rule could result in loss not just of tax-exemption rights but also of charitable status. However, in some jurisdictions the judiciary would now seem to regard it as a redundant threshold, not necessarily rendering impermissible trading that is neither incidental nor ancillary: in Australia, for example, prior to *Word* it was the scale of the trading enterprise that was all-important, but after the decision neither "incidental" nor "ancillary" was sufficient to prevent feeder entities acquiring tax-exempt status.

B. Contemporary Judicial/Regulator Rules

Understandably, in the absence of legislative updating, regulators and the judiciary have been formulating their own jurisdiction-specific rules to guide determination of charitable trading issues. Mostly these have been forged in the United States and remain contained within that domestic context (e.g., the "community benefit" standard and the "convenience doctrine"). Some, regardless of their originating jurisdiction, have now acquired a varying degree of international currency as instruments to be applied in the regulatory process, including the "activities test," the "destination of income test," the "commerciality test," and the "commensurate test."

1. The "Activities Test"

Increasingly, in the common law world, legislative endorsement is being extended to a rule that has attracted varying judicial recognition over the years: An entity's activities must further its charitable purpose, and the reality and substance of its declared purpose must be substantiated (i.e., confirmed, corroborated, or demonstrated) by its actual activities. First established by the judiciary in England and Wales,[58] and subsequently confirmed by the Charity Commission,[59] the rule holds that it is not just the nature of the activity that is important, but also its role in supporting the charitable purpose. In the recent Australian case *Navy Health Ltd v. DFC of T*,[60] Jessop J. explained the task facing the court in terms of the activity test:

> To determine whether it was "charitable" requires a consideration of its objects, to be discerned from its constitution, its rules and its activities. As stated in its constitution, the single purpose of the applicant was to conduct a health benefits fund. To secure a finding that its objects were charitable, therefore, the applicant needs to go beyond the constitution to its rules and activities.

[57] Certainly this remains the governing principle in the U.K. jurisdictions, Ireland, New Zealand, Singapore, and Canada.

[58] See Inland Revenue Commissioners v. City of Glasgow Police Athletic Association [1953] 1 All ER 747.

[59] See the Charity Commission, [1996] Ch Com Rep 79.

[60] [2007] FCA 931 at para. 25.

Subsequently, in the *Aid/Watch* case, the Australian judiciary's adoption of the test was put beyond doubt by the explicit endorsement by Gummo J.[61] In the United States, the test has long been applied by the courts and by the Internal Revenue Service,[62] but in Canada a good deal of ambiguity is still apparent,[63] whereas New Zealand has given the test legislative authority. In Europe, the effect of the European Commission's Sixth VAT Directive is to standardize the requirement that the status of a nonprofit is to be determined by taking all of its activities fully into account.

Although it was initially treated with considerable suspicion by the judiciary and regulators due to the traditional rule that a charity's purpose was to be established by reference to its objects as stated in its governing instruments, the activities test is now becoming accepted as a supplementary method of confirming or challenging the actual nature and extent of the charity's work. It has proved valuable in estimating the weight a charity gives to activity that furthers its trading as opposed to its charitable purpose.

2. The "Destination of Income Test"

This rule, which emerged as such in the United States, allows charities to engage in any form of income-generating activity provided that the proceeds are wholly directed to a charitable purpose. The "destination of income test" has never played any part in the charity law of the U.K. or Ireland. It was similarly denied in Australia until the recent decision in the *Word Investments*[64] case, which has now entrenched the test in that jurisdiction unless or until it is legislatively repealed. In the United States, its nemesis came with the *Mueller Macaroni*[65] case, which triggered its displacement by UBIT. It has no place in New Zealand charity law. In Canada, following a period of acceptance,[66] it was decisively rejected by the court in the *Earth Fund* case.[67]

[61] Aid/Watch Incorporated v. Commissioner of Taxation [2010] HCA 42; [2009] FCAFC 128 per Gummo J. when he commented: "It is one thing to have objectives. Another question is what you are actually doing."

[62] See, e.g., B.S.W. Group, Inc. v. Commissioner, 70 T.C. 352, 356–57 (1978).

[63] See, e.g., Phillips, J., "The Federal Court of Appeal and the Legal Meaning of Charity: Review and Critique," in Phillips, J., Chapman, B., and Stevens, D. (eds.), *Between State and Market: Essays on Charities Law and Policy in Canada*, McGill-Queen's University Press, Montreal, 2002, at pp. 219–50: "the Court has been inconsistent in how it has distinguished between charitable 'activities' and charitable 'purposes' and, more important, that in practice it has given too much weight to an organisation's 'activities' as opposed to the broader issue of charitable 'purposes,'" at p. 220; see further at pp. 229–34.

[64] Commissioner of Taxation of the Commonwealth of Australia v. Word Investments Ltd (2008) 236 CLR 204.

[65] C. F. Mueller Co. v. Commissioner of Internal Revenue, 190 F.2d 120 (3rd Cir. 1951).

[66] See Alberta Institute on Mental Retardation v. The Queen [1987] 2 C.T.C. 70, 87 D.T.C. 5306 (F.C.A.).

[67] Earth Fund/Fond pour la Terre v. Minister of National Revenue, 2002 FCA 498, 2003 D.T.C. 5016 (Eng.), 298 N.R. 391, [2003] 2 C.T.C. 10.

The revival of the test in Australia brings with it the legitimation of "feeder" organizations as charitable and the concern that this will promote unfair competition with for-profit companies. It is unlikely to transcend that jurisdiction or, indeed, survive long within it. The test still applies in parts of continental Europe, for example in Poland and Germany where income from the economic activity of nonprofits is tax-exempt to the extent that it is dedicated to pursuit of public benefit activities as specified in law.

3. The "Commerciality Test"

This test, applied in order to determine whether a charity or other nonprofit is operating in such an excessively commercial manner that its activities are in competition with those of for-profits, is used to identify those organizations that are driven by commercial rather than public benefit concerns. It will look for indications that a charity or other nonprofit is operating in a non-commercial manner by not providing services at substantially below cost (preferably to charitable recipients), or by advertising in a commercial manner, or operating in such a way, as to suggest that its primary purpose is to maximize profits. Essentially, where the evidence shows an organization to be operating in a commercial manner, it will have failed the test. Used often in the United States,[68] it has also gained credence in New Zealand[69] and Canada,[70] but there are no specific references to it in U.K. case law. In addition, the test does not appear to have been wholly embraced by the Australian judiciary where it can have no relevance in the immediate post-*Word* era in the absence of legislative intervention repealing the basis of that decision.

4. The "Commensurate Test"

Whether a charity undertakes, through contributions and grants, a charitable purpose commensurate in scope with its financial resources is likely to become a matter of increasing interest to governments. Essentially, the commensurate test requires organizations to conduct charitable activities to a scale in keeping with their resources. The intention is to prompt charities to spend their annual income rather than simply amass funds. For endowed foundations, the implications of the test are that they must ensure their expenditure policy allows for an appropriate annual rate of asset depletion. This is fixed at 5 percent in the United States but, significantly, endowed universities are exempt from this percent ceiling. So, for example, universities such as Harvard (which had an endowment fund of $34.6 billion in 2007) are

[68] See, e.g., Presbyterian and Reformed Publishing Co. v. Commissioner, 743 F.2d 148, 153 (3d Cir. 1984) and Living Faith, Inc. v. Commissioner, 60 T.C.M. 710, 713 (1990).

[69] See Re Education New Zealand Trust, HC, Wellington, CIV-2009-485-2301 (June 29, 2010).

[70] See Earth Fund/Fond pour la Terre v. Minister of National Revenue, 2002 FCA 498, 2003 D.T.C. 5016 (Eng.), 298 N.R. 391, [2003] 2 C.T.C. 10.

not required to reduce the fee level that the beneficiaries of its educational mission must pay in order to access their services. Arguably, some tend to focus more on "growing" their assets than on facilitating their intended beneficiaries.

In the United States and U.K., charities are required to develop written reserves policies justifying the levels of reserves held. This is not the case in New Zealand, and there are no references to the test playing a significant role in the Australian regulation of charities. Canada removed the mandatory disbursement quota in 2010, leaving charitable foundations with the option of "growing assets." The observation made by Hopt and Hippel in relation to continental Europe that "while fundraising is regulated in many countries, asset management of nonprofit organizations is neglected by law"[71] would seem to hold good as a general truth. This is due, as they point out, to regulatory attention being given to the effects of chronic mismanagement rather than to passive or nonmanagement of assets.

C. Charities, Altruism, and the Constraints on Profiting

Altruism is clearly represented in some of the above rules. The relative jurisdictional stringency constraining the opportunities for charities to pursue profit partially reflects a corresponding jurisdictional interest in protecting for-profit interests, but it also says something about their willingness to provide charities with opportunities for altruism. As Hippel and Walz explain:[72]

> This does not mean that a profit motive or motive of personal advantage has to be absent, but the profit that a public benefit organization, its finances and its management can earn has to be subjected in a clear-cut way to the services of a dominant idealistic mission which embodies the public purpose recognized by law...the important question concerns *what rule dominates the activity, the organization and the financing of the organization.*

It is to be expected that in regulating the trading environment, a somewhat different balance will be struck in relation to the respective profit opportunities for charity and business. The fact that this differs on a jurisdictional basis is perhaps, also, not unexpected.

1. The Charitable Purpose Priority

The "primary purpose test" coupled with the "incidental and ancillary rule," and underpinned by the "exclusivity" requirement, together form the clearest expression

[71] Hopt and Von Hippel (eds.), *Comparative Corporate Governance of Non-Profit Organisations*, at p. xlii.

[72] See Von Hippel, T. and Walz, W. R., "Tax Law as an Instrument to Strengthen Governance," in Hopt and Von Hippel, *Comparative Corporate Governance of Non-Profit Organisations*, at pp. 942–43.

of a regulatory concern to ensure that priority is given to charitable purpose over all other considerations. An award of charitable status, and the subsequent attraction of public donations and tax-exempt privileges, requires the organization to accept the need to remain within the confines of charitable purpose and ensure that all its activities remain subordinate to and in furtherance of charity. This combination of rules remains intact throughout the jurisdictions studied, but their capacity to prevail over commercial considerations is more compromised in the United States, and now also in Australia. Moreover, the public benefit synergy between government and charity, as promoted by the former, is everywhere eroding the capacity of the latter to maintain a strategic, mission-led direction rather than being sidetracked into remunerative service provision contracts.

2. Profit Constraints

The rules governing the safeguarding of assets for the benefit of intended recipients, the distribution of profits, and the requirement that the activities of charity are not dominated by a commercial purpose are all constraints that favor altruism. The first is a long-standing strict obligation, rooted in the history of trusts, which appears to be assured of continuing respect in all jurisdictions studied. The corollary, however, that assets should be efficiently managed and income routinely expended in furtherance of charitable purpose, is not always evident, particularly in some private U.S. charities, also in New Zealand, and to some extent in continental Europe. The second finds expression in the nondistribution constraint, which forms the distinguishing characteristic of all nonprofits, and is upheld in all jurisdictions, and also in the rule against private inurement toward which the U.S. regulatory regime takes a relaxed approach, allowing individual profit where this is incidental, necessary, and reasonable in amount. In recent years, the previous prohibition on U.K. charity trustees acquiring any form of remuneration for their responsibilities has also been relaxed to some degree. The third continues to be enforced in all jurisdictions studied except in the United States, where the UBIT regime allows commerce more scope but the proceeds are taxed, and in Australia where "feeder" organizations in the post-*Word* era were briefly free to be wholly driven by profit acquisition concerns without any charitable purpose constraint, provided that the profits ultimately went to a charity.

Arguably, the traditional common law regulatory constraints remain intact, and would seem to be not dissimilar to those that prevail in continental Europe. The continued ability of these constraints to ring-fence altruism and protect the identity of charity from dilution by creeping commercialization is diminishing.

V. CHARITY TRADING AND THE TAX REGIME

The relationship between tax and public benefit provision is complicated. Maintaining the balance between favoring tax-exempt charities and at the same time ensuring sufficient tax revenue to finance an acceptable level of public services, while avoiding de-incentivising those private sector entrepreneurs wishing to compete or contribute, is a political minefield. Again, balancing tax benefits accruing to a charity or other nonprofit on the revenue received from public donations, service delivery contracts, and commercial ventures with tax benefits awarded to private and corporate donors through incentive schemes is politically fraught. For the governments of "advanced" democratic nations, the complexities of tax regimes have offered relatively opaque means of juggling the interests of the parties concerned with minimum direct political exposure through ongoing adjustments to VAT/GST or corporate tax, etc. In the present economic climate, however, this has become a highly sensitive political area with fewer hiding places for any government sleight of hand intended to favor charity at the expense of tax revenues or business opportunities; in fact, the reverse has proven to be more likely.

A. Charitable Purpose and Tax

Although in the U.K. and Irish jurisdictions, the line between charities and other nonprofits is quite clearly drawn, and charitable status does carry definite tax privileges and a distinctive cachet that confers a market advantage, this distinction is less clear-cut in other jurisdictions—particularly in continental Europe, the United States, Australia, and, to some extent, Canada. In all jurisdictions, the growing spread of social enterprises and experiments with new hybrid models for philanthropy launched by entrepreneurs are bringing added contention to the debates regarding the privileged status of charity, and exactly what it is that sets charity apart from other nonprofits and entitles it to preferential treatment. For tax purposes, the differentiating feature in practice is the distinction between public benefit service provision that is tax-exempt because it fits within judicially defined charitable purposes, and other such provisions that are statutorily defined or otherwise encoded in regulatory instruments. The former owes its origins to case law derived from the Preamble/*Pemsel* formulation, and has expanded organically and exponentially largely free from government direction. The latter are wholly government determined. In some respects these two strands are now converging.

1. The Charitable Purpose Jurisdictions

As mentioned in previous chapters, for a core group of the jurisdictions studied, tax exemption was tied to specified charitable purposes: either limited to the four *Pemsel* heads or to the newly statutorily extended *Pemsel*-plus list of purposes from which the charities with donor-favored status were also selected. History had ensured that tax exemption for this group remained within common law definitional parameters, addressed the Preamble/*Pemsel*-identified areas of public benefit, and left government to legislate when it wished to extend exemption on charitable grounds. As Justice Iacobucci commented in *Vancouver Society*, when considering an expansion of the definition of charity, the courts must consider whether what was being proposed was an incremental change or one with such complex ramifications that it should be left to Parliament.[73] The latter option was taken in many common law countries in relation to recreation,[74] and it has been applied more recently to child care services provided on a nonprofit basis in Australia.[75] Moreover, the charitable purposes limitation brought with it the common law constraints of public benefit, "exclusivity," and others that were employed to deny charitable status to mutual benefit entities while serving to reinforce the separate and somewhat elitist image of charity. Although in the United States the line between mutual benefit and public benefit has never been as rigidly drawn, there is a basic structural distinction built into the tax code represented by the defined term "charitable organization," which refers to both public charities and private foundations.[76] Under the tax code, public charities include schools, hospitals, churches, and other charities that receive a third of their funding from a broad public group of donors or patrons; these are treated preferentially for tax purposes.[77]

Charitable purpose has also provided the basis for establishing charity subsets in some common law countries. In Australia and Singapore, for example, a distinction is drawn between charities and entities called, respectively, public benefit institutions (PBIs) or institutions of a public character (IPCs). This tiered approach to tax exemption on charitable grounds enables government to give fiscal preference to certain charities and their purposes, usually those committed to relieving the greatest need in society; for instance the status of PBI is restricted to the approximately one-third of Australian charities judged to be "organized for the relief of poverty, sickness, destitution or helplessness."[78] As with IPCs in Singapore, PBIs are authorized to receive tax-deductible donations, as are PBOs in South Africa. This is highly relevant to the present context as preferred charities already benefit from tax dividends not available to other charities and nonprofits, and are well positioned to use their tax privileged leverage to gain further advantages by competing for service provision or commercial contracts.

[73] See *Vancouver Society of Immigrant and Visible Minority Women v. M.N.R.* [1999] 1 S.C.R. 10, per Iacobucci J., at p. 21.

[74] See, most recently, A.Y.S.A. Amateur Youth Soccer Association v. Canada Revenue Agency [2007] 3 S.C.R. 217.

[75] The shift to a legislative platform, in the jurisdictions of the U.K. and Ireland, leaves open the possibility of a further extension or retraction in specified charitable purposes there, as and when deemed politically desirable.

[76] See s.509(a)(1) of the Internal Revenue Code. This distinction originated in the Tax Reform Act 1969, which added s.509 and the private foundation penalty taxes to the tax code. It has carried over for tax purposes (but not for purposes of the corporate law) to some 48 states.

[77] See s.509(a)(1) of the Internal Revenue Code.

[78] See Perpetual Trustee Co. Ltd. v. Federal Commissioner of Taxation [1931] 45 CLR 224 per Starke, J., at p. 232.

2. The Non-Charitable Purpose Jurisdictions

Most countries in continental Europe have laws providing exemption from income and other taxes for a broad range of nonprofits, including public benefit and mutual benefit organizations.[79] As in the common law countries, governments have determined that tax exemption is necessary and a justifiable inducement if nonprofits are to be encouraged to develop a diversified funding base. Thus, not only are contributions, grants, and member dues free from tax, but under certain conditions, so also is income from economic activities.

3. Regulatory Changes

The charity law reform outcomes introduced the possibility of government management of tax exemption for public benefit entities in the jurisdictions concerned. As Rosenman warns, the inherent power of "legislators" to define the nature of charitable purposes—and of organizational practices and program activities in their service—could bring profound shifts in the nonprofit sector.[80] It also would bring them into closer alignment with the corresponding tax administration systems in the United States and continental Europe, which have long relied on categories of public benefit as encoded in statute or in regulatory instruments.

Another important result of charity law reform has been the introduction in some jurisdictions of a "Charity Commission type" body. Although this development has strengthened the hand of those governments with an agenda for sharing more responsibility for public benefit services with charity, it has also served to distance them from their counterparts in North America and continental Europe. In the U.K., Ireland, Singapore, and New Zealand (and soon Hong Kong), a charity-specific Commission now intercedes between charity and Revenue to moderate on any tax exemption issues, whereas a more revenue-driven approach predominates in North America and continental Europe. Indeed there is, perhaps, a linkage between a legacy more oriented toward trust and charitable purpose, a commitment to charity law reform, and a reform outcome that includes the "Charity Commission model" as the key component in a new regulatory regime for charities. The result, however, is unmistakable: A group of common law jurisdictions, following the lead provided by the government of England and Wales, are setting off on a different route from that currently taken in North America and continental Europe by anchoring the further development of their regulatory regimes for charity to *Pemsel*-based, statutorily defined charitable purposes as administered by a Charity Commission–type agency. Australia would appear to be

[79] See further ICNL, "Survey of Tax Laws Affecting NGOs in Central and Eastern Europe," *International Center for Not-for-Profit Law*, Washington, D.C., 2002.

[80] Rosenman, M., "Independence: A Matter of Definition—The Charitable Sector in the United States," in Smerdon, M. (ed.), *The First Principle of Voluntary Action*, Baring Foundation, London, October 2009, at pp. 99–120, at p. 110.

intent on forging its own path, which, although leaning more toward North America and continental Europe in its broad and more inclusive approach toward nonprofits, will also incorporate *Pemsel* charitable purposes and a Commission. It would seem likely that the attraction of the package of charitable purposes plus Commission is that it builds on an already-established government/charity public benefit agenda, and offers a basis for consolidating that agenda and extending that relationship into a government/sector public benefit partnership.

B. Charity Law Reform, Tax, and Trading

The definition of a taxable entity, the range of taxes it may be subject to, and the actual meaning given to a named tax (e.g., corporate tax), varies considerably across the jurisdictions studied. In the U.S. and Canada, for example, the status of an entity as a company or individual is irrelevant; all are uniformly treated as taxable entities and are equally subject to such taxes albeit at different rates, such as property tax, payroll tax, withholding tax, excise tax, customs duties, value added tax, and others. Elsewhere a tax differentiation between corporations, individuals, and unincorporated entities is not unusual.

While some of the tax related outcomes of law reform have increased the tendency towards convergence between the jurisdictions concerned and the established approach in the U.S., others have had the reverse effect.

1. Tax Neutrality

The principle that taxes should be applied in a policy-neutral fashion, free of incentives or constraints intended to favor any particular entities or enterprises, and leaving the market to sort out the winners and losers, is one that has been most vigorously asserted in the United States. It stands as a polar opposite to the legacy of market fixing, so characteristic of the former east European states and the corporatism of the European welfare state economies, where citizens are accustomed to government manipulation of market and tax regimes to further social policy objectives.

However, the citizens of all advanced economies are now becoming increasingly familiar with the policy-driven cost implications of taxing commodities such as cigarettes and alcohol, or congestion charges in central city areas, or carbon emissions, etc. There is a general acceptance that public benefit policies come with a tax price tag, and, although not universally popular, a broad consensus prevails that meeting such a cost is the socially responsible option, a response strengthened when that policy is operationalized by a charity (e.g., in health care or education). In like fashion, the business community in all the jurisdictions studied have accommodated, with varying degrees of discomfort, the distortion to neutrality caused by the tax preference of charities as a price worth paying in the interests of furthering the common good. As the creeping commercialization of charities and nonprofits eats further into the profit margins of for-profit entities, the protests of the latter are getting louder. They complain, with some justification, about the unfairness of having to compete on a like-for-like basis with tax-subsidized entities that use their social cachet of charitable branding to gain an unwarranted market advantage for the sale of goods or services that are identical in most respects to those on offer from for-profits.[81] Sadiq and Richardson have recently and very reasonably expressed the problem as follows:[82]

> The tax concessions and exemptions granted to charitable organisations are generally provided on the basis that these organisations provide goods and services with a broad public benefit. Part of the rationale for granting tax concessions is that charitable organisations have historically operated alongside the for-profit sector by meeting the demands of a different segment of the market. Traditionally, charitable organisations have not operated in direct competition with for-profit organisations that could not access any tax exemptions. This is evidenced by long-established commercial activities undertaken by charitable organisations, such as second hand goods stores and employment opportunities for the disabled and disadvantaged. However, entities with charitable status for taxation purposes are increasingly engaging in commercial activities that potentially place them in direct competition with the for-profit sector...concerns arise about the integrity and fairness of the taxation regime where charitable organisations, which avail themselves of the tax exemption status while undertaking commercial activities, compete directly with the for-profit sector.

There are good reasons for now querying whether the policy of tax subsidies to trading charities, giving them an edge in competing with commercial enterprises, is a socially responsible option, particularly when the trade in question has been chosen by the charity purely on the basis of potential profit margins, and is neither ancillary nor incidental to its charitable purpose. There is "no obvious rationale for the subsidisation of (charities) commercial output."[83]

Tax neutrality has also been a contentious issue, for the EU. Member States have been slow to implement the EU Tax Merger Directive (90/434/EC, as amended by Directive 2005/19/EC) in relation to commercial companies.[84] This requires

[81] As Blake Ratcliff points out, however, "beyond the social cachet of a nonprofit label, a consumer can find very real value in a venture not driven by a profit motive and a fealty to investment dividends but by mission or purpose, leading to a higher level of transparency, trust, integrity, environmental concern, etc." (Ratcliff's note to author, February 8, 2012).

[82] See, e.g., Sadiq, K. and Richardson, C., "Tax Concessions for Charities: Competitive Neutrality, the Tax Base and "Public Goods" Choice," in *Australian Tax Forum*, Vol. 25, No. 4, 2010, at pp. 597–612.

[83] See Schiff, J. and Weisbrod, B., "Competition between For-Profit and Nonprofit Organizations in Commercial Markets," in Ben Ner, A and Gui, B. (eds.), *The Nonprofit Sector in the Mixed Economy*, University of Michigan Press, Ann Arbor, 1993, at p. 636.

[84] Belgium, for example, doing so in January 2010.

Member States to ensure their laws facilitate cross-border mergers, divisions, partial divisions, transfers of assets, and exchanges of shares between companies within the EU. It is intended that such operations be treated in a tax-neutral fashion by the countries concerned, and that any profits derived are exempted from capital gains tax. The prospect of laws being introduced transferring the same requirements, and providing tax neutrality for the cross-border activities of nonprofit entities in all Member States, would seem to be some years away.

2. Mission-Related Trading and Tax Exemption

In the U.K. jurisdictions, following charity law reform, where a charity is engaged in both primary purpose and non-primary purpose trading, tax exemption is applied accordingly: the former being tax-exempt provided the proceeds are applied exclusively to the charitable purpose; the latter are fully taxable.[85] This apportionment approach effectively frees charitable trading from the ancillary and incidental rule, again bringing U.K. law closer to alignment with the UBIT regime in the United States. This change, as has been pointed out, may amount to a "surreptitious introduction of an American UBIT equivalent into U.K. law."[86]

C. Donor Incentive Schemes

Given the increased need for charity to find substitute sources of funding to replace government grants, it is to be expected that tax incentives to encourage and direct donor giving would be important. There are significant jurisdictional differences in donor incentive schemes, and not all would seem wholly compliant with the spirit of altruism that rests on an element of self-sacrifice for the benefit of a "stranger."

1. Altruism and Incentivizing Donors

Charitable purposes form the basis for donor incentive schemes in most of the jurisdictions studied (U.K., Ireland, Singapore, Australia, and New Zealand), with donor-favored status being usually awarded in respect of donations made for charities addressing the more basic forms of social need (relief of poverty, illness, etc). In the United States, Canada, and much of continental Europe, such preferential tax treatment is awarded to government-selected areas of social need, rather than charitable purposes, addressed by nonprofits including but not confined to charities.

In Australia, the introduction of Deductible Gift Recipient enables taxpayers to claim a deduction for certain donations. In the U.K. jurisdictions, the Gift Aid scheme and "Getting Britain Giving" campaign are donor incentive schemes,

85 See the Corporations Taxes Act 1988 as amended by the Finance Act 2006.

86 See Breen, O., "Holding the Line: Regulatory Challenges in Ireland and England when Business and Charity collide," in McGregor-Lowndes, M., and O'Halloran, K., *Modernising Charity Law: Recent Developments and Future Directions*, Edward Elgar, Cheltenham, 2010, at p. 144.

although it is the National Lottery that provides government with various opportunities for channeling tax revenues toward its favored forms of public service. Donor incentive schemes are amenable to government manipulation, as illustrated in New Zealand when, in the context of the 2007 budget, the Minister responsible announced the removal of the cap on rebates for charitable donations from individuals and companies to "donee organizations," which immediately made that jurisdiction a more attractive environment for philanthropic investment. In Singapore, at much the same time and in the same context, the relevant Minister announced the removal of the rule requiring a charitable institution to spend within the jurisdiction, in any year of assessment, at least 80 percent of its received donations and income on charitable causes or lose its rights to tax exemption. These were both politically motivated adjustments of the tax code calculated to attract foreign philanthropists. Most recently, in the UK, a government initiative taken to increase the tax revenue needed to manage its public debt crisis will have a negative effect on the philanthropic environment. In response to a confidential report by HM Revenue and Customs that the use of tax relief on charitable donations was among the top three tax loopholes used to legally reduce income tax bills, the U.K. government announced its intention to impose a £50,000 cap on tax relief, or 25 percent of income if that is higher, effective from April 2013. This will curtail the present regime that permits higher-rate taxpayers to make unlimited donations to charity, then offset this against their tax bill and reduce the amount payable, sometimes to zero. Instead, the cap will remove wealthy donor discretion regarding the public benefit destination of taxable income, leaving them with the option of donating more but only from their taxed income.

In the United States, it has been argued that:[87]

> The key feature of U.S. tax incentives for giving is that they directly benefit the donor. Donors who itemise deductions (in practice those who own homes and are thereby able to qualify for the mortgage interest deduction) are able to deduct the full charitable value of their contributions from their taxable income.

Although unadorned altruism may well be the incentive for those donors making Gift Aid donations (where the tax dividend goes to the charity), this would seem less likely in relation to tax-offset schemes, capped or uncapped, in the United States, Canada, the U.K., and other jurisdictions where the incentive lies in benefits to the donor. In continental Europe much the same donor incentive schemes are in operation: Tax benefits are provided in the form of either a deduction or credit for the donor; the former reduces the amount of income subject to tax, and are the most common; the latter reduces the amount of tax owed and are used less frequently. In Central and Eastern Europe, only Hungary provides for tax credits, and there,

[87] See Howard, C., *The Hidden Welfare State: Tax Expenditures and Social Policy in the United States*, Princeton, Princeton University Press, 1997.

only for donations by individuals.[88] Donor incentive schemes such as Gift Aid, or systems for matching government grants to the contributions of individual donors, clearly allow more room for altruism than those relying on government credits or tax offsets.

VI. CHARITIES AND THE ANTITERRORISM CONSTRAINTS

It was somewhat ironic that charity law reform, initiated by governments to liberate philanthropy from some of the more constricting aspects of its common law legacy, and to lay the foundations for a new era of partnership with charity, should conclude in circumstances where government was simultaneously introducing tough legislative provisions designed to tighten its surveillance and control of the sector. The increasing volume of national and international measures intended to address the growing international security imperative is of little direct significance for present purposes, but it is worth noting how these efforts affect the new national charity law constraints, as they will undoubtedly also inhibit charities and impact upon their capacity to raise funds through commerce as well as by other means.

A. Regulatory Constraints

The governments in all jurisdictions studied have both introduced domestic antiterrorism legislation and subscribed to international conventions, pacts, protocols, and other instruments specifically intended to detect subversive activity. Those charity law reform processes that concluded with new charity-specific legislation also contained provisions designed to allow the monitoring of a registered charity's activities and the use of its funds by the relevant regulatory body.

1. National Legislative Constraints

Measures designed to improve the regulation of fund-raising and to reduce opportunities for channeling funds for terrorist use were part of the legislative outcomes achieved, to a varying extent, by the charity law reform processes.[89] In Australia, for example, the government announced its intention to amend the "in Australia" special conditions in Division 50 of the Income Tax Assessment Act 1997 to ensure that Parliament retains the ability to fully scrutinize those organizations seeking to

[88] See ICNL, "Survey of Tax Laws Affecting NGOs in Central and Eastern Europe," *International Center for Not-for-Profit Law*, Washington, DC, 2002, at p. 9.

[89] For England and Wales, see the Charities Act 2006, sections 45–69; for Scotland, the Charities and Trustee Investment (Scotland) Act 2005, sections 79–92; for Northern Ireland, the Charities Act (Northern Ireland) 2008, sections 131–59; for Ireland, the Charities Act 2009, sections 93–97; for New Zealand, the Income Tax Act 2004, as amended by the Income Tax Act 2007.

pass money to overseas charities and other entities. The "in Australia" special conditions provide additional measures to address possible abuse of nonprofit entities for the purposes of money laundering and terrorist financing, and ensure the proper operation of nonprofit entities, their use of public donations and funds, and the protection of their assets. In both the United States and Canada, a rash of terrorism-related polices and laws have been adopted since the 9/11 attacks.[90] In England and Wales, as highlighted in the Kennedy report,[91] government has introduced new control measures not just in the form of antiterrorism legislation, but including a range of other powers such as "stop and search" and restrictions on broadcasting, advertising, and public demonstrations.[92] The consequence of imposing such a legislative blanket of restrictions in this jurisdiction, as in others, is that the work of charity is being impeded, and mutual trust between government and the sector, essential for any future public benefit service provision partnership, is at risk of being eroded. In 2010, for example, considerable controversy was generated in the U.K. by the decision of the Charity Commission not to suspend registration of the charity Muslim Aid despite allegations of its links to terrorist organizations.[93] Subsequently, the ECtHR upheld the Commission's suspension of Mustapha Kamal Mustapha as Imam of Finsbury Park Mosque on grounds of his alleged terrorist connections.[94]

2. International Constraints

National constraints are further compounded by international initiatives as governments acknowledge the global presence of many charities, some of which have built up operational networks in precisely the same underdeveloped countries identified as containing terrorist networks, and coordinate multinational agreements to intercept their activities. So, for example, the Financial Action Task Force (FATF), an

[90] See, e.g.: in the United States, The USA Patriot Act 2001, Executive Order 13224 2001, and the Anti-Terrorist Financing Guidelines 2002; in Canada, the Anti-Terrorism Act 2001, the Foreign Missions Amendment Act 2002, and the Public Safety Act 2004. See generally Carters Professional Corporation, "Anti-Terrorism Law.ca," http://www.antiterrorismlaw.ca. See also McCullough J. and Pickering S., "Suppressing the Financing of Terrorism," in *British Journal of Criminology*, Vol. 45, No. 4, 2005, at pp. 470–86.

[91] See Kennedy, H., *Report of the Advisory Group on Campaigning and the Voluntary Sector*, London, 2007.

[92] Kennedy, *Report of the Advisory Group on Campaigning and the Voluntary Sector*, citing in particular the Protection from Harassment Act 1997, Terrorism Act 2000, the Communications Act 2003, and the Serious Organised Crime and Police Act 2005.

[93] See Rickets, A., "Charity Commission Rejects Criticism Over Muslim Aid Allegation" at: http://thirdsector.co.uk/news/Article/1047280/Charity-Commission-rejects-criticism-Muslim-Aid-investigation.

[94] See Mustafa Kamal Mustafa (Abu Hamza) (No. 1) v. the United Kingdom—31411/07 [2011] ECHR 211.

intergovernmental body established to combat money laundering and the financing of terrorism, has led the way in negotiating such agreements because:[95]

> terrorists and terrorist organizations exploit the NPO sector to raise and move funds, provide logistical support, encourage terrorist recruitment or otherwise support terrorist organizations and operations. This misuse not only facilitates terrorist activity but also undermines donor confidence and jeopardizes the very integrity of NPOs. Therefore, protecting the NPO sector from terrorist abuse is both a critical component of the global fight against terrorism and a necessary step to preserve the integrity of NPOs.

The willingness of governments to increase regulatory control over charities and other nonprofits "for their own good" does not augur well for future public benefit partnership arrangements and can only impede the flow of funds to and from charities.

VII. CONCLUSION

In *Government versus Markets,* Tanzio makes the point that[96] the "government must play a far more vigilant and effective supervisory and regulatory role than in the past. This is a fundamental role in a market economy, one that the state has not played well or has not played at all in past years." The recent excesses in the under-regulated financial sector, which triggered a market collapse that has put the global economy on the brink of recession, lends weight to Tanzio's argument. In the years leading up to the 2008 crisis, it seemed as though a doctrine of market fundamentalism[97] was allowed free rein: The market knew best and was self-correcting, and intervention by government was futile as it normally would fail, and in failing would exacerbate the problem it sought to correct. The problem is that government lacks the tools to regulate to the degree of depth, refinement, and responsiveness likely to prove effective.

The charity law reform processes were initiated primarily with a view to improve the regulatory framework for charity, and to some extent they were successful. Progress was particularly made in those jurisdictions where a charity-specific regulator was introduced alongside a registration system. However, it is hard to avoid the conclusion that a charity-specific focus is itself flawed as a regulatory strategy. Charity has become enmeshed in other spheres of activity, and any regulatory frame of reference must now not only take this into account, but must functionally address that fact and its ramifications. The public benefit principle and designated charitable

[95] FATF:GAFI—*Interpretative Note to Special Recommendation VIII Non-Profit Organisations.* See further at www.fatf-gafi.org

[96] Tanzio, V., *Government versus Markets: The Changing Economic Role of the State,* Cambridge, Cambridge University Press, 2011, at p. 31.

[97] See, e.g., Van Overtveldt, J., *The Chicago School,* Agate, Chicago, 2007; and Ebenstein, L., *Milton Friedman,* Palgrave Macmillan, New York, 2007.

purposes accompanied by related activity are key, but when they lead charity into the public and private sectors, the regulatory arm must follow. It is very evident from the charity law reform outcomes that this was viewed as a step too far for all legislators.

In the absence of any legislative initiative to provide a regulatory capacity to supervise charity involvement in public benefit service provision or in commercial ventures, the judiciary and the Revenue are left to apply such common law rules and tax regulations as may fit, but without the guidance of a framework of principles. The judiciary in particular has been formulating its own jurisdiction-specific rules to guide determination of charitable trading issues. It is likely that in the interests of creating a more effective regulatory system, allowing government to rigorously supervise and protect charity as it becomes subsumed into the market, a further phase of law reform will be necessary.

13

NEW FRONTIERS AND LEGAL STRUCTURES

I. INTRODUCTION

The ebb and flow of boundaries between government, commerce, and the nonprofits is creating uncertainty for charities. The evolving/mutating legal structures, now emerging in response to the associated market opportunities, are adding to that uncertainty. For the charitable trust, established to exist in perpetuity, these are just further challenges to overcome like the many others already encountered over the centuries. Although there is no serious threat to the future of "charity," as it has been known to the common law jurisdictions, it would be a mistake to underestimate the importance of the difficulties it now faces. The new era opening up for charity will require compromises and adjustments.

This final chapter considers the impact of current socioeconomic changes on the role and functions of charity. It begins by noting the influence of the common law legacy of principles and regulatory framework. It examines the fissures that would seem to be splitting charities into different camps, particularly the separation into those primarily oriented toward public benefit service delivery and those with a dominant commercial orientation. It then identifies the new legal structures, assesses their relative merits, and notes their current distribution across the jurisdictions studied, giving particular attention to the community foundations, the community interest company and charitable incorporated organization, the L3C; and the Social Impact Bonds. The challenge presented to the future of charities by social enterprises and by the myriad range of hybrid legal structures now flourishing, particularly in the United States, is assessed.[1]

[1] See further, Billitteri, T., "Mixing Mission and Business: Does Social Enterprise Need a New Legal Approach?," *Highlights from an Aspen Institute Roundtable,* January 2007, available at: http://www.aspeninstitute.org/sites/default/files/content/docs/pubs/New_Legal_Forms_Report_FINAL.pdf.

The chapter closes by giving some consideration to the probable future funding streams for charity and the compromises that may need to be made to ensure financial security. It suggests that this may have a considerable influence on the traditional hallmarks of charity, particularly its capacity for asserting independence and fostering altruism. The wider implications for the nonprofit sector are also considered.

II. CHARITY AND ITS FRONTIERS: FROM OLD TO NEW

The common law has long provided a protected environment for charity, particularly in the U.K. and Irish jurisdictions where the charitable trust has been the dominant legal form, enabling it to survive and flourish, if unevenly, across the many nations that share the same legal heritage. In recent times this has been changing in keeping with the fading significance of the common law as a sufficient regulatory framework for charity. Change has also come about as a consequence of charities opting for corporate status, developing commercial and competitive trading arms, or becoming deeply enmeshed in government public service provision. The move in several nations—from the Preamble/*Pemsel* body of case law to statutory law as the source of authority, from adjudication to administration as the method, and from Revenue to Commission as the operative means for deciding issues relating to charitable purpose and status—does signify a new era for charity, and one in which its common law origins, while of continuing importance, is likely to be offset in the future by statute-based regulatory adjustments. The nature and scale of these changes will also have implications for the future relationship between charity and the nonprofit sector.

A. New Structures and Old Regulatory Principles

The regulatory means for monitoring charities in the 21st century is largely predicated on legal structures designed for an earlier era. The charity law struggle to accommodate a dichotomy that allows charities to be structured as trusts and as corporations, without providing the necessary legal linkages between them, has long been divisive. Arguably, the surge of interest in new legal structures is partly attributable to the underlying mismatch between equitable principles and company law, the consequences of which have included frustrating the efforts of charities to blend trade with mission.

1. Trust and Company

The law relating to charity contains a fundamental definitional problem. The primarily trust-led charity law culture (rooted in equity principles and tied to related regulatory agencies, etc.) operates in tandem with a corporate-led charity culture (in which charities are essentially treated the same as any other corporation).

There is thus an inbuilt tension between trust and company law: Although underpinning common law principles distinguish charities defined as trusts, the regulatory machinery defines charities as just another species of corporation. This tension between corporate form and trust principles does not assist philanthropic functionality.

The extent to which the trust rather than the company, the latter with its corresponding emphasis on formal governance arrangements and reporting requirements, prevailed as the preferred structure differed considerably in the jurisdictions studied. Instead of the forced choice between the two, neither of which quite had the capacity to equally address both the protection of charitable purpose and the requirements of company law—or more bluntly to marry social mission with business methods—some jurisdictions have chosen to create specially designated legal structures by legislation, usually accompanied by incentives to encourage their use, with the intention that these should in time displace the need for the present bifurcated regulatory approach. Recently there has also been some experimentation with new and varied hybrid structures as will be discussed later in the chapter, which may suggest a different way forward.

2. Charity Commission and Revenue

The realignment, in some jurisdictions, of the regulatory regime for charities with a Charity Commission–type of overseeing body, corresponds to a shift in government emphasis from tax exemption to a charitable purpose orientation. The transition seemed to come more naturally in those jurisdictions where the trust legacy was strongest.

It remains the case, however, that so far most common law countries maintain a tax-driven approach to charitable activity with the Revenue as sole regulator. This may change as governments everywhere turn to a steadily strengthening and increasingly more cohesive and coherent nonprofit sector for assistance in meeting expectations regarding future public benefit service provision.

3. Nonprofits, Charities, and the Regulator

If the U.S. tax-driven approach to charities and other nonprofits represents one model, and the U.K. Charity Commission another, then the model being proposed in Australia would seem to offer an interesting compromise located somewhere between the two on the same spectrum. In Australia, the intention is to switch from the ATO to a Commission regulator but the latter, instead of being charity-specific, will be a Commissioner for Charities and Not-for-profits. It would seem wholly appropriate that a government, which aims to engage with the sector in its entirety, should establish a new regulatory body that while giving specific recognition to charities also embraces all other sector entities. This is in keeping with its National Compact strategy (see chapter 9). Neither in Australia nor anywhere else is there any suggestion that the charities should lose their separate and distinct charitable status and be treated as just another tax-exempt entity in the nonprofit sector.

B. Charities and Their Contemporary Social Role

The spectrum of nonprofit activity has expanded in keeping with the contraction of the public sector. The general impermanence of sectoral boundaries has, for charities, also led to a certain amount of drifting into separate blocs. The established foundations have maintained their institutional character and social role, particularly so in continental Europe, but many mission-specific charitable trusts and corporations have changed considerably as they adapted to changes in their funding environment.

1. Institutional and Grassroots

The institutional range of charities—that is, churches, schools, universities, hospital complexes, etc.—continue to comprise the core of charitable activity and act as a repository for most charitable assets in all jurisdictions as they have done for generations. They are virtually part of the public sector. Institutional charities have become such established components of our social infrastructure, relatively impervious to political turmoil (at least in the common law countries) and yet accustomed to working alongside government, that their future seems safely assured. At the other extreme, the grassroots charities—welfare agencies for children, the aged, sick, and disabled, etc.—that have long been closely enmeshed with their socially disadvantaged constituencies, also form a distinct group. Although they too have funding issues, both groups and their associated legal structures (foundation, charitable trust, and association) have a reasonably secure future in all the jurisdictions studied.

2. Civil Society

For some years, and in some jurisdictions more than in others, there has been a flowering of what might be termed "civil society organizations," that is those charities and other nonprofits that have as their raison d'être the building of a greater sense of civic responsibility and that foster the engagement of citizens in public benefit activity on a local, national, and international basis. The legislative outcomes of charity law reform gave recognition and encouragement to this development by listing new charitable purposes such as the advancement of civil society and the promotion of multiculturalism. This group is mostly evident in the more mature democracies. Because they draw their principles and members from vaguely ideological sources, civil society organizations are vulnerable to changes in the political environment. Support for this group may wilt due to the continuation of common law constraints on political activity coupled with the imposition of modern antiterrorism restraints, particularly in the current climate of financial stringency when government and the general public tend to be faced with pressures requiring their more immediate attention. Indeed, the concept of "civil society" itself becomes suspect as evidence from contemporary events in places such as Norway, England, Wall Street, and the Middle East suggests that the mutual bonds of trust and compassion, without which no society can be held to be "civil," are too amorphous, patchy, and susceptible to rupture, to provide a sound basis for social cohesion.

3. Public Benefit Service Provision

Many charities have aligned themselves and their resources more closely to government public benefit service provision, becoming, in varying degrees, extensions of government as the latter's funds and service contracts largely dictate their activities insofar as charitable purposes and objects permit. These tend to differ from the other groups of charities not only in that service delivery constitutes by far the largest part of their charitable activities, but also as their management style and governance arrangements have acquired the characteristics of government bodies. This group contains a subgroup of faith-based charities, particularly strong in education services and health care, which is gradually acquiring a higher social profile, and in so doing is raising questions as to the propriety of such church/state linkages that are especially evident in the United States. Although this group is relatively secure and prosperous due to growth opportunities resulting from its close relationship with governments, in the process it has perhaps become distanced from its original constituency, is less in touch with the pattern of needs outside its servicing remit and less attuned to the merits of a strategic approach, and is more restrained in objectively and assertively advocating on behalf of the socially disadvantaged.

However, it has yet to be determined where the line may be safely drawn between the public benefit responsibilities that charities may undertake and those which, being inherent to government, cannot be divested to charity or other nonprofits. There are indications from decisions of the judiciary in the U.K., Australia, United States, and EU that attention is beginning to focus on the legitimacy of some government outsourcing of public benefit responsibilities. It can be anticipated that some key precedents are due in the not-too-distant future, which could help clarify boundaries and set realistic expectations for further growth opportunities. In the meantime, in all jurisdictions, the charitable and other nonprofit public benefit service providers constitute a sizeable and distinct group.

4. Commerce

Another group, growing fast and by no means wholly separate from the others, is comprised of those that have turned to commerce as a means of securing funds. This group is clearly subdivided into charities that have restricted trading to activities that relate to their charitable purposes and others that have pursued profit-making opportunities unrelated to those purposes. Unlike the other charitable groupings, this one has ventured furthest into the marketplace. Their extensive participation gives rise to questions as to the balance struck between charity and business. It can be argued that altruism can have little place, other than as a marketing device, in the competition for profits; merchandising rather than mission can become the focus of staff attention; and users or recipients have little say in product appropriateness. The tests now being introduced by the U.S. judiciary, especially in the wake of the *Provena* case,[2] are probably a fair guide to the approach likely to be taken in due course by the judiciary and regulators in other jurisdictions as they too confront the balance issue (see chapter 7).

C. Charities and the Nonprofit Sector

For some time, there has been a growing disquiet regarding the rationale, underpinned by charity law, for maintaining a firm distinction between charities and the rest of the nonprofit sector.[3] This debate should perhaps now be broadened to take account of the above fracture lines that are gradually splitting the world of charities into recognizably separate and distinct blocks. The justification for continuing to treat them as a discrete, coherent, and relatively small category of nonprofits with unique tax privileges, among the myriad forms of organizations that constitute the sector, diminishes as their activities become more like those of government departments or commercial enterprises. Arguably, charities should no longer be viewed as a "stand alone" species of nonprofit, with its self-contained body of law and institutional infrastructure, cohering around an immutable but ever-extending band of charitable purposes. Instead they should be regulated in a manner that recognizes their particular cross-sectoral linkages and accords with the nature of their main activities. This challenge was not taken up by any of the reforming nations, though such a model has for some time been operational in the United States and may yet be addressed in the latest and ongoing phase of reform in Australia.

1. Values and the Sector

Of all the common law legacies inherited by the sector, probably none are as important as the principles forged in the Courts of Equity and ultimately bequeathed to charity. These have come to shape the values that now set the nonprofit sector apart from the public and business sectors. The above divisions are, however, also beginning to corrode the distinctive values of the nonprofit sector, and for that reason alone perhaps the charity/nonprofit relationship needs to be reconsidered.

Both government and commerce have used the leverage of funding to prod charities into building cross-sectoral alignments and to become more like the sector entities with which they aspire to collaborate or compete. This is evident not only in terms of models of management and governance, improved efficiency, and effectiveness, etc., but also in the assumption of aggressive competitive tactics, "hard sell"

[2] Provena Covenant Medical Center v. Department of Revenue, 236 Ill. 2d 386 (2010).

[3] A distinction greatly reduced in the United States by the tax code approach.

advertising, increased attention to service or product specification and less to need, reduced involvement of volunteers, and a fading grasp of the context and causes of problems in the disadvantaged community to which their charitable purpose is linked. The sector's distinctive attributes of a "strongly idealism-based ethos which places highest priority on responding to need or producing social good, and doing so via indigenous, cooperative, mostly layperson- or community-based action"[4] is in some danger of incremental corruption.

D. Reconfiguring Charities and the Sector

One possible means of protecting core values and reinforcing sector parameters might lie in a clearer delineation, in law and tax terms, between different categories of public benefit entities. Given the existing division between charity and other nonprofits, together with the above fault lines within charity itself, and bearing in mind the lateral tax differentiation applied by the IRS in its treatment of all nonprofits, such a step would not be too difficult for most jurisdictions studied should they wish to pursue it. However, for Judt the contemporary approach of U.S. government toward public benefit provision is attributable to reasons of culture and history, rather than to any economic rationale, and is rooted in "the American combination of economic insecurity, social inequality, and reduced or minimal government intervention in the field of welfare legislation."[5] His conclusion that due to such singular causal features "the U.S. model is not exportable"[6] is open to challenge as evidence mounts that in the U.K., and arguably at least in countries such as Australia and to a lesser degree Canada, there are indications of a gradual convergence toward the U.S. approach.

1. Existing Tiered Tax Definitional Systems

The sense in which the concept of "charity" is a tax-driven definition is particularly evident in some of the jurisdictions studied that have subdivided the concept to earmark a category of charities as eligible for preferential tax treatment. In Canada, for example, a distinction is made between "charitable organisation," "private foundation," and "public foundation," all of which can be a "registered charity," whereas in the United States a "charitable organisation" may be a corporation, community chest, fund, foundation, or sports association.

In some jurisdictions, notably Australia, Singapore, and South Africa, where the trust failed to become the main legal structure for charities, the definitional focus on charitable purposes has been further compromised. For tax purposes, a subset of "charity" (PBI in Australia, IPC in Singapore, and PBO in South Africa) has been identified as a category entitled to receive tax-deductible donations from the public

[4] See Reed, P. and Howe, V., "Publicly Available Data Resources on the Nonprofit Sector in Canada," Nonprofit Sector Knowledge Base Project, Statistics Canada, 1998, at p. 52.

[5] Reed and Howe, "Publicly Available Data Resources on the Nonprofit Sector in Canada."

[6] Judt, T., *Reappraisals*, Vintage Books, London, 2008, at p. 420.

and to confer tax-deductible privileges on donors. This requires an organization to first satisfy the definitional requirements of a "charity" and then satisfy additional requirements if it is to be granted the enhanced status. Such a transparent acknowledgement that specified entities are of such public benefit so as to warrant additional tax concessions has much to commend it, as it clearly and candidly prioritizes some charitable entities and directs revenue streams accordingly. In Singapore, for example, the following nonprofits are singled out as IPCs: hospitals; a public authority or society engaged in research or other work connected with the causes, prevention, or cure of disease in human beings; a university or a public fund for the establishment, maintenance, enlargement, or improvement of a university; an educational institution or a public fund for the establishment, maintenance, enlargement, or improvement of such an educational institution; a public or private fund for the provision, establishment, or endowment of a scholarship, exhibition, or prize in a university, or an educational institution not operated or conducted for profit; a public fund established and maintained for the relief of distress among members of the public; an institution that is established for charitable, benevolent or philanthropic purposes only; or an organization not operated or conducted for profit that is engaged in or connected with the promotion of culture, the arts, or sports.[7] In Australia, the definition of Public Benevolent Institution (PBI) is a nonprofit institution organized for the direct relief of such poverty, sickness, suffering, distress, misfortune, disability, destitution, or helplessness as arouses compassion in the community. The PBI approach also provides a mechanism for the adjustment of status by the government: Charitable purposes and their associated charities may be moved into and out of the enhanced status as warranted by changing circumstances. For the future, the Australian government has announced its intention to design a better system for the targeting of nonprofit tax concessions.[8] It has been suggested that such a tiered approach could be beneficial if introduced to charity law in the U.K.[9]

2. Prospective Multitiered Definitional System

Arguably, the charity "brand" now needs protection. Where charities have opted to compromise their independence and their activities by having become largely tied to commerce, government-type service delivery, institutional infrastructure, or the pursuit of civil society goals, there is an argument for giving these arrangements formal recognition by making legal and tax adjustments to their charitable status. It might be appropriate to consider restricting the full status of "charity" to those entities that continue to satisfy all of the common law benchmarks—exclusivity, independence,

[7] Reed and Howe, "Publicly Available Data Resources on the Nonprofit Sector in Canada."

[8] Australian Government, Office of Assistant Treasurer, press release: The Hon Tanya Plibersek MP, Minister for Human Services and Social Inclusion—"Making it Easier for Charities to Help Those Who Need it" (10.05.2011).

[9] See Chesterman, M., "Foundations of Charity Law in the New Welfare State," in Mitchell, C. and Moody, S. (eds.), *Foundations of Charity*, Hart Publishing, Oxford, Portland, OR, 2000.

and altruism—and where their activities are confined to charitable purposes but are largely and directly applied to prevent or address the more traditional "welfare" aspects of social need. Other organizations that rely on commercial activity for funds would be free to do so while either foregoing their charitable status, or having it formally registered as compromised, and being subject to tax on that activity.

If the same approach was then applied to the nonprofit sector in general, a distinction could at least be drawn between those nonprofits that in reality, due to funding, accountability, and policy control reasons, may be considered to function more as members of the "public sector" rather than as "nonprofit" sector entities. This "public sector" category could appropriately accommodate those nonprofit entities that have responsibility for utilities (e.g., power plants and pipelines), transportation and warehousing establishments (e.g., harbor authorities and municipal bus lines), certain construction establishments (e.g., bridge, street, and sewer construction) and waste-disposal establishments.[10]

The case for constructing a web of legislative provisions that differentiates between and governs charities and all other types of nonprofits in an organized fashion shows every sign of steadily becoming irrefutable.

3. Advocacy and Human Rights

Any reconfiguration of the sector will have to address the currently compromised position of advocacy groups, some of which now opt to avoid charitable status in some states so that they may campaign unhindered on behalf of the socially disadvantaged. This aspect of charitable activity, proudly associated with a history of campaigns for equality and equity such as the antislavery and universal suffrage movements, now needs to legislatively reaffirmed.

It has to be acknowledged, however, that the tradition of advocacy, which has most often served to give the sector a binding sense of solidarity, has also been weakened in recent years by the number and sometimes conflicting nature of new associational forms that have sprung up to assert the separate identity of minority groups. Sector coherence has always been riven to some degree by the separate sets of needs of special interest groups. This is now becoming further endangered by the splintering effect of minority groups (e.g., gay/lesbian, disabled, faith-based) asserting their separate rights against the collective values of historically disadvantaged communities (e.g., poor, racially distinct). It is a sad irony that some of the more basic principles underpinning the Human Rights Convention—equality, nondiscrimination—deployed to gain justifiable recognition for the singular identity of a group with shared interests would now seem to be licensing incremental sector fragmentation. Given that older social groupings always have to make room for newcomers, this process should not be perceived as necessarily reductive. On the contrary, the fact that an ever more pervasive human rights ethos encourages the self-affirmation

[10] See further, Osborne, D. and Gaebler, T., *Reinventing Government*, Plume, New York, 1993.

of minority interest groups is to be expected and welcomed. Nonetheless, the political effect of competing minority interests is currently detracting from attaining sector cohesion. This development would seem to be of a piece with the more general move away from the collectivist approach to public benefit provision, which, in many of the jurisdictions studied, had seen 20th-century governments assume responsibility for standardized public service silos that delivered fairly similarly packaged educational, health, and other services to matching client groups.

III. NEW LEGAL STRUCTURES

The time-honored boundaries of charitable purpose and the nondistribution constraint, of exclusivity and relative scale, are being questioned and are in danger of being seen as obstructive and redundant. Does it matter whether public benefit outcomes are achieved by commerce or charity, or by a mix of both? Should any associated tax exemption entitlement be dependent upon legal status? Such questions are leading some to argue that public benefit entities should receive tax-exempt recognition on the basis of function rather than structure,[11] whereas others make a case for new structures specifically designed to blend nonprofit purposes with for-profit form,[12] as we move away from the familiar touchstones that have traditionally demarcated sector boundaries.

A. Foundations

Far from being a new legal structure, foundations have long formed the basic unit for organized charitable activity and the backbone of the nonprofit sector in all the jurisdictions studied. The signature characteristic of the modern foundation, its independence both from market considerations and election politics, means that it is among the most autonomous institutions of modern societies. Foundations may take the long-term view, can afford to be less swayed by the vagaries of economic and political pressures, and need not be beholden to populist expectations. Although foundations generally continue to play their customary institutional role, the community foundation and the corporate foundation have emerged as relatively new structures that are responsive to local need, and they are rapidly spreading from the United States, Canada, and the U.K., and from their foothold in Australia and New Zealand, into continental Europe.

1. Community Foundations

A community foundation is an independent philanthropic organization working in a specific geographical area. Typically, a community foundation provides grants

[11] See, e.g., Malani, A. and Posner, E. A., "The Case for For-Profit Charities," in *Virginia Law Review*, Vol. 93, 2007, at p. 2017.

[12] See, e.g., Yunus, M., "Nobel Peace Prize 2006: The Nobel Lecture," in *Law and Business Review of the Americas*, Vol. 13, 2007, at pp. 267, 272.

and other services to assist other charitable organizations in meeting local needs, and also offers services to help donors establish endowed funds for specific charitable purposes. It identifies local needs, mobilizes local resources to strengthen communities, and, over time, it builds up a collection of endowed funds from many donors for grantmaking. A variety of different contributions and funding sources are utilized ranging from individuals, commercial companies, and charitable trusts to government agencies. Though generally incorporated in most states, community foundations in Australia are always in the form of a charitable trust.

The community foundation has become widespread and is now, for example, the fastest-growing philanthropic entity in Canada.[13] Since the 1980s, a number of private foundations in the United States have created initiatives to develop community foundations in various states. Community foundation giving dipped 2.1 percent to $4.1 billion in 2010, the first consecutive-year decline on record.[14] There are approximately 60 community foundations in the U.K., and the community foundation concept is now taking root in many other countries, particularly in central and eastern Europe.

2. Corporate Foundations

Also known as a company-sponsored foundation, corporate foundations are private foundations that receive their primary funding from a profit-making business. The foundation is a legally separate charitable organization, even though it often maintains close ties with the founding company. It must abide by the same rules and regulations as other private foundations, meaning that it must exist only to further charitable purposes for the public benefit and not the purposes of the company.[15] The strength of corporate foundations lies in their ability to provide a structure and focus for corporate giving as a means of engaging with the nonprofit sector, and the opportunity to share and apply expertise in an effort to tackle challenging social issues.[16]

[13] See Wayne, S., Canadian Council for International Co-operation, *A Profile of Planned Giving and Endowments within the Canadian International NGO Community*, 1999. This form of charity recorded 83.2 percent growth in assets between 1994 and 1997.

[14] See Foundation Center, *Foundation Growth and Giving Estimates: Current Outlook (2011 Edition*, April 2011 at: http://foundationcenter.org/gainknowledge/research/nationaltrends.html.

[15] There are over 50,000 foundations in the United States with $448 billion in assets in 1999 (somewhat less now). When the federal government launched its War on Poverty, foundations' assets were then valued at less than $30 billion. The Bill & Melinda Gates Foundation started in 1999 with $21 billion is now the biggest U.S. foundation. John Walters, publisher of *Philanthropy*, estimates that foundation assets alone may easily grow to between $4 trillion and $5.9 trillion by 2035, "Come the Revolution," in *Philanthropy*, July–August 1999, at pp. 25–26.

[16] See further, Charity Commission, *A Guide to Corporate Foundations*, Feb. 2010, at: http://www.charitycommission.gov.uk/Charity_requirements_guidance/Specialist_guidance/corporate_foundations/default.aspx.

Corporate foundations are well established in the United States, where their level of giving remained basically unchanged at $4.7 billion in 2010.[17] In England and Wales, there are over 100 corporate foundations.

In central and eastern Europe, corporate giving is still in its infancy though growing rapidly: in Slovakia, for example, 43 corporate foundations were established in the period 2003–2006, twice as many as in the period 1993–2001.

B. New Statutory Structures Linking For-Profits with Public Benefit Provision

There has been no rush to legislate into existence legal structures that might grow to displace the role occupied by charity in its various forms. Those jurisdictions with a heavy reliance upon the traditional trust and unincorporated association have found it expedient to redress the balance by introducing new incorporated structures, whereas Australia, New Zealand, and Singapore have so far found it unnecessary to create new structures. In Ireland, for example, there are plans to introduce a Charitable Designated Activity Company (CDAC), which will be allowed to lock its profits into the company, to ensure not-for-profit purposes, and is intended for groups such as non-charitable community interest groups, social enterprises, and/or trading subsidiaries of charities.

In a small minority of the jurisdictions studied, tentative steps have been taken to create new statutory structures that blend commerce and charitable purpose. Whereas Ireland and other states are seeking to create new structures for charities, other jurisdictions such as the U.K. and the United States have been developing legal structures out of the corporate tradition for companies that pursue socially beneficial goals.

1. The Community Interest Company

The U.K. government recently introduced the community interest company (CIC), which in essence is a normal limited company established to pursue socially beneficial ends rather than profits for individuals. This new legal structure has several crucial features: It is deliberately designed to marry public benefit with for-profit rewards; although it is not eligible for charitable status, a CIC may be owned and directed by a charity; and it is not itself entitled to tax exemption. A charity, including one structured as a limited company, may convert to CIC status. The advantages of this form over a charity include the fact that a CIC may pay its directors without having either a constitution that specifically allows payment or the prior consent of the Charity Commission, and it can obtain outside equity investment. As the inability to receive equity investment has proven to be a serious obstacle for charities, this latter advantage is particularly important. The U.K. government has explained that

[17] Charity Commission, *A Guide to Corporate Foundations.*

although it views them as suitable for assisting in the delivery of social services at the local authority level, it did not envisage that CICs should be used to deliver centrally directed public services such as health and education.

However, unlike charities, community interest companies are unable to use tax relief to raise capital through social impact bonds. Moreover, the amount of profit that CICs are allowed to distribute is limited, and they are ineligible for the tax relief that applies to charities, although a recent government concession now allows CICs to be able to keep community investment tax relief (CITR), which allows investors in community development finance institutions to reclaim up to 25 percent of their investment over five years. In total, only some 3000 CICs have been established, which is considerably fewer than anticipated and at a rate that bears no resemblance to the comparatively massive growth in social enterprises. This slow take-up has been attributed to difficulties with the dividend cap imposed on CICs, which has made equity investment difficult—meaning that the profit margins for potential shareholders have proved unattractive.

2. The L3C

The low-profit limited liability company (L3C) is a relatively new legal structure that has been created in the United States specifically to bridge the gap between nonprofit and for-profit investing by providing a structure that is intended to make it easier for companies with a social mission to receive investments, including loans and grants, from charitable foundations. Like a nonprofit, the L3C's primary purpose must be to promote a charitable purpose but, unlike the traditional limited company, the L3C must be formed to accomplish a charitable purpose in addition to a business purpose. Although the L3C must have a charitable purpose, donations to it are not deductible as a charitable contribution because the L3C is a for-profit entity. By becoming an L3C, a business is better positioned to receive a mix of investments from both traditional sources and nonprofit foundations. This taxable for-profit business, the primary goal of which is to achieve a stated social mission, is perhaps best defined in the Vermont legislation that first gave statutory authority to the L3C in 2008:[18]

> "L3C" or "Low-profit limited liability company" means a person organized under this chapter that is organized for a business purpose that satisfies and is at all times operated to satisfy each of the following requirements.
>
> (A) The Company significantly furthers the accomplishment of one or more charitable or educational purposes within the meaning of Section 170(c)(2)(B) of

[18] T.11, Ch 21 Section 3001(27). Note that the referenced "charitable or educational purposes" as noted in 26 U.S.C. § 170(c)(2)(B) are: "organized and operated exclusively for religious, charitable, scientific, literary, or educational purposes, or to foster national or international amateur sports competition (but only if no part of its activities involve the provision of athletic facilities or equipment), or for the prevention of cruelty to children or animals."

the IRS Code of 1986, 26 U.S.C. Section 170(c)(2)(B); and (ii) would not have been formed but for the company's relationship to the accomplishment of charitable or educational purposes.

(B) No significant purpose of the company is the production of income or the appreciation of property; provided, however, that the fact that a person produces significant income or capital appreciation shall not, in the absence of other factors, be conclusive evidence of a significant purpose involving the production of income or the appreciation of property.

(C) No purpose of the company is to accomplish one or more political or legislative purposes within the meaning of Section 170(c)(2)(D) of the IRS code of 1986, 26 U.S.C. Section 170(c)(2)(D).

(D) If a company that met the definition of this subdivision (27) at its formation at any time ceases to satisfy any one of the requirements, it shall immediately cease to be a low-profit LLC, but by continuing to meet all the other requirements of this chapter, will continue to exist as a limited liability company. The name of the company must be changed to be in conformance with subsection 3005(a).

The L3C facilitates investments in socially beneficial, for-profit ventures while simplifying compliance with Internal Revenue Service rules for Program Related Investments (PRIs), which are loans or investments private foundations can offer for charitable or educational projects such as affordable housing or health clinics, even if they are run by for-profit entities. To qualify as a PRI, the IRS requires that the primary purpose of the investment must be to accomplish a charitable or educational purpose, the production of income or capital appreciation of property cannot be a significant purpose of the investment, and the investment cannot be used for political or legislative purposes.[19] A PRI allows private foundations to make investments in the form of loans, grants, and equity purchases in socially motivated for-profit entities.

In theory, the L3C should be attractive to foundations as they are obliged to make annual program-related investments of at least 5 percent of their assets in order to keep their tax-exempt status, and it allows foundations to recoup their outlays; the same funds may be recycled and loaned out multiple times. The involvement of a foundation as the "anchor tenant" in a project is also attractive to L3C owners as it then provides an incentive for private investors to participate, and a spread of investment can be secured. Usually the L3C is structured so that the private foundation accepts the highest risk while receiving a lower rate of return on its investment. This permits an L3C to offer layered ownership in which the investment risk and return are distributed unevenly among its members.

However, although L3Cs generally serve as tailor-made vehicles for private foundations to facilitate their annual PRI obligations, foundations have so far been

[19] See IRS, "Program-Related Investmentsm" at http://www.irs.gov/charities/foundations/article/0,,id=137793,00.html.

unwilling to make such investments: the New York-based Foundation Center estimates that PRIs made up less than 1 percent of the charitable distributions made by foundations in 2006 and 2007. In the main this would seem to be due to the uncertainty surrounding the status of the L3C: The IRS has still not ruled on whether a private foundation's investment in an L3C will automatically qualify as a PRI, despite the above-three IRS requirements now being routinely included in most L3Cs governing documents.

Given the steady spread of legislation authorizing the use of L3Cs, often incorporating clauses that provide specifically for their use of PRIs and that reiterate the IRS requirements regarding such use, it would seem likely that in due course the IRS will issue guidance allowing a standardized process of recognition for this hybrid entity.[20] When that time comes, the L3C may well quickly become a significant legal structure, at least in the United States, as a means whereby charities and business interest can simultaneously pursue both the advancement of charitable purposes and profit. It might be useful as a wholly owned subsidiary of a charity, or it could have a place within certain partially charitable structures such as hospital–physician joint ventures. In terms of public benefit service provision, this vehicle lends itself particularly well to community-based projects such as developing affordable housing for the poor. In terms of commerce it has already proven to be successful for investors and those in need by returning failing family farms to viability.[21] However, there remains the fact that an L3C is required to ensure that its profit purpose remains secondary to the charitable purpose. Given that in the spread of investors some will be attracted primarily by the prospects of profit, it is unclear how L3Cs will be monitored to make sure that, in strategic or even routine management decisions, charity prevails over profit.

C. New Statutory Structures for Trading Charities

Innovatory steps have been taken in this area in the U.K., where a new structure, the charitable incorporated organisation, will shortly be on the statute books.

1. The Charitable Incorporated Organisation

In the U.K., the Charities Act 2006 provided authority for the Charitable Incorporated Organisation (CIO), a new form that has yet to be introduced and

[20] However, there has recently been criticism surrounding L3Cs, and a high level of uncertainty as to whether this form will be accepted across many more U.S. states and at the federal level by the IRS. Some groups, including a few committees of the American Bar Association, have urged state legislatures not to adopt L3Cs, prompting recent exchanges by academics and practicing attorneys. There is an interesting debate as to whether L3Cs have peaked, have been overtaken by other structures in some states, or will continue to spread (author acknowledges with gratitude the contribution made by Blake Ratcliff to this subject in note to author on February 8, 2012).

[21] See, further, at: http://www.nonprofitlawblog.com/home/2008/07/l3c.html.

implemented. This long-awaited structure is intended to provide some of the benefits of being a company without many of the associated burdens. A CIO will be a corporate body with a constitution, and will be registered with and regulated by the Charity Commission, enabling that regulator to protect the integrity of charitable purpose and police charitable status.

The CIO, which can be established with limited or unlimited liability but only for charitable purposes, has several advantages for charities, the main ones being that the trustees will have limited liability and that the trustees and members can be the same people. This is likely to make it significantly easier to find trustees with professional skills.

This form of organization is designed exclusively for registered charities (though why it is not equally available to all nonprofits is unclear), and may be suitable for a charity wishing to engage in charitable activities involving commercial risks. Its introduction signifies government recognition that charity will need to be housed in a range of different legal structures if it is to have the flexibility needed for operating jointly with government and for-profit bodies. In the U.K., as in Ireland following the introduction of the CDAC, the principal regulator will be neither the Revenue nor the company registrar, but a different regulating body with a concern for charitable purpose. This should facilitate the marrying of trust principles to company rules within a new legal structure that is flexible enough to attract innovative entrepreneurs and to address emerging areas of social need. Such limited liability corporate structures may be sufficient to allow philanthropy to bridge the for-profit/charity dichotomy and encourage the forming of partnerships or joint ventures among commercial, nonprofit, and charitable entities.

D. Social Enterprises

The "social enterprise" is an amorphous, ill-defined concept that seems capable of accommodating a loose assortment of interpretations. They are businesses with primarily social objectives that direct their profits toward furthering public benefit in the community, rather than toward the private benefit of those running the business: They use the principles, skills and resources of business to help communities. The Community Interest Company (CIC) is a good example of a legal structure that has been developed as a vehicle to facilitate social enterprises.

In the United States, social enterprise embraces a wide range of entities engaged largely in public benefit service delivery. In continental Europe, the concept indicates a much more restricted range of public benefit activity in which, unlike the United States, there is normally a high level of user involvement. There are also differing views on the social significance of this growing phenomenon: Some see it as having a democratizing effect by breaking down institutionalized structures and replacing them with organizations concerned to have more direct involvement with areas and people suffering social disadvantage; others take the view that it poses a threat to civil society[22] as encouraging the involvement of nonprofits in trading corrupts their value base, diverting them from tending to their traditional stakeholders and networks, distorting their capacity to promote social capital, and diluting their public benefit contribution.[23] There is also a fear that any such shift in nonprofit interest from mission to market may be followed by a shift in board members from those connected to the community to those connected to business, though some rebalancing will clearly be necessary and advantageous.[24]

For present purposes, however, the term "social enterprise" is taken to refer broadly to recent entities and methods that pursue both commercial profit and social mission, but where the emphasis lies more on the latter.

1. Social Impact Bonds

There are now many forms of finance that aim to achieve social outcomes, including mainstream public spending of all kinds, grants, loans, equity investments, and convertible grants. In the U.K., some local tax tools—such as Tax Increment Financing and Development Taxes, are also employed to serve the same ends. There is a growing interest in more innovative approaches to finance ranging from advance market commitments for purchasing of pharmaceuticals to local bonds, to the burgeoning world of "social funds" and "social investment funds." In this world, the Social Impact Bonds (SIBs) in the U.K. show particular promise with considerable implications for charity.

The Social Impact Bond is a financial tool designed to attract new investment in outcomes-based contracts that benefit individuals and communities. Social Finance,[25] an organization set up in 2007 to help build a social investment market in the U.K., and that recommended the establishment of a Social Investment Bank in March 2007, launched the first SIB in September 2010. As Social Finance then explained, the goal was to provide a new way to invest money in social outcomes, and the key innovation of an SIB was to link three elements: investments (by commercial investors or foundations); a program of action to improve the prospects of a group; and commitments by national government to make payments linked to outcomes achieved in improving the lives of the group. The SIB provides private

[22] See, e.g., Eikenberry, A. and Kluver, J., "The Marketization of the Nonprofit Sector: Civil Society at Risk?," *Public Administration Review*, Vol. 64, No. 2, 2004, at pp. 132–40.

[23] Eikenberry, A. and Kluver, J., *The Nonprofit Sector and the Market: Opportunities and Challenges*, Aspen Institute, Washington, DC, 2001.

[24] Backman, E. and Smith, S. R., "Healthy Organizations, Unhealthy Communities?," in *Nonprofit Management and Leadership*, Vol. 10, No. 4, 2000, at pp. 355–73.

[25] As explained on its website, http://www.socialfinance.org.uk/sib:

> Social Finance is building a pioneering organisation to develop financial products that marry the ambitions of investors and the sector. We support social organisations to raise and deploy capital; we work with government to deliver social change; and we develop social investment markets and opportunities.

investment to pay for interventions, which are delivered by service providers with a proven track record, and financial returns to investors are made by the public sector on the basis of improved social outcomes. If outcomes do not improve, then investors do not recover their investment. The central idea is that investors buy bonds, and their money funds preventive social intervention. The bond issuer (usually a government department) will repay the bond with profit premium at a later date, after the benefits of the scheme have started to feed through. This model for more effective social intervention is currently being developed in collaboration with national and local government as well as with charities.

The first SIB project was piloted in the criminal justice sector in March 2010, when Social Finance arranged that the charity St Giles Trust would deliver a program intended to reduce the rate of recidivism for convicted prisoners (currently about 60 percent of prisoners in that category re-offend) following their discharge from Peterborough Prison. The project requires measurable outcomes to be achieved in respect of a fixed number of prisoners over a specific time period, through methods such as mentoring and drug counseling. The scheme is financed by £5 million worth of SIBs sold to charitable trusts and private enterprises (in fact, largely to the former). If the target of a 10 percent reduction in recidivism is met, the investors could receive £8 million after six years (an annual rate of return of 7.5 percent); if not, they stand to lose their investment. Significantly, the contribution of the investors was not limited to funding: They also played a role in designing the program, and identifying and negotiating with the service delivery partners—just as they would with any form of investment. Currently, Social Finance is negotiating with government departments for employing SIBs to address issues such as improving the outcomes for children in and on the edge of state care, reducing substance addiction, and reducing hospital waiting lists. They may also be used in projects designed to cut school truancy and exclusion, increase youth employment, reduce acute hospital care by improving community support, and improve provision of fostering to cut the cost of residential placements for children in care. Other initiatives could include investments in domiciliary care for the terminally ill and in making the homes of elderly people more livable, resulting in savings on palliative care and long-term hospital stays.

SIBs provide a mechanism for aligning the interests of investors, government, and charity around specific aspects of public benefit provision. In theory they can be used to address the causes rather than the symptoms of pernicious social problems that have proved resilient to other forms of intervention by incentivizing investors with the offer of a financial return based on successful social impact. In practice, although SIBs have a relatively straightforward application to matters such as re-offending and hospital bed–occupancy, they are likely to have less relevance for the type of embedded social problems that require early preventative intervention, such as avoiding admissions to the child care or juvenile justice systems, because in that context measuring prospective outcomes is a good deal more problematic. Indeed, many social problems are immensely complicated and tend to include an array of crosscutting issues that have successfully resisted years of professional intervention; "problem families," for example, is a term that usually embraces a constellation of challenging issues, including mental health, addiction, disability, violence, school aversion, etc. For investors, the risk factor being greater, the incentive to invest is correspondingly reduced. Either way, however, it is very much in the interests of government to defer payments for some years (in a manner not dissimilar to its management of PFI schemes), and then pass to a third party the responsibility and risk of public opprobrium in the event of failure. It remains to be seen, in practice, what proportion of the investment comes from private businesses and what from charitable foundations, how expensive it is to run in terms of administrative costs and professional siphoning, and how sustainable the end results will prove to be. It will also be interesting to see where the courts will eventually draw the line demarcating the responsibilities that government may and may not devolve in this way. Calibrating the risk-and-reward balance will be crucial to the success of a mechanism that owes more to profit than to altruism.

2. B Corporations

In the United States, despite corporate law imposing a fiduciary obligation on trustees to maximize shareholder return, B Corporations have become part of the growing sector of mission-driven businesses with their launch in 2010.[26] This new legal structure permits corporate owners to subordinate profit maximization to social goals: They serve social and environmental purposes while also generating profits and shareholder value, and fiduciaries are protected from lawsuits alleging they did not maximize profits.[27] The idea of B Corporations (an abbreviation for "Benefit Corporations") was conceived by B Lab, a Pennsylvania-based nonprofit organization, which coordinates the B Corporation certification procedure that ensures that each B Corporation has a purpose of creating general public benefit, defined as a material positive impact on society and the environment. B Lab also leads a nationwide lobbying effort to have B Corporation legislation enacted in every state.

The designation "B Corporation" can signify a particular legal structure, but it above all signifies a seal of approval that the company has been certified as having committed to pursuing public benefit as well as profit, functioning autonomously on the basis of income generated by commerce without the need for external funding whether from government or public donations. The certification requires the companies to consider

[26] See further, B Lab, "Become a B Corp," http://www.bcorporation.net/become-a-b-Corp.

[27] B Lab describes itself as a nonprofit organization dedicated to using the power of business to solve social and environmental problems. B Lab drives systemic change through three interrelated initiatives: (1) building a community of Certified B Corporations to make it easier for all of us to tell the difference between "good companies" and just good marketing; (2) accelerating the growth of the impact investing through use of B Lab's Global Impact Investing Rating System (GIIRS); and (3) promoting supportive public policies, including legislation that would create Benefit Corporations in all 50 states. Its mission is to institutionalize social entrepreneurship and create legal space for mission-driven companies. See further B Lab, "B Lab—The Nonprofit Behind B Corps," http://www.bcorporation.net/The-Non-Profit-behind-B-Corps.

all stakeholders, not just shareholders, in their decisions and operations, and to protect the social missions of their businesses in the event of something such as an acquisition. Certified B Corporations must also prepare an annual Benefit Report to B Lab's independent, transparent third-party standards for social and environmental impact, to be made public and filed with appropriate state incorporating agencies. Tax credits may also be available to B Corporations in certain jurisdictions (e.g., Philadelphia, Pennsylvania). In states that have enacted B Corporation legislation, a new business can incorporate as a B Corporation, and existing corporations can amend their governing documents to include the interests of their employees, the community, and the environment. All corporate forms can become B Corporations: partnerships, limited liability corporations, etc.

Maryland became the first state in the United States to enact a B Corporation law in 2010, and soon afterward Vermont, New Jersey, Virginia, Hawaii, California, and New York passed legislation to govern this new kind of corporation. Consequently, more than 400 companies drawn from over 60 industries are now so certified; Most are consumer products companies, but also included are organic restaurants, financial firms, and some law firms. Additionally, Pennsylvania, Colorado, North Carolina, and Michigan all have related legislation pending. In an effort to market the products and services of B Corporations directly to nonprofits, B Corporations for Nonprofits was launched in January, 2011,[28] which highlights certified B Corporations that earn more than 50 percent of their revenue from nonprofit clients and/or that have a client base that consists largely of nonprofit organizations (in itself, an interesting attempt to clarify the designation "nonprofit").

IV. THE FUTURE FUNDING OF CHARITY: BALANCING PROFIT AND LOSS

Charities face serious financial challenges today. This situation is unlikely to improve in the short-term. Most of the jurisdictions studied will probably continue to experience a low rate of economic growth, while some may drift into recession, which will reduce funding streams from government and the general public while increasing the drain on charity resources. If they are to be equipped to deal effectively with mounting social problems at home and abroad, charities must have both sustainable income revenue and spare capacity to invest in organizational development. Given that the status quo of tax-exempt status and the general switch from government grant aid to contract funding is pretty certain to be maintained, where can charities hope to find the necessary new sources of funding?

To some extent this challenge has already been taken up. In recent years, the world of charities has become enmeshed in commerce and compromised by newly emergent hybrid entities with roots in both public and private sectors. The future, therefore, probably lies in charities negotiating collaborative, income-generating

[28] See further at: www.bcorpsfornonprofits.com.

arrangements, with a mix of the same public, private, and nonprofit organizations with which it is now engaged. The terms on which it does so, and the balance then struck between scale of profit-making activity and compromised independence, will be crucial. The "gift relationship" that for so long served to fairly conceptualize the traditional transaction between charity, donor, and beneficiary may well need to be reviewed depending on the source of future funding.

A. Leave It to the Market

As charity copes with the victims of recent market failure, attributable to the reckless risk management of financiers, it is simultaneously being induced to trust the same market and financiers as offering a safe haven for its investments. There are grounds for skepticism.

1. The Corporate Donor

There is a steadily unfolding narrative, most clearly articulated in the U.K. and the United States, but also evident in most if not all of the countries studied, in which the traditionally profit-driven business sector in a capitalist-oriented marketplace is acquiring a broader social awareness and is increasingly prepared to make room for a public benefit contribution to run alongside its profit-generating goals. Self-evidently, there are business owners who do indeed believe that the forces of capitalism can be harnessed to promote positive change in their communities and elsewhere: Many high-value business entrepreneurs have demonstrated that philanthropic capitalism can work, and many businesses and nonprofits have added an explicitly social or environmental dimension to their commercial goals. Where for-profit corporations elect, for bona fide philanthropic reasons, to pursue public benefit purposes, this can be a self-sustaining and effective strategy. The income from the business can fund the public benefit activities as a deductible expense, and tax deductions used to achieve a public benefit purpose can be just as tax efficient as a charitable donation deduction. The problem arises when the for-profit corporation is merely using the charity "brand" as a for-profit marketing device. Close regulatory supervision is all-important.

In this context, the B Lab initiative (mentioned above) in the United States looks promising. It requires B Corporations to build-in transparent accountability measures for the attainment of social and environmental objectives that are required to be clearly stated in their governing documents. As the B Lab "branding" spreads, at least in the United States, it may leverage a culture shift in business that will see significant resources added to the efforts of charity and other public benefit nonprofits.

2. Financial Investment Market

Charities have traditionally had a passive investment policy whereby they settled for a low rate of return on safe investments. More recently, the general trend has seen charity, mainly the large charitable foundations, being drawn further into the more speculative end of the investment market as a means of utilizing equity locked up in their trust assets. This is a strategy that carries obvious high risks. In the current economic climate, where governments in many of the jurisdictions studied are struggling with massive public debt and the business sector is in the doldrums, the very considerable assets entrusted to and protected by charitable foundations over many generations are likely to be viewed with interest by both public and private sectors.

Perhaps the most invidious aspect of charity turning to the market as a funding source lies in the differentiated market valuation that is then likely to be placed on charitable purposes: Solid brands with secured assets and a high profile provide an attractive risk/profit balance for investors and will grow to have a stronger presence in the market; this will happen at the expense of all other charitable purposes, which will be correspondingly diminished. The experience, for example, of Harvard University—a tax-exempt public charity with its $24.7 billion endowment fund and with its investments in hedge funds and private equity funds, which retuned a dividend of 11 percent in the fiscal year ending in June 2010—is far from being representative of other charitable institutions.[29] The prospect of returns such as this is unlikely to deter many other endowed foundations, and nonprofits more generally, from turning to the market and seeking to gain sufficient income from investments to be self-sustaining. However, although those charities that are market leaders in education and health care may do well when they turn to the market for funding, others may not. The consequence of leaving the market to decide funding is that the equation for determining charity viability shifts from social need plus recipient satisfaction to the profit and risk margins of investors.

3. Social Finance

In recent years, a variant of the above investment market has been emerging to provide funding specifically for charities and other nonprofits. A number of countries, most notably the United States and the U.K., have seen a range of social finance initiatives launched to inject market principles and investment funding into the burgeoning social enterprise field in order to generate positive social and financial outcomes.

Social bonds, the key concept in this new financial market, originated in 2006 with the creation of the GAVI Alliance (formerly the Global Alliance for Vaccines and Immunisation), a partnership of public and private sectors that borrows against government promises of future aid to fund vaccination programs.[30] So far it has raised more than $2 billion and the fourth issue of "vaccine bonds" was issued in March 2011. The International Finance Facility for Immunisation was created to devise the public/private financial structures; it brings together developing country

[29] Harvard has been one of the pioneer investors in hedge funds and private equity. See further at: http://richard-wilson.blogspot.com/2010/09/harvard-endowment-hedge-funds.html.

[30] See further at: http://www.gavialliance.org/.

and donor governments, the World Health Organization, UNICEF, the World Bank, the vaccine industry in both industrialized and developing countries, research and technical agencies, NGOs, the Bill & Melinda Gates Foundation, and private philanthropists. This very successful initiative makes vaccines cost effective and scales up their delivery, and has transformed the vaccine market. Its model has since been extended to address other problem areas such as public toilets and fertilizer production. The various national experiments with social finance are largely attempts to replicate and apply the GAVI model to deal with domestic problems such as the high costs associated with prisons. Where the contribution from charity is service delivery, private finance covers the cost and reimbursement plus any profit coming from government, and such a model is one that may well serve as a useful funding source for charity.

Social procurement schemes, which came in varying shapes and sizes, are also becoming more popular. These schemes are arrangements between government and businesses whereby they jointly agree to source a certain percentage of procurement from social enterprises rather than from the market.

4. Microfinance Schemes

Microcredit blends nonprofit purposes with for-profit form, and is generally considered to have originated with the Grameen Bank in Bangladesh, where it successfully enabled extremely impoverished people to engage in self-employment projects. In the lecture given after his receipt of the Nobel Peace Prize for his pioneering work on microfinance and with the Grameen Bank, Professor Muhammed Yunus called for the creation of a new legal form to better account for charitable businesses.[31] Essentially, he called for the provision of small loans at low interest rates to an organized group in order to help create a social business that will be self-sustaining and create surplus for expansion because it is a non-loss enterprise. The finance for such schemes is typically provided by a microcredit organization funded by government, banks, NGOs, or by a combination of bodies that might include a private entrepreneur. Once it is recognized in law, many existing companies then come forward to create social businesses in addition to their corporate foundation activities. For charities and other nonprofits, this is an attractive public benefit scheme as it helps the socially disadvantaged to escape the trap of poverty and relieves pressure on the nonprofit sector. For charities, microfinance schemes may also offer access to consistent funding rather than having to rely on donations.

B. Leave It to Government

Funding for the public benefit activities of charities and other nonprofits has traditionally come largely from this source. It continues to do so, albeit more often in the

[31] See Yunus, "Nobel Peace Prize 2006," at p. 272.

form of contacts for service delivery than in grant aid, and is likely to be maintained if reduced as governments struggle to cope with massive public debt problems. In countries such as Australia, which has not suffered the same degree of economic slowdown and is less burdened by public debt than other jurisdictions, government would seem able to maintain established levels of grant aid. Some governments, however, have been experimenting with new ways of channeling funds to charity.

1. Commissioning for Social Outcomes

In the U.K. and the United States, there has long been a particular interest in designing new financial tools to address misaligned incentives in social policy. For example, local government has not necessarily received any direct financial benefit from reducing the running costs of social institutions such as prisons, day care facilities, hospitals, etc. In fact, where these are funded wholly or partially from central government funds through recurring budgets, a counterincentive has been in play at the local level to protect that budget so as to facilitate future planning, by ensuring that running costs are at least maintained; this phenomenon known as "path dependency" has become a particular problem in public service provision. In order to address this recidivism in a functional manner, direct financial incentives would need to be injected into the system.

The United States, always more market-oriented than other jurisdictions when considering such social policy issues, became many years ago the first to impose a business—profit and loss—model on the running of prisons and other institutions. In one example, the adoption of children from the public care system was transformed at the end of the 20th century by the introduction of a schedule of increased payments per head for every child adopted above a set quota to the authorities at the city or county level. This approach has been recently similarly applied to adoption in the U.K. The realigning of desired social outcomes with direct financial incentives, within a frame of reference that targets areas of high public spend, has since gone from strength to strength in both jurisdictions.

The introduction in the U.K. of Social Impact Bonds, which provide up-front funding for prevention and early intervention services and remove from government the risk that its interventions do not deliver desired outcomes (as detailed in chapter 5), is in many ways simply the latest example of government's commitment to this approach and a variation of PFI. The intervention is undertaken by the charity or other nonprofit with the expertise and funded by investors buying bonds, which are redeemed at a later fixed date from government finances. The more money the organization saves the government, the higher the return the bond will pay investors. This goes beyond the standard public–private partnership model, which aims to provide the same service as the state but at a lower cost. Social Impact Bonds are intended to reward better social outcomes, not merely cut costs. There is every indication that this form of indirect funding for charity is set to become the centerpiece of U.K. government strategy for producing more cost effective public benefit outcomes in targeted areas of social need. In the United States, an equivalent scheme featuring Pay for Success Bonds[32] was introduced in Spring 2011. This type of initiative is likely to spread to most jurisdictions studied.

2. Tax Incentives

As mentioned above, a tiered or multitiered tax exemption framework for charities and other nonprofits, calibrated but adjustable across the sector in accordance with prioritized areas of social disadvantage, may offer one way forward. Domestic social policy is now more often given effect, where possible, through the manipulation of the tax regime rather than through the more politically exposed route of preparing legislation and having to justify the need for change. It may well be that introducing such a policy through the tax system would be a pragmatic option for government.

Given that many governments are moving rapidly towards more targeted and cost-effective social intervention, there would be a logical consistency in adopting this approach to direct a differentiated flow of tax revenues to charities and other nonprofits.[33] Full tax exemption linked to donor incentive schemes would then be restricted to those entities that continue to satisfy all the common law benchmarks of "charity" and the charitable purpose and activities of which are focused on areas of core public benefit provision. This would return "charity" to its initial role of supplementing government by doing that which government would otherwise be obliged to do or have done: both standing clearly and unequivocally on the same public benefit platform, with charities assured of secure funding derived from their preferential tax status and from government service contracts. Such charities would not be proxy government agents as they would retain their hallmark characteristic of independence, which they could and should exercise by assertive advocacy on behalf of the socially disadvantaged. They would also continue to stimulate innovatory government provision by pioneering new forms of services. This would clearly differentiate and financially secure the charity "brand."

The above approach would allow for charities and other nonprofits to be, in effect, mapped across a spectrum of social disadvantage, with tax privileges and charitable status awarded accordingly. A variation on this theme could see charities and other nonprofits receiving preferential tax treatment for intervention in geographical areas, domestic and overseas, of concentrated social disadvantage.

C. Leave It to Charity and the Nonprofit Sector

As economic growth tails off and more citizens in the jurisdictions studied slide toward poverty, charities and other nonprofits are coming to terms with declining fund-raising revenues. Although it is true that a growing cohort of high value donors

[32] See further at: http://economix.blogs.nytimes.com/tag/pay-for-success-bonds/.

[33] See, e.g., Commonwealth of Australia, The Treasury, *Consultation Paper: Better Targeting of Not-for-Profit Tax Concessions*, Canberra, May 2011.

is offsetting this trend to some degree, and natural disasters still elicit a generous public response, it remains the case that fund-raising is declining somewhat just at the time when more funds are needed. However, in some of the jurisdictions studied the nonprofit sector has become a mature, cohesive, and politically adept entity. In many, for all its "nonprofit" status, the statistics also reveal the extent to which the sector has grown to become a significant wealth-generating part of the national economy. It is not impossible that securing future funding arrangements for charity may now be a matter that the sector and charity itself could resolve.

1. Charity, Social Finance, and Public Service Provision

There seems to be no insuperable obstacle to charity itself directly accessing the new sources of social finance, although where equity release is a key factor, this may have to be underpinned by a sizeable charity foundation that could provide insurance against possible payment default. Microlending schemes, SIBs, and utilization of the bond market, together with emerging statutory legal structures, offer new opportunities for charities to generate funds. Charities, for example, may not need to rely on the extra partners and complicated finance arrangements of SIB schemes in order to fit within government's "commissioning for social outcomes" program. As a contractor, the charity with relevant expertise could raise its own capital through the social finance sources now more available within the sector, and rely on government bonds for eventual repayment with profit. Alternatively, the contracting charity could seek a straightforward no-interest loan from the city council or local government authority in order to undertake a social intervention project. For example, a London-based charity could borrow £X million from the City for an intensive program of work with a cohort of potential young offenders, over a fixed period of time, with payment to be made at the end of that period according to the numbers without a criminal conviction who had achieved educational qualifications relative to an agreed-upon baseline. The repayments would represent a proportion of the lifetime savings to national government (primarily through tax and benefits). In all such schemes, essentially finance is raised from investors who bear some of the risk for any nonachievement of social outcomes, the charity delivers or manages the delivery of agreed intervention services, and payment is based on results against agreed benchmarks.

Similar ideas are getting attention around the world. Such models are apparently relatively easy to design and implement, and involve relatively few players and transaction costs, though they require clear protocols on design, and the establishment of baselines and success measures. They also require an awareness of the realities of risk transfer and of where accountability lies. However, in short, the new social finance initiatives offer opportunities for charity to step into the market, negotiate on its own terms for the necessary funding to retain independence, provide for organizational growth, and pursue its charitable purposes through public service provision as an independent contractor.

2. Charity, New Legal Structures, and Supplementary Commercial Ventures

The "user pays" ethos is likely to become more prominent in the years ahead. Utilizing this approach, it is probable that many charity or nonprofit hospitals, other health and social care facilities and educational establishments etc., will increasingly seek to at least cover running costs by requiring payment for services. The arrival of new and designed-for-the-purpose legal vehicles, such as the CIC and the L3C, reinforces the capacity of charity to retain and grow its presence in the market, and strengthens the probability of a further expansion in business activity unrelated to charitable purpose. It remains to be seen, however, where the judiciary or legislators ultimately fix the boundaries that will enable charities and other nonprofits to compete with for-profits in the market on terms that do not unduly disadvantage any of the parties involved, not least the taxpayer.

D. Charities and the Nonprofit Sector: Integrity of Status

As the boundary between charity and commerce becomes increasingly blurred, questions inevitably arise as to the rationale for continuing to treat both as separate and distinct.[34] Such a question cannot be raised without also considering the corollary as to why the status of "nonprofit" and "nonprofit sector" should retain their distinctiveness and be treated differently, for purposes of law and tax, from their for-profit counterparts. Once the profit motive gains traction in the activities of charities and nonprofits, then the justification for requiring the taxpayer to subsidize their capacity to compete with for-profits and pocket the proceeds is not obvious. Nor can public or political respect for the value base of the nonprofit sector hope to survive.

1. For-Profit Charities

An argument can, perhaps, be made that in some circumstances, commercial and charitable purpose activities are in practice indivisible, and it would be best to treat them similarly for law and for tax reasons accordingly. So, in some jurisdictions, although a registered charity remains subject to charity law, a proportionate accounting process is then applied to calculate the approximate extent of its commercial activity and the amount of associated income that is not tax-exempt. Where the balance between charitable and profitable activity remains firmly in favor of the former, this relatively straightforward approach can be commended.

[34] Sugin, L., "The Increasing Resemblance of Nonprofit and Business Organizations Law: Resisting the Corporatization of Nonprofit Governance: Transforming Obedience into Fidelity," in *Fordham Law Review*, Vol. 76, 2007, at pp. 893–927.

However, the case has also been made for going a step further and recognizing "for-profit charities."[35] Although there is no denying that some charities are gradually becoming more profit-conscious and acquisitive, and some charitable institutions such as Harvard seem to have already fully embraced the for-profit ethos, it cannot be legitimate, in accepted charity law terms, for an entity with charitable status to give as much attention to making profit as to furthering its charitable purpose. Where such institutions (mainly in education and health care) have acquired substantial assets and deliver user pays services largely to high end clientele then, unless an "activities test" discloses other ways in which the "public" are receiving a proportionate amount of related "benefit" (e.g., reduced or no-fees service access for the poor), the argument for gifting them with tax-exempt privileges is difficult to sustain. If the point is ever reached where profit has become a primary purpose, the institution is then in breach of the exclusivity rule, and for that reason it should not gain or retain charitable status. The concept of "for-profit charities" is therefore suspect.

2. Public Benefit Regardless of Organizational Status

A more radical argument is sometimes advanced that advocates dispensing altogether with organizational status as a determinant of tax liability because it is becoming increasingly difficult to be certain of the parameters of "public benefit," and difficult also to be confident of the circumstances in which public benefit and private interest are actually in conflict. Given that public benefit activity may be carried out by for-profits, charities, other nonprofits, and government bodies, all of which may also be engaged in some degree of for-profit activity, it might be simpler to remove the existing relatively exclusive association between legal structure and tax exemption and instead substitute a rule that enables any organization to claim tax exemption to the extent that its activities deliver public benefit outcomes.[36] So, charities would free to engage in commercial activity and for-profits in charitable activity, and both would be equally eligible for tax exemption and donation deductibility, but only in proportion to activity constituting public benefit as currently defined in law.[37] This approach would apply to all organizations including social enterprises, L3Cs, and emerging hybrids. A paramount legislative weighting could then be given to the "public benefit," preferably as encoded in a designated list of charitable or public benefit purposes, accompanied by a tight regulatory framework

[35] See Malani and Posner, "The Case for For-Profit Charities"; see also Rose, H., "Comment, The Social Business: The Viability of a New Business Entity Type," *Willamette Law Review*, Vol. 44, 2007, at p. 131.

[36] An approach not unlike that adopted in the EU; see, e.g., European Court of Justice: Case C-180/98 to C-184/98—Pavel Pavlov and Others v. Stichting Pensioenfonds Medische Specialisten, para. 108. See also European Court of Justice, Case C-41/90, Klaus Hofner at para. 21.

[37] See Hines, J. R., Horwitz, J. R., and Nichols, A., "The Attack on Nonprofit Status: A Charitable Assessment," in *Michigan Law Review*, Vol. 108, No. 7, 2010, at pp. 1179–220.

that will apply a fixed set of indices to identify and weigh the public benefit component in any set of circumstances and regardless of the status of the entity.

The rationale for such an approach rests on the view that existing charities and nonprofits can often be less efficient and effective than their for-profit counterparts,[38] so the latter should be given tax incentives to encourage their involvement in public benefit activity; also, charities and nonprofits are currently constrained by the rules governing their organizational status from acquiring the capital they need for organizational growth, so they should be freed up from that status and its constraints. Such a radical step would extinguish the charity "brand."

3. Nonprofits: Status and Sector

The case for valuing and preserving charities, other nonprofits, and the integrity of the nonprofit sector has been cogently made by academics. Sugin, for example has argued that "the crucial difference between for-profit social entrepreneurship and nonprofit philanthropy is that only those in control of charitable organizations have the privilege and responsibility of subordinating all interests to the charitable mission of the organization...with the rise of for-profit philanthropy, increasing the resemblance of nonprofit governance to for-profit governance is a mistake because it fosters a type of accountability that is more suited to serving the private goal of profit than the public goal of mission."[39] Arguably, however, it has also been convincingly made by the consequences of poor regulatory control exercised in the public and for-profit sectors in recent years. There is a sense in which charities, other nonprofits, and the nonprofit sector more generally are now viewed as the preferred custodians of public benefit. The case for preserving the separateness and integrity of the sector and its entities has become more compelling than ever: Current social circumstances can only benefit from the affirmation of legally designated charitable purposes; allowing the market or government to absorb "charity" may further accentuate the "public" at the price of the private, and there may well be a hidden cost attached to not setting aside opportunities for altruistic activity to be undertaken by individuals and communities.

V. CONCLUSION

There is every sign that commerce, as a mode of generating supplementary funding, will continue to be employed and be further developed as a resource for charity well into the foreseeable future. This can only be accelerated by the rapid spread and

[38] See, e.g., Young, D. R., "Alternative Perspectives on Social Enterprise," in Cordes, J. J. and Steuerle, C. E (eds,), *Nonprofits & Business*, Urban Institute Press, Washington, D.C., 2008; Billitteri, "Mixing Mission and Business."

[39] See Sugin, "The Increasing Resemblance of Nonprofit and Business Organizations Law." See also Atkinson, R., "Altruism in Nonprofit Organisations," in *BCL Review*, Vol. 31, at pp. 501, 605 (1990) at: http://lawdigitalcommons.bc.edu/bclr/vol31/iss3/1.

diversity of new legal structures designed to merge the interests of charity and commerce and by the emergence of social finance initiatives. The challenge presented by social enterprises, those businesses with primarily social objectives that invest any surpluses to address their objectives, is also likely to add pressure on charities to seek from commerce the funding they need to compete effectively. However, the more charity and other nonprofits become involved in commerce, the stronger the protests will be from the business sector, particularly small businesses. Also, this would strengthen the case for questioning whether they should be subsidized by tax exemptions and would question also the standing of the nonprofit sector.

The recent history of market collapse sounds a cautionary note. There are risks, and a price to be paid in terms of compromised independence, that could prove prohibitive for charity. It may not be in the interests of charity or the sector for the sectoral boundaries to become more fudged. A way forward may lie in giving formal recognition to the existing main divisions in charitable activity and, by utilizing the tiered approach to tax exemption, differentiate between charities and other nonprofits as well as among charities themselves so as to identify, secure, and protect the core public benefit charities and ensure they receive adequate government funding. Arguably, the point has now been reached where statutory intervention is required to recognize and protect the values that set the nonprofit sector apart from the public and business sectors.

CONCLUSION

Tanzi, in his most recent book,[1] provides a wealth of statistical information to illustrate the extent to which government in the "advanced" nations, having greatly expanded its intervention in the economic life of the state, was beginning to wind back on the eve of the 2008 financial crisis. He refers to "the phenomenal increase in public spending that took place in industrial countries from the first to the second half of the 20th Century, the government became a huge insurance company and intermediary for the citizens."[2] By the late 20th century, he notes that public spending in several European countries approached, or in some cases exceeded, 59 percent of GDP,[3] and in several European countries tax levels had their fastest rate of increase in public spending in the period 1960 to the mid-1990s: "practically all the countries reached the highest level of taxation some time before 2008 . . . during the first decade of the 21st century, and until the crisis, many tried to reduce the tax burden."[4] The experiments in large-scale collectivism, which for the past century and a half had seen a transfer of responsibility from private to public for a vast range of public benefit services—including health, water supply, sewage disposal, housing, schools, burials, transport, and public safety—had run its course and was in the process of being reversed. Following the crisis, and faced with the resulting weight of barely manageable public debt, government is now being forced to cut the coat of its public services in accordance with the cloth of public debt, as tax revenues are swallowed up by the demands of debt management.

Galvanized by debt repayment concerns, coupled with the additional stress of having to cope with the increased expenditure on welfare benefits resulting from surging unemployment, and the persistent drain of paying in various ways for wars in Muslim countries, containing Eurozone economic instability, and managing widespread creeping inflation, government now readily accepts that it has no future as "a huge insurance company and intermediary for the citizens." As in the U.K. during the 1980s and 90s, government must disengage from the burden of being the direct provider of general public benefit services. Specifically, as much as possible of health, social care, education, and general utility provision has to be transferred from the public sector to the nonprofit and business sectors; the degree of transfer varies according to jurisdictional

[1] Tanzi, V., *Government versus Markets: The Changing Economic Role of the State*, Cambridge, Cambridge University Press, 2011.

[2] Tanzi, *Government versus Markets*, at p. 13.

[3] Tanzi, *Government versus Markets*, at p. 61.

[4] Tanzi, *Government versus Markets*, at p. 105.

differences in culture and politics. Management rather than ownership of public benefit provision, other than that considered vital to the national interest, is the preferred way forward for modern common law government.

Charity, other nonprofits, and the sector as a whole have no alternative but to step up to the plate. Being mission-driven, their value base demands that charities respond to the opening opportunities for a greater contribution to public benefit provision. To do so, when hindered by a decrease in government grants and public donations, they have had to turn to the market for the additional funding needed to maintain accustomed levels of functioning and fuel a capacity to undertake additional responsibilities. As they are, of necessity, lured deeper into the market, retaining a balance between the pursuit of purposes of charity and of profit becomes correspondingly more fraught. This is the dilemma to which Titmuss[5] first alluded some 40 years ago.

If, as Titmuss then said, "the social relations set up by gift-exchange are among the most powerful forces which bind a social group together,"[6] in that case the time is now undoubtedly right for charity, other nonprofits, and the sector as a whole to demonstrate how this might be achieved. It would be hard to overstate the harm caused to public confidence in government and business by the consequences of poor leadership in those sectors in recent years. Public trust in government has clearly been damaged by government's failure to safeguard standards in basic areas of public benefit such as safety from international terrorism. It has also been affected by issues of economic stability and the value of currencies, as well as by its failure to provide protection from prolonged institutionalized abuse by religious bodies; by withdrawal from traditional health, social care, and education responsibilities; by the selling off of public utilities; and by the cavalier use of high tech weaponry in some of the poorest countries on earth. It has similarly been damaged in relation to the for-profit sector by the failings of prominent banks, financial institutions, and some leading companies amid depressing evidence of a reckless disregard for public benefit and avaricious behavior by those entrusted with the funds of others. The murky closed cultures that emerged from government and business, spawning suspect concepts such as "drones," "extraordinary rendition," and "derivatives," brought both into considerable disrepute.

More recently, public disenchantment has been exacerbated by government austerity measures imposed to manage the financial crisis and reduce the burden of national public debt. These have involved: making drastic cuts in public service programs, diverting revenues from health and social welfare to the banking and financial institutions, and spreading the tax net to increase gross contributions while easing the liability of high earners to stimulate economic growth. Government recourse to national measures such as arbitrarily selling off choice parts of the social infrastructure to the highest bidder, and to international measures such as erecting

[5] Titmuss, R. A., *The Gift Relationship: From Human Blood to Social Policy*, Allen & Unwin, London, 1970.

[6] Titmuss, *The Gift Relationship*, at p. 73.

firewalls to halt the spreading contagion of financial instability, have not helped to build any sense of social partnership. Indeed, protracted government avoidance of measures that might curb the persistent bonus culture of bank executives, the mercenary operations of hedge funds, or the gambling on the bond markets, or require some public recompense from those whose dealings brought them disproportionate rewards and triggered global recession, may well have a lasting deleterious effect on its aspirations to promote civil society. Any such aspirations can only be further damaged by the measures currently being taken to rescue the euro: as governments indulge in the "blame game", some maneuver to protect national interests, and others are forced to cede sovereignty to the financial dictates of the IMF and central banks. The altruistic spirit that inspired EU growth is unlikely to survive an enforced contraction. For some European countries in particular (viz. Greece, Spain, Italy, Portugal, and Ireland) the consequences of such government action and inaction have included a sharp rise in levels of unemployment and poverty and a widening of the social gap between rich and poor but no relief from domestic recession. The prospect of a deepening crisis in the international currency and financial markets, prompting further government retrenchment accompanied by a more general erosion of living standards, threatens to turn the prevailing public mistrust in government and the financial sectors into widespread social unrest.

In the wake of a not-inconsequential collapse of public trust in traditional institutions, there is now a need for socially unifying initiatives. Perhaps, also, there is a greater public readiness to place trust in charity, other nonprofits, and the sector more generally as fit custodians of the public benefit on a growing range of matters central to the well-being of contemporary society. This would not be a bad time for the introduction of an improved regulatory framework that would instill public confidence that the failings allowed to tarnish other sectors will not transfer to charities, would be able to prevent or detect systemic abuse and misuse of funds, and could provide some coherence for the sector as a whole.

The Titmuss concept of "the gift relationship," offering "the moral choice of giving to strangers"[7] and underpinning the social role of charity, stands as a polar opposite to the approach recently pursued in the public and private sectors. It positively advances the public benefit agenda and, by pointing toward a more caring society, may counterbalance the dangerous levels of disenchantment and alienation now very evident in some of the jurisdictions studied. Rather than allowing charity to be absorbed by government or market, it suggests preventing further drift in either direction and rescuing charity from the additional danger of being lost to the fund-raising and tax benefits industry. Instead, charity might be legislatively established in a sector leadership role with state-funded responsibility (protected from manipulation by the government-of-the-day) for promoting public benefit exclusively and independently through the pursuit of designated charitable purposes. This might allow the harnessing of selflessness,

[7] Titmuss, R. A., *The Gift Relationship*, at p. 12.

goodwill, and resources to achieve public benefit outcomes while providing opportunities for demonstrating the virtue and effectiveness of altruism, adding value to a shared sense of civic responsibility, and strengthening society as well as assisting intended beneficiaries. The consequent reshaping of relationships between governments, business, charity, and citizens might do much to repair public trust and consolidate the civil society ethos.

Not to take the Titmuss approach would seem to suggest settling for a spectator role while the increasing involvement of charity, other nonprofits, and the sector with commerce would steadily detract from the gift-exchange transaction that he saw as a sine qua non for building trust relationships. Whether this takes the form of reliance upon government contracts for public service delivery or dependency upon commercial trading, it can lead to profit margins becoming a primary concern. In the former case, there are risks for those charities that become immersed as government contractors in public service delivery: The boundaries between government and charity, entitlement to tax exemption and donor gift, and between legal rights and handouts, becomes uncertain; the traditional bond of mutual understanding between charity and the socially disadvantaged becomes weakened as treating the effects of their plight displaces the capacity to address its causes, while the traditional inputs of support and advocacy become less available. For those that turn to trading the value problems can be more acute: The concepts of "charity" and "competition" do not sit comfortably together, and reconciling the values traditionally associated with charity—compassion, generosity, selflessness, respect for the indigent, etc.—with those seemingly necessary to succeed in the modern marketplace is not easily done. In either context, as competitiveness increases, there is less room for altruism.

Moreover, in legal terms charity stands aside from other nonprofits and the sector. This has long been evident in the tax regime, which was statutorily structured so as to incentivize donors to give to charity while limiting the latter's capacity to use its tax-exempt status to unfair advantage in competing with for-profits. Charity's most distinctive characteristics, however, derive from its U.K. roots in the law of trusts, which, for many centuries, provided the means for giving effect to charitable gifts. For more than 900 years in that jurisdiction, until the introduction in 1862 of companies limited by guarantee and the resulting incorporation of some trusts,[8] it was the trust rather than the charitable corporation that prevailed as the preferred legal form for charities.

For present purposes, three consequences of note are attributable to this trust legacy: an abiding state apprehension that charity may again cultivate measures to extend the inalienability of property; an entrenchment of the obligation to conserve and distribute the benefits of a trust, fairly, among present and future beneficiaries; and the gradual evolution of a set of equitable principles applied in the Chancery Division

[8] See the Companies Act 1862.

of the High Court to resolve disputes.[9] The first has ensured that charity remains as inhibited in the 21st century as previously by the rules directing it exclusively toward defined charitable purposes to be pursued for the public benefit. The asset lock and equity access constraints, the limits imposed upon perpetuity privileges, together with a general absence of "ownership" attributes, have held charity back, preventing it from evolving and engaging equally with other entities as modern markets have developed. The second, which requires an intergenerational approach to the management of trust assets, prohibits any undue risk taking that may reward contemporary recipients at the expense of jeopardizing the rightful and intended entitlement of future beneficiaries. It is an approach that should restrain charity from engaging in short-term investment and trading activity for immediate profit yields, or in collaborative public/private finance initiatives that defer costs for future payment, and would instead suggest that charity focus on such long-term non-remunerative or low-profit activity as environmental protection and sustainable development ventures. The third has for centuries prescribed a principled regime to guide the actions of trustees and the governance of charities. This has been particularly evident in the strict obligation to protect assets, and to maintain the independence of a charity and its trustees while also eschewing opportunities for private profit.

For these and other reasons, charity, to a greater extent than other nonprofits and the sector in general, has always been legally restricted in its capacity to utilize the market. Arguably, this is a unique strength to be valued as offering an intergenerational approach to the management of resources based on principles of equity

[9] The Chancery Division, which can trace its roots back 1000 years to Norman times, did not begin to develop its modern jurisdiction over trusts and land until the 15th century. One of three divisions of the High Court since 1875, the Chancery Division still retains its 400-year-old jurisdiction as a Court of Equity. The following maxims of equity stand as powerful reminders of the principled basis on which Chancery resolved disputes, and continue to inspire lawyers and influence contemporary judicial decision making:

Equity follows the law.
Equity will not suffer a wrong to be without a remedy.
Equity acts in personam.
He who seeks equity must do equity.
He who comes into equity must come with clean hands.
Delay defeats equity.
Equality is equity.
Equity looks to the intent rather than the form.
Equity looks on that as done which ought to have been done.
Equity imputes an intention to fulfill an obligation.
Where the equities are equal, the first in time prevails.
Where the equities are equal, the law prevails.

These maxims reflect the traditional common law judicial approach to charity, they differentiate charitable trusts from other organizational forms and distinguish the regulatory regime of charity law from company law, and, arguably, they may provide charities with a distinctive equitable basis for exercising leadership of the nonprofit sector that would clearly affirm its independence and its differences from other sectors.

and fairness, which contrasts with the present short-term focus of management in the public and private sectors. To now abandon charity to find such security of funding as it can in the marketplace may well entail allowing it to become part of the problem: associated with the recent institutional failings, vulnerable to future market failures, accepting a corresponding diminution in its capacity to attract public trust and demonstrate positive civic values, all accompanied by a downgrading of altruism.

Titmuss and the market offer diametrically opposed approaches. Although both have advantages, neither would seem sufficient in itself to cope with the complexities of contemporary dense intersectoral linkages: The gift relationship and its contractual counterpart are transactional models that are steadily becoming less representative as modes of public benefit service provision become more complex; similarly, the apparent dichotomy between shareholder and stakeholder can be seen as redundant in circumstances where, for example, environmental concerns ensure that the shareholder is also a stakeholder. When tax revenues can be used to bail out banks, to revive for-profit companies, and generally to shore up market institutions that are too big to fail, as well as to assist charities, then the concept of "public benefit" has developed considerable elasticity. Nor does it make much sense to continue construing charity as merely the foil of capitalism, a proposition dependent upon their continued separation. The clear differentiation between "public" and "private" interests that allowed Titmuss to develop his thesis and the market to be anchored on an ethos of competition for private profit seems increasingly dated.

An unmistakable air of excitement, however, is currently energizing the nonprofit sector across the common law world. Arguably, it emanates from precisely this sense of being caught up in a process of quite radical change in the accepted public/private balance: of growth opportunities that may be in the offing as sectors realign; or, perhaps, as a new "public benefit provider" paradigm emerges to carve its own course without regard for either sector boundaries or the legal status of the entities concerned. There is mounting evidence that such a new approach, deliberately blending public/private and charity/commerce, is becoming a driving force for innovative interventions and is building in momentum. This is particularly evident in the rapid spread of corporate social responsibility that is gaining real traction in some jurisdictions. The initiative of successful entrepreneurs such as Gates and Buffett in diverting their profits into schemes such as developing a cure for malaria may well have triggered the wave of "high-value donors" that are now becoming entry-level contributors to philanthropy. Similarly, corporate philanthropy—whereby for-profit entities commit resources to pursuing public benefit purposes alongside profit acquisition—is becoming de rigueur for companies with any level of social profile that wish to retain the loyalty of contemporary politically aware customers: Competing in their appeals to the conscience of consumers is bringing additional resources and methods of intervention into charitable activity and is the new added value for customers. In addition, charities, government, and business are now combining resources to address long-standing pernicious social problems such as those of criminal recidivism through the use of newly forged tools such as Social

Impact Bonds. As social enterprises proliferate and a range of new legal structures allow charities and other nonprofits to develop evermore complex partnerships with government and business, while the latter find new ways to integrate sustainable versions of corporate social responsibility into their for-profit enterprises, it is clear that the economies of the modern states are fast moving away from accepted sectoral divisions. This is important because—if for no other reason—the legal framework for charity and the entire taxation regime have long rested upon those divisions and the distinction between public and private interests they embody. A more nuanced approach is now necessary, but a schematic for this is at present far from obvious.

In the meantime, the rules and tests being applied by the judiciary in the many cases discussed in this book are beginning to sketch out parameters for eventual legislative intervention. Although it is reasonably certain that charity—having weathered passing trends, fads and market innovations over many generations—will continue to do so in the future, it is also clear that it will need to adapt to yet more changes in its operating environment. The various charity law reform processes can be seen as initial steps that have taken us some way down what could indeed be a long and winding road.[10]

[10] See Morris, D., "Public Benefit: The Long and Winding Road to Reforming the Public Benefit Test for Charity: A Worthwhile Trip or 'Is Your Journey Really necessary?,'" in McGregor-Lowndes, M. and O'Halloran, K. (eds.), *Modernising Charity Law*, Elgar, Cheltenham, 2010.

BIBLIOGRAPHY

Aimers, J. and Walker, P., "Alternative Models of Accountability for Third Sector Organisations in New Zealand," paper presented at the International Society for Third Sector Research, Barcelona, 2008.

Alesina, A., Glaeser, E. and Sacerdote, B., "Why Doesn't the United States Have a European-Style Welfare State?," in *Brookings Papers on Economic Activity*, Vol. 2, 2001, at pp. 187–254.

Alexander, J., Nank, R., and Stivers, C., "Implications of Welfare Reform: Do Nonprofit Survival Strategies Threaten Civil Society?," in *Nonprofit and Voluntary Sector Quarterly*, Vol. 28, No. 2, 1999, at pp. 452–75.

Anheier, H. K., "The Global Economic Downturn, Philanthropy and Nonprofits: Reflections on What It Means, and What to Do." Paper presented at Philanthropy and Nonprofits conference, University of Heidelberg, January 2009.

Anheier, H. and Daly, S., *The Politics of Foundations: A Comparative Analysis*, Routledge, London and New York, 2007.

Anheier, H. and Leat, D., *From Charity to Creativity: Philanthropic Foundations in the 21st Century*, Comedia, Stroud, U.K., 2002.

Anheier, H. and Leat, D., *Creative Philanthropy: Toward a New Philanthropy for the 21st Century*, Routledge, 2005.

Anheier, H. and Seibel, W., *Defining the Nonprofit Sector: Germany*, The Johns Hopkins Comparative Nonprofit Sector Project, 1993.

Anheier, H. and Toepler, S. (eds.), *International Encyclopedia of Civil Society*, Vol. 3, "Umbrella Organizations," Springer, New York, 2010.

Arnsberger, P., "Charities, Social Welfare, and Other Tax-Exempt Organizations, 2004," in *Statistics of Income Bulletin*, September 22, 2007, at pp. 231–45, 2007.

Atkinson, R., "Altruism in Nonprofit Organisations," in *BCL Review*, Vol. 31, No. 3, 1990, at pp. 501–639, 501, 605.

Austin, R. P., "The Impact of the Human Rights Act on Administrative Law," in *Current Legal Problems*, 1999, at pp. 200–10.

Backman, E. and Smith, S. R., "Healthy Organizations, Unhealthy Communities?," in *Nonprofit Management and Leadership*, Vol. 10, No. 4, 2000, at pp. 355–73.

Barker, S. and Yesberg, K, "Charities Act Review," *NZLawyer Online*, Chen Palmer, Wellington, April 8, 2011.

Barraket, J. (ed.), *Strategic Issues for the Not-For-Profit Sector*, UNSW Press, Sydney, 2008.

Barraket, J., *Finding Australia's Social Enterprise Sector*, Australian Centre for Philanthropy and Nonprofit Studies (ACPNS), Brisbane, June 2010.

Bartholomew, J., *The Welfare State We're In*, Methuen, London, 2006.

Baxter, K., "Community-Government Relationships: Issues in Establishing Formal Linkages between Central Government and the Community Sector', paper for presentation at the *Strengthening Communities through Local Partnerships Symposium,* University of Auckland, April 12, 2002.

Benn, M., *School Wars: The Battle for Britain's Education,* Verso Books, London, 2011.

Ben-Ner, Avener, "Outsourcing by Nonprofit Organisations," in Young, D. (ed.), *Effective Economic Decision-Making by Nonprofit Organisations,* The Foundation Center, New York, 2004, at pp. 67–83.

Beveridge, W.H., *Voluntary Action: A Report on Methods of Social Advance,* Allen and Unwin, London, 1948.

Billitteri, T., "Mixing Mission and Business: Does Social Enterprise Need a New Legal Approach?" in *Highlights from an Aspen Institute Roundtable,* January 2007.

Blair, T., *The Third Way: New Politics for the New Century,* Fabian Society, London, 1998.

Bloche, M. G., "PERSPECTIVE: Tax Preferences for Nonprofits: From Per Se Exemption to Pay-for-Performance," in *Health Affairs,* Vol. 25, 2006, at w304.

Blumberg, M., "Canadian Charity Law," CRA letter in response to query (August 18, 2009) at http://www.canadiancharitylaw.ca/index.php/blog/comments/canadian_charities_and_holding_shares_of_subsidiary.

Bode, I., "Creeping Marketization and Post-Corporatist Governance: The Transformation of State-Nonprofit Relations in Continental Europe', in Phillips, S. D. and Rathgeb Smith, S. (eds.), *Governance and Regulation in the Third Sector,* Routledge, London, 2011, at pp. 115–41.

Bothwell, J., "Indicators of a Healthy Civil Society," in Burbridge, J. (ed.), *Beyond Prince and Merchant: Citizen Participation and the Rise of Civil Society,* Institute of Cultural Affairs International, Brussels, 1997, at pp. 249–51.

Bourgeois, D. J., *The Law of Charitable and Not-for-Profit Organizations* (3rd ed), Butterworths, Toronto, 2002.

Bourgeois, D. J., "Business Activities—Raising Revenue through Business Activities without Violating Legal Principles," in *Charity Law Bulletin,* No. 196, February 25, 2010.

Bradford, N., "Place-Based Public Policy: Towards a New Urban and Community Agenda for Canada," Research Report F/51, Family Network, *CPRN,* March 2005.

Bradford, S. and Nowland-Foreman, G., *Mahi Tahi Working Together: Civil Society in Aotearoa/New Zealand,* Association of Non-Governmental Organizations of Aotearoa, Wellington, 1999.

Brady, J., "The Law of Charity and Judicial Responsiveness to Changing Need," in *Northern Ireland Legal Quarterly,* Vol. 27, No. 3, at pp. 198–216, 1976.

Brady, J. J., *Religion and the Law of Charities in Ireland,* W&S Magowan, Belfast, 1975.

Brakman, R. D., "For Profit Philanthropy," in *Fordham Law Review,* Vol. 77, 2009, at pp. 2437, 2472.

Breen, O., "Holding the Line," in McGregor-Lowndes, M. and O'Halloran, K. (eds.), *Modernising Charity Law,* Elgar, Cheltenham, 2010, at pp. 136–63.

Breiteneicher, C. K. and Marble, M. G., "Strategic Programme Management," in A. Schluter, V. Then, and P. Walkenhorst, (eds.), *Foundations in Europe, Society, Management and Law,* Directory of Social Change, The Brookings Institution, London.

Brindle, D., "The Worst Is Yet to Come," *The Guardian,* February 18, 2009.

Brody, E., "All Charities Are Property-Tax Exempt, but Some Charities Are More Exempt than Others," in *New England Law Review,* Vol. 44, at pp. 621–732, 2010.

Brody, E. (ed.), *Property-Tax Exemption for Charities: Mapping the Battlefield,* The Urban Institute Press, Washington, DC, 2002.

Brody, E., "Business Activities of Nonprofit Organisations: Legal Boundary Problems," in Cordes, J. J. and Steuerle, C. E. (eds.), *Nonprofits and Business,* Urban Institute Press, Washington, DC, 2009, at pp. 83–127.

Brody, E., "The Ambitions and Limitations of U.S. Nonprofit Law Reform Projects," in *NVSQ,* September 2011.

Brody, E. and Cordes, J., *The Unrelated Business Income Tax: All Bark and No Bite?* The Urban Institute, Washington, DC, 2001.

Bromley, B., "The 1601 Preamble: The State's Agenda for Charity," in *Charity Law & Practice Review,* Vol. 7, Issue 3, 2002, at pp. 140–59.

Brooks, N., "The Tax Credit for Charitable Contributions: Giving Credit Where None Is Due," in Phillips, J., Chapman, B., and Stevens, D. (eds.), *Between State and Market: Essays on Charities Law and Policy in Canada,* McGill-Queen's University Press, Montreal, 2002, at pp. 457–81.

Brown, E. and Silvinski, A., "Nonprofit Organisations and the Market," in Powell, W. W. and Steinberg, R. (eds.), *The Nonprofit Sector: A Research Handbook (2nd ed.),* Yale University Press, New Haven, CT, 2006, at pp. 3–23, 2006, at: http://www.thephilanthropist.ca/index.php/phil/article/download/510/515.

Brown, M., *Giving USA 2005,* the Annual Report on Philanthropy for the Year 2004 (50th ed.), Giving USA Foundation, AAFRC Trust for Philanthropy, New York, 2005.

Burrows, M. D., "Charitable Tax Incentives in Canada: Overview and Opportunities for Expansion," in *The Philanthropist,* Vol. 22, 2009, at pp. 510–15.

Carpenter, M., *Reformatory Schools for the Perishing and Dangerous Classes and for the Prevention of Juvenile Delinquency,* C Gilpin, London, 1851.

Carreyrou, J., "Nonprofit Hospitals, Once for the Poor, Strike It Rich," *Wall Street Journal,* April 4, 2008.

Carter, E., "Nonprofit Law Jargon Buster: The Commensurate Test," in *Charity Lawyer,* August 16, 2010, http://charitylawyerblog.com/2010/08/16/nonprofit-law-jargon-buster-the-commensurate-test/#ixzz18lqfWpkb.

Castles, F. G., *The Wage Earners' Welfare State Revisited,* Australian National University, Graduate Program in Public Policy, Sydney, 1994.

Charlesworth, L., "England's Early "Big Society": Parish Welfare under the Old Poor Law," in *History & Policy,* December 2010.

Chesterman, M., "Foundations of Charity Law in the New Welfare State," in Mitchell, C. and Moody, S. (eds.), *Foundations of Charity,* Hart Publishing, Oxford, Portland Oregon, 2000, at pp. 249–69.

Clarke, J. and Newman, J., *Publics, Politics and Power: Remaking the Public in Public Services,* Sage, London 2009.

Clery, C., *The Billionaire Who Wasn't: How Chuck Feeney Made and Gave Away a Fortune without Anyone Knowing,* Public Affairs, New York, 2007.

Clotfelter, C., "Tax-Induced Distortions in the Voluntary Sector," in *Case Western Law Review,* Vol. 39, 1988/1989, at pp. 663–94.

Cohen, L. and Arato, A., *Civil Society and Political Theory,* MIT Press, Cambridge, MA, 1992.

Colombo, J. and Hall, M., *The Charitable Tax Exemption,* Westview Press, Boulder, CO, (1995).

Colombo, J. D., "Commercial Activity and Charitable Tax Exemption," in *William and Mary Law Review*, Vol. 4, 2002, at pp. 487–567.

Colombo, J. D., "Private Benefit, Joint Ventures and the Death of Health Care as an Exempt Purpose," in *Journal of Health Law*, Vol. 34, 2001, at pp. 505, 521.

Colombo, J., "The Role of Tax Exemption in a Competitive Health Care Market," in *Journal of Health, Politics, Policy & Law*, Vol. 31, 2006, at pp. 621–625.

Cook, L., *"Good Intentions": An Assessment of the Statement of Government Intentions for an Improved Community-Government Relationship*, Association of Non-Governmental Organizations of Aotearoa (ANGOA), January 2009, available at: http://www.angoa.org.nz/angoa_docs/SOGI-Full-Review.pdf.

Commission on the Future of the Voluntary Sector in England, *Meeting the Challenge of Change: Voluntary Action into the 21st Century*, NCVO Publications, London, 1996.

Corbet, C., "Stewardship of Public Assets under Nonprofit Conversion Models: New York's Empire Blue Cross Blue Shield Case Study," in *Nonprofit Management & Leadership*, Vol. 16, No. 2, 2005, at pp. 153–69.

Cordery, C. and Baskerville, R., "Charity financial reporting regulation: a comparative study of the UK and New Zealand," in *Accounting History*, Vol. 12, No. 1, February 2007, at pp. 7–27.

Cordes, J., Gantz, M., and Pollack, T., "What Is the Property-Tax Exemption Worth," in Brody, E. (ed.), *Property-Tax Exemption for Charities: Mapping the Battlefield*, The Urban Institute Press, Washington, DC, 2002, at pp. 81–112.

Cordes, J. J. and Steurle, C. (eds.), *Nonprofits and Business*, Urban Institute Press, Washington, DC, 2008.

Cordes, J. and Weisbrod, B., "Differential Taxation of Nonprofits and the Commercialization of Nonprofit Revenues," in Weisbrod, B. (ed.), *To Profit or Not to Profit: The Commercial Transformation of the Nonprofit Sector*, Cambridge University Press, Cambridge, 1998, at pp. 97–100.

Crampton P., Dowell A., and Woodward A., "Third Sector Primary Care for Vulnerable Populations," *Social Science and Medicine*, Vol. 53, No. 11, 2001, at pp. 1491–502.

Cribb, J., "Accounting for Something: Voluntary Organisations, Accountability and the Implications for Government Funders," in *Social Policy Journal of New Zealand*, Vol. 26, 2005, at pp. 43–51.

Cutlip, S. M., *Fund Raising in the United States*, first published (by Rutgers U.P.) in 1965, Transaction Publishers, New Brunswick, NJ, 1990.

Dadelszen, M., "Economic Development—Charitable?," *NZLawyer Online*, May 7, 2011.

Dale, H. P., "The Crux of Charity: Inurement, Private Benefit, and Excess Benefit Transactions," October 28, 2004. Conference paper, accessible at: http://www1.law.nyu.edu/ncpl/bibliography/index.html.

Dal Pont, G., *Charity Law in Australia and New Zealand*, Oxford University Press, Melbourne, 2003.

Dal Pont, G., *Law of Charity*, LexisNexis Butterworths, Sydney, 2010.

Dalton, B. and Green, J., "Sweet Charity and Filthy Lucre: The Social Construction of Nonprofit Business Venturing in Australia, the United Kingdom and the United States of America," Working Paper No. 72, *Centre for Australian Community Organisations and Management*, 2005.

Dalton, B. and Lyons, M., "Advocacy Organisations in Australian Politics: Governance and Democratic Effects," University of Technology Sydney, in *Third Sector Review*, Vol. 11, No. 2, 2006, at pp. 11–23.

Dart, R., "Charities in Business, Business in Charities, Charities and Business—Mapping and Understanding the Complex Non-Profit/Business Interface," in *The Philanthropist*, Vol. 18, No. 3, 2004, at pp. 181–84.

Deakin, N., *In Search of Civil Society*, Palgrave, Hampshire, 2001.

De Borms, L. T., *Foundations: Creating Impact in a Globalized World*, John Wiley, Chichester, UK, 2005.

De Mandeville, B., *Essay on Charity Schools* (1723) (no details known).

De Tocqueville, A., *Democracy in America* (1835), trans. George Lawrence, New York, Harper Collins, 1988.

Doberstein, C., "Institutional Creation and Death: Urban Development Agreements in Canada," paper for Canadian Political Science Association Conference, 2011.

Dobkin Hall, P., "An Historical Overview of the Private Nonprofit Sector," in Powell, W. W. (ed.), *The Nonprofit Sector—A Research Handbook*, Yale University Press, New Haven, CT, 1987, at pp. 3–26.

Driver, S. and David Robinson, C., *Voluntary Social Services: A Review of Funding*, Planning Paper No. 28, New Zealand Planning Council, Wellington, 1986.

Dunn, A. (ed.), *The Voluntary Sector, the State and the Law*, Hart Publishing, Oxford, 2000.

Eakin, A., "We Can't Afford to Do Business This Way: A Study of the Administrative Burden Resulting from Funder Accountability and Compliance Practices," *Wellesley Institute*, 2007.

Eakin, L. "Community Capacity Draining: The Impact of Funding Practices on Community Organizations." *Community Social Planning Council of Toronto*, Toronto, 2004.

Ebenstein, L., *Milton Friedman*, Palgrave Macmillan, New York, 2007.

Eikenberry, A. and Kluver, J., *The Nonprofit Sector and the Market: Opportunities and Challenges*, Aspen Institute, Washington, DC, 2001.

Eikenberry, A. and Kluver, J., "The Marketization of the Nonprofit Sector: Civil Society at Risk?," in *Public Administration Review*, Vol. 64, No. 2, 2004, at pp. 132–40.

Elson, P. R., "Independence in a Cold Climate: A Profile of the Nonprofit and Voluntary Sector in Canada," in Smerdon, M. (ed.), *The First Principle of Voluntary Action*, Baring Foundation, London, October 2009.

Emerson, J. and Twersky, F., *New Social Entrepreneurs: The Success, Challenge and Lessons of Nonprofit Enterprise Creation*, The Roberts Foundations, San Francisco, 1996.

Etzioni, A., "The Third Sector and Domestic Missions," in *Public Administration Review*, Vol. 33, 1973, at pp. 314–23.

Evers, A. and Sachße, C., "Social Care Services for Children and Older People in Germany: Distinct and Separate Histories," in Anttonen, A., Baldock, J., and Sipilä, J. (eds.), *The Young, the Old and the State: Social Care Systems in Five Industrial Nations*, Edward Elgar, Cheltenham, 2003, at pp. 55–70.

Ferguson, A., "Charity Cases," *Business Review Weekly*, March 24, 2005.

Fishman, J., "Nonprofit Organisations in the United States," in Hopt, K. J. and Von Hippel, T. (eds.), *Comparative Corporate Governance of Non-Profit Organisations*, Cambridge, Cambridge University Press, 2010, at pp. 129–69.

Fishman, J. J., "The Development of Nonprofit Corporation Law and an Agenda for Reform," in *Emory Law Journal*, Vol. 34, 1985, at pp. 619–83.

Fishman, J. J. and Schwarz, S., *Nonprofit Organizations* (2nd ed), Foundation Press, New York, 2001.

Ford, H. A. J., "Dispositions for Purposes," in Finn, P. (ed.), *Essays in Equity*, Law Book Company Limited, Sydney, 1985, at pp. 159–78.

Forder, J., Knapp, M., "Social Care Markets: The Voluntary Sector and Residential Care for Elderly People in England," in Saxon-Harrold, S., and Kendall, J. (eds.), *Researching the Voluntary Sector*, Charities Aid Foundation, Tonbridge, U.K., 1993.

Foundation Center, *Foundation Growth and Giving Estimates: Current Outlook (2011 Edition)*, Foundation Center, New York, April 2011. See further at: http://foundationcenter.org/.

Fox, D. M. and Schaffer, D. C., "Tax Administration as Health Policy: Hospitals, the Internal Revenue Services and the Courts," in *Journal of Health Politics, Policy, and Law.*, Vol. 16, 1991, at pp. 251, 255–56.

Frank, R. G. and Salkever, D. S., "Nonprofit Organizations in the Health Sector," in *Journal of Economic Perspective*, Vol. 8, 1994, at pp. 129, 130.

Frank, R. G., Salkever, D. S., and Horwitz, J., "*PERSPECTIVE: Nonprofit Ownership, Private Property, and Public Accountability*," Health Affairs, Vol. 25, 2006, at w308.

Fremont-Smith, M. R., *Governing Nonprofit Organizations*, Harvard University Press, Cambridge, MA, 2004.

Freund, E., "Legal Aspects of Philanthropy," in Faris, E., Laune, F., and Todd, A. J. (eds.), *Intelligent Philanthropy*, Chicago, University of Chicago Press, 1930, at pp. 133–48.

Giddens, A., *The Third Way: The Renewal of Social Democracy*, Polity Press, Cambridge, 1998.

Gilbert, N. and Bridge, R., "Helping Charities Speak Out: What Funders Can Do," in *The Philanthropist*, Vol. 20, No. 2, 2005, at pp. 153–57.

Goddeeris, J. H. and Weisbrod, B. A., "Conversion from Nonprofit to For-Profit Legal Status: Why Does It Happen and Should We Care?," Institute for Policy Research at Northwestern University, 1998.

Gordon, L., *Mary Wollstonecraft: A New Genus*, Little Brown, London, 2004.

Gousmett, M. J., "Charity and Economic Development," in *New Zealand Law Journal*, March 2011, at pp. 63–68.

Gousmett, M. J., "Economic Development Corporations as Charitable Trusts," in Maples, A. and Sawyer, A. (eds.), *Taxation Issues: Existing and Emerging*, The Centre for Commercial & Corporate Law Inc., Wellington, 2011, at pp. 101–34.

Grant, S., "Contextualising Social Enterprise in New Zealand," in *Social Enterprise Journal*, Vol. 4, No. 1, 2008, at pp. 9–23.

Grant, W., *The Common Agricultural Policy*, Macmillan Press Ltd., Basingstoke, U.K, 1997.

Gugerty, M. K. and Prakash, A. (eds.), *Advocacy Organizations and Collective Action*, Cambridge University Press, New York, 2010.

Gunn, T. J., "Adjudicating Rights of Conscience under the European Convention on Human Rights," in Van der Vyver, J. D. and Witte, J. D. (eds.), *Religious Human Rights in Global Perspective: Legal Perspectives*, Martinus Nijhoff, The Hague, 1996, at pp. 305–30.

Guo, B., "Charity for Profit? Exploring Factors Associated with the Commercialization of Human Service Nonprofits," in *Nonprofit and Voluntary Sector Quarterly*, Vol. 35, 2006, at p. 123.

Gurin, M. G. and Van Til, J., "Philanthropy in Its Historical Context," in Van Til, V. and Assocs. (eds.), *Critical Issues in American Philanthropy, Strengthening Theory and Practice*, Jossey-Bass, San Francisco, 1990, at pp. 3–18.

Haag, M. and Richter, A., "Legal Standards for Capital Investments by Foundations in Hedge Funds According to German and American Law," in Hopt, K. J. and Von Hippel, T. (eds.), *Comparative Corporate Governance of Non-Profit Organizations*, Cambridge, Cambridge University Press, 2010, at pp. 710–39.

Hall, M. H., Barr, C. W., Easwaramoorthy, M., Sokolowski, M. S. W., and Salamon, L., *Canada's Nonprofit Sector in Comparative Perspective*, John Hopkins Comparative Nonprofit Sector Project, John Hopkins University, Baltimore, MD, 2005.

Handy, C., "The Privatisation of Social Housing: Capture and Commercialisation of the Voluntary Sector," in Dunn, A. (ed.), *The Voluntary Sector, the State and the Law*, Hart Publishing, Oxford, 2000, at pp. 107–19.

Hansmann, H., "The Rationale for Exempting Nonprofit Organisations from Corporate Income Taxation," in *Yale Law Journal*, Vol. 91, No. (1), 1981, at pp. 54–100.

Hansmann, H., "The Role of Nonprofit Enterprise," in *Yale Law Journal*, Vol. 89, No. 5, 1980, at pp. 835–902.

Hansmann, H., "Unfair Competition and the Unrelated Business Income Tax," in *Virginia Law Review*, Vol. 75, No. 3, 1989, at p. 605.

Hart, H. L. A., *The Concept of Law* (2nd ed.), Clarendon Law Series, Oxford University Press, Oxford, 1994.

Hartnell, C., "European Foundations' Support for Civil Society: A Means to an End or an End in Itself?," in MacDonald, N. and de Borms, L. T. (eds.), *Philanthropy in Europe: A Rich Past, a Promising Future*, Alliance Publishing Trust, London, 2008, at pp. 245–59

Hemstrom, C., "Nonprofit Organisations and Economic Activities/Enterprises," in Hopt, K. J. and Von Hippel, T. (eds.), *Comparative Corporate Governance of Non-Profit Organisations*, Cambridge, Cambridge University Press, 2010, at pp. 740–69.

Hill, O., *Homes of the London Poor*, Macmillan, London, 1875.

Hines, J. R., Horwitz J. R., and Nichols, A., "The Attack on Nonprofit Status: A Charitable Assessment," in *Michigan Law Review*. Vol. 108, No. 7, 2010, at pp. 1179–220.

Hitchcock, T., "Paupers and Preachers: The SPCK and the Parochial Workhouse Movement," in Davison, L. et al. (eds.), *Stilling the Grumbling Hive: The Response to Social and Economic Problems in England, 1689–1750*, Stroud, UK, Alan Sutton/St. Martin's Press, New York, St. Martin's Press, 1992, at pp. 145–66.

Hodgkinson V.A. et al, *A Portrait of the Independent Sector: The Activities and Finances of Charitable Organizations*, the *Independent Sector*, Washington DC, 1993.

Hood, C., "The New Public Management in the 1980s: Variations on a Theme, Accounting Organizations and Society," Vol. 20, No. 3, 1995, pp. 93–109.

Hopkins, B. R., "The Most Important Concept in the Law of Tax Exempt Organizations Today: The Commerciality Doctrine," in *Exempt Organisation Tax Review*, 1992, at p. 459.

Hopkins, B. R., *The Law of Tax-Exempt Organizations*, Wiley, New York, 1998.

Hopt, K. J., "The Board of Nonprofit Organisations: Europe," in Hopt, K. J. and Von Hippel, T. (eds.), *Comparative Corporate Governance of Non-Profit Organisations*, Cambridge, Cambridge University Press, 2010, 531–63.

Hopt, K. J. and Von Hippel, T. (eds.), *Comparative Corporate Governance of Non-Profit Organisations*, Cambridge, Cambridge University Press, 2010.

Howard, C., *The Hidden Welfare State: Tax Expenditures and Social Policy in the United States*, Princeton University Press, Princeton, NJ, 1997.

Hyman, D. A. and Sage, W. S., "PERSPECTIVE: Subsidizing Health Care Providers Through the Tax Code: Status or Conduct?," *Health Affairs*, Vol. 25, at w312 (2006).

ICNL, "Survey of Tax Laws Affecting NGOs in Central and Eastern Europe," *International Center for Not-for-Profit Law*, Washington, DC, 2002.

John, R., *Venture Philanthropy: The Evolution of High Engagement Philanthropy in Europe*, Skoll Centre for Social Entrepreneurship, Saïd Business School, Oxford University, 2006.

Jones, G., *History of the Law of Charity 1532–1827*, Wm. W. Gaunt & Sons, Inc., Holmes Beach, FL, 1986.

Judt, T., *Postwar: A History of Europe since 1945*, Vintage Books, London, 2010.

Judt, T., *Reappraisals*, Vintage Books, London, 2008.

Judt, T., *The Memory Chalet*, Heinemann, London, 2010.

Karl, B. D. and Katz, S.N. "The American Private Philanthropic Foundation and the Public Sphere, 1890–1930," in *Minerva*, Vol. 19, 1981, at pp. 236–70.

Kelley, T., "Rediscovering Vulgar Charity: An Historical Analysis of America's Tangled Nonprofit Law," in *Fordham Law Review*, Vol. 73, No. 6, 2005, at pp. 2437–99.

Kendall, J., "Revisiting the Loose and Baggy Monster," in *Charity Finance*, November 2003.

Kendall, J. and Knapp, M. R. J., "Measuring the Performance of Voluntary Organizations," in *Public Management*, Vol. 2, No. 1, 2000, at pp. 105–32.

Kendall, J. and Taylor, M., "On the Interdependence between Politics and Policy in the Shaping of English Horizontal Third Sector Initiative," in Gidron, B. and Bar, M., (eds.), *Policy Initiatives towards the Third Sector in International Perspective*, Springer Publishing, The Netherlands, 2009, at pp. 189–212.

Kennedy, H., *Report of the Advisory Group on Campaigning and the Voluntary Sector*, published by the Advisory Group on Campaigning and the Voluntary Sector, London, 2007

Kerlin, J. A., "Social Enterprise in the United States and Europe: Understanding and Learning from the Differences," in *Voluntas*, Vol. 17, 2006, at pp. 247–63.

Kirkman Gray, *Philanthropy and the State*, B. L. Hutchins Publishers, London, 1908.

Kleis, M. and Nicolaides, P., "The Concept of Undertaking in Education and Public Health Systems," European Institute of Public Administration, Maastricht, The Netherlands, June 9, 2006.

Kramer, M. and Cooch, S., *Investing for Impact*, Foundation Strategy Group, Boston, 2006.

Krull, W., "Encouraging Change, the Role of Private Foundations in Innovation Processes," in Albers, Sönke (ed.), *Cross-Functional Innovation Management: Perspectives from Different Disciplines*, Wiesbaden, 2004, at pp. 407–20.

Krull, W., "Encouraging Change: European Foundations Funding Research," in MacDonald, N. and de Borms, L.T. (eds.), *Philanthropy in Europe: A Rich Past, a Promising Future*, Alliance Publishing Trust, London, 2008, 235–45.

Lake, P. and Pincus, S., "Rethinking the Public Sphere in Early Modern England," in *Journal of British Studies*, Vol. 45, 2006, at pp. 270–92.

Lambie, G., "Nemesis of 'Market Fundamentalism'? The Ideology, Deregulation and Crisis of Finance," in *Contemporary Politics*, Vol. 15, 2009, at pp.157–77.

Lansley, J., "Changing Concepts of Charity 1700–1900," paper presented to NCVO conference, Birmingham, September 2000.

Lavarch, L., "Equal Pay and Pay Equity," in McGregor-Lowndes, M. (ed), *The Australian Nonprofit Sector Legal and Accounting Almanac 2011*, the Australian Centre for Philanthropy and Nonprofit Studies (Working Paper No. ACPNS 55), Brisbane, March 2012.

Lea, R. and Lewis, D., *The Larceny of the Lottery Fund*, Centre for Policy Studies, London, 2006.,

Leat, D., "Foundations and Policy Influence in Europe," in MacDonald, N. and de Borms, L. T. (eds.), *Philanthropy in Europe: A Rich Past, a Promising Future*, Alliance Publishing Trust, London, 2008, at 259–73.

Leiter, J. "Structural Isomorphism in Australian Nonprofit Organizations," in *Voluntas: International Journal of Voluntary and Nonprofit Organizations*, Vol. 16, No. 1, March 2005, at pp. 1–31.

Leonard, E. M., *The Early History of the English Poor Relief*, Cambridge University Press, Cambridge, 1900.

Letts, C., Ryan, W., and Grossman, A., "Virtuous Capital: What Foundations Can Learn from Venture Capitalists," in *Harvard Business Review*, March/April 1997, at pp. 36–44.

Lewis, D. J., "Principled Approach to the Law of Charities in the Face of Analogies, Activities and the Advancement of Education," in *Queen's Law Journal*, Vol. 25, 1999–2000 at p. 679.

Lipman, H., "Health-Conversion Funds Hold $16 Billion in Assets," in *Chronicle of Philanthropy*, May 4, 2000, at p. 12.

Lloyd, S. and Walker, A. F., *Charities, Trading and the Law* (2nd ed), Jordans, Bristol, 2009.

Lucas, B. and Robinson, A., "Religion as a Head of Charity," in McGregor-Lowndes, M. and O'Halloran, K. (eds.), *Modernising Charity Law*, Elgar, Cheltenham, 2010, at pp. 187–204.

Ludlum, M., "Unrelated Business Income Tax Returns, 2005," in *Statistics of Income Bulletin*, Department of the Treasury, Internal Revenue Service, Winter 2009.

Lunder, E. K. and Liu, E. C., *501(c)(3) Hospitals and the Community Benefit Standard*, Congressional Research Service, Washington, DC, November 2009.

Luxton, P., *The Law of Charities* (1st ed.,), Oxford, Oxford University Press, 2001.

Luxton, P. *Making Law? Parliament v The Charity Commission*, Politeia, London, 2009.

Lyons, M., "Defining the Nonprofit Sector: Australia," in Salamon, M. and Anheier, H. (eds.), *The Johns Hopkins Comparative Nonprofit Sector Project*, The Johns Hopkins University Institute for Policy Studies, 1998.

Lyons, M., *Third Sector: The Contribution of Nonprofit and Cooperative Enterprises in Australia*, Allen & Unwin, Crows Nest, 2001.

Lyons, M., "What Do We Know of Corporate Support for Australian Nonprofits? A Research Note," in *Third Sector Review*, Vol. 5, No 2, 1999, pp. 71–80.

Lyons, M., and Hocking, S., *Dimensions of Australia's Third Sector*, Centre for Australian Community Organisations and Management, University of Technology, Sydney, 2000.

Malani, A. and Posner, E. A., "The Case for For-Profit Charities," *Virginia Law Review*, Vol. 93, 2007, at p. 2017.

Marmot, M., *Fair Society, Healthy Lives: Strategic Review of Health Inequalities in England Post-2010*, Government Publications, London, February 2010.

Martin, M., "Engaged Philanthropy and Market-Based solutions," in MacDonald, N. and de Borms, L. T. (eds.), *Philanthropy in Europe: A Rich Past, a Promising Future*, Alliance Publishing Trust, London, 2008, at pp. 273–89.

McGregor-Lowndes, M. (ed), *The Australian Nonprofit Sector Legal and Accounting Almanac 2011*, the Australian Centre for Philanthropy and Nonprofit Studies (Working Paper No. ACPNS 55), Brisbane, March 2012.

McGregor-Lowndes, M. and O'Halloran, K. (eds), *Modernising Charity Law: Recent Developments and Future Directions*, Elgar, Cheltenham, October 2010.

McGregor-Lowndes, M. and Turnour, M., "Recent Developments in Government Community Service Relations: Are You Really My Partner?," in *The Journal of Contemporary Issues in Business and Government*, Vol. 9, No. 1, 2003, at pp. 31–42.

McGregor-Lowndes, M., Turnour, M., and Turnour, E., "Not for Profit Income Tax Exemption: Is There a Hole in the Bucket, Dear Henry?," *Australian Tax Forum*, Vol. 26, 2011, at pp. 601–31.

McIntosh, M. K., "Poverty, Charity and Coercion in Elizabethan England," *Journal of Interdisciplinary History*, Vol. 35, 2005, at p. 3, 2005.

McMullen, K. and Schellenberg, G., CPRN Research Series on Human Resources in the Non-Profit Sector, "Mapping the Non-profit Sector," Appendix 2, *Canadian Policy Research Networks*, Ottawa, December 2002.

Melville, R. "Australian Peak Bodies and the Market Policy Culture," in *Social Policy for the 21st Century: Justice and Responsibility*, Proceedings of the National Social Policy Conference, Sydney, July, 21–23 1999, Vol. 1. (eds. Shaver, S. & Saunders, P.), Social Policy Research Centre, Reports and Proceedings No. 141, December, 1999.

Melville, R., "Nonprofit Umbrella Organisations in a Contracting Regime: A Comparative Review of Australian, British and North American Literature and Experience," in *International Journal of NotforProfit Law*, 1999.

Melville, R. "The State and Community Sector Peak Bodies: Theoretical and Policy Challenges," in *Third Sector Review*, Vol. 3, 1999, at pp. 41–65.

Melville, R., "Voice and the Role of Community Sector Peak Bodies," in *Third Sector Review*, special issue, Vol. 7, No. 2, 2001, at pp. 89–110.

Melville, R. and Perkins, R., "Changing Roles of Community Sector Peak Bodies in a Neo-Liberal Policy Environment in Australia," NCOSS Conference Paper, University of Wollongong, NSW March 12, 2003.

Mill, J. S., *Principles of Political Economy* (1848), Longmans, Green and Co, London, 1909.

Ministry of Social Policy, *Models of Community-Government Partnerships and Their Effectiveness in Achieving Welfare Goals: A Review of the Literature*, Ministry of Social Policy, Wellington, 2000, at p.7.

Monbiot, G., *Captive State—The Corporate Takeover of Britain*, Macmillan, London, 2000.

Moore, D., Hadzi-Miceva, K., and Bullain, N., "A Comparative Overview of Public Benefit Status in Europe," in *The International Journal of Not-for-Profit Law*, Vol. 11, No. 1, November 2008.

Morris, D., "Fee-Paying Hospitals and Charitable Status: A New Dawn or Lost Opportunities?," in *Kings Law Journal*, Vol. 18, 2007, at pp. 455–79.

Morris, D., "Paying the Piper: The 'Contract Culture' as Dependency Culture for Charities," in Dunn, A. (ed.), *The Voluntary Sector, the State and the Law*, Hart Publishing, Oxford, 2000, at pp. 123–41.

Morris, D., "Public Benefit: The Long and Winding Road to Reforming the Public Benefit Test for Charity: A worthwhile trip or 'Is your journey really necessary?,'" in McGregor-Lowndes, M. and O'Halloran, K. (eds.), *Modernising Charity Law*, Elgar, London, 2010, at pp. 103–27.

Mulgan, G., *The Art of Public Strategy,* Oxford University Press, Oxford, 2009.

Nowland-Foreman, G., "Can Voluntary Organizations Survive the Bear Hug of Government Funding under a Contracting Regime? A View from Aotearoa/New Zealand," in *Third Sector Review,* Vol. 3, 1997, at pp. 5–39.

Nowland-Foreman, G., "No Longer Overlooked and Undervalued," at the launch of *The New Zealand Non-Profit Sector in Comparative Perspective,* Wellington, August 12, 2008.

O'Brien, M., Sanders, J., and Tennant, M., *The New Zealand Non-Profit Sector and Government Policy,* Office for the Community and Voluntary Sector, Wellington, 2009.

O'Halloran, K., *Charity Law and Social Inclusion: An International Study,* Routledge, London, 2006.

O'Halloran, K., *The Politics of Charity,* Routledge, London, 2011.

O'Halloran, K., McGregor-Lowndes, M., and Simon, K., *Charity Law & Social Policy: National and International Perspectives on the Functions of the Law Relating to Charities,* Springer, The Netherlands, 2009.

Olsen, O., Guthrie, J., and Humphrey, C., "International Experiences with Financial Management Reforms in the World of Public Services: New World?," in Olsen, O., Guthrie, J., and Humphrey, C. (eds.), *Global Warning: Debating International Developments in the New Public Financial Management,* Cappelen Akademisk Forlag, Bergen, 1998, at pp. 49–75.

Ong, D. S. K., *Trusts Law in Australia,* Federation Press, Sydney, 2007.

Osborne, D. and Gaebler, T., *Reinventing Government,* Plume, New York, 1993.

Owen, D., *English Philanthropy 1660–1960,* Oxford University Press, London, 1965.

Paines, A., "Grant-Making Charities and the NHS," in Garton J. and Mitchell, C. (eds.), *Charities and the NHS,* King's Law Journal, Vol. 18, No. 3, Hart Publishing, London, 2007, at pp. 503–15.

Parachin, A., "The Definition of Charity and Public Law Equality Norms,", paper presented at the conference *Private and Public Law—Intersections in Law and Method,* Brisbane, July 2011.

Parham, D., "Microeconomic Reforms and the Revival in Australia's Growth in Productivity and Living Standards," Conference of Economists, Adelaide, October 1, 2002.

Phillips, J., "The Federal Court of Appeal and the Legal Meaning of Charity: Review and Critique,", in Phillips, J., Chapman, B., and Stevens, D. (eds.), *Between State and Market: Essays on Charities Law and Policy in Canada,* McGill-Queen's University Press, Montreal, 2001, at pp. 219–50.

Phillips, J., Chapman, B., and Stevens, D. (eds.), *Between State and Market: Essays on Charities Law and Policy in Canada,* McGill-Queen's University Press, Montreal, 2001.

Picarda, H., *The Law and Practice Relating to Charities* (3rd ed.), Butterworths, London, 1999.

Picarda, H., "Harmonising Nonprofit Law in the EU," in Hopt, K. J. and Von Hippel, T. (eds.), *Comparative Corporate Governance of Non-Profit Organisations,* Cambridge, Cambridge University Press, 2010, at pp. 170–96.

Pollitt, C., "Partnerships, Networks, Joined-Up Governance, the Information Age (and All That)," in Pollit C. (ed.), *The Essential Public Manager,* Open University Press, Philadelphia, 2003, at pp. 52–67.

Pollock, A. M., "The BetterCare Judgment: A Challenge to Health Care; European Competition Law May Cover Publicly Funded, Privately Provided Care," in *British Medical Journal,* London, February 2003, at pp. 236–37.

Pomeroy, A., "Changing the Culture of Contracting: Funding for Outcomes," in *Social Policy Journal of New Zealand*, No. 31, 2007, at pp. 158–69.

Powell, W. and Steinberg, R. (eds.), *Nonprofit Organizations and the Market, in the Non-Profit Sector* (2nd ed.), Yale University Press, New Haven, CT and London, 2006.

Puttnam, R., *Bowling Alone*, Simon and Schuster, New York, 2000.

Quint, F. and Spring, T., "Religion, Charity Law and Human Rights," in *Charity Law & Practice Review*, Vol. 5, No. 3, 1999, at pp. 153–86.

Reid, M., "Community Councils and Public Sector Reform—A Case of Conflicting Signals," paper delivered at ANZTSR Conference, Victoria University, Wellington, 1996.

Reed, P. and Howe, V., "Publicly Available Data Resources on the Nonprofit Sector in Canada," Nonprofit Sector Knowledge Base Project, Statistics Canada, 1998.

Reis, T. and Clohsey, S. J., "Unleashing New Resources and Entrepreneurship for the Common Good: A Philanthropic Renaissance," in Schluter, A., Then, V., and Walkenhorst, P. (eds.), *Foundations in Europe, Society, Management and Law*, London, Directory of Social Change, 2001.

Rickett, C., "A Statutory Charitable Trust," in *New Zealand Law Journal*, March 2000, at pp. 59–61.

Robinson, D. and Hanley, P., *Funding New Zealand 2002: Resource Flows to the Community Nonprofit Sector in New Zealand*, Philanthropy New Zealand, Wellington, 2002.

Rockefeller, J. D., *Random Reminiscences of Men and Events*, Doubleday, Page and Company, New York, 1909.

Rose, H., "Comment, The Social Business: The Viability of a New Business Entity Type," in *Willamette Law Review*, Vol. 44, 2007, at p. 131.

Rosenman, M., "Independence: A Matter of Definition—The Charitable Sector in the United States," in Smerdon, M. (ed.), *The First Principle of Voluntary Action*, Baring Foundation, London, October 2009, at pp. 99–120.

Rutzen, D., Moore, D., and Durham, M., "The Legal Framework for Not-for-Profit Organizations in Central and Eastern Europe," in *IJNL*, Vol 11, Issue 2, 2009.

Ryan, W. P., "The New Landscape for Nonprofits," in *Harvard Business Review*, January–February 1999, at pp.127–36.

Sadiq, K. and Richardson, C., "Tax Concessions for Charities: Competitive Neutrality, the Tax Base and 'Public Goods' Choice," in *Australian Tax Forum*, Vol. 25, No. 4, 2010, at pp. 597–612.

Salamon, L., Anheier, H., and Assoc., "Civil Society in Comparative Perspective," in *Global Civil Society: Dimensions of the Nonprofit Sector*, The Johns Hopkins Center for Civil Society Studies, Baltimore, MD, 1999, at pp. 3–39.

Salamon, L., *Holding the Center: America's Nonprofit Sector at a Crossroads*, Nathan Cummings Foundation, New York, 1997.

Salamon, L. M., *Partners in Public Service: Government-Nonprofit Relations in the Modern Welfare State*, John Hopkins University Press, Baltimore MD, 1995.

Salamon, L. M. (ed.), "*The Resilient Sector: The State of Nonprofit America*, Brookings Institution Press, Washington, DC, 2002.

Salamon, L. M. and Anheier, H. K., "Social Origins of Civil Society: Explaining the Nonprofit Sector Cross-Nationally," in *Voluntas*, Vol. 9, 1998, at pp. 213–48.

Salamon, L. M. and Geller, S. L., *Nonprofit Governance and Accountability*, Johns Hopkins Nonprofit Listening Post Project Communique No. 4, 2005.

Salamon, L. M., Haddock, M. A., Wojciech Sokolowski, S., and Tice, H. S., *Measuring Civil Society and Volunteering: Initial Findings from Implementation of the UN Handbook on*

Nonprofit Institutions, Working Paper No. 23. Johns Hopkins Center for Civil Society Studies, Baltimore, MD, 2007.

Salole, G., "The Importance of There Being a European Foundation Statute," in MacDonald, N. and de Borms, L. T. (eds.), *Philanthropy in Europe: A Rich Past, a Promising Future,* Alliance Publishing Trust, London, 2007, at pp. 289–300.

Sanders, J., O'Brien, M, Tennant, M, Sokolowski J, Wojciech Sokolowski, S. and Salamon, L., *The New Zealand Non-Profit Sector in Comparative Perspective,* Office for the Community and Voluntary Sector, Wellington, 2008.

Sanders, W. M., "The Commerciality Doctrine Is Alive and Well," in *Taxation of Exempts,* Vol. 16, 2005, at pp. 212–13.

Schiff, J. and Weisbrod, B., "Competition between For-Profit and Nonprofit Organizations in Commercial Markets," in Ben Ner, A. and Gui, B. (eds.), *The Nonprofit Sector in the Mixed Economy,* University of Michigan Press, Ann Arbor, 1993, at pp. 99–125.

Scott, K., "Funding Matters: The Impact of Canada's Funding Regime on Nonprofit and Voluntary Organizations," Ottawa, *Canadian Council on Social Development,* 2003.

Scott, K., and Pike, D., "Funding Matters…for Our Communities: Challenges and Opportunities for Funding Innovation in Canada's Non-Profit and Voluntary Sector," Ottawa, *Canadian Council on Social Development,* 2005.

Scott, K. and Struthers, M., "Pan-Canadian Funding Practice in Communities: Challenges and Opportunities for the Government of Canada," Ottawa, *Canadian Council on Social Development,* 2006.

Seddon, N., *Who Cares?,* Civitas, London, 2007.

Seligman, A. B., *The Idea of Civil Society,* Princeton University Press, Princeton, NJ, 1992.

Seymour, J., "Parens Patriae and Wardship Powers: Their Nature and Origins," in *Oxford Journal of Legal Studies,* Vol. 14, No. 2, 1994, at pp. 159–88.

Sharp, A., "The History of the Taxation of Maori Authorities in New Zealand: A Unique Reflection of Law and Public Policy Working Together?," in Maples, A. and Sawyer A. (eds.), *Taxation Issues: Existing and Emerging,* The Centre for Commercial & Corporate Law Inc., 2011, at pp. pp. 163–76.

Sheppard, I., Fitzgerald, R., and Gonski, D., *Inquiry into the Definition of Charities and Related Organisations,* CanPrint Communications Pty Ltd, Canberra, June 2001.

Shipley, H. J., *Social Assistance: Welfare That Works,* Government Printer, Wellington, 1991.

Sievers, B., "If Pigs Had Wings: The Appeals and Limits of Venture Philanthropy," in the Waldemar A. Nielsen Issues in Philanthropy Seminar Series, Center for Public & Nonprofit Leadership, Georgetown University, Washington, DC, November 16, 2001.

Silk, T., "Corporate Philanthropy and Law in the United States: A Practical Guide to Tax Choices and an Introduction to Compliance with Anti-Terrorism Laws," in *The International Journal of Not-for-Profit Law,* Vol. 6, No. 3, June 2004.

Sinn, H.W, *Casino Capitalism: How the Financial Crisis Came about and What Needs to Be Done Now,* Oxford, Oxford University Press, 2010.

Smerdon, M., *Rights with Meaning,* Baring Foundation (Working Paper No. 4), London, October 2009.

Smerdon, M. (ed.), *The First Principle of Voluntary Action,* Baring Foundation, London, October 2009.

Smith, R., and Whittington, P., *Charity: The Spectre of Over-Regulation and State Dependency,* CPS, London, 2006.

Smith, V., *Contracting for Social and Welfare Services: The Changing Relationship between Government and the Voluntary Sector in New Zealand,* research paper presented at the Australian and New Zealand Third Sector Research Conference, Wellington, July 2–5, 1996.

Spencer, H., *Man versus the State,* the Contemporary Review, London, 1884.

Steinberg, R., "'Unfair' Competition by Nonprofits and Tax Policy," in *National Tax Journal,* Vol. 44, No. 3, 1991, at pp. 351–64.

Stevens, R., "'A Poor Sort of Memory': Voluntary Hospitals and Government before the Depression," in *The Milbank Memorial Fund Quarterly. Health and Society,* Vol. 60, No. 4, 1982, at pp. 551–84.

Stevens, R., *In Sickness and in Wealth* 17–51, Basic Books, New York, 1989.

Stiglitz, J., *The Economic Role of the State,* Oxford, Basil Blackwell, 1989.

St John, S., *Redesigning the Welfare State in New Zealand,* conference paper presented at School of Social Work and Social Policy, University of Queensland, Brisbane, October 4 and 5t, 2001.

Stone, E. G., "Adhering to the Old Line: Uncovering the History and Political Function of the Unrelated Business Income Tax," in *Emory Law Journal,* Vol. 54, 2005, at p. 1475.

Sugin, L., "The Increasing Resemblance of Nonprofit and Business Organizations Law: Resisting the Corporatization of Nonprofit Governance: Transforming Obedience into Fidelity," in *Fordham L. Rev.,* Vol. 76, 2007, at p. 893.

Taniguchi, Jason, *Canadian Directory to Foundations and Grants* (15th ed.), Center for Canadian Philanthropy, Toronto, 2001.

Tanzi, V., *Government versus Markets: The Changing Economic Role of the State,* Cambridge, Cambridge University Press, 2011.

Tennant, M., *Paupers and Providers: Charitable Aid in New Zealand,* Allen and Unwin/ Bridget Williams Books, Wellington, 1989.

Tennant, M., "Governments and Voluntary Sector Welfare: Historians' Perspectives," in *Social Policy Journal of New Zealand,* Vol. 17, December 2001, at pp.147–60.

Tennant, M., Sanders, J., O'Brien, M., and Castle, C., *Defining the Nonprofit Sector: New Zealand,* Working Papers of the Johns Hopkins Comparative Nonprofit Sector Project, No. 45, The Johns Hopkins Center for Civil Society Studies, Baltimore, MD, 2006.

The Economics Legislation Committee, *Tax Laws Amendment (Public Benefit Test) Bill 2010 Report,* Canberra, 2010, available via: http://www.aph.gov.au/Senate/committee/economics_ctte/public_benefit_test_10/report/index.htm

Titmuss, R. A., *The Gift Relationship: From Human Blood to Social Policy,* Allen and Unwin, London, 1970.

Torjman, S., "No Small Answers to Big Problems," OpEd, *Toronto Star,* September 17, 2007.

Tuckman, H. P. and Chang, C. F., "Commercial Activity, Technological Change and Nonprofit Mission," in Powell, W. W. and Steinberg, R. (eds.), *The Nonprofit Sector: A Research Handbook (2nd ed.),* Yale University Press, New Haven, CT, 2006, at pp. 629–45.

Tudor, O. D., Warburton, J., Morris, D., and Riddle, N. F. Tudor on *Charities,* (9th ed). Sweet & Maxwell, London, 2003.

Tull, D. L., "China's Engagement in Africa: Scope, Significance and Consequences," in *Journal of Modern African Studies,* Vol. 44, No. 3, Cambridge University Press, Cambridge, 2006, at pp. 459–79.

Turnour, M., "Modernising Charity Law: Steps to an Alternative Architecture for Common Law Charity Jurisprudence," in McGregor-Lowndes, M. and O'Halloran, K. (eds.), *Modernising Charity Law: Recent Developments and Future Directions*, Elgar, Cheltenham, 2010, at pp. 228–61.

Unwin, J., *Speaking Truth to Power: A Discussion Paper on the Voluntary Sector's Relationship with Government*, Baring Foundation, London, 2000.

Unwin, J. and Westland, P., *Health Action Zones: The Engagement of the Voluntary Sector*, the Baring Foundation, London, 2000.

Van Overtveldt, J., *The Chicago School*, Chicago, Agate, 2007.

Von Hippel, T., "Nonprofit Organisations in Germany," in Hopt, K. J. and Von Hippel, T. (eds.), *Comparative Corporate Governance of Non-Profit Organisations*, Cambridge University Press, Cambridge, 2010, at pp. 197–227.

Von Hippel, T. and Walz, W. R., "Tax Law as an Instrument to Strengthen Governance," in Hopt, K. J. and Von Hippel, T. (eds.), *Comparative Corporate Governance of Non-Profit Organisations*, Cambridge University Press, Cambridge, 2010, at pp. 942–43.

Walker, P., "Exploring Trans-Cultural Partnerships within Third Sector Organisations in New Zealand," in *International Journal of Interdisciplinary Social Sciences*, Vol. 5, No. 3, 2010, at pp. 423–34.

Wayne, S., *A Profile of Planned Giving and Endowments within the Canadian International NGO Community*, Canadian Council for International Co-operation, 1999.

Webb, S. and Webb, B., *The Prevention of Destitution*, Longmans, London. 1911.

Weisbrod, B., "The Pitfalls of Profits," in *Stanford Social Innovation Review*, Vol. 2, No. 3, 2004, at pp. 40–47.

Weisbrod, B. A. (ed.), *To Profit or Not to Profit: The Commercial Transformation of the Nonprofit Sector*, Cambridge University Press, Cambridge, 1998.

Westlake, H. F., *The Parish Gilds of Mediaeval England*, Society for Promoting Christian Knowledge, London, 1919.

Whelan, R., *Helping the Poor*, Civitas, London, 2001.

Whiteford, P., "Pulling Our Welfare Weight," in Uniken, University of NSW, Social Policy Research Centre, August 2009.

Wilson, C., *The Changing Face of Social Service Volunteering: A Literature Review*, Ministry of Social Development, Wellington, 2001.

Wing, K. T., Roeger, K. L., and Pollak, T.H., *The Nonprofit Almanac 2010*, Urban Institute Press, Washington, DC, September 2010.

Wing, K., Roeger, K. L., and Pollak, T. H., *The Nonprofit Sector in Brief: Public Charities, Giving and Volunteering, 2010*, Urban Institute Press, Washington, DC, September 2010.

Wohl, A. S. (ed.), *The Victorian Family: Structure and Stresses*, Croom Helm Ltd., London, 1978.

Wolfenden, J., *The Future of Voluntary Organisations*, Croom Helm, London, 1978.

Woodward, S. and Marshall, S., *A Better Framework: Reforming Not-for-Profit Regulation*, Centre for Corporate Law and Securities Regulation, University of Melbourne, 2004.

Woolley, F., "The Strengths and Limits of the Voluntary Sector," in *Isuma: Canadian Journal of Policy Research*, Vol. 2, Issue 2, 2001, at pp. 21–27.

Wright, K., "Generosity vs. Altruism: Philanthropy and Charity in the United States and United Kingdom," in *Voluntas: International Journal of Voluntary and Nonprofit Organizations*, Vol. 12, No. 4, 2002.

Wuthnow, R., "The Voluntary Sector: Legacy of the Past, Hope for the Future?," in R. Wuthnow (ed.), *Between States and Markets: The Voluntary Sector in Comparative Perspective*, Princeton University Press, Princeton, NJ, 1991, at pp. 3–29.

Wyatt, B. and Hunter, L., "Charity Law Reforms: Overview of Progress since 2001," in McGregor-Lowndes, M. and O'Halloran, K. (eds.), *Modernising Charity Law*, Elgar Publications, Cheltenham, 2010.

Young, D., "Social Enterprise in the United States: Alternate Identities and Forms," paper presented at The EMES Conference, The Social Enterprise: A Comparative Perspective, Trento, Italy, December 13–15, 2001.

Young, D. R., "Alternative Perspectives on Social Enterprise,", in Cordes, J. J. and Steuerle, C. E. (eds.), *Nonprofits & Business*, Urban Institute Press, 2008, at pp. 21–46.

Young, D. and Salamon, L., "Commercialization, Social Ventures, and For-Profit Competition," in Salamon, L. (ed.), *The State of Nonprofit America*, Brookings Institution Press, Washington, DC, 2002, at pp. 425–48.

Yunus, M., "Nobel Peace Prize 2006: the Nobel Lecture,", Law and Bus. Review of the Americas, Vol. 13, 2007, at pp. 267, 272.

Zappalà, G. and Lyons, M., "Non-Profit Organizations and Business: Mapping the Extent and Scope of Community–Business Partnerships in Australia," in Barraket, J. (ed.), *Strategic Issues for the Not-For-Profit Sector*, UNSW Press, Sydney, 2008, at pp. 16–44.

Zelinsky, E., "Are Tax 'Benefits' Constitutionally Equivalent to Direct Expenditures?,", *Harvard Law Review*, Vol. 112, No. 2, 1998, pp. 379–433.

TABLE OF CASES

H

I

N

O

P

Q

R

Y

INDEX